Digital Transformation in Public Sector Human Resource Management

Elvin Shava
University of KwaZulu-Natal, South Africa

Nduduzo Ndebele
University of KwaZulu-Natal, South Africa

A volume in the Advances in Human Resources Management and Organizational Development (AHRMOD) Book Series

IGI Global
PUBLISHER of TIMELY KNOWLEDGE

Published in the United States of America by
IGI Global
Business Science Reference (an imprint of IGI Global)
701 E. Chocolate Avenue
Hershey PA, USA 17033
Tel: 717-533-8845
Fax: 717-533-8661
E-mail: cust@igi-global.com
Web site: http://www.igi-global.com

Library of Congress Cataloging-in-Publication Data

CIP Pending
ISBN: 979-8-3693-2889-7
EISBN: 979-8-3693-2890-3

British Cataloguing in Publication Data
A Cataloguing in Publication record for this book is available from the British Library.

For electronic access to this publication, please contact: eresources@igi-global.com.

Advances in Human Resources Management and Organizational Development (AHRMOD) Book Series

Patricia Ordóñez de Pablos
Universidad de Oviedo, Spain

ISSN:2327-3372
EISSN:2327-3380

Mission

A solid foundation is essential to the development and success of any organization and can be accomplished through the effective and careful management of an organization's human capital. Research in human resources management and organizational development is necessary in providing business leaders with the tools and methodologies which will assist in the development and maintenance of their organizational structure.

The **Advances in Human Resources Management and Organizational Development (AHRMOD) Book Series** aims to publish the latest research on all aspects of human resources as well as the latest methodologies, tools, and theories regarding organizational development and sustainability. The **AHRMOD Book Series** intends to provide business professionals, managers, researchers, and students with the necessary resources to effectively develop and implement organizational strategies.

Coverage

- Employment and Labor Laws
- Collaborative Method
- Job Enrichment
- Recruitment Process
- E-Human Resources Management
- Human Relations Movement
- Personnel Retention
- Diversity in the Workplace
- Worker Behavior and Engagement
- Performance Improvement

IGI Global is currently accepting manuscripts for publication within this series. To submit a proposal for a volume in this series, please contact our Acquisition Editors at Acquisitions@igi-global.com or visit: http://www.igi-global.com/publish/.

The Advances in Human Resources Management and Organizational Development (AHRMOD) Book Series (ISSN 2327-3372) is published by IGI Global, 701 E. Chocolate Avenue, Hershey, PA 17033-1240, USA, www.igi-global.com. This series is composed of titles available for purchase individually; each title is edited to be contextually exclusive from any other title within the series. For pricing and ordering information please visit http://www.igi-global.com/book-series/advances-human-resources-management-organizational/73670. Postmaster: Send all address changes to above address.

Titles in this Series

For a list of additional titles in this series, please visit: www.igi-global.com/book-series

Enhancing Employee Motivation Through Training and Development
Tricia Mazurowski (Adler University, USA)
Business Science Reference • copyright 2024 • 309pp • H/C (ISBN: 9798369316740) • US $205.00 (our price)

Global Practices on Effective Talent Acquisition and Retention
Bryan Christiansen (Southern New Hampshire University, USA) Muhammad Abdul Aziz (University of Greenwich, UK) and Elle Lily O'Keeffe (Rasmussen University, USA)
Business Science Reference • copyright 2024 • 531pp • H/C (ISBN: 9798369319383) • US $295.00 (our price)

Convergence of Human Resources Technologies and Industry 5.0
Pawan Kumar (Lovely Professional University, India) Sunil Kumar (Shoolini University, India) Rajesh Verma (Lovely Professional University, India) and Sumesh Dadwal (London South Bank University, UK)
Business Science Reference • copyright 2024 • 363pp • H/C (ISBN: 9798369313435) • US $290.00 (our price)

Building Sustainable Human Resources Management Practices for Businesses
Cristina Raluca Gh. Popescu (University of Bucharest, Romania & The Bucharest University of Economic Studies, Romania) Javier Martínez-Falcó (University of Alicante, Spain & University of Stellenbosch, South Africa) Bartolomé Marco-Lajara (University of Alicante, Spain) Eduardo Sánchez-García (University of Alicante, Spain) and Luis A. Millán-Tudela (University of Alicante, Spain)
Business Science Reference • copyright 2024 • 364pp • H/C (ISBN: 9798369319949) • US $275.00 (our price)

Demystifying the Dark Side of AI in Business
Sumesh Dadwal (Northumbria University, UK) Shikha Goyal (Lovely Professional University, India) Pawan Kumar (Lovely Professional University, India) and Rajesh Verma (Lovely Professional University, India)
Business Science Reference • copyright 2024 • 268pp • H/C (ISBN: 9798369307243) • US $275.00 (our price)

Organizational Management Sustainability in VUCA Contexts
Rafael Perez-Uribe (Universidad de la Salle, Colombia) David Ocampo-Guzman (Santo Tomas University, Colombia & EAN University, Colombia) Carlos Salcedo-Perez (Politecnico Grancolombiano, Colombia) and Andrés Carvajal-Contreras (EAN University, Colombia)
Business Science Reference • copyright 2024 • 435pp • H/C (ISBN: 9798369307205) • US $275.00 (our price)

IGI Global
PUBLISHER of TIMELY KNOWLEDGE

701 East Chocolate Avenue, Hershey, PA 17033, USA
Tel: 717-533-8845 x100 • Fax: 717-533-8661
E-Mail: cust@igi-global.com • www.igi-global.com

Table of Contents

Preface xvi

Chapter 1
Streamlining Public Sector Human Resource Recruitment and Selection Processes Through Digitalisation: Prospects and Challenges for African Bureaucracies 1
Leon Poshai, Midlands State University, Zimbabwe
Kudakwashe Intauno, University of Duisburg-Essen, Germany

Chapter 2
Digital Workforce Planning and Management in the Public Sector 21
Ayler Beniah Ndraha, Universitas Nias, Indonesia

Chapter 3
Drivers of Digital Transformation and Their Efficacy in Public Sector Human Resource Management 39
Andrew Enaifoghe, University of Zululand, South Africa
Nduduzo C. Ndebele, University of KwaZulu-Natal, South Africa
Anuoluwapo Durokifa, University of Johannesburg, South Africa
Xolani Thusi, University of Limpopo, South Africa

Chapter 4
Examining the Challenges of Adopting Modern Technologies in Public Sector Human Resource Management 60
Standa Sani, Africa University, Zimbabwe
Siphiwe Plaxedes Mandina, De Montfort University, Zimbabwe

Chapter 5
Leveraging Human Resource (HR) Analytics for Effective Talent Management in Public Sector Organisations 90
Blessing Takawira, University of Johannesburg, South Africa
Misheck Musaigwa, University of Johannesburg, South Africa
Vivence Kalitanyi, University of Johannesburg, South Africa

Chapter 6
Digital Transformation in Hiring and Selection Processes: A Ugandan Public Sector Perspective... 115
Alexander Markey Oluka, European University Viadrina, Germany
Elvin Shava, University of KwaZulu-Natal, South Africa

Chapter 7
Embracing Transformative Digital Human Resource Management in the Nigerian Public Sector ... 130
Oluwaseun Temitope Ojogiwa, University of KwaZulu-Natal, South Africa
Sibongile Ruth Nhari, University of KwaZulu-Natal, South Africa

Chapter 8
Navigating the Future! Exploring the Impact of Digital Hiring and Selection Processes in South African Municipalities ... 145
Beauty Zindi, University of Johannesburg, South Africa

Chapter 9
Performance Contracts for Senior Administrators in "Unsettled" Political and Economic Contexts: A Zimbabwean Local Government Perspective ... 162
Tawanda Nyikadzino, University of Johannesburg, South Africa
Shikha Vyas-Doorgapersad, University of Johannesburg, South Africa

Chapter 10
Revolutionizing Public Sector Human Resources: A Digital Frontier for Innovative Transformation ... 185
Vumani Mbatha, University of KwaZulu-Natal, South Africa
Andrisha Beharry Ramraj, University of KwaZulu-Natal, South Africa
Idris Ganiyu, York St. John University, UK

Chapter 11
Digitalisation of Employee Performance Evaluation to Advance Public Sector Human Resource Management ... 202
Syanda A. Mthuli, School of Management, University of KwaZulu-Natal, South Africa

Chapter 12
The Impact of Talent Retention and Management Practices on Service Delivery Outcomes in the South African Public Service ... 222
Thokozani Ian Nzimakwe, University of KwaZulu-Natal, South Africa
Sindy Olive Mbele, University of KwaZulu-Natal, South Africa

Chapter 13
Positioning Digital Transformation of Public Sector Human Resources in Zimbabwe and South Africa: Challenges and Opportunities ... 239
Lewis Edwin Chigova, North-West University, South Africa
Costa Hofisi, North-West University, South Africa

Chapter 14
Talent Management in the Digital Age: Leveraging Technology to Enhance Public Sector Recruitment and Retention in Zimbabwe 259
Raymond Mapuranga, Midlands State University, Zimbabwe
Kebiat Mukuze, Midlands State University, Zimbabwe
Abigail Maravanyika, Reformed Church University, Zimbabwe

Compilation of References 278

About the Contributors 323

Index 327

Detailed Table of Contents

Preface..xvi

Chapter 1
Streamlining Public Sector Human Resource Recruitment and Selection Processes Through Digitalisation: Prospects and Challenges for African Bureaucracies 1
Leon Poshai, Midlands State University, Zimbabwe
Kudakwashe Intauno, University of Duisburg-Essen, Germany

The Fourth Industrial Revolution (4IR) has had a profound impact on technological advancements in different development sectors around the world through digitalisation. In public sector human resource management, particularly in the areas of recruitment and selection of employees, the deployment of technology has enabled human resource managers to eliminate physical interactions in the processes of hiring employees through the digitalisation of the human resource management function. Through a desktop review methodology, which is anchored on the conceptual content analysis technique, this chapter argues that the digitalisation of recruitment and selection processes has created opportunities to curb challenges such as bureaucratic delays, nepotism and corruption which undermine fairness in the hiring processes. However, as the chapter reveals, challenges such as underdeveloped technological infrastructure, resistance to change, lack of digital literacy skills and the digital divide continue to plague the efforts to digitalise recruitment and selection processes in public sector institutions in African bureaucracies.

Chapter 2
Digital Workforce Planning and Management in the Public Sector 21
Ayler Beniah Ndraha, Universitas Nias, Indonesia

This chapter offers a comprehensive guide for public sector professionals, scholars, and policymakers, delving into the challenges and opportunities brought about by digital transformation in Human Resource Management (HRM). The chapter provides a nuanced understanding of theoretical foundations, practical strategies, and real-world implications in digital workforce planning and management. By emphasizing talent management, technological integration, and strategic decision-making, it inspires proactive approaches to thrive in the digitally-driven landscape. Through integration of insights from the African public sector, it highlights the importance of aligning digital strategies with ethical considerations and leveraging technological capabilities. In conclusion, the chapter aims to empower public sector entities to adapt and succeed in the digital era, fostering organizational resilience and long-term success while addressing societal needs.

Chapter 3
Drivers of Digital Transformation and Their Efficacy in Public Sector Human Resource Management 39
Andrew Enaifoghe, University of Zululand, South Africa
Nduduzo C. Ndebele, University of KwaZulu-Natal, South Africa
Anuoluwapo Durokifa, University of Johannesburg, South Africa
Xolani Thusi, University of Limpopo, South Africa

The chapter examines digital transformation drivers and their efficacy in improving public sector human resource management in the digital age. Implementing Digitalisation in the public sector opens up possibilities for human resource management (HRM) to reform and accelerate the delivery of services using the most advanced digital technologies. Although digital transformation is expected to offer change in the public sector, various challenges may require significant backing to support the HRM function amid waves and shocks posed by digital transformation. The chapter employs a qualitative research methodology drawn from a systematic literature review to comprehensively evaluate the literature on digital transformation and its role in public sector HRM. Search engines such as Scopus, google, and Google Scholar were used to find relevant information on the role of digital transformation in enhancing public sector HRM. Keywords such as "digital transformation", "public sector", "HRM", "were used in streamlining the search for the study for the study. Findings from the literature indicated several impediments, such as unreformed bureaucratic culture, staff resistance to change, and budget constraints that threaten digital transformation in public sector HRM. The conclusions drawn for this chapter suggest optimisation techniques, which include strengthening the HRM's information security system while encouraging a digitally-driven culture among staff members, which is key to improving digital skills and accelerating the public sector HRM for improved service delivery.

Chapter 4
Examining the Challenges of Adopting Modern Technologies in Public Sector Human Resource Management 60
Standa Sani, Africa University, Zimbabwe
Siphiwe Plaxedes Mandina, De Montfort University, Zimbabwe

HRM in the public sector is undergoing digital transformation, presenting opportunities and challenges. This chapter examines ethical considerations, strategic planning, teamwork, monitoring, and adaptation. It addresses algorithmic bias, emphasizing transparency, accountability, and fairness. The digital divide and equal access are crucial. Interagency collaboration and compatibility enable effective information exchange. Ongoing monitoring and adaptability maximize technology usage and employee satisfaction. Recruitment, Onboarding, Performance Management, and Engagement Technologies are explored. Communication, change leadership, and legal factors are highlighted. This chapter provides a roadmap for successful digital transformation, encompassing ethics, collaboration, inclusivity, and technology integration.

Chapter 5
Leveraging Human Resource (HR) Analytics for Effective Talent Management in Public Sector Organisations 90
Blessing Takawira, University of Johannesburg, South Africa
Misheck Musaigwa, University of Johannesburg, South Africa
Vivence Kalitanyi, University of Johannesburg, South Africa

The book chapter explores how HR analytics may improve talent management in the African public sector. Through case studies and theoretical insights, the chapter emphasises the adoption and influence of HR analytics on many aspects of talent management, such as recruiting performance evaluation, employee retention, and leadership development. The chapter explores the advantages and obstacles of adopting HR analytics, including issues like data protection, the need for HR professionals to enhance their analytical skills, and opposition to data-driven methods due to cultural factors. The implications for public sector HR management are significant, indicating a trend towards evidence-based HR approaches that closely align with organisational goals and strategic imperatives. The chapter ends by highlighting the importance of further research in HR analytics to gain a more profound insight into its lasting effects, addressing obstacles to its adoption and ethical concerns, and investigating regional differences in the African setting.

Chapter 6
Digital Transformation in Hiring and Selection Processes: A Ugandan Public Sector Perspective... 115
Alexander Markey Oluka, European University Viadrina, Germany
Elvin Shava, University of KwaZulu-Natal, South Africa

The study explores the digital transformation of public sector hiring in Uganda, highlighting the potential of digital technologies to revolutionise recruitment by enhancing efficiency, accessibility, and transparency. Automation, online platforms, and data-driven decision-making serve to streamline administrative tasks, expand candidate outreach, and promote merit-based hiring. Despite these benefits, significant challenges including data security risks, technological failures, digital divides, and algorithmic biases necessitate strategic intervention. Through document analysis and qualitative research, this study draws on policy documents and government reports to outline current practices and future prospects. It emphasises the need for robust infrastructure, improved digital literacy, and clear policy frameworks to support digital adoption while mitigating risks. Effective leadership and a supportive organisational culture are crucial to successfully navigating the digital shift, aiming to achieve an effective, inclusive, and transparent public sector hiring process in Uganda.

Chapter 7
Embracing Transformative Digital Human Resource Management in the Nigerian Public Sector ... 130
Oluwaseun Temitope Ojogiwa, University of KwaZulu-Natal, South Africa
Sibongile Ruth Nhari, University of KwaZulu-Natal, South Africa

The Fourth Industrial Revolution is generating changes in every element of society. The implication of this digital transformation continues to vary based on the readiness, available resources, and the level of development of each nation and organisation. Digital transformation is anticipated to have a far-reaching positive effect of modernising public organisations through the HR element. This chapter, based on a desktop review, explores the adoption of digital HRM in the unique context of the Nigerian public sector, characterised by inefficient bureaucratic structures, obsolete methods that foster nepotism, and limited innovation. The literature presents opportunities for transforming the longstanding HRM challenges in the sector. However, the adoption of digital HRM is faced with resistance from the workforce, political interference, inadequate infrastructures, and a lack of necessary digital skills. Digital HRM can be propelled by a strong will and commitment from all stakeholders to align with technological change imperatives and foster a more responsive sector.

Chapter 8
Navigating the Future! Exploring the Impact of Digital Hiring and Selection Processes in South African Municipalities 145
Beauty Zindi, University of Johannesburg, South Africa

As South African municipalities navigate the complexities of modern workforce dynamics, the adoption of digital hiring and selection processes emerges as a critical strategy to address recruitment challenges and drive organizational success. This paper explores the impact of digital transformation on hiring practices within South African municipalities. Through a comprehensive analysis of the benefits, challenges, and future outlook of digital hiring, this study sheds light on the transformative potential of technology in municipal recruitment processes. Drawing on practical examples and case studies, the paper examines the role of digital tools and platforms, the implications on municipalities, and the strategies for overcoming barriers to adoption. Furthermore, article discusses emerging trends, such as AI-driven recruitment, virtual assessments, and remote work adaptation shaping the future landscape of municipal hiring practices.

Chapter 9
Performance Contracts for Senior Administrators in "Unsettled" Political and Economic Contexts: A Zimbabwean Local Government Perspective............ 162
Tawanda Nyikadzino, University of Johannesburg, South Africa
Shikha Vyas-Doorgapersad, University of Johannesburg, South Africa

Zimbabweans are interested in seeing how local governments will perform in providing services in the era of devolution and digital transformation. Scholars have begun to examine and evaluate the significance of devolution and digital transformation in a nation with a history of dictatorship and centralised authorities in decision-making processes. To enhance the performance of devolved local governments, the Government of Zimbabwe (GoZ) introduced a performance management system in 2020 as a Human Resources Management reform that mandates all local governments to have performance contracts for senior administrators. The introduction of performance contracts for senior administrators arose from the need to address persistent service delivery and administrative challenges in local governments, particularly urban local authorities. Policymakers believed that the introduction of a performance management system for senior administrators would enhance digital transformation, public value and fundamental principles of local governance, namely, effectiveness, efficiency, economy, accountability, responsiveness, and integrity. There have been relatively few studies investigating implementation experiences since a performance management system that placed senior local government administrators on performance contracts was introduced. Consequently, the topic of performance contracts and how Zimbabwe's unstable political and economic environment affects their execution is covered in this chapter. Data to address the preceding question was generated qualitatively through documentary reviews and key informant interviews. Since the performance contract system is relatively new, the authors conducted some key informant interviews to gain insights into the implementation experiences. The chapter found that the unsettled economic and political contexts and sluggish digital transformation pose an existential threat to its implementation. Economic instability, poor revenue generation, brain drain and associated human capacity constraints, political influence and the nature of performance contracts and assessment framework compromise the viability of performance contracts. To improve the implementation of performance contracts, the chapter recommends the Office of the President and Cabinet (OPC) review the performance contracts in light of implementation experiences. The review process should be done in a participatory manner so that the views of the implementing agencies are heard and factored in. The chapter also recommends the use of digital systems to enhance the implementation of performance contracts.

Chapter 10
Revolutionizing Public Sector Human Resources: A Digital Frontier for Innovative Transformation 185
Vumani Mbatha, University of KwaZulu-Natal, South Africa
Andrisha Beharry Ramraj, University of KwaZulu-Natal, South Africa
Idris Ganiyu, York St. John University, UK

The Industrial Revolution 4.0 sometimes known as the Fourth Industrial Revolution (4IR) has gathered momentum, and it calls for faster production rates, more flexible scheduling, and better customer services. The advent of automated and digital technologies has already revolutionised many private industries and has the potential of revolutionising public sector human resource management in South Africa. However, the South African public sector has been lagging in digital transformation. The integration of digital advancements in Human Resource Management (HRM) within the South African public sector is imperative considering the need to improve the delivery of public goods and services. The existing Human Resource Management (HRM) processes used in the recruitment of public officials are outdated and prone to biases, which can negatively impact talent acquisition, diversity, inclusion, and employee morale. This chapter aims to delve into specific strategies and approaches necessary for effectively implementing digital transformation initiatives in HRM within the public sector context. The chapter utilised a document analysis and conceptual analysis, where traditional scholarly and peer-reviewed sources on public sector human resource management and digital examination were examined. The analysis of documents pointed to key findings regarding the pivotal role of revolutionising Public Sector HRM through digital skills development which is critical in driving the transformation of the public sector in the 4IR. The findings reflected further the underlying impact of revolutionising public sector HRM which lies in enhancing individual and organizational productivity. Human Resources (HR) emerges as a strategic facilitator in this process, necessitating job redesign and organizational restructuring to foster readiness and innovation. However, there is a notable gap in understanding tailored strategies for the unique challenges faced by the South African public sector. Policy frameworks are identified as critical enablers of ethical and effective digital transformation in HR processes.

Chapter 11
Digitalisation of Employee Performance Evaluation to Advance Public Sector Human Resource Management 202
Syanda A. Mthuli, School of Management, University of KwaZulu-Natal, South Africa

The evaluation of the performance of government remains one of the most fiercely debated in democracies and problematic in countries. While today's digital age affects all aspects of life, necessitates change including the integration of advanced technologies to aid policy implementation & public service delivery performance. The efficiency of governments and the positive develop of humans is said to be tied to innovation and technological progress. This study explores the digitalisation of employee performance evaluation in human resource management in South Africa's bureaucracy, with an objective to explore its contribution as a panacea for policy implementation & public service delivery ills in the country. The findings point to that in the public service in the country employee performance evaluation remains outdated though policy documents call for the integrating information communication technology. A digitalised performance measurement (e-performance management and e-HRM) in the country would add value and have a positive impact as has been long established in the private sector.

Chapter 12
The Impact of Talent Retention and Management Practices on Service Delivery Outcomes in the South African Public Service 222
Thokozani Ian Nzimakwe, University of KwaZulu-Natal, South Africa
Sindy Olive Mbele, University of KwaZulu-Natal, South Africa

Talent management requires the identification of talented employees who work in the organisation. The South African public service continues to have a high concentration of an ageing workforce within its management and leadership occupational levels which poses a risk to business continuity. Poor recruitment practices linked to political interference have led to the appointment of inadequate leaders in key positions thus stifling leadership potential and service delivery outcomes. The South African public service aims to develop talent for service excellence which drives all talent-related initiatives within the organisation. This chapter explores variables such as compliance with regulatory provisions, talent acquisition, talent development, employee performance, digital hiring, digital workforce and succession planning, and digital transformation. Digital transformation influences human resource factors and contributes to enhancing productivity.

Chapter 13
Positioning Digital Transformation of Public Sector Human Resources in Zimbabwe and South Africa: Challenges and Opportunities... 239
Lewis Edwin Chigova, North-West University, South Africa
Costa Hofisi, North-West University, South Africa

This chapter notes that in Zimbabwe and South Africa, where challenges such as service delivery, economic instability, and technological disruptions are prevalent, the potential of advanced technologies to reshape the public service workforce is recognised. However, very few studies position the digital transformation of HRM within these countries' contextual constraints and opportunities necessitating a need for more systematic inquiries. The study draws from various peer-reviewed articles and expansive policy documents on the digital transformation of HRM in the public sector in South Africa and Zimbabwe. It found that while the two countries have recognised the importance of digital transformation in HRM and laid down frameworks to support this transition, their paths diverge on implementation effectiveness and the challenges faced. Strategic and administrative hurdles impede South Africa's journey, whereas infrastructural and HR constraints deeply challenge Zimbabwe's. The study recommends that these countries must establish solid digital transformation strategies for HRM.

Chapter 14
Talent Management in the Digital Age: Leveraging Technology to Enhance Public Sector Recruitment and Retention in Zimbabwe 259
Raymond Mapuranga, Midlands State University, Zimbabwe
Kebiat Mukuze, Midlands State University, Zimbabwe
Abigail Maravanyika, Reformed Church University, Zimbabwe

Using the integrative literature review as the research methodology, this chapter explores the role of technology in talent management within the public sector, specifically focusing on recruitment and retention strategies. The chapter highlights the unique challenges faced by public sector organizations in talent acquisition and retention, such as limited budgets, bureaucratic processes, and the perception of a less dynamic work environment. The chapter revealed that various technologies can be utilized to improve recruitment efforts in the public sector including the use of applicant tracking systems, online job portals, and social media platforms. The study concluded that technology could contribute to talent retention in the public sector through the role of digital platforms in fostering employee engagement, facilitating knowledge sharing and collaboration, and providing continuous learning opportunities. Lastly, the chapter provides practical recommendations for public sector organizations looking to leverage technology for recruitment and retention.

Compilation of References 278

About the Contributors 323

Index 327

Preface

As editors of "Digital Transformation in Public Sector Human Resource Management," we are delighted to present this comprehensive exploration of the intersection between modern digital technologies and the evolving landscape of public sector human resources management. In an era marked by the pervasive influence of the Fourth Industrial Revolution (4IR), the imperative for digital transformation in African public institutions cannot be overstated.

The digital age, characterized by an array of transformative technologies such as cloud computing, artificial intelligence, big data, blockchain, and the Internet of Things (IoT), has fundamentally altered the dynamics of public sector human resources management. This book delves into the imperative for reform within human resources management processes, aligning them with emerging concepts and models in the rapidly evolving technological environment.

Our aim is to provide insights into how digital transformation can render public sector human resources management more responsive to evolving stakeholder needs, enhance performance evaluation mechanisms, cultivate conducive workplace environments, promote digital competitiveness, and facilitate informed decision-making in hiring, selection, training, and development.

Drawing on diverse examples and case studies from public administration, we examine existing impediments that may hinder the effective implementation of digital reforms, the adoption of modern technologies, and the implementation of innovative strategies aimed at enhancing efficiency and effectiveness in the delivery of public goods and services.

This book is designed to serve as a valuable resource for a wide range of professionals and individuals engaged in the field of public sector human resources management. From scholars and consultants to researchers, analysts, public managers, policy makers, and students, the insights offered here are relevant to anyone seeking to understand and navigate the complexities of digital transformation in the public sector.

The chapters within this book cover a broad spectrum of topics, including understanding digital transformation, drivers and challenges, the role of HRM in driving change, deployment of modern digital technologies, digital workforce planning and management, talent acquisition and retention, performance evaluation, diversity and inclusion, HR analytics, disruptive innovations, and best practices for implementing digital technologies.

We extend our gratitude to all the contributors who have enriched this volume with their expertise and insights. It is our hope that this book will serve as a catalyst for informed discourse and action, ultimately contributing to the advancement of public sector human resources management in the digital age.

In this edited reference book on "Digital Transformation in Public Sector Human Resource Management," we have gathered insightful contributions from scholars and experts in the field. Each chapter offers a unique perspective on the challenges and opportunities presented by the integration of digital technologies into various aspects of public sector HRM. Here's an overview of the chapters:

The first chapter by Leon Poshai and Kudakwashe Intauno examines the impact of digital technologies on recruitment and selection processes in African public sector institutions, highlighting both opportunities and challenges. They argue that in public sector human resource management, particularly in the areas of recruitment and selection of employees, the deployment of technology has enabled human resources managers to eliminate physical interactions in the processes of talent acquisition through the digitalization of the human resource management function.

The second chapter by Ayler Beniah Ndraha offers a comprehensive guide for public sector professionals, scholars, and policymakers, delving into the challenges and opportunities brought about by digital transformation in Human Resource Management (HRM). The chapter further provides a comprehensive guide to navigating digital transformation in HRM, emphasizing talent management, technological integration, and strategic decision-making.

In chapter three, Andrew Enaifoghe, Nduduzo Ndebele, Anuoluwapo Durokifa and Xolani Thusi broadly explore the drivers of digital transformation in HRM, assessing their effectiveness and addressing challenges such as corporate culture and resistance to change. These authors argue that better protections for the public sector are required as a result of the combination of digital transformation and HRM ideas, which provide new difficulties for employees to overcome.

Chapter four, Standa Sani and Siphiwe Plaxedes Mandina explore the classification of modern technologies commonly adopted in public sector HRM and examine various types of modern technologies used in recruitment, on-boarding, performance management, and employee engagement within the public sector.

In chapter five, Blessing Takawira, Misheck Musaigwa and Vivence Kalitanyi explore how HR analytics may improve talent management in the African public sector. The chapter emphasizes the adoption and influence of HR analytics on many aspects of talent management, such as recruiting performance evaluation, employee retention, and leadership development. The chapter ends by highlighting the importance of further research in HR analytics to gain a more profound insight into its lasting effects, addressing obstacles to its adoption and ethical concerns, and investigating regional differences in the African setting.

Chapter six, Alexander Markey Oluka and Elvin Shava explore the digital transformation of public sector hiring in Uganda, highlighting the potential of digital technologies to revolutionize recruitment by enhancing efficiency, accessibility, and transparency. The chapter argues that effective leadership and a supportive organizational culture are crucial to successfully navigating the digital shift, aiming to achieve an effective, inclusive, and transparent public sector hiring process in Uganda.

In chapter seven, Oluwaseun Temitope Ojogiwa and Sibongile Ruth Nhari explored the adoption of digital HRM in Nigeria, highlighting opportunities and challenges in the context of bureaucratic structures and limited innovation. These authors argue that digital HRM can be propelled by a strong will and commitment from all stakeholders to align with technological change imperatives and foster a more responsive sector.

Chapter eight, Beauty Zindi explores the impact of digital transformation on hiring practices within South African municipalities. Through a comprehensive analysis of the benefits, challenges, and future outlook of digital hiring, this chapter sheds light on the transformative potential of technology in municipal recruitment processes. Drawing on practical examples and case studies, the paper further examines the role of digital tools and platforms, the implications on municipalities, and the strategies for overcoming barriers to adoption.

In chapter nine, Tawanda Nyikadzino and Shikha Vyas-Doorgapersad evaluate the implementation of performance contracts in Zimbabwean local governments, addressing challenges and opportunities in an environment of political and economic instability. They argue that the introduction of performance contracts for senior administrators arose from the need to address persistent service delivery challenges in local governments, particularly urban local authorities.

Chapter ten, Andrisha Beharry Ramraj and Idris Ganiyu explore strategies for bolstering digital capabilities in South African public sector HRM. These authors suggest strategies for bolstering digital capabilities in public sector HRM and the key policy considerations for digital transformation. In conclusion, the chapter emphasise the need for the South African public sector to embrace digital advancements in HRM and address challenges like ICT illiteracy through targeted training.

Chapter eleven, Syanda Mthuli investigates the digitalization of employee performance evaluation in human resource management in South Africa's bureaucracy, with an objective to explore its contribution as a panacea for policy implementation & public service delivery ills in the country. He concludes that the public service in the country employee performance evaluation remains outdated though policy documents call for the integration of information communication technology.

In chapter twelve, Thokozani Ian Nzimakwe and Sindy Olive Mbele explore talent management practices in South Africa, addressing challenges and opportunities in the context of an ageing workforce and political interference. These authors conclude that digital transformation influences human resource factors and contributes to enhancing productivity.

In chapter thirteen, Lewis Edwin Chigova and Costa Hofisi evaluate digital transformation within public sector HR in Zimbabwe and South Africa by highlighting contextual constraints and opportunities for implementation. They contextualise digital transformation efforts within the unique country characteristics of public sector HRM. The authors recommend that these countries establish solid digital transformation strategies for HRM.

In chapter fourteen, Raymond Mapuranga, Kebiat Mukuze and Abigail Maravanyika explore the role of technology in talent management within the public sector, specifically focusing on recruitment and retention strategies. These authors provide practical recommendations for recruitment and retention strategies.

Each chapter contributes valuable insights to the discourse on digital transformation in public sector HRM, offering a roadmap for navigating the complexities of the digital age and enhancing organizational effectiveness and efficiency.

In compiling "Digital Transformation in Public Sector Human Resource Management," our aim was to provide a comprehensive exploration of how modern digital technologies intersect with the evolving landscape of public sector HRM. As we conclude this edited reference book, we reflect on the wealth of insights shared by our contributors across diverse topics.

From the examination of digital workforce planning and management to the exploration of talent acquisition, retention, and performance evaluation, each chapter has contributed valuable perspectives and practical strategies for navigating the challenges and opportunities presented by digital transformation.

Through case studies, theoretical analyses, and practical recommendations, our contributors have shed light on the imperative for reform within HRM processes, aligning them with emerging concepts and models in the rapidly evolving technological environment.

As editors, we are grateful to all the contributors who have enriched this volume with their expertise and insights. It is our hope that this book serves as a catalyst for informed discourse and action, ultimately contributing to the advancement of public sector HRM in the digital age.

We believe that the insights offered in this book will be valuable to a wide range of professionals and individuals engaged in the field of public sector HRM, from scholars and consultants to policymakers and practitioners. By embracing digital transformation, we can enhance organizational effectiveness, promote inclusivity and diversity, and ultimately improve the delivery of public goods and services to citizens.

We extend our gratitude to all who have contributed to this project, and we look forward to the continued dialogue and collaboration in the ongoing journey of digital transformation in public sector HRM.

Editors:

Elvin Shava
University of KwaZulu Natal, South Africa

Nduduzo C. Ndebele
University of KwaZulu Natal, South Africa

Chapter 1
Streamlining Public Sector Human Resource Recruitment and Selection Processes Through Digitalisation:
Prospects and Challenges for African Bureaucracies

Leon Poshai
https://orcid.org/0000-0003-1829-6025
Midlands State University, Zimbabwe

Kudakwashe Intauno
https://orcid.org/0000-0003-4305-5709
University of Duisburg-Essen, Germany

ABSTRACT

The Fourth Industrial Revolution (4IR) has had a profound impact on technological advancements in different development sectors around the world through digitalisation. In public sector human resource management, particularly in the areas of recruitment and selection of employees, the deployment of technology has enabled human resource managers to eliminate physical interactions in the processes of hiring employees through the digitalisation of the human resource management function. Through a desktop review methodology, which is anchored on the conceptual content analysis technique, this chapter argues that the digitalisation of recruitment and selection processes has created opportunities to curb challenges such as bureaucratic delays, nepotism and corruption which undermine fairness in the hiring processes. However, as the chapter reveals, challenges such as underdeveloped technological infrastructure, resistance to change, lack of digital literacy skills and the digital divide continue to plague the efforts to digitalise recruitment and selection processes in public sector institutions in African bureaucracies.

DOI: 10.4018/979-8-3693-2889-7.ch001

INTRODUCTION

The public sector refers to the collection of institutions that are managed and controlled by the government (Ansell & Torfing, 2021). Institutions in the public sector include central government ministries, departments, agencies and the local government. Public sector institutions provide a wide range of services to the citizens, including but not limited to education, public healthcare, electricity, water and sanitation, transport, defence, policing and law enforcement (Kuwali, 2024). The public sector is regarded as the biggest employer in any country as it requires many employees (Erin et al., 2024). Many people often prefer to work in the public sector because of the high job security and tenure of employment in comparison to the private sector. In the same vein, many experienced workers often leave public sector institutions to search for better salaries in the private sector. Moreover, public sector institutions continue to expand their mandate and size, which makes them require more personnel. For these reasons, public sector institutions never stop recruiting. The role of human resource managers in the public sector is highly demanding as they deal with many applications throughout the year.

In the 4IR era, which is characterised by rapid technological advancements, the public sector urgently needs to modernise its human resource recruitment and selection processes through digitalisation. Digitalisation depicts the augmented use of digital and computer technologies to facilitate work processes (Dabić et al., 2023). Recruitment is concerned with attracting qualified candidates for a vacant or newly formed job role while selection entails the systematic process of selecting the right candidate for the job from the pull of applicants (Metz, 2022). As governments across the African continent strive to establish more efficient, transparent, and meritocratic systems for hiring talent, it is crucial to understand the transformative potential of digitalisation in recruitment and selection. This chapter provides a unique analysis that not only highlights the benefits of embracing digital tools in human resource management but also recognises the unique challenges that undermine digitalisation initiatives in the African context.

The emergence of digital technologies offers an opportunity to enhance public sector human resource recruitment and selection by addressing biases embedded in talent hiring through human interface platforms (Singh & Sahoo, 2023). Habitually, in African countries such as Nigeria, Tanzania, Zimbabwe and South Africa, the competition for jobs is intense because of high job demands, which leaves job seekers susceptible to fraudulent or clandestine recruitment and selection practices (Okolie & Irabor, 2017; Zinyama, 2021; Mokgolo & Dikoltla, 2023; Saad & Itika, 2024). Subsequently, by being the key human resource management functions, responsible for deciding who joins the organisations and who does not, the recruitment and selection process is often infested by nepotism and corrupt tendencies (Mugari et al., 2023). In some cases, formal recruitment is never done, or when it is done, it is only a formality because the advertised jobs would have been 'taken' already by those with 'effectual ties' with the human resource managers (Choto & Poshai, 2023; Metz, 2022). Thus, the use of technology can enable applicants to send their job applications directly to the human resource managers or recruitment and selection officers. While these benefits are glaring, implementing digital solutions in the African context comes with challenges. These challenges include underdeveloped technological infrastructure, socio-economic disparities, and cultural distinctions.

The digitalisation of recruitment and selection procedures in the public sector is one of the essential transformations in contemporary African bureaucracies. Previous research has concentrated on the utilisation of big data to inform human resource management practices like recruitment and selection in the public sector (Majam & Jarbandhan, 2022) and the integration of Artificial Intelligence in these processes (Chilunjika et al., 2022). Majam and Jarbandhan (2022) also emphasise the benefits of employing big data in human resource management, including improved talent retention, selection, recruitment, and performance management, as well as addressing legal and ethical concerns. Furthermore, Chilunjika et al. (2022) contend that adopting digital tools in recruitment can diminish bureaucratic obstacles and enhance the responsiveness of public sector human resource organisations in Africa. However, existing literature primarily discusses the use of digital capabilities in the public sector and its impact on human resource practices, with limited studies specifically investigating how digital methods can usher total optimisation of recruitment and selection processes in public sector human resources. Consequently, there is a gap in the extant literature concerning the evaluation of the current state of the digitalisation of public sector human resource recruitment and selection in African contexts.

This chapter contributes to the current literature and the academic discourse on human resource management by providing a guide for understanding the opportunities and challenges associated with digitalising public-sector human resource practices in Africa. Given the many job applications received by public sector institutions, the chapter will expose how the paper-based approach recruitment and selection strategies have become inefficient in managing the hiring process in the public sector. Specifically, it offers enlightening perspectives on the advantages of digitalising public sector recruitment and selection in Africa, such as increased efficiency, reduced time-to-hire, and improved transparency and accountability. In addition, it acknowledges the challenges that arise, such as concerns related to the digital divide, data security issues, and the potential for biases in algorithmic decision-making. By doing so, the chapter aims to inform policymakers, HR professionals, and technology developers on how to navigate the complexities of digital transformation for optimal outcomes in the public sector across the African continent. The chapter argues that digitalisation has become a critical reform strategy for streamlining human resource recruitment and selection processes in the public sector, which helps to create a competent workforce for improving the effectiveness of public sector institutions in Africa.

METHODOLOGY

This study aimed to understand the strategies, opportunities and challenges associated with streamlining public sector human resource recruitment and selection in Africa. The study used a scoping review approach in which sources of secondary data were analysed. Document analysis, which is the systematic procedure for reviewing or evaluating documents in both printed and electronic formats (Bowen 2009; Morgan, 2022) enabled the researchers to analyse a diverse body of purposefully selected extant literature such as research papers, books, and Internet sources. In selecting the secondary documents for analysis, the researchers used a dual strategy. The first step in this strategy was to set the criteria for source identification and the criteria for source screening for eligibility and inclusion into the sampled documents for review. The secondary sources were identified from academic repositories such as Web of Science databases, and Google Scholar among others. The criteria for identifying the sources were based on themes such as merits of public sector digital recruitment and selection, challenges of public sector digital recruitment and selection, and platforms for public sector digital recruitment and selection among other themes germane to the topic under investigation. Key phrases such as digitalisation of public sector human resource recruitment and selection were used to identify key sources. This first step generated a total of 167 documents, and the next step was to set the criteria for screening the most relevant documents from the initial 167 documents.

The second step was to set the eligibility criteria for the selection of documents for the sample. This criterion involved a perusal of the abstracts, title and introduction of identified documents to check their relevance to the subject investigated. After this perusal, 98 documents were found relevant to the subject matter of digitalising public sector human resource recruitment and selection. However, this number was considered too high for the review; hence, the publication timeframe criterion was applied to further screen the documents. The timeframe of the publications was also considered in the second step as priority was given to sources from 2014-2024. This helped to capture contemporary debates and developments on the use of technology to facilitate recruitment and selection processes in the context of the public sector in Africa since the dawn of the 4IR. Nevertheless, literature from 2020 was prioritised based on the fact that 2020 was the year when digital recruitment and selection dominated many institutions because of the COVID-19 pandemic constraints which halted the physical submission of job application documents and physical interview sessions. After applying this criterion, 56 research papers met the criteria set. Inductive content analysis, which refers to the systematic and rigorous examination of purposefully sampled secondary material (Anderson & Lemken, 2023; Vears & Gillam, 2022), was employed to interpret data from the documentary review with relevant themes developed through the coding process. The 56 research papers were then reviewed using thematic analyses to distil relevant information on the scope of streamlining public sector human resource recruitment and selection through digitalisation as presented in this chapter.

RESULTS AND DISCUSSION

This section presents and discusses the main findings on streamlining public sector human resource recruitment and selection processes through digitalisation the context of African bureaucracies. The section begins with an analysis of the state of digitalisation in the African public sector.

The State of Digitalisation in the African Public sector

Public sector digitalisation refers to the adoption of information technology to transform service delivery processes (Alvarenga et al., 2020). Digitalisation in African bureaucracies started at the beginning of the twentieth century, and since then, it has taken an upward trajectory although the pace of digitalisation is different from country to country (Rademacher & Grant, 2019). In Kenya, for example, digitalisation in the public sector has resulted in the turnaround of government functions such as tax administration, justice delivery and general public service delivery (Meru & Kinoti, 2022). In the pre-digital era, the administrative operations of public sector institutions in Africa were largely manual and public administrators were inundated with laborious paperwork which made their roles cumbersome (Senyo et al., 2021). In countries such as Rwanda, digitalisation, dubbed as the paperless regime, brought about efficiency, and innovation in the operations of the public sector by removing the red tape that plagues the pre-digital era (Mukamurenzi et al., 2019). In Ghana, for example, the adoption of digital technologies in the public sector has brought opportunities for improved service delivery in areas such as national health insurance, public finance management and education delivery (Ayakwah et al., 2021).

However, the current state of digitalisation in Africa reflects that the full utilisation of digital systems is being marred by many obstacles. In Zimbabwe, the rising cybersecurity threats are also impeding the digitalisation of the public sector as citizens fear that their safety may be infringed on cyberspace (Poshai et al., 2023). In other parts of Africa, such as Nigeria, Tanzania, Ghana and South Africa, challenges such as the lack of adequate ICT resources, lack of funds to subscribe to ICT functional software applications, inadequate system upgrades, the lack of ICT training, the lack of understanding of existing and emerging digital tools have all contributed to the underutilisation of the digital systems in Africa's public sector (Camngca et al., 2024).

To improve the digitalisation of public sector institutions in Africa, there is a need to invest in ICT infrastructure developed to enable uninterrupted Internet connection for public administrators. In addition, governments must adequately support their agencies, units and departments with sufficient digital devices to enable them to transform their administrative functions from analogue to digital. In addition, public sector employees must be equipped with digital skills through regular training, to enable them to obtain the required ICT competencies for using digital tools. Moreover, African governments should strengthen their cybersecurity enforcement systems to enhance data safety and the privacy of citizens when interacting with public institutions in cyberspace.

The Fourth Industrial Revolution (4IR) and the Transformation of Public Sector Recruitment and Selection Processes in African Public Sector Institutions

The use of advanced technologies, including Artificial Intelligence (AI), Robotics, and the Internet of Things (IoT), in the Fourth Industrial Revolution has the potential to significantly transform public sector recruitment and selection processes in Africa. By automating repetitive and time-consuming tasks, such as application screening and initial candidate assessments, this shift towards automation aims to streamline and optimise the recruitment process (Chilunjika et al., 2022). For example, AI systems revolutionise the recruitment process by performing tasks previously performed by professional recruiters (Chen, 2023). Consequently, the integration of these smart technologies can reduce the workload on public sector human resource personnel, leading to faster and more efficient recruitment outcomes. Below are some of the ways in which the 4IR capabilities can transform public sector human resource recruitment and selection processes.

Improved accuracy and objectivity in the evaluation of candidates: The 4IR has the potential to improve the accuracy and objectivity of candidate evaluations by utilising advanced data analytics and machine learning algorithms to process large amounts of data and identify essential skills, experience, and credentials (Majam & Jarbandhan, 2022). By adopting a data-driven approach, the 4IR capabilities such as the AI eliminate biases in the recruitment and selection process and promote fairness, inclusiveness, and efficiency, resulting in high-quality outcomes in less time and at a lower cost than humans (Raja-Santhi & Muthuswamy, 2023). In African countries such as Zimbabwe, South Africa, Tanzania and Nigeria, public sector recruitment and selection are plagued with biases, undermining the value of meritocracy and, ultimately, the quality of the public sector workforce (Chilunjika et al., 2022). However, streamlining recruitment and selection processes with cutting-edge technologies to reduce bias leads to the formation of diverse and competent teams in public sector organisations across Africa that more accurately represent the population they serve. As Nhede et al. (2022) emphasise, the functioning of public services is heavily influenced by the quality of the human resource. This makes it important for African bureaucracies to minimise shoddy hiring decisions by using technological capabilities in recruitment and selection.

Enhanced flexibility in the hiring process: In addition, the 4IR, which provides a means of conducting remote and flexible hiring processes, reduces geographical barriers to accessing recruitment offices and allows organisations to tap into a wider talent pool (Anand & Radha, 2020). For instance, smart interview and assessment tools powered by IoT devices can be integrated into virtual interview platforms to create an intelligent hiring process (Chen, 2023). With the aid of facial recognition technology and sentiment analysis, recruiters can gain deeper insights into a candidate's reactions and emotions during interviews (Nhede et al., 2022). The data can then be used to supplement traditional assessment methods, enabling recruiters to make more nuanced evaluations of a candidate's interpersonal skills and emotional intelligence. Thus, by embracing digital transformation, public sector entities in Africa can attract and engage candidates from diverse backgrounds, thereby fostering a more inclusive workforce.

Improved workforce planning and HR decision-making: Incorporating 4IR capabilities in the African public sector gives organisations a transformative opportunity to revolutionise their workforce planning and decision-making processes through AI and data-driven approaches (Nhede et al., 2022). By continuously analysing recruitment data, public sector entities can gain valuable insights into patterns and trends that enable them to evaluate the effectiveness of their strategies. For example, organisations can tailor their approaches for more targeted and efficient hiring of talent by examining the success rates of different recruitment channels or identifying key competencies in successful hires. Improved public service delivery is a direct outcome of this approach as it enables the identification and deployment of the right talent in areas critical to addressing societal needs (Strohmeier, 2020). In essence, integrating the 4IR principles empowers African public sector organisations to optimise their human resource, resulting in enhanced efficiency and effectiveness in delivering essential services to the public.

The Flaws of Paper-based Public Sector Recruitment and Selection Strategies in African Bureaucracies

Post-colonial African bureaucracies have relied heavily on traditional paper-based recruitment and selection strategies (Okeke-Uzodike & Subban, 2015). However, these methods have been hindered by several intrinsic issues that diminish efficiency and transparency (Metz, 2022). Some of the main flaws of paper-based public sector recruitment and selection strategies in African bureaucracies are presented below.

Labour-intensive and cumbersome applications processing: One notable drawback associated with paper-based public sector recruitment and selection strategies is the labour-intensive handling of applications, résumés, and other documents, which results in time-consuming and error-prone processing. In African countries such as Zimbabwe and South Africa, the recruitment and selection process of public services is notorious for being bogged down by paperwork (Chilunjika et al., 2022). This outdated approach not only extends the recruitment cycle but also raises the likelihood of misplaced or missing documents, casting doubt on the fairness and integrity of the selection process. Moreover, traditional recruitment methods are less effective because of their substantial time investment and lack of guarantee of optimal results (Chen, 2023).

Restricted accessibility to online application systems: Paper-based recruitment and selection systems are associated with restricted accessibility, particularly for applicants in remote or rural locations that have inadequate infrastructure (Chilunjika et al., 2022). Consequently, potential candidates in these areas may encounter difficulties in accessing and submitting their applications, ultimately leading to an unbalanced representation in the applicant pool (Anand & Radha, 2020). This absence of inclusivity perpetuates existing inequalities and hinders the objective of fostering a diverse and inclusive public-sector workforce in African countries. For instance, in Zimbabwe, the government is the largest employer and more than half of the population resides in rural areas where the infrastructure is inadequate to support and sustain paper-based job applications in government job openings. Most of the job seekers travel to the big towns to just be able to file their job applications physically, a process which inherently disadvantages most of them. This is against the provision of Zimbabwe's Public Service Act [Chapter 16:04] which emphasises impartial and inclusive recruitment procedures (Musopero & Lee, 2021).

Inconsistencies and biases in the evaluation and grading of candidates: Moreover, the use of traditional paper-based methods frequently results in a lack of uniformity in the evaluation and grading of applicants. The subjective nature of manual evaluations can result in biased, inconsistent, or biased results, compromising the merit-based principles that underpin public-sector recruitment (Chilunjika et al., 2022). This can erode the public's confidence and trust in the recruitment process, creating an opportunity for corruption or favouritism. For instance, in South Africa, during recruitment, interviewing and appointment stages, abuses of power, undisclosed conflicts of interest and even patronage by political heads and top-and-middle management are acutely rife in public service (Mokgolo & Dikotla, 2023).

Communication delays in the recruitment and selection process: The inefficiencies in paper-based recruitment systems in the public sector in Africa extend to the communication process between government agencies and applicants, resulting in delays in transmitting critical information to candidates (Okeke-Uzodike & Subban, 2015). Conventional methods, such as postal services or in-person notifications, are inefficient and contribute to a lack of timely communication (Saad & Itika, 2024). This not only causes frustration among applicants but also poorly reflects the government's commitment to transparency and responsiveness. For instance, in Zimbabwe, after submitting paper-based applications, candidates are expected to physically visit Public Service Commission (government's recruitment agent) offices to inquire about the status of their applications. This procedure can lead to candidates missing employment opportunities if they do not make timely and accurate guesses of the dates to check the status of their applications. This situation is even more challenging for job candidates residing in remote areas with no convenient access to government recruitment agency offices. Consequently, the civil service recruitment process involves a substantial amount of paperwork and unnecessary delays that are detrimental to the efficiency of the recruitment process (Musopero & Lee, 2021).

Corruption and nepotism: Corruption in public sector employment often manifests through patronage in the hiring of new employees or promotion of incumbents (Colonnelli et al., 2020). In Africa, patronage has been a prevalent issue in traditional paper-based human resource recruitment and selection processes. Research conducted by Chilunjika et al. (2022) highlights the extensive human interface involved in these procedures, which creates opportunities for unscrupulous practices such as kickbacks. In Lesotho, the paper-dominated public service recruitment and selection process has been marred with bias and petty corruption, resulting in the availability of job opportunities for underqualified individuals at the expense of meritocratic recruitment (Rakolobe, 2019). Similarly, nepotism has been prevalent in Malawi's manually administered public sector recruitment process especially in Malawi Energy Regulatory Authority as revealed by Mtuwa and Chiweza (2023). As evidenced by these examples, this opacity inherent in paper-based systems allows for malfeasance to flourish, as individuals exploit their positions for personal gain, compromising the integrity of the recruitment process and hampering the meritocratic principles that underpin public sector appointments. Efforts to modernise and digitise these administrative procedures, incorporating transparency measures, and reducing reliance on intermediaries may help mitigate the prevalence of petty corruption in public service recruitment and selection in African bureaucracies.

Opportunities Emerging from Digitalising Public Sector Recruitment and Selection Processes in African Bureaucracies

Utilising digitalisation to improve public sector recruitment and selection processes in Africa offers opportunities to enhance efficiency, transparency, and inclusivity (Baku, 2022). The section below presents some of the main opportunities associated with embracing digital platforms for public sector human resource recruitment and selection.

The ability to attract a larger pool of candidates: Digital systems also enable recruiters to access a broader pool of candidates through online platforms, removing geographical barriers, and ensuring equal opportunities for individuals from different regions (Anand & Radha, 2020). In Ghana's public higher education institutions, for example, digital recruitment systems have enabled universities to expeditiously disseminate information about available vacancies, thereby reaching a wider pool of potential candidates within short periods (Ayakwah, 2021). In Zimbabwe, the Public Service Commission's e-recruitment portal has also allowed the government to widen the net for potential candidates. This accessibility fosters diversity and ensures a more inclusive workforce, addressing historical issues of underrepresentation in public sector roles.

Enhanced storage of job application documents: Digitalising the recruitment process allows human resource managers to securely keep applicants' documents in case of future job openings (Bondarouk et al., 2017). Public universities such as the University of Namibia (UNAM) have an e-recruitment portal that collects and stores data on the résumés, applications, interview evaluations, reference checks, results of physical examinations, employment test reports, documentation of tests used in the recruitment process (Hashiyana et al., 2021). In addition, the organisation's e-recruitment portals can also store data for candidates who are not selected in their initial application, as their information can be used to consider them for future job vacancies.

Automation of labour-intensive HR tasks: The integration of digital technology has also facilitated the automation of labour-intensive tasks, such as applicant screening and initial evaluations, resulting in considerable time savings and increased efficiency in the recruitment process (Majam & Jarbandhan, 2022). This automation enables human resource professionals to concentrate on more strategic aspects of candidate evaluation (Chilunjika et al., 2022). By streamlining the process, public sector organisations in Africa can alleviate administrative burdens and reallocate resources to identify the most suitable candidates for various positions. For instance, countries such as Tanzania have recently modernised their public service recruitment processes by adopting digital capabilities such as e-recruitment (Saad & Itika, 2024). This transformation was necessitated by numerous instances of opacity and lack of competitiveness in the conventional recruitment method (Saad & Itika, 2024).

Reduction of operational costs: Digitalised recruitment and selection platforms reduce operational costs by eliminating paperwork and improving information processing and management (Shirase et al., 2023). For instance, advertising in print media such as newspapers and journals is expensive (Musopero & Lee, 2021). However, digitalising human resource recruitment and selection entails increased HR efficiency as this means doing more with less time as well as less operational and administrative costs. Through digital means, an organisation can receive many applications within a short space of time, unlike the traditional method where submissions can take several days. Through digital recruitment and selection platforms, the skills of applicants can also be assessed quickly and feedback can be given instantly (Setianingrum et al., 2023). Digital human resource recruitment and selection promotes flexibility and convenience in hiring employees by allowing online submission of job application documents and virtual interviewing (Gilch & Sieweke, 2021).

Combating corruption in the recruitment and selection process: Digital technologies have become essential tools for combating the prevalence of petty corruption in public sector human resource management systems (Baku, 2022). Traditional African bureaucracies, which have long been associated with manual recruitment and selection practices often create opportunities for corruption. However, the integration of digital solutions introduces transparency and accountability, thus reducing the risks associated with corrupt practices (Saad & Itika, 2024). The use of digital innovations in public sector service delivery helps to eliminate petty corruption (Sadik-Zada et al., 2022). Advanced software and online platforms streamline the entire recruitment process, from job posting to application submission, ensuring that each step is traceable and accessible. For example, the corruption associated with the human interface can be curtailed through digitalisation as physical interactions are replaced with interactive machines and ICTs as has been the case in countries such as Kenya, Nigeria and Tanzania (Kuwali, 2024). Automated recruitment systems not only expedite the process but also minimise human intervention, which could be susceptible to corruption (Baku, 2022). The use of data analytics and Artificial Intelligence enhances the effectiveness of these systems by identifying irregularities or biases in the selection process (Kshetri, 2021). Thus, the transition to technology-driven solutions is a crucial step towards building more efficient and corruption-resistant public sector recruitment and selection practices in Africa.

Enhancing fairness in the hiring process: Digital technologies play a crucial role in integrating data analytics and Artificial Intelligence into public sector recruitment and selection. This ensures fair evaluation of job applicants which is essential in maintaining integrity in human resource management (Majam & Jarbandhan, 2022). Advanced analytics allows for a comprehensive examination of large datasets, enabling the identification of trends, patterns, and correlations between candidate qualifications and performance. In the context of Africa, by incorporating cutting-edge technologies and adopting a data-driven approach, governments can make objective decisions and reduce the reliance on subjective judgments in recruitment and selection (Chilunjika et al., 2022). Thus, the use of AI ensures fairness by treating all candidates equally during résumé screening (Chen, 2023). Therefore, by leveraging these technologies, African public sector organisations can establish a more equitable and merit-based recruitment system, addressing the current challenges in public service recruitment and selection processes.

Improving communication during the recruitment and selection process: Digital platforms have transformed the recruitment process by providing real-time communication and updates to job seekers (Anand & Radha, 2020). This immediate feedback on the application status improves the overall candidate experience, while enhancing transparency and accountability (Saad & Itika, 2024). Historically, timely communication has been a challenge for African government agencies regarding the recruitment and selection of public service personnel. However, the use of digital platforms now allows applicants to receive prompt information regarding interview schedules, assessment results, and other important updates. For instance, the use of big data can be useful in reducing the time between advertising and filling a vacant post whilst the use of AI can assist in getting rid of biases in the selection process which is important in the selection of the best candidate possible based on their competencies (Majam &

Jarbandhan, 2022). This perception of the public sector as a responsive and modern employer has been strengthened.

Possible Digital Systems for Streamlining Public Sector Human Resource Recruitment and Selection Processes in African Bureaucracies

The use of digital tools not only accelerates the application and evaluation procedures but also helps overcome pervasive challenges such as bias and favouritism. This unwavering dedication to digital innovation demonstrates a strong commitment to cultivating a fair and diverse workforce, ultimately contributing to the improvement in public sector productivity and effectiveness within Africa. To achieve these objectives, African public sector human resource can utilise solutions such as Applicant Tracking Systems (ATS), Recruiter Robot, Integrated Human Resource Management Systems (IHRMS) and the Application Portal System to streamline recruitment and selection processes. These digital tools are discussed below.

Applicant Tracking Systems (ATS): Applicant Tracking Systems (ATS) play a crucial role in streamlining recruitment and selection processes in the public sector within African bureaucracies. It offers features such as résumé parsing, automated candidate matching, and reporting, which significantly streamline the recruitment process (AL-Qassem et al., 2023). These systems offer an efficient and organised way to manage large volumes of job applications, making it easier for government agencies to sift through numerous résumés and identify the most suitable candidates for vacant job positions (Memon et al., 2024). In the context of African bureaucracies, where there may be a significant number of applicants for limited positions, ATS can help eliminate manual sorting and screening, saving valuable time and resources. Additionally, ATS can be configured to ensure that recruitment processes adhere to fair and transparent practices, promoting equal opportunities for all applicants (Mansyur, 2023). This is particularly important in the public sector, where transparency and fairness in recruitment are essential for building trust and credibility within the community (Singh & Sahoo, 2023).

Furthermore, ATS in African bureaucracies can enhance collaboration among different departments involved in the recruitment and selection process. These systems enable seamless communication and data sharing, allowing HR professionals and hiring managers across various government departments to collaborate efficiently (Mansyur, 2023). This can lead to a more standardised and consistent approach to recruitment, ensuring that the selection of candidates aligns with the specific needs and criteria set by each department (Singh & Sahoo, 2023). Ultimately, the integration of ATS in the public sector of African bureaucracies not only improves the efficiency of recruitment processes but also contributes to the overall effectiveness and fairness of the selection process, fostering a more accountable and responsive government.

Recruiter Robot: The implementation of a recruitment robot in the recruitment and selection process within African public-sector bureaucracies can lead to significant improvements in terms of efficiency and fairness. Recruitment robots such as chatbots are powered by Artificial Intelligence and are capable of making real-time decisions based on pre-installed algorithms and technologies developed through data analysis to adapt and refine their responses to various situations (Martín-Hernández, 2023). First, a recruitment robot can streamline the initial stages of the hiring process by rapidly scanning through large volumes of résumé and applications and identifying the necessary qualifications and skills for specific roles (Chen, 2023). This accelerates the initial screening process, allowing human recruiters to focus on the more intricate aspects of candidate evaluation (Chilunjika et al., 2022). The use of Artificial

Intelligence algorithms in recruitment can help minimise unconscious biases in the selection process, promoting a more diverse and inclusive workforce within the public sector (Krasivskyy et al., 2023). By utilising data-driven decision-making, the recruitment process in African bureaucracies can become more transparent, reducing the likelihood of nepotism or favouritism, thereby fostering a merit-based approach to hiring.

In addition, a recruiter robot can enhance the responsiveness and accessibility of the recruitment process in African bureaucracies. In regions where bureaucratic processes may be characterised by delays and inefficiencies, an automated system can facilitate quicker communication with applicants and provide timely updates on the status of their applications (Martín-Hernández, 2023). This can lead to an overall improvement in candidate experience, potentially attracting a broader pool of qualified individuals to public sector positions. Furthermore, the use of a recruiter robot can assist in the standardisation of hiring procedures, ensuring that all candidates are evaluated against the same criteria, thereby promoting fairness and equity (Chen, 2023). Ultimately, the introduction of a recruiter robot in recruitment and selection processes in African bureaucracies has the potential to modernise and optimise these processes, contributing to the overall effectiveness and professionalism of the public sector.

Integrated Human Resource Management System (HRMS): The Integrated Human Resource Management Systems (HRMS) play a crucial role in revolutionising recruitment and selection processes within the public sector of African bureaucracies. These systems streamline and automate various HR functions, enhancing efficiency and reducing administrative burdens (Paramita, 2020). In the context of recruitment, HRMS can facilitate the creation of centralised databases that store candidate information, making it easier for hiring managers to access and evaluate candidate profiles (Bilgic, 2020). Algorithmic decision-making is becoming increasingly common as a new source of advice in HR recruitment and development, especially in trying to avoid human biases (Köchling & Wehner, 2020). In the public sector, where transparency and adherence to regulations are paramount, integrated HRMS can ensure compliance with hiring policies, monitor diversity and inclusion metrics, and generate comprehensive reports for auditing purposes. These systems go beyond recruitment, incorporating modules for talent management, performance appraisal, and workforce planning (Turnea & Aruştei, 2023). Workday, for instance, offers a unified platform for various HR functions, promoting efficiency and data consistency throughout the entire employee lifecycle (Bilgic, 2020). In African bureaucracies, these systems can incorporate Artificial Intelligence algorithms to analyse résumé, match qualifications, and identify potential candidates, thus expediting the initial screening process.

Furthermore, the use of HRMS in the selection process can lead to improved decision-making and better alignment with organisational goals (Nyathi & Kekwaletswe, 2023). These systems can standardise assessment processes, ensuring that each candidate undergoes consistent evaluations based on predetermined criteria. In the African public sector, where bureaucratic structures can be complex and multi-layered (Musopero & Lee, 2021), HRMS can help streamline communication and collaboration among various stakeholders involved in the selection process. Integration with performance management modules can also provide insights into candidates' potential for career development and long-term success within the organisation (Bilgic, 2020). Overall, the implementation of integrated HRMS in recruitment and selection in African bureaucracies can enhance transparency, reduce biases, and contribute to the overall effectiveness of the public sector in serving its constituents.

Application Portal System (APS): The APS receives, organises and securely stores electronic and digitised paper applicant records (Al-Alawi et al., 2023). The applicant can also use the same platforms to receive timely updates about their status in the recruiting process. Recruiters can instantly search and have access to the information they require about applicants and make faster and smarter hiring decisions (Dabić et al., 2023). The digital platforms for receiving applications will be set up to automatically screen out applicants who do not meet the criteria set. AI and Big Data can be used to set up such a screening criterion as these capabilities can be used to create knock-out questions for checking the documents uploaded and verify if the application should be considered further or screened out at the time of submission (Majam & Jarbandhan, 2022). Artificial Intelligence can also be used to verify an applicant's criminal record and knock out criminals at the time of applying (Ketolainen, 2018). These digital applications can help recruitment officers quickly compile a database of eligible application documents when there is an influx of résumé for vacant positions. This is beneficial for public sector human resource recruitment and selection processes in African bureaucracies as the APS creates convenience for both the job seekers and the recruitment managers in the public sector.

Obstacles Faced in Transitioning from Paper-based to Digitalised Recruitment and Selection of Human Resource in the Public Sector in African Bureaucracies

Lack of organisational preparedness: In public HRM, processes such as talent and recruitment can be digitalised to facilitate the determination of candidates with the right competencies and qualifications for a specific job. However, most public sector organisations are still at the early stages of maturity regarding the successful deployment of ICTs for recruitment and selection processes (Majam & Jarbandhan, 2022). In South Africa, for example, organisational readiness regarding the use of big data, AI and machine learning to optimise organisational effectiveness is still at an infancy stage due to departmental incapacity to absorb technology as revealed by Capelli et al. (2020) cited in Majam & Jarbandhan (2022).

Shortage of devices and undeveloped ICT infrastructure: The availability of digital tools and advanced ICT infrastructure constitute the foundation of effective digitalisation. For instance, ICT infrastructure such as computers, and Internet connection devices such as fibre optic cables and satellites are essential requirements for the successful adoption and use of digital systems in the public sector (Poshai & Vyas-Doorgapersad, 2023). However, the shortage of relevant devices and underdeveloped ICT infrastructure are the main challenges to the adoption of digitalised recruitment and selection systems in most developing countries (Singh et al., 2023). These challenges culminate in weak or unreliable Internet connectivity which negatively affects the successful transition from analogue to digital recruitment and selection. In the context of African bureaucracies, therefore, the shortage of devices and underdeveloped ICT infrastructure make it difficult for HR managers to regularly check the applications submitted on their organisations' e-recruitment portals.

Resistance to change due to lack of digital skills: Contemporary human resource managers must have relevant digital competencies and skills to navigate the evolving digital workplace environment. Relevant digital skills will help HR managers quickly embrace technological changes such as the adoption of digital recruitment and selection platforms. In many digital transformation processes, however, resistance to change is caused by the lack of digital skills and fear of the technological skills demands of the new systems adopted (Poshai, 2017). Thus, HR managers need to be able to efficiently use those technological tools that streamline the recruitment processes (Paramita, 2020). However, some HR managers may not have the relevant ICT skills to embrace digital recruitment and selection as they may not understand the process correctly. As a result, such practitioners may resist the digital transformation process as they will consider it a daunting task that may expose their ICT illiteracy (Gilch & Sieweke, 2021). Such HR managers will resist any digital innovation in recruitment and selection if they perceive it as difficult to use (Shirase et al., 2023). Thus, in the context of African bureaucracies, it is highly likely that when HR managers consider that the use of digital tools is incompatible with their technological competencies, they will not support the initiatives. This resistance should therefore be confronted with regular ICT training to enable the HR managers to obtain relevant ICT skills for using digital recruitment and selection platforms.

Inaccurate assessment of potential employees: The use of automated systems to screen applicants on the submission portal can be misleading (Shirase et al., 2023). For example, the automation screening criteria can be based on factors such as the highest qualification to determine eligibility, but this factor may not properly give an accurate reflection of the applicant's current attributes and potential. The applicant may have other superior skills such as good customer relations skills and excellent communication skills that may be required by the job, but not reflected by the level of qualification (Chigora et al., 2022). Such human skills may not be noticed by a computerised system and this may result in the rejection of potentially good candidates for the job. Thus, factors in the automated eligibility screening criteria may result in misleading decisions being made (Setianingrum et al., 2023). Owing to these challenges, human resource managers may not properly assess if the candidate uses a culture fit for the organisation since it is impossible to capture some human aspects that may be important in making the hiring decision (Okolie & Irabor, 2017).

In addition, since the résumés will be uploaded online, there is no guarantee of the authenticity and correctness of the information provided by the applicants (Okolie & Irabor, 2017). Since digital job portals cannot filter fake information, it is also difficult for HR managers to judge the personality of candidates online before shortlisting them (Gilch & Sieweke, 2021). The accuracy, verifiability, and accountability of applicants' data are also major issues for HR managers whose organisations use digital recruitment systems (Saad & Itika, 2024). Thus, some candidates applying for job positions in public sector institutions in African countries may overestimate the experience they have or other abilities to match the job requirements to get shortlisted.

Cybersecurity issues: When online recruitment is used, application documents are kept in cyberspace, in the institutional database until the processes of screening and shortlisting commence (Novac & Ciochină, 2017). However, there is no guarantee that the documents stored in online databases will be secured from unauthorised access (Poshai et al., 2023). Thus, the integrity of data in cyberspace often derails the effective adoption of digital platforms (Ketolainen, 2018) and this affects such as digital public sector human resource recruitment and selection systems. For example, cybercriminals can hack an organisation's HR database and compromise the privacy of the applicant's data (Odegov et al., 2019). The shortage of organisational cybersecurity expertise further intensifies the threats to the use of technology to facilitate HRM functions and other processes in contemporary organisations (Raja-Santhi & Muthuswamy, 2023). Thus, while organisations' recruitment sites display privacy statements that detail how the information applicants provide will be stored safely, generally, digital recruitment raises concerns among potential applicants about keeping their personal information secure and confidential (Omolawal, 2015). For African bureaucracies, therefore, digital recruitment threatens data privacy as it could expose the personal information of the applicants after unauthorised access to the databases containing the applicant's information.

Lack of user awareness: Digital awareness is required to maximise the benefits of digitalization (Chigora et al., 2022). The potential gap in technological knowledge limits the ability of human resource managers to adopt and use digital tools for recruitment and selection as well as for facilitating other human resource management functions (Njoku et al., 2019). Thus, HR managers must properly understand the digitalisation process for them to adopt digital platforms in the talent acquisition process (Shirase et al., 2023). The potential lack of awareness of digital recruitment and selection platforms by some HR managers in African bureaucracies can therefore dent the successful adoption and use of these systems.

Digital divide: The adoption of digital recruitment and selection platforms in African bureaucracies is marred by the digital divide. The digital divide refers to the gap between people who have access to modern information and communications technology (ICT) and those who do not or have restricted access to broadband Internet service and wireless technologies (Soomro et al., 2020). For example, in countries such as Zimbabwe, some government offices are located in remote rural areas where there is poor to non-existent Internet connectivity (Poshai, 2017). As a result, it is difficult for human resource managers in such areas to effectively use digital recruitment systems since these platforms require a strong internet connection. Thus, factors such as poor internet connectivity, and shortage of devices can widen the digital divide leading to the dysfunctionality of digital recruitment and selection systems in African bureaucracies.

Success Factors for Strengthening the Transition from Analogue to Digital Public Sector Human Resource Recruitment and Selection in African Bureaucracies

Leadership Commitment: Leaders in African bureaucracies should demonstrate genuine commitment towards digitalising recruitment and selection processes. The successful adoption of digital public sector human resource recruitment and selection systems is largely hinged on the commitment of top management towards the value created by digital tools in the organisation (Martinus, 2022). Top management support is an integral factor in determining the success of human resource management digitalisation processes (Bloom & Bengtsson 2017). This means that when the leadership of an organisation perceives the digital public sector human resource recruitment and selection systems as useful, then they can motivate its adoption and use in the entire human resource management department leading to the availing of resources for supporting such initiatives. Njoku et al. (2019) found a strong and positive correlation between top management's perceived usefulness of digital systems and their subsequent adoption in an organisation. For example, the setting up of an organisational portal for receiving and processing job applications depends on the leadership's view of the usefulness of such digital systems in facilitating the recruitment and selection process (Rakhy & Vijayan, 2018). Contrariwise, if the leadership of an organisation does not see value in adopting digital public sector human resource recruitment and selection systems, then the integration of technology in human resource management functions will not be motivated.

Financial resources for investing in ICT infrastructure: Public sector institutions in Africa must mobilise financial resources for investing in ICT infrastructure if the digitalisation of the recruitment and selection process is to be successful. The cost of implementing the digitalisation of HR is very high (Shirase et al., 2023). Thus, the capacity to acquire digital resources required to digitalise public sector human resource recruitment and selection systems is critical for their adoption. It can therefore be argued that if an organisation has readily available financial resources to procure digital tools and set functional portals, then it is easy for the organisation to quickly digitalise public sector human resource recruitment and selection systems. On the other hand, an organisation experiencing financial challenges will face difficulties in acquiring relevant technologies for implementing digital public sector human resource recruitment and selection systems (Novac & Ciochină, 2017). Therefore, the adoption of new digital technologies requires significant financial investments, and one of the biggest obstacles faced by organisations transforming digitally stems from insufficient budgets (Abdali, 2019). Thus, because of limited financial resources, organisations find it difficult to use digital tools (Shirase et al., 2023). In addition, financial resources are also required to procure robust software systems to guard against cybersecurity threats and related cyber-criminal activities against unauthorised access to databases (Poshai et al., 2023).

Digital literacy: Digital recruitment and selection revolve around the use of computers, smart devices and the Internet, hence the development of digital skills for employees should be a priority area in African bureaucracies. While digitalising the recruitment and selection process brings convenience and efficiency to the talent acquisition process, it requires human resource managers to become conversant with the use of digital technologies (Rakhy & Vijayan, 2018). Therefore, the transition from analogue to digital recruitment and selection is a challenging task as it requires investments in digital technology as well as upgrading the technological skills of human resource managers (Ghazzawi & Accoumeh, 2014). Institutions intending to use digital human resource recruitment systems must set up online platforms to advertise jobs and receive applications from eligible applicants (Singh et al., 2023).

The adoption of digital recruitment and selection systems in the public sector in Africa requires substantive investments in ICT training and upgrading the technological use capabilities of human resource managers. The ability of HR Managers to configure computer hardware, software and electronic networking resources for facilitating e-recruitment practices is pivotal. Thus, digital skills and talents by HR managers are a prerequisite for the digitalisation of public sector human resource recruitment and selection processes (Al-Alawi et al., 2023). Top management should organise regular refresher courses and ICT skills upgrading workshops for their HR managers. Some applicants may lack digital skills and they may make mistakes in completing the application forms thereby diminishing their chances of being selected by the automated systems (Okolie & Irabor, 2017). Therefore, African bureaucracies will not succeed if the Human resource managers do not have the requisite technological competencies to deploy technology in conducting HR functions such as recruitment and selection.

CONCLUSION

The chapter analysed the opportunities and challenges associated with the process of streamlining public sector human resource recruitment and selection processes through digitalisation in African bureaucracies. The analysis helped to dissect and appreciate the importance of adopting digital systems for facilitative public sector human resource recruitment and selection, as well as the weaknesses associated with such digital transformations. The chapter also explored opportunities that lie ahead in the public sector, with human resource managers fully embracing digitalisation for recruitment and selection processes.

REFERENCES

Al-Alawi, A. I., Messaadia, M., Mehrotra, A., Sanosi, S. K., Elias, H., & Althawadi, A. H. (2023). Digital transformation adoption in human resources management during COVID-19. *Arab Gulf Journal of Scientific Research*, 41(4), 446–461. 10.1108/AGJSR-05-2022-0069

AL-Qassem. A. H., Agha, K., Vij, M., Elrehail, H., & Agarwal, R. (2023, March). Leading Talent Management: Empirical investigation on Applicant Tracking System (ATS) on e-Recruitment Performance. In 2023 international Conference on Business Analytics for Technology and security (ICBATS) (pp. 1-5). IEEE.

Alvarenga, A., Matos, F., Godina, R., & Matias, CO, J. (. (2020). Digital transformation and knowledge management in the public sector. *Sustainability*, 12(14), 5824. 10.3390/su12145824

Anand, J., & Radha, S. (2020). E-Recruitment: An Advantage Over Traditional Recruitment. *International Journal of Advanced Research in Management, Architecture. Technology and Engineering*, 6(4), 1–15.

Anderson, M. H., & Lemken, R. K. (2023). Citation context analysis as a method for conducting rigorous and impactful literature reviews. *Organizational Research Methods*, 26(1), 77–106. 10.1177/1094428120969905

Ansell, C., & Torfing, J. (2021). *Public governance as co-creation: A strategy for revitalizing the public sector and rejuvenating democracy*. Cambridge University Press. 10.1017/9781108765381

Ayakwah, A., Damoah, I. S., & Osabutey, E. L. C. (2021). Digitalization in Africa: The Case of Public Programs in Ghana. In Abugre, J.B., L.C. Osabutey, E., P. Sigué, S. (Eds.) *Business in Africa in the Era of Digital Technology. Advances in Theory and Practice of Emerging Markets* (pp.7-25). Cham: Springer.

Baku, A. A. (2022). Digitalisation and new public management in Africa. In R.E. Hinson, N. Madichie, O. Adeola, J… (Eds.), *New Public Management in Africa: Contemporary Issues* (pp.299-316). London: Palgrave Macmillan Cham. 10.1007/978-3-030-77181-2_12

Bilgic, E. (2020). Human Resources Information Systems: A Recent Literature Survey, In M.A. Turkmenoglu, M.A. & B. Cicek, B. (Eds.), *Contemporary Global Issues in Human Resource Management* (pp. 73-87), Leeds: Emerald Publishing.

Bondarouk, T., Parry, E., & Furtmueller, E. (2017). Electronic HRM: Four decades of research on adoption and consequences. *International Journal of Human Resource Management*, 28(1), 98–131. 10.1080/09585192.2016.1245672

Bowen, G. A. (2009). Document Analysis as a Qualitative Research Method. *Qualitative Research Journal*, 9(2), 27–40. 10.3316/QRJ0902027

Camngca, V. P., Amoah, C., & Ayesu-Koranteng, E. (2024). Underutilisation of information communication and technology in the public sector construction project's implementation. *Journal of Facilities Management*, 22(1), 1–20. 10.1108/JFM-10-2021-0128

Chen, Z. (2023). Collaboration among recruiters and Artificial Intelligence: Removing human prejudices in employment. *Cognition Technology and Work*, 25(1), 135–149. 10.1007/s10111-022-00716-036187287

Chigora, P., Poshai, L., & Mcilo, A. (2022). Challenges with Online Teaching and Learning Under Covid-19 Lockdown in Selected Zimbabwean Universities. *Journal of Public Administration and Development Alternatives*, 7(2), 36–49. 10.55190/RDHC9092

Chilunjika, A., Intauno, K., & Chilunjika, S. R. (2022). Artificial Intelligence and public sector human resource management in South Africa: Opportunities, challenges, and prospects. *SA Journal of Human Resource Management*, 20(0), a197212. 10.4102/sajhrm.v20i0.1972

Choto, T. B., & Poshai, L. (2023). The Politics and Public Administration nexus in the practice of Football Administration in Zimbabwe. *Administrative Theory & Praxis*, 45(4), 1–17. 10.1080/10841806.2023.2282924

Colonnelli, E., Prem, M., & Teso, E. (2020). Patronage and selection in public sector organizations. *The American Economic Review*, 110(10), 3071–3099. 10.1257/aer.20181491

Dabić, M., Maley, J. F., Švarc, J., & Poček, J. (2023). Future of digital work: Challenges for sustainable human resources management. *Journal of Innovation & Knowledge*, 8(2), 100353. 10.1016/j.jik.2023.100353

Enaifoghe, A. (2021). Digitalisation of African Economies in the Fourth Industrial Revolution: Opportunities for Growth and Industrialisation. *African Journal of Development Studies*, 11(2), 31–53.

Erin, O., Adegboye, A., & Uwuigbe, U. (2024). Public sector transparency and sustainable development: A focus on Sub-Saharan Africa. *Journal of Public Affairs*, 24(1), e2885. 10.1002/pa.2885

Ghazzawi, K., & Accoumeh, A. (2014). Critical success factors of the e-recruitment system. *Journal of Human Resources Management and Labor Studies*, 2(2), 159–170.

Gilch, P. M., & Sieweke, J. (2021). Recruiting digital talent: The strategic role of recruitment in organisations' digital transformation. *German Journal of Human Resource Management*, 35(1), 53–82. 10.1177/2397002220952734

Hashiyana, V., Ujakpa, M. M., Suresh, N., Mukaya, K. T., & Mukupi, B. (2021, May). E-Recruitment System: A Case of Namibian Government. In *2021 IST-Africa Conference (IST-Africa)* (pp. 1-8). IEEE.

Ketolainen, N. (2018). *Digitalization of human resources – the transformation journey into an automated and data-driven service organization.* Master thesis, University of Applied Sciences Haaga, Helsinki, Finland.

Köchling, A., & Wehner, M. C. (2020). Discriminated by an algorithm: A systematic review of discrimination and fairness by algorithmic decision-making in the context of HR recruitment and HR development. *Business Research*, 13(3), 795–848. 10.1007/s40685-020-00134-w

Krasivskyy, O., Pirozhenko, N., Samborska, O., Harbusiuk, V., & Inozemtseva, O. (2023). A Model for Implementing Digital Personnel Management in Security and Safety for Engineering Enterprises. *International Journal of Safety and Security Engineering*, 13(3), 519–526. 10.18280/ijsse.130314

Kshetri, N. (2021). Evolving uses of Artificial Intelligence in human resource management in emerging economies in the global South: Some preliminary evidence. *Management Research Review*, 44(7), 970–990. 10.1108/MRR-03-2020-0168

Kuwali, D. (2024). Accountable Governance: Fighting Corruption in Africa. In Kuwali, D. (Ed.), *Corruption Proofing in Africa* (pp. 221–234). Routledge. 10.4324/9781003326649-21

Majam, T., & Jarbandhan, D. B. (2022). Data-driven human resource management in the Fourth Industrial Revolution (4IR). *Africa's Public Service Delivery & Performance Review*, 10(1), a588. 10.4102/apsdpr.v10i1.588

Mansyur, N. A. (2023). The challenges of personnel management for public service organizations in the era of technological disruption in Indonesia. *Journal of Management and Administration Provision*, 3(3), 81–92. 10.55885/jmap.v3i3.287

Martín-Hernández, P. (2023). Artificial Intelligence: The Present and Future of Human Resources Recruitment and Selection Processes. *Engineering Proceedings*, 56(1), 188–202.

Martinus, M. S. (2022). The Paradigm Shift from Traditional Public Administration to Sustainable Public Administration. *African Journal of Development Studies (formerly AFFRIKA Journal of Politics, Economics and Society), 12*(2), 99-129.

Memon, M., Soomro, N., & Qazi, S. W. (2024). Mapping Digital Recruitment Tools Using Advanced Convergent Qualitative Meta-integration. *Vision: The Journal of Business Perspective*, 09722629231220989.

Meru, A. K., & Kinoti, M. W. (2022). Digitalisation and public sector service delivery in Kenya. In Adeola, O., Edeh, J. N., & Hinson, R. E. (Eds.), *Digital Service Delivery in Africa: Platforms and Practices* (pp. 229–248). Springer International Publishing. 10.1007/978-3-030-83909-3_10

Metz, T. (2022). African Ethics and Public Governance: Nepotism, Preferential Hiring, and Other Partiality. In K, Ogunyemi, I. Adisa & R.E. Hinson (Eds.), *Ethics and Accountable Governance in Africa's Public Sector, Volume I. Palgrave Studies of Public Sector Management in Africa* (pp.109-129). Cham: Palgrave Macmillan.

Mokgolo, M. M., & Dikotla, M. (2023). Ethical violations: Shortlisting and interviewing processes in the South African public service. *Africa's Public Service Delivery & Performance Review*, 11(1), a648. 10.4102/apsdpr.v11i1.648

Morgan, H. (2022). Conducting a qualitative document analysis. *The Qualitative Report*, 27(1), 64–77.

Mtuwa, S., & Chiweza, A. L. (2023). Implications of Corruption on Public Administration in Malawi. *Journal of Humanities*, 31(1), 91–112. 10.4314/jh.v31i1.5

Mugari, I., Chigwandaza, G. S., & Obioha, E. E. (2023). Citizens' perspectives on the form, contributory factors and impacts of white-collar crimes on local authorities in Zimbabwe. *Cogent Social Sciences*, 9(2), 2248750. 10.1080/23311886.2023.2248750

Mukamurenzi, S., Grönlund, Å., & Islam, M. S. (2019). Challenges in implementing citizen-centric e-government services in Rwanda. *Electronic Government, an International Journal, 15*(3), 283-302.

Musopero, O., & Lee, G. (2021). Examining the Challenges of Implementing Merit-based Civil Servant Recruitment in Zimbabwe. *International Journal of Public Administration and Management Research*, 6(2), 84–99.

Nhede, N. T., Mazenda, A., & Masiya, T. (2022). The South African public service and the Fourth Industrial Revolution. *Africa's Public Service Delivery and Performance Review*, 10(1), 420. 10.4102/apsdpr.v10i1.420

Njoku, E., Ruel, H., Rowlands, H., Evans, L., & Murdoch, M. (2019). An Analysis of the contribution of e-HRM to sustaining business performance. In Bissola, R., & Imperatori, B. (Eds.), *HRM 4.0 For Human-Centered Organizations*. Emerald Publishing Limited. 10.1108/S1877-636120190000023003

Novac, C., & Ciochină, R. S. (2017). The Impact of The Digital Era on Human Resources Management. Social Media as Recruiting Environment for Potential Candidates. *Management and Leadership*, 2017, 97–107.

Nyathi, M., & Kekwaletswe, R. (2023). Realizing employee and organizational performance gains through electronic human resource management use in developing countries. *African Journal of Economic and Management Studies*, 14(1), 121–134. 10.1108/AJEMS-11-2021-0489

Odegov, J., Malakhova, E., & Garnov, A. (2019, February). Digitalization of Business Processes in Human Resources Management of Russian Industrial Enterprises. In *International Conference Communicative Strategies of Information Society (CSIS 2018)* (pp. 93-97). Atlantis Press. 10.2991/csis-18.2019.19

Okeke-Uzodike, O. E., & Subban, M. (2015). Public sector recruitment policies: Efficiency, effectiveness and consequences. *Problems and Perspectives in Management*, 13(1), 26–34.

Okolie, U. C., & Irabor, I. E. (2017). E-recruitment: Practices, opportunities and challenges. *European Journal of Business and Management*, 9(11), 116–122.

Paramita, D. (2020). *Digitalization in talent acquisition: A case study of AI in recruitment.* Masters Thesis. Uppsala Universitet, Sweden.

Poshai, L. (2017). *A critical assessment of the e-readiness status of Zimbabwe's public sector institutions: Exploring the Registrar General Department's level of preparedness to utilise the passport application system (2012-2016)* (Masters dissertation, University of Zimbabwe).

Poshai, L., Chilunjika, A., & Intauno, K. (2023). Examining the institutional and legislative frameworks for enforcing cybersecurity in Zimbabwe. *International Cybersecurity Law Review*, 4(4), 431–449. 10.1365/s43439-023-00093-y

Poshai, L., & Vyas-Doorgapersad, S. (2023). Digital Justice Delivery in Zimbabwe: Integrated Electronic Case Management System Adoption. *South African Journal of Information Management*, 25(1), a1695. 10.4102/sajim.v25i1.1695

Rademacher, U., & Grant, T. (2019). Out of Africa: A new perspective on digitalisation in Africa. *Journal for Technology Assessment in Theory and Practice*, 28(2), 41–47. 10.14512/tatup.28.2.s41

Raja-Santhi, A., & Muthuswamy, P. (2023). Industry 5.0 or Industry 4.0 S? Introduction to Industry 4.0 and a peek into the prospective Industry 5.0 technologies. [IJIDeM]. *International Journal on Interactive Design and Manufacturing*, 17(2), 947–979. 10.1007/s12008-023-01217-8

Rakhy, K. S., & Vijayan, S. (2018). Digitalisation in Human Resource Management Process, the Opportunity for the Competence Management in Retail Sector. *International Journal of Pure and Applied Mathematics*, 119(12), 2569–2581.

Rakolobe, M. (2019). Politicised public service and corruption in Lesotho. *The Strategic Review for Southern Africa*, 41(1), 97–121.

Saad, A., & Itika, J. (2024). An Investigation of the Transformation Process from Manual to E-Recruitment in Tanzania Public Service. *Journal of Public Policy and Administration*, 9(1), 1–19. 10.47604/jppa.2254

Sadik-Zada, E. R., Gatto, A., & Niftiyev, I. (2022). E-government and petty corruption in public sector service delivery. *Technology Analysis and Strategic Management*, 34(4), 1–17. 10.1080/09537325.2022.2067037

Senyo, P. K., Effah, J., & Osabutey, E. L. (2021). Digital platformisation as public sector transformation strategy: A case of Ghana's paperless port. *Technological Forecasting and Social Change*, 162, 120387. 10.1016/j.techfore.2020.120387

Setianingrum, H. W., Bisri, B., Widyastuti, T., & Fitra, S. (2023). Virtual reality technologies in a dynamic change of human resources management. [JMAS]. *Journal of Management Science*, 6(4), 673–678.

Shirase, R., Chhibber, P., & Narkhede, A. (2023). Factors Affecting the Successful Digitalisation of Human Resources. In P., Tyagi; N., Chilamkurti; S., Grima… (Eds.), *The Adoption and Effect of Artificial Intelligence on Human Resources Management, Part A* (pp. 99-105). Leeds: Emerald Publishing Limited. 10.1108/978-1-80382-027-920231005

Singh, A., & Sahoo, D. M. K. (2023). Revolutionizing Recruitment: Harnessing the Power of Technology. *Iconic Research and Engineering Journals*, 6(12), 1343–1355.

Singh, G., Tiwari, P., & Garg, V. (2023). HRM Digitalisation: Exploring Success and Outcomes. In P., Tyagi; N., Chilamkurti; S., Grima… (Eds.), *The Adoption and Effect of Artificial Intelligence on Human Resources Management, Part B* (pp. 199-219). Leeds: Emerald Publishing Limited.

Soomro, K. A., Kale, U., Curtis, R., Akcaoglu, M., & Bernstein, M. (2020). Digital divide among higher education faculty. *International Journal of Educational Technology in Higher Education*, 17(2), 1–16.

Strohmeier, S. (2020). Smart HRM–a Delphi study on the application and consequences of the Internet of Things in Human Resource Management. *International Journal of Human Resource Management*, 31(18), 2289–2318. 10.1080/09585192.2018.1443963

Thomas, G. (2020). Digital Maturity of HR in SMEs. *European Journal of Economics and Business Studies*, 6(1), 56–62. 10.26417/ejes.v6i1.p56-62

Turnea, E. S., & Aruştei, C. C. (2023). Augmenting HRM through enhancing the benefits of digital transformation. *Cross Cultural Management Journal*, 2, 105–111.

Vears, D. F., & Gillam, L. (2022). Inductive content analysis: A guide for beginning qualitative researchers. *Focus on Health Professional Education: A Multi-disciplinary Journal, 23*(1), 111-127.

Zinyama, T. (2021). Systemic corruption in Zimbabwe: Is the human factor the missing link? *African Journal of Public Affairs*, 12(1), 132–152.

Chapter 2
Digital Workforce Planning and Management in the Public Sector

Ayler Beniah Ndraha
https://orcid.org/0009-0007-1293-343X
Universitas Nias, Indonesia

ABSTRACT

This chapter offers a comprehensive guide for public sector professionals, scholars, and policymakers, delving into the challenges and opportunities brought about by digital transformation in Human Resource Management (HRM). The chapter provides a nuanced understanding of theoretical foundations, practical strategies, and real-world implications in digital workforce planning and management. By emphasizing talent management, technological integration, and strategic decision-making, it inspires proactive approaches to thrive in the digitally-driven landscape. Through integration of insights from the African public sector, it highlights the importance of aligning digital strategies with ethical considerations and leveraging technological capabilities. In conclusion, the chapter aims to empower public sector entities to adapt and succeed in the digital era, fostering organizational resilience and long-term success while addressing societal needs.

INTRODUCTION

This chapter examines Digital Workforce Planning and Management in the Public sector, with more focus on their impact on digital transformation on Human Resource Management (HRM) Digital transformation in HRM brings significant changes in the way public organisations manage their workforce, necessitating an in-depth understanding of the drivers, tactics applied, obstacles faced, and prospects (Nicolás-Agustín et al., 2021). On a global level, digital transformation has drastically changed the public sector HRM landscape. Digital technologies such as artificial intelligence (AI), big data, and the Internet of Things (IoT) are becoming key pillars in improving operational efficiency and data-driven decision-making in HRM. Research shows that organisations that adopt digital technologies in their HRM processes experience increased productivity and better employee engagement (Deloitte, 2020). However, challenges such as skills gaps and resistance to change are still major obstacles. At an inter-

DOI: 10.4018/979-8-3693-2889-7.ch002

national level, differences in the adoption of digital technologies across countries reflect variations in policies, infrastructure, and organisational readiness. Developed countries tend to have higher adoption rates compared to developing countries, which often face barriers such as limited digital infrastructure and lack of investment in technology (World Bank, 2021). In addition, different data privacy regulations in each country also affect how digital technologies can be applied in HRM. Regionally, especially on the African continent, the adoption of digital technology in HRM is still in its infancy. Some African countries have shown significant progress in digitalization, but challenges such as limited internet access and limited funding are still major barriers. Case studies from various countries in Africa show how governments and public sector organisations are working to overcome these challenges through collaboration with the private sector and digital skills training initiatives (African Union, 2021). In South Africa, digital transformation in public sector HRM faces unique challenges. While the government has launched various initiatives to drive digitalization, such as the e-government strategy, there is still a significant skills gap among the workforce. Succession planning and personnel management are key in ensuring the continuity and effectiveness of digital technology implementation (South African Government, 2022).

This chapter answered the following questions: What are the key factors driving digital transformation in public sector HRM? How can CSR and HRIS contribute to the success of this transformation? What are the key challenges faced by public sector organisations in Africa, particularly South Africa, in adopting digital technologies? These research gaps will be filled with empirical analysis and relevant case studies. To understand digital transformation in HRM, this chapter will use the theoretical framework of the technology adoption model and organisational change theory. This framework will help link the role of CSR in shaping organisational culture and increasing employee engagement and the role of HRIS in streamlining HRM processes and data-driven decision-making. This chapter includes statistics and empirical evidence that support the claims made, such as data on the adoption of digital technologies in public sector HRM, the impact of CSR on employee engagement, and the effectiveness of HRIS. For example, a report from McKinsey (2021) showed that organisations that adopted HRIS experienced a 40% reduction in administrative processing time. The findings from this research have significant practical implications for public sector organisations. By understanding the factors that drive and hinder digital transformation, organisations can develop more effective strategies to improve operational efficiency and employee engagement. In addition, effective CSR implementation can improve organisational culture and overall workforce well-being. This introduction provides a comprehensive foundation for further exploration of digital workforce planning and management in the public sector. By emphasising the relevance of CSR, HRIS, and African case studies, this chapter aims to provide valuable insights and practical strategies for public sector entities in navigating the complexities of the digital age and driving organisational resilience and long-term success.

CONCEPTUAL AND THEORETICAL FOUNDATIONS

In exploring the theoretical foundations of digital workforce planning and management, it is imperative to delve into fundamental concepts of Human Resource Management (HRM), trace its evolution in the digital context, and examine contemporary models shaping workforce planning and management strategies.

1. Basic Concepts of HRM: HRM encompasses a spectrum of principles, policies, and practices aimed at effectively managing an organization's human capital. Fundamental concepts include recruitment, selection, training, performance management, compensation, and employee relations (Gomathy, 2024; Marhil et al., 2023; Järlström et al., 2023; Zhang & Chen, 2023; Sakib, 2023). In the digital era, HRM extends beyond traditional administrative functions to encompass strategic initiatives focused on leveraging technology, fostering innovation, and enhancing employee experiences. The foundation of Human Resource Management (HRM) lies in its fundamental concepts, which encompass a wide array of principles and practices essential for managing an organization's workforce. Recruitment and selection, training and development, performance management, compensation and benefits, and employee relations are fundamental concepts in HRM that underpin strategies for attracting, developing, and retaining talented employees (Konateh et al., 2023). Rigorous selection and recruitment, along with extensive training, are crucial for ensuring a skilled workforce (Sánchez-Marín, 2023). Effective HR strategies significantly impact employee performance (Marhil et al., 2023). In times of crisis, such as during a recession, restructuring and alternatives to downsizing are essential aspects of HRM (Johnstone, 2023). By fostering an innovative culture and utilising innovation-based HR practices, public sector organisations can enhance employees' innovative behaviors (AlMunthiri, 2023).
2. Evolution of HRM in the Digital Context: The evolution of HRM in the digital context signifies a shift from transactional to strategic paradigms. Historically, HRM primarily focused on administrative tasks such as payroll processing and record-keeping. However, advancements in technology have revolutionized HRM practices, enabling the automation of routine tasks and the emergence of data-driven decision-making. The digital transformation has significantly impacted Human Resource Management (HRM), leading to a shift from administrative tasks to strategic functions such as talent management, workforce analytics, and organisational agility. By utilising digital platforms and tools, HRM has been able to automate routine tasks, allowing professionals to focus on strategic initiatives like talent acquisition and development. Data-driven HRM practices, enabled by digitalization, offer valuable insights into workforce trends and performance metrics. This evolution underscores the importance of aligning HR strategies with broader organisational goals, driving digital change, fostering innovation, and enhancing employee experiences (AbdulKareem, 2024; Sposato, 2024; Bonilla-Chaves & Palos-Sanchez, 2023).
3. Contemporary Models in Digital Workforce Planning and Management: Contemporary models in digital workforce planning and management reflect the dynamic nature of the digital landscape and the evolving needs of organisations. Contemporary models in digital workforce planning and management have evolved to incorporate advanced technologies such as artificial intelligence, predictive analytics, and machine learning to enhance HRM processes and decision-making capabilities (Subbaiah, 2024). These models, which include agile workforce planning, predictive workforce analytics, and talent marketplace platforms, aim to improve organisational agility, flexibility, and adaptability in response to the dynamic digital landscape (Gibson, 2024). By utilising advanced technologies and data-driven insights, organisations can optimize their workforce planning processes and enhance overall performance (Heger, 2024). Agile workforce planning, a fundamental aspect of these contemporary models, focuses on continuous iteration and adjustment based on real-time data and feedback, departing from traditional rigid annual planning cycles (Gibson, 2024). Predictive workforce analytics allows organisations to predict future workforce trends and outcomes by analyzing historical data, demographic shifts, and external factors, enabling them to anticipate talent

shortages, identify high-potential employees, and predict turnover risks (Heger, 2024). Additionally, talent marketplace platforms play a vital role in facilitating the agile deployment of talent across projects and initiatives by establishing centralized marketplaces where employees can showcase their skills and interests, while project managers can recruit talent based on specific project requirements (Heger, 2024). These platforms streamline the talent allocation process and ensure that organisational goals align effectively with workforce capabilities in real-time. Incorporating human-centered design principles in these models ensures that HRM initiatives are user-friendly, intuitive, and effective by prioritizing the needs and preferences of employees (Heger, 2024). This approach emphasizes empathy, collaboration, and iteration in designing HRM processes, systems, and experiences, ultimately enhancing employee engagement and satisfaction. Overall, contemporary models in digital workforce planning and management offer organisations a comprehensive framework to navigate the complexities of managing a digital workforce in the modern era, fostering innovation, efficiency, and strategic alignment with organisational goals.

The theoretical foundation underpinning the management and planning of digital workforces in public sectors traces its roots to the evolutionary trajectory of Human Resource Management (HRM), progressing from transactional to strategic paradigms (Wang et al., 2022). This evolutionary journey forms the bedrock for comprehending the intricate dynamics of digital transformation within HRM. Moreover, the integration of Corporate Social Responsibility (CSR) principles into contemporary HRM models is underscored, accentuating stakeholder orientation and its relevance to the themes discussed in this chapter. The infusion of CSR into HRM underscores the ethical and societal dimensions inherent in managing and planning workforces within public sectors. Furthermore, the pivotal role played by Human Resources Information Systems (HRIS) in facilitating digital transformation for efficient HR management is duly acknowledged (Stachová et al., 2019). Leveraging HRIS enables public sector entities to streamline HR processes, fortify data-driven decision-making capabilities, and optimize workforce planning strategies.

Additionally, fostering external partnerships emerges as a crucial strategy for addressing challenges associated with Industry 4.0 within the public sector. Collaborative endeavours with external stakeholders such as industry partners, academic institutions, and non-governmental organisations yield valuable insights and resources to bolster initiatives for digital workforce planning and management. Moreover, the theoretical underpinnings encompass the effective management of human and structural capital for fostering sustainable HRM practices. This entails recognizing the value of human capital in enhancing organisational performance and the imperative of investing in developing digital skills within the workforce (Obermayer-Kovács et al., 2022).

The integration of programs aimed at digital skills development and training initiatives is deemed essential to equip public sector employees with the competencies requisite for excelling in the digital age. Furthermore, the significance of case studies and best practices drawn from African public sector organisations is underscored within the theoretical framework. By incorporating case studies and examples from African contexts, the framework acknowledges the diverse and dynamic nature of challenges and opportunities inherent in the public sector. Drawing upon African experiences in digital workforce planning and management furnishes valuable insights into innovative strategies, cultural considerations, and contextual factors enriching the comprehension of digital transformation in HRM within the public sector.

Moreover, the role of Chief Human Resources Officers (CHROs) in harnessing AI-powered Human Capital Management (HCM) and Human-Computer Interaction (HCI) emerges as a critical aspect of the theoretical framework (Prakash et al., 2021). Integrating AI technologies into HCM and HCI presents opportunities for enhancing talent management, optimizing employee experiences, and informing strategic decision-making within public sector organisations.

In summary, the theoretical foundations of digital workforce planning and management in the public sector constitute a multifaceted framework integrating Corporate Social Responsibility, Human Resources Information Systems, digital skills development, external partnerships, African case studies, and AI-powered technologies. This comprehensive theoretical framework offers a nuanced understanding of the complexities and opportunities associated with digital transformation in public sector HRM. By synthesizing theory, case studies, and innovative strategies, the theoretical foundations illuminate a pathway for public entities to thrive in the digital era, ensuring organisational resilience and sustained success. Furthermore, incorporating African case studies and best practices underscores the global relevance of the theoretical framework and highlights the diverse perspectives enriching the discourse on digital workforce planning and management in the public sector.

UNDERSTANDING DRIVERS OF DIGITAL TRANSFORMATION

The transition to digital HRM within the public sector is influenced by a variety of factors, such as shifts in workforce expectations, technological advancements, and the pursuit of greater efficiency. Additionally, the emphasis on data-driven decision-making and the presence of a digitally savvy workforce accelerates the need for innovative HR practices (Satispi et al., 2023). Furthermore, the drive for digital transformation is amplified by desires for cost reduction, increased agility, and societal movements toward digital governance. Recognizing these drivers is crucial for developing adaptable approaches that align public sector human resource management with the ever-changing landscape of digital revolutions.

In the context of digital workforce planning and management within the public sector, Corporate Social Responsibility (CSR) plays a crucial role in aligning organisational strategies with ethical, social, and environmental considerations. By integrating CSR principles, public sector entities can enhance talent acquisition, retention, and development while fostering a positive work environment and improving their reputation (Roffia & Dabić, 2023). Moreover, the Human Resources Information System (HRIS) serves as a pivotal component in the digital transformation of workforce planning and management. HRIS enables the consolidation of various HR functions into a centralized platform, facilitating data-driven decision-making, operational efficiency, and strategic workforce planning (Kamalakannan, 2024). Through analytics and reporting, HRIS empowers organisations to optimize talent management strategies and adapt to the evolving digital landscape, thereby streamlining HR processes and aligning practices with organisational objectives (Kamalakannan, 2024). Furthermore, examining case studies and best practices from the African public sector enriches the understanding of digital workforce planning and management. Real-world examples offer insights into contextual challenges, innovative solutions, and lessons learned in implementing digital HRM strategies, serving as benchmarks for assessing the effectiveness of initiatives in unique socio-economic and technological dynamics (St-Hilaire, 2024). By incorporating best practices from the African public sector, a diverse perspective on digital transformation is gained, contributing to a more comprehensive exploration of the subject matter (St-Hilaire, 2024).

Based on the review of literature understanding the drivers of digital transformation in the public sector, such as shifts in workforce expectations and technological advancements, is essential for shaping effective digital workforce planning and management strategies. The integration of CSR principles and HRIS capabilities underscores the importance of ethical considerations and technological advancements in HRM practices within the public sector. Additionally, leveraging insights from case studies and best practices from the African public sector enhances the exploration of digital workforce planning and management, offering valuable insights for professionals, scholars, and policymakers in the public sector (Roffia & Dabić, 2023; Kamalakannan, 2024; St-Hilaire, 2024).

STRATEGIES FOR DIGITAL WORKFORCE PLANNING

Strategies for digital workforce planning in the public sector involve a multifaceted approach aimed at aligning organisational objectives with the evolving demands of the digital landscape (Nair, 2019). This entails assessing current and future skill requirements, identifying talent gaps, and implementing targeted training programs to ensure workforce readiness for the digital age. Effective tactics leverage robust HRM systems and analytical technologies to enable well-informed decision-making. Adopting a proactive stance towards talent acquisition and retention is essential for cultivating a workforce capable of driving innovation and fostering sustainable growth.

Digital workforce planning and management in the public sector are increasingly reliant on various strategies and technologies to enhance efficiency and effectiveness. Integrating Corporate Social Responsibility (CSR) principles into workforce planning not only influences talent acquisition and retention strategies but also contributes to building a positive employer brand, crucial for attracting top talent (Rönnblom et al., 2023). Moreover, the utilization of Human Resources Information Systems (HRIS) streamlines HR processes, enables data-driven decision-making, and enhances workforce management efficiency by providing insights for strategic talent planning (AlMunthiri, 2023). In the context of the public sector, the practical application of digital workforce planning strategies can benefit from case studies and best practices, particularly from the African context. These insights offer valuable strategies to address unique challenges and opportunities in digital transformation and workforce management in Africa (Curzi, 2023). Additionally, leveraging Digital HRM Systems is essential for effective digital workforce planning, as these systems optimize talent management strategies and align HR practices with organisational goals (Gintova, 2023). Furthermore, integrating Analytical Technologies for Strategic Planning enhances digital workforce planning efforts by providing valuable insights into trends, skill gaps, and performance metrics, enabling informed decision-making for talent acquisition and development (St-Hilaire, 2024). Highlighting best practices in digital technology implementation offers valuable lessons for public sector organisations embarking on digital transformation journeys, optimizing digital workforce planning efforts and driving positive outcomes in the digital era (Patterson, 2023).

In this sense, a comprehensive approach to digital workforce planning and management in the public sector integrates strategies such as utilising Digital HRM Systems, integrating Analytical Technologies for Strategic Planning, and highlighting Best Practices in Digital Technology Implementation. By leveraging these strategies and insights, public sector organisations can navigate the complexities of digital transformation, enhance workforce readiness, and drive sustainable success in the digital age.

IMPLEMENTATION OF DIGITAL TECHNOLOGY IN HRM

The integration of digital technology into Human Resource Management (HRM) has transformed conventional practices, boosting efficiency, data-driven decision-making, and employee experiences (Halid et al., 2020). This shift enables organisations to strategically plan, utilize talent more effectively, and adapt to evolving workforce needs. Moreover, it cultivates an innovative culture, positioning HRM as a catalyst for organisational flexibility and long-term success in the modern digital landscape. The successful implementation of digital HRM systems hinges on managerial capabilities. The process of converting analog human resource data into digital format for operational and strategic HRM objectives is termed the "digitalization of HRM."

Corporate Social Responsibility (CSR) holds significant relevance in the realm of digital workforce planning and management, particularly in the public sector. As organisations embrace digital HRM transformation, it becomes crucial to consider the ethical and social ramifications of these changes. CSR initiatives encompass various aspects such as environmental sustainability, diversity and inclusion, and ethical technology use. In the public sector, where organisational actions directly impact society, integrating CSR into digital workforce planning and management is imperative.

Ethical technology use is a key facet of CSR in the context of digital workforce planning and management. Public sector entities must ensure that the technologies they adopt adhere to ethical standards and uphold employee privacy and rights. This involves transparent communication regarding data collection and usage, along with implementing safeguards to protect sensitive employee information. Furthermore, CSR initiatives related to diversity and inclusion are highly pertinent to digital workforce planning and management. Organisations leveraging digital technologies must ensure these systems promote diversity and inclusivity, free from bias and discrimination, while actively fostering an inclusive work environment through digital means.

Moreover, environmental sustainability intersects with digital workforce planning and management as a critical aspect of CSR. The integration of digital technologies should aim to minimize the environmental impact of administrative processes, such as adopting paperless HR operations and facilitating remote work through digital tools. By incorporating environmental sustainability into digital workforce planning and management, public sector organisations can demonstrate their commitment to CSR while contributing to broader sustainability goals.

The Human Resources Information System (HRIS) stands as a foundational element in digital workforce planning and management within the public sector. HRIS encompasses the software and systems used for HR processes, including employee data management, payroll, benefits administration, and performance management. In the context of digital transformation, HRIS plays a pivotal role in streamlining HR operations, enhancing data-driven decision-making, and improving overall workforce management.

In the public sector, where efficient HRM is essential for delivering public services, the relevance of HRIS in digital workforce planning and management cannot be overstated. By leveraging HRIS, public sector entities can centralize and automate HR processes, leading to increased efficiency and accuracy in managing workforce data. This not only reduces administrative burden but also enables HR professionals to focus on strategic talent management initiatives.

Moreover, HRIS facilitates data-driven decision-making in HRM by providing comprehensive insights into workforce metrics, performance indicators, and talent analytics. Through the integration of digital technologies, HRIS enables public sector organisations to make informed decisions regarding workforce planning, talent acquisition, and performance optimization. Furthermore, HRIS supports the digitalization of HRM by enabling seamless integration with other digital tools and systems. This interoperability is crucial for public sector organisations seeking to create a cohesive digital ecosystem for workforce planning and management. By integrating HRIS with talent management platforms, learning management systems, and performance evaluation tools, public sector entities can establish a comprehensive digital infrastructure that optimizes HR processes and enhances employee experiences.

Examining case studies and best practices from the African public sector provides valuable insights into the unique challenges and opportunities faced by public sector organisations in the region regarding digital workforce planning and management. African countries present diverse landscapes of public sector operations, with varying levels of digital maturity and distinct socio-economic factors influencing HRM practices. One notable case study is the digital transformation initiatives undertaken by the South African government to modernize its HRM processes. These initiatives highlight the strategic use of digital technology to overcome administrative inefficiencies and enhance HR service delivery in the public sector. Furthermore, best practices in digital workforce planning and management from African public sector organisations emphasize the importance of contextualizing digital strategies to address local workforce dynamics. For instance, mobile-enabled HRIS solutions have been instrumental in extending HR services to remote areas and facilitating access to training and development opportunities in countries with significant rural workforces.

Additionally, the adoption of digital technologies for talent management and capacity building in African public sector organisations has shown promising outcomes. By leveraging e-learning platforms, digital performance management tools, and talent analytics, public sector entities in Africa have enhanced employee skills, improved performance evaluation processes, and identified talent gaps for targeted development interventions.

Incorporating CSR principles and strategically utilising HRIS in digital workforce planning and management are crucial considerations for public sector entities navigating digital transformation. Case studies and best practices from the African public sector offer valuable lessons to inform the development of tailored digital strategies that address the specific needs and challenges of the region. The convergence of CSR, HRIS, and contextual best practices contributes to a holistic approach to digital workforce planning and management, fostering organisational resilience and sustainable success in the public sector.

DIGITAL TALENT MANAGEMENT

Talent management in the digital era represents a critical aspect of organisational success, particularly for entities navigating the complexities of today's workforce landscape. It encompasses a strategic approach to acquiring, nurturing, and retaining individuals with digital proficiency, essential for propelling technological advancement and aligning personal goals with organisational objectives. In this competitive era, the deliberate cultivation of talent is paramount for sustained innovation and prosperity. Establishing robust talent development programs and fostering an environment conducive to talent growth are crucial endeavours. Employers must prioritize attracting individuals with specialized digital skills and implement strategies to bridge talent gaps, thereby enhancing productivity and maintaining a competitive edge in the market.

Moreover, Corporate Social Responsibility (CSR) significantly influences organisational culture and values, particularly within the public sector context. In the realm of digital talent management, leveraging CSR initiatives can serve as a powerful tool for attracting and retaining top digital talents. Organisations committed to CSR are often perceived as desirable employers, especially among younger demographics valuing social and environmental impact. Integrating CSR principles into talent management strategies can contribute to building a compelling employer brand for public sector entities, fostering employee engagement and retention, thereby supporting long-term digital workforce planning and management success.

Furthermore, the Human Resources Information System (HRIS) plays a pivotal role in optimizing digital talent within the public sector. Serving as a centralized platform, HRIS facilitates the collection, storage, and analysis of employee data, including skills and career aspirations. In the realm of digital talent management, HRIS serves as a valuable tool for identifying existing skills, assessing skill gaps, and planning targeted development initiatives. Additionally, it enables the tracking of individual career progression, facilitating personalized development aligned with organisational goals. Leveraging HRIS enables public sector organisations to effectively manage their digital talent pool, ensuring the presence of necessary skills for driving digital transformation and innovation.

In expanding upon the discourse, it is imperative to delve into specific strategies for acquiring and retaining digital talent. Organisations must employ proactive approaches such as targeted recruitment efforts, offering competitive compensation packages, and providing continuous learning opportunities to attract and retain digital-savvy individuals. Moreover, implementing strategies for upskilling and re-skilling existing employees to meet evolving digital demands is essential for maintaining a competitive workforce. Furthermore, managing talent for digital transformation involves aligning talent management strategies with organisational objectives for digitalization. This entails identifying key digital competencies required for successful transformation, developing a talent pipeline equipped with these skills, and fostering a culture of innovation and adaptability within the organization.

Additionally, linking talent management to organisational performance involves establishing metrics and Key Performance Indicators (KPIs) to measure the impact of talent management initiatives on key business outcomes. By aligning talent management efforts with organisational performance goals, public sector entities can demonstrate the value of investing in digital talent and drive continuous improvement in workforce capabilities.

Examining case studies and best practices from diverse global contexts, including the African public sector, is crucial for gaining insights into effective strategies for digital workforce planning and management. Insights from African examples highlight unique challenges and opportunities in digital talent management, offering valuable lessons applicable to similar contexts worldwide. By leveraging successful strategies for identifying, developing, and retaining digital talents within African public sector organisations, entities can enhance their understanding of global digital workforce planning and management best practices, fostering resilience and long-term success.

CHALLENGES IN IMPLEMENTING DIGITAL WORKFORCE MANAGEMENT

Implementing digital workforce management in the public sector poses numerous challenges across technical integration, change management, and legal compliance. Overcoming these hurdles necessitates a holistic strategy merging technological prowess with strategic planning. This complexity is compounded by the imperative for collaboration between the public sector and other entities (Bryson et al., 2015). Additionally, the urgency for a digitally proficient workforce in transforming digital health underscores the need for preparedness and governance. Establishing institutions and policies in the digital economy also proves challenging for the public sector. To address these intricacies and cultivate a technologically empowered workforce, a flexible strategy incorporating change management, legal compliance, and technological capabilities is imperative.

Implementing digital workforce management in the public sector involves various challenges that necessitate a strategic and comprehensive approach. Corporate social responsibility (CSR) plays a crucial role in this process by ensuring ethical practices and social responsibility are upheld during digital transformation (Kiadaliri et al., 2023). By prioritizing CSR, public sector entities can maintain a positive organisational culture amidst technological advancements. Additionally, integrating a robust Human Resources Information System (HRIS) is essential for overcoming challenges associated with digital workforce management (Gani, 2024). HRIS serves as a foundational tool that streamlines processes, enhances data-driven decision-making, and optimizes workforce management in the digital era. Furthermore, insights from case studies and best practices in the African public sector offer practical applications of digital workforce management strategies (He, 2024). Real-world examples provide valuable insights into the unique challenges faced and innovative solutions implemented, enriching the discourse with a global perspective. By examining experiences from the African public sector, the relevance of context-specific approaches in navigating digital transformation complexities is highlighted.

It can be argued that, by emphasising CSR initiatives, leveraging HRIS capabilities, and drawing insights from the African public sector, public sector entities can effectively navigate the challenges of digital workforce management and cultivate organisational resilience in the digital era. This comprehensive approach addresses the multifaceted nature of challenges in implementing digital workforce management, ensuring a nuanced strategy that considers ethical, technical, and legal aspects while leveraging HRIS and contextual insights for successful digital transformation.

OPPORTUNITIES FOR INNOVATION AND IMPROVEMENT

In the realm of digital workforce planning and management within the public sector, integrating cutting-edge technologies such as artificial intelligence and predictive analytics is paramount for enhancing decision-making processes. Collaborative platforms can foster employee knowledge sharing, cultivating a culture of continuous learning and adaptation. Strategic alignment with government agendas for digital transformation can promote efficiency and synergy, as highlighted by Väyrynen et al. (2022). Leveraging data-driven insights enables optimal resource allocation, ultimately enhancing organisational performance. By seizing these opportunities, human resource management (HRM) in the public sector can pioneer innovative techniques that equip employees for long-term success in an increasingly digital environment.

In the public sector, Human Resource Management (HRM), the integration of Corporate Social Responsibility (CSR) and the Human Resources Information System (HRIS) plays a pivotal role in fostering innovation and improvement. CSR initiatives within public sector organisations are instrumental in promoting employee well-being, diversity, ethical utilization of digital technologies, and aligning workforce strategies with broader societal and environmental goals (AlMunthiri, 2023). On the other hand, HRIS serves as a foundational element in the digital transformation of HRM, offering advanced technological capabilities for talent management, performance evaluation, and decision-making processes (Todisco et al., 2023). By leveraging HRIS, public sector entities can streamline HR processes, enhance data-driven decision-making, and facilitate continuous learning and adaptation. The relevance of CSR and

HRIS in the public sector is further enriched by theoretical exploration alongside case studies and best practices from the African public sector. Real-world examples from African public sector organisations provide valuable insights into contextual nuances and practical challenges associated with implementing innovative HRM strategies within a specific regional context (Alkhalaf, 2023). These case studies offer actionable lessons and recommendations for public sector entities, facilitating knowledge exchange and cross-regional learning to inspire proactive approaches and innovative techniques for long-term success in an increasingly digital environment. By incorporating CSR, HRIS, and regional case studies, public entities can navigate digital transformation's multifaceted challenges and opportunities.

The inclusion of CSR fosters positive organisational culture, employee engagement, and community welfare, while HRIS revolutionises talent management, decision-making processes, and strategic planning (AlMunthiri, 2023; Todisco et al., 2023). The synthesis of theoretical insights with practical examples from the African public sector illuminates a pathway for public organisations to thrive in the digital era, ensuring organisational resilience and sustained success through innovative HRM strategies tailored to regional contexts.

CASE STUDIES

Case A. Successful Implementation of Digital Workforce Management in the Public Sector

In the realm of successful implementation of digital workforce management in the public sector, the integration of Corporate Social Responsibility (CSR) and Human Resources Information System (HRIS) plays a pivotal role in driving organisational transformation. CSR initiatives are not merely about fulfilling ethical obligations; they encompass a broader commitment to societal well-being and environmental sustainability. Within the public sector, these initiatives are instrumental in shaping organisational culture, fostering employee engagement, and contributing to the attainment of broader societal goals. For instance, a government agency in South Africa prioritized CSR-focused talent management strategies, leading to enhanced employee morale and productivity. By emphasising diversity and inclusion programs, environmental sustainability efforts, and community engagement activities, the organization demonstrated its commitment to social responsibility while fostering a positive work environment. Similarly, Human Resources Information System (HRIS) serves as the technological backbone of digital workforce management, facilitating the integration, automation, and optimization of HR processes. HRIS enables organisations to streamline recruitment, training, performance management, and payroll processes, leading to improved operational efficiency and data-driven decision-making. For example, in Nigeria, a government agency implemented an HRIS solution to centralize employee data, automate routine tasks, and enhance reporting capabilities, resulting in significant cost savings and improved workforce planning accuracy.

Moreover, examining case studies and best practices from the African public sector provides valuable insights into the unique challenges and opportunities associated with implementing digital workforce management strategies. For instance, Rwanda's investment in digital skills development and ICT infrastructure has transformed the public sector workforce, enabling greater efficiency, transparency, and citizen engagement. By leveraging digital technologies such as e-government platforms and mobile applications, Rwandan public sector organisations have been able to improve service delivery and enhance citizen satisfaction. Similarly, in South Africa, the adoption of innovative HRIS solutions has revolutionized talent management practices within the public sector, empowering employees to take ownership of their career development and advancement opportunities.

The successful implementation of digital workforce management in the public sector requires a holistic approach that integrates CSR, HRIS, and contextual best practices. By prioritizing CSR-driven workforce management initiatives, leveraging advanced HRIS solutions, and drawing insights from African case studies and best practices, public sector organisations can navigate the complexities of digital transformation while fostering organisational resilience and long-term success.

Case B. Learning from Challenges and Failures in Digital Workforce Management Projects

In the landscape of digital workforce management projects, lessons gleaned from challenges and failures are as instructive as successes. Despite the best intentions, organisations often encounter hurdles that impede the smooth implementation of digital initiatives. In such instances, the integration of Corporate Social Responsibility (CSR) and Human Resources Information System (HRIS) can provide valuable insights into addressing these challenges and mitigating potential failures.

CSR, beyond its ethical connotations, serves as a guiding principle for navigating the complexities of digital workforce management projects. By prioritizing CSR-driven initiatives, organisations demonstrate a commitment to ethical practices, employee well-being, and community engagement, fostering a positive organisational culture conducive to project success. For example, a public sector entity in Kenya faced challenges during the implementation of a digital workforce management system due to resistance from employees unfamiliar with the technology. However, by incorporating CSR principles into the project framework and emphasising employee training and support, the organization was able to overcome resistance and achieve successful adoption of the new system.

Similarly, HRIS emerges as a critical component in addressing challenges and failures encountered during digital workforce management projects. By leveraging HRIS functionalities such as data analytics, process automation, and talent management, organisations can streamline project workflows, enhance decision-making, and optimize resource allocation. For instance, in Ghana, a government agency experienced difficulty in managing a digital workforce planning project due to inadequate data infrastructure and a lack of HRIS integration. However, by investing in HRIS solutions tailored to the organization's needs and capabilities, the agency was able to overcome these challenges and achieve project objectives effectively.

Moreover, examining case studies and best practices from the African public sector offers valuable insights into addressing challenges and failures in digital workforce management projects. For instance, in Tanzania, a public sector organization encountered setbacks during the implementation of a digital talent management system due to insufficient stakeholder engagement and resistance to change. However, by learning from past failures and adopting a collaborative approach that prioritized stakeholder involvement, the organization successfully implemented the system, leading to improved employee satisfaction and organisational performance.

In conclusion, learning from challenges and failures in digital workforce management projects requires a strategic approach that integrates CSR, HRIS, and contextual best practices. By leveraging CSR-driven principles to foster a positive organisational culture and prioritizing HRIS functionalities to streamline project workflows, organisations can address challenges effectively and mitigate potential failures. Moreover, drawing insights from African case studies and best practices offers valuable lessons for navigating the complexities of digital transformation in the public sector, ultimately fostering organisational resilience and long-term success.

CONCLUSION

The imperative for public sector organisations to embrace digital transformation in HRM is underscored by the critical need to navigate digital skill identification, cutting-edge technology implementation, and strategic talent management. This chapter synthesizes theoretical frameworks, real-world case studies, and innovative strategies, illuminating a pathway for public entities to not merely adapt but thrive in the digital era. The integration of digital workforce practices emerges as pivotal for organisational resilience. It provides insights into the transformative potential and strategic implications of digital HRM. Real-world case studies offer practical lessons for effective digital workforce planning and management in the public sector, ensuring sustained success.

In the dynamic landscape of the public sector, digital transformation has become a driving force reshaping workforce planning and management paradigms. This chapter has explored the multifaceted aspects of digitalization within Human Resource Management (HRM), identifying key factors, challenges, opportunities, and strategies crucial for navigating this transformative journey. Drawing insights from theoretical frameworks, practical examples, and case studies from the African public sector, we have outlined a comprehensive roadmap for embracing innovation and improving organisational resilience in the face of digital disruption.

Our exploration began by establishing the theoretical foundations of digital workforce planning and management, emphasising the evolution of HRM paradigms and the integration of Corporate Social Responsibility (CSR) principles and Human Resources Information Systems (HRIS) in facilitating digital transformation. Subsequently, we delved into the drivers of digital transformation, highlighting the urgency for innovative HR strategies driven by shifts in workforce expectations, technological advancements, and societal movements towards digital governance. Throughout, we underscored the critical roles of CSR initiatives and HRIS integration in addressing ethical, social, and environmental dimensions of digital transformation.

Moving forward, strategies for digital workforce planning were elucidated, emphasising the alignment of organisational objectives with digital demands, talent acquisition, and targeted training programs. The crucial roles of CSR and HRIS in shaping effective workforce planning strategies were highlighted, with insights from African case studies providing practical applications of these strategies in diverse contexts. The successful implementation of digital technology in HRM, challenges, opportunities for innovation and improvement were also discussed, offering public sector entities a holistic approach to navigate the digital future of workforce management, ensuring organisational resilience and sustained success in an increasingly digital environment.

REFERENCES

AbdulKareem, A. (2024). Investigating ICT adoption and public value of e-recruitment in the public sector: The role of social media use. *International Journal of Public Sector Management, 37*(2), 284-304. https://doi.org/10.1108/IJPSM-10-2023-0307

African Union. (2021). *Digital transformation strategy for Africa (2020-2030)*. Retrieved from https://au.int/en/documents/20200518/digital-transformation-strategy-africa-2020-2030

Alkhalaf, T. (2023). The effect of ability, motivation and opportunity (AMO) on SMEs' innovation performance. *Creativity and Innovation Management, 33*(1), 21-38. https://doi.org/10.1111/caim.12578

AlMunthiri, O., Bani-Melhem, S., Mohd-Shamsudin, F., & Raziq, M. M. (2023). Fostering innovative behaviours of public sector employees: The potency of innovation-based HR practices, risk propensity and error tolerance. *. *International Journal of Public Sector Management*, 37(2), 159–182. 10.1108/IJPSM-08-2023-0242

Bonilla-Chaves, E., & Palos-Sanchez, P. (2023). Exploring the evolution of human resource analytics: A bibliometric study. *Behavioral Sciences, 13*(3), 244. https://doi.org/10.3390/bs13030244

Bryson, J., Crosby, B., & Stone, M. (2015). Designing and implementing cross-sector collaborations: Needed and challenging. *Public Administration Review, 75*(5), 647-663. https://doi.org/10.1111/puar.12432

Curzi, Y. (2023). High-performance work systems and firm innovation: The moderating role of digital technology and employee participation. Evidence from Europe. *Management Research Review, 47*(13), 51-67. https://doi.org/10.1108/MRR-11-2022-0751

Deloitte. (2020). *Global human capital trends 2020: The social enterprise at work: Paradox as a path forward*. Deloitte Insights. Retrieved from https://www2.deloitte.com/us/en/insights/focus/human-capital-trends/2020.html

Gani, N. (2024). Optimising human resource information systems in the context of MSME technology management. *Jurnal Informasi Dan Teknologi, 6*(1), 302-309. https://doi.org/10.60083/jidt.v6i1.519

Gibson, A. (2024). Agile workforce planning. In Harper, S. M., & Marshall, C. J. (Eds.), *Strategic workforce planning: Concepts, theories, and applications** (pp. 116–139). Oxford University Press., 10.1093/oso/9780197759745.003.0007

Gintova, M. (2023). Understanding public servants' perspectives on return to office and digital government: Lessons learned from Canada. *Transforming Government People Process and Policy, 18*(1), 118-130. https://doi.org/10.1108/TG-07-2023-0091

Gomathy, D. (2024). Human resource management: Case study with solutions. *International Journal of Scientific Research in Engineering and Management, 08*(03), 1-11. https://doi.org/10.55041/IJSREM23383

Halid, H., Yusoff, Y., & Somu, H. (2020). The relationship between digital human resource management and organisational performance. https://doi.org/10.2991/aebmr.k.200514.022

He, T. (2024). Digital health integration for noncommunicable diseases: Comprehensive process mapping for full-life-cycle management. *Journal of Evidence-Based Medicine, 17*(1), 26-36. https://doi.org/10.1111/jebm.1258

Heger, B. (2024). Enabling strategic workforce planning through skills, artificial intelligence, and internal talent marketplace. In Harper, S. M., & Marshall, C. J. (Eds.), *Strategic workforce planning: Concepts, theories, and applications** (pp. 164–197). Oxford University Press., 10.1093/oso/9780197759745.003.0009

Järlström, M., Saru, E., & Pekkarinen, A. (2023). Practices of sustainable human resource management in three Finnish companies: Comparative case study. *South Asian Journal of Business and Management Cases, 12*(1), 31-51. https://doi.org/10.1177/22779779231154656

Johnstone, S. (2023). Human resource management in recession: Restructuring and alternatives to downsizing in times of crisis. *Human Resource Management Journal, 34*(1), 138-157. https://doi.org/10.1111/1748-8583.12512

Kamalakannan, D. (2024). The integration of digital transformation with human resource management – a theoretical point of view. *International Journal of Scientific Research in Engineering and Management, 08*(02), 1-13. https://doi.org/10.55041/IJSREM28895

Kiadaliri, A., Dell'Isola, A., Lohmander, L., Hunter, D., & Dahlberg, L. (2023). Assessing the importance of predictors of adherence to a digital self-management intervention for osteoarthritis. *Journal of Orthopaedic Surgery and Research, 18*(1). https://doi.org/10.1186/s13018-023-03562-6

Konateh, H., Duramany-Lakkoh, E., & Udeh, E. (2023). Cost and administrative effectiveness of recruitment and selection practices on public service delivery in public sector institutions. *European Journal of Business Management and Research, 8*(2), 21-30. https://doi.org/10.24018/ejbmr.2023.8.2.1814

Marhil, M., Masaud, K., & Majid, N. (2023). The mediating role of job satisfaction on the relationship between human resources management strategies and employees performance in Waha Oil & Gas Company in Libya. *American Journal of Economics and Business Innovation, 2*(1), 63-69. https://doi.org/10.54536/ajebi.v2i1.1437

McKinsey & Company. (2021). *The future of work after COVID-19*. Retrieved from https://www.mckinsey.com/featured-insights/future-of-work/the-future-of-work-after-covid-19

Nair, K. (2019). Overcoming today's digital talent gap in organisations worldwide. *Development in Learning Organisations an International Journal, 33*(6), 16-18. https://doi.org/10.1108/DLO-02-2019-0044

Nicolás-Agustín, Á., Jiménez, D., & Maeso-Fernandez, F. (2021). The role of human resource practices in the implementation of digital transformation. *International Journal of Manpower, 43*(2), 395-410. https://doi.org/10.1108/IJM-03-2021-0176

Nicolás-Agustín, D., Ramírez-Correa, P. E., & Alfaro-Perez, J. (2021). Digital workforce planning and management in the public sector: Drivers, strategies, and challenges. In Tan, B. B. T., & Dahlin, P. A. (Eds.), *Digital transformation in public sector organisations** (pp. 101–120). Springer.

Obermayer-Kovács, N., Csizmadia, T., & Banász, Z. (2022). Companies on thin ice due to digital transformation: The role of digital skills and human characteristics. *International and Multidisciplinary Journal of Social Sciences, 11*(3), 88-118. https://doi.org/10.17583/rimcis.10641

Patterson, E. (2023). Reducing the gap between rhetoric and reality: Use of digital service standards for public service innovation through digital transformation in Australia. *Australian Journal of Public Administration, 82*(4), 557-589. https://doi.org/10.1111/1467-8500.12615

Prakash, K., Reddy, A., & Yasaswi, R. (2021). AI-powered HCM: The analytics and augmentations. https://doi.org/10.5772/intechopen.100475

Roffia, P., & Dabić, M. (2023). The role of management control and integrated information systems for the resilience of SMEs. *Review of Managerial Science, 18*(5), 1353-1375. https://doi.org/10.1007/s11846-023-00657-6

Rönnblom, M., Carlsson, V., & Öjehag-Pettersson, A. (2023). Gender equality in Swedish AI policies. What's the problem represented to be? *Review of Policy Research, 40*(5), 688-704. https://doi.org/10.1111/ropr.12547

Sakib, M. (2023). Industry 4.0 and its implications on human resource management practices: A systematic literature review and bibliometric analysis. *Dhaka University Journal of Management, 15*(1&2). https://doi.org/10.57240/DUJMV15A8

Sánchez-Marín, G. (2023). Linkages between high-performance work practices and family-centered goals: Implications for financial performance in family firms. *Journal of Small Business and Enterprise Development, 31*(1), 126-151. https://doi.org/10.1108/JSBED-03-2023-0117

Satispi, E., Rajiani, I., Murod, M., & Andriansyah, A. (2023). Human resources information system (HRIS) to enhance civil servants' innovation outcomes: Compulsory or complimentary? *Administrative Sciences, 13*(2), 32. https://doi.org/10.3390/admsci13020032

South African Government. (2022). *South African e-Government strategy 2022-2025*. Retrieved from https://www.gov.za/documents/e-government-strategy-2022-2025

Sposato, M. (2024). Editorial. *Strategic HR Review, 23*(1), 40-42. https://doi.org/10.1108/SHR-02-2024-204

St-Hilaire, W. (2024). The public sector value-based management: Effect of the digital matrix on the optimisation of resources for micro-organisations. *SEDME (Small Enterprises Development Management & Extension Journal) a Worldwide Window on MSME Studies, 51*(1), 17-26. https://doi.org/10.1177/09708464231223485

Stachová, K., Papula, J., Stacho, Z., & Kohnová, L. (2019). External partnerships in employee education and development as the key to facing industry 4.0 challenges. *Sustainability, 11*(2), 345. https://doi.org/10.3390/su11020345

Subbaiah, D. (2024). AI-powered strategies for talent management optimization. *Journal of Industrial Engineering Research, 4*(2). https://doi.org/10.52783/jier.v4i2.848

Todisco, L., Tomo, A., Canonico, P., & Mangia, G. (2023). The bright and dark side of smart working in the public sector: Employees' experiences before and during COVID-19. *Management Decision, 61*(13), 85-102. https://doi.org/10.1108/MD-02-2022-0164

Väyrynen, H., Helander, N., & Jalonen, H. (2022). Public innovation and digital transformation. https://doi.org/10.4324/9781003230854

Wang, J., Bai, W., & Liu, Y. (2022). Optimization for the human resources management strategy of the IoT industry based on AHP. *Computational Intelligence and Neuroscience, 2022*, 1-10. https://doi.org/10.1155/2022/3514285

World Bank. (2021). *World development report 2021: Data for better lives*. Retrieved from https://www.worldbank.org/en/publication/wdr2021

Zhang, J., & Chen, Z. (2023). Exploring human resource management digital transformation in the digital age. *. *Journal of the Knowledge Economy*. Advance online publication. 10.1007/s13132-023-01214-y

KEY TERMS AND DEFINITIONS:

Digital Transformation: Digital transformation refers to the integration of digital technologies into various aspects of organisational operations, processes, and strategies to fundamentally change how they operate and deliver value to stakeholders (Nicolás-Agustín et al., 2021).

Human Resource Management (HRM): Definition: Human Resource Management (HRM) involves the planning, recruitment, selection, training, development, and management of an organization's workforce to achieve its goals effectively and efficiently (Nair, 2019).

Corporate Social Responsibility (CSR): Corporate Social Responsibility (CSR) encompasses a company's initiatives to assess and take responsibility for its impact on social and environmental well-being, aiming to contribute to sustainable development while considering the interests of stakeholders (Bryson et al., 2015).

Human Resources Information System (HRIS): Human Resources Information System (HRIS) is a software solution that automates and integrates various HR functions, such as payroll, benefits administration, recruiting, training, and performance management, into one system for efficient management of human resources (Halid et al., 2020).

Talent Management: Talent management involves the strategic planning and implementation of processes to attract, develop, retain, and maximize the potential of employees with the required skills and competencies to achieve organisational objectives (Wang et al., 2022).

Digital Workforce Planning: Digital workforce planning refers to the process of strategically forecasting and managing the talent needs of an organization in the context of digital transformation, ensuring the alignment of workforce capabilities with technological advancements and organisational goals (Satispi et al., 2023).

Change Management: Change management is a structured approach to transitioning individuals, teams, and organisations from their current state to a desired future state, aiming to minimize resistance and maximize adoption of new processes, technologies, or strategies (Väyrynen et al., 2022).

Predictive Analytics: Predictive analytics involves the use of data, statistical algorithms, and machine learning techniques to analyze current and historical facts to make predictions about future events or behaviors, enabling organisations to anticipate trends and make proactive decisions (Prakash et al., 2021).

Chapter 3
Drivers of Digital Transformation and Their Efficacy in Public Sector Human Resource Management

Andrew Enaifoghe
https://orcid.org/0000-0003-4890-9179
University of Zululand, South Africa

Nduduzo C. Ndebele
https://orcid.org/0000-0001-5938-5011
University of KwaZulu-Natal, South Africa

Anuoluwapo Durokifa
https://orcid.org/0000-0001-5378-1056
University of Johannesburg, South Africa

Xolani Thusi
https://orcid.org/0000-0001-7316-6165
University of Limpopo, South Africa

ABSTRACT

The chapter examines digital transformation drivers and their efficacy in improving public sector human resource management in the digital age. Implementing Digitalisation in the public sector opens up possibilities for human resource management (HRM) to reform and accelerate the delivery of services using the most advanced digital technologies. Although digital transformation is expected to offer change in the public sector, various challenges may require significant backing to support the HRM function amid waves and shocks posed by digital transformation. The chapter employs a qualitative research methodology drawn from a systematic literature review to comprehensively evaluate the literature on digital transformation and its role in public sector HRM. Search engines such as Scopus, google, and Google Scholar were used to find relevant information on the role of digital transformation in enhancing public sector HRM. Keywords such as "digital transformation", "public sector", "HRM", "were used in streamlining the search for the study for the study. Findings from the literature indicated several im-

DOI: 10.4018/979-8-3693-2889-7.ch003

pediments, such as unreformed bureaucratic culture, staff resistance to change, and budget constraints that threaten digital transformation in public sector HRM. The conclusions drawn for this chapter suggest optimisation techniques, which include strengthening the HRM's information security system while encouraging a digitally-driven culture among staff members, which is key to improving digital skills and accelerating the public sector HRM for improved service delivery.

INTRODUCTION

The wave of change has engulfed public sector institutions globally with digital transformation taking a leading role in disrupting the existing status allowing new ideas, innovation and models to be implemented to enhance the delivery of public goods and services. Public Sector Human Resource Management is a key functional department in the public sector that was and is still being affected by trends in the technological environment as digital transformation takes shape and form. While various definitions are proposed in the literature regarding digital transformation, our study describes "digital transformation" as the ways in which digital technology has impacted all aspects of life for humans, or the continual process by which businesses employ their digital capabilities to create innovative companies, goods, and services in response to market and customer disruptions (Al-Ruithe et al., 2018; Vial, 2019). The merits of digital transformation in the public sector are many with Enaifoghe & Ndebele (2023) attesting to the benefits of digitalising the public sector and related institutions locally and globally.

Pockets of excellence in digitalising the public sector, for example, were noted in South Africa following the digital overhaul of the public sector revenue service. Over the past decade, the South African Money Service has deployed various innovative digital solutions that have improved the user experience, enhanced its ability to collect money, and empowered its employees (Ndebele & Enaifoghe, 2023). As a form of development triggered by modern technologies, the money service almost eliminated the use of paper, considerably accelerated its procedures, and increased risk management. As commonly understood in public sector innovation studies, HRM departments operate with dedicated budgets to ensure they deliver on their mandates. The effective revenue collection assures tax compliance, leading to an enhanced budget, which is reinvested in the country through capital projects that benefit local communities. Adapting to digital trends within public sector HRM is crucial to ensure that public sector organisations align their systems and structures to the demands of modern digital technologies.

The widescale use of "digital transformation tools such as 5G, cloud computing, big data, artificial intelligence, IoT, blockchain, and others" (Enaifoghe et al., 2020: 3) can help leverage efficiency in public sector HRM. It is imperative to note that digitalising information in the public sector is crucial for improving and using data-driven insights to achieve efficiency and productivity. Studies indicated that technology now plays a crucial role in delivering services, supporting growth, and assuring efficiency in both public and commercial sectors (Enaifoghe, 2021; Yu & JInajun, 2020; Banga, 2018). The reappearance of the COVID-19 pandemic in 2020 posed a threat to organizations worldwide, including the South African Public Service. To prevent the spread of the virus, organizations needed to use Fourth Industrial Revolution (4IR) technology to maintain HRM continuity during curfews and lockdowns. As a result, quick 4IR technologies transformed how the Public Service learns, lives, works, conducts business, and serves its stakeholders.

The National Development Plan, Vision 2030, referred to the 4IR and warned government agencies that the technological revolution had deepened and expedited the world's interconnectivity (Enaifoghe, 2021). To prevent a "digital divide" in South Africa, departments should invest in appropriate systems and manage the ICT environment effectively. Siyaya et al. (2023), argued that the government must design and implement policies to regulate actions in areas where the digital revolution will have the most significant influence. The transition from manual to knowledge-intensive production involves diverse abilities, including digital, analytical, technical, and management expertise (Banga & Velde, 2018).

We noted that organizational success relies on effective policies and institutional capacity, including knowledge, skills, talents, and behaviour. As Ndebele and Enaifoghe (2023) indicated, public sector departments should prioritize talent development and system adoption to accelerate the shift from manual to digital formats. Digitising information in the public sector is crucial for improving operations, increasing efficiency, and leveraging data insights. Following the key arguments this chapter examines the drivers of digital transformation and their efficacy in public-sector human resource management. This chapter further assesses the roles of digital transformation in advancing public-sector human resource management (HRM) to improve service delivery.

LITERATURE REVIEW

Drivers of Digital Transformation in the Public Sector

The penetration of digital transformation in the past two decades has seen the widespread use of contemporary information and communication technologies (ICTs) and digital technologies which have prompted public and private institutions to devise strategies to exploit and harness the benefits of modern technology. Some public sector organisations adopted these modern technologies to enhance customer relations, public service delivery and human resource development. These strategies involve the explicit change of essential HRM operations such as organizational structures, product creation, internal workflow processes, public sector values, and fundamental concepts (Al-Alawi & Al Showmali, 2019; Betchoo, 2016).

Achieving public sector reforms using ICTs has been examined extensively in the literature from two fundamental approaches (Luna-Reyes & Gil-Garcia, 2014, p. 546), such as: 'Technological determinism views technology as a powerful tool for transforming social systems and driving new interactions. Social determinism refers to how social groups assign meaning to technological artifacts, choose which technologies to adopt, and influence success. A unified approach suggests a complex interplay between technology and social elements'.

Drawing from the aforementioned assertions, it is crucial to note that digital transformation in public sector HRM "can occur in two ways: either through the change of internal processes or through the transformation of external links between governments and other political, economic, and social players" (Luna-Reyes & Gil-Garcia, 2014: 5). Arguably the interplay of various factors contributes to the success or failure of public sector HRM in rendering public services. As confirmed by Mergel (2015), the rise of new technologies enables new types of open cooperation and alternative forms of innovation creation); including collaborative governance, coproduction, collective action and collaborations (Linders, 2012, p.447), however for technology to bring a change a cultural transformation is required (Serrat, 2017).

The importance of the above attributes has been noted and Mergel (2014) believes that public administrations are shifting from a "need-to-know" to a "need-to-share" paradigm, which encompasses features such as openness, discussions, inclusiveness, co-creation, and real-time feedback cycles. For example, social media was initially viewed and used for amusement and youth activities, driven mostly by inventive citizen use, but the popularity of social networking sites has greatly led to a shift in HRM models and industries (Mergel 2014). In improving communication public sector HRM could tap into the use of new digital platforms such as Facebook to effectively deliver change messages and ensure that public officials are well-capacitated to respond to the needs of the people.

Social Media in Transforming Public Sector HRM

Social media may play a crucial role in the public sector's digital transformation. According to Serrat (2017), social media platforms ought to be employed in the public sector for several reasons:

> "First, the public sector bears social responsibility for embracing change, and in turn, social media will be used to evaluate the public sector; second, the applications offer opportunities to achieve user-oriented, transparent, accountable, participative, inclusive, responsive, joined-up, networked, and efficient government; third, public-sector organizations" (Serrat, 2017, p. 3).

Based on the above, scholars argue that the role of Digitalisation is essential for collaboration, interactivity, re-shaping the relationship, co-creation between government and other stakeholders (Criado, Rojas-Martín, Gil-Garcia (2017), Mergel, 2016), cumulative smartness of public action (Bertot, Jaeger, Hansen, 2012), and helping the public sector find "innovative new ways to deliver public value" (Linders, 2012, p. 446). Besides, to "increase participation, transparency, and interagency collaboration in the public sector" (Mergel, 2014, p. 33). The use of social media in the public sector necessitates a plan, as well as daily use and monitoring, which entails observing its use to correct faults or operational inadequacies (Linder, 2012).

While it is important to understand what stimulates employees to contribute to innovation, adjusting to new Human Resources (HR) regulations, measuring social media use and evaluating activities that spearhead service delivery is critical in reaching specified goals. In implementing digital transformation, measurements and evaluation are crucial components of social media implementation, as they can help HRM practitioners in the public sector to increase citizen interaction and engagement (Criado, Rojas-Martin, Gil-Garcia, 2017; Mickoleit, 2014). Many indicators can be employed; typically, the goal is to measure online activities and interactions, but it is vital to consider network effects, which may not always be apparent but impact participation, engagement, and collaboration.

Advent of Digital Transformation in the Public Service Sector

A study conducted by Heavin & Power (2018) indicated that digital transformation has altered, how public sector organisations operate as they seek to align institutional strategies to the possible demands of meeting technology expectations. To take advantage of the exponential changes brought about by the complete advent of the digital era, public service managers are expected to modify their human resource management models so that efficiency and effectiveness can be attained in the digital age while striving to respond more swiftly to changing market and technological conditions. It was observed in the study of Mosca (2020) that the effects of digital transformation in public sector HRM result in modifications of customer behaviour, and assessments of public goods and services including citizen expectations Due to the dynamic state in which public sector HRM operates there is a need to stay ahead of the digital trends and use of modern technologies in the private sector which be adopted to transform public sector HRM in the digital age. Becoming technologically competitive can be an advantage for public sector organisations as they seek to remain relevant and responsive to service delivery demands.,

Digital transformation has arguably, revolutionised every element of our lives, but it has also had significant effects on how the tasks and procedures of HRM (Schmid & Pscherer, 2021). Research done on digital transformation revealed that effective leaders are required in the public sector to support the HRM function to deliver on its key mandate (Enaifoghe & Zenzile, 2023; McKinsey, 2020). In the contemporary public sector, HRM can now interact with data and information in a unique way as new digital technologies develop to achieve efficiency (Yu & JInajun, 2020). While research does not fully elucidate the merits of digital transformation on public sector HRM, Mocsa (2020) affirms that using digital technologies has significantly transformed specific HRM procedures, such as hiring new employees, developing human resources and evaluating employee performance, which enhances service delivery to stakeholders.

The use of modern technologies in public sector HRM saves time as HRM functions can become more productive in the delivery of services. In another research, Démeijer (2017), argues that digital transformation has made HRM procedures simpler and quicker which is advantageous to HRM specialists who can focus on projects that are relevant to their functional areas. The review of documents indicated that digital HRM techniques are becoming increasingly critical as, can influence both HR strategy and the organisational settings as a whole. Researchers such as Parry (2012), emphasise in the future HRM will likely face the disruptive shocks triggered by the digital revolution. In this case, the modern concepts, drivers of transformation and ramifications of digital HRM must be explained in light of recent advancements in digital technology and how the public sector can benefit to achieve quality service delivery.

Digital HRM and Digital Transformation Strategy in the Public Sector

In today's digital age, the public sector should prioritise digital transformation to remain competitive in the dynamic service delivery landscape (Kraus et al., 2022). The broad adoption of digital technologies has fundamentally altered public sector organisations' nature, functions, and citizen interactions. As alluded to in this chapter, digital transformation is a wide phenomenon that can impact all organisations globally, regardless of size or location. A study conducted by Kazançoglu and Ozkan-Ozen, (2018) attests to the improved production that could be attained when digital technologies are used in public sector HRM. For Enaifoghe & Zenzile (2023) a social and economic shift brought about by advancements affects how individuals HRM in public sector organisations should respond to changing job hiring conditions as digital hiring among other modernise methods is fast transforming.

The public sector HRM landscape the evolvement of digital transformation in public sector organisations provides HRM, with a competitive edge to revamp the workplace and developing new competencies that align with the latest technological innovations (Mazurchenko and Marsıkova, 2019). To help secure employee well-being and organisational sustainability in the digital era, Cantoni and Mangia (2019) suggest that HR professionals should be positioned to adopt new roles and acquire new capabilities which can help in improving their efficiency and effectiveness in public service delivery. The study of

Sharma (2015) holds the same sentiments that restructuring the HRM function in the public sector can help increase organisational efficiency and growth while leveraging digitalisation opportunities.

Apart from achieving efficiency in the digital transformation era, Ulrich and Dulebohn (2015) contend that accountability of HRM operations can be achieved by using digital technologies that help management performance and track the actions of public officials in executing their public duties. Accountability can further be achieved in various administrative units which makes it easier for HR departments to navigate key areas of public organisations that require HR attention.

Digital Transformation and Technological Advancement of HRM in the Public Sector

Globally public sector HRM has already felt the effects of digitisation and technological advancements on public service delivery (see Sharma, 2015; Kavanagh and Johnson, 2018). HRM techniques are beginning to shift in favour of increased digital innovation and creativity (Chytiri, 2019; Salamzadeh et al., 2019). For public sector HRM to be sustained, there is a need to adjust to the quick changes brought about by technological advancements as they have a disruptive manner to 'unprepared' public institutions in today's digital world. Vial (2019) claims that the growing adoption of digital technology in many industries, especially the public sector, has sparked an increase in the amount of study being done on this topic. However, because the research on this topic is varied and there is not a clear, shared understanding of the notion, there is still a lot of confusion and misunderstandings surrounding digital transformation in the public sector.

There is no single accepted definition of digital transformation in the literature; thus, scholars often describe it according to their areas of specialisation and interest. A more cohesive and thorough knowledge of this phenomenon is becoming more and more necessary as digital transformation continues to affect many facets of society (Komarčević et al., 2017). Goran et al., (2017) reiterate that digital transformation encompasses more than integrating digital tools to promote innovation and serve the interests of the organisation's stakeholders. In addition, digital transformation includes a thorough reorganisation of HRM processes, culture, and strategy (Horlacher & Hess, 2016; João Catarino et al., 2018; Kutnjak et al., 2019; Tumbas et al., 2017).

Public sector organisations are therefore positioned to accept digital transformation which is widely regarded as having the capacity to accomplish the service delivery goals within HRM departments. Many researchers have confused digital technologies with the digitisation or digitalisation process in the past. Consequently, the phrase "digital transformation" was misconstrued, resulting in divergent interpretations. Digital transformation was described by Lankshear & Knobel (2008) as the achievement of notable change in a knowledge or professional domain through digital tools that support creativity and innovation. In a similar vein, digital transformation is defined by Westerman et al. (2014) and Bekkhus (2016) as the use of technology to improve corporate performance and broaden reach. The term "digital transformation" describes how digital technology influences all facets of human life or the ongoing process by which companies use their digital competencies to develop new HRM models, products, and services in response to market and customer disruptions (Vial, 2019).

Several authors, notably Al-Ruithe et al. (2018), have advocated this definition. Elizabeth Robinson (2017) states that firms must possess digital competency to remain competitive. For organisations to prosper in the long run, they must constantly adapt to digital advancements and be receptive to new technology (McKinsey, 2018). The scientific community has recognized that digital transformation requires more than just a technology transition (Verhoef et al., 2021). To achieve this, several other components, including as strategy, human resources, culture, talent development, and leadership, must be altered (Al-Alawi et al., 2023; Bharadwaj et al., 2013; Cortellazzo et al., 2019; Goran et al., 2017; Guerra et al., 2023). Digital transformation enables cross-border interaction with suppliers, customers, and competitors, giving organizations a competitive edge by leveraging current core competencies or developing new ones (Elizabeth Robinson, 2017; Komarčević et al., 2017; Verhoef et al., 2021; Vial, 2019).

Adopting digital transformation is critical because it changes the way human resource management operates and acts in the public sector, increasing output and providing a more productive work environment (John Metselaar, 2021). Consequently, for the public service sector to benefit from digital transformation, it must recognise that it is a comprehensive organisational shift that calls for significant adjustments in leadership, culture, and mindset (Behnam Tabrizi et al., 2019). This is because digital transformation is not just a technological process (Goran et al., 2017; Korhonen & Halén, 2017; Singh & Hess, 2017). Some authors (Cozza, 2020; John Metselaar, 2021) concentrate on how digital transformation affects managerial decisions and how it might expedite decision-making processes. The methodology adopted by modern digital technologies enables sophisticated data collecting and analysis, hence supporting decision-making, is consistent with this. These writers do stress, though, that utilising cutting-edge tools and techniques is not the only factor in the success of the digital transition.

Application of Digital Workplace in Public Sector HRM

Professionals in a digital workplace have access to new form of technology such as computers and access to the internet. The convergence of the information age and the technological revolution in offices, shop floors, and boardrooms around the world has changed the function and nature of work that human resources managers perform in guaranteeing the successful operation of organizations, processes, and people (Benson, Johnson, & Kuchinke, 2002). Job transformations are defined as using digital technologies to enhance employee experience and performance. Digital workplaces are cultural digital and physical frameworks that facilitate working life in complex, dynamic, and frequently unstructured work environments (Zimmer, Baiyere, & Salmela, 2020). Digital workplace transformation, which helps to improve employee performance and organisational effectiveness, is also an important component of HRM digital transformation.

Digital transformation in the workplace incorporates digital technology, including ICT and web technologies, into the work process (Fabbri et al., 2019). The digital workplace fosters an environment that encourages employee involvement, collaboration, team productivity, and transparency. However, the expectations established by digital technology have resulted in a substantial demand for workplace reform (Betchoo 2016). Many employees' desks now have computers with Internet connections, allowing them to access a world of informal learning. Employee-initiated informal learning can be as simple and unstructured as conducting a web search to acquire background material for a specific job task, or as complex and structured as joining an online community of practice (Benson et al, 2002).

Through the application and adoption of digital transformation of HRM in the public service sector, data and digital tools are now essential for showcasing value and helping people make the correct decisions. Likewise, management technologies have made data and processes swift regarding HRM (Kavanagh and Johnson, 2018). The progress of digitisation involves more than just task reduction and automation, as Samson and Rathee (2018) point out. As Samson and Rathee (2018) point out, the influence can be seen in all aspects of human capital management, including hiring, training and development, efficient workforce management, productivity optimisation, performance management procedures, administrative procedures, data visualisation, and fostering interpersonal experiences. Digitalising HRM was developed as a result of the integration of HRM with contemporary digital technology (Bondarouk and Brewster, 2016).

Although this phrase has other definitions, Strohmeier (2020) highlights the concept's macro-level aspect. For example, Fisher and Cassady (2019) propose deepening the understanding of eHRM, whereas Kavanagh and Johnson (2019) see it as a digital means to apply HRM utilising information technology. The broadening of perspectives on e-HRM as a means of enhancing and fortifying employee relations at the workplace. It is also important to highlight how new technologies affect personnel management procedures within the public service sector (Waters-Sobkowiak et al., 2018). The growth of talent management systems is aided by technological advancements that make it possible to integrate cutting-edge hiring, development, assessment, and compensation procedures (Pauli and Pocztowski, 2019).

Mainly focused on expansion, the creation of new technologies can help alleviate access-related constraints and give human resource management a competitive edge (Brandt and Suonp€a€a, 2020). Finally, it should be noted that the impact of technology has altered the organisational requirements and services in human resource management. Technological advancement has brought about a shift in converting manual, antiquated HR procedures into electronic, cutting-edge ones, which has led to the modification, acceleration, and termination of certain HR procedures.

RESEARCH METHODOLOGY

The study uses a qualitative methodology to collect data through a systematic literature review to accomplish the study objectives. In support, Borrego, Foster & Froyd (2014), expound that a systematic literature review is a review that adopts systematic approaches to gather secondary data, critically evaluate research articles, and qualitatively synthesise findings. A comprehensive literature evaluation on digital transformation in the public service sector was conducted. Search engines such as Scopus, google, and Google Scholar were used to find relevant information on the role of digital transformation in enhancing public sector HRM. Keywords such as “digital transformation”, “public sector”, “HRM”, “were used in streamlining the search for the study for the study. The exclusion and inclusion in the review process were done following the topic and research questions regarding exclusions and inclusions. Peer review journals pertinent to the subject were transferred and selected, as were periodicals, newspapers, and internet material. Articles relevant to the study were carefully examined to develop themes to address the topic and research objectives. The data were analysed using the themes that emerged. Procedures were followed to provide systematic narrative reviews and guidelines for integrative write-up reviews. The search streamlined its search to studies published between 2014 and 2024. However, in exceptional cases, the study went over and beyond the estimated years based on how pertinent the information was to the study.

DISCUSSION OF FINDINGS

This section discusses the chapter findings derived from systematic literature review analysis.

The Role of Digital Transformation in Public Sector Human Resource Management

The survey of literature has shown various roles that digital transformation could play in improving the operations of public sector HRM. Harnessing the Digitalisation of public sector HRM through "innovative technologies such as artificial intelligence, big data, cloud computing", and ChatGPT is key to improving service delivery and transforming society's lifestyle, learning, and working styles. The increased demand to utilise digital technologies has significantly impacted the functioning of public organisations as HRM departments find it hard to integrate technologies fully in conducting public sector business. To improve the role of HRM in the public sector researchers argue for a policy framework that supports technology adoption and implementation. For example in China, legislative frameworks for adopting and implementing technologies were developed which significantly improved HRM in various government departments.

Furthermore, such a gesture dramatically lowered the cost of HRM in public service departments while consistently improving work efficiency, service quality, and management levels. Due to limited resources, HRM practices are often modest, especially in African countries where public sector organisations are rigid in accepting change. Madhavkumar (2023) argues that developing and preserving people's assets through effective HRM practices is fundamental when deciding on utilising digital transformation tools in the public sector. From these arguments, one can suggest that the public sector human resource management must adapt to the "rolling wave" of digital reform to align its policies and systematic to the transformative agenda ordered by digital transformation.

Digitalisation Accelerates Reforms in Public Sector Human Resources Management

The analysis of the chapter documents indicated that rapid intensification of technological advancement and the growing popularity of digital transformation provide a new achievable strategy for transforming human resource management in the public service sector. The study by Nicoletti (2021) claims that the digital transformation of public sector HRM offers an excellent foundation for accelerating system reforms and enhancing public sector performance). The review of documents further indicates that digital transformation can potentially minimise the costs related to hiring and selection of candidates including performance management in public-sector human resource management. Through digital performance management public services, such as "running at most once," use the Internet and big data to lay the groundwork for decentralising and reforming public sector tasks.

A study by Borkowska & Wilczewska (2018) revealed that digital transformation and the use of new technologies in the public sector can provide more reliable and transparent data that reduce human error, promote informed decision-making and speed up management operations. Utilising digital transformation tools further helps in streamlining and improving the sometimes complex processes involved in effectively eliminating redundancy, bureaucracy in public sector HRM. Adhering to the strategic use of modern technology significantly improves the quality of public sector HRM and increases the performance of public sector employees by providing strong support for accelerating service delivery reforms in the public sector.

The Dilemma of HRM in the Public Sector Organisations

Digital transformation in the public service sector provides an innovative approach to resolving public departments' human resource management challenges. Human resource management in the public sector confronts considerable challenges due to a lack of readiness to change, limiting its ability to adapt internally and keep up with the rapidly changing external environment. However, the introduction of digital transformation addresses this issue by transforming public-sector human resource management from administrative experts to strategic partners (Nemanja & Bilana, 2018). On the one hand, digitalization streamlines office procedures in the public sector by leveraging internet-based platforms, reducing the complexities of workflows and cumbersome administrative practices.

It increases "the perspective of human resource management departments and the interaction and flexibility of human resource management in the public service sector. A more comprehensive human resource management system provides" better employee data access and increases performance review openness (Lim, Wang & Lee, 2017: 9). As a result, strategic cooperation activities enable the public sector to make more flexible and accurate decisions and adapt quickly to the ever-changing external environment. On the other hand, digitalization has broadened the scope of public-sector human resource reform to include both departments and personnel. This broader approach expands on personnel as "the first resource, capital, and driving force." The public sector can promptly detect changes in personnel circumstances through digital transformation by evaluating large amounts of data (Enaifoghe, 2021).

As a result, interventions such as support, dispute resolution, employee well-being, and stress reduction can help to boost productivity and job satisfaction (Zhou, 2017). In the digital age, although the public sector focuses on technical HRM reform, it is critical to recognize that people are the fundamental force behind attaining organizational goals and ensuring long-term development.

Development of HRM System in the Public Sector

The role of digital transformation provides power for the long-term development of the public sector's human resource management system. Given an ever-changing and demanding external environment, it is critical to address the issue of achieving sustainable development in HRM in the public sector. Enaifoghe et al. (2023) noted that digital technology is essential to respond to these changes appropriately. As a result, it considerably improves the ability of public sector human resource management to manage crises, assisting the system in meeting its sustainable development goals. Furthermore, it contributes to mitigating the detrimental consequences of external environmental changes.

The use of digital technology in the public sector has various benefits. Firstly, it minimises the time required for staff to obtain information, enabling adequate support for sectors based in remote areas. Furthermore, it allows the analysis of previous examples and the calculation of the probability of various situations in the shortest time, resulting in intelligent solutions with valuable references (Zhao, 2019). Furthermore, it promotes the development of pre-established crisis response methods, significantly improving the public sector's ability to handle crises. Moreover, digital HRM enables the personalization of training programs by conducting complete employee evaluations. This guarantees that employees' requirements and strengths are identified and merged into various training programs. As a result, it contributes to enhancing employees' skills and job capabilities, delivering support for the future growth of human resource management within government agencies from both corporate and personal points of view.

Digital Technology and Transformation of Experiences in Public Sector HRM

Research has shown that digital technology can transform public sector HRM which is fundamental for citizens to have value for their money. According to studies, digital technology has dramatically influenced consumers' behaviour. As a result, public service must provide greater levels of customer support. This is demonstrated by the DBS Bank case study (Sia et al., 2016), where Asian customers anticipate using mobile digital banking solutions for most of their banking needs. Banks are now pressured to implement digital reforms and adjust to the market's shifting dynamics. Enhancing the digital customer experience through realignment and investment in digitalised solutions and models can lead to the success of a digital transformation (Shrivastava, 2017).

Rethinking relationships with customers is a key driver of digital transformation (Shrivastava, 2017). Because they use innovations on a regular basis, their expectations are always changing, influencing how users perceive their services (Chanias, 2017; Hong and Lee, 2017). The digital transformation must affect an organization's production and support activities (Battistoni et al., 2023; Bun et al., 2021). According to Lin et al. (2009), these changes are necessary for human resource management to remain competitive in an increasingly digital environment for efficiency and productivity. One advantage of the digital transformation process is the ability to collect additional information on customer behavior every time a client chooses a digital service over a traditional one (Roedder et al., 2016). Using this data, the service can be made more flexible to satisfy the user's specific requirements (Chen et al., 2012; Wang & Ji, 2010).

Learning about clients' needs and preferences allows the public sector to tailor its services to provide a more personalized experience. This may increase client satisfaction and loyalty. Additionally, firms can find opportunities for process improvement using data collection and analysis, which can result in increased productivity and cost savings (Alexopoulos et al., 2022; Alvaro & Challener, 2022). But digital transformation also has drawbacks (Ana Kutnjak & Igor Pihir, 2019; Komarčević et al., 2017). Organisations must guarantee they possess the requisite infrastructure, expertise, and procedures to efficiently gather, examine, and utilise data (Benevene & Cortini, 2010).

To safeguard client information, they must also be aware of data security and privacy issues (Pramanik, 2016; Trung et al., 2021). Ultimately, digital transformation is a complicated and continuous process that calls on firms to be flexible and agile in their strategies. According to Gölzer and Fritzsche (2017), firms can effectively position themselves for success in the digital age by adopting digital technology and data-driven insights.

Digital Transformation of HRM and Citizen Experience

Human resource management in the public sector refers to the collection of management actions and processes that plan, hire, appoint, use, pay, and assure the legal compliance of the human resources to which they belong. Human resource management in the public sector is based on wholly new modern ideas and management concepts. It provides a comprehensive overview of the philosophy and practice of public sector personnel administration (Kavanagh and Johnson, 2018). It deviates greatly from standard personnel administration in terms of management content, management principles, management methods, and departmental status. When considering supporting the public sector, we must do it from a functional perspective.

The functional perspective always keeps the end user and optimisation in mind. It is helpful to distinguish various government domains - local, provincial, and national - in terms of how they operate, their mandates, and the services they provide to citizens to evaluate how technology may best serve them (Samson and Rathee, 2018). There are apparent opportunities to empower public servants, such as allowing them to report on revenue and expenditures more readily and accurately. You can also empower citizens by implementing a fault-reporting mechanism that will enable them to readily report potholes, power outages, and other daily issues in their communities.

Digital Transformation of HRM and Enhanced Public-Private Partnerships

One fundamental impediment to the merger of state and technology is that our structure for public-private partnerships (PPPs) must be revised to meet the special needs of large-scale digital initiatives. The existing legislative PPP framework is designed to support large-scale physical infrastructure investments. Another impediment to successful digital-oriented PPPs is a reduction in technological skills in the public sector. The IT landscape is highly competitive. Financial and other institutions frequently hire talented government employees. The best path ahead is to implement an outcomes-based approach in which public and private entities share risk, capacity, and expertise. The private sector would supply funds; there currently would be agreed-upon results and outcomes. There are also systems in place to protect intellectual property. The latter is a contentious but significant issue. There is a contradiction between transparency in the bid and tender processes and the preservation of competitive advantage, which is critical in this sector.

Investing in the Digitalisation of Public Sector HRM

Digitalisation is a resource-intensive, innovative method, to digitise public HRM fully, the government needs to invest in human resources who will lead the digitisation initiative. According to Bell, Lee, & Yeung (2006), technological expenditures aim to improve operational efficiency. There are digital tools particularly created for each HRM function, whether operational, relational, or strategic. The use of digital technology in organisations has improved the productivity, effectiveness, and efficiency of human resource tasks. It entails redesigning conventional HR management tasks based on modern digital business thinking, focusing on people and work efficiency that benefits all stakeholders (Samson & Agrawal, 2020).

Organisations can capitalise on the potential of digital technologies to drive organisational performance and improve service delivery to citizens by investing in training and development programmes to enhance digital skills among HR professionals and fostering an innovative and collaborative culture (De Pril., 2020). Investment and the necessary skills to design and implement digitisation into HRM are required to integrate digitisation into HRM. Employers must invest in digital technology and prepare their managers to use these digital tools (Samson & Agrawal,2020). Taking advantage of the technological developments of the fourth industrial revolution requires a digitally skilled workforce (Hazafi & Kajtár, 2022). Organisations should emphasise investing in human capital via training as soon as possible. Implementing Digitalisation in organisational operations might prevent potential complications (Štaffenová & Kucharčíková, 2021).

Keep up With the Digital Revolution

To keep up with digital developments such as "recruiting and selection, performance and reward management, career management, and learning and development" of public sector organisations must restructure essential HR operations. Thite (2022) highlighted that web-based technologies have transformed the learning and development role. The digital revolution has a significant influence on human resources. Such consequences will undoubtedly "have an impact on human resource performance and quality. If digital transformation has a beneficial influence on human resources, there will likely be obvious changes in performance, production, service quality, talent development, and other areas" (Kumar, 2016).

Digital governance has the potential to provide significant advantages to citizens by allowing for more prompt, personalised, and cost-effective public services. As one of the largest employers in most countries and with a critical role to play in allowing a well-functioning society, governments must accelerate the transformation of their workforces to give long-term value to people. As new digital technologies emerge, the way HR interacts with information and data has altered. Some HRM procedures, such as employee recruitment, performance evaluation, and human resource development, have been extensively changed utilising digital technology to improve stakeholder service delivery (Mosca, 2020).

The digital revolution has brought about workplace changes ranging from mechanical to computerised, information-based to knowledge-based, individualised to team-based, and hands-on to minds-on (Thite, 2022). According to Smith (2019), the current landscape of public sector management is rapidly being defined by the fast growth and integration of digital and information communication technologies (ICT). In response to changing social requirements and expectations, governments throughout the world are embracing technology advancements to improve the efficiency and effectiveness of their operations, including HRM procedures.

Foster a Culture of Innovation

The government should foster an environment that stimulates innovation and experimentation with emerging technology. Establish procedures for gathering feedback from HR experts about their experiences with digital technologies and incorporating ideas for improvement (Nosike, 2023). Technological innovation is an important strategic tool for organisations seeking to increase competitiveness and performance. Organisations that can produce digital innovation are expected to become the greatest and compete in the present period (Yusuf, Satia Bernardianto, Nurhasanah, Irwani, Kurniasih, & Setyoko,2023).

The culture of innovation is the product of a set of integrated HRM practices rather than a single policy. This foundation is built on visionary leadership and open communication, which are critical to engaging people to actively participate in innovation (Susantinah & Krishernawan, 2023). According to Chen & Huang (2009), knowledge management and HRM practices are positively related, favouring workers' creative actions. Furthermore, knowledge-sharing shapes and strengthens a creative culture. An organisation's management must support and grow its human resources to make innovation effective by fostering an inventive culture.

Employees in such an innovative culture are encouraged to offer new and exciting enhancements to HRM procedures that foster innovation (Opoku et al., 20220). Several strategic initiatives must be taken to improve organisational innovation via HRM strategy. First and foremost, it is critical to implement long-term skill development programmes that focus on skills relevant to technology improvements and market trends. Furthermore, the creation of creative pay systems, such as special bonuses or rewards for inventive contributions, can act as powerful motivators for employees (Susantinah & Krishernawan, 2023).

CONCLUSION

This chapter examines the drivers of digital transformation and their efficacy in enhancing public-sector Human Resource Management. The study highlighted Digitalisation's role in reshaping HRM practices in public agencies while offering better ways and methods for managing human capital. Undoubtedly, digital technology serves as a significant enabler for HRM reform in the public sector, facilitating the execution of swift and efficient services. However, the full utilization of digital technologies is still hindered by a bureaucratic culture that is resistant to change among public officials, budgetary constraints including data security. The chapter observes the public sector must the smooth integration of digital technologies within the HRM function. The chapter emphasises that public sector organisations should foster a culture of digital fluency among staff, enhance digital skills through training, and more importantly, redesign the HR system from the conventional approach to the digital way of doing things.

Based on the conclusion derived from this chapter, the researchers suggest that public sector organisations should foster an environment that stimulates human resource innovation and experimentation with emerging technology. By establishing procedures for gathering feedback from HR experts about their experiences with digital technologies and incorporating ideas for improvement, technological innovations could be used effectively to transform public sector HRM which may ultimately lead to improved service delivery.

Further review of other studies has shown various existing impediments that may threaten the digital transformation of public sector human resources. These include unreformed bereacratic culture, personnel opposition to change, budget limits, and so on. This chapter advocates for optimisation techniques, such as strengthening the public sector's information security system, encouraging a digitally-driven culture among staff members, improving digital skills, and accelerating the transformation and smooth integration of public sector tasks to enhance effectiveness and efficiency in public sector HRM.

RECOMMENDATIONS AND DIRECTION FOR FURTHER RESEARCH

This study found that budgetary restrictions, particularly data security, and bureaucratic cultures that are resistant to change among public officials continue to impede the full utilisation of digital technologies. The study suggests that future research concentrates more intently on what the public sector can do to prevent bureaucratic culture, budgetary restrictions, and data security from impeding the much-needed reform. The study suggests that the government establish boundaries between public administration and political administration and implements the professionalisation framework in crucial positions brought about by the digital era. The study concludes that for HRM practitioners to embrace innovation and change, governments should provide them with the necessary digital skills that could help enhance efficiency in service delivery.

REFERENCES

Africa, S. (2012). National Development Plan. Retrieved from www.gov.za/issues/national-developmentplan2030

Al-Alawi, A. I., & Al Showmali, Z. (2019). Role of human resource management in the learning organization: An empirical study of public sector in the Kingdom of Bahrain. In *Proceedings of the 33rd IBIMA Conference*.

Al-Alawi, A. I., Messaadia, M., Mehrotra, A., Sanosi, S. K., Elias, H., & Althawadi, A. H. (2023). Digital transformation adoption in human resources management during COVID-19. *Arab Gulf Journal of Scientific Research*, 41(4), 446–461. 10.1108/AGJSR-05-2022-0069

Al-Ruithe, M., Benkhelifa, E., & Hameed, K. (2018). Data Governance Taxonomy: Cloud versus Non-Cloud. *Sustainability (Basel)*, 10(1), 95. 10.3390/su10010095

Al-Ruithe, M., Benkhelifa, E., & Hameed, K. (2018). Key Issues for Embracing the Cloud Computing to Adopt a Digital Transformation: A study of Saudi Public Sector. *Procedia Computer Science*, 130, 1037–1043. 10.1016/j.procs.2018.04.145

Banga, K. (2018). Digitalisation and the future of industrialisation in Africa. Economic Transformation, Science, Technology and Innovation for Development. https://set.odi.org/wp-content/uploads/2018/06/ATF-2018-presentation_KB.pdf

Banga, K., & Velde, D. W. (2018). Digitalisation and the future of manufacturing in Africa. *Supporting Economic Transformation* (SET). https://set.odi.org/wp-content/uploads/2018/03/SET_Future-of-manufacturing_Brief_Final.pdf

Behnam, T. Ed Lam, Girard, K., & Irvin, V. (2019 March 13). Digital Transformation Is Not About Technology. https://hbr.org/2019/03/digital-transformation-is-not-about-technology

Bekkhus, R. (2016). Do KPIs used by CIOs Decelerate Digital Business Transformation? The Case of ITIL. DIGIT 2016 Proceedings. https://aisel.aisnet.org/digit2016/16

Bell, B. S., Lee, S., & Yeung, S. K. (2006). The impact of e-HR on professional competence in HRM: Implications for the development of HR professionals. *Human Resource Management*, 45(3), 295–308. 10.1002/hrm.20113

Benson, A. D., Johnson, S. D., & Kuchinke, K. P. (2002). The use of technology in the digital workplace: A framework for human resource development. *Advances in Developing Human Resources*, 4(4), 392–404. 10.1177/152342202237518

Bertot, J. C., Jaeger, P. T., & Hansen, D. (2012). The Impact of Polices on Government Social Media Usage: Issues, Challenges, and Recommendations. *Government Information Quarterly*, 29(1), 30–40. 10.1016/j.giq.2011.04.004

Bertrand, A. A., & McQueen, J. (2022, October 11). *How governments can foster a digital-first culture in their workforce*. https://www.ey.com/en_za/government-digital-innovation/how-governments-can-foster-a-digital-first-culture-in-their-workforce

Betchoo, N. K. (2016, August). Digital transformation and its impact on human resource management: A case analysis of two unrelated businesses in the Mauritian public service. In *2016 IEEE International Conference on Emerging Technologies and Innovative Business Practices for the Transformation of Societies (EmergiTech)* (pp. 147-152). IEEE. 10.1109/EmergiTech.2016.7737328

Betchoo, N. K. (2016). Digital transformation and its impact on human resource management: A case analysis of two unrelated businesses in the Mauritian public service. 2016 IEEE *International Conference on Emerging Technologies and Innovative Business Practices for the Transformation of Societies* (EmergiTech), 147-152. 10.1109/EmergiTech.2016.7737328

Bharadwaj, A., El Sawy, O. A., Pavlou, P. A., & Venkatraman, N. (2013). Digital Business Strategy: Toward a Next Generation of Insights. *Management Information Systems Quarterly*, 37(2), 471–482. 10.25300/MISQ/2013/37:2.3

Borrego, M., Foster, M. J., & Froyd, J. E. (2014). Systematic literature reviews in engineering education and other developing interdisciplinary fields. *Journal of Engineering Education*, 103(1), 45–76. 10.1002/jee.20038

Cantoni, F., & Mangia, G. (Eds.). (2018). *Human Resource Management and Digitalization* (1st ed.). Routledge., 10.4324/9780429425288

Chanani, U.L., & Wibowo, U.B. (2019). A learning culture and continuous learning for a learning organization. *KnE Social Sciences*, 591-598.

Chen, C. J., & Huang, J. W. (2009). Strategic human resource practices and innovation performance – the mediating role of knowledge management capacity. *Journal of Business Research*, 62(1), 104–114. 10.1016/j.jbusres.2007.11.016

Chytiri, A. P. (2019). "Human Resource Managers' Role in the Digital Era," SPOUDAI Journal of Economics and Business, *SPOUDAI Journal of Economics and Business* [January-J.]. *University of Piraeus*, 69(1-2), 62–72.

Cortellazzo, L., Bruni, E., & Zampieri, R. (2019). The Role of Leadership in a Digitalized World: A Review. *Frontiers in Psychology*, 10, 1938. https://www.frontiersin.org/articles/10.3389/fpsyg.2019.01938. 10.3389/fpsyg.2019.0193831507494

Cozza, M. (2020). Course: Bachelor thesis in Business Administration Course code: FOA230 15 cr.

Criado, J. I., Rojas-Martín, F., & Gil-Garcia, J. R. (2017). Enacting social media success in local public administrations: An empirical analysis of organizational, institutional, and contextual factors. *International Journal of Public Sector Management*, 30(1), 31–47. 10.1108/IJPSM-03-2016-0053

Ctarino, J., Rosa, I., & Da Silvi, M. M. (2018). Defining the Chief Digital Officer Using COBIT 5. *ISACA J*, 6, 41–48.

Démeijer, D. (2017). Making digital HRM work: A study in changes in perceived consequences of e-HRM in the past decade. https://essay.utwente.nl/71821/1/Demeijer_BA_BMS.pdf

Elizabeth, R. (2017, October 10). Increasing competitive threats are driving digital transformation. *Technology Record.*https://www.technologyrecord.com/Article/increasing-competitive-threats-are-driving-digital-transformation-6044

Enaifoghe, A. (2021). Digitalisation of African Economies in the Fourth Industrial Revolution: Opportunities for Growth and Industrialisation. *African Journal of Development Studies*, 11(2), 31–53.

Enaifoghe, A., Dlamini, N.P., & Agwuna, L.U. (2020). African Economic Integration Development in Technological Transformation: Accessing the Importance of Ethical Leadership for Policy Implementation in SADC. *Journal of Economics and Behavioral Studies, 12*(6 (J), 11-20.

Enaifoghe, A., Dlamini, N. P., Jili, N. N., & Mthethwa, R. (2023). The role of e-government as enabler of good governance for socio-economic development in South Africa. *International Journal of Social Science Research and Review*, 6(1), 493–508.

Enaifoghe, A., & Ndebele, N. (2023). Examining the barriers to adopting and integrating information communication technologies as e-Government in Africa. *International Journal of Research in Business and Social Science (*2147-4478), *12*(7), 383-393.

Enaifoghe, A., & Zenzile, N. (2023). The rapidly evolving situation of employee work-from-home productivity and the integration of ICT in Post-COVID-19 pandemic. *Scientific African*, 20, e01709. 10.1016/j.sciaf.2023.e01709

Fabbri, T., Mandreoli, F., Martoglia, R., & Scapolan, A. C. (2019, July). Employee attitudes and (digital) collaboration data: A preliminary analysis in the HRM field. In *2019 28th International Conference on Computer Communication and Networks (ICCCN)* (pp. 1-6). IEEE.

Goran, J., LaBerge, L., & Srinivasan, R. (2017). *Culture for a digital age*. 10.

Guerra, J., Danvila del Valle, I., & Méndez-Suárez, M. (2023). The impact of digital transformation on talent management. *Technological Forecasting and Social Change*, 188, 122291. 10.1016/j.techfore.2022.122291

Hazafi, Z., & Kajtár, E. (2022). The Impact of COVID on the Development of HRM in Public Service. *Belügyi Szemle, 70*(1. ksz.), 88-106.

Heavin, C. M., & Power, D. J. (2018). Challenges for digital transformation – towards a conceptual decision support guide for managers. *Journal of Decision Systems*, 27(sup1), 38–45. 10.1080/12460125.2018.1468697

Horlacher, A., & Hess, T. (2016). *What Does a Chief Digital Officer Do? Managerial Tasks and Roles of a New C-Level Position in the Context of Digital Transformation.* 5126–5135.10.1109/HICSS.2016.634

Kavanagh, M. J., & Johnson, R. D. (2018). *Human resource information systems: Basics, applications, and future directions* (4th ed.). Sage.

Kazançoğlu, Y., & Ozkan-Özen, Y. D. (2018). Analyzing workforce 4.0 in the fourth industrial revolution and proposing a road map from operations management perspective with fuzzy DEMATEL. *Journal of Enterprise Information Management*, 31(6), 891–907. 10.1108/JEIM-01-2017-0015

Komarčević, M., Dimić, M., & Čelik, P. (2017). Challenges and impacts of the digital transformation of society in the social sphere. *SEER: Journal for Labour and Social Affairs in Eastern Europe*, 20(1), 31–48. 10.5771/1435-2869-2017-1-31

Korhonen, J. J., & Halén, M. (2017). Enterprise Architecture for Digital Transformation. *2017 IEEE19th Conference on Business Informatics* (CBI), 01, 349–358.10.1109/CBI.2017.45

Kraus, S., Durst, S., Ferreira, J., Veiga, P., Kailer, N., & Weinmann, A. (2022). Digital transformation in business and management research: An overview of the current status quo. *International Journal of Information Management*, 63, 63. 10.1016/j.ijinfomgt.2021.102466

Kumar, B. N. (2016). Digital revolution in the mauritian public service: A human resource development perspective in two unrelated companies. *International Journal of Novel Research in Interdisciplinary Studies*, 3(5), 1–10.

Kutnjak, A., Krizanic, S., & Pihir, I. (2019). *Educational And Practical View Ofknowledge, Skills And Experience Needed By A Chief Digital Officer*. 5711–5718. 10.21125/edulearn.2019.1389

Lankshear, C., & Knobel, M. (2008). *Digital Literacies: Concepts, Policies and Practices*. Peter Lang.

Lim, S., Wang, T. K., & Lee, S. (2017). Shedding new light on strategic human resource management: The impact of human resource management practices and human resources on the perception of federal agency mission accomplishment. *Public Personnel Management*, 46(2), 91–117. 10.1177/0091026017704440

Linders, D. (2012). From e-government to we-government: Defining a typology for citizen coproduction in the age of social media. *Government Information Quarterly*, 29(4), 446–454. 10.1016/j.giq.2012.06.003

Luna-Reyes, L. F., & Gil-García, J. R. (2014). Digital government transformation and internet portals: The co-evolution of institutions, technology, and organizations. *Government Information Quarterly*, 31(4), 545–555. 10.1016/j.giq.2014.08.001

Madhavkumar, V. (2023). Human resource management practices as determinants of organizational performance. *Productivity*, 63(4), 465–477. 10.32381/PROD.2023.63.04.9

Mazurchenko, A., & Maršíková, K. (2019). "Digitally-Powered Human Resource Management: Skills and Roles in the Digital Era," *Acta Informatica Pragensia, Prague University of Economics and Business, vol.* 2019(2), 72-87.

McKinsey. (2018, October 29). The keys to a successful digital transformation.https://www.mckinsey.com/capabilities/people-and-organizational-performance/our-insights/unlocking-success-in-digital-transformation

McKinsey. (2020). How COVID-19 has pushed companies over the technology tipping point—and transformed business forever. https://www.mckinsey.com/capabilities/strategy-and-corporate-finance/our-insights/how-covid-19-has-pushed-companies-over-the-technology-tipping-point-and-transformed-business-forever#/

Mergel, I. (2015). Open collaboration in the public sector: The case of social coding on GitHub. *Government Information Quarterly*, 32(4), 464–472. 10.1016/j.giq.2015.09.004

Mergel, I. (2016). Agile innovation management in government: A research agenda. *Government Information Quarterly*, 33(3), 516–523. 10.1016/j.giq.2016.07.004

Mergel, I., & Desouza, K. (2013). Implementing open innovation in the public sector: The case of Challenge.gov. *Public Administration Review*, 73(6), 882–890. 10.1111/puar.12141

Metselaar, J. (2021). The Impact of Digital Transformation on Business: A Detailed Review.https://www.proudpen.com/book/strategic-management-in-the-age-of-digital-transformation/the-impact-of-digital-transformation-on-business-a-detailed-review/

Mickoleit, A. (2014). "Social Media Use by Governments: A Policy Primer to Discuss Trends, Identify Policy Opportunities and Guide Decision Makers," OECD Working Papers on Public Governance 26, *OECD Publishing*.

Mosca, M. (2020). *Digitalization of HRM: A study of success factors and consequences in the last decade* (Master's thesis, University of Twente).

Ndebele, N. C., & Enaifoghe, A. (2023). The Adoption of Innovative Strategies for Enhanced Service Delivery in the South Africa Public Sector. *Social Sciences And Education Research Review*, 10(2), 114–121.

Neeley, T., & Leonardi, P. (2022). Developing a digital mindset. *Harvard Business Review*, 100(5-6), 50–55.

Nemanja, B., & Bilana, S. M. (2018). Electronic Human Resource Management: A New Concept for the Digital Age. *Strategic Management*, 2018(2), 22–32.

Nicoletti, B. (2021). *Banking 5.0: How Fintech Will Change Traditional Banks in the 'New Normal' Post Pandemic*. Springer Nature. 10.1007/978-3-030-75871-4

Nosike, C. J. (2023). Deployment Of Modern Digital Technologies And Icts In Public Sector Hrm: Benefits And Challenges. *Interdisciplinary Journal Of African & Asian Studies (Ijaas), 9*(3).

Opoku, S. T., Apenteng, B. A., & Boakye, K. G. (2022). Rewards and employee creativity among rural healthcare employees: The mediating role of organizational support for innovation and the moderating impact of supervisory support. *International Journal of Quality and Service Sciences*, 14(1), 37–53. 10.1108/IJQSS-11-2020-0187

Perry, J. L. (2012). How can we improve our science to generate more usable knowledge for public professionals? *Public Administration Review*, 72(4), 479–482. 10.1111/j.1540-6210.2012.02607.x

Rode, J. C., Huang, X., & Schroeder, R. G. (2022). Human resources practices and continuous improvement and learning across cultures. *Journal of International Management*, 28(4), 100972. 10.1016/j.intman.2022.100972

Rodrigues da Fonseca, L., Silva, M. R., Silva, S. W., & Pereira, G. M. (2019). Continuous-Learning Work Environment: A Study with Developers in Software Development Organizations. *Knowledge Management & E-Learning*, 11(3), 281–303.

Roedder, N., Dauer, D., Laubis, K., Karaenke, P., & Weinhardt, C. (2016). The digital transformation and smart data analytics: An overview of enabling developments and application areas. *2016 IEEE International Conference on Big Data (Big Data)*, 2795–2802.10.1109/BigData.2016.7840927

Salamzadeh, A.The Emergence of Media Entrepreneurship as a Promising Field of Research. (2020). *Journal of Organizational Culture, Communications and Conflict, 24* (2), 1-2. https://ssrn.com/abstract=3674356

Samson, H., & Agrawal, V. (2020). Effectiveness of digitalization in HRM: An emerging trend. *Journal of Critical Reviews*, 7(4), 4082–4088.

Schmid, Y., & Pscherer, F. (2021). Digital transformation affecting human resource activities: A mixed-methods approach. Human Interaction, Emerging Technologies and Future Systems V: Proceedings of the 5th International Virtual Conference on Human Interaction and Emerging Technologies, IHIET 2021, August 27-29, 2021 and the 6th IHIET: Future Systems (IHIET-FS 2021), October 28-30, 2021, France 543-549). *Springer International Publishing.*10.1007/978-3-030-85540-6_68

Serrat, O. (2017). Understanding and Developing Emotional Intelligence. In *Knowledge Solutions* (pp. 329–339). Springer., 10.1007/978-981-10-0983-9_37

Sharma, O. P. (2015). Ethics in Science. *Indian Journal of Microbiology*, 55(3), 341–344. https://www.ncbi.nlm.nih.gov/pmc/articles/PMC4456506/https://doi.org/10.1007/s12088-015-0532-x. 10.1007/s12088-015-0532-x26063945

Singh, A., & Hess, T. (2017). How Chief Digital Officers Promote the Digital Transformation of their Companies. *MIS Quarterly Executive*, 16, 1–17.

Siyaya, M. C., Enaifoghe, A., Uleanya, C., & Gamede, B. T. (2023). The Impact of Information Communication Technology in teaching accounting in South African secondary schools. *Social Sciences And Education Research Review*, 10(2), 270–279.

Smith, L. N., Vician, C., & Derwent, G. (2019). Public Sector Innovation and Organizational Change: Examining the Role of Leadership and Organizational Culture. *International Public Management Journal*, 22(4), 532–556.

Štaffenová, N., & Kucharčíková, A. (2021). Digitalization and human capital. *Journal of HRM*, 24(1).

Susantinah, N., Krishernawan, I., & Murthada, . (2023). Human Resource Management (HRM) Strategy in Improving Organisational Innovation. [ADMAN]. *Journal of Contemporary Administration and Management*, 1(3), 201–207. 10.61100/adman.v1i3.80

Thite, M. (2022). Digital human resource development: Where are we? Where should we go and how do we go there? *Human Resource Development International*, 25(1), 87–103. 10.1080/13678868.2020.1842982

Tumbas, S., Berente, N., & vom Brocke, J. (2017). Three types of chief digital officers and the reasons organizations adopt the role. *MIS Quarterly Executive*, 16, 121–134.UiPath. (2021). What is Robotic Process Automation—RPA Software | UiPath.https://www.uipath.com/rpa/robotic-process-automation

Verhoef, P. C., Broekhuizen, T., Bart, Y., Bhattacharya, A., Qi Dong, J., Fabian, N., & Haenlein, M. (2021). Digital transformation: A multidisciplinary reflection and research agenda. *Journal of Business Research*, 122, 889–901. 10.1016/j.jbusres.2019.09.022

Vial, G. (2019). Understanding digital transformation: A review and a research agenda. *The Journal of Strategic Information Systems*, 28(2), 118–144. 10.1016/j.jsis.2019.01.003

Westerman, G., Bonnet, D., & McAfee, A. (2014). *The Nine Elements of Digital*. 8

Yusuf, M., Satia, H. M. R., Bernardianto, R. B., Nurhasanah, N., Irwani, I., Kurniasih, D., & Setyoko, P. I. (2023). Investigating the Effect of Digital HRM and Digital Innovation and the SMEs Performance in Indonesia. *International Journal of Professional Business Review*, 8(6), e02751–e02751. 10.26668/businessreview/2023.v8i6.2751

Zhao, Y. (2019). Research on the Evaluation System of Local Government Human Resources Management in the New Era [J]. *China Administration, 2019*(5).

Zhou, C. (2017). On how to improve the efficiency of human resource management in government departments [J]. *Commercial Times,* 2010 (5).

Zimmer, M. P., Baiyere, A., & Salmela, H. (2020). Digital Workplace Transformation: The Importance of Deinstitutionalising the Taken for Granted. In *ECIS*.

Chapter 4
Examining the Challenges of Adopting Modern Technologies in Public Sector Human Resource Management

Standa Sani
https://orcid.org/0000-0002-4195-6178
Africa University, Zimbabwe

Siphiwe Plaxedes Mandina
De Montfort University, Zimbabwe

ABSTRACT

HRM in the public sector is undergoing digital transformation, presenting opportunities and challenges. This chapter examines ethical considerations, strategic planning, teamwork, monitoring, and adaptation. It addresses algorithmic bias, emphasizing transparency, accountability, and fairness. The digital divide and equal access are crucial. Interagency collaboration and compatibility enable effective information exchange. Ongoing monitoring and adaptability maximize technology usage and employee satisfaction. Recruitment, Onboarding, Performance Management, and Engagement Technologies are explored. Communication, change leadership, and legal factors are highlighted. This chapter provides a roadmap for successful digital transformation, encompassing ethics, collaboration, inclusivity, and technology integration.

INTRODUCTION

Recent technological advancements have significantly impacted various industries, including human resource management (HRM) (Kim, Wang & Boon, 2021). Public sector organisations recognise the need to leverage technological advancements to enhance HRM effectiveness, efficiency, and employee satisfaction (Ogedengbe et al., 2023). However, implementing modern technologies in public sector HRM comes with unique challenges that require careful planning (Cho, Choi & Choi, 2023). This chapter aims to provide an overview of the digital transformation taking place in public sector HRM and to establish

DOI: 10.4018/979-8-3693-2889-7.ch004

the context and importance of digital transformation in public sector HRM processes. The chapter also explores the classification of modern technologies commonly adopted in public sector HRM and examines various types of modern technologies used in recruitment, on-boarding, performance management, and employee engagement within the public sector. It also identifies the challenges in implementing modern technologies in public sector HRM. The chapter further discusses the common obstacles faced by public sector organisations when implementing digital HRM initiatives, including resource constraints, cultural barriers, data privacy concerns, digital skills gaps, compatibility issues, and ethical considerations.

Strategies for successful implementation of modern technologies in public sector HRM are provided through guidance on building a digital readiness framework, change management, stakeholder engagement, and upskilling HR professionals to overcome implementation challenges and ensure successful adoption of modern technologies. The chapter highlights real-world examples of public sector organisations that have effectively implemented digital HRM processes, offering insights and lessons learned and provides insights on globalisation of such HRM processes in the global south. The chapter explores the potential impact of emerging technologies, such as artificial intelligence, robotic process automation, enhanced data analytics, virtual and augmented reality, blockchain, and the ethical and social implications of technology adoption.

Public sector organisations have a critical role in delivering public services to citisens (Wirtz & Müller, 2023). The adoption of modern HRM technologies can greatly impact their efficiency, effectiveness, and employee satisfaction (Agustian, Pohan & Zen, 2023). Kambur and Yildirim (2023) highlight that digital transformation in HRM enables public sector organisations to improve data management, automate administrative tasks, and streamline processes. By leveraging these technologies, talent acquisition and retention can be enhanced through optimised workforce planning, recruitment, and selection procedures. Digital HRM tools, as mentioned by Shukla, Mishra, and Agnihotri (2023), enable easier access for employees to update personal data, submit leave requests, and manage performance.

The adoption of contemporary HRM technologies in the public sector enables data-driven decision-making (Colombari & Neirotti, 2023). Analytics and predictive modelling provide insights into skill gaps, inform targeted training programs, and offer workforce trend analysis. This data-driven approach improves decision-making and enables efficient resource allocation. Digital HRM technologies also contribute to increased employee engagement and satisfaction (Mer & Srivastava, 2023). User-friendly self-service platforms empower employees to manage their HR-related responsibilities, reducing administrative workloads, enhancing accessibility, and fostering transparency and empowerment.

Overview of Digital Transformation in Public Sector HRM

Public sector HRM differs from the private sector as it prioritises the public interest and social responsibility. Transparency, fairness, and equity are crucial in Human Resources (HR) practices (Hammon, Gillis & Icenogle, 2023). Legal and regulatory complexities are prominent, requiring compliance with various laws and guidelines (Shahaab et al., 2023). Budgetary constraints, political influence and public scrutiny are common issues that the public sector must contend with (Di Carlo, 2023). Balancing efficiency, talent retention, and high performance is difficult due to diverse employee skills and motivations in the public sector. Therefore, managing a multi-generational workforce, promoting diversity, and fostering engagement are essential to strike the balance, (Kirtzalidou, 2023). Research has shown that digital transformation offers both opportunities and challenges for public sector HRM. Utilising modern technologies such as data analytics, machine learning, and artificial intelligence (AI) enables data-driven decision-making, process optimisation, and improved service delivery. However, data privacy, security, and the digital divide must be addressed alongside other HRM aspects (Konateh, Duramany-Lakkoh & Udeh, 2023).

Digital transformation in public sector HRM presents numerous opportunities and challenges. Embracing digital technologies enables data-driven decision-making, streamlined HR procedures, improved service delivery, and enhanced collaboration. HR professionals can leverage data analytics to gain insights into workforce trends and make informed decisions. Automation of routine tasks reduces administrative burdens and allows HR teams to focus on strategic initiatives. Digital platforms enhance service delivery by providing self-service options and facilitating seamless communication. Integration of HR data promotes collaboration and coordination across departments and agencies. However, challenges must be addressed to ensure a successful digital transformation. Data privacy and security are crucial, requiring compliance with regulations and the establishment of robust protocols. Bridging the digital divide is essential to ensure equitable access to technology and digital HR services. Change management strategies and upskilling initiatives are needed to facilitate the transition and overcome resistance. Ethical considerations, such as algorithmic bias, must be addressed through transparent guidelines and monitoring.

Public sector organisations should adopt a holistic approach that combines technological advancements with governance, change management, privacy, and ethics. Stakeholder engagement and collaboration are vital for successful implementation. Legacy system integration should be carefully planned to minimise disruptions. By navigating these opportunities and challenges, public sector HRM can harness the full potential of digital transformation to drive efficiency, effectiveness, and employee well-being.

Importance of Technology in Public Sector HRM

Technology such as AI-powered Applicant Tracking Systems (ATS), Video Interviewing Platforms, Digital on-boarding Platforms, Performance Management Software, Virtual Reality (VR) Training Platforms, E-Learning Systems, Self-Service Portals, Communication and Collaboration Tools and Recognition Programs have revolutionised public sector HRM procedures in numerous ways, including expediting hiring, enhancing on-boarding, transforming performance management, revolutionising training and development, and increasing employee engagement (Mer & Virdi, 2023). The hiring process has become more inclusive and efficient through digital platforms and applicant tracking systems (ATS) that automate resume parsing, candidate tracking, and interview scheduling (Bhanumathi Jeevitha & Rema, 2023). Artificial Intelligence (AI)-powered technologies analyse resumes and evaluate candidate fit, while video interview platforms facilitate remote evaluations (Veglianti et al., 2023). Digital on-boarding platforms streamline paperwork and deliver training modules centrally, ensuring a uniform process (Cranfil et al., 2023). Automated workflows and reminders monitor new hires' progress and enhance engagement (Islam & Tamzid, 2023).

Technology is fast replacing traditional performance management with continuous, data-driven procedures, offering real-time feedback and analytics in public sector HRM although due to varying factors discussed in this chapter, public sector organisations are at different developmental stages that are not uniform (Aldoseri, Al-Khalifa & Hamouda, 2023). Employee training and development have been transformed through learning management systems (LMS) and e-learning platforms that provide customised, adaptable learning experiences in public sector organisations that have adopted HRM technologies (Chen, 2023). AI-driven adaptive learning systems tailor training materials to each learner's requirements and learning preferences (Thimmanna et al., 2024).

A study conducted by Daher & Ziade (2024) indicates that technology can be used to promote employee engagement through internal communication platforms, recognition tools, and feedback mechanisms. Technology has significantly improved HRM procedures, benefiting organisations in hiring, on-boarding, performance management, training, and employee engagement.

Classification of Modern Technologies in the HRM Context

With cutting-edge tools and solutions to improve decision-making, expedite procedures, and enhance employee experiences, modern technologies have completely transformed the field of human resource management (HRM), (Shukla, Mishra & Agnihotri, 2023). These technologies include a broad spectrum of online programs and tools created to assist human resources operations. Here, we define and categorise contemporary technologies within the framework of HRM. Within HRM, the term "modern technologies" refers to digital tools, software, and platforms that help businesses automate, optimise, and improve a range of HR applications, (Pandey et al. 2024). Through the use of innovations in artificial intelligence, data analytics, cloud computing, and mobile applications, these technologies are revolutionising traditional HR procedures and enhancing productivity, efficacy, and retention.

The rapid evolution of HRM's digital transformation is driven by technology breakthroughs and shifting labour dynamics (Galanti et al., 2023). To promote organisational success, public sector HRM should stay updated on emerging technologies, evaluate their suitability for specific HR needs, and strategically adopt and integrate them. Utilising modern technologies enables improved employee experiences, streamlined HR procedures, and organisational advancement. However, it is essential to align an organisation's HR strategy and objectives with the adoption and application of these technologies. Given the unique technological requirements and priorities of each public sector entity, it is crucial to assess the specific requirements and potential benefits before implementing any particular technology. The continuous emergence of new technologies, such as talent acquisition, HR Information Systems, learning and development, virtual reality training platforms, and people analytics tools, further enhances the transformation of public sector HRM. Organisations can evaluate their specific requirements and better align their technology investments with their HR goals and objectives by classifying technological needs and priorities into categories such as, Operational Efficiency, Data Management and Analytics, Talent Acquisition and Recruitment, On-boarding and Training, Performance Management and Employee Development, Employee Engagement and Collaboration and so forth.

TYPES OF MODERN TECHNOLOGIES COMMONLY ADOPTED IN PUBLIC SECTOR HRM

Incorporating digital technologies into contemporary HRM practices has become essential, as it allows HR practitioners to optimise workflows, improve employee satisfaction, and propel organisational achievements. To guarantee successful implementation and utilisation, organisations can select the technologies that best fit their unique HR needs, goals, sise, integration capabilities with the current HR systems, and budget. The following are types of technologies commonly adopted in public sector HRM.

Recruitment Technologies

The unique demands and specifications of the hiring and recruiting processes in government agencies and organisations are specifically addressed by public sector HR recruitment technologies (Cho, Choi & Choi, 2023). These technologies are specifically designed to tackle the difficulties and intricacies of hiring in the public sector, which frequently entails adhering to rules, managing high applicant volumes, and guaranteeing justice and transparency. Typical instances of these technologies are as follows.

(a) Job Portals and Online job Boards

Public sector organisations utilise dedicated job boards and online portals, providing a centralised location for job seekers to access and apply for positions (Napierala & Kvetan, 2023). These platforms automate processes, streamline hiring, and save time and money for employers and job seekers (Aisa, Cabeza & Martin, 2023). Advanced search options help job seekers find opportunities aligned with their preferences, while employers can attract suitable candidates (Habbal, Ali & Abuzaraida, 2024). Detailed information promotes transparency and attracts applicants who share organisational goals. Some portals offer career development tools and networking features for job seekers (Sidoti et al., 2023). Accessibility and equity considerations are important, ensuring inclusivity and mitigating biases (Raghavan et al., 2020). Job portals have transformed recruitment, fostering openness and accessibility in the public sector (Raghavan et al., 2020).

However, job portals often provide a standardised application process, which may lack the personal touch of traditional recruitment methods. Candidates may feel disconnected or perceive a lack of individual attention during the application process. Job portals can generate a large volume of applications for each job posting, especially if they have a wide reach. Managing and reviewing a high number of applications can be time-consuming for HR professionals. Job portals depend on the accuracy and quality of the data provided by job seekers. However, there can be instances of inaccurate or incomplete information in candidate profiles, which can lead to inefficiencies in the recruitment process. Job portals often rely on keyword-based searches or algorithms to match candidates to job postings. This approach may not effectively capture the nuances of candidates' skills, experiences, and suitability for a particular role. Job portals primarily attract candidates who are actively seeking employment and actively using the platform. This may exclude passive job seekers who are not actively searching for jobs or may not be aware of the specific job portal being utilised.

Saad and Itika, (2024) posit that the Zimbabwean government implemented online job portals to streamline the recruitment processes. By digitising job advertisements and applications, this initiative aimed to expedite the hiring process and improve access to job opportunities for applicants. The online portals allowed HR practitioners to efficiently manage job vacancies, review applications, and select candidates, ultimately speeding up the on-boarding of employees.

(b) Applicant Tracking Systems (ATS)

Public sector organisations commonly use customised Applicant Tracking Systems (ATS) platforms to streamline their hiring process (Laurim et al., 2021). These systems automate job posting, application management, candidate screening, and interview scheduling. ATS platforms simplify candidate data examination and evaluation for hiring managers (Shruthi & Poornima, 2023). Automated resume screening and talent pools aid in efficient candidate selection (Laurim et al., 2021). The successful implementation of HRIS can bring several benefits to organisations, including improved data management, streamlined administrative processes, enhanced reporting capabilities, and increased efficiency in HR operations. By centralising employee information, automating routine tasks, and facilitating data-driven decision-making, HRIS can contribute to better workforce management and strategic planning. The study by Midio (2015) found that HRIS (Human Resource Information System) was serving its intended purpose in the Kenyan and Zimbabwean health sectors where the implementation of HRIS in those institutions was successful in achieving its objectives.

However, the public sector needs to be cautious about potential biases and continually improve ATS procedures to mitigate potential biases and ensure fair and equitable recruitment processes (Laurim et al., 2021). ATS platforms offer automation, efficiency, and organisation in managing large volumes of applications although there can be potential drawbacks or challenges associated with managing large volumes of applications, particularly if not handled effectively. (Laurim et al., 2021).

(c) Electronic Document Management Systems

To enhance record-keeping and compliance, public sector HR departments utilise electronic document management systems (EDMS) (Alkashami, 2023). EDMS platforms provide a secure and centralised repository for storing, organising, and retrieving candidate and employee records (Alkashami, 2023). They offer structured categorisation, version control, and robust search capabilities (Alade, 2023). Document formats like Word, Excel, PDF, and multimedia files can be stored, while version control tracks and archives previous versions (Alade, 2023). Efficient search functions reduce retrieval time (Alade, 2023).

EDMS platforms enable collaboration, allowing multiple users to view, edit, and comment on documents simultaneously (Alade, 2023). Workflow management tools automate approval processes, ensuring efficiency and auditability. Document security is ensured through permissions, access controls, audit trails, user authentication, and encryption (Ndebele, 2021).

Integration with other systems like ERP and CRM is possible, facilitating data synchronisation and exchange (Aleksandrova, 2023). EDMS systems are adaptable to an organisation's evolving needs (Sternad Zabukovšek et al., 2023). Implementing an EDMS improves document organisation, reduces physical storage requirements, enhances collaboration, increases productivity, and strengthens information security (Alade, 2023). Considerations for effective implementation include system compatibility, user training, change management, and data migration (Alade, 2023).

Chikomba, Rodrigues and Ngoepe (2021) state that the increased use of ICTs in public sector institutions in Zimbabwe, with the aim of promoting accountability, transparency, and service delivery, has led to the generation of a significant volume of digital records. However, effectively managing these digital records in public sector HRM has been a challenge for many public sector institutions, not just in Zimbabwe but globally. The transition to a digital environment requires careful attention to records management practices to ensure the long-term preservation, accessibility, and integrity of these records.

(d) Talent Pool and Succession Planning Software

Public sector organisations can use talent pool and succession planning software to identify and develop internal candidates for future leadership roles (Padma, 2023). This software assesses employees based on performance, skills, and growth potential, creating succession plans and personalised development opportunities (Al Awadhi & Muslim, 2023). It addresses skill gaps, integrates with performance management systems, and encourages internal career advancement (Al Awadhi & Muslim, 2023). Analytics and integration with HR systems provide insights and accurate talent data (Wheeler & van de Haterd, 2024). Further the implementation requires alignment with talent management strategy, data accuracy, privacy, and user support to ensure that efficiency is improved within public sector HRM (Padma, 2023).

On-boarding Technologies

Public sector HR on-boarding technologies are devices and software designed to enhance and speed up the on-boarding process for new employees in government agencies and enterprises, (Biea et al. 2023). These technologies facilitate communication and training, expedite administrative tasks, and ensure a smooth on-boarding process for new hires. Mutegi (2021) postulate that Kenya has indeed made significant progress in digital innovation and e-government services, and platforms like Huduma Kenya have the potential to enhance various aspects of public sector HRM, including the on-boarding process. Huduma Kenya, for instance, serves as a centralised portal for citisens to access a wide range of government services. This type of platform can potentially be extended to include HRM functionalities, such as digital on-boarding processes. By integrating on-boarding technologies into the Huduma Kenya platform, the government can streamline the on-boarding process for new employees in the public sector. The following are most of the on-boarding tools used in public sector HRM.

(a) Digital on-Boarding Platforms

Digital on-boarding platforms streamline and enhance the on-boarding process for public sector new hires (Chaturvedi, 2023). They offer centralised access to forms, training materials, and resources, replacing paper-based procedures. New hires can complete paperwork online, customise their on-boarding experience, and access the platform remotely (Chang, 2023). Integration with HR systems ensures data accuracy and transfer (Prokopenko, Garafonova & Zhosan, 2023). Data security, privacy compliance, and personalised engagement are prioritised (Henry et al., 2024). Implementing a digital on-boarding platform improves efficiency and enhances the on-boarding experience (Chaturvedi, 2023).

Government agencies, such as ministries, departments, and regulatory bodies, can benefit from digital on-boarding platforms. These platforms streamline the on-boarding process by providing new employees with centralised access to essential information, policies, and training materials. They expedite administrative tasks, reduce paperwork, and ensure a smooth transition into the organisation. Public Service Commissions responsible for recruiting and appointing employees in the public sector can utilise digital on-boarding platforms. These platforms facilitate efficient communication with newly appointed individuals, provide access to necessary forms and documents, and guide them through the on-boarding process. This helps in expediting the administrative procedures and ensuring compliance with regulations.

Local government authorities, including municipalities, city councils, and regional bodies, can leverage digital on-boarding platforms to enhance efficiency and improve the on-boarding experience. These platforms enable new employees to access relevant information, complete required forms, and familiarise themselves with local policies and procedures. They can also provide training modules specific to the local government's functions and responsibilities. Public schools, colleges, and universities can adopt digital on-boarding platforms to streamline the on-boarding process for new faculty and staff members. These platforms can provide access to academic policies, curriculum materials, and training resources.

They can also facilitate communication between new hires and relevant departments, ensuring a smooth integration into the educational institution. Public healthcare organisations, such as hospitals, clinics, and public health agencies, can benefit from digital on-boarding platforms. These platforms can provide new healthcare professionals with access to patient care protocols, medical guidelines, and training modules. They can also streamline the collection of necessary credentials and certifications, ensuring compliance with healthcare regulations.

(b) Workflow Automation Tools

Workflow automation tools automate and enhance HR workflows in the public sector, increasing efficiency and reducing errors (Kumar et al., 2024). They streamline employee on-boarding, off boarding, performance management, and training processes (Thakur, 2024; Dhanalakshmi et al., 2024). Employee self-service portals empower employees, while analytics enable data-driven decision-making (Hartono, Tijahyadi & Cassandra, 2021; Pillai & Sivathanu, 2022). Integration with HR systems ensures data consistency (Kumar et al., 2024). Implementing automation tools improves productivity and accuracy (Kumar et al., 2024).

(c) Virtual On-boarding and Orientation Tools

HRM software streamlines remote on-boarding in the public sector, using video conferencing platforms and virtual tools (Majam & Jarbandhan, 2022). Virtual sessions and online portals automate paperwork and provide interactive orientation, training, and collaboration opportunities (Citrin & deRosa, 2021; Alkhalil et al., 2021). Gamification and feedback enhance engagement and evaluation (Shuster, 2023). Virtual on-boarding fosters connection, knowledge transfer, and engagement in the public sector (Majam & Jarbandhan, 2022).

(d) Interactive on-boarding modules

Interactive on-boarding modules in public sector HRM enhance the on-boarding process using multimedia, simulations, and gamification (Chaturvedi, 2023). They deliver engaging content tailored to new hires' needs, foster critical thinking, and offer mobile accessibility (Haswani & Erlita, 2023). Integration with HR systems ensures seamless access and tracking (Islam & Tamzid, 2023). Interactive modules improve understanding, participation, and knowledge retention in public sector on-boarding (Chaturvedi, 2023).

Performance Management Technologies

Public sector HR performance management technologies are software programs designed to aid performance management in government agencies and organisations. These tools assist in performance evaluations, goal-setting, progress monitoring, feedback giving, and facilitation of performance discussions, making them popular in the public sector.

(a) Performance Management Platforms

Performance management platforms in public sector HRM automate and streamline performance monitoring, goal-setting, feedback, and reviews (Cho, Choi & Choi, 2023). They enable clear performance targets, continuous coaching, and real-time feedback. These platforms simplify the review process, generate reports, and integrate with LMS for employee development (Varma, Budhwar & DeNisi, 2023; Upadhyay, 2024). Integration with HR systems ensures data consistency (Varma, Budhwar & DeNisi, 2023). Implementing performance management platforms enhances efficiency and effectiveness (Cho, Choi & Choi, 2023).

(b) Continuous Feedback Tools

Continuous feedback tools in public sector HRM enable real-time communication, feedback exchange, and performance improvement (Cho, Choi & Choi, 2023). These tools foster open communication, ongoing feedback, and goal tracking. Features like comment threads and 360-degree feedback enhance collaboration and accountability (Das & Rajini, 2023). Automatic notifications and analytics support evaluation and improvement. Continuous feedback technologies strengthen relationships, cultivate a feedback-rich culture, and enhance performance in the public sector (Cho, Choi & Choi, 2023).

(c) Real-time Performance Analytics Platforms

Real-time performance analytics platforms in public sector HRM provide data analytics and insights into employee performance (Khatri, 2023). These platforms collect and analyse data from various sources, offering reporting tools, visual dashboards, and alerts (Cho, Choi & Choi, 2023; Fagarasan et al., 2023). Real-time metrics, visualisations, and benchmarks support decision-making and improvement. Integration with relevant systems enables comprehensive analysis and predictive capabilities (Cho, Choi & Choi, 2023). Implementing real-time performance analytics enhances decision-making and performance development in the public sector (Khatri, 2023).

(d) 360-Degree Feedback tools

360-degree feedback instruments in HRM gather and report feedback from multiple sources, providing a comprehensive perspective on employee performance (Ali, Abdalgani & Dahlan, 2023). Customised questionnaires align with company values and goals, supporting development planning (Cho, Choi & Choi, 2023). Integration with performance management systems ensures feedback is considered in performance discussions (Varma, Budhwar & DeNisi, 2023). Integrating a 360-degree feedback tool in public sector HRM enhances employee development and performance management. Effective utilisation requires clear instructions, training, and emphasising its constructive nature (Ali, Abdalgani & Dahlan, 2023).

Employee Engagement Technologies

Tools and software programs intended to improve employee engagement, communication, and the development of a healthy work environment inside government agencies and enterprises are known as public sector HR employee engagement technology. Effective employee recognition, feedback, cooperation, communication, and engagement are all made possible by these tools. These are a few typical HR employee engagement tools used in the public sector.

(a) Internal Communication and Collaboration Platforms

Internal communication and collaboration platforms (ICM) in public sector HRM enhance employee engagement, information sharing, and teamwork. These platforms provide a centralised digital workspace for communication, collaboration, and access to information (Nguyen & Ha, 2023). Features such as chat, instant messaging, and file sharing facilitate real-time communication and collaboration. Dedicated spaces for teams and projects support collaboration, task management, and document sharing (Vignesh Saravanan et al., 2023). News and announcements can be disseminated, and employee directories promote networking (Prebreza, 2021). Mobile accessibility ensures connectivity beyond the office (Nguyen & Ha, 2023).

Integrating an ICM platform in public sector HRM improves collaboration, communication, and productivity. Selecting the right platform, providing training, and ensuring data security and privacy are essential. Fostering an open communication environment and motivating employee participation contribute to the success of these platforms (Nguyen & Ha, 2023).

(b) Employee Recognition Platforms

Employee recognition platforms in public sector HRM aim to acknowledge and value employee accomplishments, contributions, and behaviours (Reina & Scarozza, 2021). These platforms support peer-to-peer, management, and incentive programs, utilising elements like badges, point systems, and social recognition feeds. Peer-to-peer recognition promotes appreciation, cooperation, and teamwork (AlSaadoon, 2020). Company-wide recognition fosters employee pride and unity (Beer, 2022). Employee recognition platforms can include social features, gamification elements, and virtual rewards. Implementing these platforms in public sector HRM reinforces positive work culture, enhances engagement and motivation, and improves retention. Careful platform selection, integration, and communication are important for effective implementation. Fair and consistent recognition aligned with performance expectations is crucial (Reina & Scarozza, 2021).

(c) Pulse Survey Tools

Pulse survey tools in public sector HRM collect employee feedback on engagement, work experience, and happiness (Salvadorinho & Teixeira, 2023). These tools enable quick and easy gathering of insights through sentiment analysis, analytics dashboards, and pre-made survey templates. Conducting shorter questionnaires more frequently increases participation rates (Brown, 2022). Pulse surveys cover various topics, providing insights into communication, leadership, teamwork, work-life balance, job satisfaction, and corporate culture. Regular feedback helps identify patterns and opportunities for development (Salvadorinho & Teixeira, 2023). Real-time insights facilitate data-driven decision-making (Mukuze, 2023).

Pulse survey tools provide instantaneous insights into employee opinions and comments, allowing HR professionals to measure progress, monitor trends, and make quick responses (Mukuze, 2023). Anonymous feedback options encourage participation. Survey data generates actionable outcomes and suggestions for improvement, enhancing employee engagement and happiness. Benchmarking features enable comparisons with industry standards or historical data. Pulse surveys streamline staff follow-up and communication, ensuring employees feel heard and engaged. Implementing pulse survey tools in public sector HRM boosts engagement, identifies areas for development, and regularly gauges employee opinions (Salvadorinho & Teixeira, 2023).

(d) Employee Feedback Mechanisms

Public sector HRM employs various employee feedback mechanisms, including surveys, focus groups, interviews, suggestion boxes, town hall meetings, exit interviews, and digital platforms. These mechanisms enable the collection of input on organisational factors, ensuring confidentiality, anonymity, open communication, and active participation (Tensay & Singh, 2020). HR professionals should explain the purpose, provide updates, and involve employees in the feedback process (Turesky, Smith & Tureski, 2020).

CHALLENGES IN IMPLEMENTING MODERN TECHNOLOGIES IN PUBLIC SECTOR HRM

Public sector companies are becoming more aware of the necessity of utilising contemporary technology to improve their HRM procedures in the current era of technological breakthroughs (Zhang & Chen, 2023). Nevertheless, the implementation of these technologies poses distinct difficulties that are exclusive to the public sector (Giulio & Vecchi, 2023).

Resource Constraints

Budgetary restrictions are a common problem for public sector enterprises, which makes it difficult to invest in and implement innovative HRM technology (Glyptis et al. 2020). The procurement of sophisticated software solutions or the infrastructure required to install and maintain these technologies may be hampered by a lack of funding. When contemplating technology expenditures, public sector enterprises need to carefully weigh the cost-benefit ratio and look into cost-effective choices.

Organisational Culture and Resistance to Change

Comprehensive training programs and efficient change management techniques are necessary for the implementation of new technology (Molino, Cortese & Ghislieri, 2020). Workers might be resistant to change or find it difficult to get used to new systems. To get staff buy-in, public sector firms need to give change management initiatives top priority, offer sufficient training and support, and clearly explain the advantages and goals of adopting new technologies.

Data Privacy and Security Concerns

Ensuring the privacy and security of sensitive employee data is crucial for public sector firms that manage such data, (Masilela & Nel, 2021). Concerns of data breaches, illegal access, and adherence to data protection laws may arise from the use of new technology. To protect employee information, public sector firms need to emphasise strong security measures and set tight procedures.

Lack of Digital Skills and Technological Literacy Among HR Professionals

A major challenge in adopting and utilising HRM technology in the public sector is the lack of digital skills and technical literacy among HR professionals (Sharma et al., 2022). To address this issue, public sector enterprises need to allocate resources for professional development and training programs. These programs can include workshops, webinars, online courses, and certifications focused on relevant HR tools and technology. By equipping HR professionals with the necessary skills, organisations can enhance their ability to effectively utilise HRM technology.

Promoting cooperation and information exchange among HR professionals is another way to address digital skill shortages (Kolot et al., 2020). Creating internal networks, online communities, or communities of practice allows HR practitioners to share best practices, experiences, and knowledge about HRM technology. Peer-to-peer learning and mentorship play a crucial role in upskilling HR professionals. Collaboration between HR and IT departments can provide technical support, system deployment guidance, and insights into emerging technology trends, fostering a better understanding of HRM technology and improving digital capabilities.

When hiring new HR personnel, public sector organisations should prioritise applicants with digital skills and technical literacy. Job descriptions can specify these abilities as preferences or requirements, attracting candidates already proficient in HRM software. Cross-training opportunities should be provided for current HR employees to develop digital proficiency and adapt to new technologies. Creating a culture of learning, providing access to relevant resources, and offering ongoing professional development are essential for HR professionals to stay updated on emerging technologies. Seeking guidance from external consultants, suppliers, or industry experts with expertise in HRM technologies can also help navigate the challenges of adopting and effectively using HRM technology.

A comprehensive strategy that includes training, cooperation, recruitment tactics, and continuous learning is necessary to address the lack of digital skills and technical literacy among HR professionals. By investing in the development of digital skills, public sector companies can empower HR professionals to fully leverage HRM technology and achieve positive outcomes for both the organisation and its workforce.

Compatibility and Integration Challenges with Existing HRM Systems

Implementing new technology in public sector HRM systems can often lead to compatibility issues, (Rahman & Aydin, 2020). Legacy systems may not be easily integrated with contemporary HRM solutions. To overcome these issues, careful planning, teamwork, and technological expertise are needed. Public sector companies can optimise HR procedures by evaluating their current systems, using integration tools, and prioritising data transfer and compatibility.

Ethical Considerations in Adopting Modern Technologies in Public Sector HRM

Ethical considerations are of paramount importance in the field of Public Sector HRM. The following are some of the common ethical pitfalls that take place in public sector HRM and how they can be avoided.

Algorithmic Bias and Fairness

The government sector should prioritise fairness and equity in HRM for all personnel management tasks, including selection, hiring, advancement, pay, performance reviews, and disciplinary measures, regardless of an employee's origin, ethnicity, gender, age, religion, or protected trait, to ensure equal opportunities and treatment (Kruyen & Sowa, 2023).

Ethical Use of Technology

Public sector organisations must consider the moral implications of integrating technology into HRM, ensuring the appropriate application of data analytics, AI, and automated procedures to prevent discriminatory or prejudiced behaviours (Sakka, Maknouzi & Sadok, 2022). HR practitioners should be aware of potential bias in algorithms or AI-driven systems and act to reduce it.

Ethical Leadership and Governance

Public sector HRM requires leaders to uphold ethical standards, conduct ethically, and commit to moral principles (Atthahiru, 2021). They should create a culture that values ethics and integrity, setting an example for their staff. Ethical governance tools like codes of conduct and ethics training can guide HR professionals in making moral judgments. Establishing HRM-specific ethical standards, training practitioners, and regularly evaluating the ethical implications of HRM procedures are crucial steps for public sector firms to foster an environment of honesty, equity, and responsibility.

STRATEGIES FOR SUCCESSFUL IMPLEMENTATION OF PUBLIC SECTOR HRM

Building a Digital Readiness Framework

Building a Digital Readiness Framework in public sector HRM involves establishing a structured approach to assess and enhance the organisation's readiness to embrace and leverage digital technologies. The following is a framework for assessing an organisation's digital readiness, including infrastructure, skills, and change management capabilities.

Technology Infrastructure in Public Sector HRM

Examine the organisation's current IT setup, considering networks, hardware, software, and data storage capacity. Examine the infrastructure's security, dependability, and scalability to support digital activities. Determine any weaknesses or potential areas for development, such as out-of-date software, limited bandwidth, or weak cybersecurity safeguards.

Digital Skills and Competencies

Evaluate workers' digital abilities and competencies at all organisational levels and for all functions. Determine the digital competencies needed for a variety of positions in fields including digital marketing, data analytics, and new technologies. Assess the tools and training programs that are available to improve digital competency and close skill gaps.

Data and Analytics

Examine the company's data management procedures, considering data integration, storage, gathering, and analysis skills. Evaluate the quality and accessibility of the data for strategic planning and decision-making. Examine how well the company can use data analytics tools and methods to gather information and promote evidence based HRM practices.

Change Management Capabilities

Evaluate the organisation's capacity for managing change to successfully traverse digital changes. Examine the leadership's support for change, the organisation's culture, and its openness to it. Assess how well training, engagement, and communication strategies are working to encourage the adoption and acceptance of digital projects.

Digital Governance and Policies

Examine whether the company has any rules, processes, or structures for digital governance. Examine how well digital efforts adhere to ethical, legal, and regulatory standards. Consider the organisation's capacity to handle privacy and digital technology threats.

External Collaboration and Partnerships

Evaluate how the company interacts with outside partners including academic institutes, industry groups, and IT vendors. Assess the organisation's capacity to improve digital preparedness by utilising outside knowledge, resources, and cooperative possibilities. Consider the company's participation in projects or industry networks that support knowledge-sharing and digital innovation.

Measurement and Evaluation

Establish key performance indicators (KPIs) to gauge the organisation's overall level of digital readiness. Provide systems for continuing to track and assess the advancement of digital readiness. Review and update the assessment framework on a regular basis to consider evolving organisational needs, trends, and technology.

This framework offers a comprehensive method for evaluating the digital readiness of a company and pinpointing areas in need of development. It makes sure businesses are ready for the possibilities and challenges of the digital age by helping them create focused strategies and action plans to improve their digital capabilities.

Change Management and Stakeholder Engagement

Change management strategies and effective stakeholder engagement are essential for successful technology implementation within the public sector (Lauer, 2020). Employee resistance to change, particularly regarding technology, is common (Warrick, 2023). Change management techniques address this by raising awareness, promoting understanding, and managing emotions associated with change. Proactively addressing resistance reduces disruptions and increases the chances of successful implementation. Engaging stakeholders effectively ensures their involvement in the process, fostering buy-in and facilitating decision-making.

Clear communication plays a crucial role in change management, helping stakeholders understand the benefits, reasons, and impact of the technology on their jobs (Martínez-Peláez et al., 2023). Timely and accurate information manages expectations, addresses uncertainties, and builds stakeholder confidence. Investing in training and skill development decreases resistance and increases acceptance by equipping employees with the necessary knowledge and abilities to utilise the technology. Change management techniques also involve assessing the technology's impact on various organisational components, creating mitigation plans, and establishing support systems to prevent productivity losses and ensure a smooth transition.

Continuous support and feedback systems are vital during and after technology deployment. Prompt assistance, coaching, and troubleshooting help employees overcome obstacles and build confidence in using the technology (Reunamäki & Fey, 2023). Regular feedback loops enable organisations to address issues, adjust, and continuously improve system efficacy. Identifying change champions and influencers within the company is a common practice in change management, as they can promote adoption and support colleagues throughout the implementation phase. Change management recognises that technology implementation is an ongoing process, requiring flexibility and adaptability to respond to evolving demands, challenges, and feedback. In summary, effective stakeholder engagement and change management techniques are crucial for the successful deployment of technology. They help overcome resistance, gain stakeholder support, minimise disruptions, and create an environment conducive to accepting and utilising new technology.

Upskilling HR Professionals

Employee resistance to change, particularly regarding technology, is common (Warrick, 2023). Change management techniques address this by raising awareness, fostering understanding, and controlling change-related emotions. Proactively addressing opposition reduces interruptions and improves the chances of successful implementation. Effective stakeholder engagement involves involving those affected by the technology deployment, increasing buy-in and facilitating decision-making.

Clear communication is essential in change management, helping stakeholders understand the benefits, reasons, and impact of the technology on their jobs. Timely and accurate information manages expectations, handles uncertainties, and builds stakeholder confidence. Investing in training and skill development decreases resistance and increases acceptance by equipping staff with the necessary skills and knowledge to utilise the technology (Bozkus, 2023). Change management techniques also anticipate and resolve interruptions by assessing the technology's effects on various organisational components, creating mitigation plans, and setting up support systems to ensure a smooth transition. Continuous assistance and feedback systems are crucial during and after technology deployment, enabling employees to overcome obstacles and gain confidence through prompt assistance, coaching, and troubleshooting. Regular feedback loops help organisations solve problems, adjust, and continuously improve system efficacy.

Identifying change champions and influencers is a common practice, as they encourage adoption and support colleagues throughout the implementation phase (Moran, 2023). Change management emphasises that technology implementation is an ongoing process, requiring flexibility and adaptability to respond to changing demands, obstacles, and feedback. In conclusion, effective stakeholder involvement and change management techniques are critical for successful technology deployment. They help overcome resistance, gain stakeholder support, minimise interruptions, and create an environment conducive to accepting and using new technology.

CASE STUDIES AND BEST PRACTICES OF PUBLIC SECTOR HRM

The following is an exploration of a range of case studies and best practices that showcase successful initiatives and strategies employed by public sector organisations to enhance their HRM practices, foster employee engagement, and drive overall organisational performance. These examples provide valuable insights into real-world implementations and highlight the positive outcomes achieved by public sector entities through their HRM endeavours. These case studies and best practices foster a deeper understanding of the effective strategies that have been employed in the public sector to optimise HRM processes and create a thriving work environment that contributes to organisational success in different countries.

City of Edmonton, Canada

A thorough talent management system was put in place by the City of Edmonton to streamline HR procedures and raise worker satisfaction, (Roy, 2017). There were components in the system for learning and development, succession planning, performance management, and recruiting. The city increased operational efficiency and realised considerable cost savings by offering employees self-service options and streamlined HR procedures. Enhancing workforce planning and talent development initiatives through data-driven decision-making was another benefit of the system. Establishing an integrated talent management system may improve employee engagement, expedite HR procedures, and enable public sector organisations to make well-informed talent management choices.

While the City of Edmonton's talent management system may not be directly replicable, it can serve as a reference point for organisations in the global South. It is essential to understand the local context, cultural nuances, and specific HR challenges in the target region. Leveraging technology is crucial for streamlining HR procedures and enabling self-service options, as demonstrated by the City of Edmonton. In the global South, organisations can explore technology solutions that are suitable for their context and budget. This could include utilising existing digital platforms or investing in cost-effective HR software that offers self-service capabilities, performance management modules, and recruitment functionalities. Workforce planning and talent development are critical aspects of the City of Edmonton's talent management system. To glocalise this approach, public sector organisations in the global South can focus on understanding their specific workforce needs and aligning talent development initiatives accordingly.

The City of Edmonton's talent management system emphasises data-driven decision-making. Public sector organisations in the global South can adopt a similar approach by leveraging data analytics to inform HR strategies. Engaging stakeholders, including employees, unions, and relevant government bodies, is vital for successful implementation. Public sector organisations in the global South should involve key stakeholders in the design and implementation of the talent management system. This ensures buy-in, addresses concerns, and enhances the system's acceptance and effectiveness. Capacity building and knowledge sharing initiatives can facilitate the adoption of effective HRM practices in the global South. Organisations can collaborate with international partners, attend conferences, participate in training programs, and leverage resources provided by global HRM networks to enhance their understanding and implementation of talent management systems.

Government of Singapore

To improve service delivery and transform HR practices, the Singaporean government unveiled PS21, a digital HRM platform, (Yeo et al. 2015). PS21 integrated payroll, leave management, and performance reviews into a unified system that is accessible to managers and employees. The solution reduced administrative effort, improved data accuracy, and automated manual tasks. To facilitate continuing education and employee upskilling, the government also introduced the online learning platform Skills Future. Enhancing efficiency, precision, and employee experience in public sector HRM may be achieved through the implementation of a centralised digital HRM platform and the provision of self-service capabilities.

Public sector organisations in the global South may have existing HR systems or processes in place. To globalise the digital HRM platform, it is important to consider integration with these systems to ensure smooth data flow and minimise disruption during the transition. To ensure successful adoption and utilisation of the digital HRM platform, public sector organisations in the global South should invest in training programs and provide ongoing support to employees. This includes training sessions, user guides, and help-desk support to address any challenges or questions that may arise during implementation. Translating the digital HRM platform into local languages and incorporating region-specific content can enhance accessibility and user experience for employees in the global South. Providing multilingual support and culturally relevant resources can help overcome language barriers and improve engagement. Ultimately, public sector organisations in the global South should choose digital HRM solutions that are scalable and affordable, considering the available resources and technological infrastructure in the region. This may involve exploring cloud-based solutions or partnering with technology providers that offer cost-effective options.

City of San Diego, United States

A data analytics project was launched by the City of San Diego to enhance workforce planning and decision-making (Tripathi & Goel, 2022). Through the integration of data from many HR systems and other sources, the city was able to learn more about patterns in hiring, retention, and employee performance. These insights aided HR managers in determining talent shortages, putting targeted training programs into place, and allocating resources sensibly. The workforce planning process was enhanced by the data-driven approach, which also decreased recruitment and turnover expenses. Using data analytics to improve workforce planning and guide HR decisions can save costs and produce better results for public sector HRM.

African governments should begin by assessing their current HRM systems and data infrastructure. This includes evaluating the availability, quality, and accessibility of HR data. Identifying any gaps or areas for improvement will inform the steps needed to adopt data analytics technologies effectively. Establishing data governance policies is crucial to ensure data privacy, security, and compliance. African governments should create frameworks that outline data collection, storage, access, and usage guidelines. This helps build trust and confidence in data analytics initiatives. Governments need to invest in building data analytics capabilities within their HR departments. This may involve training HR professionals in data analysis and interpretation, hiring data analysts or data scientists, or partnering with external organisations that specialise in data analytics. Choosing the right analytics tools and technologies is critical. African governments should consider user-friendly and scalable analytics platforms that suit their specific needs and adhere to budget constraints. Cloud-based solutions can be particularly beneficial in terms of accessibility and flexibility.

Defining relevant KPIs is important to measure the effectiveness of data analytics initiatives. African governments should identify HR metrics aligned with their strategic goals, such as employee turnover rates, talent shortages, or training program effectiveness. These KPIs will help monitor progress and assess the impact of data-driven HR decisions. African governments can learn from successful data analytics implementations in other regions. Engaging in partnerships, attending conferences, and participating in knowledge-sharing networks can provide valuable insights and best practices. Collaboration with international organisations can help build capacity and accelerate the adoption of data analytics technologies. Ongoing monitoring and evaluation of data analytics initiatives are essential. African governments should regularly assess the impact of these technologies on HR decision-making, cost savings, and overall organisational performance. This allows for continuous improvement and refinement of data analytics practices.

Government of New South Wales, Australia

"Activity Based Working" (ABW) is a flexible work strategy that the government of New South Wales established to improve employee happiness and productivity (Theresianto, 2017). Employees at ABW were given the freedom to select their workplace, with a range of options catered to specific job requirements. Employee cooperation and knowledge exchange were also promoted by the policy. The program enhanced work-life balance, decreased absenteeism, and raised employee engagement.

In the public sector, implementing flexible work policies such as activity-based working can improve employee engagement, productivity, and work-life balance. For public sector organisations looking to hire and retain top people, especially in areas where there is a skills shortage, digital platforms and focused recruiting efforts may be very helpful. In public sector HRM, these case studies showcase effective programs and industry best practices. Public sector companies may optimise worker results, streamline HR procedures, and provide people with improved services by embracing new ideas, utilising technology, and emphasising employee involvement and data-driven decision-making.

FUTURE TRENDS AND EMERGING TECHNOLOGIES IN PUBLIC SECTOR HRM

The rapid advancement of technology has made it imperative for HRM practitioners in the public sector to be up-to-date on emerging trends and technologies that might significantly impact HR practices. The fascinating opportunities and foreseeable difficulties related to the integration of contemporary technology in public sector HRM are examined in this section. It also explores the possibilities and factors that are particular to the public sector setting.

The Impact of Artificial Intelligence (AI) and Machine Learning

Artificial intelligence (AI) and machine learning technologies, according to Chilunjika, Intauno and Chilunjika (2022), have the potential to revolutionise HR processes in the public sector. AI-driven recruitment and selection systems can efficiently analyse large volumes of candidate data, improving the accuracy and speed of hiring decisions. Rodgers et al. (2023) affirm that machine learning algorithms can assist in employee performance evaluation and workforce analytics, enabling HR professionals to gain valuable insights for informed decision-making. However, the ethical considerations of AI implementation, such as privacy, bias, and transparency, must be carefully addressed in the public sector.

Robotic Process Automation (RPA) and Process Optimisation

It is possible to automate tedious administrative processes in public sector HRM with robotic process automation (RPA), (Eikebrokk & Olsen, 2020). Employers may automate tasks like benefit administration, leave management, and payroll processing by implementing software robots. Cost reductions, accuracy, and efficiency may all be improved via RPA. But companies also need to think about retraining staff for more strategic positions, applying change management techniques, and addressing the possibility of job displacement.

Enhanced Data Analytics and Predictive HR

The use of advanced data analytics has the potential to revolutionise public sector HR procedures. Organisations can forecast and maximise HR outcomes, such as workforce planning, talent retention, and employee engagement, by utilising big data. Proactive interventions can be made possible by using predictive analytics to assist detect possible challenges before they develop (Ramírez, 2024). Public sector organisations must, however, manage data security and privacy issues while guaranteeing that pertinent laws are followed and that confidential employee data is protected.

Virtual and Augmented Reality in Training and Development

The public sector has tremendous prospects for training and development aided by virtual and augmented reality technology. Employee skills and knowledge may be improved by these technologies through the creation of remote collaboration opportunities, simulation-based training, and immersive learning experiences. According to Gromyko (2024), virtual and augmented reality are useful tools that public sector firms may use to better prepare staff for high-risk situations, enhance service delivery, and encourage better teamwork among geographically separated teams. Nevertheless, infrastructure, expenses, and difficulties with user acceptance must all be carefully considered before putting these technologies into practice.

Blockchain and Secure HR Transactions

Enhancing data security and integrity in HR transactions in the public sector is possible with blockchain technology. Employers may enhance the security and openness of payroll, benefits administration, and personnel information by utilising decentralised and unchangeable ledger systems. The hazards of illegal access and data manipulation can be reduced by blockchain technology (Christ & Helliar, 2021). Regulating and legal issues, guaranteeing compatibility with current systems, and controlling the intricacy of blockchain networks must all be addressed before blockchain can be used in the public sector.

Ethical and Social Implications of Technology Adoption

The public sector's HRM must carefully assess ethical issues and social ramifications as it adopts innovative technology. For HR decision-making processes to be fair, transparent, and accountable, responsible AI practices are crucial. Companies need to be aware of any potential biases included in data sets and algorithms. To preserve public confidence, user privacy, data protection, and informed consent must also be given top priority. In the context of public sector HRM, technological development and implementation should be guided by ethical issues (Bankins, 2021).

Chatbots and Virtual Assistants

The utilisation of chatbots and virtual assistants in public sector HRM can provide substantial benefits by augmenting employee self-service and assistance. These tools may help employees navigate HR procedures, give immediate answers to frequently asked questions about HR, and provide information on rules and procedures. Suta et al. (2020) postulate that chatbots and virtual assistants may offer accurate and tailored support by utilising machine learning and natural language processing. This improves employee experience and lessens the administrative load on HR professionals.

Cybersecurity and Data Protection

The growing dependence on technology has made cybersecurity and data protection crucial factors in public sector human resource management. HR departments manage private employee data, such as financial records, health information, and personal data. Strong cybersecurity measures must be put in place to protect this data from cyber-attacks, illegal access, and breaches. To guarantee data safety and uphold public confidence, secure data storage, encryption, frequent security audits, and staff training on cybersecurity best practices are essential.

Remote Work and Digital Workforce Management

In the public sector, remote work is becoming more popular as a result of the COVID-19 epidemic. HR divisions must change to efficiently manage a dispersed workforce. One way to do this is by putting in place digital workforce management solutions, which enable HR specialists to keep tabs on worker output, evaluate performance, and promote cooperation and dialogue. Technologies that facilitate remote collaboration and keep workers connected and focused on their job include project management software and video conferencing platforms (Mitchell, 2023).

Mobile HR Applications

Employees now have mobile access to HR services and information thanks to the growing popularity of mobile HR applications. Through these applications, staff members may access training materials, see their pay stubs, request time off, and have critical HR notifications sent straight to their mobile devices. Public sector companies may improve communication, boost employee happiness, and promote employee self-service by implementing mobile HR apps.

Diversity, Equity, and Inclusion (DEI) Technologies

In the public sector, HRM initiatives about diversity, equity, and inclusion may be greatly aided by technology. DEI technologies can assist lessen unconscious biases and encourage fair and inclusive behaviours (Dick, 2021). Examples of these technologies include blind recruiting platforms and AI-based solutions for minimising bias in hiring and performance evaluation. Analytics tools may also reveal areas for development and offer insights into diversity measures, allowing businesses to create focused plans for promoting inclusion and diversity in the workplace.

Human-Centric Design and User Experience

The public sector must integrate HR technology with a focus on user experience and human-centric design principles. HR software needs to be simple to use, straightforward, and available to all workers, including those with impairments. It is important to put simplicity, clarity, and ease of navigation at the top of user experience design so that employees can use HR platforms and products efficiently. Organisations may improve employee acceptance, engagement, and happiness with HR technology by implementing a human-centric design approach (Wadhwa, Wadhwa & Khalique, 2024).

Collaboration and Knowledge Sharing Platforms

In the context of public sector HRM, collaboration and knowledge sharing platforms are critical for promoting cooperation, communication, and information exchange. Knowledge exchange, cross-functional involvement, and seamless collaboration may all be facilitated via intranets, social collaboration platforms, and virtual workplaces. These platforms may increase information accessibility, expedite decision-making procedures, and foster creativity and productivity in the HR department.

CONCLUSION

This chapter provides a road-map for navigating digital HRM in the public sector and has explored the challenges and opportunities associated with the adoption of modern technologies in public sector HRM. It has highlighted the importance of digital transformation in enhancing HRM effectiveness, efficiency, and employee satisfaction in the public sector. The chapter began by establishing the context and significance of digital transformation in public sector HRM processes, acknowledging the need for public sector organisations to leverage technological advancements. It provided an overview of the classification of modern technologies commonly adopted in public sector HRM, focusing on recruitment, on-boarding, performance management, and employee engagement. The challenges in implementing these technologies were thoroughly examined, including resource constraints, cultural barriers, data privacy concerns, digital skills gaps, compatibility issues, and ethical considerations. However, the chapter also presented strategies for successful implementation, emphasising the importance of building a digital readiness framework, change management, stakeholder engagement, and upskilling HR professionals. Real-world examples were provided to illustrate effective implementation of digital HRM processes in public sector organisations, offering valuable insights and lessons learned. The chapter also discussed the potential impact of emerging technologies, such as artificial intelligence, robotic process automation, enhanced data analytics, virtual and augmented reality, and blockchain, while addressing the ethical and social implications of technology adoption. By adopting modern HRM technologies, public sector organisations can enhance their efficiency, effectiveness, and employee satisfaction. These technologies enable improved data management, automation of administrative tasks, streamlined processes, and data-driven decision-making. They also contribute to enhanced talent acquisition and retention, increased employee engagement, and user-friendly self-service platforms that empower employees. The successful adoption of modern technologies in public sector HRM therefore requires careful planning, change management strategies, and upskilling of HR professionals. The chapter, "Examining the Challenges of adopting modern technologies in Public Sector HRM" concludes that by embracing digital transformation and leveraging emerging technologies, public sector organisations can deliver improved public services, make data-driven decisions, and foster a more engaged and satisfied workforce.

REFERENCES

Agustian, K., Pohan, A., Zen, A., Wiwin, W., & Malik, A. J. (2023). Human Resource Management Strategies in Achieving Competitive Advantage in Business Administration. [ADMAN]. *Journal of Contemporary Administration and Management*, 1(2), 108–117. 10.61100/adman.v1i2.53

Aisa, R., Cabeza, J., & Martin, J. (2023). Automation and aging: The impact on older workers in the workforce. *The Journal of the Economics of Ageing*, 26, 100476. 10.1016/j.jeoa.2023.100476

Al Awadhi, T. H., & Muslim, S. B. (2023). Reviewing the relation between human resources practices, talent management and succession planning in UAE public sector. *Information Sciences Letters*, 12(4), 1271–1283. 10.18576/isl/120442

Alade, S. (2023). Design and Implementation of a Web-based Document Management System. *Information Technology and Computer Science*, 2, 35–53.

Aldoseri, A., Al-Khalifa, K., & Hamouda, A. (2023). A road-map for integrating automation with process optimisation for AI-powered digital transformation. *Preprints*.org.

Aleksandrova, S. V. (2023, September). Implementation of Digital Technologies in Production Processes. In *2023 International Conference on Quality Management, Transport and Information Security, Information Technologies (IT&QM&IS)* (pp. 104-108). IEEE. 10.1109/ITQMTIS58985.2023.10346533

Ali, M. S., Abdalgani, S. A., & Dahlan, D. (2023). Assessing the Effectiveness of 360-Degree Performance Appraisal System to Enhance Employees' Productivity in Jordanian Listed Banks. In *Artificial Intelligence (AI) and Finance* (pp. 164–174). Springer Nature Switzerland. 10.1007/978-3-031-39158-3_15

Alkashami, M. (2023). Human Resource Information Systems (HRIS) in the 21st Century: A Critical Appraisal: . *Baltic Journal of Law & Politics, 16*(1), 375-388.10.2478/bjlp-2023-0000026

Alkhalil, Z., Hewage, C., Nawaf, L., & Khan, I. (2021). Phishing attacks: A recent comprehensive study and a new anatomy. *Frontiers of Computer Science*, 3, 563060. 10.3389/fcomp.2021.563060

AlSaadoon, A. (2020). *A Design Research Approach to Enhance the Peer-to-peer Recognition and Appreciation Among Employees and Develop a Better Relationship to Boost Employee Motivation.* California (Doctoral dissertation, The Claremont Graduate University).

Bankins, S. (2021). The ethical use of artificial intelligence in human resource management: A decision-making framework. *Ethics and Information Technology*, 23(4), 841–854. 10.1007/s10676-021-09619-6

Bhanumathi, P., Jeevitha, R., & Rema, V. (2023). Embedding Technology in Human Resource Management. In *Managing Technology Integration for Human Resources in Industry 5.0, 1-19*. IGI Global.

Biea, E. A., Dinu, E., Bunica, A., & Jerdea, L. (2023). Recruitment in SMEs: The role of managerial practices, technology and innovation. *European Business Review*, 36(3), 361–391. 10.1108/EBR-05-2023-0162

Bozkus, K. (2023). Organisational Culture Change and Technology: Navigating the Digital Transformation. In Sarfraz, M., & Hassan Shah, W. U. (Eds.), *Organisational Culture - Cultural Change and Technology* (pp. 1–22). Intechopen.

Brown, M. I. (2022). Investigating the promise and pitfalls of pulse surveys. *Industrial and Organizational Psychology: Perspectives on Science and Practice*, 15(1), 137–149. 10.1017/iop.2021.124

Chang, Y. J. (2023). *Building an effective hiring and smooth employee boarding process: company X.* Turku and Salo (Master's Thesis, Turku University Of Applied Sciences).

Chaturvedi, V. (2023). Role of Cognitive Technology for Improving Human Resource Management Experience: A Multi-Dimensional Perspective. *Data Science and Intelligent Computing Techniques; Nanda, SJ, Yadav, RP, Eds*, 13-25.

Chen, Z. (2023). Artificial intelligence-virtual trainer: Innovative didactics aimed at personalised training needs. *Journal of the Knowledge Economy*, 14(2), 2007–2025. 10.1007/s13132-022-00985-0

Chikomba, A., Rodrigues, A., & Ngoepe, M. (2021). Management of digital records in selected financial services parastatals in Zimbabwe. *Information Development*, 37(2), 245–257. 10.1177/0266666920906858

Chilunjika, A., Intauno, K., & Chilunjika, S. R. (2022). Artificial intelligence and public sector human resource management in South Africa: Opportunities, challenges and prospects. *SA Journal of Human Resource Management*, 20, 1–12. 10.4102/sajhrm.v20i0.1972

Cho, W., Choi, S., & Choi, H. (2023). Human Resources Analytics for Public Personnel Management: Concepts, Cases, and Caveats. *Administrative Sciences*, 13(2), 1–22. 10.3390/admsci13020041

Christ, K. L., & Helliar, C. V. (2021). Blockchain technology and modern slavery: Reducing deceptive recruitment in migrant worker populations. *Journal of Business Research*, 131, 112–120. 10.1016/j.jbusres.2021.03.065

Citrin, J. M., & DeRosa, D. (2021). *Leading at a distance: Practical lessons for virtual success.* John Wiley & Sons.

Colombari, R., & Neirotti, P. (2023). Leveraging Frontline Employees' Knowledge for Operational Data-Driven Decision-Making: A Multilevel Perspective. *IEEE Transactions on Engineering Management*, •••, 1–12.

Daher, M. M., & Ziade, F. (2024). Technology, Workforce, and the Future of Sustainable Work. In *Navigating the Intersection of Business, Sustainability and Technology* (pp. 119–136). Springer Nature Singapore.

Das, B. K., & Rajini, G. (2023). Leadership development through 360-degree multi-rater feedback—An experience sharing of need, approach, roll-out, and the impact. *Environment and Social Psychology*, 9(2), 1–20. 10.54517/esp.v9i2.2000

Dhanalakshmi, R., Cherukuri, D. M., Ambashankar, A., Sivaraman, A., & Sood, K. (2023). Smart Analytics and AI for Managing Modern Performance Management Systems. In *Smart Analytics, Artificial Intelligence and Sustainable Performance Management in a Global Digitalised Economy,110, 243-263.* Emerald Publishing Limited. 10.1108/S1569-37592023000110B016

Di Carlo, D. (2023). Beyond neo-corporatism: State employers and the special-interest politics of public sector wage-setting. *Journal of European Public Policy*, 30(5), 967–994. 10.1080/13501763.2022.2036791

Di Giulio, M., & Vecchi, G. (2023). Implementing digitalisation in the public sector. Technologies, agency, and governance. *Public Policy and Administration*, 38(2), 133–158. 10.1177/09520767211023283

Dick, E. (2021). *Current and potential uses of AR/VR for equity and inclusion. Information Technology and Innovation Foundation, 1-12*. ITIF Publications.

Eikebrokk, T. R., & Olsen, D. H. (2020). Robotic process automation and consequences for knowledge workers; a mixed-method study. In *Responsible Design, Implementation and Use of Information and Communication Technology: 19th IFIP WG 6.11 Conference on e-Business, e-Services, and e-Society, I3E 2020, Skukuza, South Africa, April 6–8, 2020* [Springer International Publishing.]. *Proceedings*, 19(Part I), 114–125.

Fagarasan, C., Cristea, C., Cristea, M., Popa, O., & Pisla, A. (2023). Integrating Sustainability Metrics into Project and Portfolio Performance Assessment in Agile Software Development: A Data-Driven Scoring Model. *Sustainability (Basel)*, 15(17), 13139. 10.3390/su151713139

Galanti, T., De Vincenzi, C., Buonomo, I., & Benevene, P. (2023). Digital Transformation: Inevitable Change or Sisable Opportunity? The Strategic Role of HR Management in Industry 4.0. *Administrative Sciences*, 13(2), 1–19. 10.3390/admsci13020030

Glyptis, L., Christofi, M., Vrontis, D., Del Giudice, M., Dimitriou, S., & Michael, P. (2020). E-Government implementation challenges in small countries: The project manager's perspective. *Technological Forecasting and Social Change*, 152, 119880. 10.1016/j.techfore.2019.119880

Gromyko, I. (2024). Organisational support for leadership and teamwork in international virtual project teams. Vilnius (Doctoral dissertation, Vilniaus Universitetas).

Habbal, A., Ali, M. K., & Abuzaraida, M. A. (2024). Artificial Intelligence Trust, risk and security management (AI trism): Frameworks, applications, challenges and future research directions. *Expert Systems with Applications*, 240, 122442. 10.1016/j.eswa.2023.122442

Hartono, S., Tjahyadi, R., & Cassandra, C. (2021, August). Analysis of Employee and Manager Self Service Module on SAP Portal (A Case Study Approach). In *2021 International Conference on Information Management and Technology (ICIMTech), 1*, 93-98. IEEE. 10.1109/ICIMTech53080.2021.9535090

Haswani, F., Erlita, Y., & Rika, . (2023). Integrating extensive and intensive reading worksheets on digital platforms. [Journal of Applied Linguistics and Literature]. *JOALL*, 8(2), 415–432. 10.33369/joall.v8i2.28043

Henry, L. M., Hansen, E., Chimoff, J., Pokstis, K., Kiderman, M., Naim, R., Kossowsky, J., Byrne, M. E., Lopez-Guzman, S., Kircanski, K., Pine, D. S., & Brotman, M. A. (2024). Selecting an Ecological Momentary Assessment Platform: Tutorial for Researchers. *Journal of Medical Internet Research*, 26(1), e51125. 10.2196/5112538175682

Islam, M. T., & Tamzid, M. (2023). Artificial Intelligence in Human Resource Management. *the Book "Management Education for Achieving Sustainable Development Goals in the Context of Bangladesh*, 61-80.

Kambur, E., & Yildirim, T. (2023). From traditional to smart human resources management. *International Journal of Manpower*, 44(3), 422–452. 10.1108/IJM-10-2021-0622

Khatri, M. R. (2023). Integration of natural language processing, self-service platforms, predictive maintenance, and prescriptive analytics for cost reduction, personalisation, and real-time insights customer service and operational efficiency. *International Journal of Information and Cybersecurity*, 7(9), 1–30.

Kim, S., Wang, Y., & Boon, C. (2021). Sixty years of research on technology and human resource management: Looking back and looking forward. *Human Resource Management*, 60(1), 229–247. 10.1002/hrm.22049

Kirtzalidou, A. (2023). Factors Affecting Human Resource Motivation in The Public Sector. Thessaloniki (Master's Thesis, International Hellenic University).

Konateh, H., Duramany-Lakkoh, E. K., & Udeh, E. (2023). Cost and Administrative Effectiveness of Recruitment and Selection Practices on Public Service Delivery in Public Sector Institutions. *European Journal of Business and Management Research*, 8(2), 21–30. 10.24018/ejbmr.2023.8.2.1814

Kruyen, P. M., & Sowa, J. E. (2023). Essential but ignored: Including blue-collar government workers into human resource management research. *Public Personnel Management*, 52(4), 521–542. 10.1177/00910260231187540

Kumar, M. D., Yap, A. C. T., Govindarajo, N. S., Tamah, A., & Sharma, V. (2024). Intelligent Industry 4.0: Artificial Intelligence and Robotic Process Automation as Tendsetters. In *AI and Data Analytics Applications in Organisational Management* (pp. 249–273). IGI Global.

Lauer, T. (2020). *Change management: fundamentals and success factors*. Springer Nature.

Laurim, V., Arpaci, S., Prommegger, B., & Krcmar, H. (2021). Computer, whom should I hire?–acceptance criteria for artificial intelligence in the recruitment process. In *Proceedings of the 54th Hawaii International Conference on System Sciences,* 5495-5504. Scholar Space. 10.24251/HICSS.2021.668

Majam, T., & Jarbandhan, D. B. (2022). Data driven human resource management in the Fourth Industrial Revolution (4IR). *Africa's Public Service Delivery & Performance Review*, 10(1), 1–12. 10.4102/apsdpr.v10i1.588

Martínez-Peláez, R., Ochoa-Brust, A., Rivera, S., Félix, V. G., Ostos, R., Brito, H., Félix, R. A., & Mena, L. J. (2023). Role of digital transformation for achieving sustainability: Mediated role of stakeholders, key capabilities, and technology. *Sustainability (Basel)*, 15(14), 11221. 10.3390/su151411221

Masilela, L., & Nel, D. (2021). The role of data and information security governance in protecting public sector data and information assets in national government in South Africa. *Africa's Public Service Delivery and Performance Review*, 9(1), 385. 10.4102/apsdpr.v9i1.385

Mer, A., & Srivastava, A. (2023). Employee Engagement in the New Normal: Artificial Intelligence as a Buzzword or a Game Changer? In *The Adoption and Effect of Artificial Intelligence on Human Resources Management, Part A* (pp. 15–46). Emerald Publishing Limited. 10.1108/978-1-80382-027-920231002

Mer, A., & Virdi, A. S. (2023). Navigating the paradigm shift in HRM practices through the lens of artificial intelligence: A post-pandemic perspective. *The Adoption and Effect of Artificial Intelligence on Human Resources Management, Part A*, 123-154.

Midiwo, J. (2016). Influence of Human Resource Information Systems on the Performance in Kenyan Public Universities (Doctoral dissertation, Jomo Kenyatta University of Agriculture and Technology).

Mitchell, A. (2023). Collaboration technology affordances from virtual collaboration in the time of COVID-19 and post-pandemic strategies. *Information Technology & People*, 36(5), 1982–2008. 10.1108/ITP-01-2021-0003

Molino, M., Cortese, C. G., & Ghislieri, C. (2020). The promotion of technology acceptance and work engagement in industry 4.0: From personal resources to information and training. *International Journal of Environmental Research and Public Health*, 17(7), 2438. 10.3390/ijerph1707243832260142

Moran, R. (2023). An investigative analysis of how influential leadership and change management strategies were during the transitional phase to a Technological University.

Mukuze, K. (2023). *Developing a predictive model for human capital analytics adoption in Zimbabwean State Universities.* Chinhoyi (Doctoral dissertation, Chinhoyi University of Technology).

Mutegi, F. M. (2021). Influence of Strategic Human Resource Practices on Public Service Delivery of Huduma Centres in Kenya (Doctoral dissertation, KeMU).

Napierala, J., & Kvetan, V. (2023). Changing job skills in a changing world. In *Handbook of Computational Social Science for Policy* (pp. 243–259). Springer International Publishing. 10.1007/978-3-031-16624-2_13

Ndebele, I. (2021). *Management's support and implementation of electronic document and records management systems in government departments.* Durban (Doctoral dissertation, Durban University of Technology).

Nguyen, C. M. A., & Ha, M. T. (2023). The interplay between internal communication, employee engagement, job satisfaction, and employee loyalty in higher education institutions in Vietnam. *Humanities & Social Sciences Communications*, 10(1), 1–13. 10.1057/s41599-023-01806-837361101

Ogedengbe, D. E., James, O. O., Afolabi, J. O. A., Olatoye, F. O., & Eboigbe, E. O. (2023). Human Resources In The Era of The Fourth Industrial Revolution (4ir): Strategies and Innovations In The Global South. *Engineering Science & Technology Journal*, 4(5), 308–322.

Padma, S. (2023). Securing Organisational Sustainability: The Vitality of Succession Planning in Indian Public Sector Enterprises. *International Development Planning Review*, 22(2), 187–195.

Pandey, A., Grima, S., Pandey, S., & Balusamy, B. (Eds.). (2024). *The Role of HR in the Transforming Workplace: Challenges, Technology, and Future Directions*. CRC Press.

Pillai, R., & Sivathanu, B. (2022). Measure what matters: Descriptive and predictive metrics of HRM-pathway toward organisational performance. *International Journal of Productivity and Performance Management*, 71(7), 3009–3029. 10.1108/IJPPM-10-2020-0509

Prebreza, B. (2021). *Towards a blended working environment*. Thuringia, Erfurt (Master's Thesis, University of Applied Sciences Ltd.).

Prokopenko, O., Garafonova, O., & Zhosan, H. (2023). Digital tools in human resource management: how digitisation affects personnel management. *Socio-economic relations in the digital society, 4*(50), 84-94.

Raghavan, M., Barocas, S., Kleinberg, J., & Levy, K. (2020, January). Mitigating bias in algorithmic hiring: Evaluating claims and practices. In *Proceedings of the 2020 conference on fairness, accountability, and transparency* (pp. 469-481). 10.1145/3351095.3372828

Rahman, M., & Aydin, E. (2020). Benefits, barriers and risks–the role of technology in e-HRM implementations in public sector organisations: Evidence from Bangladesh. *International Journal of Human Resources Development and Management*, 20(3-4), 252–268. 10.1504/IJHRDM.2020.107976

Ramírez, J. G. C. (2024). AI in Healthcare: Revolutionising Patient Care with Predictive Analytics and Decision Support Systems. *Journal of Artificial Intelligence General science (JAIGS)* 3006-4023, 1(1), 31-37.

Reina, R., & Scarozza, D. (2021). Human Resource Management in the Public Administration. In Decastri, M., Battini, S., Buonocore, F., & Gagliarducci, F. (Eds.), *Organisational Development in Public Administration* (pp. 61–101). Palgrave Macmillan. 10.1007/978-3-030-43799-2_3

Reunamäki, R., & Fey, C. F. (2023). Remote agile: Problems, solutions, and pitfalls to avoid. *Business Horizons*, 66(4), 505–516. 10.1016/j.bushor.2022.10.003

Rodgers, W., Murray, J. M., Stefanidis, A., Degbey, W. Y., & Tarba, S. Y. (2023). An artificial intelligence algorithmic approach to ethical decision-making in human resource management processes. *Human Resource Management Review*, 33(1), 100925. 10.1016/j.hrmr.2022.100925

Roy, J. (2017). Smart cities in Canada: An examination of progress and impediments in Halifax, Canada. *International Journal of Services Technology and Management*, 23(5-6), 361–380. 10.1504/IJSTM.2017.088944

Saad, A., & Itika, J. (2024). An Investigation of the Transformation Process from Manual to E-Recruitment in Tanzania Public Service. *Journal of Public Policy and Administration*, 9(1), 1–19. 10.47604/jppa.2254

Sakka, F., El Maknouzi, M. E. H., & Sadok, H. (2022). Human resource management in the era of artificial intelligence: Future HR work practices, anticipated skill set, financial and legal implications. *Academy of Strategic Management Journal*, 21(1), 1–14.

Salvadorinho, J., & Teixeira, L. (2023). Happy and Engaged Workforce in Industry 4.0: A New Concept of Digital Tool for HR Based on Theoretical and Practical Trends. *Sustainability (Basel)*, 15(3), 2781. 10.3390/su15032781

Shahaab, A., Khan, I. A., Maude, R., Hewage, C., & Wang, Y. (2023). Public service operational efficiency and blockchain–A case study of Companies House, UK. *Government Information Quarterly*, 40(1), 101759. 10.1016/j.giq.2022.101759

Sharma, M., Luthra, S., Joshi, S., & Kumar, A. (2022). Analysing the impact of sustainable human resource management practices and industry 4.0 technologies adoption on employability skills. *International Journal of Manpower*, 43(2), 463–485. 10.1108/IJM-02-2021-0085

Sharma, P. (2023). Innovations in Human Resource Management: Adapting to the Future of Work. *Journal of Informatics Education and Research*, 3(2), 1–11.

Shruthi, K., & Poornima, A. S. (2023, September). A Transparent and Privacy-Preserving Job Search Platform Built on the Ethereum Blockchain Framework. In *2023 IEEE 2nd International Conference on Industrial Electronics: Developments & Applications (ICIDeA)* (pp. 235-242). IEEE.

Shukla, A., Mishra, L., & Agnihotri, A. (2023). A Comprehensive Review of the Effects of Digital Technology on Human Resource Management. *Technology. Management and Business*, 31, 7–19. 10.1108/S1877-636120230000031002

Sidoti, B. J., Walsh, L. L., Parsley, K. M., Callis-Duehl, K., Hove, A. A., Liu, H., Uzcategui, M., Sternad Zabukovšek, S., Jordan, S., & Bobek, S. (2023). Managing Document Management Systems' Life Cycle in Relation to an Organisation's Maturity for Digital Transformation. *Sustainability*, 15(21), 1–35.

Suta, P., Lan, X., Wu, B., Mongkolnam, P., & Chan, J. H. (2020). An overview of machine learning in chatbots. *International Journal of Mechanical Engineering and Robotics Research*, 9(4), 502–510. 10.18178/ijmerr.9.4.502-510

Tensay, A. T., & Singh, M. (2020). The nexus between HRM, employee engagement and organisational performance of federal public service organisations in Ethiopia. *Heliyon*, 6(6), 1–15. 10.1016/j.heliyon.2020.e0409432577549

Thakur, A. (2024). Implementation of Artificial Intelligence in Human Resource Management in Asia-Pacific. In *Exploring the Intersection of AI and Human Resources Management* (pp. 30–46). IGI Global.

Theresianto, S. (2017). *Activity-Based Workplace Design: An Australian Perspective*. Sydney (Doctoral dissertation, The University of New South Wales, Sydney).

Thimmanna, A. V. N. S., Naik, M. S., Radhakrishnan, S., & Sharma, A. (2024). Personalised Learning Paths: Adapting Education with AI-Driven Curriculum. [EEL]. *European Economic Letters*, 14(1), 31–40.

Tripathi, N. G., & Goel, M. (2022). Citisen-Centric Smart Planning: Case Study San Diego, California. In *Smart Master Planning for Cities: Case Studies on Domain Innovations* (pp. 271–300). Springer Nature Singapore. 10.1007/978-981-19-2386-9_8

Turesky, E. F., Smith, C. D., & Turesky, T. K. (2020). A call to action for virtual team leaders: Practitioner perspectives on trust, conflict and the need for organisational support. *Organizational Management Journal*, 17(4/5), 185–206. 10.1108/OMJ-09-2019-0798

Upadhyay, P. (2024). Industry 4.0 Inducing Paradigm Changes in Human Resources. In *The Role of HR in the Transforming Workplace* (pp. 1-9). Productivity Press.

Varma, A., Budhwar, P. S., & DeNisi, A. (Eds.). (2023). *Performance management systems: A global perspective*. Taylor & Francis. 10.4324/9781003306849

Veglianti, E., Trombin, M., Pinna, R., & De Marco, M. (2023). Customised Artificial Intelligence for Talent Recruiting: A Bias-Free Tool? In *Smart Technologies for Organisations: Managing a Sustainable and Inclusive Digital Transformation* (pp. 245–261). Springer International Publishing. 10.1007/978-3-031-24775-0_15

Vignesh Saravanan, K., Jothi Thilaga, P., Kavipriya, S., & Vijayalakshmi, K. (2023). Data Protection and Security Enhancement in Cyber-Physical Systems Using AI and Blockchain. In *AI Models for Blockchain-Based Intelligent Networks in IoT Systems: Concepts, Methodologies, Tools, and Applications* (pp. 285–325). Springer International Publishing. 10.1007/978-3-031-31952-5_13

Wadhwa, S., Wadhwa, P., & Khalique, F. (2024). Explorative Study on Understanding the Human-Centred Design to Nurture the Employee Experience. In *Humanising Businesses for a Better World of Work* (pp. 109–126). Emerald Publishing Limited. 10.1108/978-1-83797-332-320241008

Warrick, D. D. (2023). Revisiting resistance to change and how to manage it: What has been learned and what organisations need to do. *Business Horizons*, 66(4), 433–441. 10.1016/j.bushor.2022.09.001

Wheeler, K., & van de Haterd, B. (2024). *Talent Acquisition Excellence: Using Digital Capabilities and Analytics to Improve Recruitment.* Kogan Page Publishers.

Wirtz, B. W., & Müller, W. M. (2023). An integrated framework for public service provision in smart cities. *International Journal of Public Sector Performance Management*, 11(3), 310–340. 10.1504/IJPSPM.2023.130260

Yeo, M., Ananthram, S., Teo, S. T., & Pearson, C. A. (2015). Leader–member exchange and relational quality in a Singapore public sector organisation. *Public Management Review*, 17(10), 1379–1402. 10.1080/14719037.2013.806573

Zhang, J., & Chen, Z. (2023). Exploring Human Resource Management Digital Transformation in the Digital Age. *Journal of the Knowledge Economy*, 1–17. 10.1007/s13132-023-01214-y

Chapter 5
Leveraging Human Resource (HR) Analytics for Effective Talent Management in Public Sector Organisations

Blessing Takawira
https://orcid.org/0000-0002-1633-8693
University of Johannesburg, South Africa

Misheck Musaigwa
https://orcid.org/0000-0002-1474-5949
University of Johannesburg, South Africa

Vivence Kalitanyi
https://orcid.org/0000-0002-0140-6649
University of Johannesburg, South Africa

ABSTRACT

The book chapter explores how HR analytics may improve talent management in the African public sector. Through case studies and theoretical insights, the chapter emphasises the adoption and influence of HR analytics on many aspects of talent management, such as recruiting performance evaluation, employee retention, and leadership development. The chapter explores the advantages and obstacles of adopting HR analytics, including issues like data protection, the need for HR professionals to enhance their analytical skills, and opposition to data-driven methods due to cultural factors. The implications for public sector HR management are significant, indicating a trend towards evidence-based HR approaches that closely align with organisational goals and strategic imperatives. The chapter ends by highlighting the importance of further research in HR analytics to gain a more profound insight into its lasting effects, addressing obstacles to its adoption and ethical concerns, and investigating regional differences in the African setting.

DOI: 10.4018/979-8-3693-2889-7.ch005

INTRODUCTION

Human Resource (HR) analytics involves the collection and implementation of talent data to enhance critical talent and business outcomes, promoting data-driven insights and positive employee experience (Elrehail, 2023; Gupta, 2023). The use of HR analytics is crucial for organisations striving to attract and retain skilled individuals in a competitive global environment, aiding in strategic workforce management decisions such as talent acquisition, retention, training, and development (Elrehail, 2023). The public sector in Africa experiences talent management obstacles that necessitate the implementation of equitable appraisal systems, the cultivation of leadership skills, and the proactive prediction of future human resource requirements (Ali & Elias, 2023; Anlesinya, Amponsah-Tawiah & Dartey-Baah, 2019a; Musakuro & De Klerk, 2021).

Talent management research in Africa is at an embryonic stage, with under-researched areas in North, West, and Eastern African sub-regions (Anlesinya *et al.*, 2019a). The South African public sector faces talent management challenges affecting workforce planning, compensation, training, and performance management (Musakuro & De Klerk, 2021). The future of HR analytics is linked to understanding data analytics, focusing on connecting data to HR policies and practices to influence overall business performance (Diez, Bussin & Lee, 2019). HR analytics is an emerging field with substantial practitioner and academic attention, contributing to the emerging subfield of HRM (Edwards, Charlwood, Guenole & Marler, 2022). This chapter addresses the prevailing deficiency of equitable and transparent appraisal systems within the public sector, which are essential for upholding integrity and fostering employee motivation. This gap has been addressed through the adoption of technology, specifically by leveraging digital transformation initiatives. These initiatives facilitate the implementation of data-driven performance management systems, thereby ensuring objectivity and fairness in the evaluation of employee performance. In addition, the study identified a gap in proactive human resources (HR) planning within public sector organisations, which typically respond to HR demands reactively rather than anticipating them. To bridge this gap, the implementation of digital tools and predictive analytics could revolutionize HR management. These technological advancements facilitate enhanced workforce planning and management by forecasting future HR needs based on observed trends and organisational objectives. Drawing from this background the chapter objectives are to:

- To establish the impact of HR analytics on public sector HRM in public sector organisations;
- To explore the adoption of HR analytics in talent management practises of public sector organisations; and
- To explore the impact of HR analytics on talent management

This section of the chapter begins with a theoretical background on HR Analytics, discussing its evolution and integration into talent management strategies within public sector HRM. It contextualizes the application of HR Analytics in African public sectors, tracing the evolution of talent management influenced by digital advancements. Methodology is detailed through a systematic literature review, examining key aspects from search strategies to data synthesis. The final sections explore the implications of digital transformation on HR practices, the role of HR Analytics in enhancing talent management, and the practical challenges and benefits observed in African public sector institutions. The chapter concludes by summarising the impact of HR Analytics on talent management and offering recommendations for future research and practice, aiming to enhance HR processes and address the strategic needs of the public sector.

THEORETICAL BACKGROUND

Overview of HR Analytics

This section explores HR Analytics, a rapidly evolving domain that intersects data science with human resource management to enhance talent management practices. Organisations can glean valuable insights into workforce dynamics by systematically analysing HR data, enabling evidence-based decision-making. This section discusses the progression of HR analytics from a novel concept to a fundamental HR function, emphasising its role in optimising talent acquisition, development, and retention strategies.

HR Analytics is a rapidly evolving field that uses data science and analytics to enhance organisational talent management practices. By systematically analysing HR data, organisations can gain valuable insights into their workforce, enabling evidence-based decision-making to optimise talent acquisition, development, and retention strategies (Qamar & Samad, 2021; Bonilla-Chaves & Palos-Sanchez, 2023). The evolution of HR analytics has led to a shift in understanding, emphasising the importance of utilising data-driven approaches to address HR challenges effectively (Ben-Gal, 2019). To effectively implement HR analytics in the public sector, it is crucial to start by defining specific business problems that need to be addressed and aligning analytics initiatives with organisational goals (Fernández & Gallardo-Gallardo, 2020). Moreover, adopting HR analytics in the public sector can contribute to organisational performance by capturing team proactivity and enhancing content validity through technological applications (Ontrup, Schempp & Kluge, 2021).

In the context of competence management, HR analytics plays a pivotal role in identifying and developing competencies within the workforce (Karwehl & Kauffeld, 2021; Klepić & Klepić, 2023). By utilising HR analytics, organisations can determine the required competencies for improved business performance, particularly in small and medium enterprises (Klepić & Klepić, 2023). Additionally, the application of HR analytics in monitoring employee performance can be influenced by the organisational, market, and country context, highlighting the importance of considering cultural values and norms in analytics implementation (Bechter, Brandl & Lehr, 2022).

Furthermore, the successful implementation of HR analytics is contingent on overcoming challenges such as resistance to change and the lack of confidence among HR professionals (Arora, Prakash, Mittal & Singh, 2022). By addressing these challenges and emphasising the value proposition of HR analytics, public sector organisations can harness the full potential of analytics to drive talent management practices (Likhitkar & Verma, 2019). Additionally, the integration of HR analytics with evidence-based human resource management can provide valuable insights for line managers in addressing workforce-related challenges (Cavanagh, Walker, Pariona-Cabrera, Bartram & Halvorsen, 2022).

Figure 1 below addresses the key components of HR analytics, its contribution to talent management in the public sector, the theoretical foundations of HR analytics, and the challenges of implementing HR analytics in the African public sector.

Figure 1. Key Components of HR Analytics

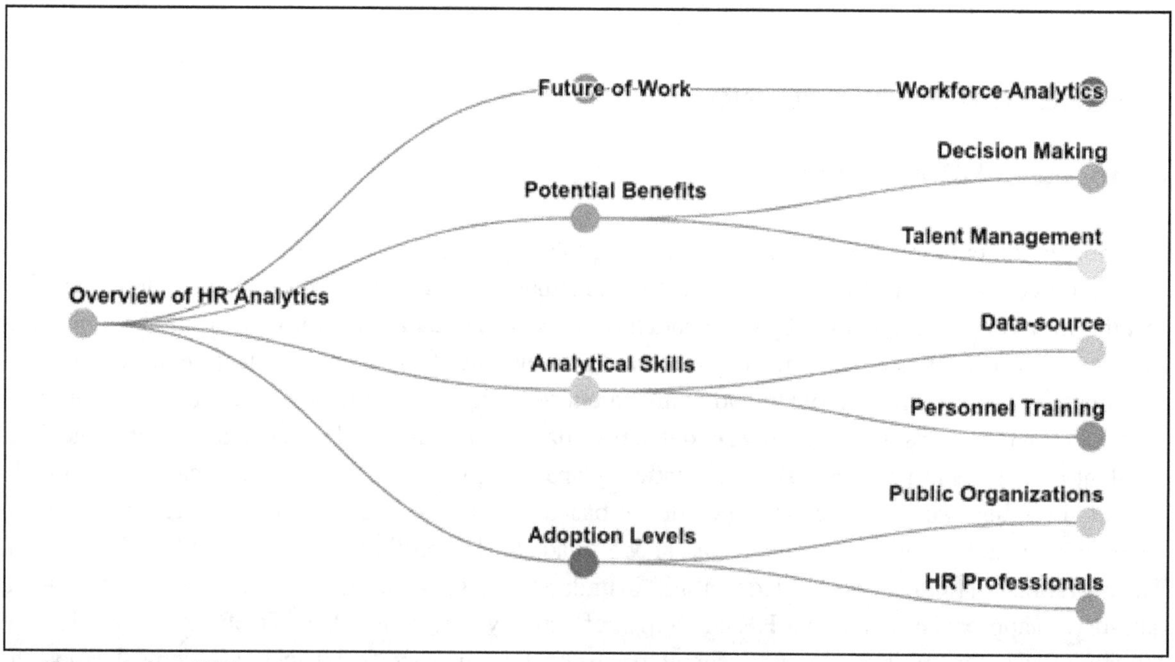

(Source: Authors, 2024)

Figure 1 offers a comprehensive representation of the essential elements that make up HR analytics within the context of public sector talent management. This diagram highlights how HR analytics serves as a pivotal tool for enhancing decision-making processes and aligning HR strategies with overall organizational goals. The diagram categorizes the key components of HR analytics into several primary domains, emphasizing their interconnectedness and the role each plays in fostering an effective and data-driven HR management environment.

HR analytics encompasses measuring performance metrics, workplace and recruitment analytics, and talent retention practices (Sripathi & Madhavaiah, 2018). It involves the collection and implementation of talent data for enhancing critical talent and business outcomes, aiding in effective decision-making by HR managers and boosting employee performance (Sripathi & Madhavaiah, 2018). HR analytics contributes to talent management in the public sector by aiding HR professionals in making informed decisions and aligning HR strategies with overall organisational goals (Gupta, 2023). It is crucial for optimising HR processes and enhancing workforce productivity, ultimately leading to better talent management and organisational performance (Gupta, 2023). The use of HR analytics in the public sector can assist in making more data-driven and strategic workforce management decisions such as talent acquisition, retention, training, and development (Angrave, Charlwood, Kirkpatrick, Lawrence & Stuart, 2016; Elrehail, 2023).

HR analytics is based on a data-driven approach that aids HR professionals in making informed decisions and aligning HR strategies with overall organisational goals (Gupta, 2023). It involves the application of the analytical process to the organisation's human resources, focusing on the relationships between work behaviour/skills of employees, HRM/leadership practice, and company-related performance variables (Marler & Boudreau, 2017).

CONTEXTUALISING HR ANALYTICS IN PUBLIC SECTOR HRM

Implementing HR analytics in the African public sector for talent management is a complex process that requires careful consideration of various factors. Ali and Elias (2023) emphasise the need for a fair appraisal scheme and leadership development. Meanwhile, Jayasena, Rajasekera and Wenkai (2023) suggest a talent management model that includes gap analysis, acquisition, development, assessment, retention, and transition. Chilunjika, Intauno and Chilunjika (2022) highlight the potential of AI in public sector HR management, particularly in improving service delivery and minimising bias. However, the transferability of talent management strategies to the public sector is a critical issue, as discussed by Kravariti and Johnston (2019a). The potential of HR analytics in enhancing business performance is underscored by Madhani (2022a) and Rana, Sharma and Goel (2018), focusing on data-driven decision-making and strategy realisation. Further, Abdeldayem and Aldulaimi (2020) acknowledge the opportunities and challenges of AI in HR management, particularly in Bahrain's public sector. These studies collectively suggest that the effective implementation of HR analytics in public sector organisations in Africa requires a comprehensive approach that addresses the unique challenges and opportunities in the region.

EVOLUTION OF TALENT MANAGEMENT IN THE PUBLIC SECTOR

Talent management in the public sector has undergone significant transformations, particularly in response to the digital advancements of the Fourth Industrial Revolution. This subsection traces the historical trajectory of talent management, from its roots in the planning functions of HR to its current emphasis on strategic alignment with organisational goals. The discussion extends to the unique challenges and advancements within the African public sector, highlighting the regional disparities in talent management practices.

Talent management has become increasingly crucial in the public sector, especially in the context of the Fourth Industrial Revolution (4IR) (Shava, 2022). The roots of talent management practices in the public sector can be traced back to the planning function of HR, indicating its integral role in every HR function (Kumar, 2021). Despite the emphasis on talent management, research in Africa has shown disparities in the attention given to different sub-regions, with Southern Africa being more researched compared to North, West, and East Africa (Anlesinya, Amponsah-Tawiah & Dartey-Baah, 2019b). The historical developments in talent management in the public sector have been under-researched, particularly in the African context (Kravariti & Johnston, 2019a; Ali & Elias, 2023). However, it is noted that talent management has evolved in response to global trends such as economic globalisation, cultural diversity, and technological advancements (Kravariti & Johnston, 2019a; Musakuro & De Klerk, 2021). The evolution of talent management in the African public sector has been shaped by the colonial, post-colonial, and modern periods, responding to global influences, reforms, and digitalization (Musakuro & De Klerk, 2021).

In the public sector, the transferability of talent management strategies from the private sector has been critically appraised, highlighting the need for a tailored approach for public institutions (Kravariti & Johnston, 2019b). Talent management concepts in the public sector must be adaptable and applicable across various public organisations (Kozjek & Franca, 2020). The advent of the knowledge economy and the need for strategic competitiveness have underscored the importance of talent management in modern organisations (Ndou, Mofokeng & Khosa, 2021).

Moreover, the evolution of talent management in the public sector has faced challenges due to the bureaucratic nature of public service, hindering effective implementation (Mukwawaya, Proches & Green, 2021). The mediating role of line managerial support has been identified as crucial in enhancing talent management practices and, ultimately, organisational performance in the public sector (Semaihi, 2023). Additionally, the relationship between talent management and job satisfaction has been highlighted as a critical factor in influencing turnover intentions in government institutions (Barkhuizen & Gumede, 2021). The challenges and opportunities in talent management in the public sector, especially in Africa, are highlighted. These include the need for fair appraisal schemes, leadership development, and the use of HR analytics to forecast and prepare for future human resource demands (Al Jawali, Darwish, Scullion & Haak-Saheem, 2022; Musakuro, 2022; Vaiman & Collings, 2023). The considerations for leveraging HR analytics in talent management in the African public sector include the need for more training in leadership development, the potential benefits of HR analytics utilisation, and the importance of good governance and ethical leadership in public sector management (Al Jawali *et al.*, 2022; Musakuro, 2022; Vaiman & Collings, 2023).

Importance of Talent Management in Public Sector HRM

Talent management is pivotal in organisational success and sustainability in the contemporary digital age. Organisations are increasingly recognising talent as a critical asset that can provide a sustainable competitive advantage (Saadatmand, Safaie & Dastjerdi, 2022). Talent management is strategically significant for organisations across the globe, emphasising its role in driving competitiveness and innovation (Jayaraman, Talib & Khan, 2018). The digital era presents unique challenges and opportunities for talent management, requiring individuals to adapt to evolving roles and market demands continuously (Macedo, Veloso, Pinsky & Trevisan, 2023). Moreover, talent retention is crucial for establishing sustainable employment relationships in the digital era, highlighting the importance of effective talent management strategies (Lin & Wang, 2022).

In the context of multinational corporations, the translation of corporate talent management strategies into subsidiaries is essential for knowledge sourcing and organisational success (Napathorn, 2020). Talent management serves as a solution to poor task performance, particularly in industries undergoing digital transformations (Jimoh & Kee, 2022). The successful management of talent is imperative for public service delivery in the Fourth Industrial Revolution, emphasising the need for skilled expertise in managing digital technologies (Shava & Doorgapersad, 2021). Public sector talent management systems are vital for enhancing state functionality and development (Kozjek & Franca, 2020).

Talent management is intricately linked to organisational performance and human capital development (Leskina, 2022). As organisations strive for digital transformation, talent management becomes a critical component in attracting and retaining digital talent (Maharani & Wang, 2022). The management of older talents in an ageing society underscores the importance of mentoring and talent adaptation for organisational success (Vilčiauskaitė, Savanevičienė & Navickas, 2020). Talent management is crucial for acquiring a high-performance and reliable workforce, contributing to organisational effectiveness (Dwiputrianti, Sutiyono, Suryanto, Rachmawati & Purba, 2023).

METHODOLOGY

Systematic Literature Review Approach

This study adopts a systematic literature review (SLR) methodology, which is ideal for comprehensively gathering and synthesizing evidence on the integration and impact of HR analytics in public sector talent management. The SLR approach is instrumental in understanding the depth and breadth of the existing academic and practitioner insights, identifying gaps in current knowledge, and providing a rigorous evaluation of the research findings.

Search Strategy

The SLR was conducted following a clearly defined search strategy to ensure the comprehensiveness and relevance of the literature collected. Key electronic databases such as Scopus, Web of Science, Google Scholar, and specific HR and public administration journals were searched. The search was limited to works published in English from 2000 to 2023 to capture the most relevant and contemporary practices and theories in HR analytics. The search strategy employed combinations of the following keywords and phrases: "HR analytics," "human resource analytics," "public sector," "talent management," "digital transformation in HR," "performance management," and "operational efficiency." Boolean operators (AND, OR) were used to combine these terms effectively and broaden the search scope.

Inclusion and Exclusion Criteria

Studies were included based on their focus on HR analytics, relevance to public sector organizations, and contributions to talent management strategies. The inclusion criteria were, peer-reviewed journal articles and conference papers, studies focusing on the application or impact of HR analytics in the public sector and articles providing insights into both the challenges and benefits of HR analytics. Exclusion criteria ruled out, non-English articles, and publications before 2000, as the focus is on contemporary practices.

Data Extraction and Synthesis

Data from the selected articles were extracted systematically, focusing on authors, year of publication, research objectives, methodologies, key findings, and conclusions. This process was aided by bibliographic software and involved recording details in a standardized form to facilitate analysis and synthesis.

A thematic analysis was employed to synthesise the findings, grouping them into themes according to similarities in outcomes, challenges, strategies, and implications for practice and policy in the public sector. This approach allowed for a detailed examination of the landscape of HR analytics in public sector talent management, identifying trends, gaps, and areas requiring further research. The systematic literature review methodology is particularly relevant to this study as it allows for a structured exploration of how HR analytics can transform talent management in public sector organizations. Given the strategic importance of HR analytics in improving decision-making and organisational efficiency, the SLR provides a solid foundation to evaluate existing research, guiding future empirical studies and practical implementations in public sector contexts.

DISCUSSION OF FINDINGS

The implementation and application of HR analytics in the African public sector face challenges such as the need for a shift to a more process-oriented perspective, defining the actual roles in the process of implementing and applying HR analytics addressing competency requirements and refining strategies for harnessing the full potential of HR analytics (Margherita, 2022). The public sector is not proactive in forecasting and preparing for future human resource demands, and there is a need for more training for leadership development and addressing the potential challenges of privacy, integrity, algorithmic bias, and publicness (Angrave *et al.*, 2016; Elrehail, 2023). This section focuses on the challenges of implementing HR analytics in the African public sector.

Impact of Digital Transformation and Analytics on Public Sector HRM

The analysis of literature sources has shown that digital transformation has redefined the landscape of HRM by integrating digital technologies into traditional HR practices. This section delves into how digitalisation has facilitated a shift towards more dynamic and efficient HR operations. It examines the impact of digital tools and platforms on recruitment, selection, training, compensation systems, and performance management, illustrating the substantial benefits and challenges accompanying this transformation.

Digital transformation in HRM is significantly reshaping the operations of HR functions within the public sector organisations. Literature has highlighted that, integrating digital technologies in HRM processes has become increasingly crucial, particularly accelerated by the COVID-19 pandemic (Zavyalova, Sokolov, Kucherov & Lisovskaya, 2022). Research has further indicated that, digitalisation in HRM involves utilising electronic media, mobile platforms, analytics, and information technology to enhance the efficiency of HR practices and processes (Halid, Yusoff & Somu, 2020). This transformation encompasses technological advancements and the overhaul of outdated practices to instigate organisational change (Naidoo & Ndlovu, 2022).

The impact of digital transformation on HRM practices is substantial, with research indicating that various dimensions of digital transformation have a statistically significant positive direct effect on the development of HRM practices such as recruitment, selection, training, compensation systems, and performance management (Abugabel, 2023). Moreover, the implementation of digital HRM strategies throughout the HR value chain has been shown to contribute to the achievement of business objectives (Chapano, Mey & Werner, 2022). Digital HRM methods play a crucial role in evaluating employee and company performance, thereby assisting managers in making informed strategic decisions (Haque & Nishat, 2022).

A key challenge in the digital transformation of HRM is the necessity for HR professionals to acquire competencies suitable for the digital era (Kapitanov, Osipova & Chikileva, 2021). Additionally, the adoption of HR analytics has been demonstrated to enhance business performance by optimising the influence of various HR activities on organisational performance (Madhani, 2022b). It was found that the utilisation of big data analytics in talent management is identified as a promising area that can positively impact HR performance (Saputra, Wang, Zhang & Behl, 2021).

Figure 2 below illustrates the key components of digital transformation in HRM and its impact on talent management in African public sector organisations can include elements such as:

- Digital technologies (e.g., AI, IoT);
- HR analytics;
- Recruitment and selection processes;
- Training and development initiatives;
- Performance management systems; and
- Organisational performance and efficiency.

This diagram visually represents how the integration of digital technologies and analytics in HRM processes can improve talent management practices and overall organisational success.

Figure 2. Digital Transformation in HRM

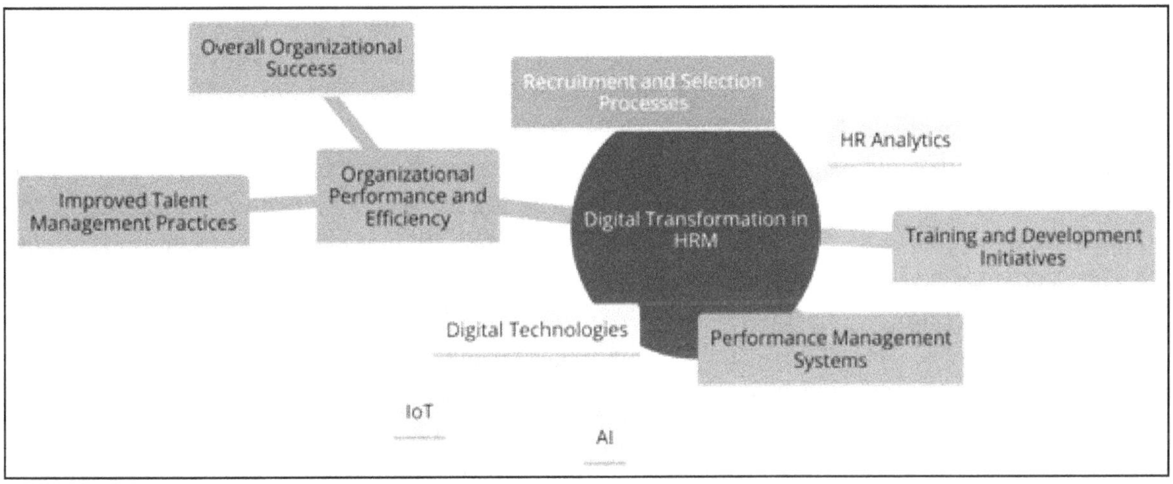

Source: Authors

Figure 2 above presents a conceptual model that encapsulates the essence of digital transformation within the realm of HRM and delineates its multifaceted impact on the operational facets of the organisation. The central theme, depicted as a large blue circle, is 'Digital Transformation in HRM', representing the nucleus of change that radiates outward, influencing various components of HR practices. The model identifies 'Digital Technologies' as a cornerstone of digital transformation in HRM, highlighting the role of the Internet of Things (IoT) and Artificial Intelligence (AI) as critical enablers that drive innovation within the HR function. These technologies underpin the other elements within the framework, revealing their foundational importance in the digitisation of HR processes. Surrounding the core concept are pivotal areas of HRM that are directly influenced by digital transformation. 'Recruitment and Selection Processes' are positioned as key beneficiaries of digital transformation, suggesting that modernising these processes is crucial for attracting and selecting the best talent. 'Performance Management Systems' are also emphasised, indicating that digital tools are integral to objectively assessing and managing employee performance.

The model includes 'Training and Development Initiatives' and 'HR Analytics', signifying their enhanced role in a digitally transformed HR landscape. Training and development are vital to maintaining a competent and adaptive workforce to changing business needs. At the same time, HR analytics provides the data-driven insights necessary for strategic decision-making. On the periphery of the model, 'Organisational Performance and Efficiency' and 'Improved Talent Management Practices' are shown as outcomes of digital transformation, which ultimately lead to 'Overall Organisational Success'. This causal relationship underscores the strategic importance of embracing digital transformation in HRM to achieve superior organisational performance and a competitive edge in the marketplace.

In essence, the diagram encapsulates the transformative impact of digital technologies on HRM and its subsequent influence on recruitment, performance management, and development initiatives. It underlines the criticality of HR analytics in shaping strategic HR decisions and illustrates the overarching goal of digital transformation in driving organisational success through improved talent management practices.

The findings highlighted that digital transformation in HRM is driven by factors such as internal customer digital needs, industry digital innovation, competitor challenges, digital innovation governance, and digital era needs (Adisa & Mordi, 2022). It involves the implementation of selection, training and development, and assessment functions leveraging state-of-the-art digital technologies (Adisa & Mordi, 2022). The essence of digital transformation in HRM includes the digital workplace, digital human resource management processes, and digital employee services (Adisa & Mordi, 2022).

Digital transformation in HRM was found to have a profound impact on talent management, affecting job setting, labour demand, and talent structure of enterprises (Verma, Rana & Meher, 2024). It shifts HR management from control to empowerment, emphasising the need for adaptive adjustments in corporate management methods (Verma *et al.*, 2024). The digitalisation of HR processes aims to improve workforce productivity and performance management, with a focus on attracting and retaining skilled individuals (Ali & Elias, 2023; Verma *et al.*, 2024).

The African Public Sector faces challenges in the acceptability and practicability of digital HRM, including organisational attachment to old methods, lack of required skills, and a fixed mindset hindering adaptability to digital HRM (Gobble, 2017). Opportunities lie in the necessity for effective public sector HRM to integrate all functions with digital technology, invest in automation and digital HR technologies, and build capacities to support e-HR systems (Zhang & Chen, 2023).

HR analytics is becoming crucial for organisations to make more data-driven and strategic workforce management decisions such as talent acquisition, retention, training, and development (Ali & Elias, 2023). A shift to a more process-oriented perspective on HR analytics is needed, defining the roles in the process of implementing and applying HR analytics, including the interaction between the specialist department, the HR business partner, and the HR analytics function (Elrehail, 2023). The data-driven approach of HR analytics aids in making informed decisions and aligning HR strategies with overall organisational goals, ultimately leading to better talent management and organisational performance (Rasmussen & Ulrich, 2015).

HR ANALYTICS IN TALENT MANAGEMENT: AN AFRICAN PERSPECTIVE

Case Studies from African Public Sector Institutions

Case Study: Building Capacity of Government Leaders in Egypt

The policy paper on building the capacity of government leaders in Egypt, prepared under the supervision of Dr Shahjahan Bhuiyan at The American University in Cairo in 2018, critically examines the Egyptian civil service sector's inefficiencies and proposes a comprehensive reform strategy aimed at enhancing the capabilities of mid- and senior-level management within the public service.
The document draws upon international best practices and lessons learned, proposing a reform path based on preparing, training, and retaining capable civil servants.
The paper begins by contextualising the historical development of the Egyptian civil service, highlighting how various political regimes have impacted its structure and efficiency. It critically evaluates the current legal framework, particularly the Civil Service Law 81/2016, discussing its ambitions and shortcomings in reforming the bureaucracy. The methodology relies on secondary data and international case studies to propose a framework for effective human resource management (HRM) in the civil service.
Key issues identified include the civil service's size, inefficiency, and lack of merit-based promotion and performance systems, contributing to widespread corruption and favouritism. The paper advocates for a reform focused on mid and senior management levels, outlining steps to revolutionise their preparation, training, and retention.
Drawing lessons from Singapore, France, and India, the paper suggests models for Egypt's HRM reform. Singapore's success story emphasises the importance of a comprehensive public service reform program, continuous training opportunities, and technology for talent management. France's centralised approach to managing high positions and constant education and training programs offers insights into leadership development. India's rigorous selection process through competitive exams highlights the value of merit-based recruitment.
The paper concludes with a call for reform based on international experience, emphasising the need for a clear and operational framework to effectively enforce Civil Service Law 81/2016. It suggests developing a Public Servant Competency Framework, employing technology for standardised training and management, and instituting a merit-based selection and promotion system to retain qualified personnel.
This case study serves as a roadmap for revitalising the Egyptian civil service, aiming to enhance efficiency, reduce corruption, and improve public service delivery. By aligning HR practices with strategic development policies and international best practices, Egypt can ensure the development of a competent, motivated, and ethical civil service workforce.

Source: Shariuda, El Tanany and Maraiyesa (2018)

ADOPTION AND IMPLEMENTATION OF HR ANALYTICS IN PUBLIC SECTOR INSTITUTIONS

Implementing HR analytics in institutions is a multifaceted process driven by several aspects. Ramachandran, Babu and Murugesan (2023) and Mukuze, Chavunduka, Manuere and Ndhlovu (2023) stress the significance of trained experts and management assistance in promoting adoption. Mukuze *et al.* (2023) also underscore the importance of clear knowledge of HRA. Rex, Bhattacharya, Narayanan and Budhwar (2020) and Zeidan and Itani (2020) warn that while HRA has potential, it is hindered by a lack of data analytics expertise and inadequate IT infrastructure. Boakye and Ayerki Lamptey (2020) and Mohammed (2019) delve deeper into the consequences of HR analytics with Boakye and Ayerki Lamptey (2020) concentrating on its possibilities in developing nations and (Mohammed, 2019) on its function in predictive decision-making. Muscalu and Anca (2014); and Fernandez and Gallardo-Gallardo (2020) offer practical insights. Fernandez and Gallardo-Gallardo (2020) discuss obstacles to adoption and suggest critical success criteria while Muscalu and Anca (2014) highlight the importance of HR's strategic involvement in enhancing organisational performance.

Integrating HR analytics in institutions presents numerous challenges that need to be addressed for successful implementation. Dahlbom, Siikanen, Sajasalo and Järvenpää (2019) identified that obstacles such as outdated HR processes, legacy information systems, and poor data quality hinder using contemporary HR analytics. It emphasises the importance of overcoming technical and data-related challenges to fully leverage the benefits of HR analytics effectively. Chugunova and Danilov (2022) suggested various barriers to adoption, including a lack of experienced professionals, high costs, and unclear legal regulations. These challenges underscore the significance of companies allocating resources towards training and development, cost-efficient strategies, and regulatory adherence to encourage the implementation of HR analytics. Chapano, Mey and Werner (2023) discussed the challenges of implementing digital HRM practices in automotive manufacturing organisations. Public sector organisations nonetheless implemented digital HRM methods despite the constraints. The findings indicate that public organisations organisations must address challenges and persist with digitalisation projects in HRM to showcase resilience. Greasley and Thomas (2020) situated HR analytics within the broader HRM and data development framework, highlighting the predominance of a positivist approach and the promotion of evidence-based management. Understanding HR analytics adoption's epistemic and political dimensions is crucial for successfully integrating analytics into HR procedures. Ramachandran *et al.* (2023) investigated the potential influence of blockchain technology on decision-making in HRM, emphasising the challenges that need to be addressed and proposing a study plan for using blockchain in HRM. Emerging technology could present both possibilities and challenges when implementing new HR practices.

Figure 3 illustrates a conceptual diagram showing the connections between adopting and implementing HR Analytics and several aspects of human resource management in businesses. The network diagram visually displays the relationship between HR Analytics and essential human resource concepts, with each idea represented by a node of a unique colour and labelled accordingly. The main components, HR Analytics, Adoption, and Implementation, create the fundamental sequence that outlines the progression of the analytics process inside an institutional setting.

HR Analytics is identified as the fundamental starting point in analysing Figure 3. Two crucial pathways branch out from this node, leading towards Adoption and Implementation, indicating a step-by-step process where analytics is initially embraced inside an organisation and subsequently used. The Implementation node then extends into different HR areas that could be affected by HR Analytics. The domains encompass HR Information Systems, HR Metrics, Quantitative Data, People Analytics, Talent Management, Human Capital Management, Organisational Effectiveness, Strategic HRM, and Decision-making. HR Information Systems, HR Metrics, and Quantitative Data are crucial components for implementing HR Analytics, highlighting the significance of information systems and measurable metrics. This highlights the dependence on data-driven methods in HR operations. The diagram links HR Analytics with People Analytics, emphasising the importance of data in comprehending and enhancing workforce productivity. Analytics is believed to improve plans for employee development and recognise individuals as essential assets in Talent Management and Human Capital Management. The diagram indicates that HR Analytics contributes to public sector organisation's Effectiveness, Strategic HRM, and Decision-making. This demonstrates how analytics may enhance public sector organisations' strategy and the efficiency of HR management, therefore impacting strategic decision-making.

Figure 3. Adoption and implementation of HR Analytics

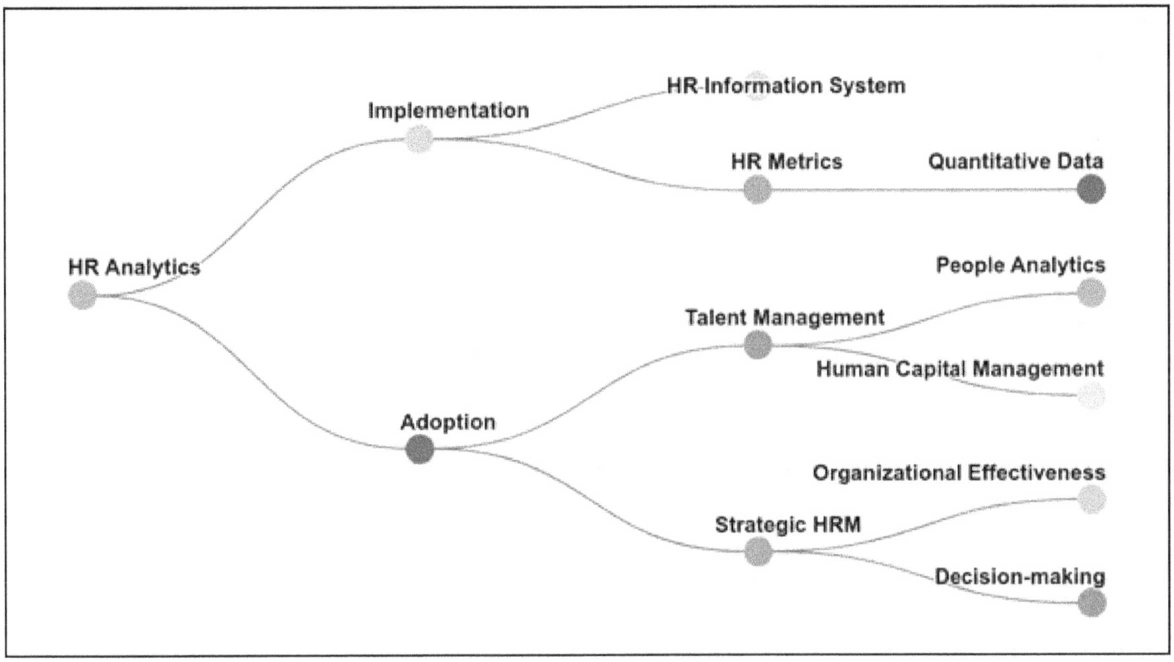

Source: Authors

IMPACT OF HR ANALYTICS ON TALENT MANAGEMENT

HR analytics using advanced data mining and business analytics methods in the HR profession (Ben-Gal, 2019). It involves utilising information technology to analyse data about HR processes, human capital, organisational performance, and external economic benchmarks through descriptive, visual, and statistical methods. This analysis aims to determine business impact and facilitate decision-making based on data (McCartney & Fu, 2022). Studies have shown that Workforce Analytics (HR Analytics, Talent Analytics, or People Analytics) is becoming increasingly popular in modern Human Resource Management (Fernandez & Gallardo-Gallardo, 2020). HR analytics is crucial in talent management since it helps organisations make well-informed decisions about their people resources. By utilising data-driven insights, HR managers may enhance their understanding and optimise several aspects of personnel management, including hiring, retention, training, and performance evaluation. Public sector organisations may identify patterns, trends, and correlations by examining HR data to forecast future personnel requirements, evaluate employee engagement, and create successful talent development strategies. HR analytics is essential in modern Human Resource Management because it enables the transition of HR practices from reactive to proactive and strategic. Public sector organisations can transition from intuition-based decision-making to evidence-based approaches that promote success by using analytics. HR analytics allows HR professionals to assess the effectiveness of HR programmes, align HR strategies with public sector goals, and efficiently allocate resources to enhance the productivity of their employees. Research has shown that HR analytics improves the accuracy and reliability of HR activities in businesses (Belizón & Kieran, 2021). HR professionals can enhance their strategic position in the organisation by demonstrating the tangible impact of HR initiatives on business outcomes through data-driven research. Adopting evidence-based HR practices improves decision-making and fosters a culture of ongoing enhancement and innovation in talent management operations.

Dutta (2018); and Chethana and Noronha (2022) highlight the significance of incorporating HR analytics in recruitment strategies. The public sector organisations may improve their recruitment processes by utilising data insights to select the most suitable candidate for each position. The findings highlight that technology solutions and data insights have revolutionised talent acquisition practices, resulting in improved recruitment strategies. Chen, Lee and Ahlström (2019) conducted research emphasising how strategic talent management systems impact employee behaviours and performance assessment. Public sector organisations can enhance employee commitment and achieve sustained competitive advantage by utilising talent management strategies such as strategic job identification, competence training, and performance evaluation. Public sector organisations can use HR analytics to identify factors affecting employee retention and create strategies to improve employee engagement, satisfaction, and loyalty, leading to lower turnover rates. Coculova and Tomčíková (2021); and Mohana and Subramanyam (2021) investigate talent management approaches to organisational performance and talent development. Public sector organisations may establish an atmosphere that fosters talent growth and success by recognising important aspects of talent management processes such as talent acquisition, performance management, and career development. Research conducted by Filippus and Schultz (2019); and Musakuro and De Klerk (2021) offers valuable information on the difficulties faced in talent management within the African public sector. The studies emphasise how workforce planning, remuneration, training, and development negatively affect talent management methods in the South African higher education sector and the Namibian public sector. Comprehending these challenges can assist HR professionals in comparable situations to effectively tackle talent management issues.

HR analytics has considerably changed talent management practices, resulting in enhanced outcomes in recruitment, employee engagement and retention, leadership development, and workforce planning. Ahmed, Kura, Umrani and Pahi (2019); and Rahi (2023) emphasised the positive impact of modern HR methods on improving employee engagement. Public sector organisations may enhance employee engagement, productivity, and job satisfaction by establishing a friendly atmosphere, providing feedback, and fostering a service-oriented culture. He, Morrison and Zhang (2021) highlight the significance of effective HR methods and leader-member interactions in promoting employee engagement and creativity to identify and cultivate leadership capabilities. These habits are crucial for establishing a leadership development-supportive environment that fosters business talent development, resulting in creativity and organisational success. HR analytics has significantly improved workforce planning strategies. Studies by Jasni, Mahadi, Yaakop and Baskaran (2022); and Saxena, Bagga, Gupta and Mittal (2022) have shown the advantageous use of analytics in talent acquisition, attrition risk management, and capacity planning. Public sector organisations can utilise HR analytics to inform decisions based on data for workforce planning, aligning human requirements with organisational objectives. Furthermore, HR analytics has significantly enhanced employee engagement and retention. Research conducted by Luu (2018); and Opoku, Kwao and Johnson (2023) indicate that human resources policy, psychological empowerment, and disability-inclusive practices can positively influence employee engagement. Public sector organisations can cultivate a supportive work environment that promotes employee engagement and decreases turnover rates by emphasising psychological well-being, empowerment, and inclusivity.

HR analytics in the African public sector has significantly influenced personnel management outcomes, leading to a mix of successes and challenges. Chilunjika *et al.* (2022) studied how Artificial Intelligence (AI) was integrated into the human resources management of South Africa's public sector. The study highlighted the advantages of AI in enhancing HR processes and identified challenges in its implementation and integration. Using AI in talent management can improve recruitment, performance evaluation, and workforce planning. However, obstacles such as data security, skill gaps, and ethical issues need to be addressed. A study examined the significance of talent management strategies in the public health sector using a case study of a well-known hospital in Zimbabwe (Nkala, Mudimu & Mbengwa, 2021). The study emphasised the need for effective personnel management to improve health service delivery while pinpointing challenges in implementing holistic people management techniques. Obstacles to obtaining optimal personnel management results in the public health sector included talent shortages, skills mismatches, and restricted resources. Boakye and Ayerki Lamptey (2020) studied the impact of HR analytics in a developing country, focusing on Ghana's organisations. The study highlighted the growing significance of HR analytics in shaping strategic decision-making in talent management. Obstacles such as data quality, technology maturity, and organisational culture were discovered to hinder the effective utilisation of HR analytics in talent management procedures.

The literature highlights the challenge of data quality as a vital issue. Anlesinya *et al.* (2019a) and Nocker and Sena (2019) researched the accuracy, thoroughness, and reliability of HR data in the African public sector. Poor quality data can lead to inaccurate findings and decision-making, hindering the effectiveness of HR analytics. Data privacy regulations must be complied with to protect employee data, and analytics must be used for talent management initiatives. Conte and Siano (2023) found that skill shortages hinder the successful adoption of HR analytics in talent management. The lack of expertise in data analysis, interpretation, and application can impede the success of HR analytics projects. Cultural barriers, such as resistance to change, organisational hierarchy, and entrenched traditions, must be overcome to foster a culture that values data-driven approaches and analytics. Barkhuizen and Gumede (2021) emphasise the need to overcome cultural barriers. Limited resources, including technical infrastructure and financial investments, can impede the effective use of HR analytics in talent management within the African public sector. Mukwawaya *et al.* (2021) highlight that resource limitations pose a significant challenge in conducting comprehensive HR analytics initiatives.

While offering numerous benefits, adopting HR Analytics in the public sector is not without significant challenges. These obstacles can hinder the effective implementation and utilisation of data-driven approaches to human resource management. This section discusses the primary challenges faced, supplemented by references to relevant literature that further elucidate these issues. Figure 4 below visualises the HR Analytics Adoption Challenges.

Figure 4. HR Analytics Adoption Challenges

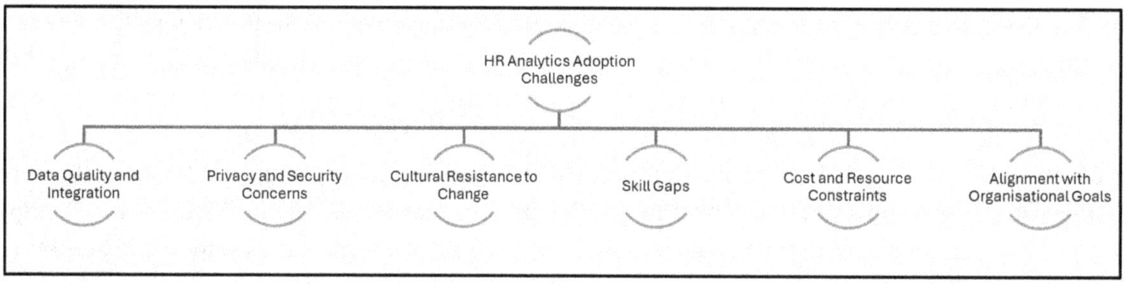

(Source: Authors, 2024)

The diagram in Figure 4 effectively encapsulates the common obstacles such as data quality issues, skill shortages, cultural resistance, and infrastructural limitations. Each of these challenges is interconnected, indicating that addressing one may impact the ability to overcome others, thereby stressing the complexity of implementing advanced analytical tools in a sector often characterized by rigid, traditional practices. The relevance of this diagram lies in its ability to provide a structured depiction of these challenges, offering a clear pathway for the study's discussion on strategies to mitigate these barriers. It serves as a foundation for recommending actionable steps that public sector entities can take to embrace HR analytics fully, such as investing in skills development, enhancing IT infrastructure, and fostering a culture that values data-driven decision-making.

CONCLUSION

This chapter investigated the influence of HR analytics on talent management in the public sector. HR analytics revolutionises talent management through data-driven decision-making, enhancing recruiting and selection, improving performance evaluation, and strengthening employee retention tactics. The case studies from African public sector organisations highlighted the practical use and advantages of using HR analytics to address conventional issues in talent management. Implementing HR analytics effectively faces hurdles like data protection issues, the need for HR workers to learn analytical abilities, and the cultural acceptance of data-driven processes. The results of this chapter have several consequences for public sector HRM. Integrating HR analytics can enhance the precision and effectiveness of personnel management procedures, leading to improved organisational performance and service provision. To properly leverage HR analytics, HRM requires investment in HR technology infrastructure, professional development in data analytics for HR practitioners, and a culture that prioritises evidence-based decision-making. Public sector organisations must address the ethical implications of HR analytics, prioritising data protection and security. Future research should investigate the enduring effects of HR analytics on talent management results in the African public sector, emphasising their role in organisational efficiency and employee welfare. Additional research might explore the obstacles hindering the acceptance and utilisation of HR analytics in more detail, pinpointing methods to address these difficulties. Comparative studies across various African countries could provide insights into regional differences in HR analytics techniques and their efficiency. Research on the ethical implications of HR analytics is necessary, focusing on data protection, employee permission, and the potential bias in algorithmic decision-making.

Ultimately, utilising HR analytics has great potential for improving talent management in the African public sector. Public sector organisations can enhance their HR management framework and increase organisational performance by implementing a strategic approach to HR analytics, resulting in more dynamic and responsive operations and better public service delivery.

RECOMMENDATIONS AND FUTURE DIRECTIONS

Future research should focus on improving data quality in HR analytics within the African public sector by examining data cleansing, integration, and validation techniques. This will enhance the accuracy and dependability of HR data, which is essential for effective decision-making. Additionally, studies should establish frameworks that ensure ethical data usage and adhere to increasingly important data privacy regulations. Addressing the skill gap in data analysis is also crucial and requires training programs and capacity-building to enhance HR professionals' analytical abilities. Research should also investigate cultural factors affecting the adoption of HR analytics and develop strategies to foster a data-driven culture. Furthermore, cost-effective solutions like open-source tools and cloud-based systems can help overcome resource constraints. Longitudinal studies tracking the impact of HR analytics on talent retention and overall organisational performance will provide valuable insights into its effectiveness and sustainability in improving HR processes in the African public sector.

REFERENCES

Abdeldayem, M. & Aldulaimi, S. 2020. Trends And Opportunities Of Artificial Intelligence In Human Resource Management: Aspirations For Public Sector In Bahrain.

Abugabel, A. 2023. The Impact of Digital Transformation on Sustainable Development: The Mediating Role of Development of Human Resources Management Practices "An Empirical Study on Private Hospitals. *Journal of Alexandria University for Administrative Sciences,*https://doi.org/10.21608/acj.2023.294133

Adisa, T. A. & Mordi, C. 2022. *HRM in the Global South: A Critical Perspective,*https://doi.org/10.1007/978-3-030-98309-3

Ahmed, U., Kura, K. M., Umrani, W. A., & Pahi, M. H. (2019). Modelling the Link Between Developmental Human Resource Practices and Work Engagement: The Moderation Role of Service Climate. *Global Business Review*. Advance online publication. 10.1177/0972150919837813

Al Jawali, H., Darwish, T. K., Scullion, H., & Haak-Saheem, W. (2022). Talent management in the public sector: Empirical evidence from the Emerging Economy of Dubai. *International Journal of Human Resource Management*, 33(11), 2256–2284. 10.1080/09585192.2021.2001764

Ali, E., & Elias, H. Potential Application of HR Analytics to Talent Management in the Public Sector: a Literature Review. *2023 International Conference on Cyber Management and Engineering, CyMaEn 2023*, 2023. 8-11 https://doi.org/10.1109/CyMaEn57228.2023.10051107

Angrave, D., Charlwood, A., Kirkpatrick, I., Lawrence, M., & Stuart, M. (2016). HR and analytics: Why HR is set to fail the big data challenge. *Human Resource Management Journal*, 26(1), 1–11. 10.1111/1748-8583.12090

Anlesinya, A., Amponsah-Tawiah, K., & Dartey-Baah, K. (2019a). Talent management research in Africa: Towards multilevel model and research agenda. *African Journal of Economic and Management Studies*, 10(4), 440–457. 10.1108/AJEMS-12-2018-0371

Anlesinya, A., Amponsah-Tawiah, K., & Dartey-Baah, K. (2019b). Talent Management Research in Africa: Towards Multilevel Model and Research Agenda. *African Journal of Economic and Management Studies*, 10(4), 440–457. Advance online publication. 10.1108/AJEMS-12-2018-0371

Arora, M., Prakash, A., Mittal, A., & Singh, S. 2022. Moderating Role of Resistance to Change in the Actual Adoption of HR Analytics in the Indian Banking and Financial Services Industry. *Evidence-Based HRM a Global Forum for Empirical Scholarship,*https://doi.org/10.1108/EBHRM-12-2021-0249

Barkhuizen, N., & Gumede, B. (2021). The Relationship Between Talent Management, Job Satisfaction and Voluntary Turnover Intentions of Employees in a Selected Government Institution. *SA Journal of Human Resource Management*, 19. Advance online publication. 10.4102/sajhrm.v19i0.1396

Bechter, B., Brandl, B., & Lehr, A. (2022). The Role of the Capability, Opportunity, and Motivation of Firms for Using Human Resource Analytics to Monitor Employee Performance: A Multi-level Analysis of the Organisational, Market, and Country Context. *New Technology, Work and Employment*, 37(3), 398–424. Advance online publication. 10.1111/ntwe.12239

Belizón, M. J., & Kieran, S. (2021). Human Resources Analytics: A Legitimacy Process. *Human Resource Management Journal*. Advance online publication. 10.1111/1748-8583.12417

Ben-Gal, H. C. (2019). An ROI-based Review of HR Analytics: Practical Implementation Tools. *Personnel Review*, 48(6), 1429–1448. Advance online publication. 10.1108/PR-11-2017-0362

Boakye, A., & Ayerki Lamptey, Y. (2020). The Rise of HR Analytics: Exploring Its Implications from a Developing Country Perspective. *Journal of Human Resource Management*, 8(3), 181. 10.11648/j.jhrm.20200803.19

Bonilla-Chaves, E. F., & Palos-Sanchez, P. R. (2023). Exploring the Evolution of Human Resource Analytics: A Bibliometric Study. *Behavioral Sciences (Basel, Switzerland)*, 13(3), 244. Advance online publication. 10.3390/bs1303024436975268

Cavanagh, J., Walker, M., Pariona-Cabrera, P., Bartram, T., & Halvorsen, B. (2022). Health Services in Australia and the Impact of Antiquated Rostering Practices on Medical Scientists: A case for HR Analytics and Evidenced-Based Human Resource Management. *Personnel Review*. Advance online publication. 10.1108/PR-09-2021-0690

Chapano, M., Mey, M. R., & Werner, A. (2022). Adoption of Digital Strategies Across the Human Resource Value Chain. *SA Journal of Human Resource Management*, 20. Advance online publication. 10.4102/sajhrm.v20i0.1992

Chapano, M., Mey, M. R., & Werner, A. (2023). Perceived Challenges: Unfounded Reasons for Not Forging Ahead With Digital Human Resource Management Practices. *SA Journal of Human Resource Management*, 21. Advance online publication. 10.4102/sajhrm.v21i0.2085

Chen, S., Lee, A. Y., & Ahlström, D. (2019). Strategic Talent Management Systems and Employee Behaviors: The Mediating Effect of Calling. *Asia Pacific Journal of Human Resources*. Advance online publication. 10.1111/1744-7941.12229

Chethana, K. M., & Noronha, S. D. (2022). *A Descriptive Study of Talent Management Practices Followed by Wipro LTD*. International Journal of Case Studies in Business It and Education., 10.47992/IJCSBE.2581.6942.0221

Chilunjika, A., Intauno, K., & Chilunjika, S. R. (2022). Artificial intelligence and public sector human resource management in South Africa: Opportunities, challenges and prospects. *SA Journal of Human Resource Management*, 20. Advance online publication. 10.4102/sajhrm.v20i0.1972

Chugunova, M., & Danilov, A. 2022. Use of Digital Technologies for HR Management in Germany: Survey Evidence. SSRN *Electronic Journal,*https://doi.org/10.2139/ssrn.4010539

Coculova, J., & Tomčíková, Ľ. (2021). *Innovative Human Resource Management Practices for the Talent Management Implementation*. Marketing and Management of Innovations., 10.21272/mmi.2021.4-04

Conte, F., & Siano, A. (2023). Data-Driven Human Resource and Data-Driven Talent Management In internal and Recruitment Communication Strategies: An empirical Survey on Italian Firms and Insights for European Context. *Corporate Communications*, 28(4), 618–637. Advance online publication. 10.1108/CCIJ-02-2022-0012

Dahlbom, P., Siikanen, N., Sajasalo, P., & Järvenpää, M. (2019). Big Data and HR Analytics in the Digital Era. *Baltic Journal of Management*, 15(1), 120–138. Advance online publication. 10.1108/BJM-11-2018-0393

Diez, F., Bussin, M. & Lee, V. 2019. *Fundamentals of HR analytics: A manual on becoming HR analytical,*https://doi.org/10.1108/9781789739619

Dutta, D. 2018. Social Media and Technology Trends in HRM: Cases in Recruitment and Talent Management. https://doi.org/10.5772/intechopen.79342

Dwiputrianti, S., Sutiyono, W., Suryanto, A., Rachmawati, T., & Purba, C. O. (2023). *Understanding Indicators of Talent Acquisition and Retention of Different Generations in Building Talent Management: A Case Study of DKI Jakarta Provincial Government.* Policy & Governance Review., 10.30589/pgr.v7i1.646

Edwards, M. R., Charlwood, A., Guenole, N., & Marler, J. (2022). HR analytics: An emerging field finding its place in the world alongside simmering ethical challenges. *Human Resource Management Journal*. Advance online publication. 10.1111/1748-8583.12435

Elrehail, H. HR Analytics and Future of Work: A Systematic Literature Review. *2nd International Conference on Business Analytics for Technology and Security, ICBATS 2023*, 2023. https://doi.org/10.1109/ICBATS57792.2023.10111370

Fernandez, V., & Gallardo-Gallardo, E. (2020). Tackling the HR digitalization challenge: Key factors and barriers to. *Competitiveness Review*, 31(1), 162–187. 10.1108/CR-12-2019-0163

Fernández, V. & Gallardo-Gallardo, E. 2020. Tackling the HR Digitalization Challenge: Key Factors and Barriers to HR Analytics Adoption. *Competitiveness Review an International Business Journal Incorporating Journal of Global Competitiveness,*https://doi.org/10.1108/CR-12-2019-0163

Filippus, K., & Schultz, C. (2019). Exploring Talent Management Execution in the Ministry of Justice in the Namibian Public Sector. *SA Journal of Human Resource Management*, 17. Advance online publication. 10.4102/sajhrm.v17i0.1162

Gobble, M. M. (2017). The Datification of Human Resources. *Research Technology Management*, 60(5), 59–63. 10.1080/08956308.2017.1348143

Greasley, K., & Thomas, P. (2020). HR Analytics: The Onto-epistemology and Politics of Metricised HRM. *Human Resource Management Journal*, 30(4), 494–507. Advance online publication. 10.1111/1748-8583.12283

Gupta, P. 2023. HR analytics: An effective tool for performance management and business development. *HR Analytics in an Era of Rapid Automation.*https://doi.org/10.4018/978-1-6684-8942-0.ch008

Halid, H., Yusoff, Y. & Somu, H. 2020. The Relationship Between Digital Human Resource Management and Organizational Performance. https://doi.org/10.2991/aebmr.k.200514.022

Haque, M. A., & Nishat, S. S. (2022). *The Impact of HRM Digitalization on Employee Performance in the RMG Industry of Bangladesh.* European Journal of Business Management and Research., 10.24018/ejbmr.2022.7.4.1540

He, J., Morrison, A. M., & Zhang, H. (2021). How High-Performance HR Practices and LMX Affect Employee Engagement and Creativity in Hospitality. *Journal of Hospitality & Tourism Research (Washington, D.C.)*, 45(8), 1360–1382. Advance online publication. 10.1177/1096348021996800

Jasni, N. N., Mahadi, N., Yaakop, A. Y., & Baskaran, S. (2022). *People Analytics: An Evidence-Based Approach in Managing Employees*. International Journal of Academic Research in Progressive Education and Development., 10.6007/IJARPED/v11-i3/15086

Jayaraman, S., Talib, P., & Khan, A. N. (2018). Integrated Talent Management Scale: Construction and Initial Validation. *SAGE Open*, 8(3). Advance online publication. 10.1177/2158244018780965

Jayasena, S. D. N. S., Rajasekera, J., & Wenkai, L. (2023). Talent Management for Enhancing the Efficiency of Human Resources in the Public Sector of Sri Lanka: A Comparative Study. *Kelaniya Journal of Human Resource Management*, 18(2), 1–11. 10.4038/kjhrm.v18i2.108

Jimoh, L. A., & Kee, D. M. H. (2022). Talent Management: The Way Out of Poor Task Performance. *Industrial and Commercial Training*, 54(4), 623–636. Advance online publication. 10.1108/ICT-03-2022-0016

Kapitanov, V. A., Osipova, O., & Chikileva, L. S. 2021. Promising Areas for Developing HR Managers' Competencies in the Digital Age. *SHS Web of Conferences*, https://doi.org/10.1051/shsconf/20219101016

Karwehl, L. J. & Kauffeld, S. 2021. Traditional and New Ways in Competence Management: Application of HR Analytics in Competence Management. *Gruppe Interaktion Organisation Zeitschrift Für Angewandte Organisationspsychologie (Gio)*, https://doi.org/10.1007/s11612-021-00548-y

Klepić, I. & Klepić, Z. 2023. The Influence of Determination of the Required Competencies on the Business Performance of Small and Medium Enterprises. https://doi.org/10.20867/thi.26.5

Kozjek, T., & Franca, V. (2020). *Talent Management in the Public Sector*. Central European Public Administration Review., 10.17573/cepar.2020.2.03

Kravariti, F., & Johnston, K. (2019a). Talent management: A critical literature review and research agenda fo r public sector human resource management. *Public Management Review*, 22(1), 75–95. 10.1080/14719037.2019.1638439

Kravariti, F., & Johnston, K. (2019b). Talent Management: A Critical Literature Review and Research Agenda for Public Sector Human Resource Management. *Public Management Review*. Advance online publication. 10.1080/14719037.2019.1638439

Kumar, S. R. (2021). The Impact of Talent Management Practices on Employee Turnover and Retention Intentions. *Global Business and Organizational Excellence*. Advance online publication. 10.1002/joe.22130

Leskina, E. I. 2022. Digital Talent Management for Human Capital Development. https://doi.org/10.15405/epsbs.2022.01.62

Likhitkar, P. & Verma, P. 2019. HR Value Proposition Using Predictive Analytics: An Overview. https://doi.org/10.1007/978-981-13-9330-3_15

Lin, L.-H., & Wang, K.-J. (2022). Talent Retention of New Generations for Sustainable Employment Relationships in Work 4.0 Era—Assessment by Fuzzy Delphi Method. *Sustainability (Basel)*, 14(18), 11535. Advance online publication. 10.3390/su141811535

Luu, T. T. (2018). Engaging Employees With Disabilities in Vietnamese Business Context. *Employee Relations*, 40(5), 822–847. Advance online publication. 10.1108/ER-06-2017-0134

Macedo, R. R. d., Veloso, E. F. R., Pinsky, V. C., & Trevisan, L. N. (2023). *Career Management in Digital Age: A Study of Leadership's Competencies and Practices Applied for IT Professionals*. Revista De Administração Da Ufsm., 10.5902/1983465969082

Madhani, P. M. (2022a). Human Resources Analytics: Leveraging Human Resources for Enhancing Business Performance. *Compensation &amp. Compensation and Benefits Review*, 55(1), 31–45. 10.1177/08863687221131730

Madhani, P. M. (2022b). Human Resources Analytics: Leveraging Human Resources for Enhancing Business Performance. *Compensation and Benefits Review*. Advance online publication. 10.1177/08863687221131730

Maharani, M. & Wang, G. 2022. The Use of Gamification for Pre-Recruitment System in Tax Consulting Company. *Journal of Information Systems and Informatics,*https://doi.org/10.51519/journalisi.v4i3.320

Margherita, A. (2022). Human resources analytics: A systematization of research topics and directions for future research. *Human Resource Management Review*, 32(2), 100795. Advance online publication. 10.1016/j.hrmr.2020.100795

Marler, J. H., & Boudreau, J. W. (2017). An evidence-based review of HR Analytics. *International Journal of Human Resource Management*, 28(1), 3–26. 10.1080/09585192.2016.1244699

McCartney, S., & Fu, N. (2022). Bridging the Gap: Why, How and When HR Analytics Can Impact Organizational Performance. *Management Decision*, 60(13), 25–47. Advance online publication. 10.1108/MD-12-2020-1581

Mohammed, A. Q. (2019). HR ANALYTICS: A MODERN TOOL IN HR FOR PREDICTIVE DECISION MAKING. *Journal of Management*, 10(3). Advance online publication. 10.34218/JOM.6.3.2019.007

Mohana, S., M, R. K. & Subramanyam, P. N. V. B. 2021. Talent Management Practices and Sustainable Organizational Performance in Cement Industry. *Journal of Management and Science,*https://doi.org/10.26524/jms.11.24

Mukuze, K., Chavunduka, D., Manuere, F., & Ndhlovu, P. (2023). An Integrative Review of HR Analytics Implementation. *Management and Economics Research Journal*, 9(1), 1–7. 10.18639/MERJ.2023.9900076

Mukwawaya, O. Z., Proches, C. G., & Green, P. (2021). Perceived Challenges of Implementing an Integrated Talent Management Strategy at a Tertiary Institution in South Africa. *International Journal of Higher Education*, 11(1), 100. Advance online publication. 10.5430/ijhe.v11n1p100

Musakuro, R. (2022). TALENT MANAGEMENT PRACTICES IN A SELECTED SOUTH AFRICAN HIGHER EDUCATION INSTITUTION. *Problems and Perspectives in Management*, 20(1), 532–542. 10.21511/ppm.20(1).2022.42

Musakuro, R. N., & De Klerk, F. (2021). Academic talent: Perceived challenges to talent management in the south african higher education sector. *SA Journal of Human Resource Management*, 19, 1–13. 10.4102/sajhrm.v19i0.1394

Muscalu, E. (2014). *Anca, e.* HR ANALYTICS FOR STRATEGIC HUMAN RESOURCE MANAGEMENT.

Naidoo, R. & Ndlovu, S. W. 2022. Stickiness Impediments in Digital HRM. https://doi.org/10.24251/HICSS.2022.638

Napathorn, C. 2020. How Do MNCs Translate Corporate Talent Management Strategies Into Their Subsidiaries? Evidence From MNCs in Thailand. *Review of International Business and Strategy,*https://doi.org/10.1108/RIBS-04-2020-0043

Ndou, M. M., Mofokeng, J. T., & Khosa, D. (2021). *Exploring the Role of Management in the Implementation of Talent Management.* Technium Social Sciences Journal., 10.47577/tssj.v26i1.4887

Nkala, B., Mudimu, C., & Mbengwa, A. M. (2021). *Human Resources for Health Talent Management Contribution: A Case for Health Systems Strengthening in the Public Health Sector.* World Journal of Advanced Research and Reviews., 10.30574/wjarr.2021.9.2.0062

Nocker, M., & Sena, V. (2019). Big Data and Human Resources Management: The Rise of Talent Analytics. *Social Sciences (Basel, Switzerland)*, 8(10), 273. Advance online publication. 10.3390/socsci8100273

Ontrup, G., Schempp, P. S. & Kluge, A. 2021. Choosing the Right (HR) Metrics: Digital Data for Capturing Team Proactivity and Determinants of Content Validity. *Journal of Organizational Effectiveness People and Performance,*https://doi.org/10.1108/JOEPP-03-2021-0064

Opoku, F. K., Kwao, I. T., & Johnson, A.-P. (2023). Human Resource Policies and Work–life Balance in Higher Education: Employee Engagement as Mediator. *SA Journal of Human Resource Management*, 21. Advance online publication. 10.4102/sajhrm.v21i0.1939

Qamar, Y., & Samad, T. A. (2021). Human Resource Analytics: A Review and Bibliometric Analysis. *Personnel Review*. Advance online publication. 10.1108/PR-04-2020-0247

Rahi, S. (2023). Fostering Employee Work Engagement and Sustainable Employment During COVID-19 Crisis Through HR Practices, Employee Psychological Well-Being and Psychological Empowerment. *Industrial and Commercial Training*, 55(3), 324–345. Advance online publication. 10.1108/ICT-04-2022-0023

Ramachandran, R., Babu, V., & Murugesan, V. P. (2023). Human resource analytics revisited: A systematic literature review of its adoption, global acceptance and implementation. *Benchmarking*. Advance online publication. 10.1108/BIJ-04-2022-0272

Rana, G., Sharma, R., & Goel, A. K. (2018). *Unraveling the Power of Talent Analytics: Implications for Enhancing B usiness Performance. Business Governance and Society*. Springer International Publishing., 10.1007/978-3-319-94613-9_3

Rasmussen, T., & Ulrich, D. (2015). Learning from practice: How HR analytics avoids being a management fad. *Organizational Dynamics*, 44(3), 236–242. 10.1016/j.orgdyn.2015.05.008

Rex, T., Bhattacharya, S., Narayanan, K., & Budhwar, P. (2020). *Opportunities and Barriers in the Practice of Human Resource Analytics. Human & Technological Resource Management (HTRM): New Insights int o Revolution 4.0.* Emerald Publishing Limited., 10.1108/978-1-83867-223-220201004

Saadatmand, M., Safaie, N., & Dastjerdi, M. (2022). Presenting a Structural Model of Digitalised Talent Management in a New Age: A Case Study on the Mobile Telecommunication Industry in Iran. *SA Journal of Human Resource Management*, 20. Advance online publication. 10.4102/sajhrm.v20i0.1894

Saputra, A., Wang, G., Zhang, Z., & Behl, A. (2021). The Framework of Talent Analytics Using Big Data. *The TQM Journal.* Advance online publication. 10.1108/TQM-03-2021-0089

Saxena, M., Bagga, T., Gupta, S., & Mittal, A. (2022). Employees' Experiences of Accepting and Adopting HR Analytics: A Phenomenology Study. *The Open Psychology Journal*, 15(1), e187435012208040. Advance online publication. 10.2174/18743501-v15-e2208040

Semaihi, S. O. 2023. Talent Management and Performance in the Public Sector: The Mediating Role of Line Managerial Support. *Journal of Organizational Effectiveness People and Performance,*https://doi.org/10.1108/JOEPP-09-2022-0274

Shariuda, M. A., El Tanany, S. & Maraiyesa, Y. 2018. Building Capacity of Government Leaders in Egypt/ .

Shava, E. 2022. Talent Management: A 'Recipe' for Public Service Delivery in the Fourth Industrial Revolution. *International Journal of Research in Business and Social Science (2147-4478),*https://doi.org/10.20525/ijrbs.v10i8.1504

Shava, E. & Doorgapersad, S. V. 2021. Talent management: A'recipe'for public service delivery in the fourth industrial revolution. *International Journal of Research in Business and Social Science (2147-4478),* 10, 138-148

Sripathi, K., & Madhavaiah, C. (2018). Are HR professionals ready to adopt HR analytics? A study on analytical skills of HR professionals. *Journal of Advanced Research in Dynamical and Control Systems*, 10, 303–308.

Vaiman, V., & Collings, D. G. (2023). *GLOBAL TALENT MANAGEMENT: Past, Present, and Future* (7th ed.). Readings and Cases in International Human Resource Management., 10.4324/9781003247272-3

Verma, S., Rana, N., & Meher, J. R. (2024). Identifying the enablers of HR digitalization and HR analytics using ISM and MICMAC analysis. *The International Journal of Organizational Analysis*, 32(3), 504–521. 10.1108/IJOA-01-2023-3611

Vilčiauskaitė, B., Savanevičienė, A., & Navickas, V. (2020). *Managing Older Talents in the Context of Aging Society.* Economics & Sociology., 10.14254/2071-789X.2020/13-4/13

Zavyalova, E., Sokolov, D., Kucherov, D. & Lisovskaya, A. 2022. The Digitalization of Human Resource Management: Present and Future. *Foresight and Sti Governance,*https://doi.org/10.17323/2500-2597.2022.2.42.51

Zeidan, S. & Itani, N. 2020. HR Analytics and Organizational Effectiveness.

Zhang, J., & Chen, Z. (2023). Exploring Human Resource Management Digital Transformation in the Digital Age. *Journal of the Knowledge Economy*. Advance online publication. 10.1007/s13132-023-01214-y

Chapter 6
Digital Transformation in Hiring and Selection Processes:
A Ugandan Public Sector Perspective

Alexander Markey Oluka
https://orcid.org/0000-0001-7632-1490
European University Viadrina, Germany

Elvin Shava
https://orcid.org/0000-0001-8721-4666
University of KwaZulu-Natal, South Africa

ABSTRACT

The study explores the digital transformation of public sector hiring in Uganda, highlighting the potential of digital technologies to revolutionise recruitment by enhancing efficiency, accessibility, and transparency. Automation, online platforms, and data-driven decision-making serve to streamline administrative tasks, expand candidate outreach, and promote merit-based hiring. Despite these benefits, significant challenges including data security risks, technological failures, digital divides, and algorithmic biases necessitate strategic intervention. Through document analysis and qualitative research, this study draws on policy documents and government reports to outline current practices and future prospects. It emphasises the need for robust infrastructure, improved digital literacy, and clear policy frameworks to support digital adoption while mitigating risks. Effective leadership and a supportive organisational culture are crucial to successfully navigating the digital shift, aiming to achieve an effective, inclusive, and transparent public sector hiring process in Uganda.

INTRODUCTION

African bureaucracies are destined to be the epitome of rendering public goods and services. To achieve this public sector human resource management is one of the key functions that enables employee development, and wellness and ensures that all the needs of public sector officials is catered to enhance quality service delivery. For many years government bureaucracies in Africa have been operating in a more rigid manner that resists change in the process instilling red tape as a measure to ensure that bu-

DOI: 10.4018/979-8-3693-2889-7.ch006

reaucratic decisions are hierarchically carried out. Nevertheless, due to the trends emanating from the technological environment globally, public sector organisations are forced to transform and align with the use of modern technologies which the Fourth Industrial Revolution believe is a drastic game changer in rendering quality goods and services. The digital transformation orchestrated by the fusion of various modern technologies has also awakened African bureaucracies of which Uganda's public sector is not spared from this transformative wave. Research done in the past decade has shown that digital transformation has altered the landscape of public sector operations worldwide. The paradigm shift, driven by technological advancements, has been pivotal in reshaping government functions, including hiring and selection processes. Globally, the public sector is increasingly adopting digital technologies to enhance operational efficiency, improve service delivery, and foster transparency (Heeks & Bailur, 2007). Public sector transformation is not simply a technological upgrade but represents a fundamental change in how public institutions engage with technology to meet their objectives (Mergel, 2016).

In public sector human resource management, digitalisation has introduced innovative approaches to recruitment and selection of candidates. According to a study by Prabhu et al. (2020), digital tools and platforms are revolutionising public sector hiring by streamlining processes, enabling data-driven decision-making, and expanding the reach to a broader pool of candidates. Moreover, the integration of digital practices in the public sector is not a trend limited to developed nations. Emerging economies are also embracing these changes, albeit at varying paces and scales (UN, 2020). The case of Uganda presents a unique perspective in this global narrative as a developing country with an expanding digital infrastructure. Uganda is at a critical juncture where the adoption of digital practices in public sector hiring could significantly influence its administrative efficacy and governance outcomes (Osborne et al., 2022). The study focuses on the benefits and risks of implementing digital transformation in Uganda's public sector hiring processes. It examines the disparity between the potential benefits of digitalisation, such as efficiency and transparency, highlighted by Debrah et al. (2019) and the existing challenges related to infrastructure, digital literacy, and policy frameworks, as noted by (Falloon, 2020). The central issue is understanding the impact of these factors on the successful integration of digital practices in hiring, providing critical insights into the obstacles and opportunities in this significant administrative evolution. The chapter answers the following objectives. To examine the benefits of digital transformation in hiring and selection and to assess the challenges associated with digital transformation in hiring and selection in the Ugandan public sector.

The next section reviews the literature by synthesising global trends and local initiatives in Uganda's digital hiring practices. Following this, the section explores traditional hiring practices in Uganda, discussing their limitations and inefficiencies. It then examines global digital hiring trends and their relevance to Uganda, highlighting case studies of successful digital initiatives within the Ugandan public sector. The discussion extends to the challenges of digital transformation, focusing on infrastructural, literacy, and policy barriers alongside political and economic factors. The methodology section describes the research methods employed, while subsequent sections discuss the opportunities digital transformation can bring and strategic recommendations for overcoming existing challenges. The conclusion summarises key findings and reflects on the potential future of digital HR practices in Uganda.

6.2 LITERATURE REVIEW

Global Trends In Digital Hiring And Their Relevance To Uganda

Globally, digital hiring practices are increasingly becoming the norm in public sector recruitment. A shift towards technology-based solutions, such as online job portals, digital application tracking systems, and virtual interviews, is evident. Bissola and Imperatori (2019) note that there is a growing adoption of Artificial Intelligence (AI) and machine learning in screening applicants, which enhances the efficiency and effectiveness of the recruitment process. Furthermore, social media platforms are being leveraged for employer branding and reaching potential candidates, as discussed in a study by Van Hoye et al. (2019) in the International Journal of Selection and Assessment.

Digital hiring trends are undergoing significant transformations due to the rapid digitalisation of the economy. The Information and Communications Technology (ICT) sector is experiencing labour market volatility, leading to challenges for both companies seeking to hire specialists and for the specialists themselves in terms of job retention (Brabete, 2023). Academic libraries are increasingly interested in hiring digital scholarship librarians to support digital scholarship initiatives (Hannah et al., 2020). Moreover, there is a noticeable cross-hiring trend between journalism and human rights sectors, with human rights professionals joining digital investigation teams at news organisations.

The digitalisation of hiring processes offers numerous benefits in public sector HRM. Firstly, it significantly increases efficiency by automating and streamlining recruitment tasks, as highlighted by Stone et al. (2023) in their book on Human Resource Management. Digital methods also foster greater transparency in recruitment, reducing the potential for bias and corruption, as noted in the World Economic Forum's Future of Jobs Report (2020). Moreover, digital platforms expand the reach of job advertisements, enabling access to a broader talent pool, including remote and international applicants.

Applying these global trends to Uganda's context offers promising prospects. Uganda, with its growing internet penetration and digital literacy, is well-positioned to adopt these practices. A study by Nguimkeu and Okou (2021) in the review of policy research highlights Uganda's potential to leverage digital platforms to overcome traditional recruitment challenges. For instance, introducing online job portals and digital application systems can significantly reduce the time and resources required for hiring. Moreover, as Castro and Lopes (2022) argue, digital methods can help mitigate issues of transparency and nepotism in Uganda's public sector, aligning with the government's efforts towards good governance and public service improvement. Thus, integrating digital hiring practices in Uganda can streamline recruitment processes and enhance the overall governance quality.

6.2.2 Digital Transformation in Uganda's Public Sector HRM

The World Bank's World Development Report (2021) indicates that Uganda has made notable strides in integrating digital technologies into various government functions, signalling a commitment to modernising its public services. The integration of modern technologies into hiring is imperative in a country where the public sector is a significant employer and plays a pivotal role in economic stability and development. The Uganda Bureau of Statistics (2020) reports that the government's digital initiatives have been focused on improving efficiency and transparency, especially in areas like public sector hiring. These efforts are backed by the National Development Plan III (2020/21 – 2024/25), which emphasises the importance of digital skills and infrastructure in enhancing service delivery. The plan recognises the potential of digitalisation to streamline recruitment processes, reduce bureaucratic delays, and mitigate corruption risks.

Uganda's increasing internet penetration, which as per the Uganda Communications Commission (2020), stands at approximately 40%, provides a solid foundation for digital ventures in public sector hiring. However, challenges such as limited digital literacy and infrastructure disparities between urban and rural areas persist, as highlighted in the National Information Technology Authority-Uganda (NITA-U) report (2019). The transition to digital hiring processes in Uganda's public sector is a technological shift and an economic and social imperative. It holds the promise of enhancing the efficiency of public sector operations and driving broader socio-economic development by leveraging technology for more inclusive and equitable government practices.

Uganda's Traditional Public Sector Hiring Practices

Uganda's public sector hiring process has historically followed a conventional, manual approach. The Civil Service College Uganda (2018) in their study highlights that recruitment typically involves several stages, including job advertisement, manual application submission, shortlisting, interviewing, and final selection. The Public Service Commission (PSC), as indicated in its annual reports, plays a central role in overseeing and conducting these processes. Traditional methods heavily rely on paper-based applications and face-to-face interactions, which, while functional, are often protracted and resource-intensive (Kiggundu, 2017). The manual processes, as described by Yiga and Wandiba (2017), involve significant bureaucratic procedures. Job advertisements are primarily disseminated through print media and government bulletins, limiting their reach to a broader audience. The PSC's mandate, as detailed in the Uganda Public Service Standing Orders (2020), includes ensuring fairness and meritocracy in hiring. However, the implementation of these principles often encounters challenges in the manual system.

One of the primary issues, as identified by Wright (2019) in his study on public sector reforms, is the lengthy duration of the recruitment process. This delay often results from the manual handling of applications and the need to convene various committees and panels for decision-making. In addition, there is a lack of transparency and the potential for corrupt practices in traditional hiring and selection practices. As noted by Transparency International's Corruption Perceptions Index (2020), Uganda faces a considerable challenge with corruption, which can infiltrate hiring processes. The manual system, with its limited oversight mechanisms, is susceptible to nepotism and favouritism, as argued by the Council of Europe (2019) in their analysis of public sector governance. In addition, the manual approach limits the pool of potential candidates. As Singh (2017) notes, the reliance on traditional media for job advertisements may not effectively reach the increasingly tech-savvy and geographically dispersed population. This limitation potentially excludes qualified candidates, particularly the youth and those in remote areas, from public sector opportunities.

Owing to the trends in the technological environment the current state of digital transformation in Uganda's public sector has been promising for human resources practitioners. The National Information Technology Authority-Uganda (NITA-U) report (2020) reveals that there has been a gradual implementation of digital tools in public recruitment processes. This includes the use of online job portals and electronic application systems in some government agencies. However, the adoption is not uniform across all sectors. The Ministry of Public Service's digital strategy (2019) articulates a plan to integrate more robust digital platforms and database systems for recruitment, but actual implementation varies significantly among different government departments. Despite these advancements, there remain gaps in comprehensive digital adoption. The Uganda Public Service Commission Annual Report (2020) highlights the need for broader infrastructure development and more consistent application of digital tools across all recruitment stages. Limited digital literacy among both applicants and hiring staff, as well as inconsistent internet access across the country, are cited as key barriers in the report.

RISKS ASSOCIATED WITH DIGITAL TRANSFORMATION IN HIRING AND SELECTION

The digital transformation of public sector hiring also raises concerns about data security and privacy. For example, when the public sector collects and processes a significant amount of personal information, safeguarding this data against breaches is paramount. Duggineni (2023) stresses the importance of robust cybersecurity measures to protect sensitive data. Without adequate security protocols, there is a risk of data breaches, leading to loss of trust and potential legal repercussions. Moreover, over-reliance on digital systems can pose risks, particularly when these systems fail. Debrah, Effah and Owusu-Mensah (2019) note that technical glitches or system breakdowns can disrupt the recruitment process, leading to delays and inefficiencies. Moreover, in the absence of manual backup processes, such failures can bring recruitment activities to a standstill.

The UN (2020) highlights the digital divide between demographic groups and geographic regions. Applicants lacking access to digital technologies and the necessary digital literacy may be unfairly disadvantaged, undermining the equity of the recruitment process. This reveals that the transition to digital hiring may exacerbate existing inequalities. While digital tools aim to reduce human bias, they are not immune to biases. Yarger, Cobb Payton and Neupane (2020) warn of the potential for algorithmic bias, where automated systems replicate and even amplify existing prejudices, leading to discriminatory hiring practices. Moreover, the use of algorithms and digital tools in benchmarking and peer selection can obscure the decision criteria, making it difficult to identify and rectify instances of bias or unfair practices in candidate selection (Agostino et al., 2021). Ensuring that digital hiring tools are unbiased and fair is a significant challenge.

The rapid acceleration of digital transformation in response to events like the COVID-19 pandemic can result in inadequate planning and control mechanisms in the hiring process (Gabryelczyk, 2020). The rush to adopt digital solutions may overlook critical aspects of candidate evaluation, such as ensuring data privacy and security, which can compromise the integrity of the selection process. Tangi et al. (2020) indicate that external pressures may drive transformation without addressing internal readiness. In the context of hiring, this could translate to the adoption of digital tools without adequate training for staff involved in the selection process, leading to errors and misuse of technology that impacts candidate assessments. The reliance on digital platforms for hiring may introduce challenges in maintaining agility and responsiveness in the selection process (Tate et al., 2018). The "fuzzy front end" of digital innovation in the public sector may lead to rigid processes that hinder adaptability to changing hiring needs or emerging candidate profiles.

The introduction of digital hiring processes may require significant changes in organisational culture and practices. As Scholkmann (2021) observe, resistance to change is a common risk in digital transformation. Employees may be hesitant to adopt modern technologies due to fear of job displacement or a lack of confidence in using digital tools. Furthermore, digital hiring must comply with various laws and regulations, including those related to employment, data protection, and accessibility. Non-compliance can result in legal challenges and reputational damage. The Public Service Commission's guidelines (2020) indicate that navigating this complex legal landscape is a critical aspect of implementing digital hiring.

BENEFITS OF DIGITAL TRANSFORMATION IN HIRING AND SELECTION

The digital transformation of public sector hiring processes offers a plethora of benefits by impacting the efficiency, accessibility, and transparency of recruitment. Stone et al. (2023) discuss how digital tools, such as Applicant Tracking Systems (ATS) and online testing platforms, streamline recruitment by automating tasks like resume screening and candidate assessment. The automation speeds up the selection and hiring process and reduces the workload of human resource departments, allowing them to focus on more strategic aspects of recruitment.

Digital platforms extend the reach of public sector job advertisements, enabling organisations to attract a broader and more diverse applicant pool. Koch, Gerber and De Klerk (2018) note that online job portals and social media channels provide access to job opportunities for individuals who might not be reached through traditional means. This inclusivity is particularly important for public sector organisations aiming to reflect the diversity of the communities they serve. Digital hiring processes can significantly improve transparency and fairness in recruitment. Yarger, Cobb Payton and Neupane (2020) highlight how digital tools offer better documentation and tracking of recruitment activities, reducing the risks of bias and corruption. Public sector agencies can use data-driven approaches to ensure a fairer, merit-based selection process, promoting equal opportunity and trust in public institutions.

The use of digital platforms enables the collection and analysis of vast amounts of data on recruitment processes and outcomes. As argued by Wang (2021), this data can be leveraged to make informed decisions about hiring practices, identifying trends, and addressing gaps. It also allows for continuous improvement in recruitment strategies by ensuring they align with the organisation's goals and workforce needs. Digital tools reduce the need for physical space, paper-based materials, and manual labour, as pointed out by the United Nations (UN) E-Government Survey (2020). These savings are beneficial for public sector organisations, which often operate under budget constraints, revealing that while the initial investment in digital hiring systems may be significant, the long-term cost savings are considerable.

METHODOLOGY

The chapter employed document analysis which involves systematic evaluation and interpretation of documents on digital hiring and selection to glean meaningful information and insights on how the public sector in Uganda is undertaking strategies to embrace digital transformation. This technique is advantageous as it provides access to data that is non-reactive and unobtrusive, ensuring that the research process does not influence the information. The chapter utilised documents such as policy papers, digital strategy outlines, government reports, and even internal communications that can serve as rich data sources on the subject matter in Uganda. Tracy (2019) explains that documents can reveal the historical and current state of digital hiring practices, policy orientations, and strategic planning, offering a contextual backdrop against which other qualitative data (like interviews or surveys) can be interpreted.

DISCUSSION OF FINDINGS

This section discusses the challenges of digital transformation in Uganda's public sector HRM

Technological inadequacy and cultural adaptation of digital transformation

The core impediment to digital transformation in Uganda's public sector hiring is the inadequacy of technological infrastructure. As observed by the World Bank's Digital Economy for Africa (DE4A) Initiative (2021), many regions in Uganda still face significant challenges in terms of reliable internet access and modern ICT facilities. The digital divide hampers the implementation of online recruitment processes and limits the potential applicant pool to those with internet access, as noted in a study by Semyachkov (2019) focusing on digitalisation in developing countries.

Africa is home to various cultural beliefs and traditions that may act as barriers to the adoption of modern digital technologies if they are not adhered to properly. The Ugandan public is one typical example which subscribes to various cultural traditions that perceive the adoption of foreign or Western innovations as a threat to existing cultural beliefs among other patriarchal reasons. Although modernisation has been evident in Uganda through the use of modern digital devices, the penetration is still slow which may affect the work of human resource practitioners in the public sector to render change. A study conducted by Eyamu et al. (2021), has shown that cultural adaption impedes as there is often resistance to change among both public sector employees and job seekers in Uganda. The resistance stems from a lack of familiarity with digital tools, apprehension about the transparency of digital processes, and concerns about job security in the face of automation. Further due to existing societal problems such as inequalities and absence of economic opportunities, the adoption of digital hiring and selection has adverse implications on job seekers in Uganda which is a wakeup call for the state institutions to educate the masses but most importantly leverage access to modern digital devices to transform the role of HRM. Public sector employees on the one hand still believe in the traditional hiring methods which they perceive as fair and cannot be superseded by modern digital hiring methods that impact negatively on potential candidates. Research done in Uganda has not yet solidified the role of digital transformation in embracing change in public sector organisations. The need for advanced studies are required to ensure that the government of Uganda can develop programmes that empower citizens most importantly rural youth to ensure that they have access to modern digital devices to explore employment opportunities while embarking on other entrepreneurial programmes. The HRM practitioners on the one hand are pivotal in emphasising the merits of digital transformation which is critical in learning new things, methods, strategies and mechanisms to revamp the existing public structure for effective public service delivery.

Political Factors

The political will and commitment of the government are necessary to foster a conducive environment for digital advancements. In Uganda, the government's endorsement and support through initiatives like the National Development Plan III influence the pace and extent of digital transformation. However, political instability or leadership changes can lead to shifts in priorities and disruptions in ongoing projects, which may slow down or alter the course of digital initiatives (Mergel, 2016). Moreover, political interests might affect the allocation of resources, where digital transformation competes with other national priorities for funding and attention. This competition can limit the financial and institutional support necessary to sustain long-term digital projects, which are essential for transforming HR practices. Additionally, regulatory environments and government policies directly impact the implementation of digital HR systems. For instance, the effectiveness of digital transformation in public sector HR is contingent upon the establishment of supportive legal frameworks that ensure data protection and cybersecurity (Baum & Maio, 2020). Inconsistencies or delays in formulating these regulations can hinder the adoption of digital tools, leaving sensitive HR data vulnerable and undermining trust in digital systems. Furthermore, political agendas may influence the focus areas of digital transformation, potentially skewing developments towards politically beneficial regions or demographics, thereby exacerbating the digital divide. As such, for digital transformation to be effective and equitable, political actions and policies must be aligned with the principles of transparency, inclusiveness, and sustainability, ensuring that all regions and sectors benefit from digital advancements in HR.

Economic Environment

Economic stability provides the necessary resources for investment in technology and infrastructure, which are necessary for digital initiatives. However, Uganda, like many developing countries, faces budget constraints that can limit the ability to allocate sufficient funds to digital projects. Economic fluctuations and priorities may divert funds towards more immediate needs such as healthcare and education, leaving less capital available for the technological advancements needed in HR systems. Moreover, a constrained economic environment can lead to underinvestment in critical areas such as internet connectivity and digital literacy programs, which are essential for the successful implementation of digital HR practices (Mergel, 2016). The availability of economic resources influences the capacity to maintain and upgrade digital infrastructure, which is necessary to keep pace with evolving technological standards and security demands.

Additionally, the broader economic context affects workforce dynamics and the labour market, which in turn impacts digital transformation in HR. In an economy struggling with high unemployment rates, there may be increased pressure on public sector HR departments to streamline recruitment and make it more accessible through digital platforms (da Silva et al., 2022). Conversely, economic challenges can exacerbate the digital divide, as individuals in lower economic brackets may lack access to digital tools and the internet, making it difficult for them to participate in digitalised recruitment processes. This necessitates targeted economic policies that support both digital transformation and inclusion. For instance, economic incentives for businesses to develop digital skills among their employees or subsidies for digital device purchases could help mitigate some of these challenges. Ensuring that the economic policies align with the goals of digital transformation can facilitate a more cohesive and inclusive approach to modernising public sector HR practices in Uganda.

OPPORTUNITIES FOR DIGITAL TRANSFORMATION IN UGANDA PUBLIC SECTOR HRM

Digital transformation in the public sector presents numerous opportunities for enhancing service delivery, organisational efficiency, and citizen engagement. The Uganda Communications Commission (2020) reported that increasing internet penetration provides a growing platform for online recruitment initiatives. Furthermore, as Castro and Lopes (2022) note, digital platforms offer the potential for greater transparency and efficiency in the recruitment process, which can help mitigate corruption and improve governance. Leveraging online platforms for recruitment has become increasingly popular due to its efficiency and effectiveness.

The digital platformisation strategy, as observed in Ghana's paperless port, exemplifies the potential for technology and transformational leadership in the public sector (Senyo et al., 2021). Furthermore, the outbreak of the COVID-19 pandemic has accelerated digital transformation in public service delivery by revitalising the focus on digital initiatives and e-government. Digital transformation has led to a departure from mere digitisation to a comprehensive redesign of government services to meet evolving user needs, as seen in the case of hybrid organisational forms in the public sector. Therefore, digital transformation in the public sector requires a complete overhaul of work processes, service delivery, and departmental operations, extending beyond technology to encompass organisational and operational changes. The adoption of digital processes and practices is fundamental for public organisations to provide social value in an increasingly digital world (Sánchez, 2020). However, barriers to digital transformation in public organisations necessitate a deeper understanding of the transformational efforts and the empirical evidence supporting real public sector transformation.

Social media platforms like Facebook and LinkedIn have also proven valuable tools for recruiting participants (Ali et al., 2021). The speed of recruitment, cost-efficiency, and accessibility to a wide range of potential participants are key advantages of using social media for recruitment purposes. Additionally, online recruitment methods are superior in terms of time efficiency and cost-effectiveness compared to traditional recruitment approaches (Upadhyay & Lipkovich, 2020). Online recruitment practices contribute to improving diversity and inclusion in research studies by reaching out to underrepresented groups (Rehman et al., 2022). By utilising online technologies, researchers can engage with a more diverse pool of participants, enhancing the representativeness of their studies.

The adoption of digital tools can also enhance the reach of public sector job advertisements, attracting a more diverse and qualified applicant pool. This expansion is particularly beneficial for engaging the youth demographic, which is increasingly tech-savvy and represents a substantial portion of the Ugandan population. While Uganda faces infrastructural, cultural, and policy challenges in its journey towards digital transformation in public sector hiring, the opportunities presented by this shift are considerable. The potential for improved efficiency, transparency, and inclusivity in recruitment processes can significantly contribute to the overall effectiveness and integrity of Uganda's public administration.

CONCLUSION

The study of digital transformation within Uganda's public sector hiring illustrates a path filled with benefits and risks. The shift towards digitalisation heralds significant improvements in the efficiency, accessibility, and transparency of recruitment processes. This transition aligns with a broader global movement towards leveraging technology to enhance public service delivery, promising a more inclusive and streamlined approach to attracting a diverse workforce. The potential to automate and digitise various stages of the hiring process could markedly reduce the time and resources traditionally required, offering an avenue to widen the talent pool and ensure public sector roles are accessible to a broader segment of the population.

Conversely, the transition towards digital platforms introduces critical challenges related to data security and privacy, underscoring the importance of robust cybersecurity measures to protect sensitive information. Furthermore, the reliance on digital systems raises concerns about technology failures and their potential to disrupt recruitment activities. This stresses the need for resilient systems and backup processes. The digital divide remains a significant barrier, with disparities in access to technology and digital literacy potentially exacerbating inequality in the recruitment process. Additionally, there is the risk of algorithmic bias in automated selection tools, which could replicate or amplify existing prejudices if not carefully monitored and managed.

The successful navigation of Uganda's public sector towards digital hiring thus requires a balanced approach that harnesses the benefits of digitalisation while mitigating its risks. Addressing the challenges of infrastructure readiness, digital literacy, and policy development is paramount to creating an equitable and efficient digital hiring environment. Moreover, the shift necessitates a cultural and organisational transformation championed by leadership committed to fostering a digital-friendly ethos within the public sector. This involves investing in the necessary technological infrastructure and the people who will use and be affected by these digital systems, ensuring they are equipped with the skills and support needed to adapt to new working methods.

The potential of digital transformation in public sector hiring in Uganda is vast and offers opportunities to enhance efficiency, expand access, and improve the fairness of recruitment practices. However, realising this potential requires careful consideration of the associated risks, particularly those related to data security, technology dependence, the digital divide, and potential biases in digital tools. As Uganda continues to advance its digital agenda, it will be crucial to adopt a comprehensive strategy that addresses these challenges, supported by robust policies, continuous capacity building, and a culture of innovation and adaptability. With thoughtful implementation and leadership, digital transformation can significantly improve the public sector hiring landscape in Uganda, making it more inclusive, efficient, and transparent.

REFERENCES

African Tax Administration Forum. (2021). Case Study: Uganda Revenue Authority's Digital Transformation. Available at: Revenue mobilisation through tax transparency (ataftax.org) [Accessed 21 December 2023]

Agostino, D., Bracci, E., & Steccolini, I. (2021). Accounting and accountability for the digital transformation of public services. *Financial Accountability & Management*, 38(2), 145–151. 10.1111/faam.12314

Ali, Z., Valk, T. J., Bjerre-Christensen, T., Brandt, S., Isberg, A. P., Jensen, M. L., Helledi, L. S., Kaas, A., Thomsen, S. F., Andersen, A. D., & Robert Zibert, J. (2021). Exploring decentralized glucose and behaviometric monitoring of persons with type 2 diabetes in the setting of a clinical trial. *Journal of Diabetes Science and Technology*, 17(1), 117–124. 10.1177/1932296821104565634553637

Arundel, A., Bloch, C., & Ferguson, B. (2019). Advancing innovation in the public sector: Aligning innovation measurement with policy goals. *Research Policy*, 48(3), 789–798. 10.1016/j.respol.2018.12.001

Bissola, R., & Imperatori, B. (2018). HRM 4.0: The digital transformation of the HR department. In *Human Resource Management and Digitalization. The Effects of Industry 4.0 on Human Resource* (pp. 51-69). Routledge.

Brabete, V. (2023). Assessing and forecasting current and future trends of ict employment in european enterprises. *Brain Broad Research in Artificial Intelligence and Neuroscience*, 14(4), 1–40. 10.18662/brain/14.4/489

Castro, C., & Lopes, C. (2022). Digital government and sustainable development. *Journal of the Knowledge Economy*, 13(2), 880–903. 10.1007/s13132-021-00749-2

Civil Service College Uganda. (2018). Report on Public Sector Recruitment Practices. Available at: Annual Report 2018 - 2019 Civil Service College Annual Report for the Year Ended 31 March 2019 - DocsLib [Accessed 12 January 2024]

Council of Europe. (2019). Public ethics: fighting nepotism within local and regional authorities. Available at: ES274310_PREMS 072519 GBR 5001 Combattre le nÃ©potisme au sein des pouvoirs locaux et rÃ©gionaux TXT BAT A6.pdf (coe.int) [accessed 22 December 2023]

da Silva, L. B. P., Soltovski, R., Pontes, J., Treinta, F. T., Leitão, P., Mosconi, E., de Resende, L. M. M., & Yoshino, R. T. (2022). Human resources management 4.0: Literature review and trends. *Computers & Industrial Engineering*, 168, 108111. 10.1016/j.cie.2022.108111

Debrah, E., Effah, J., & Owusu-Mensah, I. (2019). Does the use of a biometric system guarantee an acceptable election's outcome? Evidence from Ghana's 2012 election. *African Studies*, 78(3), 347–369. 10.1080/00020184.2018.1519335

Deloitte. (2022). Government Trends 2022. Available at: 2022 Government Trends I Deloitte Insights [Accessed 12 January 2024]

Duggineni, S. (2023). Impact of Controls on Data Integrity and Information Systems. *Science and Technology*, 13(2), 29–35.

Eyamu, S., Wanyama, S. B., Ndanyi, D. M., & Sansa, A. (2021). A Critical Analysis of New Public Management, Human Resource Practices and Operational Performance in Uganda's Public Sector. *Journal of Human Resource Management*, 9(4), 102–114.

Falloon, G. (2020). From digital literacy to digital competence: The teacher digital competency (TDC) framework. *Educational Technology Research and Development*, 68(5), 2449–2472. 10.1007/s11423-020-09767-4

Gabryelczyk, R. (2020). Has covid-19 accelerated digital transformation? initial lessons learned for public administrations. *Information Systems Management*, 37(4), 303–309. 10.1080/10580530.2020.1820633

Hannah, M., Heyns, E., & Mulligan, R. (2020). Inclusive infrastructure: Digital scholarship centers and the academic library liaison. *Portal (Baltimore, Md.)*, 20(4), 693–714. 10.1353/pla.2020.0033

Harvard Business Review. (2021). Insights on Digital Transformation. Available at: The Essential Components of Digital Transformation (hbr.org) [Accessed 12 January 2024]

Heeks, R., & Bailur, S. (2007). Analyzing e-government research: Perspectives, philosophies, theories, methods, and practice. *Government Information Quarterly*, 24(2), 243–265. 10.1016/j.giq.2006.06.005

Hujran, O., Alarabiat, A., Al-Adwan, A. S., & Al-Debei, M. (2023). Digitally transforming electronic governments into smart governments: SMARTGOV, an extended maturity model. *Information Development*, 39(4), 811–834. 10.1177/02666669211054188

International Labour Organization. (2020). Guidelines on Fair Recruitment. Available at: FAIR III brochure (ilo.org) [Accessed 12 January 2024]

Kentenyingi, R. (2022). Closing the growing digital skills gap in Uganda. Available at: https://www.uncdf.org/article/7859/closing-the-growing-digital-skills-gap-in-uganda [Accessed 15 April 2024]

Kiggundu, M. N. (2017). Alternative service delivery in Africa: The case for international regional organisations. *Africa's Public Service Delivery & Performance Review*, 4(2), 283–311. 10.4102/apsdpr.v4i2.114

Koch, T., Gerber, C., & De Klerk, J. J. (2018). The impact of social media on recruitment: Are you LinkedIn? *SA Journal of Human Resource Management*, 16(1), 1–14. 10.4102/sajhrm.v16i0.861

McKinsey & Company. (2020). The next chapter: Driving technology leadership in the public sector. Available at: McKinsey & Company Article [accessed 05 January 2024]

Mergel, I. (2016). Agile innovation management in government: A research agenda. *Government Information Quarterly*, 33(3), 516–523. 10.1016/j.giq.2016.07.004

Mergel, I. (2021). Open innovation in the public sector: drivers and barriers for the adoption of Challenge.gov. In *Digital Government and Public Management* (pp. 94–113). Routledge. 10.4324/9781003258742-6

Ministry of Public Service. (2019). Public Service Digital Strategy. Available at: Ministry of Public Service Strategic Plan 2015/2016 – 2019/2020 – Ministry of Public Service [Accessed 20 December 2023]

National Information Technology Authority-Uganda (NITA-U). (2019). National IT Survey Report. Available at: Final NITA-U ANNUAL REPORT FY2019-20 Ver.1.2 Final Report -2020-08-04.pdf [Accessed 12 Jan. 2024]

National Information Technology Authority-Uganda (NITA-U). (2020). National IT Survey Report. Available at: National IT Survey Report 2022 - Final.pdf (nita.go.ug) [Accessed 2January 2024]

National Planning Agency. (2020). National Development Plan III (NDP III). Available at: NDP-3-Report.pdf (health.go.ug) [Accessed 10 January 2024].

National Planning Authority. (2020). National Development Plan III (2020/21 – 2024/25). Available at: THIRD NATIONAL DEVELOPMENT PLAN (NDPIII) 2020/21 – 2024/25 - Ministry of Health | Government of Uganda [Accessed 04 January 2024]

Nguimkeu, P., & Okou, C. (2021). Leveraging digital technologies to boost productivity in the informal sector in Sub-Saharan Africa. *The Review of Policy Research*, 38(6), 707–731. 10.1111/ropr.12441

Osborne, S. P., Cucciniello, M., Nasi, G., & Zhu, E. (2022). Digital transformation, artificial intelligence and effective public services: Challenges and opportunities. *Global Public Policy and Governance*, 2(4), 377–380. 10.1007/s43508-022-00058-7

Prabhu, U., Fathima, Y., Sathyanarayana, N., Srikumar, M. S., & Cavaliere, L. P. L. (2024). Emerging Digitalization Trends in Human Resource Management. In *Data-Driven Intelligent Business Sustainability* (pp. 214–234). IGI Global.

Public Procurement and Disposal of Public Assets Authority (PPDA). (2020). Report on e-Government Procurement System. Available at: PPDA-Annual-Report-2020-2021.pdf [Accessed 12 January 2024]

Sánchez, M. (2020). University e-readiness for the digital transformation: The case of universidad nacional del sur. *Revista Gestão & Tecnologia*, 20(2), 75–97. 10.20397/2177-6652/2020.v20i2.1848

Scholkmann, A. B. (2021). Resistance to (digital) change: Individual, systemic and learning-related perspectives. *Digital transformation of learning organizations*, 219-236.

Semyachkov, K. A. (2019). May. Digital economy in developing countries: problems and prospects. In *1st International Scientific Conference" Modern Management Trends and the Digital Economy: from Regional Development to Global Economic Growth"(MTDE 2019)* (102-106). Atlantis Press.

Senyo, P., Effah, J., & Osabutey, E. (2021). Digital platformisation as public sector transformation strategy: A case of ghana's paperless port. *Technological Forecasting and Social Change*, 162, 120387. 10.1016/j.techfore.2020.120387

Singh, S. (2017). E-Recruitment: A new dimension of human resource management in India. *International Journal of Advance Research in Computer Science and Management Studies*, 5(3), 99–105.

Stone, R. J., Cox, A., Gavin, M., & Carpini, J. (2023). *Human resource management*. John Wiley & Sons.

Tangi, L., Janssen, M., Benedetti, M., & Noci, G. (2020). Barriers and drivers of digital transformation in public organizations: Results from a survey in the Netherlands. In *Electronic Government: 19th IFIP WG 8.5 International Conference, EGOV 2020, Linköping, Sweden, August 31–September 2, 2020* [Springer International Publishing.]. *Proceedings*, 19, 42–56.

Tate, M., Bongiovanni, I., Kowalkiewicz, M., & Townson, P. (2018). Managing the "fuzzy front end" of open digital service innovation in the public sector: A methodology. *International Journal of Information Management*, 39, 186–198. 10.1016/j.ijinfomgt.2017.11.008

Tracy, S. J. (2019). *Qualitative research methods: Collecting evidence, crafting analysis, communicating impact*. John Wiley & Sons.

Transparency International. (2020). Corruption Perceptions Index. Available at: 2020 Corruption Perceptions Index - Explore the… - Transparency.org [Accessed 30 December 2023]

Uganda Bureau of Statistics. (2020). Statistical Abstract. Available at: 11_2020STATISTICAL__ABSTRACT_2020.pdf (ubos.org) [Accessed 10 December 2023]

Uganda Communications Commission. (2020). Communications Market Performance Report. Available at: UCC-September-2020-Market-Intelligence-Report.pdf [Accessed10 January 2024]

Uganda Public Service Commission. (2021). Annual Report. Available at: Consolidated Annual Inspection and PAIPAS Report FY 2021-22.pdf [Accessed 12 January 2024]

Uganda Public Service Standing Orders. (2020). Available at: https://publicservice.go.ug/download/the-uganda-public-service-standing-orders-2021-edition/ [Accessed 12 Jan. 24]

United Nations. (2020). E-Government Development Index. Available at: EGOVKB | United Nations > About > Overview > E-Government Development Index [Accessed 12 January 2024]

United Nations Development Programme. (2023). Uganda's Digital Transformation Journey. Available at: Uganda's Digital Transformation Journey | United Nations Development Programme (undp.org) [Accessed 15 April 2024]

United Nations E-Government Survey. (2020). E-Government in the Digital Era: Challenges and Opportunities. United Nations. Available at: Regional Challenges and Opportunities | United Nations iLibrary (un-ilibrary.org) [accessed 15 December 2023]

Van Hoye, G., Van Hooft, E. A., Stremersch, J., & Lievens, F. (2019). Specific job search self-efficacy beliefs and behaviors of unemployed ethnic minority women. *International Journal of Selection and Assessment*, 27(1), 9–20. 10.1111/ijsa.12231

Wang, Y. (2021). When artificial intelligence meets educational leaders' data-informed decision-making: A cautionary tale. *Studies in Educational Evaluation*, 69, 100872. 10.1016/j.stueduc.2020.100872

World Bank. (2021). Digital Economy for Africa (DE4A) Initiative. Available at: Digital Economy for Africa Initiative (worldbank.org) [Accessed 12 January 2024]

World Bank. (2021). World Development Report 2021: Data for Better Lives. Available at: World Development Report 2022: FINANCE for an Equitable Recovery (worldbank.org) [Accessed 12 Jan. 24]

World Economic Forum. (2020). The Future of Jobs Report 2020. Available at: WEF_Future_of_Jobs_2020.pdf (weforum.org) [accessed 11 January 2024]

Wright, V. (2019). Reshaping the state: the implications for public administration. In *The State in Western Europe* (pp. 102–137). Routledge. 10.4324/9781315037479-6

Yarger, L., Cobb Payton, F., & Neupane, B. (2020). Algorithmic equity in the hiring of underrepresented IT job candidates. *Online Information Review*, 44(2), 383–395. 10.1108/OIR-10-2018-0334

Yiga, I., & Wandiba, A. (2017). Recruitment and Selection Process and Local Government Performance in Kiboga District, Uganda. *KIU Journal of Social Sciences*, 2(2), 71–82.

Chapter 7
Embracing Transformative Digital Human Resource Management in the Nigerian Public Sector

Oluwaseun Temitope Ojogiwa
University of KwaZulu-Natal, South Africa

Sibongile Ruth Nhari
University of KwaZulu-Natal, South Africa

ABSTRACT

The Fourth Industrial Revolution is generating changes in every element of society. The implication of this digital transformation continues to vary based on the readiness, available resources, and the level of development of each nation and organisation. Digital transformation is anticipated to have a far-reaching positive effect of modernising public organisations through the HR element. This chapter, based on a desktop review, explores the adoption of digital HRM in the unique context of the Nigerian public sector, characterised by inefficient bureaucratic structures, obsolete methods that foster nepotism, and limited innovation. The literature presents opportunities for transforming the longstanding HRM challenges in the sector. However, the adoption of digital HRM is faced with resistance from the workforce, political interference, inadequate infrastructures, and a lack of necessary digital skills. Digital HRM can be propelled by a strong will and commitment from all stakeholders to align with technological change imperatives and foster a more responsive sector.

INTRODUCTION

The Fourth Industrial Revolution (4IR) represents a stage of technological advancement that is transforming lives and workplaces through digitalisation, including the use of the internet and the incorporation of unified devices as real-time online applications (Palos-Sánchez et al., 2022). The digital era is defined by various terms and concepts such as e-government, Information technology (IT), digitalisation, and the 4IR among others. Nalubega and Uwizeyimana (2019) assert that 4IR is a revolution propelled by

DOI: 10.4018/979-8-3693-2889-7.ch007

Artificial Intelligence (AI) and cyber-physical systems. This revolution is marked by the introduction of digital business models and digitalised human endeavours and product and service offerings. The 4IR is primarily driven by mobile internet and cloud technology, advanced manufacturing and 3D printing, big data analytics, biotechnology, advanced robotics, autonomous transport, machine learning, new technologies and energy supplies, as well as the Internet of Things (IoT) (Ojogiwa et al., 2023). The digital transformation has implications for many fields of activity and every aspect of human life. The transformative era is reshaping the global workplace, and it offers both prospects and challenges for Human Resource Management (HRM) in organisations, either in the public or private sector (Fenwick et al., 2024). This infers that smart technologies are altering existing norms of professions such as HR to improve their functions.

Nigeria has an opportunity to leverage the prospects of digitalisation to reform its public sector that is reported to be burdened by entrenched inefficiencies, nepotism and corruption, and influenced by political machinations. These challenges are connected to the existing HRM practices in the sector (Orga & Ogbo, 2012; Nosike, 2023). The Nigerian public sector struggles with outdated HRM systems, which impede both the sector's effectiveness and the country's sustainable development. Existing opaque procedures and skills gaps continue to erode the efficiency of civil servants and hinder the effective delivery of public services. Its traditional recruitment and selection processes, as well as its performance management and talent development strategies, are often flawed by bias and nepotism, requiring a paradigm shift to keep pace with global advancements (Fiias & Augustine, 2020; Yaro, 2014). The Nigerian public sector presents a unique context marked by bureaucratic structures, diverse demographics, and historical challenges. This chapter acknowledges the distinctiveness of this context, recognising that effective digital HRM strategies must be tailored to address specific contextual nuances for successful implementation.

Employees, also referred to as a human resource or human capital, are considered valuable assets for an organisation, and have been emphasised to be a country's most crucial asset, whose development and well-being should be invested in, as they make valuable contributions in accomplishing organisational objectives (Aroge & Hassan, 2011). It is evident that people are essential to the means of organisations' production. Regardless of digitisation and automation, people are still essential for setting up, operating, and maintaining machinery. Although this has generated arguments and further studies among scholars, Nardo et al. (2020) emphasised that human resources must have new skills to comprehend and analyse the growing need for innovation. An argument by Budhwar et al. (2023) indicated that the initial designs and operating procedures are often engineered by humans who have experiential knowledge of the problems that the machinery is intended to solve. Therefore, it could be inferred that with advanced algorithms, human judgement and adaptation are required in the event of unforeseen circumstances. Humans ensure that ethical issues are not overlooked and adhere to the environmental and social responsibility. The concept of Human Resource Management (HRM) transcends mere employee handling; it is a strategic and organised approach to maximise an organisation's workforce (Majam & Jarbandhan, 2022). HRM oversees the various factors, strategies, practices, principles, operations, activities, functions, decisions and processes related to employees in an organisation. The growing technological landscape also associated HRM's responsibility with maintaining employment relationships and their ensuing dynamics (Van der Esthuizen, 2021). The effective management of limited talents and skills, and the recruitment and retention of trained employees are paramount issues in HRM. The quality of employment stands out as a fundamental concern for HRM, while it faces the critical challenges of framing an active work system and flexibility, reward systems, and employee or political influence in the public sector (Salau et al., 2020). This necessitates research on how the opportunities that are associated with digital HRM could be harnessed in the Nigerian public sector that continually strives for improvement in response to citizens' demands and globalisation trends.

Against this backdrop, this chapter explores the existing HRM practices in Nigeria's public sector. It sheds light on undermining factors like corruption, resistance to change, and the digital skills gap towards the adoption of digital HRM in the public sector. Ultimately, the chapter highlights the transformative opportunities of digitalisation for public sector HRM and offers actionable recommendations that will help technology experts, policymakers, government organisations, and HRM professionals to successfully traverse the adoption of digital HRM. Realising the full potential of 4IR in the Nigeria public sector HRM could considerably transform the sector for optimal performance.

The Nature of Nigerian Public Sector HRM Practices

The Nigerian public service inherits its structure and principles from the colonial era. The inherited British structure reflects the model employed in managing public undertakings (Ofoma, 2021). The sector is designed to cater to the needs of all citizens through the formulation and implementation of policies and is sustained and administered through shared resources. According to Adekunle (2018), the government's workforce is usually referred to as the civil service or the public service. The public service or civil service represents the entire workforce that drives the policy landscape, and it plays a vital role in the success of the public sector, as it functions as the operational drivers of governments' goals and drives the country's development.

The public sector employs a vast workforce with diverse skill levels across different categories. This diversity encompasses the unskilled and under-skilled, underscoring the need to upskill these employees for organisational success. Nigeria's public sector plays a vital role in national development, but its HRM practices frequently face criticisms surrounding its inefficiency, which affects the credibility of the sector. The sector faces significant challenges of limited stakeholder involvement and high levels of corruption, for instance, which are additionally compounded by the complex socioeconomic, cultural, and historical context in which policy decisions are made and enacted (Ofoma, 2021; Aroge & Hassan, 2011).

Employee engagement, talent management, and public service delivery in the sector are considered flawed (Yaro, 2014; Ukeje et al., 2020). These factors collectively contribute to the Nigeria's public sector inefficiency and credibility challenges. According to Wurim (2012), the personnel employed within the Nigerian public sector across various levels of government is excessive, cumbersome, and inefficient. As highlighted in literature, high unemployment rates and pressure from political parties have been known to lead to a tendency within the public sector to engage in over-employment practices, where more than one individual is hired to fill a role that a single person would typically occupy. What was once an instrumental force in driving progressive policy development and execution, as well as the primary supplier of essential social services sustaining livelihoods and fostering economic growth in the country, has regrettably deteriorated into a dilapidated system of political favouritism that neglects meritocracy. Ironically, the procedures outlined in the Civil Service policy guidelines and the Constitution underscore crucial attributes like uniformity, transparency, meritocracy, and standardization of the recruitment process. However, the staffing composition of most government agencies, departments, and ministries shows the appointment of many unqualified personnel (Adenugba et al., 2017).

The poor quality of talent in the sector is informed by traditional recruitment practices, where standardised tests rarely figure in the selection of the best candidates (Adegboye & Akinyemi, 2014). Recruitment advertisements often lack transparency, perpetuating a culture of exclusion and unfairness.

Additionally, the perception of technology within the public sector is polarised, with public servants exhibiting contrasting views about it. While younger employees appear to embrace it without much resistance, the older personnel are attached to familiar traditional HRM procedures, further widening the digital generational divide. Also, a deficiency of digital literacy and training on digital tools such as Integrated HRM Systems and Applicant Tracking systems often creates anxiety and signals unpreparedness for the adoption of digital HRM (Sarker et al., 2018; Nosike, 2023). Zhang and Chen (2023), however, noted that for HRM to play an active role in the digital sphere, HR professionals need to develop the required skills to manage the evolving workforce and acquire tools to adapt activities and strategies to the digital workspace. It was emphasised that digitisation is more than the use of digital tools and is a powerful lever for organisation to transform their mode of operations for more excellent optimisation.

Significant challenges faced by public sector HR managers are political interference and constant policy changes. The *godfatherism* culture, as identified by Orga and Ogbo (2012), creates an environment that lacks continuity. This is due to existing corruption, lack of transparency, and unequal power dynamics, which together pose as challenges for HR managers to maintain professionalism. Bawalla & Rufai (2021) attest to the influence of the political system, involving government policies, power play and regulations, on HRM in organisations. HR managers are often placed in a state of perpetual adaptation, confounding their responsibility of making long-term planning decisions. The employment process lacks due diligence as recruitment often bypasses standard procedures to favour political loyalists above qualified candidates. Consequently, HR managers become ineffective and lack a fair process to attract and retain skilled and needed talent. Vacancy announcements are mere formalities and applicants' confidence in interviews dwindles, with interview results considered inconsequential (Orga and Ogbo, 2012). Nonetheless, according to Nosike (2023), through the use of digital technologies, the public sector HRM will be able to simplify administrative duties, enhance staffing process, support training efforts and improve employee morale and engagement.

While traditional HRM might have sufficed in the past for issues such as inadequate feedback mechanisms and subjectivity, the growing complexity of the public sector coupled with citizens' insatiable needs demand a transformative approach (Christian, 2022). Hence, digital transformation emerges as a promising solution to propel Nigerian public sector HRM into the 21st century, with the possibility of offering improved efficiency, effectiveness, and transparency (Ogedengbe et al., 2023). For instance, the infusion of AI into HRM practices represents a transformative trend with the potential to revolutionise how the Nigerian public sector manages its workforce. AI applications in HRM range from talent acquisition management to employee engagement and performance management.

METHODOLOGY

This study adopted a qualitative approach through a desktop review of relevant and extant literature by using key phrases such as digital HRM in the public sector, HRM and 4IR, and Nigerian public sector HR, among others. The adopted qualitative approach allows for a comprehensive understanding of the complex context, laying the groundwork for further empirical research. Due to the emerging trend of digitalisation in the Nigerian public sector HRM and motivated by the need to understand the dynamics surrounding the adoption of 4IR in HRM within the public sector, the study relied on secondary data from Google Scholar databases. Peer reviewed articles and book chapters were studied to gain insights into the prevailing HRM landscape in the country and particularly the public sector. The qualitative analysis involved synthesising information, identifying patterns, and drawing themes from the diverse perspectives presented in the literature.

RESULT AND DISCUSSION

This ensuing section presents the findings and discussion from different sources that were extensively reviewed. Each section is uniquely identifiable with its aim.

Potential Opportunities of Digital HRM in the Nigerian Public Sector

As the Nigerian public sector grapples with embracing digital transformation in HRM, opportunities have been identified to leverage emerging technologies to enhance various aspects of HR practices (Oyebanji & Kassim, 2017). Studies (Majam & Jarbandhan, 2022; Nosike, 2023) revealed that big data could improve transparency, internal efficiency, and communication in government agencies. For instance, HR practitioners in countries like New Zealand have recognised the benefits of big data in areas such as succession, training, planning, and workforce productivity. Big data is recognised to support workforce planning and identify skills gaps in some occupations. This section explores prospects that are derivable from adopting digital technologies within the Nigerian public sector HRM, emphasising strategic considerations that are associated with integrating these technologies.

Enhanced Public Sector Recruitment and Retention Processes

According to Chilunjika et al. (2022) and Majam and Jarbandhan (2022), the public sector HRM process could benefit from using big data, AI and other components of 4IR in areas such as recruitment, performance monitoring and appraisal, and talent acquisition, through data analysis. Noske (2023) emphasised that the process of attracting and retaining top talent will continue to be a challenge without the embrace of digitalisation in public sector HRM as prospective employees anticipate intuitive and seamless experiences that are similar to those provided by the private sector.

Leveraging Technology for Efficient Hiring processes: Emerging technologies offer the potential for employing optimising and streamlining the hiring process in the public sector. AI is confirmed to have upgraded the traditional recruitment procedures in South Africa. It is considered useful in managing time and cost throughout the automation of employment (Chilunjika et al., 2022). Ukeje et al. (2020) referenced the use of online assessments, data analytics, and applicant tracker systems as significant tools to enhance the efficiency of recruitment processes in Nigeria. By automating routine tasks, public sector HR professionals could focus more deeply on strategic aspects of candidate evaluation, ensuring a more thorough and efficient hiring process with less administrative burdens and reduced application processing time. Adekunle (2018) alludes to digital hiring tools like cloud-based hiring and RoboRcruiter that could make the recruitment process of the Nigerian public sector to be devoid of nepotism and HR personnels' subjective decisions. Majam and Jarbandhan (2022) underscore that data-driven HRM is useful for evaluation and monitoring purposes, with indicators focusing on innovation in HR plans, staff awareness of training interventions, professional standards for performance management, and a flexible working environment.

Improving Inclusion and Diversity in Recruitment: Technology provides possibilities for addressing inclusion and diversity challenges in recruitment within the Nigerian public sector. Biases in recruitment practices could be identified and mitigated while ensuring a fair and inclusive selection process (Yaro, 2014). Technology-driven platforms for job adverts and candidate outreach could reach a broader audience, promoting diversity in the applicant pool and fostering a more inclusive workforce. The talent pool could be expanded beyond geographical limitations, encouraging more involvement with video conference tools (Majam & Jarbandhan, 2022).

Improved Employee Engagement

Enhancing Employee Experience: The traditional public sector experience, often characterised by cumbersome processes and limited communication, can dampen employee morale and stifle engagement (Fajana et al., 2011). Digital HR applications such as self-service portals are designed to empower employees, manage personal information, provide access to learning resources, and submit feedback conveniently. These efforts have often been supported by gamified online training and learning platforms for employees to further enhance their experience, turning professional development into an interactive and rewarding endeavour (Bella et al., 2023). The efficient use of these technologies has been noted as contributing to building a positive work environment (Salau et al., 2020).

Optimising Effective Feedback and Recognition: Feeling valued and heard is crucial for employee engagement. Online performance management and real-time performance feedback systems offer a structured way for employees to receive constructive feedback and express their perspectives without fear of being victimized. Moreover, these improve communication and mutual understanding in the public service (Ogedengbe et al., 2023). According to Majam and Jarbandhan (2022), feedback and incentives are provided based on performance without bias, through big data integration in HR practices. Digital platforms for recognition programs can further create a culture of collaboration and boost morale within the workforce. HR technology could be leveraged for continuous feedback loops and to enhance employee engagement, satisfaction, and performance in the Nigerian public sector (Orga & Ogbo, 2012).

Data-Driven Management

Affording Analytics in HRM: Analytics facilities that are data-driven provide insights into workforce trends, employee performance, and overall HR effectiveness (Christian, 2022). By leveraging reliable data and analytical tools, HR professionals have the opportunity to make evidence-based decisions, while having insightful viewpoints and reports on talent acquisition, development, and gaps, resource allocation, workforce planning, and retention strategies, contributing to the overall efficiency and effectiveness of the public sector HR functions (Majam & Jarbandhan, 2022). Modern HR analytics tools have potent data visualisation and predictive capabilities to detect workforce strengths, needs, and weaknesses. Majam and Jarbandhan (2022) identified predictive analytics, statistical models, and forecasts as helpful in anticipating future workforce trends, allowing for better planning and cost reduction.

Making Informed Policy and Strategic Decisions: Beyond operational matters, modern technologies enable HR professionals to make cost-effective decisions with precision, based on comprehensive data analysis. According to Chilunjika et al. (2022), AI technologies is incredibly useful and the future of complex HRM decision. Evidence-based decision provides time-conscious and cost-benefit benefits for HR professionals. Therefore, HR managers can reshape public sector strategy and policy, assess the impact of policies, identify areas for improvement, and align HR strategies with organisational goals (Salau et al., 2020). Budhwar et al. (2022) also noted that AI algorithms helps HR professionals to make excellent decisions beyond human capacity to perform their responsibilities such as the identification of an appropriate job candidate. Asides from enhancing overall effectiveness, digital HRM helps to drive responsive policies to the evolving needs and dynamics of the public sector. For instance, Majam and Jarbandhan (2022) attest that big data benefits public HRM by offering data-driven decision-making and analytic metrics for managing turnover rates, human capital risks, talent recruitment, and training efficiencies. Therefore, data on service delivery, public value, and citizens' satisfaction can guide HRM's adjustments to public service design and resource allocation.

Alignment of HRM with Organisational Goals

Integrating HRM processes with the Public Sector's Objectives: Digitalisation of HRM processes is capable of seamlessly integrating and aligning HR practices with the broader goals of the public sector. This involves the strategic integration of workforce data across HR functions, and the use of digital tools that facilitate talent development, goal-setting, and performance management (Nosike, 2023). Digital HRM, according to Adekunle (2018), forms an unbiassed HR planning to establish and sustain the personnel management practices in the public service. Consequently, this can foster a more cohesive and goal-oriented workforce, contributing to bridging skill gaps, harnessing the full potential of available human capital, and improving the sector's performance (Majam & Jarbandhan, 2022).

Ensuring Strategic HRM Practices: Strategic HRM practices within the Nigerian public sector involve the systematic alignment of HR functions with the overall strategic direction of the sector. This requires the incorporation of digital tools that facilitate strategic succession and workforce planning (Wurim, 2012). Digital transformation in HRM would ensure that this sector's operations are future-oriented and contribute to the resilience and adaptability of the public sector in the face of evolving challenges and opportunities. The absence of the digital tools for automation will burden the HR experts in the public sector with processes that are labour-intensive and tedious, which can result to delays, mistakes and inefficiencies (Nosike, 2023).

Regardless of the potential benefits of digital HRM, there are challenges to harnessing its full potential from organisational and personnel perspectives.

Potential Obstacles to Adopting Digital Technologies in Nigerian Public Sector HRM

In the Nigerian context, transformative HRM, which embraces the deliberate and direct use of digital technology to implement HR strategies, practices, and policies, would encounter challenges in adapting to various challenges that could affect the effectiveness of personnel and organisational performance. As attested by Nosike (2023), the adoption of digital HRM in the Nigerian public sector is influenced by complex perspective from the individual to organisational levels. Organisational' factors include support from the organisational leaders, organisational culture and resource readiness while individual factors include their technical skills and attitudes. Oyebanji & Kassim (2017) emphasised that the 4IR, from an HRM perspective, will necessitate a re-invention that could transform organisational structures to counter present threats and obstacles, aside from its highlighted benefits. Despite the prospective advantages of digital HRM, the readiness of organisations to embrace AI, machine learning, big data and other component of 4IR to optimise the organisational effectiveness is still in its early stages. Many organisational leaders report being unprepared to leverage new data analytic tools, highlighting challenges in building data analytics capabilities (Majam and Jarbandhan, 2022). The Nigerian public sector is challenged in redesigning and reengineering HR functions with the introduction of 4IR as a result of some of the following.

Inadequate Technological Infrastructure

The Nigerian public sector's disposition to embrace digital transformation in HRM is inherently connected to the state of infrastructural availability in the country. Fajana et al. (2011) and Ogedengbe et al. (2023) highlight that inadequate technological infrastructure continue to undermine the optimisation of HRM practices, personnel's productivity, and the public sector outputs. This demands a thorough assessment of existing software, hardware, and networking capabilities within the public sector to identify the areas where improvement is required for the seamless adoption of digital HRM systems. The derisory state of infrastructure directly impacts the effective deployment of digital tools. This leads to performance bottlenecks and system inefficiencies that continue to promote existing corrupt practices (Ikyanyon et al., 2020). Addressing poor infrastructure is pivotal to realise an optimal deployment of 4IR in HRM, and thus supporting the overall objectives of the sector to achieve societal well-being. Limited internet connectivity, unreliable power grids, and data inconsistencies, particularly in rural areas covered by the public sector, restrict access to online platforms and impede data transfer, significantly hindering the potential of digital HR solutions (Ogedengbe et al., 2023; Ojogiwa et al., 2023).

Managerial Issues and Resistance to Change

Resistance to change is a recurrent challenge within the Nigerian public sector and a significant hurdle to adopting digital technologies in HRM. While Inakefe et al. (2023) underline that public servants' corruptive interests are motivators of their resistance to digital transformation, Ogedengbe et al. (2023) underscore the importance of understanding the sources of their resistance, which may stem from cultural factors, a lack of adequate knowledge about the 4IR, fear of job displacement, or concerns about unfamiliar technology (Fajana et al., 2011). Resistance from some different stakeholders such as service recipients and public servants suggest a need for a cultural transformation that would recognise and emphasise the benefits of 4IR for it to be embraced (Chashi & Mwanza, 2022; Inakefe et al., 2023). This is buttressed by Singh et al. (2023) argument that the immune system of an organisation includes its personnel, policies, culture and procedures, which are often resistant to any change. Some managers accustomed to the traditional paper-based methods view digital HRM with scepticism, perceiving it as an unnecessary disruption to established routines (Meiyanti et al., 2018). Therefore, concerns about stored data and potential job losses due to automation trigger resistance to digital HRM initiatives.

Data Security and Privacy Concerns

Although security is highlighted as one of the vital skills for digital competence in Nigeria (Inakefe et al., 2023), the integration of digital technologies in HRM systems within the Nigerian public sector introduces significant concerns regarding data security. With the increasing reliance on cloud-based solutions and the storage of sensitive employee information, safeguarding data becomes vital. Studies such as Oyebanji & Kassim (2020) and Orga and Ogbo (2012) emphasise the need to address data security challenges in HRM systems to prevent unauthorised access, data breaches, and the potential misuse of sensitive information. There is a need to implement robust cybersecurity measures, encryption protocols, regular audit steps to fortify the security of HRM systems in the Nigerian public sector. In addition, digital literacy is alleged necessary to dispel the fears regarding data security (Inakefe et al., 2023). Security protection measures must operate within a legal and regulatory framework that would mandates the protection of individual and organisational privacy. As digital HRM systems collect, store, and process public servants' personal data, ensuring compliance with privacy regulations is imperative. HR professionals must navigate the nuances of data protection regulations to establish systems that enhance efficiency of their operations (Oyebanji & Kassim, 2020).

Digital Skills Gap

Digital literacy is vital to drive the reception and adoption of any components of 4IR. The successful adoption of digital HRM technologies in the Nigerian public sector hinges on the existing skills within the HR workforce. Nosike (2023) identified a lack of familiarity with HRM platforms and digital literacy, which might hinder the effective use of digital tools. This confirms the possible absence of proficient data analytics and navigation skills required for using complex HRM software. Ofoma (2021) acknowledged an existing digital divide in embracing digital transformation in the Nigerian public sector as a result of education, location and income gap. Inakefe et al. (2023) noted that the wide knowledge gap in the public sector is also due to the high turnover rate of personnel who have been trained in the sector. Recognising the skills required for digitalisation is a foundational step for targeted capacity-building initiatives. Wurim (2012) emphasised the need for workshops, training programs, and continuous professional development opportunities to equip HR professionals with the competencies required for digital HRM adoption.

Drivers of Digital Transformative HRM in the Nigerian Public Sector

In the dynamic landscape of the Nigerian public sector, digital transformation within HRM is propelled by a convergence of factors. The ongoing transformative digital revolution excludes no sector and nation. Therefore, embracing modern technologies in HRM has become essential particularly in the public sector that is greatly burdened to service many with limited resources. The drivers for steering this transformation, with an emphasis on the reality and impact of globalisation, technological advancement, and government policies, are further explored.

Technological Advancement and Globalisation

The evolution of the technological landscape in Nigeria is a pivotal driver of digital transformation in public sector HR. The proliferation of internet connectivity and the rise of mobile technologies and cloud computing have fundamentally altered HRM functions (Aro-Gordon, 2016; Eze & Omena, 2019). Technological advancements profoundly influence HRM practices within the Nigerian public sector. As elucidated by the empirical studies of Oyebanji and Kassim (2020) in Nigeria, integrating digital tools enhances recruitment processes, facilitates real-time communication, and streamlines administrative tasks.

Furthermore, public sector institutions in Nigeria constantly compete with private sector companies and international organisations for skilled professionals. Globalisation acts as a catalyst for redefining recruitment and selection practices within the public sector. The interconnectedness of the global economy, as discussed by Yaro (2014), demands a more dynamic and competitive approach to talent acquisition. Hence, it becomes imperative to be able to attract a diverse pool of candidates, with a shift towards a more inclusive strategy, to ensure the public sector attracts and retains the best talent. Talent retention is a critical aspect of public service HRM, and big data analytics could help to identify factors contributing to employee attrition and retention. Analytical tools like logistic regressions could be employed to understand the reason behind employee resignation, allowing for adjustments in workplace conditions to retain talent (Majam & Jarbandhan, 2022). According to Wurim (2012), there is a need for a strategic approach to talent management, which aligns with global best practices. Digital transformation enables adopting talent management systems that facilitate continuous learning, cross-cultural collaboration, and career development.

Changing Demographics of Employees

The demographic makeup of the Nigerian workforce is undergoing substantial shifts, with implications for HRM practices. A diverse and multi-generational workforce necessitates a re-evaluation of HRM practices. Adopting digital technologies in public sector HRM is a strategic imperative to adapt to ongoing demographic changes, as rigid, traditional HR practices may not resonate with the work preferences of younger generations, who are accustomed to technology and seek flexible work arrangements (Yoon, 2019). From recruitment to talent management, HR professionals in the public sector must leverage digital tools to accommodate the needs and expectations of a workforce that spans various skillsets and age groups. However, demographic changes according to Yoon (2019) will have great impact on the hiring process as older civil servants retires and create the need for a suitable replacement for the job with the contemporary demand of digital literacy. Ikyanyon et al. (2020) emphasise the role of technology in bridging generation gaps that coexist among the Nigerian public sector employees, that reflects their diverse values, technological receptive levels, and varying expectations. Digital HRM tools are considered helpful in facilitating communication, collaboration, and knowledge sharing, to foster a harmonious and productive work environment that aligns with the diverse expectations of the citizens and the workforce.

Government Support, Policies, and Initiatives

The role of government policies in steering digital transformation within the Nigerian public sector HRM is fundamental. With recent globalisation and growing technological changes, governments, including the government of Nigeria, are required to redesign their HR processes, strategies and structures to exploit emerging digital tools and development (Yoon, 2019). Policies that promote the integration of digital technologies, cybersecurity measures, and data privacy would, for instance, form the conducive environment for digital HRM to thrive. Beyond policies, active government support is crucial to accelerate HR technology adoption. Financial support and training initiatives for both capacity and infrastructural development are vital investments as support from the government (Ladimeji, 2020). For instance, the E-government Department in Nigeria is recognised for implementing initiatives such as the National

E-government master plan, government service portal, Electronic Document Management system among others (Ofoma, 2021). Aro-Gordon (2016) highlights the importance of government-backed initiatives to nurture a culture of innovation within the public sector. The recognition of the strategic value of digital HRM, government support is an essential catalyst to overcome probable implementation barriers and ensure the sustainable adoption of transformative technologies.

CONCLUSION

This chapter investigates diverse challenges, opportunities and enablers of adopting digital transformation in Nigeria's public sector HRM. Practical insights and recommendations are provided to guide policymakers, HR practitioners and other relevant stakeholders in their effort to navigate the crucial shift for digitalisation. The findings from the desktop review are presented to easily identify required factors to successfully traverse ongoing digital transformation process and realise the full potential of 4IR in the public sector HRM. It is anticipated that digital HRM will foster transparency, efficiency, and the citizen-orientation of the public sector.

The historical context of the Nigerian public sector influences the current challenges and practice within the public service. Despite the diverse workforce employed in the sector, many lack the digital skills required and some got employed through defective HR processes, which could be restrained by the adoption of digital HRM. While this suggests an urgent need to invest in training and upskilling programs to improve effectiveness and productivity of the employees, digital transformation, augmented by the adoption of AI, big data and other components in HRM practices, is a practical approach to reforming the Nigerian public sector. With an apparent generational gap in the public sector, where younger generations are more inclined towards technology use compared to older personnel, efforts should focus on digital literacy training to bridge this gap.

The findings revealed that integrating 4IR technologies into public sector HRM offers many benefits such as streamlining recruitment and selection processes through online platforms and automated candidate assessments to foster meritocratic hiring and eliminate systemic biases. Also, talent management will be strengthened through digital learning platforms, personalised employee development plans, and performance management systems powered by big data analytics and other components of 4IR. This could develop a more engaged and productive workforce. It is anticipated that services delivered by the public service will be transformed through e-government solutions, enhancing responsiveness, and realising citizens' satisfaction. By embracing emerging technologies, the public sector could revolutionise its HRM practices and unleash its full potential as public machinery. Moreover, the adoption of 4IR technologies has the potential to promote cost-effectiveness in HRM, streamline administrative tasks, and combat corruption.

This chapter identified contributors to the ongoing need for embracing for 4IR in HRM such as government's commitments towards development and growing citizens' demands for digital interactions and technologies. However, significant challenges such as inadequate infrastructure, digital skills gap, resistance to change, perceived threats to jobs, and concerns around data privacy and security are acknowledged as barriers. To overcome these challenges and harness the potential of 4IR, this chapter recommends a sectoral readiness and digital transformation strategies supported by the government, HR professionals and civil servants with concrete action plans and dedicated funding. Asides investing in digital infrastructure, capacity-building programs to upskill and reskill personnel are essential to bridge the digital skills gap and foster a culture of innovation. Additionally, robust data governance frameworks are needed to safeguard data privacy and security, mitigate public concerns, and promote responsible data use. By addressing the existing obstacles to adopting 4IR and capitalising on the opportunities it presents, it is anticipated that the Nigerian public sector HRM will be transformed into a dynamic and efficient instrument for national progress.

REFERENCES

Adekunle, A. A. (2018). Digital HR, public service and sustainable governance. *IOSR Journal of Humanities and Social Science (IOSR-JHSS), 23*(12), 61-65.

Adenugba, A. A., Fadoju, O., & Akhuetie, R. E. (2017). Non-meritocratic factors and the recruitment process in Oyo State Civil Service, Nigeria. *African Sociological Review/Revue Africaine de Sociologie, 21*(2), 115-133.

Aro-Gordon, S. (2016). Leveraging Information Technology for Effective Performance Appraisal in the Nigerian Public Service. *SDMIMD Journal of Management, 7*(2).

Aroge, S. T., & Hassan, M. A. (2011). The responsibility of human resource management and development professionals in the development of low-skilled workers in the Nigeria public sector. *International Journal of Business and Management*, 6(11), 227–233.

Bawalla, O. G., & Rufai, D. O. (2021). Technological Advancement: Issues, Challenges and Perspectives for Human Resource Practice in Nigeria. *KIU Journal of Social Sciences*, 7(3), 47–55.

Bella, K. M. J., Ramyasri, M. D., & Vijayashree, P. (2023). Revolutionizing HR Management: Embracing Technology for Enhanced Efficiency and Employee Engagement. *International Journal of Scientific Research in Modern Science and Technology*, 2(3), 28–34.

Budhwar, P., Chowdhury, S., Wood, G., Aguinis, H., Bamber, G. J., Beltran, J. R., Boselie, P., Lee Cooke, F., Decker, S., DeNisi, A., Dey, P. K., Guest, D., Knoblich, A. J., Malik, A., Paauwe, J., Papagiannidis, S., Patel, C., Pereira, V., Ren, S., & Varma, A. (2023). Human resource management in the age of generative artificial intelligence: Perspectives and research directions on ChatGPT. *Human Resource Management Journal*, 33(3), 606–659. 10.1111/1748-8583.12524

Budhwar, P., Malik, A., De Silva, M. T., & Thevisuthan, P. (2022). Artificial intelligence–challenges and opportunities for international HRM: A review and research agenda. *International Journal of Human Resource Management*, 33(6), 1065–1097. 10.1080/09585192.2022.2035161

Chashi, K., & Mwanza, B. G. (2022). The Influence of the Fourth Industrial Revolution on Human Resource within the Zambian Banking Sector. SSRN *Electronic Journal*. 1-16. 10.2139/ssrn.4190617

Chilunjika, A., Intauno, K., & Chilunjika, S. R. (2022). Artificial intelligence and public sector human resource management in South Africa: Opportunities, challenges and prospects. *SA Journal of Human Resource Management*, 20, 12. 10.4102/sajhrm.v20i0.1972

Christian, C. C. (2022). Artificial intelligence in human resources management and human resource accounting in Nigerian public sector. *Management and Human Resource Research Journal, 11*(01).

Fajana, S., Owoyemi, O., Elegbede, T., & Gbajumo-Sheriff, M. (2011). Human resource management practices in Nigeria. *Journal of Management and Strategy*, 2(2), 57–62. 10.5430/jms.v2n2p57

Fatile, O. J., & Igbokwe-Ibeto, C. J. (2012). Nigerian public sector and the challenges of human capital development: The way forward. *Scottish Journal of Arts. Social Sciences and Scientific Study*, 1(2), 11–23.

Fenwick, A., Molnar, G., & Frangos, P. (2024). Revisiting the Role of HR in the age of AI: Bringing humans and machines closer together in the workplace. *Frontiers in Artificial Intelligence*, 6(1272823), 1–10. 10.3389/frai.2023.127282338288334

Fiias, O. C., & Augustine, A. C. (2020). Promoting Human Resource Management Practice in Public Organisations in Nigeria. *SGI-Journal of Social Science and Humanities*, 2(5), 118–128.

Ikyanyon, D., Johnson, P., & Dawson, J. (2020). Institutional context and human resource management in Nigeria. *Employee Relations*, 42(1), 1–16. 10.1108/ER-03-2017-0056

Inakefe, G. I., Bassey, V. U., Ikeanyibe, O. M., Nwagboso, C. I., Agbor, U. I., Ebegbulem, J., Mbonu, F. I., & Ike, G. U. (2023). Digital Literacy and E-Governance Adoption for Service Delivery in Cross River State Civil Service. [IJEGR]. *International Journal of Electronic Government Research*, 19(1), 1–23. 10.4018/IJEGR.328327

Ladimeji, O. A. (2020). The Fourth Industrial Revolution and Nigeria: A Policy Conundrum and High Stakes for the Future of the African Continent. *Think (London, England)*, 83(1).

Majam, T., & Jarbandhan, D. B. (2022). Data driven human resource management in the Fourth Industrial Revolution (4IR). *Africa's Public Service Delivery & Performance Review*, 10(1), 12. 10.4102/apsdpr.v10i1.588

Meiyanti, R., Utomo, B., Sensuse, D. I., & Wahyuni, R. (2018, August). e-Government challenges in developing Countries: A literature review. In *2018 6th International Conference on Cyber and IT Service Management (CITSM)* (pp. 1-6). IEEE.

Nalubega, T., & Uwizeyimana, D. E. (2019). Public sector monitoring and evaluation in the Fourth Industrial Revolution: Implications for Africa. *Africa's Public Service Delivery and Performance Review*, 7(1), 1–12. 10.4102/apsdpr.v7i1.318

Nardo, M., Forino, D., & Murino, T. (2020). The evolution of man–machine interaction: The role of human in Industry 4.0 paradigm. *Production & Manufacturing Research*, 8(1), 20–34. 10.1080/21693277.2020.1737592

Nosike, C. J. (2023). Deployment of modern digital technologies and ICTs in Public Sector HRM: Benefits and challenges. [IJAAS]. *Interdisciplinary Journal of African & Asian Studies*, 9(3), 1–13.

Ofoma, C. (2021). Digitalization driven public service and service delivery: The Nigeria's experience. *Journal of Public Administration. Finance and Law*, 10(22), 73–80.

Ogedengbe, D. E., James, O. O., Afolabi, J. O. A., Olatoye, F. O., & Eboigbe, E. O.Damilola Emmanuel Ogedengbe1Oladapo Olakunle JamesJennifer Osayawe Atu AfolabiFunmilola Olatundun OlatoyeEmmanuel Osamuyimen Eboigbe. (2023). Human Resources in the Era of the Fourth Industrial Revolution (4IR): Strategies and Innovations in the Global South. *Engineering Science & Technology Journal*, 4(5), 308–322. 10.51594/estj.v4i5.617

Ojogiwa, O. T., Sokfa, F. J., & Qwabe, B. R. (2023). Exploring the Capabilities of the Fourth Industrial Revolution for Improved Public Service Delivery in Nigeria. *International Journal of Environmental, Sustainability, and Social Science*, 4(4), 952–962.

Orga, C. C., & Ogbo, A. I. (2012). Evaluating the challenges of human resource management in Nigeria. *European Journal of Business and Management*, 4(13), 78–86.

Oyebanji, B. K., & Kassim, R. N. M. (2017). Technology (ICT) Perception of Employee Towards E-HRM Practices in Public Sectors: A Case Study of Nigeria. *World Journal of Research and Review*, 4(6), 262790.

Palos-Sánchez, P. R., Baena-Luna, P., Badicu, A., & Infante-Moro, J. C. (2022). Artificial intelligence and human resources management: A bibliometric analysis. *Applied Artificial Intelligence*, 36(1), 2145631. 10.1080/08839514.2022.2145631

Salau, O. P., Osibanjo, A., Adeniji, A., Falola, H., Igbinoba, E., Atolagbe, T., & Ogueyungbo, O. (2020). Crystalising employment quality and behavioural outcomes of employees in the public service. *Heliyon*, 6(12), 1–11. 10.1016/j.heliyon.2020.e0561933364474

Sarker, M. N. I., Wu, M., & Hossin, M. A. (2018, May). Smart governance through bigdata: Digital transformation of public agencies. In *2018 international conference on artificial intelligence and big data (ICAIBD)* (pp. 62-70). IEEE.

Singh, P. S. J., Oke, A. E., Kineber, A. F., Olanrewaju, O. I., Omole, O., Samsurijan, M. S., & Ramli, R. A. (2023). A mathematical analysis of 4IR innovation barriers in developmental social work—A structural equation modeling approach. *Mathematics*, 11(4), 1–7. 10.3390/math11041003

Ukeje, I. O., Ndukwe, C., Emma, C., Ogbulu, U., & Onele, J. C. (2020). Public service recruitment practices and implications for sustainable development in Ebonyi State, Nigeria. *International Journal of Public Administration*, 43(4), 361–372. 10.1080/01900692.2019.1636394

Van der Westhuizen, E. J. (Ed.). (2016). *Human resource management in government: A South African perspective on theories, politics and processes*. Juta and Company, (Pty) Limited, Capetown.

Wurim, B. P. (2012). Talent management and employee productivity in public sector organizations of Nigeria. *Journal of Management and Corporate Governance*, 4(1), 1–13.

Yaro, I. (2014). Recruitment and selection in the Nigerian public service: Nature, challenges and way forward. *British Journal of Economics. Management and Trade*, 4(7), 1005–1017.

Yoon, B. S. (2019). The Role of Civil Service and the Human Resource Management Policies Required for the Government of the Future. *Public Service Excellence in the 21st Century*, 169-202.

Zhang, J., & Chen, Z. (2023). Exploring human resource management digital transformation in the digital age. *Journal of the Knowledge Economy*, •••, 1–17. 10.1007/s13132-023-01214-y

Chapter 8
Navigating the Future!
Exploring the Impact of Digital Hiring and Selection Processes in South African Municipalities

Beauty Zindi
https://orcid.org/0000-0003-4790-5379
University of Johannesburg, South Africa

ABSTRACT

As South African municipalities navigate the complexities of modern workforce dynamics, the adoption of digital hiring and selection processes emerges as a critical strategy to address recruitment challenges and drive organizational success. This paper explores the impact of digital transformation on hiring practices within South African municipalities. Through a comprehensive analysis of the benefits, challenges, and future outlook of digital hiring, this study sheds light on the transformative potential of technology in municipal recruitment processes. Drawing on practical examples and case studies, the paper examines the role of digital tools and platforms, the implications on municipalities, and the strategies for overcoming barriers to adoption. Furthermore, article discusses emerging trends, such as AI-driven recruitment, virtual assessments, and remote work adaptation shaping the future landscape of municipal hiring practices.

Navigating the Future! Exploring the impact of digital hiring and selection processes in South African municipalities

INTRODUCTION

In the era of rapid technological development, the use of digital technologies in public sector human resources management has become a game-changing phenomenon. Many aspects of people's daily live, including communication and employment procedures, have transformed with the arrival of digital technologies (Halid, Yusoff & Somu, 2020). In South Africa, municipalities are spearheading digital transformation, in about recruitment and selection practices to enhance the role of public sector HRM. A study conducted by Aggarwal & Sharon (2017) asserts that as digital transformation developments grow more prevalent, investigate the public sector hiring and selection climate in South African munic-

DOI: 10.4018/979-8-3693-2889-7.ch008

ipalities is to understand how modern digital technologies affect the work of Human Resources (HR) practitioners. South African municipalities, as enshrined in legislation such as White Paper on Local Government (1998) among other pieces of legislation are regarded as the backbone of local governance and are tasked with delivering essential services and goods to their communities. In the past, municipalities conducted hiring through in-person meetings, paperwork, and manual processes (Strohmeier, 2020) although such a tradition has since changed due to trends triggered by digital transformation. The use of digital technologies to hire and select public officials has been enabled a paradigm shift in the employment procedures which is critical to enhancing efficiency and effectiveness in public sector HRM.

As the digital transformation wave gathers momentum in the South African public sector, a several modern techniques are used in digital hiring processes. These include artificial intelligence-powered tests, video interviews, and online applications. The use of these digital techniques enhances the competence and confidence of public sector HRM which results in improved service delivery. The transition from traditional hiring to digital hiring can be attributed to several factors, including the need for increased efficiency, the ability to access a wider talent pool, and the potential for more objective decision-making (Wang, Zhou, & Zheng, 2022). As local municipalities in South Africa move across this digital terrain, the worry about how these advancements can impact the fairness, practicality, and overall effectiveness of the hiring process is something to talk about. This is because no research has yet clarified that using digital technologies in hiring and selection guarantees efficiency and effectiveness in public sector HRM. An evident gap exists in the literature where modern digital technologies are not the panacea to several administrative and political problems experienced in public sector HRM in South African municipalities. Based on these arguments this chapter examines the implications of digital hiring and selection processes on public sector HRM. The chapter further discusses the challenges of implementing digital hiring and selection processes in public sector HRM in local municipalities while seeking to identify the opportunities and proposing solutions to enhance the role of HRM in the digital transformation era.

THE DEVELOPMENT OF DIGITAL HIRING AND SELECTION PROCESSES IN SOUTH AFRICAN MUNICIPALITIES

In South Africa, the municipal hiring and staffing procedures were based on traditional processes before the advent of technology. These traditional processes include newspapers, bulletin boards, and word-of-mouth, for advertising any employment opportunities. Okemwa (2016), affirms that in the past, applicants used to mail or bring their resumes or paper application forms in person. Traditional hiring and recruiting channels include print media, physical ads, job fairs, and networking events. Recruiters conduct in-person interviews, carefully review each application, and rank applicants according to their views (Choung & Manamela, 2018). Applications were contacted primarily through mail and phone. For example, municipalities used to hire people for municipal jobs by placing physical job ads and advertisements in newspapers. Recruiters interviewed the shortlisted individuals in-person after carefully sorting through piles of paper resumes. However, the advent of digital technology has facilitated the transition to online application processes. Municipalities now commonly use their websites or dedicated online portals to advertise vacancies and allow candidates to submit applications electronically. For instance, the City of Johannesburg now primarily advertises job vacancies on its website and accepts online applications through its e-Recruitment portal.

In South African municipalities, the shift from conventional employment techniques to digital hiring and selection procedures has had a revolutionary impact, bringing efficiency, accessibility, and transparency to recruitment procedures (Clarke, Lindquist & Roy, 2017). South African municipalities have been implementing digital hiring and selection procedures to improve hiring efficiency, expedite the hiring process, and guarantee equity and openness. Municipalities are moving more and more of their hiring procedures online. With this change, candidates can now electronically submit their applications, check the progress of their applications, and apply for jobs. The City of Cape Town established an online employment platform where prospective employees can browse open vacancies, apply, and follow the status of their applications in real-time (Tan, 2021). This platform minimizes paperwork and streamlines the application process.

In the past, municipalities handled employment applications manually by organizing physical resumes and keeping spreadsheets. Digital screening technologies are being used by many municipalities to quickly evaluate applicants' qualifications and fit for open posts. Online tests, pre-employment exams and resume screening software with automation are some of these tools. The use of applicant tracking systems has completely changed the hiring process by automating a number of functions like resume parsing, application management, and candidate communication (Kshetri, 2021). Tan (2021) mentioned that the human resource at the eThekwini Municipality in Durban, for instance, can effectively handle applications and track candidate progress and streamline the system's recruitment workflow using the applicant tracking system.

Municipal employment procedures now frequently use virtual interviews, which let hiring managers interview applicants from a distance. Through the use of video conferencing technology, municipalities may interview applicants from anywhere in the world, promoting a more inclusive hiring process. Johansson & Herranen (2019) affirm in Nelson Mandela Bay Municipalities if a candidate is unable to attend in-person interview because of scheduling issues or distance, virtual interviews are offered. This method guarantees that every eligible applicant will be given a chance to take part in the selection procedure.

Municipalities can use data analytics to monitor important recruiting indicators, examine the demographics of applicants, and pinpoint areas where their hiring procedures need to be strengthened. Municipalities can pinpoint areas for development and enhance their hiring practices by examining data such as time to hire, applicant demographics, and candidate experience feedback. To attract and retain top personnel, the Tshwane Metropolitan Municipality, for example, tracks recruitment parameters, like application flow and selection rates, using data analytics to find hiring process bottlenecks and provide targeted interventions to increase hiring efficiency and diversity (Tan, 2021).

The introduction of technology has, however, prompted several inquiries about how the labour force of today will adapt to these developments. Will the current workforce be able to transition to digital operations without any problems, or will programs for training and upskilling be required? These are the main research questions that demonstrate how complex the digital transformation is in South African municipalities. However, not enough research has been done on how digital hiring practices might help with these issues. By examining the precise impact of digital recruiting on recruitment effectiveness and the ensuing performance of employees in South African municipalities, this study aims to close this performance gap. The chapter's primary goal is to investigate how digital hiring and selection procedures have affected South African municipalities. The chapter answers following objectives:

- To understand how digital hiring and selection can enhance the role of human resources management in municipalities.
- To identify challenges associated with the adoption of digital selection methods and explore the opportunities that can be derived for improved pubic sector HRM.

The article consists of eight sections, in the first section is the introduction where digital hiring and selection processes in in public sector HRM. The second section discusses the development of digital hiring and selection processes in South African municipalities. The third section focuses on theoretical and empirical perspectives on the implementation of digital hiring and selection processes in public sector HRM in local municipalities, followed by a discussion in the fourth section on contextualising digital hiring and selection processes in South African municipalities. The fifth section discusses the methodology used to collect data on the implementation of the digital hiring and selection processes on public sector HRM. The sixth section discusses the benefits of digital hiring and recruitment processes in South African municipalities followed by challenges associated when implementing digital hiring and selection processes in public sector. The seventh section draws conclusion while the last section offers recommendations to improve digital hiring and selection processes on public sector HRM.

THEORETICAL AND EMPIRICAL PERSPECTIVES

Technology Acceptance Model (TAM)

The Technology Acceptance Model (TAM) was developed by Fred Davis in the late 1980s to understand and predict users' acceptance of technology (Chesney, 2006). According to Kumar & Priyanka (2013), the theory suggests that users' attitudes and intentions towards adopting a technology are significantly influenced by perceived ease of use and utility. TAM indicates that people are more inclined to accept and use technology if they believe it will help them perform better or be more productive (Udovita, 2020). South African municipalities have to evaluate hiring managers' perceptions of the value of digital tools and platforms in the context of digital hiring and selection procedures. For instance, they might think about how well these technologies streamline the application screening process, lessen the workload for administrative tasks, or give access to a larger pool of potential candidates. Job seekers can also assess how helpful digital platforms are in making it simpler to locate job prospects, expediting the application process, and enhancing hiring process transparency.

According to the TAM theory, people are more likely to embrace a technology if they think it's simple to use (Bagozzi, 2007). South African municipalities should think about how user-friendly the digital tools and platforms they utilize are when it comes to digital hiring and selection procedures. This covers elements including how user-friendly the technology interface is, how well users are instructed, and whether training and assistance are offered. When choosing whether to use these digital platforms for recruitment, hiring managers and job searchers will evaluate how user-friendly they are. Through the utilization of TAM, stakeholders can evaluate the adoption of digital recruiting and selection procedures in South African municipalities and obtain valuable insights into the elements impacting users' perceptions and intentions towards these technologies (Strohmeier, 2020; Mohanty & Mishra, 2020). This knowledge can help design tactics that will maximize the success of digital recruitment initiatives while addressing possible adoption barriers and improving user approval.

The TAM highlights how people's intentions and attitudes toward a technology affect how they use it (Kumar & Priyanka, 2013). In light of this, South African municipalities can employ TAM to evaluate and comprehend the elements impacting user approval and adoption of digital employment and selection procedures. Municipalities can create plans to overcome obstacles to digital recruitment campaigns and encourage a wider acceptance of these efforts by identifying hurdles to adoption, such as resistance to change or worries about data security. According to TAM, a person's intention to utilize technology is a major factor in determining how they use it (Lumunon, Massie & Trang, 2021). Evaluating the intent of candidates and human resource managers to utilize digital recruitment platforms in the context of digital hiring in South African municipalities might shed light on the chances of acceptance and successful implementation. By tracking actual use behaviour over time, governments may pinpoint adoption barriers and places where the digital hiring process needs to be improved.

CONTEXTUALISING DIGITAL HIRING AND SELECTION PROCESSES IN SOUTH AFRICAN MUNICIPALITIES

The effectiveness of public service delivery depends on the hiring and selection of qualified employees and their willingness to perform their duties (Udovita, 2020). With the adoption of modern technology hiring and selection of qualified candidates becomes very easy as candidates can apply via online platforms and conduct virtual interviews in their comfort zones. While digital hiring practices have advantages, there are drawbacks and challenges associated with this technological change. Accessibility becomes crucial, especially for people who do not have much access to technology or who do not have knowledge of how to use it well (Strohmeier, 2020).

In Public sector HRM, the term "digital hiring" describes the application of digital tools and technologies to optimise and expedite an organisation's hiring and selection procedures. This method attracts, evaluates, and selects potential employees by utilising a variety of digital platforms, software, and data-driven tactics. The goal of digital recruiting is to improve the hiring process's effectiveness, economy, and alignment with the changing needs of the digital era (Al-hassi, 2021). Digital solutions are being implemented to monitor and control the entire recruitment process. Applicant Tracking Systems assist in managing applications, organizing candidate data, and promoting communication among members of the hiring team (Calvard & Jeske, 2018). Municipalities can increase their chances of drawing in a diverse pool of candidates by using online job portals to make job vacancies easily accessible to a wider audience. According to Wang et al. (2022) candidates can submit applications electronically through digital platforms, which minimizes paperwork and streamlines the initial application process for both applicants and municipal officials. Deng, Duan & Wibowo (2022) are of the view that recruiting methods can be improved by municipalities using data analytics tools to examine vast amounts of candidate data by finding trends, evaluating the efficacy of recruitment channels, and making data-driven decisions. By integrating hiring procedures with smart city efforts, digital hiring demonstrates a dedication to efficiency and technological improvement in the larger context of municipal services (Halid, Yusoff & Somu, 2020).

In the current technological era, internet technologies are used for hiring and selecting the best applicants. To reach a wider audience, digital hiring involves posting job openings online on social media, employment portals, and official websites (Al-hassi, 2021). Udovita (2020) reports that application forms and digital resumes from candidates are electronically sent. These materials are often sent via email or specialized online portals such as job boards, social networking platforms (Facebook, Twitter, and LinkedIn), municipal websites, and online job boards. Recruiters administer online tests, schedule video conferences for interviews, and automatically review resumes using Applicant Tracking Systems (Debasis, 2019). Contacting candidates from a distance is possible through email, chat, video calls, and other channels. The eThekwini Municipality for an example, modified its digital hiring practices by posting job openings on its website and social media (Bejakovic & Mrnjavac, 2020).

Like many other municipalities throughout the world, South African municipalities are modernizing their operations through digital transformation projects. This entails utilizing digital technologies to enhance service delivery, efficiency, and transparency. When it comes to hiring, digital transformation includes using online platforms and technologies to post job openings, collect applications, and oversee the hiring procedure (Strohmeier, 2020). The use of an online job portal by the City of Johannesburg allows job seekers to see open positions, apply, and follow the status of their applications in real-time (Calvard & Jeske, 2018).

Municipalities are beginning to implement e-recruitment strategies to reach a wider pool of candidates and expedite the application process in response to the rapid growth of technology. This entails utilizing tools like social media, recruiting websites, and online job boards to draw in and interact with possible applicants (Al-hassi, 2021). The City of Cape Town's e-Recruitment System enables applicants to make profiles, look for job openings, and submit applications online (Udovita, 2020). Several steps in the hiring process are automated by this system, which minimizes the amount of paperwork and administrative burden.

With the introduction of digitization, South African municipalities frequently work with partners in the private sector, colleges, and non-governmental organizations to innovate in their hiring practices. This partnership encourages the exchange of knowledge and the adoption of industry best practices. One example is the collaboration between eThekwini Municipality and nearby colleges to create online assessment instruments customized for certain job positions, enhancing the efficacy and efficiency of applicant screening (Zuiderwijk, Chen & Salem, 2021). More specifically, employment decisions are being made by governments using data analytics to find areas for improvement in the hiring strategies. Data-driven insights improve hiring outcomes and optimize recruitment adoption. This can be accomplished by looking for hiring process bottlenecks and implementing focused interventions by analyzing the recruitment data such as reducing turnaround times for application review or addressing biases in candidate selection.

Digital recruiting and selection facilitate the online completion of activities through job portals, career websites, and social networking sites (Debasis, 2019). There is a claim that the success of an organization is directly impacted by digital hiring and selection. The HRM teams' time and expenses are reduced when screening, interviewing, shortlisting, and giving feedback to applicants and interviewers are done digitally. This frees up time for the completion of more strategically important duties (Ivarsson & Svahn, 2020). For example, using artificial intelligence to search and filter resumes would make it easy to identify candidates from a range of databases that match the job description and the organization's culture.

Social media can be used to network with potential talent and assess their profiles, while mobile applications could be leveraged to create customized hiring and onboarding processes. This improves employee involvement and communication throughout the organization. However, Rykun (2019) argues that because hiring managers and candidates need to have the necessary digital skills and applications to use the system's many digital channels, using digital technology increases the complexity and cost of recruitment and selection.

Technological Tools and Platforms Used in Digital Hiring Processes.

Municipalities can use Applicant Tracking Systems (ATS) software to manage job advertising, keep track of candidate applications, and speed up the hiring process. According to Clarke (2017), automated resume parsing, keyword matching, and application status tracking can help recruiters manage many applications efficiently. Another kind of technology that can be used in online employment processes are platforms for video interviews. Municipalities can conduct remote interviews with candidates using video interviewing platforms by utilizing video conferencing technology (Siemens, 2017). This eliminates the need for in-person interviews, reduces travel costs, and enables efficient evaluation of applications regardless of where they are.

By employing artificial intelligence-based assessment tools to analyze candidate data, municipalities can also forecast job fit and performance. Jacobs (2021) noted that assessments of skills, personality, and cognitive ability may be included in these exams. By using predetermined criteria, they help to identify qualified applicants and lessen bias in the selection process. In addition to the previously mentioned, municipalities can use career websites and online job portals to advertise job openings, attract candidates, and expedite the application process (Henry, 2019). Candidates can access application forms, thorough job descriptions, and contact channels with recruiters using these platforms. According to Clarke (2017), social media recruiting platforms such as Twitter, Facebook, LinkedIn, and TikTok are utilized for corporate branding, job posting, and communication with potential candidates. Municipalities use targeted advertising and networking techniques to reach out to passive candidates and acquire specialized skills.

METHODOLOGY

This chapter is qualitative by nature and is based on secondary data which includes journal articles, internet sources and books (Nattrass, 2020). Multiple secondary sources relating to digital hiring and selection processes on public sector HRM were utilised to reduce errors as well as to ensure the validity and reliability of this chapter. The researchers gave priority to the most recent studies on South Africa's digital hiring and selection methods on public sector HRM to guarantee accuracy, trustworthiness, authenticity, representativeness and relevance to the chapter. This entailed doing content validation and scrutinizing the origins of documents to evaluate their accuracy, dependability, authenticity, and importance, as recommended by Creswell & Creswell (2018). The researchers employed many resources, including internet sources, books, journal articles and fundamental research, to acquire complete insights into digital hiring and selection practices in the public sector HRM. In addition, the researcher utilized content analysis and theme categorization methodologies to examine the gathered data, thus enhancing her comprehension of the topic and making a valuable contribution to the discussion on digital hiring and selection processes on public sector HRM.

DISCUSSIONS OF RESULTS

The adoption of digital hiring and selection processes in South African municipalities represents a significant step towards modernizing recruitment practices, improving efficiency, and fostering greater transparency and inclusivity in the hiring process. Municipalities must continue to be flexible and aggressive in utilizing digital tools to meet the changing demands of their recruitment efforts as technology advances. Despite the benefits, there are challenges associated with the adoption of digital hiring processes in South African municipalities. These include the digital divide, data privacy issues, algorithmic biases, opposition to change and poor Information and Communication Technology foundation. The following section discusses the benefits of adopting digital and recruitment processes as well as the challenges associated with it.

Benefits of Digital Hiring and Recruitment Processes in South African Municipalities

Digital portals are being implemented by local government entities for a range of services. Most municipalities in South Africa only accept applications that are filed via the most widely used portal, the building plan portal, which eliminates the need for paper-based submissions (Clarke, 2017; Sokolow, 2020). The Smart City concept prioritizes internal municipal processes just as much as electronic contact with stakeholders (Mwakatumbula & Moshir, 2020). South African municipalities stand to gain a great deal from digital hiring and recruiting, including cost savings, improved candidate experience, expanded talent pool access, decreased prejudices, and increased efficiency. According to Calvard & Jeske (2018), municipalities need to update their hiring procedures, draw in top personnel, and foster organizational success in a cutthroat market by utilising digital technologies wisely.

Increased Efficiency and Speed in the Recruitment Process

The entire recruitment process from posting jobs to selecting candidates is accelerated by digital hiring. According to Deng et al. (2022) recruiters can save a significant amount of time by automating tasks such as emailing follow-ups, scheduling interviews, and analyzing resumes. Applicant tracking systems simplify the process of managing, sorting, and filtering candidate applications, reducing human error and labour costs (Bonnet & Westerman, 2020). The City of Cape Town, one of the largest towns in South Africa, for instance, simplified its hiring process by introducing digital hiring options. By using an applicant tracking system (the municipality was able to automate job postings, application screening, and interview scheduling (Debasis, 2019). This expedited the hiring process and reduced the amount of time required for manual administrative labor. In addition, the City of Cape Town asserted that the average time-to-hire had dropped dramatically from several months to a matter of weeks. Because of this, the municipality was able to promptly fill crucial roles, ensuring service continuity and being receptive to the requirements of the community (Ivarsson & Svahn, 2020). Digital communication tools, including email and video conferencing, facilitate faster and more efficient interactions between recruiters and prospects, regardless of their geographical location (Hanekom, 2020).

Enhanced Candidate Experience

Digital recruiting offers candidates a more efficient and user-friendly application process. Candidates can easily search and apply for positions whenever and wherever they choose because of mobile-friendly application platforms and online job portals (Bejakovic & Mrnjavac, 2020). For example, Buffalo City Metropolitan Municipality in the Eastern Cape province has opened a user-friendly online application gateway for job seekers. Matli & Ngoepe (2020) state that the portal allowed candidates to track the status of their applications, gave thorough job descriptions, and allowed them to communicate directly with recruiters via email or chat. According to Henry (2019), candidates can communicate more effectively and honestly when they receive automated notification emails that update them on their application status, interview dates, and next steps. Good application feedback resulted in higher satisfaction levels and a more favourable employer brand for the municipality. As a result, more qualified candidates for municipal jobs were lured to the area. Digital tools give candidates individualized communication and feedback, demonstrating to them that their time and work are valued. This improves applicants' contentment with the recruitment procedure and the municipality's employment brand (Jacobs, 2021).

Access to a Wider Pool of Talent

Digital hiring removes geographic barriers, allowing cities to communicate with candidates who live outside of their immediate area. According to Matli & Ngoepe (2020), the utilization of social media recruitment tactics and online job posting increases visibility and attracts applicants from diverse locations and backgrounds. Through remote employment arrangements, digital technologies enable communities to access talent pools situated in rural locations or regions experiencing a skills deficit. The Johannesburg Metropolitan Municipality found it challenging to fill technical posts such as those requiring engineers and IT specialists with suitable individuals (Al-hassi, 2021). To address this issue, the municipality used social media and digital networks to increase the scope of its recruitment efforts. The HR department of the City of Johannesburg Council approved the decision to digitize the employment process. The municipality began using digital tools to replace the paper-based recruitment system with an electronic one because of the COVID-19 pandemic (Wang et al., 2022).

Furthermore, internet recruiting enables the municipality to contact a wider audience from which competent candidates can be selected, improving HR's oversight and administration of the employment process (Al-hassi, 2021). Through the JoziNet website, remote job applications can be filed. Prospective candidates visit the website, click on positions that interest them, select the role, and complete the online employment application. Using the sophisticated search and filtering features available on digital platforms, recruiters can locate candidates with specific skills or qualifications more quickly (Bejakovic & Mrnjavac, 2020). Digital hiring broadens the talent pool, which fosters innovation and organizational performance and raises the likelihood of finding the best candidates for municipal employment.

Reduction in Biases in the Selection Process

Singhavi & Basargekar (2020) claim that by emphasizing job-related criteria, structured online application forms and examinations lessen the impact of subjective factors like appearance or demographic data. The Nelson Mandela Bay Municipality employed blind recruiting processes for the first round of hiring screening (Hanekom, 2020). By keeping candidate resumes and application materials anonymous, it lessens prejudices based on factors like age, gender, or ethnicity. By removing candidate profiles that included identifying information, such as names, addresses, and demographics, the municipality ensured a more objective examination. Rather, the evaluation was predicated solely on credentials and expertise. This demonstrated the municipality's commitment to inclusion and equality by encouraging equity and diversity in the composition of their staff (Okemwa, 2016).

Cost Savings for Municipalities

Digital hiring saves money right away since it eliminates the need for manual documentation, printing, and shipping that come with traditional employment practices. Automated chores and improved workflows free up HR staff members' time and energy so they can focus on higher-value work, (Gil-Garcia, Dawes & Pardo, 2017). The availability of cloud-based hiring tools eliminates the need for expensive infrastructure upkeep and investments. The Tshwane Metropolitan Municipality, for instance, moved from conventional hiring practices based on paper to an application tracking system (ATS) housed on the Internet. As a result, there was no longer a need for actual paper storage space, printing expenses were reduced, and postal expenses for job advertisements were minimized (Jacobs, 2021).

The amount spent on hiring-related administrative overheads was significantly reduced for the municipality. By expediting the hiring process and reducing the time to hire, municipalities can decrease the cost burden of prolonged vacancies and expedite the onboarding of new hires (Sokolow, 2020). In general, municipalities can more efficiently use their resources and invest in other organizational development and service delivery sectors.

CHALLENGES ASSOCIATED WITH USING DIGITAL HIRING AND RECRUITMENT IN SOUTH AFRICAN MUNICIPALITIES

In revamping public sector HRM through digital hiring and selection, local municipalities in South Africa experience several obstacles, such as the digital divide, data privacy issues, algorithmic biases, opposition to change, poor Information and Communication Technology foundation and complex legal issues. These are discussed below:

Digital Divide

In South African public sector HRM, there is a noticeable digital divide, with disparities in digital literacy and internet access between rural and urban areas as well as between different socioeconomic classes. Such disparities trigger exclusion based on geographical location and income levels. According to Mawela, Ochara & Twinomurinzi (2017) candidates who do not have consistent internet access or a solid understanding of using digital tools may find it challenging to use online job portals, submit electronic applications, or participate in virtual interviews. The digital divide exacerbates inequality in access to job opportunities, which reduces the pool of potential candidates and upholds socioeconomic disparities. Municipalities may mistakenly reject qualified candidates from underprivileged areas, Nyagadza, Pashapa, Chare, Mazuruse & Hove (2022) contended, hindering efforts to promote diversity and inclusion in the workforce.

The lack of adequate infrastructure in impoverished municipalities results in numerous individuals being unable to access digital services and content. This lack of access hinders their involvement in the information society and impedes the overall development of public sector HRM. In certain provinces like the Eastern Cape and Limpopo, access to ICT is not readily available, particularly in rural areas (Leseame & Leopeng, 2021). Municipalities can lessen the digital divide by providing access to community centres, computer laboratories, and open Wi-Fi hotspots in impoverished areas (Vyas-Doorgapersad, 2022). To give candidates, the basic digital skills needed for job searches and application processes, they can also offer training programmes or initiatives focused on digital literacy.

Poor Information and Communication Dissemination

The issue of technological determinism in the application of information and communication technologies, whereby technologies are frequently adopted without adequate consideration of the social, cultural, and historical context, is another major obstacle to the implementation of digital hiring and recruitment (Joseph & Williams, 2022). These technologies are deployed across various societies without being customized to suit specific societal contexts, leading to challenges during implementation. These technologies tend to perform more effectively in wealthier communities. Moreover, municipalities often introduce e-government initiatives in areas where there is notable resistance to technology adoption. Consequently, it is advisable for South African municipalities to conduct an internal awareness campaign on e-government principles, particularly in centers where technology resistance is prevalent (Bojang & Bwando, 2018). Proper and sufficient development and training of municipal staff are essential, to improving their understanding and expertise in implementing e-government services. Additionally, the awareness campaign should target individuals who are hindered by socio-economic and cultural factors, such as elderly individuals and those with limited education.

Data Privacy and Security Concerns

Digital hiring processes involve the collection and management of applicants' private and sensitive personal data, including resumes, contact details, and educational history. Inadequate cybersecurity and data protection measures, however, raise the risk of data breaches, unauthorized access, and inappropriate use of candidate data, all of which can damage municipalities' reputations and infringe their right to privacy (Schäfer, 2018). For example, the City of Johannesburg experienced a data breach in its online recruitment system as a result of inadequate cybersecurity measures. The sensitivity of job candidates' personal information, such as resumes and contact details, raised concerns about identity theft and privacy (Murenzi & Olivier, 2017). According to Olaitan, Issah, and Wayi (2021), data breaches not only undermine applicant confidence in municipal recruiting practices but also expose candidates to potential harm. Municipalities must follow legislative frameworks such as the Protection of Personal Information Act (POPIA) and take stringent measures to secure sensitive information to prevent legal repercussions and damage to their reputation.

Potential Biases Embedded in Algorithms and Artificial Intelligence Systems

AI-powered recruitment tools and algorithms may inadvertently propagate preconceptions seen in past data or reflect the biases of their creators. Biased algorithms may penalize candidates from underrepresented backgrounds or favour specific demographic groups based on factors such as gender, color, or socioeconomic status (Sutcliffe & Bannister, 2020). The Ekurhuleni Metropolitan Municipality adopted an artificial intelligence (AI) resume screening tool to expedite the candidate selection mechanism. Nevertheless, an audit revealed that the algorithm displayed biases against people from historically underrepresented backgrounds and in favour of those with Westernized work experience or education (Velsberg, Westergren & Jonsson, 2020). Prejudicial algorithms uphold systemic inequities and discriminatory hiring practices. Municipalities must carefully evaluate the algorithms and AI systems used in digital hiring to guarantee equity and reduce unanticipated consequences (Wang et al., 2022). Discriminatory employment practices can also damage the reputation of towns and erode the trust of applicants and stakeholders.

Resistance to Change Among Employees and Stakeholders

Opposition to change is a prevalent barrier that South African municipalities face when implementing digital hiring procedures in public sector HRM. Employees and stakeholders may be reluctant to adopt new technology due to fears of losing their employment, losing control, or not being familiar with digital tools and processes (Udovita, 2020). Olaitan et al. (2021) revealed that a number of staff members were anxious about losing control over the hiring process or job security when the Tshwane Metropolitan Municipality introduced a new applicant tracking system (ATS).

Reluctance to adapt obstructs the efficient implementation of digital hiring initiatives, delays process improvements, and limits the realization of benefits associated with digital transformation, such as enhanced efficacy and efficiency in hiring practices (Henry, 2019, Al-hassi, 2021). Municipalities must engage in change management techniques, train and assist people, and highlight the benefits of digital transformation to gain organizational buy-in and overcome resistance.

CONCLUSION

The chapter examines digital recruiting and selection procedures in public sector HRM within South African local government. The review of documents indicates that municipal recruitment reveals a landscape full of opportunities for digital transformation as digital technologies alluded to in literature can trigger change and efficiency in public sector HRM. The analysis demonstrated further that adopting digital technologies in public sector HRM can bring equality, efficiency, and transparency in municipal hiring and selection. Further as noted in the chapter analysis, utilising digital hiring and selection procedures can help attract diverse personnel, maximize recruitment efforts, and make evidence-based decisions that propel municipal success by leveraging the power of internet platforms, automated systems, and data analytics. Despite the opportunities that digital transformation may trigger to public sector HRM, there are also challenges local municipalities may face in digital hiring and selection. The digital divide, characterized by unequal access to technology and digital literacy, poses a barrier to inclusivity and exacerbate existing disparities in employment opportunities. Moreover, concerns regarding data privacy, algorithmic bias, resistance to change by employees and the ethical use of technology underscore the need for robust regulatory frameworks and ethical guidelines to govern digital recruitment practices.

RECOMMENDATIONS

To adapt and thrive in the digital era, municipalities in South Africa can consider implementing the following recommendations:

Invest in Digital Infrastructure

To encourage the adoption of digital technology in Public Sector HRM, municipalities should give priority to investing in digital infrastructure. This entails investing in cybersecurity measures, improving internet connectivity, and giving residents and employees access to digital tools and platforms.

Promote Digital Literacy

Municipalities should provide staff and residents with educational and training opportunities to improve their digital literacy. Hiring managers and HR specialists should receive training and upskilling in diversity and inclusion programs, AI technology, and digital recruitment strategies to use digital tools efficiently and lessen prejudice. Municipalities may optimize the advantages of digitization and lower adoption obstacles by equipping people with the skills necessary to use digital technologies.

Promote Innovation and Collaboration

To promote the creation and application of novel digital solutions, municipalities must cultivate a culture of innovation and cooperation. This involves cultivating collaborations with technology companies, startups, and academic establishments to investigate inventive methods for tackling community issues and enhancing the provision of services. The collaboration with technology partners and industry experts, cities will be able to stay abreast of technological advancements, test out innovative concepts, and improve their digital recruitment practices over time. Municipalities should be informed of the moral and legal ramifications of algorithmic biases, data privacy, and labor law compliance in order to maintain transparent and equitable hiring practices.

Streamline Administrative Processes

Municipalities should digitize administrative processes to improve efficiency and reduce paperwork. This includes implementing electronic document management systems, automating routine tasks, and digitizing forms and applications. By streamlining administrative processes, municipalities can save time and resources, allowing staff to focus on delivering high-quality services to citizens.

Ensure Accessibility and Inclusivity

Municipalities should ensure that digital services and platforms are accessible to all citizens, including those with disabilities or limited access to technology. This includes designing user-friendly interfaces, providing alternative access methods, and offering support for individuals who require accommodations. The SA Connect initiative supports setting up community WiFi locations to offer internet access to disadvantaged individuals. It argues that the government should provide internet access to reduce the digital divide. However, such efforts, including the Competition Commission's mandated reductions in data retail prices, do not connect the 50% of the population who are offline, mainly due to device costs.

REFERENCES

https://www.undp.org/south-africa/blog/election-drama-promoting-civic-participation-among-youth-through-industrial-theatre (Accessed on 20 February 2024).

Aggarwal, V., & Sharon, S. D. (2017). Digital human resource management. *Gyan Management Journal*, 11(2), 23–27.

Al-hassi, A. (2021). *Digital transformation in higher education institutions and its role in achieving sustainable development (reality and obstacles)* (Unpublished thesis). Misr University for Science and Technology, Cairo, Egypt.

Bagozzi, C. (2007). The legacy of technology acceptance model and a proposal for paradigm shift. *Journal of the Association for Information Systems*, 8(4), 244–254. 10.17705/1jais.00122

Bejakovic, P., & Mrnjavac, Z. (2020). *The Importance of Digital Literacy on the labour market. Employee Relations.* [Online] Retrieved from: https://www.researchgate.net/publication/ 340515952_The_importance_of_digital_literacy_on_the_labour_market. (Accessed on 27 February 2024).

Bojang, M. B. S., & Bwando, W. (2018). *E-municipality applications in local government: Prospects and challenges*, A paper presented at 3600 with youth 4th international student conference, Manisa, 3rd–4th April 2018.

Bonnet, D., & Westerman, G. (2020). *The new elements of digital transformation.* Cambridge, MA. *MIT Sloan Management Review*, 4(2), 34–48.

Calvard, T. S., & Jeske, D. (2018). Developing human resource data risk management in the age of big data. *International Journal of Information Management*, 4(3), 159–164. 10.1016/j.ijinfomgt.2018.07.011

Chesney, T. (2006). An acceptance model for useful and fun information systems. *Human Technology*, 2(2), 225–235. 10.17011/ht/urn.2006520

Choung, M., & Manamela, M. G. (2018). *Digital inequality in rural and urban settings: Challenges of education and information in South African youth context.* [Online] Retrieved from: https://www.researchgate.net/publication/333132846_Digital_Inequality_in_Rural_and_Urban_settings_Challenges_of_Education_and_Information_in_South_African_Youth_Context. (Accessed on 19 January 2024).

Clarke, A. (2017). Digital government units: What are they, and what do they mean for digital era public management renewal? *International Public Management Journal*, 23(3), 358–379. 10.1080/10967494.2019.1686447

Clarke, A., Lindquist, E., & Roy, J. (2017). Understanding governance in the digital era: An agenda for public administration research in Canada. *Canadian Public Administration*, 60(4), 457–475. 10.1111/capa.12246

Creswell, J. W., & Creswell, J. D. (2018). *Research design: Qualitative, quantitative and mixed methods approaches* (5th ed.). SAGE.

Debasis, D. (2019). Internet of Things (IoT): The new paradigm of HRM and skill development in the fourth industrial revolution (industry 4.0). *IUP Journal of Information Technology*, 15(4), 7–30.

Deng, H., Duan, S. X., & Wibowo, S. (2022). Digital technology driven knowledge sharing for job performance. *Journal of Knowledge Management*, 2(5), 1–14. 10.1108/JKM-08-2021-0637

Gil-Garcia, J., Dawes, S., & Pardo, T. (2017). Digital government and public management research: Finding the crossroads. *Public Management Review*, 20(5), 633–646. 10.1080/14719037.2017.1327181

Halid, H., Yusoff, Y. M., & Somu, H. (2020). The relationship between digital human resource management and organizational performance. *Advances in Economics, Business and Management Research*, Series volume number 141. First ASEAN Business, Environment, and Technology Symposium (ABEATS 2019) (pp. 96-99). Atlantis Press.

Hanekom, P. (2020). *Covid-19 exposes South Africa's digital literacy divide*. Mail &Guardian. p. [Online] Retrieved from: https://mg.co.za/opinion/2020-09-08-covid-19-exposes-SouthAfricas-digital-literacy-divide (Accessed on 09 March 2024).

Henry, L. (2019). *Bridging the urban-rural digital divide and mobilizing technology for poverty eradication: Challenges and gaps.* [Online] Available from: https://www.un.org/ development/desa/dspd/wp-content/uploads/sites/22/2019/03/Henry-Bridging-the-DigitalDivide-2019.pdf (Accessed on 14 February 2024).

Ivarsson, F., & Svahn, F. (2020). *Digital and conventional matchmaking–similarities, differences and tensions*. In *Proceedings of the 53rd Hawaii International Conference on System Sciences*, Maui, HI. 10.24251/HICSS.2020.727

Jacobs, E. (2021). *Moving from Access to Accessibility: The Deception of the Digital Divide in Development*. [Online] Retrieved from: https://www.za.undp.org/content/ south_africa/en/home/blog/2021/moving-from-access-to-accessibility--the-deception-ofthe-digita.html

Johansson, J., & Herranen, S. (2019). *The application of artificial intelligence (AI) in human resource management: Current state of AI and its impact on the traditional recruitment process.* Retrieved from http://www.diva2:1322478/ FULLTEXT01.pdf (Accessed on 11 February 2024).

Joseph, J., & Williams, R. (2022). A retrospective analysis: ICT for improved municipal service delivery amidst COVID 19: ICT and Municipal Service Delivery'. *EUREKA: Social and Humanities*, 2(1), 70–85. 10.21303/2504-5571.2022.002284

Kshetri, N. B. (2021). Evolving uses of artificial intelligence in human resource management in emerging economies in the global South: Some preliminary evidence. *Management Research Review*, 44(7), 970–990. 10.1108/MRR-03-2020-0168

Kumar, A., & Priyanka, S. (2013). Understanding the evolution of technology acceptance. *International Journal of Selection and Assessment*, 1(2), 24–38.

Lederer, A. L., Maupin, D. J., Sena, M. P., & Zhuang, Y. (2000). The Technology Acceptance Model and World Wide Web. *Decision Support Systems*, 29(2), 269–282. 10.1016/S0167-9236(00)00076-2

Lumunon, D. F., Massie, J. D., & Trang, I. (2021). The Effect of Training, Digital Transformation, and Work Motivation on Employee Performance during the Covid-19 Period: A Study on Culinary UMKM Employees in Manado City. *Central Asian Journal of Literature Philosophy and Culture*, 2(8), 22–37.

Matli, W., & Ngoepe, M. (2020). Capitalizing on digital literacy skills for capacity development of people who are not in education, employment or training in South Africa. *Sabinet African Journals,* 3(7), 44-58 https://journals.co.za/doi/abs/ 10.1080/20421338.2019.1624008

Mawela, T., Ochara, N. M., & Twinomurinzi, H. (2017). *E-government implementation: A reflection on South African Municipalities.* Available at: http://www.scielo.org.za/pdf/sacj/v29n1/09. pdf. (Accessed on 20 February 2024).

Mohanty, S., & Mishra, P. C. (2020). Framework for understanding Internet of Things in human resource management. [Top of Form]. *Revista ESPACIOS*, 4(1), 1–12.

Murenzi, P., & Olivier, B. (2017). E-government challenges faced by selected district municipalities in South Africa and Rwanda. *Administratio Publica*, 25(1), 141–171.

Mwakatumbula, H., & Moshir, G. (2020). *Digital skills for gig workers in digital platforms. Digital Skills Insights.* [Online] Retrieved from: https://www.researchgate.net/publication/344927745_Digital _skills_for_gig_workers_in_di gital_platforms (Accessed on 29 January 2024).

Nattrass, N. (2020). In defence of exploratory research: A reply to critics. *South African Journal of Science, 116*(SPE), 1-36

Nel-Sanders, D., & Malomane, A. P. (2022). Challenges and best practices for e-municipalities'. *Africa's Public Service Delivery and Performance Review*, 10(1, a646), 1–15. 10.4102/apsdpr.v10i1.646

Nyagadza, B., Pashapa, R., Chare, A., Mazuruse, G., & Hove, P. K. (2022). Digital technologies, Fourth Industrial Revolution (4IR) & Global Value Chains (GVCs) nexus with emerging economies' future industrial innovation dynamics. *Cogent Economics & Finance*, 10(1), 1–15. 10.1080/23322039.2021.2014654

Okemwa, O. (2016). *Developing digital information literacy at institutions of higher learning in Sub Saharan Africa: Opportunities and Challenges.* [Online] Retrieved from: http://ir.mksu.ac.ke/handle/ 123456780/4306. (Accessed on 25 February 2024).

Olaitan, O. O., Issah, M., & Wayi, N. (2021). A framework to test South Africa's readiness for the fourth industrial revolution. *South African Journal of Information Management*, 23(1), 1–10. 10.4102/sajim. v23i1.1284

Republic of South Africa. (1998). *White Paper on Local Government.* Cape Town: Government Printers.

Rykun, E. (2019). *Artificial intelligence in HR management – What can we expect? Retrieved* from https://thebossmagazine.com/ai-hr-management/ (Accessed on 10 January 2024).

Schäfer, M. (2018). The fourth industrial revolution: How the EU can lead it. *European View*, 17(1), 5–12. 10.1177/1781685818762890

Siemens, A. (2017). *African Digitalization Maturity Report 2017.* [Online] Retrieved from: https:// www.readkong.com/page/african-digitalization-maturity-report-2017-digital – asset. (Accessed on 26 April 2024).

Singhavi, C., & Basargekar, P. (2020). *Re-imagining diffusion and adoption of information technology and systems: A continuing conversation* (pp. 650-661). [Online] Retrieved from: www.researchgate .net/publication/347648779_Implementing_ICT_at_School_Level_Facto rs_Affecting_Teachers'_Perceived_Proficiency. (Accessed on 8 April 2024).

Sokolow, A. (2020). *South Africa's Fourth Industrial Revolution limited by lack of computer literacy, access.* MEDILL Reports Chicago. [Online] Retrieved from:https://news.medill.northwestern.edu/ chicago/south-africas-fourth-industrialrevolution-limited-by-lack-of-computer-literacy-access (Accessed on 28 February 2024).

Strohmeier, S. (2020). Digital human resource management: A conceptual clarification. *German Journal of Human Resource Management*, 34(3), 345–365. 10.1177/2397002220921131

Sutcliffe, M., & Bannister, S. (2020). *Research on the 4th Industrial Revolution: Implications for Local government in the context of skills development Final Report.* City Insight. Available at https://cdn .lgseta.co.za/resources/ research_and_reports/2019%20%E2%80%93%202020%20research%20projects/ research%20project%20-%204th%20industrial%20revolution%20in%20the%20local %20govt%20sector. pdf. Accessed 8 March 2024.

Tan, E. (2021). *A conceptual model of the use of AI and blockchain for open government data governance in the public sector.* Retrieved from https://soc.kuleuven.be/io/ digi4fed/doc/d-3-2-1-a-conceptual-model-of-the-use-of-ai-and.pdf (Accessed on 11 March 2024).

Udovita, P. (2020). Conceptual review on dimensions of digital transformation in modern era. *International Journal of Scientific and Research Publications*, 10(2), 520–529. 10.29322/IJSRP.10.02.2020.p9873

Velsberg, O., Westergren, U. H., & Jonsson, K. (2020). Exploring smartness in public sector innovation – creating smart public services with the Internet of Things. *European Journal of Information Systems*, 29(4), 350–368. 10.1080/0960085X.2020.1761272

Vyas-Doorgapersad, S. (2022). The Use of Digitalization (ICTs) in Achieving Sustainable Development Goals. *Global Journal of Emerging Market Economies*, 14(2), 265–278. 10.1177/09749101211067295

Wang, L., Zhou, Y., & Zheng, G. (2022). Linking digital HRM practices with HRM effectiveness: The moderate role of HRM capability maturity from the adaptive structuration perspective. *Sustainability (Basel)*, 14(2), 10–23. 10.3390/su14021003

Zuiderwijk, A., Chen, Y.-C., & Salem, F. (2021). Implications of the use of AI in public governance: A systematic literature review and research agenda. *Government Information Quarterly*, 38(3), 34–78. https://doi.org/. giq.2021.10157710.1016/j

Chapter 9
Performance Contracts for Senior Administrators in "Unsettled" Political and Economic Contexts:
A Zimbabwean Local Government Perspective

Tawanda Nyikadzino
https://orcid.org/0000-0001-9811-6252
University of Johannesburg, South Africa

Shikha Vyas-Doorgapersad
University of Johannesburg, South Africa

ABSTRACT

Zimbabweans are interested in seeing how local governments will perform in providing services in the era of devolution and digital transformation. Scholars have begun to examine and evaluate the significance of devolution and digital transformation in a nation with a history of dictatorship and centralised authorities in decision-making processes. To enhance the performance of devolved local governments, the Government of Zimbabwe (GoZ) introduced a performance management system in 2020 as a Human Resources Management reform that mandates all local governments to have performance contracts for senior administrators. The introduction of performance contracts for senior administrators arose from the need to address persistent service delivery and administrative challenges in local governments, particularly urban local authorities. Policymakers believed that the introduction of a performance management system for senior administrators would enhance digital transformation, public value and fundamental principles of local governance, namely, effectiveness, efficiency, economy, accountability, responsiveness, and integrity. There have been relatively few studies investigating implementation experiences since a performance management system that placed senior local government administrators on performance contracts was introduced. Consequently, the topic of performance contracts and how Zimbabwe's unstable political and economic environment affects their execution is covered in this chapter. Data to address the preceding question was generated qualitatively through documentary reviews and

DOI: 10.4018/979-8-3693-2889-7.ch009

key informant interviews. Since the performance contract system is relatively new, the authors conducted some key informant interviews to gain insights into the implementation experiences. The chapter found that the unsettled economic and political contexts and sluggish digital transformation pose an existential threat to its implementation. Economic instability, poor revenue generation, brain drain and associated human capacity constraints, political influence and the nature of performance contracts and assessment framework compromise the viability of performance contracts. To improve the implementation of performance contracts, the chapter recommends the Office of the President and Cabinet (OPC) review the performance contracts in light of implementation experiences. The review process should be done in a participatory manner so that the views of the implementing agencies are heard and factored in. The chapter also recommends the use of digital systems to enhance the implementation of performance contracts.

INTRODUCTION

Around the 1990s, many countries across the globe adopted public sector reforms through the New Public Management (NPM) paradigms. The NPM (decentralisation, digital transformation, civil service reforms, contracting out, and performance management) became predominant reforms for local government (Kuhlmann, 2010; Pollitt & Bouckaert, 2004). Performance management and e-government/e-governance have been some of the widely adopted and implemented administrative reforms to improve the performance of local government in implementing development goals (Ammons & Roenigk, 2015). Performance management systems, particularly performance contracts for senior managers in local government have become a global phenomenon (Ammons & Roenigk, 2020; Chiware & Vyas-Doorgapersad, 2021).

In line with the global shift towards performance contracts, Zimbabwe introduced performance-based contracts in 2011, starting with permanent secretaries (Zinyama, Nhema & Mutandwa, 2015). Performance contracts were viewed as an important reform initiative in the country's aspiration to become an upper-middle-class economy by 2030. It was envisioned that performance contracts would enable the government to monitor how the different arms and tiers of government contribute to national development goals guided by the National Development Strategy 1 (NDS1).

The government extended the implementation of performance contracts to heads of different departments in local governments and parastatals in 2020 (Bhebhe, 2023). The Ministry of Local Government, Public Works and National Housing (MLGPWNH) Circular Number LA22 stipulates that performance contracts will be developed for each head of department. However, data on the implementation of performance contracts for senior administrators in local government in Zimbabwe is scarce. Very little is known about Zimbabwe's experiences with performance contracts in an economic and political context that reflects an *unsettled* setting with disruptive consequences on local government reform. Still, little research has been done to explore and explain how Zimbabwe's unique and *unsettled* economic and political environment has influenced the implementation and performance of performance contracts. This chapter examined the Zimbabwean local government's experiences with performance contracts for senior administrators to understand factors influencing their performance and develop tailored strategies to enhance their implementation and performance.

This chapter argues that the perception that performance contracts will enhance the performance of local government in implementing strategic plans is too simplistic. Contextual factors influence the implementation of public sector reforms profoundly. Zimbabwe's *unsettled* context influences the contribution of local government reforms profoundly. In this chapter, *unsettled* contexts imply an environment with disruptive effects on the execution of public policies, programmes and projects. It denotes a political system submerged in complex political-administrative dynamics and interconnection that may either harm or facilitate the implementation of administrative reforms (Onyango, 2020). The term captures neatly the political and economic tabulations that took place in Zimbabwe in the past three decades. Zimbabwe experienced political instability and economic crises characterized by inflation and unpredictable monetary policies. Understanding the implementation of performance contracts in local authorities under such circumstances will facilitate the development of context-specific strategies to enhance performance management for senior administrators.

This chapter is categorised into four sections. The first one reviews the literature on performance management in local government. This is followed by a methodology section that discusses the methodological orientation of the study. Last but not least is the results and discussion section. The chapter ends with conclusions and recommendations.

LITERATURE REVIEW

Local government is undoubtedly a strategic partner in realising national development plans and sustainable development goals (Pandeya & Oyama, 2019). Several countries, both developed and developing, have introduced capacity-building reforms and interventions to revamp and reinvigorate the role and contribution of local government as a strategic partner in the development endeavour (Hall, Shin & Bartels, 2022; Nyikadzino & Vyas-Doorgapersad, 2022; Onyango, 2020). Performance management is one of the popular reforms introduced under the NPM paradigm to monitor the performance of employees within local government. According to Ammons & Roenigk (2015:515) reform initiatives such as reinventing or revamping government and results-based management have also influenced the introduction and implementation of performance management in subnational governments. Performance management has been widely defined in the literature. This chapter uses Ammons & Roenigk's (2020:19) definition which views it as "the purposeful use of performance information to make decisions, including decisions to improve operations and services." A renowned performance management scholar, Moynihan (2008: 5 cited by Hall, Shin & Bartels, 2022), defines performance management as the purposive utilisation of performance management data in formulating strategic policy decisions that transform the organisation. Therefore, performance management pushes for a shift from traditional, rigid, ineffective public administration that focuses more on compliance at the expense of results (Ammons & Roenigk, 2015:515). It is a result-oriented approach to organisational management that emphasises results rather than inputs and processes (Beeri, Uster & Vigoda-Gadot, 2019; Roenigk, 2020). Beeri *et al.,* (2019) consider performance management as a three-phase process involving the following elements:

- *Planning and setting the goals and measurement process*: The stage involves setting organisational, departmental, and individual goals and targets linked to the strategic plan of the organisation, identifying performance indicators and setting a monitoring framework. Since performance management is a transparent undertaking, stakeholder engagement and involvement are critical at this stage. In the local government context, the central government should involve local government managers in developing performance goals, targets, indicators, and monitoring frameworks. The development of performance contracts should be premised on collaboration, cooperation and mutuality. This minimises implementation challenges.

- *Monitoring:* At this phase, there is a regular, continuous and systematic collection of performance data to monitor and evaluate performance. The main thrust of this stage is to identify timeously performance gaps and develop tailored interventions to address gaps and ultimately improve performance. Regular and systematic monitoring enables management to control deviant performance and behaviours. This promotes learning and continuous improvement.
- Performance review and lessons learned: This constitutes the final phase in the performance management process. It comprises the evaluation of final performance at agreed timeframes. It can take the form of an annual performance review. At this stage, those in charge of the performance management process should give feedback to the actors whose performance was evaluated. Through the feedback loop, organisations, departments and individuals can draw lessons that can improve performance going forward.

Since the introduction of performance management four decades ago, subnational governments across the world have devised and adopted digital tools of different forms to measure, monitor and manage performance (Pandeya & Oyama, 2019:877). Performance management systems in local government should be premised on a set of mutually reinforcing elements of performance management doctrine for them to achieve the desired results (Moynihan & Pandey, 2010; Chiware & Vyas-Doogapersad, 2021). Literature provides a wide range of models that guide the development and execution of performance management tools. Fryer, Antony & Ogden (2009:482) developed a framework that emphasises the following:

- Strategic integration of performance management systems and organisational systems, policies, procedures, plans and strategies.
- Leadership buy-in and commitment.
- A positive culture that views performance management as a strategy for transforming organisations and not a way to punish employees.
- Stakeholder engagement, participation and involvement; and
- Regular monitoring, evaluation, feedback, review and learning.

Ammons & Roenigk (2015, p.515-516) sum up the crucial conditions necessary for the effective implementation of performance management in local government as listed below:

- Clearly define the goals.
- Availability and use of performance information that is relevant and can be acted upon.
- Give more importance to the results or outcomes rather than inputs and procedural compliance.
- Involve executive and legislative officials in priority setting, monitoring performance reports, and data-influenced decision-making.
- Involve top executives in performance management, frequently monitor departmental performance, and provide feedback, but intervene in operating decisions only when necessary.
- Provide devolved decision authority, with operating decisions made at the departmental or program level.
- Allow managerial flexibility in using financial and human resources, with accountability for results.
- Provide incentives and sanctions linked to performance results.

The above-listed elements are mutually reinforcing, and governments should avoid focusing on one or a few, and ignore others. Performance management elements should be administered as a package. These elements are important, particularly for local governments that work as lower tiers of government under the supervision of the central government and, in some contexts, regional or provincial governments. Too much central control undermines effective management of performance in subnational governments. As recommended by Nyikadzino & Vyas-Doorgapersad (2022), decentralisation reforms should transfer financial, personnel, political and decision-making powers to local government to allow them flexibility and the decision space to make decisions and hold actors to account for their actions and inactions. In light of Kettl's (1997, p.447–448; cited by Ammons & Roenigk, 2015, p. 516) observation that organisations should create an enabling environment for managers to execute their management roles and functions, the central government should let local governments manage local government affairs. Local government autonomy will enable local government to structure performance management and measurement systems in ways that suit local contextual variables. For effective performance management, local government management should have the decision authority and space to make adjustments needed to attain the envisioned results and outcomes timeously.

Literature on performance management in local authorities highlights several challenges hampering effective implementation. Abane and Brenya (2021) conducted a study in Ghana and discovered that the execution of performance contracts was affected by environmental factors, which include social, economic, and political elements. Financial constraints have been identified as the main challenge in implementing performance contracts in Ghana's local government (Sosu, 2020; SEND-Ghana, 2015). In South Africa, Studies by Ledger and Rampedi (2019), Van der Waldt (2014) and Mamokhere (2019) revealed that financial challenges are compromising the operationalisation of the Integrated Development Plan (IDP) in local government. According to Van der Waldt (2014), municipalities in South Africa struggle to implement performance management systems because of misalignment between targets and budgets. Mohangi & Nyika (2023), found that municipalities in many African countries are failing to generate revenue to finance their development priorities. The next section presents the methodological orientation of the study.

Literature has underscored the importance of digital transformation to improve performance management processes in local authorities. Chiwawa & Wissink (2024) recommend adopting digital tools to collect performance data against indicators, monitor progress and report performance towards the set performance targets. Digital transformation has become an undeniable reform for the public sector to revamp and reinvigorate its operations (Kangethe *et al.,* 2022; Chiwawa & Wissink, 2024). Digitalisation enables public organisations to manage performance effectively and efficiently. However, regardless of the documented evidence of the benefits of the digital revolution, most public organisations in Africa are lagging in digital transformation. As aptly captured by Shopola, Mukonza & Manyaka (2024:1), "... public servants lack interdisciplinary approach needed to meet the country's complex challenges, failure to grasp new problem solving and effective governance solutions and prospects that come with technology." In light of technology skills gaps in the public sector, Shopola, Mukonza & Manyaka (2024) and Shopola, Mudau & Mukonza (2021) recommend curriculum reviews for public administration training to align the discipline to the rapidly changing technological environment. Such a review will create a talent pool of employees with the knowledge, skills and abilities to leverage digital technologies in reforming the public sector.

METHODOLOGY

The chapter is based on a qualitative research approach, which uses an inductive logic of reasoning to generate an in-depth account of a phenomenon (Leavy, 2014). The approach was used to explore and explain people's meanings and perceptions of performance contracts for senior administrators in Zimbabwe's local government. Data was generated through a combination of unobtrusive and obtrusive data collection methods. Unobtrusive data collection methods involve studying a phenomenon without affecting it. Auriacombe (2016, p.6) notes that unobtrusive research techniques are non-reactive and information about the respondent is gathered through public documents. On the other hand, obtrusive methods are reactive and involve direct interactions between researchers and participants (Babbie, 2007). From an unobtrusive perspective, the authors used a literature review and documentary search. Books and journal articles were used in the literature review. For the documentary search, the researchers used newspaper articles, local government strategic plans, the national constitution, performance contracts, and national development plans such as Vision 2030 and NDS1. However, given that performance contracts for senior administrators in Zimbabwe's local government are relatively new, the authors conducted six key informant interviews to get insights from local government top officials regarding their lived experiences with performance contracts. Key informants were purposively and conveniently selected. The primary researcher, who resides in Zimbabwe, made appointments with several local government officials, but some could not make it for the interviews due to competing responsibilities. Resultantly, the researcher ended up having interviews with those that were available. However, the researcher managed to conduct interviews with all levels of local government senior administrators who are on performance contracts, namely Chief Executive Officers (CEOs), directors, and assistant or deputy directors. The key informants also represented all the levels and types of local government in Zimbabwe, that is, city councils, municipal councils, town councils, local boards, and rural district councils.

To ensure anonymity in the presentation of findings, the researchers used the following code:

KI 1 (CEO, RDC) – Key Informant 1 (Chief Executive Officer, Rural District Council)

KI 2 (AD. MC) – Key Informant 2 (Assistant Director, Municipal Council)

KI 3 (D, CC) – Key Informant 3 (Directors, City Council)

KI 4 (CEO, LB) – Key Informant 4 (CEO, Local Board)

KI 5 (AD, MC) – Key Informant 5 (Assistant Director, Municipal Council)

KI 6 (DD, CC) – Key Informant 6 (Deputy Director, City Council)

A combination of content and thematic analysis was used to analyse data generated from documentary searches and key informant interviews, respectively. The researchers used methodological triangulation and thick descriptions to ensure the validity of the research findings. The researchers got ethical approval from the University of Johannesburg, College of Business and Economics Research Ethics Committee. In the next section, the researchers present and discuss the study's results.

RESULTS AND DISCUSSION

In this section, the researchers present the findings of the study. The section starts with the results of the structure of performance contracts for local government senior administrators and ends with a discussion and analysis of the influence of the unsettled economic and political contexts on the performance contracts in Zimbabwe.

Structure of Performance Contracts for Local Government Senior Administrators

Performance contracts for senior administrators are shaped and influenced by the WoGA which seeks to ensure linkage, alignment and coordination between the national vision and national and local development strategies. The illustration below highlights the flow of policies and programmes from the national vision to performance contracts at the local government level.

Figure 1. Flow of Performance Contracts

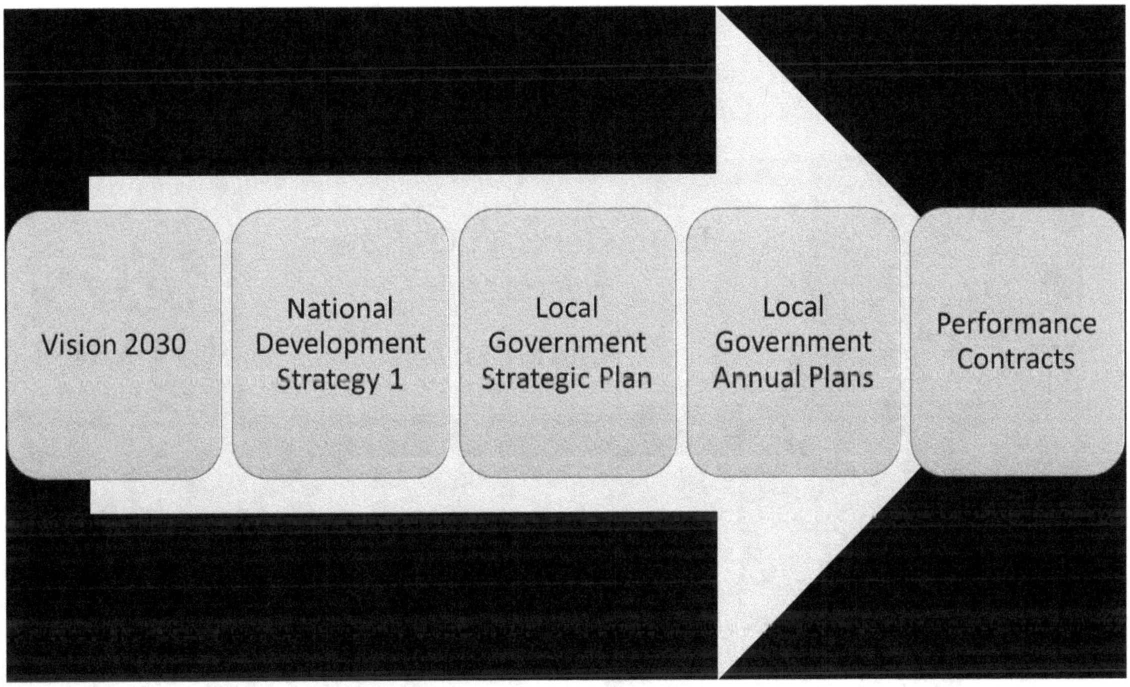

Source: Researcher's Own Illustration Informed by KIIs

As diagrammatically illustrated above, Vision 2030 sets the development trajectory for the country. The NDS1 then comes in as a five-year development strategy that provides a set of public sector reforms for the country to move towards the attainment of Vision 2030. To facilitate the realisation of Vision 2030 and NDS1, local governments are mandated to develop strategic plans, which are mostly five-year plans, strategically aligned to the preceding national policies and strategies. In implementing strategic plans, local governments develop annual plans with measurable goals, targets, outcomes and outputs. Annual plans inform the performance contracts for both the political heads (Mayors and Chairpersons) and administrative heads (town clerks and in city and municipal councils and CEOs in town councils, local boards and Rural District Councils (RDCs)) (Key Informant Interviews). KI 2(AD, MC) summed up the process followed in developing performance contracts as follows

Performance contracts are done using the integrated results-based management system where the main focus is on results. The entity starts by coming up with a five-year strategic document. From the strategic document, yearly organisational work plans are developed. Performance contracts are then crafted to meet the requirements of the organisation's yearly work plan.

Mayors and chairpersons sign performance contracts with the President. For some key informants, the involvement of the president in the signing of performance contracts for mayors and chairpersons demonstrates a political commitment not only to performance management but to the transformation of local government (KI 6, DD CC; KI 4, CEO LB).

Participants noted that for local government administrative staff, performance contracts mainly cover three levels.

Figure 2. Levels of Performance Contracts in Local Government

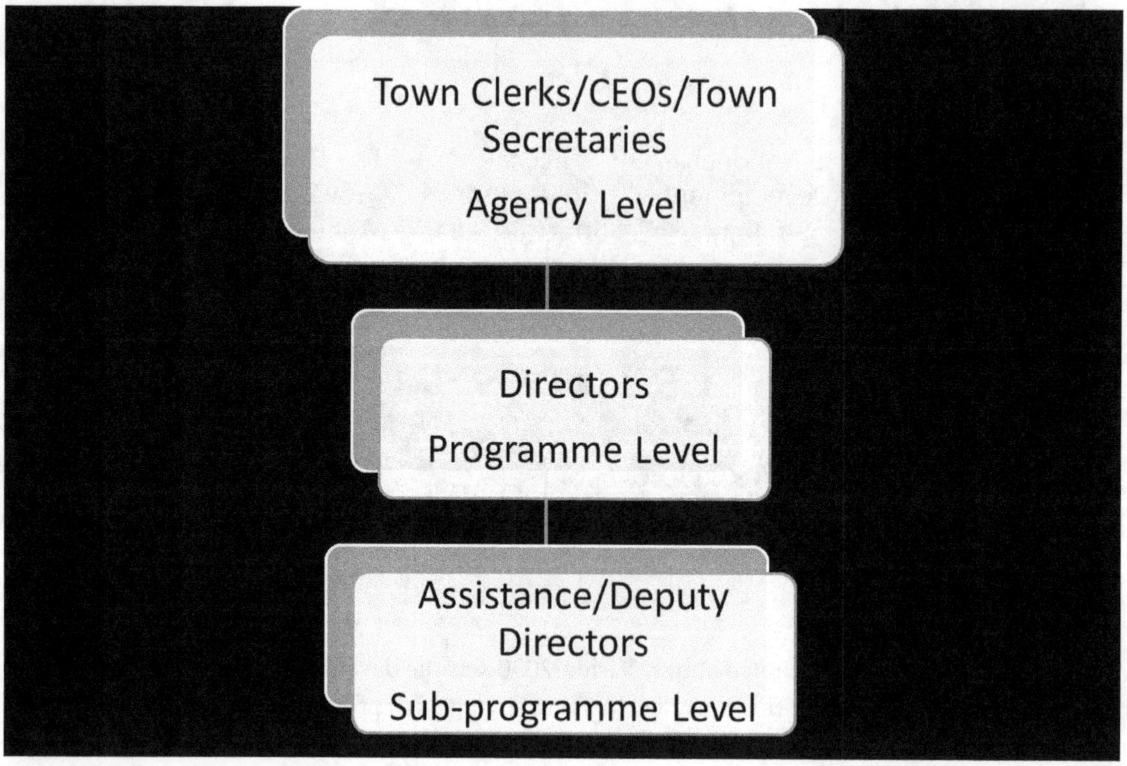

Source: Researcher's Own Illustration Informed by KIIs

Level One

It covers contracts for town clerks, CEOs and town secretaries. Town clerks, CEOs and town secretaries sign contracts with their respective mayors and chairpersons. Mayors and chairpersons represent the government. According to KI 3 (D, CC), this level is referred to as the agency level. Performance contracts for town clerks, CEOs and town secretaries, as part of the WoGA and IRBMS, are meant to:

a) "ensuring that public offices are well-managed and cost-effective in delivering efficient and quality service to the public";
b) provide "a basis for continuous improvement as we reinvent Government to meet the needs and expectations of the Zimbabwean people";
c) guide "the programmes and management priorities of the Council for the budget year" (GoZ, 2022, Performance Contract Template for Town Clerks).

The contract for town clerks, CEOs and town secretaries is in two parts. Part I shows the council's vision and mission, terms of reference/mandates (various laws guiding the operations of local government), overall functions of local government, key result areas, outcomes and outputs. The key result areas for town clerks and CEOs include a) water, sanitation and hygiene (WASH); b) social services delivery; c) roads development and maintenance; d) public safety and security services; e) governance and administration; f) natural resources conservation and management; and g) economic development. Based on the key result areas, town clerks and CEOs expected to achieve the following outcomes: a) improved corporate governance and administration; b) improved WASH; c) improved access to social services; d) improved road network; e) enhanced public safety and security; and f) improved natural resource conservation and environmental management. For performance management and scoring purposes, town clerks and CEOs are expected to provide evidence showing the following outputs: a) works council meetings conducted; b) M&E reports produced; c) stakeholder engagement programmes conducted; e) council equipment recapitalized; f) capacity building programs conducted; and g) projects completed. Part ll of the contract provides for a performance management matrix to measure performance. The matrix brings together the outcomes and outcome indicators and outputs in a table to simplify scoring and measurement of performance.

Level Two

This level covers performance contracts between the town clerk/CEO/town secretary and the directors. This level is referred to as the programme level (KI 3, D CC). Key informants interviewed in the study concurred that directors sign performance contracts with their respective town clerks or CEOs. The contract template for directors is almost the same as those for town clerks or CEOs. The only difference is that the performance contracts for directors are narrower as they focus on specific areas of specialisation. For instance, the Performance Contract for the Harare City Council Human Capital Capitals (2022) is derived from the overall functions of the human capital department including:

a) workforce planning, design and resourcing;
b) business process management;
c) remuneration and rewards administration;
d) human capital development;
e) employee performance management;
f) promotion of industrial harmony and employee wellness;

g) enforcement of safety and health legislation;
h) human capital administration;

The main key result area for the Human Capital Director is human capital management and administration, which directly feeds into the town clerk's improved governance and administration outcome. In terms of outcomes, the Human Capital Director is expected to ensure improved governance and organisational performance. These outcomes will be measured in terms of the following outputs:

a) safety programme implemented
b) performance contracts implemented
c) disciplinary cases for executives concluded
d) works council meetings conducted
e) council-wide job evaluation conducted
f) skills audit and manpower utilisation survey implemented
g) employees remunerated
h) school of excellence operationalised (phase 1)
i) occupational health and safety clinic operationalised
j) organisational restructuring completed
k) wellness programmes conducted.

Level Three

This level mainly covers contracts between directors and deputy directors or assistant directors. The level is called the sub-programme level (KI 3, D CC).

The above findings demonstrated that performance contracts in Zimbabwe's local government fraternity target senior management at the strategic apex. Although some participants expressed concern about the exclusion of the other council employees, performance contracts for senior management are crucial because senior managers are the ones who make strategic decisions regarding the operations of councils in general. It becomes the responsibility of senior managers to develop performance management systems and reporting structures for other local government employees. The literature emphasises the importance of reporting structures in the performance management process (Botlhoko, 2017; Ngqobe, 2021; Mohangi & Nyika, 2023). Ntshakala and Nzimakwe (2016) acknowledged the importance of complementary internal reporting mechanisms to monitor the performance of employees at lower levels. They indicated that reporting the performance of critical outputs and outcomes motivates employees and helps them develop tailored interventions to address performance gaps. The involvement of different levels in implementing performance contracts makes the adoption of digital systems and applications compelling. Without integrated digital platforms, data collection and management and harmonising input from different actors becomes complex. As suggested by Chiwawa & Wissink (2024), public organisations should leverage technology to mainstream performance management processes.

Influence of the *Unsettled* Economic and Political Contexts on the Performance Contracts in Zimbabwe

The question on the factors influencing the implementation and contribution of performance contracts in local government revealed three main themes as presented below.

Economic Instability

Participants cited economic instability in the country as an elephant in the room and a major hurdle in Zimbabwe's endeavour to implement performance contracts effectively. Since the 2000s, Zimbabwe has been experiencing economic challenges characterised by inflation and unemployment (Pasara & Garidzirai, 2020). Between 2008 and 2024, the GoZ through the Ministry of Finance and Economic Development and the Reserve Bank of Zimbabwe introduced several fiscal and monetary policies and currency reforms to curb inflation but to no avail. Zimbabwe is experiencing hyperinflation and there is a yawning gap between parallel and official market exchange rates (Word Bank, 2023). The inflationary environment affects economic activities in the country and local governments have not been spared. The narratives presented below demonstrate how inflation has affected the implementation of performance contracts.

> As a local authority, we develop our budget to finance the implementation of projects in our contracts between October and November every year. The budget is usually approved in January of the following year. So you can see that the gap between budget and time of implementation is wide given the rate of inflation in Zimbabwe (KI 4 CEO, LB).

KI 5 (AD, MC) had this to say

> In terms of revenue collection sometimes we will be at around 120% collection but in real terms, the value is less. The prices of goods and services are changing every day. What is planned against revenue collection doesn't match because of inflation. Because of the level of inflation and devaluation, a quarter of what is in the contract will be implemented. This performance management template works in a stable economic environment.

The study found that the economic volatility has affected local government procurement processes. Local government procurement is guided by the Public Procurement and Disposal of Public Assets Act (PPDPAA) [Chapter 22:23]. KI 3 (D, CC) queried the applicability of section 55(2)(b) in inflationary periods. The section stipulates that "the contract shall not be signed until at least fourteen days have passed following the giving of that notice". She explained that

> The Act introduced lengthy procurement processes which are okay for checks and balances in a normal economy. You know that if you advertise for tenders you will have this duration of time [14 days waiting period] and when you want to award, they introduce what they call a 14-day standstill period. This is a period when you are doing nothing. Most of our prices will be Zimbabwean dollars (ZWL) because that is the currency we collect so by the time you are done, at the award of the contract, the supplier will then tell you that prices have gone up and in terms of that Act you can only do a variation that is not more than 20%. Anything more than 20% you have to redo the tender. So some of the projects we fail to implement not because we don't have the resources but because procurement keeps failing (KI 3 D, CC)

The preceding narratives show the complexities associated with procurement processes in Zimbabwe's inflationary environment. The prolonged procurement process makes the entire procurement process vulnerable to inflation and devaluation. It makes it difficult for local governments to procure essential goods and services needed in implementing programmes in performance contracts. Participants also complained that some products, for instance, fuel and water chemicals are charged in United States of America dollars (USD) yet local governments generate revenue in ZWL. This affects the implementation of programmes that rely on fuel such as refuse collection.

However, KI 6 (AD, CC) had contrary views. He denigrated economic challenges arguing that they are a scapegoat used by managers to justify failure. He argued that

> What I know, with performance management, you can't justify not performing by citing economic factors. Performance is about you being able to innovate and strategise. You must have your own strategies to perform. For example, we have the City of Mutare which has been doing well despite what the macro environment is saying. The question is why they can perform yet they are in the same environment. It becomes the duty of the CEO to innovate and come up with ways to overcome the situation. If we consider the economy we will not be able to assess anyone because everyone will be pointing to the economy or financing. They will just say the situation was bad and there was no money.

KI 6 (AD, CC) also had contrary views regarding the effects of inflation on budgeting. He explained that

> Remember we are in a multicurrency system and like us we were the first to submit a budget in USD, which was approved two years ago. Even now our budget is in USD but when you make payments you can use any currency of your choice. Our budget is locked in USD.

From the above excerpts, it can be argued that the effectiveness of performance contracts in improving service delivery depends on the economic situation in the country. In the case of Zimbabwe, economic instability compromised the contribution of performance contracts significantly. Economic tabulations experienced since the 2000s continue to hound local governments in the country. Inconsistent monetary policies, inflations and unemployment compromised the revenue generation capacity of local governments thereby undermining the implementation of performance contracts. The central government's failure to adequately support local governments has worsened the problem. The findings of the study regarding the influence of economic factors on the implementation of performance contracts are in line with findings elsewhere. For instance, Abane & Brenya's (2021) study demonstrates that the organisation's environmental antecedents (social, economic, political) influence the implementation of performance contracts in local government. Studies by Ledger and Rampedi (2019), Van der Waldt (2014) and Mamokhere (2019) show that municipalities in South Africa struggle to implement Integrated Development Plans (IDPs) due to financial challenges. As Van der Waldt (2014) illustrates, municipalities struggle to implement performance management systems because of misalignment between the planned development targets and budgets. Municipalities in many African countries are failing to generate revenue to finance their development priorities (Mohangi & Nyika, 2023).

Poor Revenue Generation

The theme of poor revenue generation emerged as a void and crucial factor hindering the contribution of performance contracts to local and national development. There was consensus among participants that local governments are not generating adequate revenue to sustain effective implementation of performance contracts. KI 2 (AD, MC) attributed revenue collection challenges to the prevailing economic environment characterised by unpredictable monetary changes and tight controls on local government. He explained

> The environment is affecting the funding of critical programmes as some government policies are affecting revenue generation. For instance, local authorities do not have any revenue source which is strictly paid in the USD. Local authorities are also not allowed to invoice clients in USD as a way of preserving the value of the dollar whilst suppliers of goods are either demanding USD payments or those who still require payments in ZWL are inflating prices so that they can get the required USD at the black market.

Participants felt that local government should be allowed to generate revenue in USD. According to KI 3 (D, CC)

> If the Passport Office is allowed to charge in USD, why can't we be allowed to charge USD for at least those services that require the use of fuel and water chemicals which we have to buy in USD? Why can't we be allowed to at least recover the cost?

Some participants attributed low revenue collection efficiency to residents' and stakeholders' reluctance to pay rates. There was consensus among participants that residents and some government departments owed local governments huge sums of money. Due to the prevailing economic hardship and unemployment, residents have limited disposable income. Consequently, payment of council rates is seen as a luxury rather than a necessity. Economic sanctions on Zimbabwe have limited possibility for external funding for local governments.

Although the central government transfers devolution funds to augment local revenue, participants felt that the transfers were inadequate to finance critical projects (KI 1, CEO RDC; KI 3, D CC). KI 4 (CEO, RDC) also complained that devolution funds come in ZWL, which is easily eroded by inflation. He also expressed concern over delays in the disbursement of devolution funds. Delays in the disbursement of devolution funds in an inflationary environment significantly reduce the value of devolution transfers and undermine the implementation of planned projects. As explained by KI 2 (AD, MC)

> The government is also not disbursing devolution funds in time and in a stable currency. This affects the implementation of projects budgeted to be funded from devolution funds. By the time the money is disbursed, it will not be adequate to complete the budgeted programme.

The findings presented above show that the introduction of performance contracts without accompanying capacity-building mechanisms undermines effective implementation. Due to financial constraints and incapacitation, local governments struggled to implement all the planned projects outlined in their performance contracts and key result areas. These findings align with findings in other jurisdictions. Sosu

(2020) found that most of the challenges undermining the implementation of performance contracts in Ghana's local government, particularly district assemblies are attributable to financial constraints. The study also highlighted challenges associated with the disbursement of central government funds. Sosu (2020) found irregularities in the transfer of central government grants (District Assemblies Common Fund (DACF)) to local government, a situation that halted the implementation of local government projects and initiatives. Sosu (2020), succinctly argues that "the time the fund is released is a determining factor in whether or not it is possible to achieve all performance targets specified in the action plan." In support, SEND-Ghana (2015) revealed that most local governments could not effectively deliver their performance targets because of the late disbursement of central government grants.

Brain Drain and Associated Human Capacity Constraints

Due to the prevailing economic hardships and revenue generation constraints discussed above, local governments are struggling to motivate and retain critical resources. According to KI 1 (CEO, RDC) "people work to look after their families and if they feel their salary is in ZWL and as when the Finance Director has got USD you have to buy that USD using that salary. At the end of the day it's not working for us". This has resulted in high labour turnover and shortages of critical skills in some departments. The hardest hit being the health and engineering departments. KI 3 (D, CC) explained that "we are facing serious brain drains. Skills flight is now so real. We have lost so many firefighters to Saudi Arabia. We have lost so many nurses some to government some to outside." In support of the preceding view, KI 6 (AD, CC) noted that

> For our departments, the engineering department which is our service delivery department has been affected a lot by the young engineers living. You know they come as graduate trainees, you train them, you give them the job the next thing they are gone. Recently we lost our water engineer, we have lost one of the town planners, we lost a project engineer, and we have lost so many engineers.

Participants also reported staff shortages in the ICT department. The above narrative shows high employee attrition levels that threaten the implementation of performance contracts, programmes and projects. Shortages of engineers in the works department affect key service delivery areas such as water service provision, refuse collection and other related services. The other departments also rely on the works department for implementing their projects. Shortages of engineers and ICT specialists also undermine digital transformation which is critical for organisational survival in the digital era. Leveraging technology in streamlining performance management systems and processes without qualified staff becomes difficult. However, staff attrition is not unique to Zimbabwean local government. Local governments in other countries are grappling with the same challenge. Kimathi (2017) highlighted a range of challenges bedevilling devolved local governments in Kenya, chiefly among them being human resources deficiencies. Kimathi (2017) revealed cases of local governments failing to provide health services due to critical shortages of workers. Ramutsheli & Janse van Rensburg (2015) identified human resources capacity gaps and shortages as some of the major factors compromising the performance of local governments in South Africa. Their study found high vacancy rates in local government. Such gaps undermine the achievement of performance targets as local governments, just like other organisations, depend on human resources for the achievement of set objectives and targets. Without adequate human resources, performance contracts can easily become a source of frustration for local government management.

Political Influences

Participants had mixed views on how the prevailing political environment influenced the implementation of performance contracts. Some participants argued that the prevailing political context is conducive to the implementation of performance contracts. When asked about the influence of the political environment on performance contracts, KI 6 (DD, CC) said,

> The way I see those things are totally divorced from each other (politics and performance contracts). For me, political issues (recall of councillors) at local government don't have any effects on performance contracting because remember we said that the key document in performance contracting is the strategic plan. The strategic plan, which is in line with NDS1, is a five-year plan and you will also have your targets for the year, and these are moving targets and the role of the CEOs is to implement. Political issues then do not have any effect.

The above view demonstrates that political factors, particularly the recall of councillors do not change the strategic direction of the council and the implementation of already agreed annual plans. Once the plans are agreed upon, implementation goes on even after the recall of the mayor. Strategic plans and annual plans bring stability to the implementation of performance contracts. This view was also supported by KI 3 (D, CC) who explained that

> In our case, we haven't seen much changes. Yes, the Mayor that signed the performance contract was recalled but councillors agreed that we were part of the process when the strategic plan was being done and we all agreed that this is the direction we want to take so we will stick to it.

Some participants also appreciated the level of political commitment from the President, Emmerson Mnangagwa, towards the implementation of performance contracts. The study found that there is a strong political will to ensure that public organisations comply with IRBM standards and the WoGA. KI 1 (CEO, RDC) noted "Remember this whole thing of performance contracts and dashboards started in the Second Republic. This shows serious political buy in terms of ensuring that we implement performance contracting." In concurrence, KI 6 (DD, CC) indicated that "Even at the national level, we have ministers and permanent secretaries signing contracts. It's something that was never there before. Even the mayors are signing contracts before the President of the country". KI 5 (AD, MC) also cited the President's Call to Action for local authorities as an indication of political willingness to improve local government performance. The participant also shared that the President has indicated that the country is supposed to have awards for best-performing local authorities. All these pronouncements were viewed as signs of serious political commitment.

However, some participants questioned the government's sincerity and commitment to supporting local governments in the implementation of programmes and projects planned in performance contracts. Some participants felt that instead of supporting local government, the central government is rather frustrating them using supervision powers (KI 5, AD MC: KI 2, AD, MC; KI 3, D CC). Delays in the approval of local government budgets have been highlighted by participants as an instrument being used by the central government to undermine the implementation of annual plans and the performance of local governments in general. During the period of data collection (February 2024), participants indicated that 2024 budgets were not yet approved. KI 3 (D, CC) revealed that central government directives and controls undermine local innovation and creativity needed to survive in a turbulent and *unsettled* economic situation. She gave an example where their proposal to sell land in USD as a way of retaining the value of land was turned down by the Minister of Local Government. She also cited the centralisation of vehicle licenses under the Zimbabwe National Road Administration (ZINARA) and the complexities associated with road financing model. She explained that the money disbursed by ZINARA to local authorities is not enough to cover all the roads within urban local authorities. KI 5 (AD, MC) complained that ZINARA disbursements and support tend to favour rural district councils with shorter road coverage compared to urban councils. KI 2 (AD, MC) attributed the complexities to vertically divided authority. According to him "it looks like local government should not do well. If they perform, it has other connotations. Even if you consider those grants that used to support local government, they are no longer coming. It has been years now." The implications of vertically divided authority on the functionality of urban councils were supported by KI 3 (D, CC) who explained that

> I think the vertically divided authority has its challenges where the support can only be minimal because, at the same time, you have your urban councils that are dominated by oppositions. So when they thrive, it might be misconstrued to say the opposition is doing well.

The participants' views above show that political settlements have undermined local governance significantly. Central government approval is being used as a strategy of subversion to undermine local governance, particularly in urban councils. The central government is not prepared to see effective local governance in urban areas as this might give political visibility to opposition parties. This explains delays associated with central government approvals.

Recalls of mayors and councillors have also affected the implementation of performance contracts. KI 2 (AD, MC) highlighted that "the political environment in the country has caused a wave of uncertainty on sitting councillors. Councillors are not sure whether they are going to be recalled or not". High levels of uncertainty and insecurity among councillors will negatively affect the implementation of performance contracts because policymakers form part of the evaluation and oversight process.

The preceding discussion demonstrates how undue political interference in local government operations undermines the contribution of performance contracts to service delivery. Literature also highlights power politics and political interference in local government as a wicked problem hampering effective local governance in most African countries. Sosu's (2020) study in Ghana highlighted interference among policymakers in local government management. His study showed that some policymakers abused their positions to smuggle in new projects and change agreed action plans at the implementation stage. This was done without the disbursement of additional budgetary allocations, and, as a result, some departments and employees failed to fulfil their performance targets.

Nature of Performance Contract and Assessment Framework

Although participants appreciated the government's shift towards performance contracts, there were concerns over the nature of the contracts. Participants complained that the contracts were rigid and were imposed upon local authorities without any room for adjustments. KI 3 (D, CC), had this to say

> The downside of the contract is that it is a bit structured. When you query certain things or when you want certain things to appear a certain way, there isn't room for that flexibility. It is as given by the Office of the President and Cabinet (OPC). At the end of the day, you have to follow a certain format.

Some participants expressed concern over the limited scope of performance contracts. Performance contracts only cover senior management and exclude lower-level employees. According to KI 6 (DD, CC),

> There are clear performance areas, targets, and scores for senior managers. They are monitored every quarter. That system is not at the lower level. For junior employees, some kinds of performance checks are done, but in terms of the standard we are saying we need to cascade contracts downwards.

KI 3 (D, CC) supported the above view explaining that

> We have a serious appreciation of performance contracts at the top up to the assistant director level but we still have a long way to go to have that same appreciation from section heads going downwards. This affects us when we are working towards targets.

Participants also expressed concern regarding the assessment of performance contracts. The study found that the assessment of performance contracts were done by independent assessors appointed through the OPC. KI 3 (D, CC) complained that some external assessors lack knowledge and some appreciation of the local government context. She explained that

> Our experience with last time's assessments was some doctors, I don't know from which institution but then you can feel they lack the understanding of the sector and how it operates. So at the end of the day, you end up giving to what they are saying because that's what they are saying. The assessment becomes an academic exercise.

It can be inferred from the above discussion that proper understanding, monitoring and assessment of performance contracts are critical ingredients for the effective implementation of the contracts. The section also emphasised the importance of flexibility in the implementation of performance contracts. However, if implementation is rigid, people lack an in-depth understanding of the contracts and there are weak monitoring and assessment methods, performance contracts may not produce the desired results. Sosu (2020) argues that "if monitoring and supervision are inconsistent or intermittent, staff may be present at work regularly, but not working for improved service delivery". This demonstrates the centrality of proper monitoring and reporting systems linked to performance targets and indicators. Consequently, scholars (Sosu, 2020; Mohangi & Nyika, 2023) emphasise training and follow-up capacity-building initiatives to enable employees to acquire the necessary skills, knowledge and abilities to effectively implement performance contracts.

The study also revealed gaps in performance data collection and management. KI 1 (CEO, RDC); KI 3 (D, CC) and KI 6 (DD, CC), concurred that there are no systematic and digital systems and tools for effective data collection, management and reporting. KI 1 (CEO, RDC) underscored the need for leveraging technology in collecting performance data to minimise subjectivity and make decisions based on incorrect data. Because of the lack of digital data collection tools, some local authorities were reported to be making ratings that are not backed by data. Without proper data collection systems, the identification of performance gaps becomes problematic. This affects the efficacy of performance contracts as a reform strategy to improve organisational performance and facilitate the realisation of local and national development goals. Kangethe, *et al.*, (2022) hold that public organisations in Africa lag in the utilisation of digital applications in managing performance. The next section presents the conclusions and recommendations of the study.

CONCLUSIONS AND RECOMMENDATIONS

Through the WoGA and the IRBMS, the GoZ has demonstrated commitment towards implementing performance contracts. Performance contracts are seen as a way of ensuring alignment between local and national development strategies and strategically positioning the country to become an upper-middle-income economy by 2030. Indeed, if implemented to their logical conclusion, performance contracts could transform local government service delivery and facilitate the attainment of national development goals.

Although performance contracts are still at the infant stage, this chapter demonstrated that the *unsettled* economic and political contexts threaten their implementation. The chapter identified the following challenges: unpredictable monetary changes, inflation, weak local government revenue generation capacity, insufficient and unpredictable devolution funds, brain drain, tight central government controls, political recalls, rigid performance management template, and involvement of consultants with limited appreciation of local government dynamics. Since this study was done within the initial stages of implementation, the OPC in collaboration with local governments, the Ministry of Finance and Economic Development, and the Ministry of Local Government should take proactive measures to address the identified gaps.

To address the identified gaps and improve implementation, the chapter recommends the following:

- As is the case with other public organisations, the central government should permit local authorities to charge in USD and collect some tariffs in USD, for instance, land sales.
- To enhance the efficacy of performance contracts, it is important to address data collection and reporting challenges by leveraging digital technologies. Local governments and other government departments should integrate performance contracts and digital technologies to manage performance and realise local and national targets. They should establish digital tools to collect and manage data and monitor, track and report progress towards the set targets specified in the performance contracts. By prioritising digital technologies, local governments, and the government in general, will develop timely interventions to address performance gaps. The adoption of digital technologies can revolutionise how public organisations manage performance contracts and performance management in general. With digital tools, local governments can create a more streamlined and systematic approach, that is interlinked, allowing them to achieve unprecedented success. The benefits of digital technologies are widely documented and it is high time local governments embrace them to remain competitive in today's digitalised world.
- Local governments should consider alternative service delivery financing models such as public-private partnerships and crowdfunding.
- Performance contracts should be cascaded downwards to cover all council employees. This helps to promote a culture of performance across all levels.

- The central government should transfer around 50% of the devolution funds in USD as councils face difficulties in converting the ZWL to USD and councils end up buying inflated goods. In the same vein, a certain portion of ZINARA transfers to local government should be in USD. In addition, devolution funds and ZINARA transfers should be predictable and released in time so that local projects can be implemented as scheduled. Devolution funds should also be linked to the needs and uniqueness of each local government. Those with more responsibilities should receive more. They should be consultative.
- The central government in collaboration with local government and non-governmental organisations should roll out training programmes to raise awareness of performance contracts among council employees. Raising awareness of performance contracts among all council employees enhances the spirit of togetherness in chasing targets.
- To improve the assessment of performance contracts, the OPC should ensure that evaluation panels comprise academic staff and local government practitioners. This is important because some academics lack a practical appreciation of local government dynamics.
- The OPC should continuously refine the performance contracts and include consequences for performance. Good performance should be rewarded and bad performance should be punished accordingly to discourage such performance. The system should be strengthened by passing laws that deal with performers and non-performers.
- The OPC should review the performance contracts in light of implementation experiences so far. The review process should be done in a participatory manner so that the views of the implementing agencies are heard and factored in.

LIMITATION OF THE STUDY AND FUTURE RESEARCH DIRECTIONS

The study explored Zimbabwe's implementation experiences of performance contracts from a qualitative point of view. There is, therefore, a need for future studies focusing on the same issue from a quantitative point of view. Statistical analysis will help in measuring the impact of performance contracts on local government performance. Comparative studies are also necessary to explore the implementation of performance contracts in Africa.

REFERENCES

Abane, J. A., & Brenya, E. (2021). The relationship between organizational environment antecedents and performance management in local government: Evidence from Ghana. *Future Business Journal*, 7(1), 1–17. 10.1186/s43093-020-00049-2

Ammons, D. N., & Roenigk, D. J. (2015). Performance management in local government: Is practice influenced by doctrine? *Public Performance & Management Review*, 38(3), 514–541. 10.1080/15309576.2015.1006461

Ammons, D. N., & Roenigk, D. J. (2020). Exploring devolved decision authority in performance management regimes: The relevance of perceived and actual decision authority as elements of performance management success. *Public Performance & Management Review*, 43(1), 28–52. 10.1080/15309576.2019.1657918

Auriacombe, C. J. (2016). Towards the construction of unobtrusive research techniques: Critical considerations when conducting a literature analysis. *African Journal of Public Affairs*, 9(4), 1–19.

Babbie, E. R. (2007). *The practice of social research*. Thomson Wadsworth.

Beeri, I., Uster, A., & Vigoda-Gadot, E. (2019). Does performance management relate to good governance? A study of its relationship with citizens' satisfaction with and trust in Israeli local government. *Public Performance & Management Review*, 42(2), 241–279. 10.1080/15309576.2018.1436074

Bhebhe, N. (2023, February). The government insists on performance contracts for council bosses. *Chronicle (Philadelphia, Pa.)*, 17, •••. https://www.chronicle.co.zw/government-insists-on-performance-contracts-for-council-bosses/

Botlhoko, T. S. (2017). *Promoting effective financial accountability in local government in the North West Province: Developing operational guidelines for Municipal Public Accounts Committees*. Unpublished doctoral thesis. Bloemfontein: Central University of Technology.

Chikwariro, S., Bussin, M. & De Braine, R. (2021). Reframing performance management praxis at the Harare city council, *SA Journal of Human Resource Management/SA*. 19(0), a1438. https://doi.org/.10.4102/sajhrm.v19i0.1438

Chiware, M., & Vyas-Doogapersad, S. (2021). Assessing results-based personnel performance system in the Ministry of Home and Child Care, Zimbabwe. *Research in Business & Social Science*, 11(7), 321–330.

Chiwawa, N., & Wissink, H. (2024). Effective strategy execution for enhanced service delivery in South African municipalities. *Africa's Public Service Delivery and Performance Review*, 12(1), a741. 10.4102/apsdpr.v12i1.741

Di Mascio, F., & Natalini, A. (2013). Context and mechanisms in administrative reform processes: Performance management within Italian local government. *International Public Management Journal*, 16(1), 141–166. 10.1080/10967494.2013.796263

Dube, V. (2022). Mayors, council chairpersons sign performance contracts. *The Sunday News*. 1 May 2022. https://www.sundaynews.co.zw/mayors-council-chairpersons-sign-performance-contracts/

Economic Commission for Africa. (2003). *Public sector management reforms in Africa: Lessons learned.* Economic Commission for Africa.

Fryer, K., Antony, J., & Ogden, S. (2009). Performance management in the public sector. *International Journal of Public Sector Management*, 22(6), 478–498. 10.1108/09513550910982850

Government of Zimbabwe. (2013). *Constitution of Zimbabwe Amendment 20, Act 2013*. Government Publishers.

Government of Zimbabwe. (2017). *Public Procurement and Disposal of Public Assets Act* [Chapter 22:23]. Government Printers.

Government of Zimbabwe. (2018). *Vision 2030: Towards a Prosperous & Empowered Upper Middle Income Society by 2030*. Government Publishers.

Government of Zimbabwe. (2020). *National Development Strategy 1 January 2021 – December 2025: Towards a Prosperous & Empowered Upper Middle Income Society by 2030*. Government Publishers.

Government of Zimbabwe. (2022). *Performance contract*. Government Printers.

Hall, J. L., Shin, G., & Bartels, C. E. (2022). Measuring the effect of performance management in local economic development policy: The case of tax increment finance districts in the Dallas-Ft. Worth metroplex. *Local Government Studies*, 48(4), 628–654. 10.1080/03003930.2020.1869544

Kangethe, A. T. W., Njoroge, P. M., Wangombe, C. W., Munyi, C. M., & Njeru, R. G. (2022). Leveraging on Technology and Job Performance in the Public Service: A Study of Department of Finance and Economic Planning, Embu County Kenya. *International Journal of Academic Research in Business & Social Sciences*, 12(11), 2798–2813. 10.6007/IJARBSS/v12-i11/15744

Kettl, D. F. (1997). The global revolution in public management: Driving themes, missing links. *Journal of Policy Analysis and Management*, 16(3), 446–462. 10.1002/(SICI)1520-6688(199722)16:3<446::AID-PAM5>3.0.CO;2-H

Kimathi, L. (2017). Challenges of the devolved health sector in Kenya: Teething problems or systemic contradictions? *Africa Development. Afrique et Developpement*, XLII(1), 55–77.

Kuhlmann, S. (2010). New public management for the classical continental European administration. *Public Administration*, 88(4), 1116–1130. 10.1111/j.1467-9299.2010.01869.x

Leavy, P. (2014). *The Oxford handbook of qualitative research.* Oxford University Press. 10.1093/oxfordhb/9780199811755.001.0001

Ledger, T., & Rampedi, M. (2019). Mind the gap: Section 139 interventions in theory and in practise. [Online]. Available at: https://pari.org.za/reports

Loevinsohn, B. (2008). Performance-based contracting for health services in developing countries: A toolkit. https://documents.worldbank.org/curated/en/649511468314708749/Performance-based-contracting-for-health-services-indeveloping-countries-a-toolkit

Lu, J. (2015). The performance of performance-based contracting in human services: A quasi-experiment. *Journal of Public Administration: Research and Theory*, 26(2), 277–293. 10.1093/jopart/muv002

Mamokhere, J. (2019). An assessment of reasons behind service delivery protests: a case of Greater Tzaneen Municipality, *Journal of Public Affairs*. 20(2). [Online]. Available at: https://onlinelibrary.wiley.com/doi/abs/10.1002/pa.2049

Masenya, M. J., Mokoele, N. J., & Makalela, K. I. (2018). Performance management as a mechanism to effective public service delivery in South Africa. *African Journal of Public Affairs*, 10(4), 106–117.

Mohangi, P., & Nyika, F. (2023). Performance management implementation in local government: A literature review of relevant international literature. *Public Administration Journal*, 13(1), 75–86.

Moynihan, D. P., & Pandey, S. K. (2010). The big question for performance management: Why do managers use performance information? *Journal of Public Administration: Research and Theory*, 20(4), 849–866. 10.1093/jopart/muq004

Ngqobe, F., Fourie, D. J., & Tshiyoyo, M. (2021). Performance management and accountability practices in South African municipalities: Critical Considerations. *Administratio Publica*, 29(3), 109–128.

Ntshakala, T., & Nzimakwe, T. I. (2017). Performance auditing as a mechanism for effective service delivery in the South African local government. *Journal of Public Administration and Development Alternatives*, 2(1), 67–81.

Nyikadzino, T., & Vyas-Doorgapersad, S. (2022). Zimbabwe's transition to a devolved system of government: Critical factors for success. *Africa's Public Service Delivery and Performance Review*, 10(1), a604. 10.4102/apsdpr.v10i1.604

Nyikadzino, T., & Vyas-Doorgapersad, S. (2023). Collaborative governance in Zimbabwe's urban local authorities: Challenges and consideration for improved service delivery, *Social Sciences. The Humanist Educator*, 4(3). Advance online publication. 10.25273/she.v4i3.18059

Olsen, J. P. (2017). *Democratic accountability, political order, and change: Exploring accountability processes in an era of European transformation*. Oxford University Press. 10.1093/acprof:oso/9780198800606.001.0001

Onyango, G. (2020). Legislative oversight and policy-reforms in "unsettled" political contexts of public administration. *International Journal of Public Administration*, 43(3), 213–228. 10.1080/01900692.2019.1627556

Pandeya, G. P., & Oyama, T. (2019). Revitalizing local government performance management: Further dissecting the role of socioeconomic status and social mobilization policy. *Local Government Studies*, 45(6), 869–892. 10.1080/03003930.2019.1585817

Pasara, T., & Garidzirai, R. (2020). The boomerang effects: An analysis of the pre and post dollarisation era in Zimbabwe. *Economies*, 8(32), 1–20. 10.3390/economies8020032

Performance contract for the Human Capital Development Director, Harare City Council.

Pollitt, C., & Bouckaert, G. (2004). *Public Management Reform: A Comparative Analysis*. Oxford University Press. 10.1093/oso/9780199268481.001.0001

Pollitt, C., & Bouckaert, G. (2004). *Public management reform: A comparative analysis*. Oxford University Press. 10.1093/oso/9780199268481.001.0001

Ruwende, I. (2017). Performance contracts for council heads. *The Herald*. 24 May, 2017.

SEND-Ghana. (2015). *Bringing development to the doorsteps of citizens*. Ghana News Agency.

Shopola, A. M., Mukonza, R., & Manyaka, R. K. (2024). Consultocracy in South African public service: A case of repositioned public administration curricula. *Africa's Public Service Delivery and Performance Review*, 12(1), a747. 10.4102/apsdpr.v12i1.747

Shopola, M. A., Mudau, J., & Mukonza, R. M. (2021). Public administration and management training in South African technical and vocational education and training colleges: Unpacking its relevance in the contemporary time. *African Journal of Development Studies*, 2021(Special Issue (1)), 199–218. 10.31920/2634-3649/2021/sin1a11

Smith, S. R., & Smyth, J. (1996). Contracting for services in a decentralized system. *Journal of Public Administration: Research and Theory*, 6(2), 277–296. 10.1093/oxfordjournals.jpart.a024311

Sosu, J.N. (2020). Performance management in Ghana's local government: A case study of Ada East District Assembly. *Commonwealth Journal of Local Governance* 2019, 22: 7376. https://doi.org/10.5130/cjlg.vi22.7376

Van der Waldt, G. (2014). Implementation challenges facing Performance Management Systems in South African Municipalities: Selected cases. *Administratio Publica*, 22(2), 132–152.

Word Bank. (2023). https://www.worldbank.org/en/country/zimbabwe/overview (accessed on 6 March 2024).

Zinyama, T., Nhema, A. G., & Mutandwa, H. (2015). Performance management in Zimbabwe: Review of current issues. *Journal of Human Resources Management & Labour Studies*, 3(2), 1–27. 10.15640/jhrmls.v3n2a1

Chapter 10
Revolutionizing Public Sector Human Resources:
A Digital Frontier for Innovative Transformation

Vumani Mbatha
University of KwaZulu-Natal, South Africa

Andrisha Beharry Ramraj
University of KwaZulu-Natal, South Africa

Idris Ganiyu
https://orcid.org/0000-0002-7690-7886
York St. John University, UK

ABSTRACT

The Industrial Revolution 4.0 sometimes known as the Fourth Industrial Revolution (4IR) has gathered momentum, and it calls for faster production rates, more flexible scheduling, and better customer services. The advent of automated and digital technologies has already revolutionised many private industries and has the potential of revolutionising public sector human resource management in South Africa. However, the South African public sector has been lagging in digital transformation. The integration of digital advancements in Human Resource Management (HRM) within the South African public sector is imperative considering the need to improve the delivery of public goods and services. The existing Human Resource Management (HRM) processes used in the recruitment of public officials are outdated and prone to biases, which can negatively impact talent acquisition, diversity, inclusion, and employee morale. This chapter aims to delve into specific strategies and approaches necessary for effectively implementing digital transformation initiatives in HRM within the public sector context. The chapter utilised a document analysis and conceptual analysis, where traditional scholarly and peer-reviewed sources on public sector human resource management and digital examination were examined. The analysis of documents pointed to key findings regarding the pivotal role of revolutionising Public Sector HRM through digital skills development which is critical in driving the transformation of the public sector in the 4IR. The findings reflected further the underlying impact of revolutionising public sector HRM which lies in enhancing individual and organizational productivity. Human Resources (HR) emerges

DOI: 10.4018/979-8-3693-2889-7.ch010

as a strategic facilitator in this process, necessitating job redesign and organizational restructuring to foster readiness and innovation. However, there is a notable gap in understanding tailored strategies for the unique challenges faced by the South African public sector. Policy frameworks are identified as critical enablers of ethical and effective digital transformation in HR processes.

INTRODUCTION

In the wake of the Fourth Industrial Revolution (4IR) and the COVID-19 pandemic, governments worldwide adopted digital transformation as a strategic attempt to adjust to global disruption. The worldwide disruption was also highlighted by Nachit (2020) where the researcher affirms that this disruption affected both the public and the private sector. Rupeika *et al.* (2022), reiterates that the pandemic sparked a digital transformation wave across industries, giving businesses a chance to radically change their HRM processes and strategic visions, including HRM strategic business decisions to achieve long-term growth and value creation. Moreover, Juanita (2020) pointed out that the rapid advancement of information technology has made it necessary to reevaluate organizational roles, responsibilities, and HR functions.

According to Nachit (2020) numerous businesses, including state-owned enterprises, have transitioned to digital operations, spurred by the need for preventive measures amid the pandemic. The study by Brunetto and Beattie (2020) indicated that HRM in public services is significantly under-researched compared to corporate HRM, Moreover, the gap in understanding how Human Resource Management processes can be digitally transformed, particularly within the South African public sector, which is highly characterised by political interference, and corruption, is undeniable, despite extensive research based on digital transformation that has been conducted by researchers.

Continued reliance on manual HRM processes fosters biases in recruitment within the public sector, resulting in detrimental consequences. This reliance could lead to diminished public sector performance due to suboptimal talent acquisition decisions, decreased diversity and inclusion, heightened legal risks due to non-compliance with anti-discrimination laws, and erosion of employee morale and trust in the public sector.

Juanita (2020) argues that in the t digital era, technology-based HR transformation is required to meet the needs of public institutions. A handful of studies have been conducted regarding the digital transformation of Human Resource management processes in the public sector However, most of these studies have turned a blind eye to the digital transformation of the South African public sector that is characterised by, political involvement, and manipulation of public sector human resource and supply chain management processes which make it difficult to integrate new HR systems to support corrupt political appointments in the key strategic positions of the public sector.

This study aims to shed light on how public-sector HR processes can be digitally transformed by recommending strategies to enhance digital capabilities in public-sector HR, minimizing biases in recruitment and selection through technology, and proposing policy considerations for optimizing HR digital transformation in the public service. Furthermore, this study explores the challenges faced by the South African public sector and the role of digital tools in streamlining HR processes amidst those challenges. Bahiro and Imron (2024) emphasized the importance of innovative HR strategies in navigating the challenges of digital adoption.

GLOBAL TRENDS IN HR DIGITAL TRANSFORMATION

Reskilling of public sector employees for the digital era has become crucial amid new technology and changing government priorities (Forsyth, 2021). However, according to research conducted by the Organization for Economic Co-operation and Development (OECD), only 18% of employees are under the age of 34 and 24% of employees are 55 or older in jurisdictions where data on their central public administration workforces is available (Forsyth,2021). Therefore, in the context of the South African public sector, it can be argued that reskilling older employees for the digital age might not yield optimal results due to potential barriers such as technological adaptation difficulties, resistance to change, and differing learning abilities. Recruiting and training a younger, digitally fluent workforce to drive digital transformation initiatives forward.

Governments in developed countries like Germany, Ireland and Canada have shown new levels of flexibility in how their workforces and the diverse roles within them are organized and dispatched, for example managing the shift to remote and hybrid. However, this has been a challenge in developing countries because of network readiness and ICT adoption.

Morocco has advanced well in terms of network readiness and ICT adoption. Although certain sectors are undoubtedly more developed than others, Morocco's goal of having a fully digital government is generally gaining traction. (Nachit & Belhcen, 2020). Morocco's progress in network readiness and ICT adoption aligns with its aim for a fully digital government, indicating a growing momentum towards digital transformation. In Organization for Economic Cooperation and Development (OECD) countries which comprises countries like Australia, Austria, Belgium, Canada, Chile, Italy and Japan. The share of people who use the Internet grew by 30 percentage points over the last ten years and more than doubled in Greece, Mexico, and Turkey (OECD,2019) This surge in digital connectivity underscores the importance of utilising digital technologies for HR processes in the public sector, enhancing efficiency and service delivery.

LITERATURE REVIEW

According to Rainey (2009), as cited in Knies et al. (2018), organizations fall under the public sector designation when they meet certain criteria, such as being government-owned or government-funded, with political authorities holding primary stakeholder status. This aligns with the assertion by Pathirane and Blades (1982) that the public sector encompasses governments and various publicly controlled or funded entities engaged in delivering public programs, goods, or services. Therefore, the public sector comprises governmental bodies, along with any publicly controlled or funded agencies, enterprises, or entities, all working toward the provision of public goods, services, or programs.

Fitzgerald et al. (2014) defined digital transformation as the application of cutting-edge digital technologies, such as embedded devices, mobile, social media, analytics, and technology to enable significant business improvements, such as improved customer experiences, streamlined processes, or new business models. Therefore, digital transformation in the public sector means new ways of working with stakeholders, building new frameworks of service delivery, and creating new forms of relationships Mergel et al. (2019), Integral to digital transformation is HRM, defined by Susan (2019) as the thorough coordination of tasks including organizing, directing, and controlling different aspects of managing employees. Susan (2019) also highlighted the wider application of HRM, which includes hiring, training, paying, integrating, maintaining, and terminating workers. This multifaceted approach can serve as a strategic means to actualise the goals of the South African public service.

Digital Skills Development

According to Sousa & Rocha (2017), skills are regarded as organizational and individual resources that give businesses a competitive edge and boost productivity. This was confirmed by the Parliamentary Information Service (2022) by demonstrating that the purpose of the Skills Development Act of 1998 is to increase labour force knowledge and proficiency to boost employment and productivity. Furthermore, according to SITA (2023), digital transformation requires the public sector to invest in knowledge-driven digital skills first, and then start sourcing out the tools that will be used inside the various government departments. This implies that digital skills are fundamental to digital transformation and are also regarded as a significant enabler of South Africa's digitization journey (Smowtech, 2022). Therefore, the digital transformation journey necessitates the significance of developing concrete knowledge based on all the factors that are essential to the public sector environment and understanding the all-inclusive breadth of how digitization can influence these factors.

The critical function of human resources (HR) is to assist organizations in becoming ready for the Fourth Industrial Revolution (4IR), which may affect the organization and the entire workforce. According to Schultz (2021), HR practitioners must embody critical and strategic thinking skills to align the public sector with the imperatives of readiness. Schultz (2021) also emphasised the necessity for job redesign and organizational restructuring to effectively meet future demands and navigate technological advancements. This implies that HR's critical function is to drive the company to become a learning organization, support innovation, and manage ongoing development. Furthermore, in managing the ongoing digital development within the public sector, it is imperative to cultivate new capabilities across various domains. These key areas include open-source software or solution development, aimed at perpetually expanding the partner ecosystem and service repertoire for both the Government and Citizens. Moreover, the integration of software-defined networking ensures the availability of the optimal transport layer for platform-based services (SITA, 2023).

Additionally, using business intelligence and data sciences becomes crucial for drawing insightful conclusions from government data and raising public trust in general. To create the best possible digital solutions that are suited for both the government and the people, the crucial role of human resource management is brought into play. Fostering business acumen in line with new digital and on-demand services is crucial in addition to this.

SITA (2023) mentions that it is imperative to embrace artificial intelligence and machine learning to generate intelligent and predictive responses. Above all, it is critical to include strong cybersecurity safeguards to continuously protect the digital government platform environment and strengthen it against possible breaches. This holistic approach ensures that the public sector not only keeps pace with digital evolution but also operates securely and efficiently in the dynamic landscape of contemporary governance.

However, it can be argued that a limited budget from the South African National Treasury constrains funding for important components like initiatives for organizational development, modern learning technologies, and staff training in South African public sector organisations. The absence of financial support from the South African National Treasury may hinder attempts to establish a favourable learning atmosphere, restricting the availability of educational materials and impeding the adoption of creative teaching methods.

Digital technologies can help the public sector to better serve the South African public by helping employees utilise their current core competencies or develop new ones. According to Sebastian *et al.* (2020), digital transformation is intrinsically linked to strategic changes in business models due to the implementation of digital technologies. Consequently, digital skills development can be viewed as a strategic management tool to cope with the turbulence and uncertainties in the public sector environment specifically the post-COVID-19 Pandemic, and in terms of integrating public service into the requirements of the 4th industrial revolution.

This was verified by Juanita (2020), who emphasizes the significance of technology adoption in Human Resource Management by mentioning the creation of value through strategic decision-making related to human resources. This strategic decision-making process entails a clear vision and mission, particularly in the digitization of various processes within HR management. Examples include the recruitment and selection process, learning and development initiatives, and performance management. The South African Broadcasting Corporation (SABC) exemplifies this approach, articulating its mission to be a high-performing, financially sustainable, and *digitized public* broadcaster delivering compelling and informative educational content. This necessitates the integration of critical digital skills in the organization's recruitment strategy.

However, even with a clear vision and mission that takes the tremendous development of digitization into account and an agile approach to realize and encourage innovation like the one of the South African Broadcasting Corporation (SABC), some companies still struggle to tackle the challenges that come with digital transformation because human resource personnel and employees do not have the right competencies and skills to execute new digital human resource processes in the public service as stated by Vey *et al.* (2017). This is also confirmed by the study of Muzanenhamo (2023) which found that some organizations have an Employee Management System (EMS) in their human resource department. Nevertheless, significant numbers of employees are not familiar with its usage. This indicates a potential deficiency in the organization's transition to digitalization, possibly due to a lack of digital training, hindering the shift from a manual system to a more automated one as per Rankhumise (2023).

The study conducted by Vey *et al.* (2023) recommended that learning and development professionals need to critically assess the content and learning tools of any existing change management training and offerings to determine whether they are topical and correctly reflect the public sector digital needs and whether they are aligned to the strategic digital roadmap of the public service. This includes a thorough analysis of the workplace skills plan (WSP) and clear communication with other key stakeholders like the National School of Government.

Recruitment and Selection

The identification, attraction, and engagement of possible candidates for open positions within an organization is referred to as recruitment. The process of assessing the gathered candidate pool and selecting a qualified applicant is known as selection (Smowltech, 2022). The way that HR deals with information and data has changed along with the advancement of new digital technologies. Consequently, the use of digital technologies has led to a thorough revision of many HRM processes, including hiring, performance reviews, and human resource development, all of which enhance service delivery to stakeholders (Mosca, 2020).

The primary goal of recruitment is to build a pool of qualified candidates who are the possessors of the skills and qualifications necessary for the job roles. However, it is imperative to conduct a skills audit before kick-starting the recruitment process to identify the critical skills gap create a roadmap for continuous improvement and ensure the recruitment of digitally competent employees who can bear the challenges of the rapidly changing digital environment. The HR managers in the South African public sector can utilise advanced technologies such as the ATS to streamline the identification and acquisition of top-tier talent, a need that has become even more crucial in the post-COVID-19 landscape where adapting to remote work and ensuring efficient public service delivery are important. Embracing digital transformation in public human resource management processes not only aligns with the technological advancements of the 4IR, but also addresses the evolving needs of the South African public at large in a post-pandemic world, emphasizing efficiency, responsiveness, and the strategic deployment of resources.

To ensure a flexible and dynamic workforce; 4IR and digital recruitment need to work together to maximize the matching of skills to public sector needs. This strategic alignment is crucial for organizations aspiring to harness the full potential of public sector human resources in the ever-evolving digital landscape. However, it can also be argued that factors such as limited public sector budget, political involvement including the African National Congress (ANC) cadre deployment policy, and the existence of legacy systems in the public sector will hurt this transition.

Moreover, Schultz (2021) highlighted how important it is for HRM to partake in ensuring that an organization's human component is never neglected. Schultz also emphasized that human resource management plays a significant role in maintaining a balance and harmony between technology-driven advancements and the human workforce. Building upon this perspective, Juanita's (2020) study delved into the dynamics of internal business digital processes, highlighting the integral involvement of humans as the driving force. Juanita (2020) asserts that technology should be perceived as an enabler rather than a substitute for human capabilities. The researcher argued that while it is conceivable to decrease reliance on human labour in the business landscape, the human element is still essential in the world of digital business. + emphasized that the coexistence of technology and human expertise is crucial for achieving optimal outcomes in the evolving business landscape.

The Employment Equity Act no 55 of (1998) of South Africa requires that every employer take steps to promote equal opportunity in the workplace by eliminating unfair discrimination in any employment policy or practice (Labour Guide, 2023). The challenge of being vulnerable to bias and possibly omitting qualified candidates, which is against the requirements of the Employment Equity Act, remains persistent even though manual screening and recruitment have been utilised in the public service for many years. This necessitates a strategic approach to utilizing digital tools for recruitment and selection since they enable organizations to reach a broader and more diverse pool of candidates and enable the organization to minimize unconscious biases in the selection process while complying with the requirements of the Employment Equity Act.

Nonetheless, it can also be argued that while digital recruitment offers clear benefits, it also exposes the public sector to cybersecurity threats for which the government is often ill-prepared and doesn't have the capacity, both in terms of skills and resources. According to Moloi (2020), the public service had only 63 dedicated cybersecurity personnel for the 161 national and provincial departments since 2020. The shortage of cybersecurity personnel, as highlighted by the researcher emphasizes the need for strategic hiring and talent acquisition in the public service. To address this gap, recruitment efforts should focus on attracting qualified individuals with digital expertise in cybersecurity.

Moreover, selection processes should be designed to identify candidates who possess the necessary technical skills and demonstrate a deep understanding of the evolving digital landscape and potential threats. This aligns with the broader goal of strengthening the government's capacity to navigate the complexities of digital transformation securely, making effective recruitment and selection crucial components of a comprehensive cybersecurity strategy in the public service.

Human Resource Information Systems

Organizations around the world are increasingly adopting the Human Resource Information System (HRIS) to gather deeper insights into the nature and performance of their human resources as well as to identify the various means to develop the quality of these resources (Abdulrahman, 2019). However, much of the South African government's operations still rely on outdated legacy systems and paper-based processes. Nevertheless, SITA has embarked on a modernization process to ensure that new applications are written to run on the cloud and some existing applications must be migrated to the cloud. SITA (2023) indicated that those applications that cannot be migrated to the cloud in their current architecture have to be re-engineered for the new cloud platform. However, it can be argued that not all applications are suitable or cost-effective to migrate or re-engineer for the cloud. Some legacy systems may be deeply embedded in an organization's infrastructure, and attempting to migrate or re-engineer them could lead to significant disruptions and expenses that the South African National Treasury might not have budgeted for. Moreover, organisations must address security and compliance concerns when moving sensitive data and applications to the cloud. Certain industries, such as healthcare or finance, may have stringent regulations that govern data storage and processing, making it challenging to seamlessly migrate applications without careful consideration and potentially significant modifications. The complexity of upgrading or replacing these archaic setups hinders the transition to modern digital systems.

In the study that was conducted by Juanita (2020), HRIS was found to be useful in supporting the organization's Human Resources department in performing administrative and analytical tasks related to the management of human resources. Many organisations, including the SABC and other public sector organisations, have integrated SAP systems into their Human resources. Juanita (2020) explained that the advantages of utilizing HRIS are that functions are not limited to the HR department but also for employees as it enables them to self-service their respective personnel data, including accessing, updating, and validating data into the system.

Applicant Tracking Software

South Africa has the biggest unemployment rate, and the biggest challenge of screening public service resumes by far is its volume. Tiwari *et al.* (2019) stated that the number of resumes received by the Department of Public Service (DPSA) is one of the biggest time-consuming factors during the recruiting process. The applicant tracking software is a potent online recruitment and application processing support system that can be used to store and manage various user accounts, resumes, applications, jobs, and hire process steps.

Furthermore, Tiwari *et al.* (2019) mentioned that implementing applicant tracking systems to maintain an electronic record of the entire recruitment process can streamline the process. The researcher further supports this by mentioning that the automated intelligent system can take out all the vital information from the unstructured resumes and transform all of them to a common structured format which can then be ranked for a specific job position and candidate according to need.

Even so, it can be argued that older individuals who may not have grown up with digital technology may encounter challenges in adapting to digital recruitment methods, unlike digital natives. This can lead to age-related disparities in employment opportunities, which is also against the requirements of the Employment Equity Act no 55 of 1998, as the younger candidates with digital skills will have an advantage. Therefore, if a significant portion of the population is excluded from the digital recruitment process, the candidate pool becomes biased towards those with digital access. This bias can perpetuate existing inequalities and limit diversity in the public sector.

The ability of the applicant tracking software to screen applications based on predefined criteria such as education, experience, and skills, reduces the likelihood of human bias in the initial stages of screening, ensuring that all candidates are evaluated objectively. Clear and standardized evaluation criteria can be established within the ATS, ensuring all applicants are assessed on the same qualifications and competencies.

The applicant tracking system maintains an electronic record of the entire recruitment process, including communication with candidates, interview notes, and assessment results. This information can easily be utilised for audit purposes by individual audit companies such as Auditor General South Africa (AGSA) and Deloitte. This transparent and auditable record can be reviewed if any concerns about nepotism or corruption arise. Moreover, the applicant tracking software (ATS) provides real-time reporting and analytics features, allowing the organization to monitor key recruitment metrics. This enables quick identification of any anomalies or irregularities, supporting proactive intervention if needed.

Data Privacy and Security Policies

According to Lukaszewsk (2016), organizations are increasingly using HRIS to collect and store employee data to enhance employment decision-making. Data privacy refers to protecting personal information and controlling access to that information (Rashmi *et al.* 2023). The findings of the study conducted by Lukaszewsk (2016) which revealed that employees perceived that using an HRIS solely for organizational purposes instead of using it for employee benefit constituted a greater privacy violation are confirmed. In addition, the results indicated that employees believed that supervisor access to data from an HRIS constituted a greater invasion of privacy than did access by the HR department alone. Therefore, the South African public sector must implement policies defining access controls to limit who can access, modify, or view sensitive HR data. Mainly, because a high level of corruption characterizes South Africa. Some of this corruption can be linked to the African National Congress Cadre Deployment policy which was designed to appoint ANC members to key public positions. Role-based access controls can be established to ensure that only authorized personnel have appropriate levels of access. This will also prevent unauthorized people from temper with ongoing recruitment data, audit trails, and other important information. Public sector policies should mandate regular audits and monitoring of HR data to detect any unusual activities or potential breaches. This proactive approach allows the public sector to promptly identify and address security incidents.

It is of paramount importance for the public sector to establish policies outlining a clear incident response plan for data breaches, including reporting procedures, communication protocols, and steps to mitigate the impact. This ensures a swift and coordinated response to security incidents. Finally, and above all, these policies should include provisions for ongoing training programs to educate employees about data privacy and security best practices. This is necessary for building a culture of awareness and responsibility among the workforce.

Change Management Policies

The overwhelming consensus in the literature on organizational change is that employee resistance is the main reason why changes don't work out. Their fear that changes will negatively impact them is what is causing this resistance. Employees are often afraid of changes that could lead to changes in comfortable social dynamics and additional, less desirable, or even more difficult tasks (Alpopi, 2019). Moreover, digital transformation in the public sector is more likely to experience similar resistance because of the above reasons as discussed by the researcher. Information communications technology (ICT) illiteracy might also be another reason for change resistance when it comes to the digital transformation of HR processes in the public sector.

Therefore, the South African public sector needs to establish policies that mandate early and continuous engagement with key stakeholders, including employees, unions, and HR personnel. This involvement ensures that their concerns are heard, and their perspectives are considered in the Human Resource Digital transformation process. Therefore, consistent, and transparent communication must be emphasized throughout the transformation journey. This includes the provision of accessible materials to ensure that employees are well-informed about the changes and the benefits that those changes will bring. For example, Microsoft Teams meetings will allow employees to save time and money when travelling from one meeting venue to another.

These policies need to ensure that leadership is aligned with the transformation goals and serves as visible champions of the change. Policies should outline the responsibilities of leaders in fostering a positive attitude toward the transformation and addressing concerns raised by their teams. Furthermore, they need to create formal channels for collecting feedback from employees at various stages of the transformation. This feedback loop allows for the identification of issues, concerns, and potential areas for improvement, fostering a sense of ownership and involvement among employees.

Informed Consent Policies

Public Sector HR personnel need to ensure that all the drafted policies require departments to obtain informed consent from employees regarding the use of their data in HR technologies. This can include data like ID numbers, salary scale codes or levels, and other personal information. This emphasizes transparency and empowers employees to make informed decisions about how their data is utilised. It is also important that this is implemented in the applicant tracking software during the recruitment process to ensure that new applicants also make informed decisions about their data. Lastly, this should be incorporated into the performance management data collection process. For example, the performance management policy can mandate that employees are informed about the types of data collected for performance evaluations, and their explicit consent is obtained before deploying Artificial intelligence-driven tools for assessments.

Human Oversight and Intervention Policies

According to Juanita (2020), technology should be perceived as an enabler rather than a substitute for human capabilities. The researcher argued that while it is convincible to decrease reliance on human labour in the business landscape, the human element is still essential in the world of digital business. Juanita (2020) emphasized that the coexistence of technology and human expertise is crucial for achieving optimal outcomes in the evolving business landscape. Therefore, public sector human resource management policies should require human oversight in HR technologies. Automated systems should not replace human judgment entirely, and there should be mechanisms in place for human intervention when necessary. For example, the policy can stipulate that Artificial intelligence-driven recruitment tools can assist in the initial screening of resumes, but a human recruiter must review final candidate selections to ensure fairness and address any unforeseen biases.

Human Resource (HR) policies should also mandate regular training for HR professionals on the ethical considerations surrounding the use of Artificial intelligence and machine learning in HR processes. This ensures that practitioners are aware of potential ethical challenges and are equipped to make ethical decisions. For example, the policy can require HR staff to undergo annual training sessions on the ethical use of Artificial Intelligence in performance evaluations, covering topics such as bias mitigation, transparency, and the responsible handling of employee data.

By incorporating these policies, the public sector can ensure the ethical use of emerging technologies in HR processes, fostering trust among employees, mitigating biases, and promoting responsible decision-making in recruitment, performance evaluation, and other HR functions.

Drawing from the review of literature the critical role of HR in preparing public sector organizations for the 4IR and navigating the complexities of technological advancements was noted, where Schultz (2021) and Junita (2021) emphasized the importance of strategic thinking, job redesign, and organizational restructuring to align with the imperatives of readiness for the digital era. However, challenges identified by Vey *et al.* (2017) and Rankhumise (2023) highlight the need to address competency gaps in digital skills among HR personnel and employees.

Moreover, the Applicant Tracking Software (ATS) is vital in overcoming challenges like bias, improving efficiency, and supporting diversity. The integration of HRIS is also recognized as vital for administrative tasks and employee empowerment. Still, the review also draws attention to the cybersecurity challenges the public sector faces and the importance of strategic hiring to address these issues. Overall, this comprehensive literature review reinforces the significance of a strategic and adaptive approach in HR management to successfully navigate the digital landscape, foster innovation, and effectively utilise human and technological resources in the public sector.

Ultimately, given the backdrop of a corruption-prone environment and the increasing dependence on HRIS, policies should prioritize access controls, frequent audits, and proactive monitoring to prevent privacy invasions and potential breaches. Emphasizing incident response plans and ongoing employee training is important to ensure a swift and coordinated response to security incidents and foster a culture of awareness. Similarly, in Change Management, where employee resistance is a major obstacle, policies should mandate continuous stakeholder engagement, transparent communication, and leadership alignment. Recognizing the potential challenges of digital transformation and ICT illiteracy, these policies aim to address concerns and ensure a smooth transition.

E-Government

New Public Management (NPM) is a significant and ongoing improvement in public service management that is visible in a few important nations. Its ascent is frequently connected to more significant shifts in the underlying political economy that have been noticeable since the 1980s and are linked to the growth of the New Right as an intellectual and political movement (Ferlie,2017). Digital government," also known as "e-Government," refers to the creative application of websites, apps, mobile devices, and other ICT services and platforms to connect the public sector with the citizenry and promote effective and collaborative governance. According to UNESCO (2003), e-governance refers to the use of ICTs by the public sector to enhance information and service delivery, promote citizen participation in decision-making, and enhance the accountability, transparency, and effectiveness of government (Albert, 2009). E-government encompasses programs called Government to Employee (C2G), which deal with the interaction between the state and its workforce.

In the context of digital transformation, modernizing HR procedures in the public sector is essential for efficient governance and citizen involvement, not just for convenience's sake. Taking advantage of digital government initiatives, especially in e-government, has many advantages for improving citizen services as well as government agency internal operations. Government agencies can streamline their operations and reduce manual paperwork and administrative burdens.

Moreover, the South African government can benchmark with the United Nations (UN) as its members are ranked using the four-stage E-Government maturity model. The model's four phases are described as follows:

1. **Emerging information services** This is where e-Government Web sites provide static information. In the context of the South African public sector, this could mean basic details about government services, including HR-related information such as job postings and employee benefits.
2. **enhanced information services** in this stage, the presence is enhanced with one-way or simple two-way communication.
3. **Transactional services** in this stage, a two-way interaction with citizens is possible.
4. **Connected services** in this stage, websites are proactive in requesting citizens' feedback via Web 2.0 tools. Government agencies are citizen-centric, and services are customer-centric.

Therefore, as suggested above benchmarking with the UN becomes critical for the South African government. South Africa may assess its position and pinpoint areas for development in its e-government maturity by contrasting it with other UN members. The alignment of HR practices with global standards through digital transformation can improve the overall effectiveness of government operations in South Africa, given the significance of HR processes in public sector efficiency and service delivery. Insights and tactics for improving digital HR procedures to better serve both citizens and employees can also be gained by utilizing best practices from UN member states.

RESEARCH METHODOLOGY

The chapter focuses on delineating the research design employed in this study, encompassing research approaches, sample population, sampling techniques, and data collection methods. It aims to investigate the digital transformation of human resource management processes in public service, particularly addressing nepotism and bias in recruitment and selection. Additionally, it explores the influence of regulatory frameworks and government policies on digital transformation in the public sector. The research design, as per Selltiz et al. (1962) and Kumar (2014), emphasizes strategic planning tailored to the research purpose. Employing a non-empirical approach, the study conducts thorough reviews of articles and secondary data. Methodologically, qualitative research is chosen to delve into the meanings associated with societal challenges, aligning with Creswell (2014) and Denzin and Lincoln (2000). Utilizing cluster sampling, the study ensures representative subgroup selection. Data collection predominantly relies on secondary sources, including government publications, journal articles, and official statistics. The analysis follows a thematic analysis process, comprising familiarization, coding, generating themes, reviewing, defining, naming, and synthesizing findings, as outlined by Maisammaguda et al. (2022). This systematic approach enables the comprehensive interpretation of qualitative data, facilitating insights into the digital transformation of public sector human resource management.

RESULTS AND DISCUSSION

Digital Skills Development for Public Sector Transformation

The body of research highlights how crucial it is for digital skill development to propel the public sector's digital transformation. Research has drawn attention to how skills serve as both individual and organizational resources, promoting productivity and competition. The literature emphasises the importance of cultivating critical and strategic thinking skills to align with the 4IR. This includes implementing job redesign and organisational restructuring to navigate technological advancements and foster an environment conducive to ongoing development and innovation. For example, among the objectives of SABC restructuring in 2020 included being a fully digitised public broadcaster. The strategy of being a learning organisation positions HR at the forefront of readiness for the future (Schultz, 2021).

Furthermore, the researchers found that digital transformation initiatives are contingent upon investing in knowledge-driven digital skills, forming the foundation for successful digitization efforts within the public sector. The literature emphasizes the significance of digital skills for successful digital transformation, but there is a gap in understanding how to implement concrete strategies for skills development tailored to the public sector's context.

HR's Strategic Role in 4IR Readiness

Amidst the Fourth Industrial Revolution's transformative impact, HR emerges as a pivotal facilitator of public sector readiness. Scholars underscore HR's mandate in fostering strategic thinking, driving job redesign, and orchestrating organizational restructuring. By cultivating a learning culture, fostering innovation, and managing ongoing development, HR navigates organizations towards readiness for the digital era.

Despite numerous studies on digital transformation in HRM processes, there is a notable absence of attention towards the specific challenges faced by the South African public sector. This includes issues such as old-fashioned software or hardware in the public sector political interference, and corruption, which significantly impact the implementation of digital HRM processes.

Integration of Digital Technologies in HR Processes

Research indicates that incorporating state-of-the-art technologies into HR management is crucial, as Juanita's 2020 study emphasizes. The creation of a clear vision and mission that directs the digitalization of HR operations—including hiring, training, and performance evaluation is essential to this.

The literature emphasizes how digital technologies have a pervasive influence on HR procedures. Traditional practices are being reshaped by digital innovations, ranging from recruitment to HRIS. Significantly, the integration of HRIS and SAP systems improves analytical capabilities and expedites administrative tasks, which is indicative of a larger trend in HR management towards digitization.

Navigating Challenges and Opportunities in Digital Recruitment

Digital recruitment was found to present a dual landscape of challenges and opportunities. While applicant tracking software streamlines processes and mitigates biases, concerns over cybersecurity threats and inclusivity remain pertinent. This development supports hiring procedures that are more equitable and objective while also increasing efficiency, which is in line with the larger objectives of inclusivity and diversity within the organization.

Even with these advantages, there are still significant obstacles to overcome. The most important of these are worries about cybersecurity risks since hiring procedures are becoming more digital, which means that private applicant information is more vulnerable to hacks and breaches. It becomes crucial to protect the confidentiality and integrity of this data, which calls for strong cybersecurity.

Potential Limitations of the Study

The study's findings are based on the specific context of South Africa. Therefore, the conclusions are not universally applicable because different countries and continents might have their unique challenges and approaches to human resource management and digital transformation within the public sector domain, which this study does not encompass.

CONCLUSION

This comprehensive examination of digital transformation in public sector human resources management underscores the intricate interplay between skills development, technology adoption, and strategic management. The multifaceted approach outlined here, encompassing critical and strategic thinking, job redesign, and organisational restructuring, positions HR professionals at the forefront of readiness for the 4IR. The integration of advanced technologies, including HRIS and ATS, proves pivotal in streamlining processes, promoting transparency, and fostering a fair and efficient recruitment system. Challenges, such as competency gaps and cybersecurity concerns, demand strategic hiring and continuous learning initiatives. The emphasis on mitigating nepotism and bias through digital tools like the ATS highlights the transformative impact of digitalisation on creating a level playing field, ensuring fairness, and contributing to a more equitable and merit-based public sector recruitment system. As organisations navigate the ever-evolving digital landscape, these strategies collectively pave the way for a seamless transition, empowering HR professionals and employees alike.Top of Form

RECOMMENDATIONS AND FUTURE RESEARCH

Previous studies conducted on digital transformation have turned a blind eye to the challenges that come with the digitisation of Human Resource Management processes especially the implementation of Human Resource Information Systems. It is crucial that a study on how the public sector can utilise cyber security to mitigate risk during the digital transformation journey.

Studying cyber security threats and mitigation strategies that are specific to various sectors and developing proactive strategies to mitigate these risks is crucial for the South African public sector. This will be instrumental in areas that are mostly targeted by fraudsters like the Unemployment Insurance Fund (UIF) and Government Employee Pension Fund (GEPF) Research can focus on understanding emerging cyber threats, analysing successful cyber security measures implemented by other countries and during the COVID-19 pandemic, and lastly devising comprehensive frameworks for safeguarding digital infrastructure.

REFERENCES

Al Shikhy, A., Makhbul, Z. M., Rawshdeh, Z. A., Arshad, R., & Ali, K. A. M. (2019). Dispositional resistance to change and user resistance behaviour to use human resources information systems in the healthcare sector: The moderating role of conscientiousness. [IJRTE]. *International Journal of Recent Technology and Engineering*, 8(4), 565–572.

Albert, O. (2009). Whose e-governance? A critique of online citizen engagement in Africa. *African Journal of Political Science and International Relations*, 3(4), 133–141.

Alhazemi, A. (2017). Critical Analysis and Current Challenges Facing HRIS Adoption in Arab Countries Case of Saudi Arabia. *International Journal of Heritage. Tourism and Hospitality*, 11(2), 143–16.

Alpopi, C. (2019). Sustainable e-Governance and Human Resource Development European. *Journal of Sustainable Development*, 8(5), 16–20.

Babbie, L. (2014). *The Basics of Social Research.* Wadsworth: Cengage Learning.

Bahiroh, E., & Imron, A. (2024). Innovative Human Resource Management Strategies in the Era of Digital Transformation. [PRODUCTIVITY]. *Management Studies and Business Journal*, 1(2), 154–162. 10.62207/6wnrgj39

Banu, S. R. (2019). Hr digital transformation. *Journal of The Gujarat Research Society*, 21(13), 946–951.

Brunetto, Y., & Beattie, R. (2020). Changing role of HRM in the public sector. *Public Management Review*, 22(1), 1–5. 10.1080/14719037.2019.1645876

Creswell, J. W. (2014). *Research design.* Sage Publications, Inc.

Denzin, N. K., & Lincoln, Y. S. (2003). *A handbook of qualitative research.* Sage Publications.

Eurostat. (2023) Digitalisation in Europe - 2023 edition, Retrieved April 19, 2024,fromhttps://ec.europa.eu/eurostat/web/interactive-publications/digitalisation-2023

Ferlie, E. (2017, March 29). The New Public Management and Public Management Studies. *Oxford Research Encyclopedia of Business and Management.* Retrieved 23 Apr. 2024, fromhttps://oxfordre.com/business/view/10.1093/acrefore/9780190224851.001.0001/acrefore-9780190224851-e-129.

Fitzgerald, M.. (2014). Embracing digital technology: A new strategic imperative. *MIT Sloan Management Review*, 55(2), 1.

Grinell, J. R., & Unrau, Y. (2005). *The qualitative research approach in research methods for social workers. Peosta.* Eddie Bowers Publishing.

Junita, A. (2021). The Creative Hub: HR Strategic Function in The Digital Age. .10.2991/aer.k.210121.031

Kumar, L. (2014). *Research methodology.* Sage Publications.

Kumar, V., Alshazly, H., Idris, S. A., & Bourouis, S. (2021). Evaluating the impact of COVID-19 on society, environment, economy, and education. *Sustainability (Basel)*, 13(24), 13642. 10.3390/su132413642

Labour Guide. (2023). Employment Equity Act. Retrieved January 26, 2014, From https://labourguide.co.za/employment-equity/employment-equity-act

Lukaszewski, K. M., Stone, D. L., & Johnson, R. D. (2016). Impact of human resource information system policies on privacy. *AIS Transactions on Human-Computer Interaction*, 8(2), 58–73. 10.17705/1thci.00079

Mabuza, J. (2020). [Impact on digital transformation. A research report submitted to the Faculty of Commerce, Law and Management, University of the Witwatersrand, Master of Management in the field of Digital Business. From wiredspace.wits.ac.za.]. *COVID*, 19, •••.

Mergel, I., Edelmann, N., & Haug, N. (2019). Defining digital transformation: Results from expert interviews. *Government Information Quarterly*, 36(4), 101385. 10.1016/j.giq.2019.06.002

Mhlanga, D., & Moloi, T. (2020). COVID-19 and the digital transformation of education: What are we learning on 4IR in South Africa? *Education Sciences*, 10(7), 1–11. 10.3390/educsci10070180

Mosca, M. (2020). *Digitalization of HRM: A study of success factors and consequences in the last decade*. University of Twente.

Muzanenhamo, A., & Rankhumise, E. (2023). Human resource management and digitalisation in a South African public enterprise. [IJIAS]. *Indonesian Journal of Innovation and Applied Sciences*, 3(1), 31–37.

Nachit, H., & Belhcen, L. Digital Transformation in Times of COVID-19 Pandemic: The Case of Morocco (July 7, 2020). Available at *SSRN*: https://ssrn.com/abstract=3645084 or http://dx.doi.org/10.2139/ssrn.3645084

OECD. (2019). *Measuring the Digital Transformation: A Roadmap for the Future*. OECD Publishing., 10.1787/9789264311992-

Parliamentary Information Service. (2022). The Skills Development Act. Retrieved March 26, 2014, From https://static.pmg.org.za/docs/2000/appendices/000229SDASummary.htm

Pathirane, L., & Blades, D. W. (1982). Defining and measuring the public sector: Some international comparisons. *Review of Income and Wealth*, 28(3), 261–289. 10.1111/j.1475-4991.1982.tb00617.x

Prasad, S. (2023). Blockchain and Data Privacy in Human Resource Management. *3rd International Conference on Advance Computing and Innovative Technologies in Engineering (ICACITE)*

Rupeika-Apoga, R., Petrovska, K., & Bule, L. (2022). The effect of digital orientation and digital capability on digital transformation of SMEs during the COVID-19 pandemic. *Journal of Theoretical and Applied Electronic Commerce Research*, 17(2), 669–685. 10.3390/jtaer17020035

Sakarina, S., Ena, Z., Cakranegara, P. A., & Surahman, S. (2022). Digital Transformation in Human Resource Management in the Industrial Age 4.0. *Quantitative Economics and Management Studies*, 3(5), 750–756. 10.35877/454RI.qems1067

Saunders, M., Lewis P., & Thornhill, A. (2019). Research Methods for Business Students: Pearson Education Limited. Eight editions.

Schultz, C. M. (2021). The future and the role of human resource management in South Africa during the Fourth Industrial Revolution. *SA Journal of Human Resource Management*, 19, 11. 10.4102/sa-jhrm.v19i0.1624

Sebastian, I. M., Ross, J. W., Beath, C., Mocker, M., Moloney, K. G., & Fonstad, N. O. (2020). How big old companies navigate digital transformation. In *Strategic information management* (pp. 133–150). Routledge. 10.4324/9780429286797-6

SITA. (2023). Digital Transformation Strategic Plan. From https://www.sita.co.za/sites/default/files/Strategic%20Plan%202020-2024.pdf

Smowtech. (2022) Recruitment and selection: What are they, and what are their differences? Retrieved January 25, 2023, From https://smowl.net/en/blog/recruitment-selection-definition-differences/

Sousa, M. J., & Rocha, Á. (2019). Skills for disruptive digital business. *Journal of Business Research*, 94, 257–263. 10.1016/j.jbusres.2017.12.051

Susan, E. (2019). Human Resource Management. Adara. *Journal of Islamic Education Management*, 9(2), 952–962.

Tiwari, A., Vaghela, S., Nagar, R., & Desai, M. (2019). Applicant tracking and scoring system. *International Research Journal of Engineering and Technology*, 6(4), 320–324.

Verlinden, N. (2023). HR trends report Preview. From https://www.linkedin.com/posts/neelie-verlinden_aihr-hr-trends-2023-activity-7008096578326392832-bO63

Vey, K., Fandel-Meyer, T., Zipp, J. S., & Schneider, C. (2017). Learning & Development in Times of Digital Transformation: Facilitating a Culture of Change and Innovation. *International Journal of Advanced Corporate Learning*, 10(1), 22. 10.3991/ijac.v10i1.6334

Chapter 11
Digitalisation of Employee Performance Evaluation to Advance Public Sector Human Resource Management

Syanda A. Mthuli
School of Management, University of KwaZulu-Natal, South Africa

ABSTRACT

The evaluation of the performance of government remains one of the most fiercely debated in democracies and problematic in countries. While today's digital age affects all aspects of life, necessitates change including the integration of advanced technologies to aid policy implementation & public service delivery performance. The efficiency of governments and the positive develop of humans is said to be tied to innovation and technological progress. This study explores the digitalisation of employee performance evaluation in human resource management in South Africa's bureaucracy, with an objective to explore its contribution as a panacea for policy implementation & public service delivery ills in the country. The findings point to that in the public service in the country employee performance evaluation remains outdated though policy documents call for the integrating information communication technology. A digitalised performance measurement (e-performance management and e-HRM) in the country would add value and have a positive impact as has been long established in the private sector.

INTRODUCTION

Digital transformation spearheaded by the Fourth Industrial Revolution (4IR) is affecting the functioning of public sector organisations as modern technologies influence public policy-making, performance evaluations including how public data is collected and analysed to come up with data-driven decision-making in public service delivery (Benbunan-Fich, Desouza, & Andersen, 2020). Public sector human resource management (HRM) as a key functional department in public administration has continuously received immense criticism in South Africa because of poor performance which has triggered service delivery problems for the public (Khunoethe, Reddy & Mthuli, 2021). Managing the performance of

DOI: 10.4018/979-8-3693-2889-7.ch011

public officials in public sector organisations (PSOs) is the crucial role of Human Resources Management hence digitalising performance evaluation is key to enhancing service delivery in South Africa's thriving public sector. In this chapter, the term public sector encompasses public service organisations (PSOs) and agencies as well as state-owned enterprises at all government levels, namely at national, provincial and local levels established by laws applicable in South Africa. Resulting of several public sector deficiencies, scholars of Public Administration (Mello, 2015; Mkhize, Nzimakwe & Mthuli. 2021; Mthuli, Singh & Reddy, 2023b) have strongly advocated for the digitalisation of performance evaluation interchangeably used in this chapter as performance management (PM) to realign HRM with modern technologies that could be adopted to enhance change and improve performance.

Achieving efficient public sector performance remains problematic three decades after South Africa's democracy, with reports from the Auditor General of South Africa (AGSA), every year pointing to various inefficiencies within key public sector departments including HRM (Mello, 2015; Magoro, 2015; Mkhize, et al. 2021). The poor performance experienced in public sector HRM is exacerbated by limited and lack of social and digital innovations, while the use of Information Communication Technology (ICT) remains low (Nzimakwe & Pillay, 2010; Nzimakwe, 2015). The study of Biyela et al. (2018) added that poor implementation of intergovernmental relations and other service delivery models affect digital transformation in public sector HRM.

Addressing the limitations emanating from public sector HRM through employee performance management and development systems (EPMDS) has been a complex task due to poor accountability in PSOs. Although numerous regulatory and legislative frameworks to transform PSOs in South Africa have been implemented, public sector HRM continues to experience multiple challenges that may affect digital transformation in terms of employee performance evaluations (Nzimakwe, 2012). Enabling legal frameworks such as the White Paper on Transforming Public Service Delivery (1997) referred to as *Batho Pele* and the White Paper on Human Resource Management (HRM) in the Public Service (1997) in the public service (Mkhize, Nzimakwe & Mthuli, 2021), were implemented to ensure transformation and improved performance of the public sector HRM. As the desire to redirect public sector HRM and ensure improved performance, the balanced scorecard, PM agreements (PMAs) were implemented to focus on Key Performance Areas (KPAs) and Key Performance Indicators (KPIs) in PSOs.

Public sector organisations globally operate in the digital age punctuated with modern technologies such as blockchain, 3D printing, cloud computing, artificial intelligence (AI), Internet of Things (IoT) among others. This study points to limited scholarship in the field of digital performance evaluation and management in public sector HRM, which makes digital transformation a complex phenomenon in enhancing performance evaluations in South Africa. Rising from this background, the study seeks to answer the following questions: Is a digital employee performance management development system (EPMDS) a panacea for improving performance evaluation in South African public sector HRM? and what are the challenges and opportunities of digitalising employee performance evaluation to improve service delivery in PSOs?

THEORETICAL AND EMPIRICAL LITERATURE

The chapter is anchored on New Public Management (NPM) to understand the challenges and opportunities of digitalising performance evaluation towards attaining efficiency and effectiveness in the South African public sector HRM. The two core principles of NPM, the first being reducing and limiting government by letting go or offloading some of its functions to the private sector. The second, improving the performance of public institutions by importing private sector ways of doing, such as innovations and ensuring accountability, as has been witnessed in the public service of notable Western Anglo-Saxon English-speaking democracies which were large, inefficient, and unsustainable (Lapuente & Van de Walle, 2020; Mkhize et al. 2021; Mthuli, Singh & Reddy 2022).

This assumes that the adoption of private sector ways of doing such as technological innovations can contribute to a solution but are not a panacea to the public sector's challenges, such as those relating to HRM and employee evaluation. NPM has been accused of importing practices and norms from the private sector (Lapuente & Van de Walle, 2020), by adopting private sector practices and norms for performance accountability. Despite this criticism, the NPM is relevant in this chapter study as it provides for alternative principle, that of the adoption of innovations already pioneered by the private sector. The digital age today necessitates a need and urgency to digitalise employee performance evaluation in South Africa's bureaucracies as part of aligning HRM's role to the trends of digital governance practices. This study acknowledges the fiercely debated NPM and shortcomings related to issues such as copying from the private sector and pasting onto the public sector (Lapuente & Van de Walle, 2020).

DIGITALISATION OF PUBLIC SECTOR HRM AND PERFORMANCE EVALUATION

In this modern day, technological advancements are everywhere, hence it is imperative to consider the speed of progress and human technological innovation. This new era of HRM has brought with it the digitalisation of HRM in Electronic Human Resource Management (e-HRM) (Parkar, Srivastava, Kaur, Geo, Bandopadhyay & Sinha, 2021). Related concepts include Human Resource Information Systems (HRISs) (Bal, Bozkurt & Ertemsir, 2022), Human Resource Information Technology (HRIT) (Parkar et al., 2021), and Web-based HRM. The literature distinguishes three types of e-HRM: (i) operational – relating to keeping employees' data up to date through the HR website, (ii) relational - concerned with supporting business processes and (iii) transformational - relating to the HR function aligning to the organizational strategy (Phahlane, 2023). The advancements in HRM in terms of modernisation have been vital because of the role and impact the HRM function plays in the effectiveness of organisations, both private and public, but with public HRM centred on contributing to public sector institutions ensuring successful policy implementation and service delivery performance in the digital age.

The digitalisation of HRM and e-HRM would allow vacancy management, applicant management and an e-talent management feature. This is a digital process allowing public institutions to access an internet portal and use its web-enabled tools (Pantelidis, 2019). Furthermore, digitalised HRM would have an employee self-service portal which allows employees to edit their personal information. This technology is becoming more valuable and addresses the emerging trends of the digital age because e-HRM creates value for the organisation (Škudienė, Vezeliene & Stangej, 2020). The use of these systems and portals has been found to have a positive impact on the organisation's performance (Halid, Yusoff & Somu, 2020) because the HR portals greatly impact performance management and human resource planning, which is further intensely improved by digitalisation (Halid, Halim & Ravesangar, 2022).

While NPM movement's contribution to the improvement of the public service and overall public institutions in both developed and developing countries remains debated (Khunoethe et al., 2021; Mthuli et al., 2022; Mthuli, Singh & Reddy, 2023a; Mthuli, Singh & Reddy, 2023b). The issue of poor performance of government institutions is viewed as more severe in developing countries, this is where effective government performance is most needed (Reddy et al., 2015; Mthuli et al., 2023b). In Sub-Saharan Africa, countries such as South Africa with extremely high levels of inequality and myriad service delivery issues, problems as well as PSOs poor performance but with various policy and legislative interventions, a signal of governments' commitment to addressing issues tied to what it has been termed as the Triple challenge of – poverty, unemployment and inequality three decades into democracy (Mthuli et al., 2022; Mthuli et al., 2023a; Mthuli et al., 2023b).

Public Sector Performance Management and Technological Advancements

Public sector performance management is, old as the system of governance in society and remains most problematic in sub-Saharan Africa, with also the recurrence of conflicts - *coup d'états* (Mthuli et al., 2022). In the last 150 years both developed and developing worlds, postwar – World War I & II societies and bureaucracies changed and continue to do so until today about the evaluation of government performance Ranson and Stewart (1994) observed that:

> "The form in which management has served public purpose has varied radically with the nature of the polity, …in the period of social democracy, a conception of public management reflected a belief that power of the professional expertise, reinforced by the rules of fairness administration by welfare bureaucracies, could deliver the good society. The neo-liberal polity challenged those purposes, attacked the means, and substituted contract management as best suited to deliver the alternative purpose of public choice and accountability" (p.153).

The concept of PM in the public sector was introduced early in the nineteen nineties (1990s) as a way of managing the performance of government institutions specifically, to increase the performance of these institutions (Osborne & Gaebler, 1992). This was a time of dire financial pressure in the economy of the Western World, after decades of welfarism and bureaucracies' performance and accountability questioned (Ranson & Stewart, 1994; Hague, Harrop & McCormick, 2019; Mthuli et al., 2023a; Mthuli et al., 2023b).

Management in the public sector goes beyond procedures, codes, and contracts because public management is designed to serve the collective choice. This is with the activities of public organizations with a purpose to maintain, sustain life or ways of life - for what the society constitutes. Also, enables change in society by responding to the evolving needs of society and its developmental needs (Ranson and Stewart, 1994).

While the golden age of the welfare state, its end was signalled by the 1980s recessions and then financial crises which reduced the resources available to governments (Hague, Harrop & McCormick, 2019; Mthuli, Singh & Reddy, 2022; Mthuli et al., 2023a). Hence necessitating the need to within PSOs, to utilise resources effectively, efficiently and the need for accountability therein. Nevertheless, the NPM shortcomings have been evident in the developed, less developed and developing world, however, performance management is mostly needed in the developing world (Khunoethe et al., 2021; Mthuli et al., 2023a; Mthuli et al., 2023b). In the developing world is where Brent Wood institutions (the International Monetary Fund & Word Bank) promoted NPM principles (Mthuli et al., 2023a; Mthuli et al., 2023b) and NPM's eventual well-documented failure globally, but more so in the developing world.

Today the nature of the polity and professional expertise, reinforced by the rules in bureaucracies finds itself now in a digital society. We are living in a digital society that is fast evolving, and so too are societal problems. Innovations allow organizations, private or public to evolve and transform and this had been evident mostly in the turn of the Third Industrial Revolution. This relates to communications technology but some sectors not fully taking advantage, with Benbunan-Fich et al. (2020), hence observing that the public sector today is increasingly moving into the digital age but still trying to take advantage of previous Information Technology (IT) innovations.

The 1990s and 2000s were a time during which the Third Industrial Revolution was prevalent with the private sector leaping commerce innovations and the related. Although this was initially slow to take off, private sector organisations were the pioneers that encouraged the government to also pursue technological advancements for its business, which in the public sector included policy implementation and service delivery (de Vries, 2016). Nevertheless, de Vries (2017) points out that technology has been central in the government apparatus, from the traditional model of administration and the Weberian times and the bureaucratic model was an ideal fit with basic technology. Such as the quill pen to the telegram, the telephone, the use a typewriter and the plain paper photocopier as well as the fax machine, and these were major advances in the past which seem primitive today.

Public Sector Performance Management and Evaluation in South Africa

Public sector performance has long been seen as problematic in democratic South Africa which has been seen as undermining the great strides made by liberation movements leading to democracy and the democratic dispensation. At the policy design level within local bureaucracies, Khunoethe et al., (2021) observe flaws in the design and management of performance which leads to poor performance and points to a lack of alignment between the planned development and the necessary performance to achieve it. At the implementation phase, in the country's bureaucracies at varied levels, fairness and bias have indeed been featured in recent contemporary literature on public sector PM (Mkhize et al., 2021). This is the dark side of PM implementation in the country, posing challenges to be addressed, perhaps there is a need for adjustments in the existing policy and research.

The public sector's level of transparency, fairness, empathy, and professionalism, means that significant opportunities exist for information systems and for PM scholars to collaborate in this space. Benbunan-Fich et al. (2020, p.325), this because the "value analysis must go beyond utilitarian assessments". Simply evaluating value in terms of traditional measures of efficiencies (cost savings) or effectiveness (correct outputs) is not sufficient or even appropriate in the public sector. Khunoethe et al. (2021) call for the need for policy alignment based on holistic thinking in public sector performance and evaluation in local government in South Africa. This entails policy implementation and service delivery that is considerate of the environment and times, for the ideal but also exceptional performance resulting in positive policy outcomes.

The need for digitalisation of employee performance evaluation is vital since innovations are vital in addressing service delivery challenges in South Africa. While at the same time can be gradually phased in because of varied contextual reasons, similar to an empirical observation. Khanyile, et al. (2021, p. 972) found that the use of innovative participatory governance in the form of ICTs and social media platforms was being used parallel to traditional forms because of the rural and urban technological divide, to enable community participation of constituencies to improve service delivery. This is a first step signalling a commitment to policy implementation service delivery and performance in a digital age.

Public Sector HRM and Policy Implementation in South Africa

The critical need for public sector institutions to perform at the highest level possible in South Africa post-Apartheid is called for by the democratic dispensation, and its goals of public service expansion to all (Mthuli et al., 2022). The performance of public sector institutions today in the country is further tied to just administrative action. Democracy, human rights, and social justice remain vital in the country. This is evident by the existence of just administration action as a Human Right in South Africa. Pearse and Williams (2009) and Mkhize, et al. (2021) point out that the democratic government's transformation agenda has been focused on having a culture of performance. In the country however, bureaucracies' performance has remained poor at all ends, this is evident by the Supreme Audit Institution of South Africa (Khunoethe et al., 2021; Mkhize et al. 2021) and the South African Public Service Commission (Mello, 2020). The Audit institution is the only institution that has the authority to audit and report publicly on how government (at the national, provincial and local government levels) is using taxpayers' money and performing (Auditor General of South Africa (AGSA), 2020). The AGSA's reports compiled annually have long pointed to the poor performance of institutions (Mafolo, 2012; Magoro, 2015; Khunoethe et al., 2021).

South Africa when compared to its counterparts in sub-Saharan Africa has the necessary regulations and legislative frameworks in place, and a PM approach that is seen as somehow fully-fledged, however, it has not been able to enjoy benefits like Western developed countries. This is because of the contextual challenges in which the PM and systems exist considering that PM manifests differently and produces varying outcomes in countries around the world (Khunoethe et al. 2021, p.181). In South Africa, studies have found that in PM both internally and externally in bureaucracies, there is a lack of understanding of PM and what it entails. Accountability is another issue, which has been perceived as shifting around within units in bureaucracies or public agencies and resulting in its lack of ownership due to also the shifting of PM responsibilities. Across the public service in the country, the latter is tired of the lack of proper knowledge borne of limited or lack of understanding as well as low awareness. There remains also a lack of training of bureaucratic staff and proper policy compliance, with varying attitudes towards PM and PMSs, with mostly negative perceptions. Dissatisfaction is rife but there are limited positive attitudes. There is also non-alignment of policy documents, performance contracts relating to the operations of bureaucracies, and the desired institutional operations that may contribute to its ideal performance because of misalignment at varied levels (see Makasi, 2022; Khunoethe et al., 2021; Sambo & van der Waldt, 2022; Thobejane et al., 2022).

Studies by Mkhize et al. (2021) and Hadebe (2021) point to that unit supervisors in bureaucracies view PM as the responsibility of the HR unit hence the lack or limit of their ownership of the EPMDS. This has led to communication and commitment challenges between bureaucrats – from street, low, mid-level and high-level bureaucrats in these public agencies. Furthermore, this points to issues relating to a lack of appropriate communication (Moodley, 2016). Nonetheless, Mkhize, et al. (2021) note that the reason for this might be that the PM challenges are because of a PMS that is manual – paper-based, and the causes of an ineffective PMS are interconnected. Mkhize, et al. (2021) finding and of view that:

> "...to be truly result orientated and produce reliable performance information" ...the "PMS should move away from being manual, by integrating it with Information and Communication Technology" (p. 95).

When looking at performance from the angle of managing it, the use of PMSs and monitoring and evaluation therein, what is also is important are indicators because they are key to observing impact and or effectiveness in organisations. PM is led by top management, and its contribution to achieving the goals of any organisation is tied to that (Turner et al. 2004; Pulakos, & O'Leary, 2011; Khunoethe et al., 2021). This is behind a backdrop that points that PM and PMSs seem to be only implemented for regulatory compliance by bureaucrats (Mkhize et al., 2021), and managers not only lack or have a limited understanding of PM and PMSs (Makasi, 2022; Moodley, 2016; Khunoethe et al., 2021; Hadebe, 2021). Also, possessing adequate knowledge of monitoring and evaluating (M&E) performance, is necessary to take advantage of the benefits of such systems for managing performance (Govender & Reddy, 2014). Technological advancements relating to ICT, and the digitalisation of PM can play a key role in addressing the lack of adequate knowledge of M&E of performance.

In 2012, the South African Local Government Association (SALGA) released a document titled, 'A Municipal Guide/Roadmap to Successful ICT Governance'. One of its anticipated objectives is to raise the profile of ICT as a strategic enabler for effective administration and service delivery in the country (SALGA, 2021). PM and PMS challenges in South Africa undermine effective administration and ultimately service delivery. A digital ICT-enabled PM system would play a meaningful role and contribute towards addressing the challenges in the country's public sector. This argument builds up from a long-standing belief and call, that of Makasi (2011); Mello (2020); and aMkhize et al. (2021), of a new way ICT technological advancement to capture, record and use performance information with the aid of improving service delivery. Hadebe (2021) recommends an online PM and system at national and provincial levels in South Africa with a view that "an electronic automated system to be linked with all other existing ICT systems in the department, more specifically to the PERSAL system (Personal and Salary System)" - a standardized Human Resource and Payroll system. Also, other challenges related to PM are conducted inconsistently and erratically and PMSs are monetary driven, abused and seen as not used fairly (Vezi, 2017; Mkhize et al., 2021). PM being monetary driven has long been known (Makasi, 2011) and the inconsistency, erratic manner in which it is approached, the abuse and unfair use which undermine the EPMDSs purpose.

The theoretical underpinning of this study is NPM, which has long been and remains fiercely debated at either end, by both critics and advocates (see Hood & Jackson, 1992; Flynn, 2002; Osborne, 2010; Mthuli et al., 2023b), the study does not advocate for NPM but rather borrows a key principle from NPM, that of learning from the private sector. NPM while it emerged from Public Administration (PA) theory and has been seen as a transitionary phase now manifesting in the form of New Public Governance (NPG), with Osborne (2010) pointing to this transitionary phase from PA to NPG. Some have viewed today, what is now termed 'digital era governance or DEG' as having superseded NPM, with NPM declared to be dead and 'DEG' replacing it but this is possibly debatable (Dunleavy et al. 2005 as cited in de Vries, 2016, p.303).

This study however borrows from the private sector its HRM ways of employee performance evaluation today enabled by ICT to improve firm performance from productivity gains, which Bourke and Crowley (2015) found evidence of. These systems are or might not necessarily be new because they might have been in existence in the private sector for a while and from the previous industrial revolution – the Third Industrial Revolution (Hoogervorst, Koopman & Flier, 2002; Piabuo, Piendiah, Njamnshi, & Tieguhong, 2017). However, there is caution in adopting outdated systems from the private sector – to avoid one of the hazards of the NPM movement. The digitalisation of performance evaluation has been dubbed e-performance management to increase efficiency, and consistency for real-time performance data, evaluation, and feedback (Amudavi, 2018), is just one of the necessary reforms vital to ensuring effective and efficient policy implementation and public service delivery in South Africa. However, might not be the only panacea for its policy implementation and public service delivery ills but one critical competent today to addressing the issue. After varied policy, legislative and regulatory interventions to ensure ideal performance PSOs in the country (Mkhize et al. 2021; Khunoethe et al., 2021; Mthuli, Singh & Reddy, 2022; Mthuli et al., 2023a).

PSOs in South Africa are in a constantly fast-changing environment resulting in uncertainty, also borne of a liberal democratic political system, a bureaucratic machinery not ideally fit for purpose and challenged by many issues, one being the full adoption – integration of ICTs for ideal performance. The poor performance of PSOs is one shortcoming and the uncertainty of the fast-changing environment, borne of the re-emergence and rapid growth of political competitiveness – fierce political markets. Which have somehow proven problematic for local policy implementation and public service delivery. This somehow might be seen as a crisis but signals an opportunity and a drive for the digital transformation of employee performance evaluation in PSOs in the country.

Pockets of Excellence in Digital Transformation: Cases in the Developed World

Public sector agencies in their day-to-day practices are expected to leverage the latest IT innovations to sustain productivity, more so in the developed world. In the developed world, in countries such as the United States of America (USA), while public service productivity remains on legacy systems, agencies such as the Federal Communications Commission (FCC), are overhauling their legacy systems (Desouza et al., 2019). This embracing digitalisation through intelligent automation for institutional performance through the use of artificial intelligence (AI) and robotics (Coombs, Hislop, Taneva & Barnard, 2020; Vrontis et al., 2022). Khawaja and Khalid (2022) point to that in high-performing governments in the USA, the lessons are:

- The crucial role that technical developments and systems play in allowing the delivery of public services with the help of digital tools and systems; and
- Governmental systems that respond quickly and effectively while providing public services have effective decision-support systems to facilitate better planning and decision-making.

Technologies such as AI have been argued to offer a myriad of improvements in how we work and live but with a dark side in its use (Mikalef et al., 2022). Furthermore, Mikalef et al. (2022) state that AI has been featured in promoting societal well-being, particularly in government, by regulatory agencies. According to a study by Rinta-Kahila et al. (2021), the destructive effects of algorithmic decision-making in public services cause distress to citizens and employees, as well as financial damage which they found on a welfare agency. Mikalef et al. (2022) highlight empirical evidence of the dark aspects of AI and big data analysis in private organisations, governments, and society but also point to big data enabling faster, smarter, and more personal government services (Yiu, 2012). This indicates that there are both pros and cons of technology adoption.

Similarly, in the European Union (EU) digital transformation has been sought to navigate crises external to PSOs, such as the European sovereign debt crisis of 2008, and the COVID-19 outbreak and these had a direct impact on PSOs and their business (Profiroiu et al., 2023). The EU's digital decade revolves around four key points: skills, infrastructure, government, and business, to empower businesses and governance systems and people in a human-centred, sustainable and more prosperous digital future (Androniceanu et al., 2022).

In the developed world, the IoT is an emerging technology that will be also key to the realisation of smart public services (Velsberg, Westergren & Jonsson, 2020) and IoT technology, if extended to the public sector, would affect almost every public service and significantly improve processes and human efficiency (Tomar & Kaur, 2019). Innovations relating to HRM have included the Internet of Things (IoT) for which information is the backbone linked to improvements in employee performance. There is still a limited holistic understanding of the impact of the use of IoT innovations in HRM and improving employee performance (Vrontis et al., 2022, also see Strohmeier, 2020). However, what has the potential to change various HR practices is electronic performance monitoring (EPM), including evaluation with algorithmic technologies with the potential to help employers evaluate, direct and discipline workers (Kellogg, Valentine, & Christin, 2020).

Overall, in the developed world great strides have been reached in terms of technological advancements in both private and government business. For example, Government-to-employee (G2E), the reorganizing of internal operations using a computer system to ensure greater efficiency, in this case, processing PM-related forms online instead of being paper-based (de Vries, 2016). Considering that by the mid-2000s, scholars such as Pulakos (2004) observed that the employee performance evaluation process involved a considerable amount of writing, exchange of paperwork and documents, with both employees and managers spending their PM time pushing paper rather than discussing performance issues and development.

The developing world can learn considerably from the developed world's experiences in automating systems in the public sector, thus freeing resources that are much needed. Hence, there are many ways that automation can ease PM, which can result in resource-saving, such as time and the overall administrative burden which has been known for decades (Pulakos, 2004; Dobson, Myles & Jackson, 2007; Veale & Brass, 2019). While there remains what is seen as a lack of a comprehensive understanding of the impact of the use of technologies on Human Resource Management (HRM) at both organizational and individual levels, African countries should borrow lessons and best practices for their implementation of digitalisation in performance evaluation in PSOs so to improve individual and organisational performance and overall PM.

RESEARCH METHODOLOGY

The study exploring the digitalisation of employee performance evaluation in public sector human resource management in South Africa adopted a qualitative design informed by inductive reasoning. This involved collecting and analysing secondary data in the public domain and from open databases such as Google Scholar and Taylor and Francis search engines, Science Direct to facilitate a qualitative content analysis (Mthuli, 2018; Mthuli, Singh & Ruffin, 2022). The qualitative analysis enabled a systematic evaluation of the literature (Du Plooy-Cilliers, Davis & Bezuitenhout, 2014; Mthuli et al., 2023a; Mthuli et al., 2023b), identifying and synthesizing the literature to understand and analyse the specified characteristics of messages and reaching a conclusion with regards to understanding the digitalisation of employees performance evaluation and whether this provides a panacea for improving performance evaluation through a digitalised EPMDS in South Africa's public sector HRM.

FINDINGS AND DISCUSSION

This section unpacks the chapter findings derived from analysing key documents and peer-reviewed literature.

EPMDS as a Panacea for Performance Evaluation in Public Sector HRM

A digital EPMDS makes use of portals to store employees' records which employees can also store, retrieve and amend, if need be, as well as allowing them to access other PM-related data and receive feedback from line managers. This can also aid in addressing the superficial and non-SMART performance indicators, and an overall PM system that does not have a positive impact (Khunoethe et al., 2021, p.181). Non-SMART policies result in failures in basic service delivery, legal compliance, organisational policies, procedures, systems, and governance which contributes to poor performance overall, which has been observed in the local sphere of government in the country (Parliamentary Monitoring Group [PMG] 2020; Khunoethe et al. 2021). Noting Mulgan & Albury's (2003) view, what has traditionally been a problem with public sector innovation management is compliance-based box ticking exercises.

Like innovations in the participatory governance system in South Africa relating to the use of ICT platforms aimed at deepening the country's democracy but failing (Khanyile et al., 2021). The same can be cautioned on the digitalisation of employee performance evaluation in the county's public service at the varied levels (local, provincial, and national), where it might be threatened internally and externally because it would represent change. This is because change usually faces resistance and a lack of commitment, and it has been observed that:

> "...public sector innovation requires sufficient management capabilities and robust technology strategies, along with a willingness to explore and adopt new work practices rather than simply implement emerging technologies" (Velsberg, Westergren & Jonsson, 2020, p.350).

Establishing a digital EPMDS ensures accurate and safe personnel performance baseline information, which this critical in increasing accountability and productivity, to improve overall service delivery. More so because in the public sector goals are more diverse and harder to measure than in the private sector (Lapuente & Van de Walle, 2020) and monitor and track meaningful progress while constantly evaluating it too. A digital EPMDS therefore ensures the electronic archiving of document information, once digitized, can be searched and accessed anytime, in real time, anywhere simplifying procedures and efficiency. This is supported by Vrontis et al. (2022p. 1237), where intelligent automation technologies constitute a new approach to managing employees and enhancing firm performance, thus offering several opportunities for HRM this directly tied to job performance.

The digitalisation of performance data would increasingly assist supervisors and or managers at the varied levels of the bureaucracy to observe and or monitor in real-time, to assess the unit and or institutional performance, by opening the room for performance assessments and an increase in audits at individual and the organizational level. Furthermore, considering that an individual's performance is connected directly or indirectly to policies and or programmes, this data ought to evaluate policies and programs and lead to accountability. This thereby also contributes to evidence-based policymaking which is difficult (Lapuente & Van de Walle, 2020). More so in both the developing and developing world but remaining a novel trend in public policy analysis because policies fail to achieve their intended goals or are either ineffective and inefficient or both in solving problems (de Vries, 2016).

Worth noting is that there remains a growing discussion regarding the monitoring and control of online digital platforms (Parra et al., 2021). Like but not as severe in the EU (Profiroiu, 2023), there remain gaps and discrepancies in the field of digitalisation of public administration in South Africa and hence the digitalisation of bureaucrats' performance evaluation is one step towards closing that gap. A web-based or web-enabled performance measurement and evaluation system in the South African bureaucracy is ideal. This is long established in the private sector, and ought to make a meaningful contribution towards a panacea for policy implementation and public service delivery ills in the country. More so because Nurlina, Situmorang, Akob, Quilim, & Arfah (2020) observed that an e-HRM is a facility for management and employees to be more effective and efficient in measuring organizational performance, which can play a critical role in limiting or removing biases which have been perceived as evident in PM evaluations in South Africa's public sector (Vezi, 2017; Mkhize et al., 2021).

This study argues that the digitalisation of performance evaluation in PSOs is not a silver bullet but can contribute to improving performance and informing decision-making, including in institutions where employee performance evaluations tend to result in biases, mistrust, and the lack of perceived fairness. It may also help to address the lack of transparency and accountability and the existence of the 'blame game' which negatively affects policy implementation and service delivery of PSOs. Nevertheless, digitalisation ought to be "not an end goal, but a means to greater organisational effectiveness and stakeholder satisfaction" (Chapano, Mey, & Werner, 2023, p.12). Overall, not much is known about the value derived from the digitalisation of organisations, the adoption and use of e-HRM in South Africa could enhance bureaucracy and public service delivery performance.

Digitalisation of Employee Performance Evaluation to Advance Public Sector HRM

The critical examination of documents has shown that in South Africa, Human Resource and Development (HRD) units in state Departments at the National and Provincial government levels, support and ensure EPMDS cooperation among stakeholders - managers, supervisors and employees (Department of Public Service and Administration/DPSA, 2007). The EPMDS and PMDS (Performance Management and Development System) remain a source of contention in South Africa. At the local government level, it's called the PMDS, in municipalities which also need to operate optimally. A study by Kariuki and Reddy (2017) found that municipalities' evaluation capacity is usually low, and the local authorities are not inadequately resourced with competent monitoring and evaluation of human personnel in the country. The South African policymakers have answered the call for the digitalisation of performance evaluations in the public sector.

The PM call is the implementation of an online performance management and development system (PMDS) for heads of departments. Eventually issued by the Minister of the Public Service and Administration (MPSA) in terms of Regulation 88 of the Public Service Regulation (PSR) (2016). This directive requires all directors-general and heads of departments to utilise the online PMS (performance management systems) developed by the National Department of Planning Monitoring and Evaluation, with compulsory effect from the 2021/2022 performance cycle (DPSA, 2021). Arguably, this strategic intervention can be seen as a step in the right direction and an important catalyst for rethinking, accelerating, and implementing a fully digitalised employee performance evaluation system for advancing public service delivery in South Africa. Considering the sluggish adoption of digitalised HRM in the South African public and private sectors, Chapano, Mey, & Werner (2023) argue that, the value derived in the digitalisation for the latter is at operational, relational and transformational levels. This relates to keeping employees' data up to date through the HR website, supporting business processes and aligning the HR function to organisational strategies respectively.

A digital EPMDS or the PMDS ought to be the first phase in South Africa, an electronic performance monitoring (EPM), a forward-looking and optimistic view of how IT can shape the public sector, that would also direct South Africa's public sector smartness. Digitalisation is vital in bureaucracies for performance to be monitored in real-time and this improves policy implementation and service delivery. This is supported by Pulakos (2004), Bourke and Crowley (2015) and Amudavi (2018), who assert that PM workflow can greatly be facilitated by automation, substantially decrease the paperwork associated with the process and result in productivity gains if supported by investments in ICT. Furthermore, they highlight that the evaluations of automated PMSs show that such is viewed positively by both employees and managers. It streamlines PM, provides a standardized structured approach to the collecting and storing of performance data in real-time, provides feedback, reduces the workload because a paper-based PM is a heavily administrative process, and overall ensures widespread access to PM tools (Pulakos, 2004; Bourke & Crowley, 2015; Amudavi, 2018). This would enable strategic public sector management on the side of government which puts digital governance, whether e-government, e-services, or m-government at the centre of realizing a just society, social justice and contributing to just administrative action in the country. Considering the link between strategic management and public sector performance (Poister, 2010), a digital EPMDS can be seen as a first step in embracing not only the current revolution or the 4IR, but the previous one as well and this is a solid and first step towards intelligent automation of HRM at an organizational, individual, and employee level in South Africa's public service.

Digitalisation of Performance Evaluation to Enhance Data Governance

With the advancements in digitalising public sector HRM alluded to in literature, there are benefits such as improved data governance that could be realised through the utilisation of modern digital technologies and innovations. Digitalising public sector HRM challenges PSOs to uphold, data governance which Mikalef et al. (2022) confirm states "the age of AI which also imposes additional requirements around privacy and data protection, protecting against unauthorised access to data and ensuring that data is of high quality and integral". It can be argued that data governance is a critical element that HR managers need to take into consideration as it underscores the whole adoption of digital technologies to ensure public records are kept safe from hackers on any external and harmful elements. Research done in South Africa revealed the need to protect performance management and evaluation data quality and integrity. This is critical to avoid stakeholder scrutiny or criticism over the lack of quality, the design and assessment of performance in bureaucracies as well as the reliability of assessment information (Mkhize et al., 2021; Khunoethe et al., 2021). While the chapter explores more on performance evaluation, other crucial aspects around data governance can create ample opportunities for further research in South Africa and the rest of the sub-Saharan region to draw similarities and differences in the complexities being experienced so that evidence-based solutions can be sought to enhance public sector e-HRM.

Performance Evaluation and Efficiency in Public Sector HRM

Implementing performance evaluation in the public sector rests on the need to render public services adequately. The role of HRM in the public sector becomes fundamental to the reconfiguration and redirecting of skills development programmes to embrace changes triggered by digital transformation. Proper information dissemination has long been recognized as crucial to the management of the information and systems therein (Du Toit et al. 1998). The study by Thomas et al. (2019) confirms that information in public sector organisations should satisfy criteria, to value in the development and implementation of performance evaluation systems. As important that all public institutions have a management information system (MIS). Alvarenga et al. (2020) reiterate that such actions help to control *inter alia* to keep personnel, financial and financial resources, use records to not only comply with government regulations but also align data management practices with government agencies' goals including advancing knowledge on enhancing service delivery. In their study, Vrontis et al. (2022), argue that technological innovations and other information technologies offer several benefits (cost savings, harmonization and integration of HR activities, efficiency, and support strategy (but ought to also be underpinned by data management that leads to knowledge advancements and improvement in service delivery. Drawn from the literature analysis are the intricacies of digitalising performance evaluation without adequately and comprehensively conscientising public officials. This argument is derived from the fact that adopting modern technologies could advance public sector HRM through IoT or AI however Chapano, Mey & Werner (2023) warn that employees need to be prepared to embrace technological advancement that helps improve efficiency and effectiveness in service delivery.

CONCLUSION

This study chapter explored the digitalisation of employee performance evaluation in South Africa's public sector human resource management. The analysis was extended to examining the contribution of performance evaluations addressing public service delivery ills in public sector organisations. Understanding how digital transformation could be efficiently implemented helps in exploring the alternative and modern digital technologies and ICTs that have a positive bearing on improving service delivery in public sector organisations. The analysis of document understanding is critical in the digital transformation of South Africa's public sector HRM for improving and sustaining PSO performance. More so in a country where the performance of PSOs has become a wicked policy problem. The findings for this chapter affirm that employee performance evaluation in the South African public sector, is outdated, which is a clarion call for lawmakers to embrace digital transformation that could be an enabler for public sector HRM to implement change within the performance evaluation including recruitment and selection of public officials. Further, the study noted that although policy documents call for the improvement of service delivery by integrating ICTs and other related technological advancements, more still needs to be done to reinforce and empower public sector HRM to become responsive to the demand of the latest technological innovations. Arguably embracing digital transformation in South Africa's public sector HRM can be a step further in fully digitalisation of employee performance evaluation, which is key in enhancing public sector performance. As noted further in the findings, the implementation of an e-HRM, a web-enabled performance measurement and evaluation system for all employees in PSOs in the country could add value and a positive impact to public sector HRM despite the limited attention provided to this in literature. Although the merits of enhancing performance evaluation through digitalisation have been noted in the study findings, the negative and unintended consequences of modern technologies need to be explored. In this sense, future research can explore how public sector institutions can navigate digital transformation in the public sector while striking a balance to address some of the existing bureaucratic challenges that may act as hindrances to embracing technological innovations in South Africa.

REFERENCES

AGSA [Auditor General of South Africa] (2020). *Our Vision*. Available at https://www.agsa.co.za/AboutUs/OurVision.aspx (last accessed 20 January 2024).

Amudavi, E. L. (2018). Revolutionary Impact of the Advancement of Information Communication Technology (ICT) on the HRM Function. *International Journal of Innovative Information Systems & Technology Research*, 6(2), 1–7.

Androniceanu, A., Georgescu, I., & Sabie, O. M. (2022). The impact of digitalization on public administration, economic development, and well-being in the EU countries. *Central. European.Public Administration Review*, 20(2), 9–31.

Bal, Y., Bozkurt, S., & Ertemsir, E. (2022). The importance of using human resources information systems (HRIS) and a research on determining the success of HRIS. In *Strategic Human Resource Management at Tertiary Level* (pp. 197-209). River Publishers

Benbunan-Fich, R., Desouza, K. C., & Andersen, K. N. (2020). IT-enabled innovation in the public sector: Introduction to the special issue. *European Journal of Information Systems*, 29(4), 323–328. 10.1080/0960085X.2020.1814989

Biyela, A. C., Nzimakwe, T. I., Mthuli, S. A., & Khambule, I. (2018). Assessing the role of intergovernmental relations in strategic planning for economic development at local government level: A case study of Umkhanyakude District Municipality. *Journal of Gender* [JGIDA]. *Information and Development in Africa*, 7(2), 221–239. 10.31920/2050-4284/2018/v7n2a11

Bourke, J., & Crowley, F. (2015). The role of HRM and ICT complementarities in firm innovation: Evidence from transition economies. *International Journal of Innovation Management*, 19(05), 1550054. 10.1142/S1363919615500541

Chapano, M., Mey, M. R., & Werner, A. (2023). Value Derived from Digitalised Human Resource Management: Perspectives from South Africa. [-pages.]. *African Journal of Employee Relations*, 47, 29. 10.25159/2664-3731/10914

Coombs, C., Hislop, D., Taneva, S. K., & Barnard, S. (2020). The strategic impacts of Intelligent Automation for knowledge and service work: An interdisciplinary review. *The Journal of Strategic Information Systems*, 29(4), 101600. 10.1016/j.jsis.2020.101600

De Vries, M. S. (2016). *Understanding public administration*. Bloomsbury Publishing. 10.1007/978-1-137-57546-3

Department of Public Service and Administration (DPSA). (2007) Employee performance management and development System. Available from: https://www.dpsa.gov.za/dpsa2g/documents/ep/2007/EPMDS .pdf (Accessed: 11 May 2024).

Department of Public Service and Administration (DPSA). (2021). Employment practice. Available from: https://www.dpsa.gov.za/dpsa2g/documents/sms/2021/sms_30_06_2021.pdf (Accessed: 11 May 2024).

Desouza, K. C., Denford, J. S., & Krishnamurthy, R. (2019). How the US federal communications commission managed the process of IT modernization. In Urbach, N., & Röglinger, M. (Eds.), *Digitalization cases. Management for professionals* (pp. 411–428). Springer., 10.1007/978-3-319-95273-4_22

Dobson, P., Myles, J., & Jackson, P. (2007). Making the case for critical realism: Examining the implementation of automated performance management systems. [IRMJ]. *Information Resources Management Journal*, 20(2), 138–152. 10.4018/irmj.2007040109

Du Plooy-Cilliers, D., & Davis, C. (2014). *C & Bezuidenhout. Research matters* (1st ed.). Juta and Company Ltd.

Du Toit, D.F.P., van der Waldt, G., Bayat, M.S & Cheminais, J. (1998). *Public Administration and Management for effective governance*. Juta & Co Ltd: Kenwyn – South Africa.

Flynn, N. (2002). *Public Sector Management*. Prentice Hall.

Govender, I. G., & Reddy, P. S. (2014). Monitoring and Evaluation in Local Municipalities: A Case Study of KwaZulu-Natal Province. *Administration Publica*, 22(4), 160–177.

Hadebe, T. P. S. (2021). *Employee performance management and development system at the Kwa-Zulu Natal Provincial Department of Public Works*. Thesis (MPA)-Stellenbosch University, Available from: https://scholar.sun.ac.za/server/api/core/bitstreams/fabd4c7a-1ca1-44b7-9621-a5c0a5507742/content (Accessed 25 February 2024).

Hague, R., Harrop, M., & McCormick, J. (2019). *Comparative government and politics* (11th ed.). Red Globe Press.

Halid, H., Halim, S. N. A., & Ravesangar, K. (2022). Human resource management practices in the digital era. In *Technological Challenges: The Human Side of the Digital Age* (pp. 109–158). Springer International Publishing. 10.1007/978-3-030-98040-5_5

Halid, H., Yusoff, Y. M., & Somu, H. (2020, May). The relationship between digital human resource management and organizational performance. In *First ASEAN Business, Environment, and Technology Symposium (ABEATS 2019)* (pp. 96-99). Atlantis Press. 10.2991/aebmr.k.200514.022

Hood, C., & Jackson, M. (1992). *The New Public Management: A recipe for disaster*. In: Hazard Management and Emergency planning: Perspectives on Britain. London – James and James.

Hoogervorst, J. A., Koopman, P. L., & Flier, H. V. D. (2002). Human resource strategy for the new ICT-driven business context. *International Journal of Human Resource Management*, 13(8), 1245–1265. 10.1080/09585190210149501

Kariuki, P., & Reddy, P. (2017). Operationalising an effective monitoring and evaluation system for local government: Considerations for best practice. *African Evaluation Journal*, 5(2), 1–8. 10.4102/aej.v5i2.240

Kellogg, K., Valentine, M., & Christin, A. (2020). Algorithms at work: The new contested terrain of control. *The Academy of Management Annals*, 14(1), 366–410. 10.5465/annals.2018.0174

Khanyile, M., Nzimakwe, T.I. & Mthuli, S.A. (2021). Challenges of Innovations in Participatory Governance in uMshwathi Local Municipality in Kwazulu-Natal. *Journal of Public Administration, 56*(4.1), 972-985.

Khawaja, S., & Khalid, S. U. (2022). Retooling governance for improving public service delivery: Case study of right to public services commission, Khyber Pakhtunkhwa – Pakistan. *Governance: An International Journal of Policy, Administration and Institutions*, 35(2), 421–436. 10.1111/gove.12607

Khunoethe, H., Reddy, P. S., & Mthuli, S. A. (2021). Performance Management and the Integrated Development Plan of the Msunduzi Municipality in South Africa. *NISPAcee Journal of Public Administration and Policy*, 14(2), 161–187. 10.2478/nispa-2021-0019

Lapuente, V., & van de Walle, S. (2020). The effects of new public management on the quality of public services. *Governance: An International Journal of Policy, Administration and Institutions*, 33(3), 461–475. 10.1111/gove.12502

Magoro, P. (2015). Performance Management Agreements for Senior Managers in the Makhuduthamaga Local Municipality: A Case of Their Usage in Service Delivery. *Journal of Public Administration*, 50(si-1), 700–711.

Makasi, S. S. (2022). *Perspectives on the implementation of the Performance Management and Development System in the Department of Social Development in Eastern Cape*. Masters of Public Administration, University of the Western Cape. Available from: https://etd.uwc.ac.za/bitstream/handle/11394/3029/Makas_MPA_2011.pdf?sequence=1 (Accessed: 25 February 2024).

Mello, D. M. (2015). Performance management and development system in the South African public service: A critical review. *Journal of Public Administration*, 50(si-1), 688–699.

Mello, D. M. (2020). Exploring the use of information and communication technology in the implementation of a performance management and development system in the South African public service. *African Journal of Governance and Development*, 9(2), 585–598.

Mikalef, P., Conboy, K., Lundström, J. E., & Popovič, A. (2022). Thinking responsibly about responsible AI and 'the dark side' of AI. *European Journal of Information Systems*, 31(3), 257–268. 10.1080/0960085X.2022.2026621

Mkhize, L. N., Nzimakwe, T. I., & Mthuli, S. A. (2021). Bureaucrats' views on performance management in a KwaZulu-Natal Provincial Government Department. *Administratio Publica*, 21(1), 83–101.

Mofolo, M. (2012). Strengthening performance management system implementation in South African municipalities. *Africa's Public Service Delivery & Performance Review*, 1(1), 73–86. 10.4102/apsdpr.v1i1.25

Moodley, M. (2016). *Employee performance management and development system at King Edward V111 hospital as a tool for service delivery*. Master of Business Administration, University of KwaZulu-Natal. Available from: https://researchspace.ukzn.ac.za/server/api/core/bitstreams/2dbf411e-e12d-407a-b940-41d369f13bf3/content (Accessed: 25 February 2024).

Mthuli, S., Singh, N., & Reddy, p. (2022). Political leadership for improved. *Lessons from Political Leadership in Africa: Towards Inspirational and Transformational Leaders*, 15.

Mthuli, S., Singh, N., & Reddy, P. (2023b). Eroding efficiency and effectiveness: the impact of corruption on public sector performance in South Africa. In *The Nexus between Poverty and Corruption: Quo Vadis?* (pp.153. 176). Cambridge Scholars Publishing.

Mthuli, S. A. (2018). *A Systems thinking exploration of the challenges facing Maritime Education and Training: The case of public higher education institutions in KwaZulu-Natal* (Doctoral dissertation, University of KwaZulu-Natal). Available at: https://researchspace.ukzn.ac.za/items/be891477-102b-4d1f-b66d-b5675dc45d18 (Accessed: 6 May 2024).

Mthuli, S. A., Ruffin, F., & Singh, N. (2022). Define, Explain, Justify, Apply'(DEJA): An analytic tool for guiding qualitative research sample size. *International Journal of Social Research Methodology*, 25(6), 809–821. 10.1080/13645579.2021.1941646

Mthuli, S. A., Singh, N., & Reddy, P. S. (2023a). Political Leadership and *Ubuntu* for Public Sector Performance in South Africa. In *African Leadership: Powerful Paradigms for the 21st Century* (pp. 27-43). Emerald Publishing Limited.

Mulgan, G., & Albury, D. (2003). Innovation in the public sector. Strategy Unit, Cabinet Office, *1*(1), 40-. Available from: https://www.urban-response.org/system/files/content/resource/files/main/innovation-in-the-public-sector.pdf (Accessed: 25 February 2024).

Nurlina, N., Situmorang, J., Akob, M., Quilim, C. A., & Arfah, A. (2020). Influence of e-HRM and human resources service quality on employee performance. *The Journal of Asian Finance. Economics and Business*, 7(10), 391–399.

Nzimakwe, T. I. (2012). Transforming the public service through e-government: Challenges for the future. *Africanus*, 42(1), 56–68.

Nzimakwe, T. I. (2015). Adopting Innovation Strategies to Enhance Service Delivery. *Administratio Publica*, 23(2), 57–72.

Nzimakwe, T. I. (2018). Mobile technology innovations for improved governance and enhanced service delivery in South Africa. *Administratio Publica*, 26(4), 115–132.

Nzimakwe, T. I., & Pillay, P. (2010). Information and communication technology. *Administratio Publica*, 18(1), 124–138.

Osborne, D., & Gaebler, T. (1992). *Reinventing Government: How the Entrepreneurial Spirit is Transforming the Public Sector*. Addison Wesley.

Osborne, S. P. (2006). The new public governance? *Public Management Review*, 8(3), 377–387. 10.1080/14719030600853022

Osborne, S. P. (2010). *The New Public Governance? Emerging perspectives on the theory and practice of public governance*. Routledge. 10.4324/9780203861684

Pantelidis, I. (2019). Digital human resource management. In *Human Resource Management in the Hospitality Industry* (pp. 337–352). Routledge. 10.4324/9780429441400-21

Parkar, A., Srivastava, A., Kaur, A., Geo, A., Bandopadhyay, S., & Sinha, P. (2021). Digitization in Human Resource-Literature Review and Future Research Agenda. *SAMVAD*, 22(0), 21–29. 10.53739/samvad/2021/v22/164043

Parliamentary Monitoring Group [PMG]. (2020). *Report on Intervention in Msunduzi Local Municipality*. Available at https://pmg.org.za/tabled-committee-report/595/ (last accessed 20 January 2024).

Parra, C. M., Gupta, M., & Mikalef, P. (2021). Information and communication technologies (ICT)-enabled severe moral communities and how the (Covid19) pandemic might bring new ones. *International Journal of Information Management*, 57, 102271. 10.1016/j.ijinfomgt.2020.102271

Pearse, N. J., & Williams, Q. W. (2009). Organizational Culture and the Implementation of Performance Management. *Administratio Publica*, 17(1), 28–42.

Phahlane, M. M. (2023). Electronic Human Resource Management (e-HRM) in a South African Organization. In *Enhancing Employee Engagement and Productivity in the Post-Pandemic Multigenerational Workforce* (pp. 156-170). IGI Global

Piabuo, S. M., Piendiah, N. E., Njamnshi, N. L., & Tieguhong, P. J. (2017). The impact of ICT on the efficiency of HRM in Cameroonian enterprises: Case of the Mobile telephone industry. *Journal of Global Entrepreneurship Research*, 7(1), 7. 10.1186/s40497-017-0063-5

Poister, T. H. (2010). The Future of Strategic Planning in the Public Sector: Linking Strategic Management and Performance. *Public Administration Review*, 70(s1), s246–s254. 10.1111/j.1540-6210.2010.02284.x

Profiroiu, C. M., Negoi ă, C. I., & Costea, A. V. (2023). Digitalization of public administration in EU member states in times of crisis: The contributions of the national recovery and resilience plans. *International Review of Administrative Sciences*, 90(2), 336–352. 10.1177/00208523231177554

Pulakos, E. D. (2004). *Performance Management: A roadmap for developing, implementing and evaluating performance management systems*. Society for Human Resource Management (SHRM) Foundation: United States of America.

Pulakos, E. D., & O'Leary, R. S. (2011). Why is performance management broken? *Industrial and Organizational Psychology: Perspectives on Science and Practice*, 4(2), 146–164. 10.1111/j.1754-9434.2011.01315.x

Ranson, S., & Stewart, J. (1994). *Management for the Public Domain: Enabling the Learning Society*. Macmillan Press Ltd. 10.1007/978-1-349-23787-6

Reddy, P., Nemec, J., & de Vries, M. S. (2015). The State of Local Government. *Public Policy and Administration*, 14(3), 160–176. 10.5755/j01.ppaa.14.3.13430

SALGA [South African Local Government Association] (2012). A Municipal Guide/Roadmap to successful ICT governance. Available at: https://www.salga.org.za/Documents/Municipalities/Municipla%20 Focus/Municipal%20ICT/SALGA_ICT-Governance-Guidelines_revised_June2012_v1_2.pdf Accessed 23 January 24.

Sambo, N. M., & van der Waldt, G. (2022). A strategic framework for Public Performance Management and Development System implementation: The case of the National Department of Human Settlements. *Administratio Publica*, 30(2), 86–107.

Škudienė, V., Vezeliene, G., & Stangej, O. (2020). Transforming human resource management: innovative e-HRM value creation for multinational companies. In *Innovation Management* (pp. 140–166). Edward Elgar Publishing. 10.4337/9781789909814.00021

Strohmeier, S. (2020). Smart HRM–A Delphi Study on the application and consequences of the internet of things in human resource management. *International Journal of Human Resource Management*, 31(18), 2289–2230. 10.1080/09585192.2018.1443963

Thobejane, G., van der Heever, H., & Mokgatle, M. (2022). Knowledge, Understanding and Satisfaction with the Implementation of the Performance Management System at a District Hospital in the Madibeng Subdistrict, South Africa. *International Journal of Environmental Research and Public Health*, 19(1), 14461. 10.3390/ijerph19211446136361341

Thomas, M. A., Cipolla, J., Lambert, B., & Carter, L. (2019). Data management maturity assessment of public sector agencies. *Government Information Quarterly*, 36(4), 101401. 10.1016/j.giq.2019.101401

Tomar, P., & Kaur, G. (2019). *Green and smart technologies for smart cities*. CRC Press. 10.1201/9780429454837

Turner, T. S., Creighton, S., Nudurupati, S., & Bititci, U. (2004). Implementing a Web enabled performance measurement system. *Measuring Business Excellence*, 8(2), 40–54. 10.1108/13683040410539427

Veale, M., & Brass, I. (2019). *Administration by Algorithm? Public Management Meets Public Sector Machine Learning* In: Algorithmic Regulation (Karen Yeung and Martin Lodge eds., Oxford University Press, 2019), Available at *SSRN*: https://ssrn.com/abstract=3375391

Velsberg, O., Westergren, U. H., & Jonsson, K. (2020). Exploring smartness in public sector innovation-creating smart public services with the Internet of Things. *European Journal of Information Systems*, 29(4), 350–368. 10.1080/0960085X.2020.1761272

Vezi, M. J. (2017). *Nurses' Perceptions of Employee Performance Management and Development System (EPMDS) at a selected hospital in Durban, eThekwini District in KwaZulu-Natal*. Master's Degree in Nursing Administration, University of KwaZulu-Natal. Available from: https://researchspace.ukzn.ac .za/server/api/core/bitstreams/7581b2e9-a4b9-46ac-90e3 a799952cf356/content (Accessed: 25 February 2024).

Vrontis, D., Christofi, M., Pereira, V., Tarba, S., Makrides, A., & Trichina, E. (2022). Artificial intelligence, robotics, advanced technologies and human resource management: A systematic review. *International Journal of Human Resource Management*, 33(6), 1237–1266. 10.1080/09585192.2020.1871398

Yiu, C. (2012). The big data opportunity: Making government faster, smarter and more personal. The Policy Exchange:London. Available at: http://ict-industry-reports.com.au/wp-content/uploads/sites/4/2013/05/2012-The-Big-Data-opportunity-in-Government-UK-Policy-Exchange-July-2012.pdf (Accessed: 09 May 2024).

Chapter 12
The Impact of Talent Retention and Management Practices on Service Delivery Outcomes in the South African Public Service

Thokozani Ian Nzimakwe
https://orcid.org/0000-0001-5817-9910
University of KwaZulu-Natal, South Africa

Sindy Olive Mbele
https://orcid.org/0009-0004-1296-9510
University of KwaZulu-Natal, South Africa

ABSTRACT

Talent management requires the identification of talented employees who work in the organisation. The South African public service continues to have a high concentration of an ageing workforce within its management and leadership occupational levels which poses a risk to business continuity. Poor recruitment practices linked to political interference have led to the appointment of inadequate leaders in key positions thus stifling leadership potential and service delivery outcomes. The South African public service aims to develop talent for service excellence which drives all talent-related initiatives within the organisation. This chapter explores variables such as compliance with regulatory provisions, talent acquisition, talent development, employee performance, digital hiring, digital workforce and succession planning, and digital transformation. Digital transformation influences human resource factors and contributes to enhancing productivity.

INTRODUCTION

The South African public service is operating under unprecedented political conditions and economic turbulence, it is increasingly difficult to attract and retain talented employees with scarce and critical skills leading to an adverse impact on service delivery. It is, therefore, imperative that during these tough times, the government develops a purposeful process for sourcing, attracting, engaging,

DOI: 10.4018/979-8-3693-2889-7.ch012

managing, developing, and retaining key talent. Capacity constraints within the public service could hamper economic growth, therefore effective talent management is a business imperative as a lack of necessary skills could have serious consequences for South Africa's economy. It points out that Human Resources (HR) practices as part of HR strategy can "have an impact on HR outcomes such as engagement, motivation, commitment and skills," which together, can affect organisational outputs in terms of high service delivery, quality, and community satisfaction. Critical talent is becoming increasingly scarce due to rapid economic growth whilst there is also a growing skills shortage, on the other hand, HR practices are a subject of controversy. To achieve the objectives of the National Development Plan (NDP), the South African government must cultivate, retain existing talent, and grow new talent rather than rely on recruitment alone. A Talent Management Strategy must be employed to provide a pool of managers/leaders and technical specialists in all fields where there is a critical shortage of skills (NDP, 2012). This chapter analyses the importance of digital transformation within public organisations and its impact on related human resources factors like human resource development, digital talent management and performance management.

BACKGROUND OF THE STUDY

The South African government has identified areas where there has been regression in terms of service delivery. The eThekwini Municipal Services and Living Conditions survey (2019/2020) mentioned in the IDP of the municipality indicated that poor service delivery and poor provision of basic services was the highest rating in reasons for dissatisfaction with municipal services at twenty-nine-point three percent. Other reasons that were mentioned were those municipal employees are unprofessional, and the municipality does not provide basic services such as, refuse collection, water, electricity, and grass cutting. Capacity constraints within the municipality could hamper economic growth. Therefore, effective talent management is a business imperative because deficiencies in leadership and technical competencies skills could have profound consequences for the entire public service. This can be enhanced through digitalisation.

Talent management is a broad phrase with no universal definition. It depends on the context and purpose in which it will be used. The interchangeable use of talent management with succession planning and human resources planning triggers further controversies. Tetik (2016) explains talent management through various approaches, including competency, individual strength, giftedness, high potential, and high performers Gallardo et al. (2020) describe talent management as all activities that include planning, identification, engagement, retention, deployment, and developing the individual (staff) training, development, and education need systematically. Talent management is essential for attracting, motivating, and retaining productive employees in the public sector (Mehale et al., 2021).

Therefore, talent management and digital hiring should be institutionalised in municipal planning to enhance efficiency in public service delivery. Nevertheless, the chronic shortage of skills has been a barrier to effective service delivery in South African municipalities (Van Dyk, 2017). There has been a slow implementation of talent management programmes to improve the competence of officials to accelerate service delivery in communities. Gibson and McKenzie (2011) hold that skills shortage emanates from poor talent management that triggers a massive scale brain drain in South Africa.

There is no doubt that this situation has eroded and continues to erode the sector's reputation, seriously affecting not only service delivery to the community but also the capacity of an organisation to employ and retain the right talent. The sector is suffering from "reputational crisis, incompetency," and is "disorganised, and riddled with corruption" (SALGA, 2018). The chapter further suggests that political factors such as "interference in the recruitment process, policy and legislative framework, inadequate relevant HR policies, poor accountability systems, such as poor oversight and lack of or, failure to apply performance management systems plus lack of capacity and skills" are resulting in the inferior performance by municipalities and government departments.

The Municipal Staff Regulations of 2021 provide for the implementation of performance management for all employees to ensure effective service delivery. Municipalities have a performance management system in place for all their employees. The final performance assessment scores of all employees for a particular fiscal year are reviewed and the results indicate that a majority of the municipalities' workforces are meeting performance expectations, whilst a few are exceeding expectations. Despite having a performance management system in place there is a clear misalignment between people performance and organisational performance because of the increase in customer complaints and the exceptionally low customer net promoter score of the (eThekwini Municipality Services and Living Conditions Survey, 2019/2020).

RESEARCH PROBLEM

The South African public service continues to have a high concentration of an ageing workforce within its management and leadership occupational levels which poses a risk to business continuity. Poor recruitment practices linked to political interference have led to the appointment of inadequate leaders in key positions thus stifling leadership potential and service delivery outcomes (CoGTA, 2018). A shortage of management and technical skills requires an organisation-wide talent management framework and competency management process to address leadership and technical skills. The strategy will also assist in delivering against diversity and inclusion requirements through the accelerated development of successors for Senior Management and technical positions (Mehale et al., 2021). Performance management is a foundation of talent management practices, there is strong continuous misalignment between people's performance and organisational performance within the city.

Talent management flows from performance management practices and if these are not corrected the public service runs the risk of identifying, developing, and promoting incompetent people into high-impact positions with a direct impact on service delivery requirements (Warnich, Carrell, Elbert & Hatfield, 2018). Most organisations put focus on talent management and "development processes forgetting that talented and ambitious employees do not like to wait "for long to secure management positions (Ahmed, 2016). If this study is not undertaken, the organisation could lose key talent due to a lack of mobility and the current practice that sometimes rewards undeserving employees at the peril of service delivery and organisational performance (Van Zalk, 2017).

AIM OF THE STUDY

Talent management is a systematic process conducted by organisations to find, select, improve, and maintain the best talents of their employees in meeting the needs of organisations now and in the future. The government is finding it increasingly difficult to attract and retain talented employees with scarce and critical skills leading to an adverse impact on service delivery. The main aim of the study is to understand and assess the impact of organisational talent management practices on service delivery outcomes. The study uses the talent management conceptual framework which will assist the public service to better understand the impact of talent management on service delivery outcomes. The study aims to understand the impact of digital talent management practices on service delivery outcomes and seeks to propose a model for the evaluation of the effectiveness of talent management within the South African public service.

The challenge with the current trend is that few managers of municipal organisations are aware of HR approaches like digital talent management, and even when attempts have been made to include talent management in policy, there is a lack of competence to implement it. Furthermore, there is still a knowledge vacuum in this field because, so little is known about talent management as a strategic enabler in a municipal context (CoGTA, 2018). The purpose of this research is to understand the impact of organisational talent management practices on service delivery outcomes and seek to propose a model for the evaluation of the effectiveness of talent management within the public service. The theoretical tenets of this chapter are based on the most recent literature and should provide managers with the knowledge they require to conduct talent management practices effectively, the study will also propose a model for the evaluation of the effectiveness of talent management within the city.

LITERATURE REVIEW

Talent management is a systematic process conducted by the company to find, select, improve, and maintain the best talents of its employees in meeting the needs of the company today and in the future. Digital talent management requires the identification of talented employees who work in the organisation. The purpose of digital talent management is to improve employee performance, enable the company to get the right person in the right position and job, avoiding mismatch in the work in the face of increasingly fierce competition (Mitosis, Lamnisos & Talias, 2021).

Acquiring skills and professionally developing talents, managing their performance, retaining them in the organisation, and developing strategies for their future promotion and career development, also known as succession planning (Shah, Memon & Tunio, 2021). Talent management which has gradually increased in importance in recent years, can be used to find talented employees by using techniques such as career planning, career development, and training. It can provide a significant and sustainable competitive advantage, creating both operational and strategic advantages for entities (Setyawan & Nelson, 2020).

The fundamental components of successful digital talent management are basic approaches related to the employment of strategic personnel, including human resource applications, performance evaluations, reward systems, training and development, positioning, efforts to become an agent of change, and leadership development and applications. Efficient talent management provides opportunities to increase the added value created by employees by improving workforce productivity (Nicholas, 2021). Several areas of research must be pursued for talent management to grow to maturity and to gain a firm position in the field of human resource management (Charles & Onouha, 2020). A successful talent management application is not only a means of measuring performance but also provides benefits by increasing the behavioural competence of employees. Getting the right people in pivotal roles at the right time is a key factor in achieving success (Shaikh, 2021).

Talent Management from a Global Perspective

Managing talent is a challenge to all organisations in the context of globalization irrespective of the country (Adero & Odiyo, 2020). Therefore, organisations must adopt global best practices of talent management and at the same time adapt to the local requirements and local labour market (Chan, 2020). Organisations that are phenomenally successful worldwide tend to maintain local recruitment strategies, but they combine this local strategy with a more global transfer of information and best practices (Abdel, 2021).

Talent Management Strategy

Talent management strategies must be integrated and harmonized with organisational strategies, and it is also especially important to articulate talent management strategies. The recruitment of members of the talent pool is the first task of the digital talent management strategy (Sottile, 2021). The talent pool is a group of employees with special traits and is a source of future senior executives (Dalayga, Baskaran & Mahadi, 2021). The sources of talented employees can be internal or external. The best way to create a talent pool is the internal sources since the employees have already knowledge of how business processes work and can be incorporated directly into the new position and the morale of the workforce uplifted (Almatrooshi, 2016).

Talent Development

Talent development is the process of changing an organisation, its employees, its stakeholders, and groups of people within it, using planned and unplanned learning, to achieve and maintain a competitive advantage for the organisation (Almohtaseb, 2020). This implies that they identify the employees who need digital learning and development, the level of learning and development they need and the duration during which learning takes place (Dalayga, 2021).

Career Management

There are several elements of career management including career development and planning which focuses on planning employee growth and progression (Jang, Ahn, Park & Kwon, 2019). Career management consists of both formal and informal activities including employee workshops, job rotation, job enrichment, succession planning or career progression ladders. Organisations may also contribute to career identity by providing abundant opportunities for self-development, opportunities for advancement and mentors (Kusi, Opoku-Danso & Afum, 2020).

Talent Retention

To date, research indicates that talent retention practises are one of the most underutilised methods in the talent management process (Barkhuizen et al., 2020). Most government institutions lack retention practices, or management fails to have frequent talent retention conversations with employees. Dalayga, Baskaran and Mahadi (2021), believe that management should prioritise the design and implementation of digital employee retention strategies. According to Chan et al. (2020), additional factors such as digital recruitment and selection, training and development, compensation packages, working environment, recognition, and rewards, and leadership are significantly related to the institution's employee retention policies. Shiena (2019) discovered that government employees who had fewer opportunities for advancement had a weaker application of talent retention practises. Because the costs of attracting new employees are high, talent turnover is detrimental to a company's productivity. Direct costs include turnover, replacement, and transition costs, while indirect costs include lost production, lower performance levels, unnecessary overtime, and low morale (Liu, 2021).

Talent as Employee Potential

Talented employees are people who show their abilities and achievements and have the potential for promotion to higher career paths to become potential leaders in the company (Shipena, 2019). They are trained and knowledgeable not only about their work, but they can solve every situation that can occur within the organisation (Zainee, 2020). Saurombe, Barkhuizen and Schutte (2017), argued that talent can be defined as top performers, employees with high potential, senior managers qualified for directorships, or other individuals qualified for critical roles within the organisation. Taking a more analytical approach, Masri and Suliman (2019) contend that talent is the accumulation of an individual's competence, commitment to the work, the organisation, and contribution through the meaning and purpose of the work.

Talent Performance

Modern technologies and innovations can be easily replicated by competitors and generate only temporary competitive advantages, whereas talent management practises can generate the most permanent competitive advantages (Agarwal & Maurya, 2018). Sustained competitive advantage comes from talent management practices in other words, how the organisation attracts, develops, retains, motivates, manages, and rewards its talent (Gallardo-Gallardo, Thunnissen, & Scullion, 2020). The collective skills of the talent employed in an organisation comprise the organisation's core capabilities. An organisation's talent injects capabilities that are difficult for competitors to benchmark and replicate (Kamal & Lukman, 2017). More than any other asset, talent provides the potential for long-term competitive advantage. Digital talent management is important when the organisation would like to build high-performing teams which will be formed by talented people (Liu, 2021).

Few jobs allow for purely objective performance evaluations; most jobs require subjective evaluations. Concerns about disparity aversion, manifested as leniency and centrality biases, may collaborate to reduce heterogeneity in performance evaluations (Aina & Atan, 2020). It is difficult to pinpoint which strategic jobs need exceptional individual performance to have a positive effect on the company's overall performance (Dixit & Arrawatia, 2018). Organisations have attempted to address the difficulty of recognising top performers caused by performance appraisal prejudices through competency modelling.

Work performance can be evaluated more clearly using competencies (Aina et al., 2020). By being more precise about the qualities in question, they can also make it easier to distinguish between average and top performers (Pang, 2018).

CONCEPTUAL FRAMEWORK

The study uses the digital talent management conceptual framework which will assist eThekwini Municipality, and other South African public sector institutions, to better understand the impact of talent management on service delivery outcomes. In today's world of global trade, talent can guarantee the success and excellence of organisations against competitors, especially at the managerial level (Lipkie, 2018). The problem with the current trend is that few managers of municipal organisations are aware of HR practices like talent management, and even when attempts have been made to include talent management in policy, there is a lack of competence to implement it. Furthermore, there is still a knowledge vacuum in this field because, so little is known about digital talent management as a strategic enabler in a municipal context (CoGTA, 2018). According to McDonnell et al., (2020), talent consists of those individuals who can be effective in organisational performance, either through their immediate contribution or in the longer term by demonstrating the highest levels of potential. In the broadest possible terms, it is the strategic and tactical management of the flow of talent through an organisation (Senona, 2017). This emphasis on staffing and recruiting is more appropriately called the talent acquisition phase of the talent management cycle, an important but preliminary step in the overall process (Shiena, 2019).

Figure 1. Talent Management Conceptual Framework

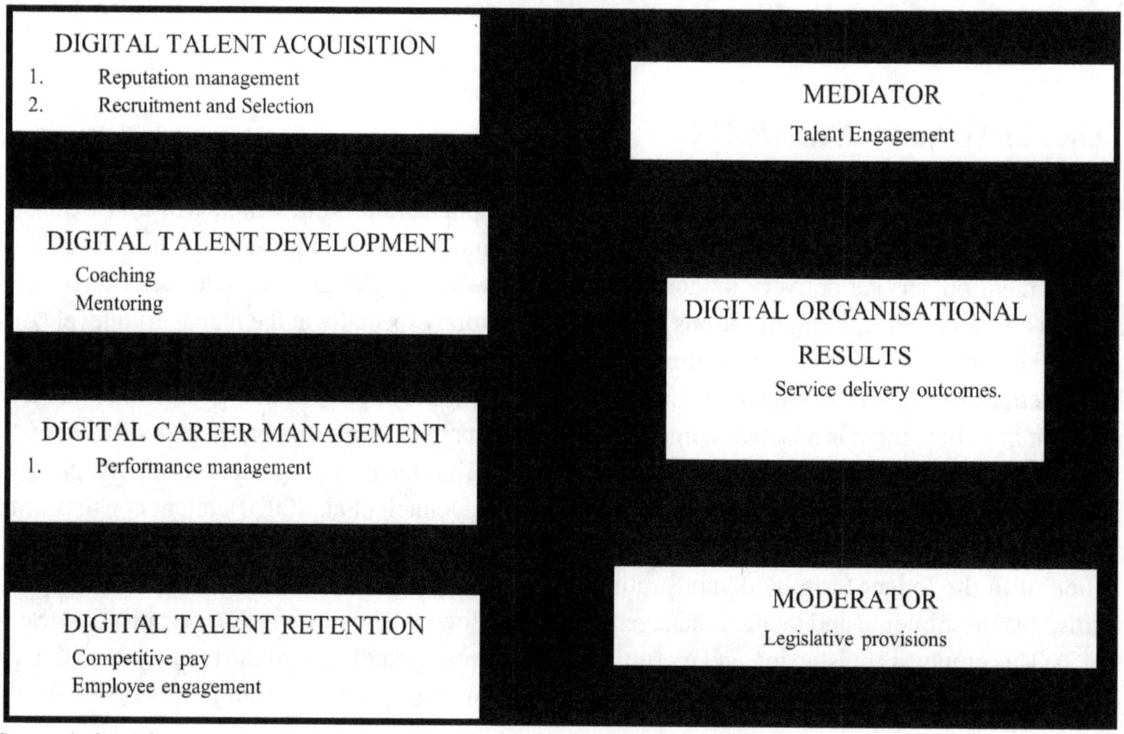

Source: Authors' diagram

The conceptual framework for the proposed study includes the proactive analysis and planning to assure long-term strategic development and deployment of critical leadership and other resources through systematic identification, assessment, planning, and developmental action. The following essential elements of the framework will be explored to better understand the phenomena under investigation (Mzezewa, 2019):

- Digital Talent Acquisition: Proactively recruiting world-class, diverse leadership talent and providing onboarding support for them to accelerate their assimilation into their roles.
- Digital Talent Development: Developing and executing learning and development programmes, processes and assessment tools to grow current and future leaders (Dalayga, Baskaran & Mahadi, 2021).
- Digital Career Management: The process of creating a work environment in which people can deliver results effectively, grow and their contribution is recognised (Charles & Onouha, 2020).
- Digital Talent Retention: This is critical towards developing a leadership pipeline or by thoughtful consideration of the availability, readiness, and development of internal talent to assume critical leadership roles (Aina et al., 2020).

- Digital Organisational Results: Achieving favourable and desired results is the outcome expected out of any effective integrated talent management system (Almatrooshi & Singh, 2016).

The flow of effective communication, the legislative environment, and the systems of recognition and rewards are integral parts of the climate which influences the talent's performance affecting productivity, creativity and driving results with the right impact (Ahmed, 2016). The risks facing municipalities include talent-related risks and are frequently identified in the risk register as the most critical issue facing the municipalities. These risks do extend to poor talent planning to support the municipalities' service delivery strategy; for example, limited leadership bench strength, reputational risk exposure, productivity risk, and inability to execute due to lack of workforce planning (South Africa Local Government Association [SALGA], 2020). This study identifies talent acquisition, talent development, career management and talent performance as an independent variable and organisational performance as a dependent variable. The review of the talent management conceptual framework will assist researchers and scholars in clarifying relationships among the research variables.

SIGNIFICANCE OF RESEARCH STUDY

The study of talent management and its value added to organisational performance is still developing. The study's contribution to the existing body of knowledge will present facts obtainable about the phenomenon relating to organisational performance. This study is driven by the desire to assist the municipality employ talent management practices to draw in, keep, and develop their personnel. The study is therefore important from a theoretical and practical point of view in that it will contribute to the understanding of the impact of digital talent management practices on eThekwini service delivery outcomes and develop a model for monitoring such practices. The problem with the current trend is that few managers of municipal organisations are aware of HR practices like talent management, and even when attempts have been made to include talent management in policy, there is a lack of competence to implement it. Furthermore, there is still a knowledge vacuum in this field because, so little is known about digital talent management as a strategic enabler in a municipal context (CoGTA, 2018).

RESEARCH METHODOLOGY

The collection of data was secondary, using desktop research and literature from South African government legislation and academic journals. Desk research is a method that explores data from existing documents and previous research, secondary data, to gather information on a particular topic. Desk research is a type of research that is based on the material published in reports and similar documents that are available in public libraries, websites, data obtained from surveys already carried out. The researcher was able to draw data from published academic papers, government documents, statistical databases, and historical records. In this study the researcher clearly defined the research topic; identified the topic and its purpose, then listed any relevant research attributes; selected appropriate resources; looked for existing data; collated, compared and assembled the facts; and analysed data. Sourcing relevant and current materials on the subject of interest paved the way for the literature review and informed the findings and recommendations.

FINDINGS OF THE STUDY

The major findings of the study indicated that the South African public service has significantly high levels of an ageing workforce in leadership and critical positions advancing capacity constraints. There is a clear misalignment between people and organisational performance which needs to be corrected. The study recommended that the South African government review the implementation of talent management initiatives with clearly stated success measures that drive organisational performance and talent retention strategies.

The research findings further revealed that participants had varying experiences with talent management, ranging from a lack of awareness of talent management to it not being consistently applied as a strategic enabler across the public service. The interviews revealed that the main reasons for implementing talent management practise were the attraction and retention of scarce and critical skills, the issue of an ageing workforce, succession management, talent performance and development, and the desire to positively impact service delivery outcomes.

DIGITAL TRANSFORMATION TO ENABLE PUBLIC SERVICE DELIVERY

Given the issues facing the public sector, technology may play an important role in improving service delivery. Citizens nowadays don't want to wait in huge lines for social and medical services. According to an international poll, 65% of public service executives believe that providing an individualized public service experience is a top priority. Transferring citizen information online is critical to digital transformation since trends demonstrate that individuals are increasingly receiving information at their fingertips via banking systems, social media platforms, websites, and other private-sector-led digital platforms. This puts the government under pressure to simplify once-implemented processes, guaranteeing a strong digital presence and social media interaction to promote citizen involvement and satisfaction (Caligiuri & Dragoni, 2019).

Current government initiatives, strategies, and plans for the use of digital platforms lack a comprehensive and integrated approach. Unified e-government ensures a seamless citizen experience. This presents itself in a variety of digital government platforms, including websites, portals, and contact centres, all of which are fragmented and lack an integrated customized public service experience. International trends indicate that there should be a single electronic public service entrance. This integrates citizen information and involvement with the government online. Citizens can examine their records and the progress of their service requests online, deal with the government by arranging appointments for services provided by the government online, submit tax filings, and keep contact and address information updated online (Elhanafy & Hessewi, 202).

As individuals become more virtual and sensitive information is shared online, cybersecurity becomes increasingly important. Cybercrime is on the rise, and there is a need for both investigative and preventive measures along the ICT value chain, which includes apps, data centres, and network connections. An integrated security monitoring/defence technological strategy is required, as is a new breed of human resource capabilities in ICT and public security. Existing government cybersecurity policies, strategies, and plans are inadequate (Cappelli, 2008). These issues require the public sector to upskill its current workforce to be technologically surveyed as well as to attract and retain highly skilled employees within the new domains and make adequate financial provisions for both infrastructural requirements as well as developmental requirements.

The government's ICT revenue isn't being utilized effectively to develop and automate its equipment. Current government ICT expenditure patterns show that up to 80% of the money is spent on sustaining outdated government machinery, with just 20% going toward innovation, research, and development. Current government ICT programmes and initiatives have become disjointed and lack the coordinated approach required to enhance service delivery. This is exacerbated by the present siloed citizen service delivery structure among government ministries, SOEs, and collaborations with businesses (Clarke, and Scurry, 2020).

PUBLIC SERVICE INTERNET OF THINGS (IOT)

The Public Service Digital Strategy intends to help enable the Government through scalable digital platforms that will provide a great service experience for the citizens. This strategy involves putting together an architecture of modern digital information technology from the available technological resources. The organisation's ambition to embark on a digital transformation journey to improve government service delivery requires digitally aware skills as well as capable and effective digital staff in core and support functions alike (Glenn, 2012).

The human capital management function should understand the strategic journey of digital transformation, be conscious of the general requirements of talent management in the digital age, possess some degree of digital skills, and run its systems and processes primarily through digital channels and toolsets like Advanced Big Data HR Analytics, Artificial Intelligence sub-capabilities like Machine Learning and Natural Language Processing to attract, create, transform, and retain such skills (Glaister, Amri, and Spicer, 2019). Furthermore, there is a skills shortage that requires active assistance with training and development to ensure that public sector organisations pursuing digital transformation initiatives incorporate a skill set matrix. In the next few years, human resources capabilities will provide an enabling environment by concentrating on the following critical areas: HR Digitalization; Digital Skills Attraction, Continuous Improvement, and Retention; HR Customer Centricity; and Transformational Leadership. The fourth industrial revolution encouraged changes in developing technology and end-user demand, producing sudden imbalances that affected the requirement for skills developed to sustain existing systems.

PUBLIC SERVICES DIGITAL TRANSFORMING CHALLENGES

With the introduction of digital technology, local governments may now provide some services to residents via a variety of channels, including online and mobile applications. Similarly, municipal governments may now leverage a variety of digital tools, including big data, cloud computing, the Internet of Things, and artificial intelligence. While these platforms and technologies offer several advantages, research on digital transformation identifies various problems for governments in areas such as public service delivery. For example, Haak-Saheem and Festing (2020) explain that digital transformation is a time-consuming and challenging process that necessitates the utilization of all business resources, including human, technological, physical, organisational, and financial. Similarly, it emphasizes that the burden extends beyond the introduction of digital technology into public service automation.

South Africa's public service must undergo digital transformation to overcome past injustices and inequality stemming from apartheid's legacy. Against this context, rethinking government and service delivery using the lens of digital transformation entails overcoming challenges such as the need for digital services to be readily available and user-friendly, the need for adaptability and versatility in delivering digital services, and the importance of cost-effective delivery methodologies. While South Africa's digital transformation needs to move quickly and with great urgency, local governments lack sufficient technological skills and skilled personnel (Dixit & Arrawatia, 2018).

The 2017 National e-Government Strategy and Roadmap emphasized the importance of highly technical professionals in delivering e-government initiatives in South Africa. Presently, many public service employees need to become better acquainted with digital technology and current digital delivery techniques. This is partly because many local public service employees require ICT training. Furthermore, digital transformation requires greater bandwidth and bandwidth-intensive applications, which may not be accessible. Meanwhile, numerous municipalities in South Africa, especially those in rural regions, require additional resources to develop and maintain digital transformation-ready infrastructure (Collings, Nyberg, Wright & McMackin, 2021).

CONCLUSION

South Africa's public sector digital talent management takes a strategic approach to human resource management, addressing large organisational concerns such as structural and cultural transformation. This strategy is directed by South Africa HR prescripts, which establish the administrative framework for talent management in the public sector. The strategic success of digital talent management in the public sector is dependent on the effective execution of strategies and plans, digital recruiting, selection, career management, and recruitment and retention practices.

These practices seek to transform the public sector into an instrument capable of performing a role in the creation of a new South Africa. Digital transformation is an ongoing process that presents a compelling argument for change inside public organisations, influencing their culture and the talent they attract and retain. The capacity to swiftly 'learn, re-learn, and unlearn' is critical to the effective completion of this journey. An organisation in this arena should be led by a leadership team with the necessary capabilities to achieve change and transformation by, amongst other things, capturing the hearts and minds of employees.

Public Service South Africa must therefore revise its leadership competence model to facilitate the attraction and retention of critical skills. Importantly, upskilling its internal personnel at all stages is not merely a corporate moral commitment, but a fundamental necessity for the organisation to stay competitive and grow now and in the future. Around the world, digital transformation has grown into a more visible reality, prompting the urgency to rethink public service delivery. This is particularly relevant for South African governments, which face a variety of service delivery issues, require assistance in keeping up with technology advances, and must move quickly to cope with a dissatisfied member of the public. According to this chapter, digital transformation may address previous challenges facing the government, find solutions for current issues as well as emerging ones, and set up government and service delivery for the future.

LIMITATIONS AND DIRECTIONS FOR FUTURE RESEARCH

The study used a qualitative approach to analyse the impact of talent retention and management practices on service delivery outcomes at the local government level. As a result, the study's findings must be restricted to South African local governments only. Furthermore, the findings reveal that talent management practices such as succession planning, competency-based recruitment, and performance management are poorly implemented due to a lack of proper monitoring and evaluation of their efficacy. As a result, this research suggests a model for tracking the impact of talent management practices on service delivery in the local government sphere. The challenge is exacerbated by the continued use of manual recruitment processes, which foster control evasion and perpetuate maladministration. Public service should investigate the automation of recruitment and selection practices to reduce political interference, and maladministration, and improve the process's effectiveness; this recommendation is closely aligned with the smart public service project, which seeks to automate major operations and service offerings within the Local Government.

REFERENCES

Abdel Azem Mostafa, H., Hassan EL-Sayed. Mahfouz, H., & Mohammed Araby Ebraheem, S. (. (2021). Effect of Educational Program about Talent Management for Nursing Managers on Their Job Affiliation and Organisational Excellence. *Egyptian Journal of Health Care*, 12(2), 718–740. 10.21608/ejhc.2021.170481

Adero, F. A., & Odiyo, W. O. (2020). Employee Characteristics, Contemporary Human Resource Management Practices and Organisation Effectiveness. *International Journal of Business Management, Entrepreneurship, and Innovation*, 2(2), 1–18. 10.35942/jbmed.v2i2.111

Ahmed, H. K. (2016). The impact of Talent management on the competitive advantage in the organisations. *UAE Proceedings of 37th ISERD International Conference*, Abu Dhabi, UAE, 6th June 2016.

Al Aina, R., & Atan, T. (2020). The Impact of Implementing Talent Management Practices on Sustainable Organisational Performance. *Sustainability (Basel)*, 12(20), 8372. 10.3390/su12208372

Almatrooshi, B., Singh, S. K., & Farouk, S. (2016). Determinants of organisational performance: A proposed framework. *International Journal of Productivity and Performance Management*, 65(6), 844–859. 10.1108/IJPPM-02-2016-0038

Caligiuri, P., & Dragoni, L. (2019). Developing global leadership talent. In Collings, D., Scullion, H., & Caligiuri, P. (Eds.), *Global talent management* (2nd ed.).

Cappelli, P. (2008). *Talent on demand: Managing talent in an age of uncertainty*. Harvard: Harvard Business Press.

Chan, J. Y., Chai, W. X., Koh, C. K., Ngo, S. L., & Teh, L. L. (2020). *The impact of talent attraction, talent development and talent retention on job satisfaction in hospitality industry*. Universiti Tunku Abdul Rahman.

Charles, K., & Onouha, B. C. (2020). *Entrepreneurial Talent Management and Organisational Agility of Construction Firms in Rivers State*.

Clarke, M., & Scurry, T. (2020). The role of the psychological contract in shaping graduate experiences: A study of public sector talent management programmes in the UK and Australia. *International Journal of Human Resource Management*, 31(8), 965–991. 10.1080/09585192.2017.1396545

Collings, N., Nyberg, A. J., Wright, P. M., & McMackin, J. (2021). Leading through paradox in a COVID-19 world: Human resources comes of age. *Human Resource Management Journal*, 31(4), 819–833. 10.1111/1748-8583.12343

Dalayga, B., Baskaran, S., & Mahadi, N. (2021). *Talent Development Practices:* A Revisit as an Imperative for Talent Retention. *International Journal of Academic Research in Business & Social Sciences*, 11(2), 330–348. 10.6007/IJARBSS/v11-i2/8578

Dixit, S., & Arrawatia, M. (2018). The impact of talent management on job satisfaction and employee performance in public sector banks of Rajasthan. *International Journal of Creative Research Thoughts*, 6(1), 425–435.

Elhanafy, E., & El Hessewi, G. (2021). Effect of talent management training program on head nurses leadership effectiveness. *Egyptian Journal of Health Care*, 12(4), 351–361. 10.21608/ejhc.2021.199134

Gallardo-Gallardo, E., Thunnissen, M., & Scullion, H. (2020). Talent management: Context matters. [REMOVED HYPERLINK FIELD]. *International Journal of Human Resource Management*, 31(4), 457–473. 10.1080/09585192.2019.1642645

Glaister, A., Amri, A., & Spicer, D. (2019). Talent management: Managerial sense making in the wake of omanization. *International Journal of Human Resource Management*, 32(3), 719–737. 10.1080/09585192.2018.1496128

Glenn, T. (2012). The state of talent management in Canada's public sector. *Canadian Public Administration*, 55(1), 25–51. 10.1111/j.1754-7121.2012.00204.x

Haak-Saheem, W., & Festing, M. (2020). Human resource management–a national business system perspective. *International Journal of Human Resource Management*, 31(14), 1863–1890. 10.1080/09585192.2017.1423366

Kamal, M., & Lukman, Z. (2017). The effects of talent management on performance management. *International Journal of Academic Research in Business & Social Sciences*, 7(9), 372–385.

Khoreva, V., Vaiman, V., & Van Zalk, M. (2017). Talent management practice effectiveness: Investigating employee perspective. *Employee Relations*, 39(1), 19–33. 10.1108/ER-01-2016-0005

Liu, M. (2021). An Empirical Study on Talent Management Strategies of Knowledge-Based Organisations Using Entrepreneurial Psychology and Key Competence. *Frontiers in Psychology*, 12, 4615.

Masri, N., & Suliman, A. (2019). Talent management, employee recognition and performance in research institution. *Studies in Business and Economics*, 14(1), 127–140. 10.2478/sbe-2019-0010

Maurya, K., & Agarwal, M. (2018). Organisational talent management and perceived employer branding. *The International Journal of Organizational Analysis*, 26(2), 312–330. 10.1108/IJOA-04-2017-1147

McCaffry, R., & Sexton, L. (2018). *Improving government performance through effective talent management*. Unpublished research report, Vol. 4, Association of International Certified Professional Accountants, Durham, NC, US.

Mehale, K. D., Govender, C. M., & Mabaso, C. M. (2021). Maximising training evaluation for employee performance improvement. *SA Journal of Human Resource Management*, 19(0), 1–11. 10.4102/sajhrm.v19i0.1473

Mitosis, K. D., Lamnisos, D., & Talias, M. A. (2021). Talent Management in Healthcare: A Systematic Qualitative Review. *Sustainability (Basel)*, 13(8), 4469. 10.3390/su13084469

Mzezewa, T. (2019). *State of staff turnover & retention in municipalities of South Africa*. Unpublished research report. Johannesburg: LGSETA

NDP. (2012). Ten Year Review of the National Development Plan: 2012-2022. https://www.nationalplanningcommission.org.za/assets/Documents/Ten%20Year%20Review%20of%20the%20National%20Development%20Plan_26%20September%202023.pdf

Nicholas, S. (2021). *Talent Management and Organisational Performance Correlation of Faculty at Community Colleges in Southern California*. ProQuest.

Pandita, D., & Ray, S. (2018). Talent management and employee engagement–a meta-analysis of their impact on talent retention. *Industrial and Commercial Training*, 50(4), 185–199. 10.1108/ICT-09-2017-0073

Pang, K., & Lu, C. (2018). Organisational motivation, employee job satisfaction and organisational performance: An empirical study of container shipping companies in Taiwan. *Maritime Business Review*, 3(1), 36–52. 10.1108/MABR-03-2018-0007

Saurombe, M., Barkhuizen, N., & Schutte, N. (2017). *Exploring the determinants of a talent value proposition for sustainable higher education institutions: A conceptual paper*. Winter London Business Research Conference. London: Proceedings of 2017 Winter London Business Research Conference.

Senona, M. E. (2017). *The relationship between talent management and job satisfaction among teachers in Limpopo Province: A case of Maleboho East Circuit*. Unpublished Masters Dissertation. Southern Business School.

Setyawan, A., & Nelson, A. (2020). Factors Affecting Talent Management Strategies in Construction Companies. *Almana: Jurnal Manajemen Dan Bisnis*, 4(3), 392–397. 10.36555/almana.v4i3.1479

Shah, G., Memon, N., & Tunio, G. (2021). Need for Talent Management and Investigating Its Impact on Organisational Performance of Higher Education Institutes. *International Review of Management and Business Research*, 10(1), 168–182. 10.30543/10-1(2021)-13

Shaikh, M. (2021). Determining the Relationship between Human Resource Practices, Employee Well-Being, and Organisational Performance. *RJ International Journal of Management Studies*, 1(1).

Sheehan, M., Grant, K., & Garavan, T. (2018). Strategic talent management: A macro and micro analysis of current issues in hospitality and tourism. *Worldwide Hospitality and Tourism Themes*, 10(1), 28–41. 10.1108/WHATT-10-2017-0062

Shipena, D. (2019). *A study of talent management practices in the Namibian Police Force*. Unpublished Masters dissertation. Krugersdorp: Southern Business School.

Sottile, S. N. (2021). *Talent Management and Organisational Performance Correlation of Faculty at Community Colleges in Southern California*. Grand Canyon University.

South African Local Government Association (SALGA). (2018). *Municipal Managers Forum*. Pretoria: SALGA.

South African Local Government Association (SALGA). (2020). *2nd Annual Local Government Talent Management Seminar*. Pretoria: SALGA.

Warnich, S., Carrell, M. R., Elbert, N. F., & Hatfield, R. D. (2018). *Human resource management in South Africa*. (6th Edition). South Western Cengage learning.

Wiblen, S., & McDonnell, A. (2020). Connecting 'talent' meanings and multi-level context: A discursive approach. *International Journal of Human Resource Management*, 31(4), 474–510. 10.1080/09585192.2019.1629988

Zaharee, M., Lipkie, T., Mehlman, S. K., & Neylon, S. K. (2018). Recruitment and Retention of Early-Career Technical Talent. *Research Technology Management*, 61(5), 51–61. 10.1080/08956308.2018.1495966

Zainee, I. A., & Puteh, F. (2020). Corporate social responsibility impact on talent retention among Generation Y. *Gestão*, 27(4), 369–392. 10.1108/REGE-06-2019-0070

Chapter 13
Positioning Digital Transformation of Public Sector Human Resources in Zimbabwe and South Africa:
Challenges and Opportunities

Lewis Edwin Chigova
https://orcid.org/0000-0001-7357-2091
North-West University, South Africa

Costa Hofisi
North-West University, South Africa

ABSTRACT

This chapter notes that in Zimbabwe and South Africa, where challenges such as service delivery, economic instability, and technological disruptions are prevalent, the potential of advanced technologies to reshape the public service workforce is recognised. However, very few studies position the digital transformation of HRM within these countries' contextual constraints and opportunities necessitating a need for more systematic inquiries. The study draws from various peer-reviewed articles and expansive policy documents on the digital transformation of HRM in the public sector in South Africa and Zimbabwe. It found that while the two countries have recognised the importance of digital transformation in HRM and laid down frameworks to support this transition, their paths diverge on implementation effectiveness and the challenges faced. Strategic and administrative hurdles impede South Africa's journey, whereas infrastructural and HR constraints deeply challenge Zimbabwe's. The study recommends that these countries must establish solid digital transformation strategies for HRM.

DOI: 10.4018/979-8-3693-2889-7.ch013

INTRODUCTION

The implementation of digital government initiatives has been a subject of scholarly inquiry, evolving through various policy paradigms and ideological trends in public administration and management (Mergel, 2019). From the early prescriptions of Woodrow Wilson and Max Weber to the New Public Management (NPM) reforms and the subsequent era of digital governance, the landscape of public sector administration has continuously evolved (Hood, 1991; Osborne & Gaebler, 1995; Dunleavy et al., 2006). Amidst these shifts, the imperative for building responsive and efficient public sector human capital remains paramount, particularly in regions like Zimbabwe and South Africa, which grapple with multifaceted challenges such as service delivery, economic instability, and technological disruptions. Bourgon (2015, p. 2) aptly captures, "In absolute terms, people in government today may not face challenges that are more difficult than the ones faced by prior generations of public sector leaders, but they sure are different". The unique challenges of the digital age, where Digital Transformation has emerged as a driving force for innovative, inclusive and sustainable growth (African Union, 2020), are particularly complex. The sudden upsurge in the use of digital technologies necessitates more systematic inquiries to understand the challenges and opportunities brought by positioning the digital transformation of public sector human resources, considering its potential to alter how people work and think within our communities (Nhede et al., 2022).

Historical imperatives and ideological currents have shaped HRM in public administration theory and practice trajectories. From the principles of bureaucracy delineated by Max Weber to the market-oriented reforms of the NPM era, successive waves of scholarship have informed the development of the public service ethos (Dunleavy et al., 2006; Hood, 1991; Weber, 2023). However, Bourgon (2015) highlights that contemporary public servants operate in a world of volatility, hyper-connectivity, and novel challenges that demand innovative responses. These new circumstances require policymakers and regulators to keep pace with technological advances, address the latest regulatory frontiers and create the foundation upon which digital transformation can achieve its full potential (African Union, 2020). However, in the context of Zimbabwe and South Africa, the imperative for digital transformation in public sector human resource (HR) is underscored by the observations of Majam and Jarbandhan (2022) regarding the inadequacy of data-driven Human Resource Management (HRM) practices and the necessity of equipping public servants with skills relevant to the 4IR. The potential of advanced technologies to reshape the public service workforce is recognised, but positioning the digital transformation of HRM within the contextual constraints and opportunities in these countries is imperative.

Furthermore, as Christensen et al. (2020) and Osborne et al. (2012) emphasise, the public sector possesses distinctive features that differentiate them from their private sector counterparts. These features include their embeddedness within the political sphere, multi-functional mandates, and obligations to serve societal interests. Hence, while lessons from the private sector can inform the positioning of digital transformation of HRM practices in the public sector, a critical scholarly perspective is warranted to ensure the applicability and effectiveness of such transfers. Currently, Majam and Jarbandhan (2022, p. 2) note that, for instance, while the private sector makes greater use of performance metrics using data science, the public sector lags. These scholars argue that this situation creates a cause of concern given that the public sector is relied on to set the policy agenda for all stakeholders (Majam & Jarbandhan, 2022, p. 2). More so, Osborne, Radnor, and Nasi (2012, p. 140) have warned against transferring lessons from the private to the public sector—whether from a manufacturing or services context, arguing the criticality of framing analyses within a critical view of the relationship between these sectors.

In light of the above, there is no doubt that the "HRM process within the government will also be a beneficiary of big data, where, for example, recruitment and selection, performance management and talent acquisition can benefit from analysing big data" (Majam & Jarbandhan, 2022, p. 1). According to Majam and Jarbandhan (2022), what is imperative is that the government's HRM component plan effectively uses data to improve performance outcomes and promote a public service that could ultimately promote the vision of a 'better life for all'. However, a previous study by Nicolás-Agustín, Jiménez-Jiménez, and Maeso-Fernandez (2022) stresses that there is still a shortage of knowledge as to what practices can cause employees to adopt behaviours that facilitate the digital transformation of an organisation.

This chapter acknowledges that the positioning of digital transformation within public sector HR in Zimbabwe and South Africa presents challenges and opportunities. It contextualises digital transformation efforts within the unique country characteristics of public sector HRM. The chapter follows a qualitative approach. It draws from various peer-reviewed articles and expansive literature on the digital transformation of HRM in the public sector. The chapter further analyses public documents, including constitutions, government regulations, white papers, policy documents, speeches, reports of meetings, and related information publicised on official government websites. It also examines the documents linked to the African Union's position on digital transformation. Content analysis is used for data analysis. The rest of the chapter is structured as follows: The following section discusses the literature on the digital transformation of HRM. The chapter comparatively examines the experiences of South Africa and Zimbabwe, analysing the related challenges and opportunities concerning digital transformation in public sector HRM. A discussion of findings follows, making a comparative exposition of the countries' experiences. Finally, the chapter provides recommendations and identifies areas for future research.

LITERATURE REVIEW

Historically, Girisha and Nagendrababu (2019) underscore that public sector organisations have increasingly incorporated information communication technology into their work processes through innovative tools and techniques since the dawn of the information era. Digital transformation implies that public sector organisations simultaneously address digitisation from several dimensions, such as strategies, organisational structure, operations or culture (Nicolás-Agustín et al., 2022). Strohmeier (2020, p. 346) observes the rising prominence in the literature of concepts such as "digitisation," "digitalisation," "digital transformation," or "digital disruption" as denoting an ever-increasing use of technology and corresponding substantial changes in numerous domains of business and society, such as HRM. Human resources studies conceptualise HRM as focussed on "how people are employed, managed, and developed in organisations" (Armstrong & Taylor, 2020, p. 3). Related studies show that the role of HRM continues to change as technology has continued to evolve throughout management practices (Girisha & Nagendrababu, 2019). Strohmeier (2020, p. 346) explains that conceptual components such as "transformation" imply substantial changes for HRM, hinting at their considerable importance. According to Nachit and Okar (2020), the digital transformation of HRM signifies the technical process of transforming manual HR information into digital form. Strohmeier (2020, p. 352) shares this view, arguing that "the digital transformation of HRM denotes the socio-technical digitalisation sub-process of exploiting digitisation potentials for strategic purposes of HRM".

At the continental level, the African Union formulated "The Digital Transformation Strategy for Africa (2020-2030)", which stresses that digital transformation drives innovative, inclusive, and sustainable growth (African Union, 2020). The African Union (2020) views digital transformation as suitable for facilitating the delivery of goods and services and contributing to achieving Agenda 2063 and the Sustainable Development Goals. Since human resources are critical to enhancing public service delivery (Nhede et al., 2022), the continuous inventions and advances in digital technologies of the Fourth Industrial Revolution (4IR) are influencing many organisational operations, including HRM (Chapano et al., 2022). In his study, Larkin (2017) argues that there is no doubt that changes in digital technologies in HR departments are all-pervasive and omnidirectional. Larkin (2017, p. 56) gives a picture of the projected impact of digital transformation of HRM in the private sector, although this study extends this notion in the public sector as follows:

> Employee engagement and learning technologies have taken a page out of social media's playbook, with many organisations pursuing strategies to roll out employee communication technology that mimics social media's quick, versatile and multi-channel approach. The employee of the future will digest information from their employer digitally, on a mobile device (typically on-the-go), in either an easy-to-digest video/audio format or as user-friendly articles. Be it a company's quarterly earnings, a message from the CEO or changes being made to the company's benefits program, such content will be consumed and shared around the organisation, like how content flows through social networks today – liked, shared and interacted with.

Thus, the analogy above suggests that HR in the public sector faces the challenging job of coping with new, innovative methods of practice, collaborating with technological support and opportunities to bring about effective performance improvement in all HR activities, and transforming and renovating the entire HRM activities (Girisha & Nagendrababu, 2019).

Digital Transformation of HRM in South Africa's Public Sector

Since the end of apartheid, South Africa has undergone significant public service reforms to address historical injustices, improve service delivery, and ensure a representative and efficient public administration. Shava and Ndebele (2023) succinctly observe that post-democracy, the South African government took various strides by formulating multiple policies to promote inclusive digital transformation and inclusion regarding ICTs and digital technologies usage. Under the Department of Public Service and Administration (DPSA), the Public Service Commission (PSC) is critical in overseeing these reforms, guided by principles embedded in the 1996 Constitution and various white papers to transform public service delivery. It derives its mandate from sections 195 and 196 of the Constitution, 1996, which enables it to investigate, monitor, and evaluate the organisation and administration of the Public Service as part of its work. According to the PSC's official web portal (2024), some of the principles and values guiding the commission, and essential for reference in this chapter, are the cultivation of good HRM and career development practices and a representative public administration with employment and personnel management practices based on ability, objectivity, fairness, and the need to redress past imbalances.

LEGAL FRAMEWORKS SUPPORTING DIGITAL TRANSFORMATION OF HRM IN SOUTH AFRICAN PUBLIC SECTOR HRM

The 1996 Constitution of South Africa in Section 195 (1d) provides that "Good human-resource management and career-development practices, to maximise human potential," is one of the principles governing public administration that "must be cultivated". Similarly, the 1995 White Paper on the Transformation of the Public Service sought to "continually improve the lives of the people of South Africa through a transformed public service which is representative, coherent, transparent, efficient, effective, accountable and responsive needs of all" (DPSA, 1995). Likewise, the 1997 White Paper on Transforming Public Service Delivery (also known as the Batho Pele White Paper) recognised the need to build a public service capable of meeting the challenge of improving the delivery of public services to the citizens of South Africa. Nhede et al. (2022) argue that the primary function of the public service is delivering public services and products to society in operationally convenient and efficient ways. Both White Papers relentlessly seek increased efficiency and the reduction of wastage within the public service. The Batho Pele White Paper clarified that money "wasted in cumbersome, inefficient processes, in delays and duplication, is money which could be invested in improving services" (DPSA, 1997). Building on this, the 2012 National Development Plan 2030 recognises that progress over the next two decades in South Africa requires doing things differently (National Planning Commission, 2012). Hence, the DPSA (2023) stresses that the government's digital transformation journey is not an option but a necessity. The Department emphasises that through digital transformation, public employees can reimagine how they interact with citizens, deliver public services, manage resources, and make data-driven decisions (DPSA, 2023). Institutionally, the State Innovation Technology Agency is responsible for driving the digital transformation of public service in South Africa.

Furthermore, the Public Service Regulations, 2016, as amended, specifically Regulation 25 (1)(e)(iii), states that "an executive authority shall prepare a strategic plan for his or her department that specifies information systems that enable service delivery through the use of information and communication technology" (PSC, 2024). The current policy framework for positioning public sector human resources' digital transformation seems outdated and incoherent. For example, the DPSA (2023) recognises the absence of a unified strategy as a hindrance to the digital transformation of human resources in public service in South Africa (Gabara, 2024). This is despite the African Union's reasoning that governments are responsible for creating an enabling environment with policies and regulations promoting digital transformation (African Union, 2020). The African Union states that policymakers and regulators must keep pace with technological advances, address the new regulatory frontiers and create the foundation upon which digital transformation can achieve its full potential (African Union, 2020). In light of these imperatives, in March 2024, the DPSA stated in its presentation to the Parliamentary Portfolio Committee on Public Service and Administration that it was finalising a policy framework to guide the digital transformation of public service (Gabara, 2024). The department stressed that the proposed Digital Government "policy framework will serve as a roadmap for the digital transformation of the public service, contributing to establishing a competent and ethical public sector in South Africa" (Gabara, 2024). It added that the framework "adopts a comprehensive approach to leverage digital technologies in the delivery of public services, enhance government operational efficiency, and foster a citizen-centric approach to governance" (Gabara, 2024).

Opportunities for Positioning Digital Transformation of HRM in South Africa

Digital transformation allows South Africa to fulfil international, regional, and national aspirations. Firstly, it prepares the public service human resources to achieve Sustainable Development Goals. Secondly, as submitted by the African Union (2020), digital HRM can facilitate the delivery of goods and services in African countries, such as South Africa, and contribute to achieving Agenda 2063 and the SDGs. One recent study by Nhede et al. (2022) argues that South Africa requires urgent and targeted action to secure advanced technologies and establish a workforce equipped with the skills to cater to the changing economic dynamics influenced by the 4IR. Thus, an action such as the digital transformation of HRM can improve the South African public service by significantly changing its attributes through information, computing, communication, and connectivity technologies (Vial, 2021). More so, the PSC (2024) explains that the relevant legislative framework, regulations, and strategic documents in South Africa show that government departments and entities must not only promote ICT and provide integrated e-services but also support and enable the digital transformation of public service delivery into an inclusive digital society. Its explanation underscores that this transformation will allow all citizens, including public servants, to benefit from the opportunities digital technologies offer to improve their quality of life (PSC, 2024).

Whilst giving a keynote address at a workshop organised by the DPSA and its partners, Mr Lucas Mogashoa, Executive for Corporate and Digital Strategy at State Innovation Technology Agency, stressed the importance of not only improving service delivery efficiencies but also deploying ICT resources to achieve cost savings in the digital transformation of the public sector (Moloi, 2023). According to Moloi (2023), Mr Mogashoa pointed out a considerable amount of duplicated effort within the government, with approximately 70% of required solutions being similar across various institutions and the remaining 30% being unique to specific entities. Digital transformation of the public sector human resources can avoid challenges such as duplication.

Chapano et al. (2022) discuss the potential digital HRM strategies that could be implemented across the HR value chain in South Africa. These include digital workforce planning (such as digital recruitment and selection), digital performance management, digital learning and development, digital reward and recognition, digital employee wellness management, digital employment relations management, and digital organisational development (Chapano et al., 2022). A 2024 PSC Report on Digitisation of Human Resources Processes in the Public Service posits that digital transformation of the public service "is critical to enhance and leverage data-driven insights to ensure continuous improvement of operations as well as increased efficiency and productivity" (PSC, 2024, p. iv). Majam and Jarbandhan (2022) give specific areas in the HRM process within the government that can benefit from digital transformation actions, like the expanded use of big data. They argue that recruitment and selection, performance management and talent acquisition are exemplary processes likely to benefit from analysing big data (Majam & Jarbandhan, 2022). Majam and Jarbandhan (2022, p. 1) further stress the importance of the government's "HRM component plan to effectively use data to improve performance outcomes and promote a public service that could ultimately promote the vision of a 'better life for all'".

Challenges of Positioning Digital Transformation of HRM in South Africa

A recent study by the PSC to "ascertain the progress made by departments in digitising HRM processes in the Public Service as well as to establish the availability of capacity and capabilities to utilise HRM digital/digitised systems" provides some interesting insights (PSC, 2024, p. vii). The study has revealed a broad understanding of the concept of digitisation amongst departments, and various legislations and frameworks have been developed to facilitate digitisation broadly within government. Nevertheless, the study exposes some key challenges. The PSC found that implementing these frameworks within the Public Service lags, whereas the full-scale adoption of and adaptation to HRM digitisation remains challenging due to multiple factors. The factors include the following: a.) centralisation of IT/ICT leadership and procurement, b.) lack of skills within HR departments, c.) non-integrated initiatives across various departments, d.) a lack of management buy-in to explore new technologies and e.) failure to nurture talent in the HRM and ICT field, inefficient and outdated ICT infrastructure, budget constraints and National Treasury restrictions to enable the interface between external systems and the transversal Persal/Persol systems (PSC, 2024). Likewise, the DPSA recognises the key challenges the public service faces in delivering high-quality services and achieving operational efficiencies (Gabara, 2024). These challenges are summed up as follows (Gabara, 2024):

i. an absence of a unified strategy;
ii. inadequate leadership in ICT e-government;
iii. adherence to governance standards;
iv. disjointed business processes;
v. outdated information systems; and
vi. a lack of digital skills and trust in government.

The National Development Plan 2030 speaks about building the capabilities of the state through making the public service a career of choice (National Planning Commission, 2012). The DPSA (2023) reiterates that the digital transformation of public service is necessary for South Africa. One essential intervention the Department acknowledges as lacking is a robust digital infrastructure connecting every corner of the nation. This intervention helps bridge the digital divide, ensuring that even remote communities can access high-speed internet (DPSA, 2023). A recent study by Shava and Ndebele (2023) noted that South Africa has data marginalisation, with citizens being excluded from using the latest digital technologies ushered in the 4IR. This challenge requires decisive government intervention to ensure that the interface between the citizens and the public service does not exclude those marginalised, for example, when recruiting and selecting for the public sector. One such intervention crucial for positioning the digital transformation of HRM is increasing digital access through investments in hard and soft digital infrastructure in places like rural areas, townships, hostels, and informal settlements.

A PSC (2024) study report provided insightful findings on the extent of digital transformation of HR processes in South Africa's public service.

- Most departments have not automated nor digitised their processes and administration about the following HRM areas: learning and development and wellness, performance management, employee relations, organisational design and monitoring and evaluation.
- Most departments depend on the State Innovation Technology Agency for ICT infrastructure, which is inadequate for large data storage, retrieval, and manipulation.

- Persal/Persol, Logistical Information System, or Basic Accounting System are the main legacy systems utilised by national and provincial departments. However, due to the restrictions of the National Treasury, they have poor interfaces with other off-the-shelves (such as the Systems Applications and Products and Oracle) and in-house-developed digital HR platforms. Some argue that since the National Treasury, Gauteng Department of eGovernment, and the Western Cape provincial departments have implemented the Systems Applications and Products/Oracle systems, the National Treasury and DPSA should learn from these institutions.
- Apart from the 2016 blanket deviation, departments have not been approved to procure any other software for modules related to the Integrated Financial Management System.
- There is no alignment between the ICT infrastructure, policy and strategy and overall strategic objectives in most departments that participated in the study to allow for large-scale information automation, digitisation, information accessibility and system scalability.

Digital Transformation of HRM in Zimbabwe's Public Sector

Following the NPM-necessitated global wave of reforms to revamp and re-engineer public sector operations, since independence, the Government of Zimbabwe (GoZ) has committed to digital transformation. This saw the introduction of various e-government and ICT systems in government departments. Human resources management operations have not been spared. Through digital transformation, almost all public sector organisations in Zimbabwe have migrated to integrated payroll and personnel management systems of different forms and shapes. However, although the GoZ has championed digital transformation in personnel management, most of Zimbabwe's human resources management systems and processes reflect the traditional public administration modus operandi. Despite the widely documented benefits of digital tools in human resources management, personnel management operations are still largely manual. This has profoundly undermined effective human resources management. The following sections provide an overview of digital transformation in Zimbabwe.

Legal Frameworks for Digital Transformation in Zimbabwe's Public Sector HRM

The Zimbabwean 2013 Constitution provides a solid base for implementing civil service reforms. Section 194 provides fundamental principles and values of public administration that make digital transformation in human resources management compelling. Of prime importance is section 194(1)(i), which states that "good HRM and career-development practices, to maximise human potential, must be cultivated." Leveraging digital transformation presents an excellent opportunity for Zimbabwe to enhance its human resources management processes and maximise human potential in achieving national and sustainable development goals. Some other Section 194(1) values and principles that underscore digital transformation include the following:

- "A high standard of professional ethics must be promoted and maintained;
- efficient and economical use of resources must be promoted;
- services must be provided impartially, fairly, equitably and without bias;
- people's needs must be responded to within a reasonable time, and the public must be encouraged to participate in policy-making and

- transparency must be fostered by providing the public with timely, accessible and accurate information."

Digital transformation is also a critical component of the 2018 Vision 2030, which seeks to propel Zimbabwe *"Towards a Prosperous & Empowered Upper Middle Income Society by 2030"* (Government of Zimbabwe, 2018). Section 219 of Vision 2030 embeds ICT across government strategies, plans and operations as a critical enabler for development (Government of Zimbabwe, 2018). The Government of Zimbabwe (2018) provides for e-government to modernise and improve the efficiency of government operations. Section 221 of the Vision 2030 states, "Efficiency of public services will be increased by applying a comprehensive e-government system. Critically, there will be the need to integrate different systems to interface." Section 222 further states, "Policies to encourage the development of smart applications that meet economic needs will be promoted" (Government of Zimbabwe, 2018). Vision 2030 encourages the adoption of digital technologies in the public sector to enhance efficiency, effectiveness, transparency, responsiveness and ease of doing business.

To facilitate the attainment of Vision 2030's aspirations, the GoZ adopted the National Development Strategy 1 (NDS1): January 2021 – December 2025 (Government of Zimbabwe, 2020). The NDS1 seeks to "Promote good governance… and … modernise the economy through the use of ICT and digital technology" (Government of Zimbabwe, 2020:x). Section 7 of the NDS1 states that the strategy "is underpinned by the Integrated Results Based Management (IRBM) system, which inculcates a culture of high performance, quality service delivery, measurement, goal clarity, continuous improvement and accountability across the public sector" (Government of Zimbabwe, 2020:x). Through the NDS1, the GoZ commits to changing the attitude and culture of public administrators across the public sector by strengthening the Personnel Performance System (PPS) (Government of Zimbabwe, 2020). It emphasises the importance of servant leadership and ethics. Adopting comprehensive digital HR systems streamlines HR functions, from recruitment to retirement.

The 2016 ICT Policy also provided a robust framework for digital transformation in the public sector. Its mission was to "Exploit the potential of ICTs for sustainable socio-economic development in Zimbabwe" (Government of Zimbabwe, 2016). The policy emphasised e-government investments to improve Government to Business (G2B), Government to Citizenry (G2C) and Government to Government (G2G) and Government to Employees (G2E) interactions and transactions to ensure

- "Convenient access to interactive information and services;
- Timely delivery of public services; and
- Efficient and effective methods of conducting business transactions" (Government of Zimbabwe, 2016).

Through the 2016 ICT Policy, the GoZ committed to deploying e-government across government institutions to "reduce government institutions operational costs and to bring Government closer to the people" (GoZ, 2016, p. 23). To strategically position Zimbabwe in the digital world, the GoZ revised the 2016 National ICT Policy and introduced the reviewed ICT Policy in March 2024. The GoZ launched the Policy together with the Smart Zimbabwe 2030 Master Plan and the National Broadband Plan to promote digital transformation and propel Zimbabwe into the digital era (Nyikadzino, 2024; Chikumira, 2024; Chitumba & Mupanedemo, 2024). During the launch of the three policy documents, the President of Zimbabwe, Emmerson Mnangagwa, encouraged government officials to use digital technologies to improve service delivery (Chikumira, 2024). Although the Government of Zimbabwe has made significant strides to promote the uptake and utilisation of ICTs in the public sector, underutilisation of e-government services and infrastructure persists.

Opportunities for Digital Transformation of HRM in Zimbabwe's Public Sector

Notwithstanding policy pronouncements encouraging digital transformation in the public sector, HRM processes in Zimbabwe remain largely traditional and manual. This section discusses HR challenges in selected areas and opportunities for digital transformation.

The public sector in Zimbabwe needs to catch up in adopting digital technologies in recruitment and selection processes. Recruitment and selection processes in the public sector are mainly conducted manually and traditionally, such as posting job opportunities in newspapers like the Herald and Sunday Mail. Such platforms have limited reach in the digital era, where people mostly rely on online sources of information. They are also associated with delays, high costs and corruption. For instance, corruption has infiltrated the recruitment of teachers and nurses (The Herald, 2019). The adoption of digital technologies can transform recruitment and selection processes significantly. As Zhang & Chen (2023) hold, adopting digital technology in HRM has made recruitment and selection the critical focus areas. They further illustrate that "the application of digital HRM practices has reduced the intensity of work in selecting candidates, analysing the skill requirements needed to fill vacant positions, and selecting whom to be recruited" (Zhang & Chen, 2023, p. 9). Given the level of recruitment and selection involved in the public sector, adopting digital tools can smoothen talent selection processes and allow HR practitioners to focus on other areas of strategic importance. As most activities are happening on the Internet, public organisations should have a paradigm shift towards the Internet of Things. Social media platforms such as LinkedIn and Facebook, among others, allow public organisations access to a vast talent pool within a short period and at reasonable costs (Khera & Gulati, 2012; Rusilowati et al., 2024).

The GoZ has been grappling with human resources planning for the past four decades. More reliance on traditional manual systems has resulted in overstaffing and, in some instances, understaffing in public sector organisations. Several media, inquiry and audit reports have flagged overstaffing and understaffing as critical factors undermining the performance of strategic public organisations. State-owned Enterprises (SOE) have become notorious for overstaffing and huge losses. According to the Herald (2020), over-staffing has led to underperformance, triggering financial bailouts. Instead of being strategic contributors to the national fiscus, SOEs have become a drain. A report by the Auditor General (2017) revealed that nearly 70% of SOEs were declared insolvent because of recurring huge losses stemming from weak corporate governance. The Auditor General (2023) also revealed cases of understaffing in SOEs, namely the Insurance and Pensions Commission (IPEC), the Air Zimbabwe Private Limited, the Nurses Council of Zimbabwe (NCZ) and the National University of Science and Technology. The Auditor General (2023) also highlighted cases of overstaffing in government ministries. The report found that the Ministry of Primary and Secondary Education had a staff shortage of 9971 (Auditor General, 2023). Other ministries, such as the Ministry of Transport and Infrastructure Development, experienced the same challenge. Local authorities were not immune to staff shortages. The Auditor General (2023) highlighted performance challenges in local authorities (Bindura Municipality, Kariba Municipality, Gokwe Town Council, among others) due to staff shortages, particularly in finance departments. The Government of Zimbabwe's (2015) civil service report highlighted cases of duplication and overstaffing that have cost the government.

Although overstaffing in the public sector can be attributed to different factors, there is no doubt that poor HR planning is a crucial contributing factor. Against this background, this chapter makes a case that leveraging digital technologies will transform HRM in the public sector. Human Resource Information Systems (HRIS) helps government departments understand their staff establishment, monitor labour turnover, and proactively manage succession planning. As Khera & Gulati (2012:6) hold, "HRIS stores ample data about the employees of the organisations that helps in escalating the snail's pace of HRP. HRIS also helps in the strategic activities of HR managers and more in training and development, succession planning, applicant tracking in recruitment and selection and manpower planning." In support, an empirical quantitative study by Rusilowati et al. (2024, p.78) revealed that the adoption and optimal use of management information systems "significantly contributes to improving efficiency in the HR planning process. Integrating information technology into HRM enables organisations to manage data more efficiently, conduct deeper analyses, and make more decisions." Therefore, for Zimbabwe to survive within the everchanging and complex digital world and realise national and sustainable development goals, there is a need to intensify the utilisation of HRISs and leverage the value of digital tools' demand and supply forecasting for human resources needs. If Zimbabwe utilises digital technologies in HRM, its public service can foster operational efficiency and effectiveness and strategically align and integrate HRM processes with business goals. In addition, digital transformation allows the public service to harness digital technology, thus ensuring business-HRM partnership and minimising human resources wastage that has characterised the public sector. Literature has documented the following benefits that Zimbabwe can realise upon digitising HRM processes:

- Efficient management of HRM data;
- Making informed, comprehensive and swift decisions;
- Precise training needs analysis;
- Smooth management of employees' organisational life from employment to retirement;
- Agility in responding to environmental changes and pressures; and
- Consolidation and integration of HRM data, systems, functions, records and organisation policies (Mobideen et al., 2019; Mogbojuri, 2024; Matimbwa, 2023)

Challenges to the Digital Transformation of HRM in Zimbabwe's Public Sector

Although the government of Zimbabwe has demonstrated a commitment to digitising government operations by adopting several policy initiatives, public organisations still need help digitalising their HRM processes. More qualified personnel are required to overcome the critical challenges hampering the adoption and implementation of digital tools in HRM in the public sector. The deficiency in the workforce also affects digital literacy levels, which, in turn, impacts the adoption and utilisation of ICT services. According to the GoZ (2016, p.31), "The number of personnel with ICT qualifications is inadequate for the country, and there is no standardised national ICT training certification. There is the need to widely expose the employed and the youth and children to ICTs". The 2018 National Critical Skills Audit Report revealed that Zimbabwe has severe ICT skills shortages that may hamper the realisation of digital transformation (Government of Zimbabwe, 2018). According to the report, the Engineering and Technology sector has a skills deficit of 93.57%. Dr Muswere, the former Minister of Information, Communication, Technology, Postal and Courier Services, quoted in (The Sunday News, 2020), expressed concern about ICT staff shortages, explaining that "The key challenges facing the ICT sector in Zimbabwe and many other countries, is the low investment in ICT technologies and the lack of a large pool of skilled ICT professionals." According to Mbiza (2021), brain drain significantly undermines government efforts to build a strong ICT skills base. Due to uncompetitive remuneration, most qualified ICT specialists are relocating to countries offering competitive remuneration packages.

In addition to skills shortages, Zimbabwe still needs to acquire adequate ICT infrastructure to sustain digital transformation across the public sector. The Government of Zimbabwe (2016) explained that "Whilst there has been significant roll-out of communications infrastructure with 2G exceeding 75% population coverage (as of 31 December 2015), high-speed broadband coverage is still patchy with most rural and remote areas remaining uncovered due to a non-holistic approach to universal service". The digital divide is still a reality in Zimbabwe. Internet connectivity in rural and hard-to-reach areas is still a challenge. Subsequently, most government departments in remote areas do not have adequate infrastructure to sustain digital transformation in the country (Chikumira, 2024; Chitumba & Mupanedemo, 2024). Electricity challenges further jeopardise the digital transformation wave. As the Government of Zimbabwe (2016) indicated, "The national power grid does not cover the whole country... Even those on the national grid experience erratic supply". Electricity shortages and outages hamper ICT deployment and utilisation in the public sector. Nyakudyaa, Jamboa, Madududu, & and Manyise (2024) identified the following challenges:

- inadequate funding of ICT development;
- Fragmented policy and institutional frameworks;
- Mobile network challenges

DISCUSSION OF FINDINGS: PITFALLS AND PROMISES

This section offers a comparative analysis of the positioning of Digital Transformation in Public Sector HRM in Zimbabwe and South Africa, examining the challenges and opportunities.

Comparative Country Analysis of Legal Frameworks for Positioning Digital Transformation or HRM in the Public Sector

Shava (2022) underscores that survival in the digital age requires governments to establish conducive policy environments that promote technology adoption and innovation. As the sections above demonstrate, South Africa and Zimbabwe have implemented significant reforms to position HRM in the public sector. The reforms seem to reflect undertones captured in past literature by Betchoo (2016), whose study focused on the Mauritian public sector. Betchoo's (2016) study concluded that digital transformation positively impacts human resource factors and is bound to play an influential role in the workplace. In South Africa and Zimbabwe, the reforms that position the digital transformation of HRM in the public sector are enabled by their constitutions and supported by different policy frameworks. South Africa has done relatively better in the digital transformation of HRM in the public service than Zimbabwe. As demonstrated above, South Africa has made considerable strides in policy development and recognises the necessity of digital transformation of HRM to enhance service delivery. The proposed Digital Government policy framework in South Africa aims to provide a comprehensive roadmap for these efforts (PSC, 2024; DPSA, 2023). On the contrary, Zimbabwe has also made significant policy pronouncements, with Vision 2030 and NDS1 emphasising the role of ICT in modernising the public sector. However, practical implementation lags due to infrastructure and skills deficits. For example, recruitment for public service in South Africa is mainly done through online platforms, compared to Zimbabwe, where paper submissions are still dominant. South Africa, unlike Zimbabwe, has a dedicated agency under the DPSA, the State Innovation Technology Agency, that is responsible for spearheading the digital transformation of the public sector HRM. Zimbabwe, on the other hand, leads in terms of national vision.

Challenges and Promises for South Africa and Zimbabwe in Positioning Digital Transformation of HRM in the Public Sector

Like Zimbabwe, South Africa faces several challenges in implementing digital HRM. These include the absence of a unified strategy, inadequate ICT leadership, outdated information systems, and a lack of digital skills and trust in government. As observed in a study by Mhlanga, Shava, and Dzingirai (2023), the Zimbabwe government understands the importance of technology development and innovation in advancing the economy. Nevertheless, as scholars observe, the policy-making institutions need to be more vital in supporting the country's vast technology and development initiatives (Mhlanga et al., 2023). Unlike Zimbabwe, the DPSA in South Africa recognises these issues and is working towards finalising a policy framework to guide digital transformation in public service. However, significant barriers such as budget constraints, inefficient infrastructure, insufficient ICT infrastructure, electricity shortage, and non-integrated initiatives across departments hinder progress in South Africa and Zimbabwe (Chikumira, 2024; Chitumba & Mupanedemo, 2024; Nyakudyaa et al., 2014; PSC, 2024). Further, the digital divide remains a significant hurdle in the two neighbourly countries, with rural and remote areas lacking connectivity (DPSA, 2023; Shava & Ndebele, 2023; GoZ, 2016). Additionally, brain drain exacerbates the skills shortage, particularly in Zimbabwe, undermining efforts to build a robust ICT workforce.

Despite legal and policy frameworks supporting the digital transformation of HRM, South Africa and Zimbabwe continue underutilising e-government services and infrastructure. For example, a recent study report by the South African PSC revealed that despite well-thought-out plans, implementation is lagging, and Public Service departments remain challenged in ensuring government continuity and resilience through the speedy adoption of and adaptation to HR digitisation processes and systems (PSC, 2024). Finally, both countries see digital transformation as improving HRM efficiency and aligning with broader development goals. As past literature by Muzanenhamo and Rankhumise (2023) aptly highlights, technology is impacting HRM roles and altering the execution of personnel activities daily. The digital transformation of HRM opportunities in both contexts reflects what is reiterated in scholarly studies, including enhanced data management, streamlined HR processes, and improved service delivery (Kambur & Yildirim, 2023; Mazurchenko & Maršíková, 2019; Bengtsson & Bloom, 2017). This study also exposes that the critical challenges in South Africa are more related to strategic and leadership issues. At the same time, Zimbabwe faces more foundational problems, such as infrastructure deficits and skills shortages.

CONCLUSION

The chapter sought to understand the challenges and opportunities of positioning digital transformation in the public sector HRM in South Africa and Zimbabwe. It argued that the proliferation of advanced digital technologies has the potential to alter how public service operates and serves communities fundamentally. For example, through digital transformation, it was argued that HR functions of government provided by the constitutions and policy frameworks could be transformed, presenting challenges and opportunities. The study found that while South Africa and Zimbabwe have recognised the importance of digital transformation in HRM and have laid down policy frameworks to support this transition, their paths diverge regarding implementation effectiveness and the nature of challenges faced. Strategic and administrative hurdles impede South Africa's journey, whereas Zimbabwe is fundamentally challenged by infrastructural and HR constraints. Addressing these issues is critical for both nations to harness the full potential of digital transformation of HRM in their public sectors.

RECOMMENDATIONS AND AREAS FOR FURTHER RESEARCH

The African Union (2020) correctly states that realising the vision of digital transformation for Africa requires appropriate policies and an enabling environment with critical policy reforms to the foundation pillars and essential sectors to drive digital transformation. Zimbabwe should follow what the DPSA in South Africa is doing to establish a comprehensive digital transformation strategy for HRM in the public sector. The study concurs with the PSC (2024) in recommending that the South African DPSA should fast-track the finalisation, adoption, and implementation of the Public Service Digital Transformation Strategy. It further suggests that the adopted strategy should address the fragmented approach in both countries and include clear guidelines, timelines, and accountability mechanisms to ensure uniform implementation across all government departments. As the African Union (2020) recommends, collaborative ICT regulatory measures and tools are the new frontier for regulators and policymakers as they work towards maximising the opportunities afforded by digital transformation across industries. Thus, to improve the adoption and utilisation of digital tools in HRM in the public sector, the GoZ should intensively retool and upskill civil servants with digital skills, knowledge, and abilities. Similarly, governments should impart relevant digital skills to employees in both countries. Such training programmes will minimise resistance to change and foster change management and adaptability to the ever-changing technological environment. In Zimbabwe, where the economic status is weaker than South Africa's, the government should leverage public-private partnerships and other alternative funding models to build digital infrastructure. Furthermore, South and Zimbabwe must continuously consider recognising the potential of emerging technologies and the impact that policy and regulatory frameworks can have on their success to encourage regulatory paradigms that push frontiers and enable digital transformation (African Union, 2020).

As digital transformation continues to play a significant role in public sector HRM, there is a need for future studies to empirically assess the impact of digital HRM systems on public sector efficiency, employee satisfaction, and service delivery quality in South Africa. It is essential to conduct comparative studies between South Africa or Zimbabwe and other countries in Africa or globally that have successfully implemented digital HRM in their public sectors to identify best practices and lessons that can be adapted to the South African context. Additionally, scholars must study public sector employees' perceptions and acceptance of digital HRM tools. Understanding their concerns and attitudes can aid in the design of user-friendly systems and effective change management strategies. Finally, longitudinal studies are required to track the progress and long-term effects of digital transformation initiatives in HRM in both countries. These studies can provide insights into the sustainability of digital tools and their evolving impact over time.

REFERENCES

African Union. (2020). *The Digital Transformation Strategy for Africa*. African Union.

Armstrong, M., & Taylor, S. (2020). *Armstrong's handbook of human resource management practice*. Kogan Page Publishers.

Auditor General. (2017). *Auditor General's Report of State-Owned Enterprises 2017*. Government Printers.

Auditor General. (2023). *Report of the Auditor General on Appropriation accounts, finance and revenue statements and fund accounts for the year ended December 31, 2022*. Government Printers.

Auditor General. (2023). *Report of the Auditor-General for the financial year ended December 31, 2020, on local authorities*. Government Printers.

Auditor General. (2023). *Report of the Auditor-General for the financial year ended December 31, 2022 on state owned enterprises and parastatals*. Government Printers.

Bengtsson, C., & Bloom, M. (2017). Human Resource Management in a Digital Era. *LUP Student Papers, 0-30*.

Betchoo, N. K. (2016, August). Digital transformation and its impact on human resource management: A case analysis of two unrelated businesses in the Mauritian public service. In *2016 IEEE International Conference on Emerging Technologies and Innovative Business Practices for the Transformation of Societies (EmergiTech)* (pp. 147–152). IEEE. 10.1109/EmergiTech.2016.7737328

Bourgon, J. (2015). Leadership for Change, Innovation for Results: A New Synthesis. Paper presented at the Distinctively Public Sector: The Case for a New Synthesis of Public Administration, Queensland, Australia.

Chapano, M., Mey, M. R., & Werner, A. (2022). Adoption of digital strategies across the human resource value chain. *SA Journal of Human Resource Management*, 20(0). Advance online publication. 10.4102/sajhrm.v20i0.1992

Chapano, M., Mey, M. R., & Werner, A. (2022). Adoption of digital strategies across the human resource value chain. *SA Journal of Human Resource Management*, 20(0), 1992. 10.4102/sajhrm.v20i0.1992

Chikumira, T. (2024, March 9). New ICT policy documents a game changer – Govt. *ZBC News*. https://www.zbcnews.co.zw/featured/new-ict-policy-documents-a-game-changer-govt/

Chitumba, P., & Mupanedemo, F. (2024, March 8). Harness ICT to improve service delivery. *The Herald*. https://www.herald.co.zw/harness-ict-to-improve-service-delivery/

Department of Public Service and Administration. (1995). *White Paper on the Transformation of the Public Service*. Pretoria: DPSA

Department of Public Service and Administration. (1995). White Paper on the Transformation of the Public Service Pretoria: DPSA

Department of Public Service and Administration. (1997). *White Paper on Transforming Public Service Delivery (Batho Pele White Paper)*. Pretoria: DPSA

Department of Public Service and Administration. (1997). White Paper on Transforming Public Service Delivery (Batho Pele White Paper) Pretoria: DPSA

Department of Public Service and Administration. (2023). Address by the Department of Communications and Digital Technologies Deputy Director-General For Information Society & Capacity Development, Mr Mlindi Mashologu, at the Digital Government Workshop at Microsoft Campus, Johannesburg. 6 September 2023. Retrieved from https://www.gov.za/news/speeches/communications-and-digital-technologies-digital-government-workshop-06-sep-2023

Department of Public Service and Administration. (2023). Address by the Department of Communications and Digital Technologies Deputy Director-General For Information Society & Capacity Development, Mr Mlindi Mashologu, at the Digital Government Workshop at Microsoft Campus, Johannesburg. 6 September 2023. Retrieved from https://www.gov.za/news/speeches/communications-and-digital-technologies-digital-government-workshop-06-sep-2023

Dunleavy, P., Margetts, H., Bastow, S., & Tinkler, J. (2006). New public management is dead—Long live digital-era governance. *Journal of Public Administration: Research and Theory*, 16(3), 467–494. 10.1093/jopart/mui057

Gabara, N. (2024). *DPSA finalising Digital Policy framework to drive public service transformation.* Retrieved from https://www.dpsa.gov.za/thepublicservant/2024/03/15/dpsa-finalising-digital-policy-framework-to-drive-public-service-transformation/

Girisha, M., & Nagendrababu, K. (2019). E-Human resource management (E-HRM): A growing role in organizations. *International Journal of Management Studies*, 6(1/5), 98–104.

Government of Zimbabwe. (2015). *Civil service report*. Government Printers.

Government of Zimbabwe. (2016). *National Informational Communication Technology Policy*. Government Printers.

Government of Zimbabwe. (2016). *Zimbabwe National Policy for Information and Communications Technology*. Government Publishers.

Government of Zimbabwe. (2018). *2018 National Critical Skills Audit Report*. Government Printers.

Government of Zimbabwe. (2018). *Vision 2030: "Towards a Prosperous & Empowered Upper Middle Income Society by 2030"*. Government Printers.

Government of Zimbabwe. (2020). *National Development Strategy 1 - January 2021 - December 2025*. Government Printers.

Hood, C. (1991). A public management for all seasons? Public administration, pp. 69, 3–19.

Kambur, E., & Yildirim, T. (2023). From traditional to smart human resources management. *International Journal of Manpower*, 44(3), 422–452. 10.1108/IJM-10-2021-0622

Khera, S., & Gulati, K. (2012). Human resource information system and its impact on human resource planning: A perceptual analysis of information technology companies. [IOSRJBM]. *IOSR Journal of Business and Management*, 3(6), 6–13. 10.9790/487X-0360613

Larkin, J. (2017). HR digital disruption: The biggest wave of transformation in decades. *Strategic HR Review*, 16(2), 55–59. 10.1108/SHR-01-2017-0006

Majam, T., & Jarbandhan, D. B. (2022). Data driven human resource management in the Fourth Industrial Revolution (4IR). *Africa's Public Service Delivery & Performance Review*, 10(1), 12. 10.4102/apsdpr.v10i1.588

Matimbwa, H. (2023). Human Resource Information System Applications: Insights from Local Government Authorities in Tanzania. *Ruaha Journal of Business. Economics and Management Sciences*, 6(1), 87–100.

Mazurchenko, A., & Maršíková, K. (2019). Digitally-powered human resource management: Skills and roles in the digital era. *Acta Informatica Pragensia*, 8(2), 72–87. 10.18267/j.aip.125

Mbiza, S. (2021). ICT Innovations Propel Local Development: Where are Zimbabwean ICT Technopreneurs? [WJRR]. *World Journal of Research and Review*, 12(6), 16–20. 10.31871/WJRR.12.6.7

Mergel, I. (2019). Digital service teams in government. *Government Information Quarterly*, 36(4), 101389. 10.1016/j.giq.2019.07.001

Mhlanga, D., Shava, E., & Dzingirai, M. (2023). Harnessing State Capability in Embracing the Fourth Industrial Revolution: Is Zimbabwe Prepared? In The Fourth Industrial Revolution in Africa: Exploring the Development Implications of Smart Technologies in Africa (pp. 239-254): Springer.

Mobideen, H., Allahawiah, S., & Alomari, K. M. (2019). The Impact of Human Resources Information Systems on Human Resources Selection and Recruitment Strategy: An applied study on Arab Potash Company in the Hashemite Kingdom of Jordan. *International Journal of Advanced Trends in Computer Science and Engineering*, 8(5), 2475–2484. 10.30534/ijatcse/2019/93852019

Mogbojuri, B. O. (2024). Unlocking the Potential: Artificial Intelligence and Machine Learning in Human Resources Information Systems. *IEEE-SEM Publications*, 12(3).

Moloi, D. (2023). *The Case for Immediate Action on Public Sector Digital Transformation is urgently needed*. Retrieved from https://www.dpsa.gov.za/thepublicservant/2023/09/06/the-case-for-immediate-action-on-public-sector-digital-transformation-is-urgently-needed/

Muzanenhamo, A., & Rankhumise, E. (2023). Human resource management and digitalization in a South African public enterprise. *Indonesian Journal of Innovation and Applied Sciences*, 3(1), 31–37. 10.47540/ijias.v3i1.692

Nachit, M., & Okar, C. (2020). Digital transformation of human resources management: A roadmap. Paper presented at the 2020 IEEE International Conference on Technology Management, Operations and Decisions (ICTMOD). 10.1109/ICTMOD49425.2020.9380608

National Planning Commission. (2012). *National Development Plan 2030: Our Future – Make it Work*. The Presidency.

Nhede, N. T., Mazenda, A., & Masiya, T. (2022). The South African public service and the Fourth Industrial Revolution. *Africa's Public Service Delivery and Performance Review*, 10(1), 420. 10.4102/apsdpr.v10i1.420

Nicolás-Agustín, Á., Jiménez-Jiménez, D., & Maeso-Fernandez, F. (2022). The role of human resource practices in the implementation of digital transformation. *International Journal of Manpower*, 43(2), 395–410. 10.1108/IJM-03-2021-0176

Nyakudya, S., Jamboa, N., Madududu, P., & Manyise, T. (2024). Unlocking the potential: Challenges and factors influencing the use of ICT by smallholder maize farmers in Zimbabwe. *Cogent Economics & Finance*, 12(1), 2330431. Advance online publication. 10.1080/23322039.2024.2330431

Nyikadzino, T. (2024). President Mnangagwa launches three ICT policies to boost the country's digital economy. *State of the Nation*. 8 March 2024.

Nyikadzino, T. (2024, March 8). President Mnangagwa launches three ICT policies to boost the country's digital economy. *State of the Nation*. https://stateofthenation.co.zw/2024/03/08/president-mnangagwa-launches-three-ict-policies-to-boost-the-countrys-digital-economy/

Osborne, S. P., Radnor, Z., & Nasi, G. (2012). A New Theory for Public Service Management? Toward a (Public) Service-Dominant Approach. *American Review of Public Administration*, 43(2), 135–158. 10.1177/0275074012466935

Public Service Commission. (2024). *Report on Digitisation of Human Resources Processes in the Public Service*. Pretoria: The Public Service Commission Retrieved from https://www.psc.gov.za/documents/reports/2024/Report_on_Digitisation_of_Human_Resource_Management_Processes_in_the_Public_Service.pdf

Public Service Commission. (2024). Report on Digitisation of Human Resources Processes in the Public Service. Pretoria: The Public Service Commission Retrieved from https://www.psc.gov.za/documents/reports/2024/Report_on_Digitisation_of_Human_Resource_Management_Processes_in_the_Public_Service.pdf

Rusilowati, U., Narimawati, U., Wijayanti, Y. R., Rahardja, U., & Arif, O. (2024). Optimizing Human Resource Planning through Advanced Management Information Systems: A Technological Approach. *Aptisi Transactions on Technopreneurship* (ATT), 72–83.

Shava, E. (2022). Survival of African governments in the Fourth Industrial Revolution. Africa and the Fourth Industrial Revolution: Curse or Cure? 125–144.

Shava, E., & Ndebele, N. C. (2023). Data marginalization in South Africa: A quest for inclusive digital participation. *Social Sciences and Education Research Review*, 10(2), 122–131.

Strohmeier, S. (2020). Digital human resource management: A conceptual clarification. *German Journal of Human Resource Management*, 34(3), 345–365. 10.1177/2397002220921131

The Herald. (2019, August 6). Editorial comment: E-recruitment of nurses will bring fairness. The *Herald*. https://www.herald.co.zw/editorial-comment-e-recruitment-of-nurses-will-bring-fairness/

The Herald. (2020, November 6). State enterprises' reform will benefit all. *The Herald*. https://www.herald.co.zw/editorial-comment-state-enterprises-reform-will-benefit-all/

The Sunday News. (2020, September 6). ICTs skills slow uptake worries Govt. *The Sunday News*. Retrieved from https://www.sundaynews.co.zw/icts-skills-slow-uptake-worries-govt/

Vial, G. (2021). *Understanding digital transformation: A review and a research agenda.* Managing Digital Transformation. 10.4324/9781003008637-4

Weber, M. (2023). Bureaucracy. In *Social theory re-wired* (pp. 271–276). Routledge. 10.4324/9781003320609-33

Zhang, J., & Chen, Z. (2023). Exploring Human Resource Management Digital Transformation in the Digital Age. *Journal of the Knowledge Economy*. Advance online publication. 10.1007/s13132-023-01214-y

Chapter 14
Talent Management in the Digital Age:
Leveraging Technology to Enhance Public Sector Recruitment and Retention in Zimbabwe

Raymond Mapuranga
https://orcid.org/0000-0002-1520-1660
Midlands State University, Zimbabwe

Kebiat Mukuze
https://orcid.org/0000-0002-0402-905X
Midlands State University, Zimbabwe

Abigail Maravanyika
Reformed Church University, Zimbabwe

ABSTRACT

Using the integrative literature review as the research methodology, this chapter explores the role of technology in talent management within the public sector, specifically focusing on recruitment and retention strategies. The chapter highlights the unique challenges faced by public sector organizations in talent acquisition and retention, such as limited budgets, bureaucratic processes, and the perception of a less dynamic work environment. The chapter revealed that various technologies can be utilized to improve recruitment efforts in the public sector including the use of applicant tracking systems, online job portals, and social media platforms. The study concluded that technology could contribute to talent retention in the public sector through the role of digital platforms in fostering employee engagement, facilitating knowledge sharing and collaboration, and providing continuous learning opportunities. Lastly, the chapter provides practical recommendations for public sector organizations looking to leverage technology for recruitment and retention.

DOI: 10.4018/979-8-3693-2889-7.ch014

INTRODUCTION

Digital transformation has disrupted the status quo of many public and private sector organisations globally. The use of modern digital technologies such as applicant tracking systems, online job portals and social media platform analytics, and artificial intelligence among others pose serious threats to public sector organizations to either 'adopt' or 'perish' if they want to sustain in conducting government business in the digital age. Public institutions cannot remain silent as trends in the technological environment stand to upset the existing bureaucratic systems and structures which at times calls for change management in public institutions to allow Human Resource Management (HRM) reforms that may be compatible with the use of modern digital technologies and other Information Communication Technology (ICT). Following, the global pandemics, economic downturns and twists have made attracting and retaining top talent a subject of growing concern, particularly in public sector organisations. Talent management, as enabled by information technology in the public sector, is important to public sector human resource practitioners. The exponential rise in the use of social media employee recruitment platforms and technology has created unprecedented recruitment opportunities for human resource managers in both private and public sectors across the globe. However, alongside the benefits, a burgeoning body of evidence (Tsamados et al., 2022) suggests that the excessive use of social media and technology in recruitment and talent management may be associated with ethical challenges to employees. While embracing digital transformation is strategic in the public sector, HRM managers need to be cognizant of other social ills that may be triggered by the use of social media in the context of Zimbabwe where data marginalization and digital disparities exist which may affect potential public sector employees in marginalised areas with poor or no internet connectivity (Mhlanga et al., 2023). The Zimbabwean public sector presents a glaring scenario in which talent management practices have been associated with traditional methods of hiring and selection which are not anywhere near the modern digital hiring techniques ushered in through digital transformation. This chapter attempts to provide a nitpicking picture of the challenges associated with public sector employee resourcing and retention, given the advancement of technology in modern-day business operations. This chapter answers the following research objectives:

- To determine the benefits of technology on talent retention in the public sector;
- To ascertain the suitable technology for recruitment and selection in the public sector; and
- To explore the talent management challenges in the public sector.

This chapter aims to contribute to the existing literature by exploring the role of technology in talent management in the Zimbabwean public sector with a focus on identifying the challenges and benefits of technology in talent management. Through a multi-dimensional approach that incorporates a systematic literature review analysis, this study seeks to shed light on the complex interplay between talent management and technology adoption in the public health sector. Ultimately, the findings are expected to inform the development of an evidence-based framework that would assist in resolving talent management challenges in the Zimbabwean public sector organisations.

THEORETICAL AND EMPIRICAL PERSPECTIVES

The researchers draw from Human Capital and Resource-Based View theories. Human capital theory was developed by Becker (1962) and Rosen (1976) as highlighted by Frese and Rauch (2001). Evidence (Utami & Alamanos, 2023) suggest that Resource-based view theory was proposed by Barney in 1991. These theories were employed to achieve theoretical triangulation such that new research data could be interpreted for future use.

Talent management is an integral part of human resource management and can be supported by Human capital theory (Becker, 1965). Human capital pertains to an individual's qualities which are valuable to production processes in organisations. This includes employee knowledge, skills, expertise, health, and education. The human capital theory assumes that each worker in the organisation possesses skills or talents (Cohen & Soto, 2007). To enhance or accumulate the traits, education is essential in employee and organisational development. Against this backdrop, managers must be able to teach, train and lead their employees appropriately. They should be saved as focal points of guidance in the organisation. Managers should seek to understand their team members in the way they operate and develop their abilities. According to this theory, sufficient investment in people will lead to economic growth through innovations and efficient work processes (Gillies, 2015). Public managers at times fail to understand the importance of employee training programs due to rigid policies crafted by top management without their involvement. Public sector organisations sometimes do not pay living wages to employees and once they receive any form of training offered by the organisation, they leave for greener pastures outside the country. Thus, this benefit and investment done by the organisation to employees renders it a training ground for other countries with better conditions of service. Such a phenomenon indicates that mere investment in people without the award of expected fringe benefits or remuneration benefits cannot assist the organisation achieve its long-term goals. Hence, motivation is an essential aspect of productivity in public sector organisations.

The Resource-Based View (RBV) is a managerial framework developed by Barney in 1991 that is used to determine the strategic resources an organisation can exploit to achieve competitive advantage. The RBV focuses managerial attention on the organisation's internal resources to identify the assets, capabilities, and competencies with the potential to deliver superior competitive advantages (Acar, 2016). Resource-based view also explains talent management and suggests that if organisations need to achieve sustainable competitive advantage, they must engage valuable resources (Barney, 2014). The organisational physical and organisational resources can be described as imitable, replicable, and substitutable. The human resources that are valuable, rare, non-substitutable, and inimitable are thought to be a source of competitive advantage for the firm. A sustainable competitive advantage can be obtained from talent-management practices which include attracting, developing, motivating, managing, rewarding, and retaining talent. In the digital transformation age, digital talent management is critical to retaining the skilled expertise in public sector organisations which will likely enable the smooth function of HRM function in delivering public services.

Justification of Theoretical Perspectives

Human capital acknowledges that not all labour is equal. Public sector employers can improve the quality of capital by investing in employees. Employees' education, experience, and abilities can be used to do this. The economic value of this is great for employers and the economy. Thus, the resource-based view theory is significant in a business as it emphasizes the importance of a company's resources and capabilities in attaining superior performance and long-term competitive advantage. It underscores the significance of a company's assets and how they can be optimally utilised. The theory emphasizes the distinctive assets and skills a company has, both physical and abstract, and how they can give it a competitive edge. By using the resource-based view, public sector Zimbabwean organisations can find and use their internal resources to gain an edge over their competitors. In addition, this theory offers a framework for management to find and use the firm's resources as ways to grow and improve. The resource-based view theory is applied in different fields to comprehend and improve performance.

CONTEXTUALIZING TALENT MANAGEMENT IN PUBLIC SECTOR ORGANISATIONS

The term talent management in public sector literature has various meanings although scholars commonly associate this term with the desire and ability of public institutions to keep a skilled workforce to render public services. A person's inborn natural ability, skills, knowledge, experience, intelligence, attitudes and entrepreneurship, as well as their ability to learn and develop, are referred to as talent (Balcerzyk & Materac, 2019). Talent in this case means something unique in most individuals because of accumulated work experience, education, and natural characteristics. Therefore, for public sector organisations to benefit from the key talents in individual employees, talent must be nurtured through various support mechanisms. Talent management in corporate organisations can be defined as the diligent placement of rightly qualified people to different business functions to achieve organisational goals (Sembiring & Damayanti, 2023). It involves the process of attracting, retaining, and developing qualified employees for open positions. Simply put, talent management covers the whole life cycle of employer-employee relations from recruitment right up to the exit stage. Thus, this definition of talent management applies to all private and public sector organisations in the corporate business world. Nevertheless, the practice of talent management varies depending on the sector of the economy. In this chapter, talent management in the Zimbabwean public sector is characterized by a shortage of personnel with the necessary electronic skills to manage digital records. The public sector in Zimbabwe is not changing fast enough to use digital tools for managing its workers. This is because of many problems, such as too many rules, not enough money, not enough knowledge, and no clear rules to follow (Mutsagondo & Khumalo, 2023). Sadly, the public sector still uses outdated, paper-based HR systems that do not help with managing employee records (Tapiwa et al., 2022).

Due to differences in the age groups of employees found in the labour market, there is a great need for organisations to develop modern-day recruitment strategies anchored on the use of technology and avoid traditional paper recruitment methods. The new generation of employees found in the present labour market are techno-savvy and have a new set of expectations different from the old people. Thus, it cannot be argued that talent management is one of the essential drivers of effective service delivery in the public sector while in businesses success and growth are derived from good recruitment policies that enable businesses to withstand competition from firms in similar lines of business. In the Zimbabwean context, talent management is better practised in the private sector than in public sector organisations due to notable "red tape" found in government departments and bureaucratic policies.

In line with the thrust of this chapter, authors saw it provident to unpack the second aspect of the book chapter title which is the public sector. All levels of governance and government-controlled enterprises make up the public sector (Wegrich, 2024). Households, privately-owned organisations, and voluntary organizations are not part and parcel of what is called the public sector. Hence, the key defining features of the public sector are government ownership and control. The public sector provides stability, direction and is responsible for providing services and managing resources to citizens and other organizations. Police force, public health services and public schools are examples of public sector institutions. On another note, the digital age refers to the present-time use of machines and computers (Denning, 2022). Societies and business organisations' day-to-day activities are being impacted by the digital age. It came with a lot of opportunities as well as costs. Professionals in digital technologies are trying to push their boundaries to become more advanced in technology even beyond imagination (ibid). Zimbabwe as a developing country, has economic stagnation and high inflation rate problems. There are various computers and technology machines in the public health services departments. Nevertheless, there is unceasing use of hard copy record keeping and traditional talent management practices this requires public sector organisations to embrace digital transformations which allow the use of modern digital technologies to enhance efficiency (Mudimu, 2013). Despite the proliferation of modern digital technologies of the Fourth Industrial Revolution (4IR), public sector organisations in Zimbabwe still struggle to adapt to modern digital techniques in hiring and selection due to various political, economic, and social issues (Mhlanga et al., 2023). The role of public sector human resource management in Zimbabwe is still constrained by the minimal or no use of modern digital hiring techniques which also has a bearing on talent management in both the long and short term. The reluctance by public sector organisations to embrace digital transformation can have adverse on talent management within Zimbabwean public sector HRM as skilled expertise in most cases is lost through the brain resulting in talent wastage.

Talent Management in Practice

Pinigis (2023) and Stuss (2020) believe that talent management is problematic for both private and public sector organisations because employees in most cases lack career satisfaction and often quit their employment. Employee turnover in public sector organisations is an ongoing issue globally. For example, in Poland, research shows that non-rational models by different organisations existed but failed to meet the existing needs of talent management (Stuss, 2020). Studies conducted by (Mutadzakupa, 2023) and (Nkala et al., 2021) revealed that tourism and public health sectors experience several challenges associated with poor practical talent management strategies which greatly affects workforce engagement. Despite the problems experienced in managing talent in public sector organisations, (Enwereji & Emmanuel, 2022) and (Mjulwa, 2023) submit that talent management can assist public sector employees to improve their work performance through advanced work skills training that helps achieve organisational goals.

A critical analysis of the body of empirical evidence (Mutadzakupa, 2023) corroborated by anecdotal evidence indicates that talent management is a thorny issue in the flesh for many public managers including HRM managers in the private sector organisations in any economy. The aspect is permeant and transcends international, regional, and local boundaries of developed and developing countries. Equally, different public sector organisations use various talent management models which involve planning, attracting, selection process, development, retention, and retirement schemes. However, there is a need for public managers in various sectors of any economy such as the health sector to utilise new technologies in the form of online talent management platforms that offer the latest trends on the job market to deal with the effects of the fast-moving digital revolution.

Talent Management and Digital Transformation in Public Sector Organisations

As compared to the private sector, empirical research on talent management in public sector organizations is still lacking (Fauzian et al., 2024). Top leadership commitment and support, HR agency capabilities, IT infrastructure support and continuous improvement are some of the key factors to consider when implementing digital talent management. According to Al Jawali et al., (2022), the public sector in Dubai lacks effective and coordinated talent management, as shown by their research findings. While research (Kravariti et al., 2023) shows that talent management practices are linked to individual and organisational outcomes, little is known about the mechanisms through which these processes unfold, especially in the public sector of emerging market economies.

(Milukutu & Siachisa, 2023) conducted a research study in Zambia and found that the public sector was struggling with poor performance, with public employees being viewed as lazy and rigid and public agencies being perceived as big, wasteful, and ineffective. The research showed that using digital tools improved how well employees did their work, especially in terms of tasks, adaptability, and context. However, there were some problems and limitations, such as poor internet connection, lack of digital tools in some areas, insufficient resources and training.

According to (Tapiwa et al., 2022), Zimbabwean research showed that the public sector in Zimbabwe is not changing fast enough to use digital tools for managing its workers. This is because of many problems, such as too many rules, not enough money, not enough knowledge, and no clear rules to follow. The public sector still uses outdated, paper-based HR systems that do not help with managing employee records, hiring, keeping, or training, despite the lack of digital HR platforms. While HR functions like payroll and pension benefits management have embraced digital adoption in the past decade, there are still unforeseen challenges and inefficiencies in meeting the needs of public service choirs and demands. The current methods of measuring and rewarding employees' work do not take advantage of the opportunities that digital technology offers to enhance efficiency and quality of service. In the same vein, (Mutsagondo & Khumalo, 2023) found that the public sector in Zimbabwe lacks the necessary electronic skills to manage digital records.

Furthermore, talent management is a problem for public sector organizations as it transcends international, regional and local boundaries. For example, the Zimbabwean public sector is adversely affected by the slow adoption of digital technologies that could be used in talent management processes. Studies done in Zimbabwe have revealed various stumbling blocks which include bureaucratic business practices, lack of training in information technology skills and brain drain challenges (Mhlanga, Shava & Dzingirai 2023). Against this backdrop, researchers opined that virtual reality, augmented reality and artificial intelligence can be used in talent management practices in Zimbabwe. Augmented reality combines real and imagined scenarios to enhance people's ways of engaging with the things around them. Public sector HR professionals can rely on augmented and virtual reality to recruit, train, onboard and engage employees (Njerekai, 2020). New employees can take a virtual tour of an organisation's offices. The employees can feel like they are in the workplace if they can understand the company culture from afar.

Ensuring that professionals know how to leverage the tools properly before using them in the real world is one of the benefits of learning how to use and deploy equipment without hands-on manipulation. This is an important technology to the Zimbabwean public sector, as it can reduce costs and train workers by replicating real-world scenarios, allowing them to make mistakes without a catastrophic impact. More engaging learning and team-building opportunities can be achieved with the use of augmented and virtual reality. Individuals can take part without leaving their couches if they are immersed in simulations.

Artificial Intelligence

One of the most sophisticated technologies brought about by digital transformation is Artificial Intelligence (AI). Artificial intelligence has a role to play in public sector talent management. Applicant tracking systems use artificial intelligence to identify qualified candidates from their resumes and application materials and find applicants who meet the specified requirements. It is possible to train it to reduce bias in the hiring process as professionals feed it more data and improve it (Jake, 2022). Artificial intelligence can help reduce time-to-hire and reduce costs associated with the hiring process. Besides the perceived advantages of using AI in the public sector, various HRM departments in Zimbabwe have not yet fully embraced this latest innovation due to institutional challenges and funding related issues. To effectively deliver services and achieve efficiency in the Zimbabwean public sector HRM, AI can be used to mitigate problems emanating from recruitment processes.

METHODOLOGY

The researchers employed an integrative systematic review methodology to synthesize data from various research designs in talent management in the digital age. This approach aimed to provide a comprehensive and reliable conclusion on the subject matter by critically evaluating and combining existing research findings. Integrative reviews, also known as orderly critical reviews, offer a thorough summary of contemporary evidence and explanations from published quantitative and qualitative investigations. Following the guidelines of (Kutcher & LeBaron, 2022), an integrative review was conducted due to the trending nature of adopting digital technologies in leveraging recruitment and retention in both business and academic domains. Kutcher and LeBaron (2022) propose five phases to work through when conducting an integrative literature review. The proposed phases include problem formulation, literature search, evaluation of data, analysis, presentation, and analysis of results. The methodology was supported by previous empirical works (Falletta & Combs, 2020). To avoid duplication and enhance credibility, a search of related literature was conducted using key terms such as talent management challenges, talent management in the digital age, and technology in recruitment and selection. Likewise, other search terms included public sector talent management, talent management, retention strategies, knowledge retention and staff retention. Recent literature within the past five years was prioritized to ensure the quality and relevance of research evidence. Recent sources were considered more reliable as they have undergone scrutiny by other scholars and are less likely to be outdated, especially in rapidly evolving fields such as technology.

Two databases, Google Scholar, and Francis and Taylor Online, were used to gather relevant information, resulting in 120 relevant results. Additionally, a search for grey literature related to leveraging digital technologies in leveraging recruitment and retention was conducted on the World Wide Web, yielding fourteen results. Grey literature refers to information obtained from sources outside of traditional indexed publishing houses, such as academic, government, and business reports available in the public domain (McKenzie, 2023). Grey literature is valuable as it provides diverse perspectives and addresses emerging research areas not covered by commercial publishers. The inclusion criteria for the articles included were guided by four key aspects.

Relevance to leveraging digital technologies to enhance recruitment and retention

- English language.
- Full-text availability.
- Scholarly nature.
- Articles that were irrelevant to the study topic (Exclusion criteria).
- Older than five years; and
- Not in English, or from pure science disciplines.

The Preferred Reporting Items for Systematic Reviews and Meta-Analyses (PRISMA) diagram illustrates the process of preparing articles for the subsequent appraisal and synthesis.

Figure 1.

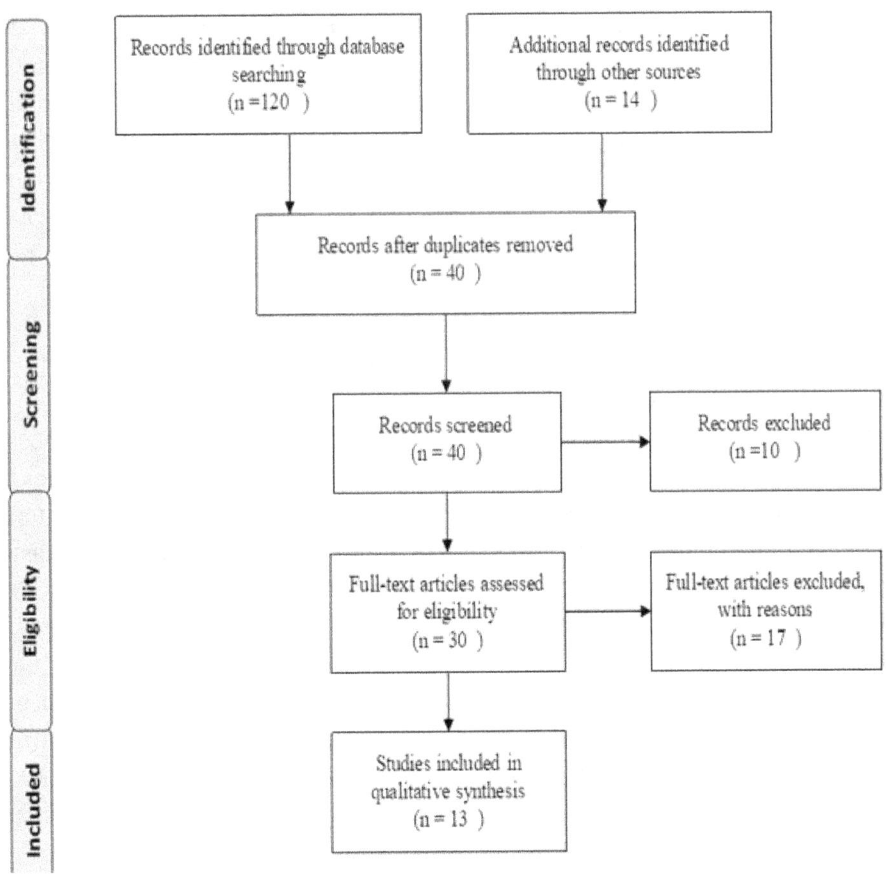

Source: *Own research*

RESULTS

The final qualitative synthesis included thirteen sources, which were then analysed thematically according to the research objectives guided by the scholarly survey. The thirteen source articles revealed three main ideas that we grouped based on our objectives.

Benefits of Technology on Talent Retention

Talent management was observed to have a positive influence on organisational performance and leadership challenges (Samidi et al., 2023). The benefits of adopting technology on talent retention in the public sector have been extensively studied, and several findings from the sources consulted highlight a positive impact of technology in this context. One study (Garcia, 2022) found that implementing technology solutions in the public sector leads to enhanced efficiency and productivity. By streamlining processes and automating tasks, technology reduces administrative burdens and allows employees to focus on more strategic work. This increased efficiency not only improves job satisfaction but also contributes to higher talent retention rates.

Furthermore, research conducted by (Johnson & Brown, 2022) reveals that technology adoption in the public sector improves work-life balance for employees. Remote work and flexible scheduling tools offered through technology enable employees to have greater control over their work arrangements. This flexibility reduces stress and enhances job satisfaction, ultimately leading to improved talent retention. In terms of professional development, the study highlights the benefits of technology-driven learning initiatives in the public sector. Online training platforms and e-learning resources provide employees with convenient access to skill-enhancement opportunities. By investing in technology-enabled learning, organizations demonstrate their commitment to employee growth, which positively influences talent retention.

Data-driven decision-making is another significant benefit of technology adoption in the public sector. According to a study by (Nguyen et al., 2023), leveraging data analytics tools enables organizations to make informed decisions. By analysing trends and patterns, public sector organizations can anticipate challenges and take proactive preventive measures. This data-driven approach enhances transparency and accountability, creating a work environment that engages employees and contributes to talent retention. Effective communication and collaboration are essential for talent retention, and technology plays a crucial role in facilitating these aspects. Research by Garcia and Smith (2020) emphasizes the role of technology platforms such as project management tools and instant messaging applications, in fostering seamless communication and collaboration among teams. These tools promote a sense of belonging and teamwork, reducing turnover rates in the public sector.

Moreover, the use of technology for employee recognition and engagement has shown positive results. A study by (Thakurta, 2024) suggests that technology-based employee recognition platforms and social intranets contribute to a positive work culture. These platforms provide channels for acknowledging and appreciating employees' contributions, fostering a sense of belonging and loyalty, which ultimately aids in talent retention.

Over and above, the findings from various studies indicate that adopting technology in the public sector has numerous benefits for talent retention. These include enhanced efficiency and productivity, improved work-life balance, opportunities for professional development, data-driven decision-making, effective communication, and collaboration, as well as recognition and employee engagement. By leveraging technology effectively, public sector organizations can create an environment that attracts and retains talented employees, leading to increased organizational success.

Suitable Technology for Recruitment and Selection

The findings from the integrative literature review on suitable technology for recruitment and selection provide valuable insights into the use of technology in optimizing these processes. Several studies have contributed to understanding the benefits and challenges associated with different technological solutions. One key finding is that applicant tracking systems (ATS) are widely recognized as a suitable technology for recruitment and selection. ATS streamline the application process by automating resume screening, managing candidate data, and facilitating communication with applicants (Potočnik et al., 2021). The use of ATS improves efficiency, reduces time-to-hire, and ensures consistency in candidate evaluation, leading to a more effective recruitment process. In their research study, (Muduli & Trivedi, 2020) explored the intricate and diverse aspects of talent and talent management, the different viewpoints that shape talent management, and the factors and results that are essential for talent management. Currently, firms primarily rely on information systems for talent management, but there has been a lack of emphasis on developing comprehensive organizational talent management systems. The study found that there is no one type of information system used in talent management. In the field of talent management, technological advancements such as data science, artificial intelligence (AI), and analytics are crucial factors to consider. According to (Kravariti & Johnston, 2020), enhancing the information systems that support the core TM practices could also help the public sector achieve TM success.

As an illustration, public sector organizations could promote their job openings on social media platforms to attract qualified candidates. Companies can employ electronic recruitment methods that facilitate the process of attracting potential employees. Information systems can also be beneficial for auditing purposes, such as tracking employee turnover rates, and can help in retaining skilled employees. Another finding suggests that video interviewing technology is gaining popularity and effectiveness in recruitment and selection (MESHRAM, 2023). Video interviews allow recruiters to assess candidates remotely, saving time and resources associated with traditional face-to-face interviews. This technology offers flexibility, particularly in global or remote hiring scenarios, and provides a standardized platform for evaluating candidate responses.

Furthermore, social media platforms have emerged as a valuable tool for recruitment and selection (Potočnik et al., 2021). Social media platforms, such as LinkedIn, Facebook, and Twitter, provide access to a large pool of potential candidates and enable recruiters to showcase job opportunities, engage with passive candidates, and assess candidates' online presence. This technology enhances employer branding, expands the reach of job postings, and enables recruiters to gather additional insights beyond traditional application materials.

Artificial intelligence (AI) and machine learning (ML) technologies have also shown promise in recruitment and selection (Muduli & Trivedi, 2020). AI-powered algorithms can analyse large volumes of candidate data, identify patterns, and predict candidate fit based on historical data. ML algorithms can be trained to screen resumes, assess candidate skills, and even conduct preliminary interviews, saving time and reducing bias in the selection process.

However, it is important to note that the integration of technology in recruitment and selection is not without challenges. Privacy concerns, data security, and potential biases embedded in technology algorithms are some of the key challenges identified (Tsamados et al., 2022). Ethical considerations need to be addressed to ensure fair and unbiased decision-making throughout the recruitment and selection process. In summary, the integrative literature review highlights several suitable technologies for recruitment and selection. Applicant tracking systems, video interviewing technology, social media platforms, and AI/ML technologies offer significant benefits in terms of efficiency, candidate reach, and data-driven decision-making.

However, organizations should be mindful of the ethical implications and potential biases associated with these technologies. By leveraging suitable technology effectively, organizations can enhance their recruitment and selection processes, attracting top talent and improving overall organizational performance.

The main idea of the text is that using information technology can help public sector organisations improve their talent management. Public sector organizations do not need to invest in specific software or technology tools, as they can benefit from the development of artificial intelligence tools and other recruitment technologies. In sum, it can be concluded that there is no one-size-fits-all kind of recruitment technology in the public sector, key elements like the culture and organisational goals would determine the form of recruitment technology to be employed.

Talent Management Challenges

Various challenges related to talent retention were noted as affecting all forms of organisations at the international level. Talent management is a serious problem that is not being handled properly even by developed countries. Several organisational leaders fail to support talent management models through watertight policies and finances. It is crystal clear that this essential facet of strategic human resource management is severely ignored and there is no value realized by top management in the practice of talent management. There is a general assumption that Millennials are a menace in the workplace and therefore succession planning is not possible with this generation.

The field of talent management in the public sector faces theoretical challenges because the existing literature on Human Resources for Health is based on limited and subjective data (Nkala et al., 2021). To make the theory that Millennials struggle with engagement less mysterious, human resource practitioners should create more interactive workplace activities. Furthermore, the public sector should have effective succession planning strategies in place to ensure that the Millennials are ready to take over from the large number of retiring employees. There is a wide range of business models and activities that enterprises use for talent management, but they do not meet the current requirements of talent. The concept of talent and how to manage it is not well-defined or followed by any common examples. Many organizations use talent management procedures on an intuitive basis (Stuss, 2020).

According to Pinigis (2023), the primary reasons for Army personnel leaving their organizations are the absence of career satisfaction and family support. It was suggested that the Army should adjust to societal transformations and seize private sector chances to efficiently handle and retain its personnel. On another note, (Ntini & Dewah, 2023) disclosed the absence of a knowledge management policy and strategies to retain valuable knowledge from their staff, which is being lost when employees resign or pass away, among other factors. It was also discovered that the backing of high-ranking officials does not guarantee sufficient resources to promote the preservation of knowledge. According to (Barkhuizen & Masale, 2022), there is a lack of strong belief in the importance of talent management among leaders. Zimbabwe's unfavourable economic situation has prompted healthcare professionals to migrate across borders and beyond in search of better opportunities. The health sector has faced difficulties in providing services and caring for patients due to this problem (Kanyumba & Msosa, 2020). (Chikwature &

Makamache, 2020) research study disclosed that the best way to keep good employees is to make the workplace appealing, supportive and rewarding for them. This encompasses a wide range of issues, such as defining the company's purpose, vision, and values, ensuring a secure and respectful workplace, and establishing clear, rational, and consistent rules and guidelines. The study uncovered that to keep employees, the institution's compensation plan must be sound.

Research (Dang et al., 2023) reveals that talent mobility, which is a talent's ability to move to different places or roles, is a talent characteristic that makes it hard to keep talent. Skilled employees are highly mobile. Industrial factors typically involve competing for skilled workers and following market trends. In addition to considering external factors like the economy and competition, strategy planners and senior managers must consider internal factors within their organizations that can directly affect the success of TM. The firm's type, the kind of work it does, how it competes, its goals, and how it manages its people affect how it finds and grows its talented workers. According to (Thakurta, 2024), the public sector's talent management is largely influenced by the bureaucratic nature of its business operations. Innovation is often hindered by bureaucracy, as the introduction of TM may not align with the sector's culture and may not meet the employees' expectations. However, a large variety of internal and external incentives could encourage public sector workers to stay motivated and work towards the organization's objectives. By implementing these methods, TM could ensure a continuous flow of skilled individuals from the public sector.

The above results indicate that the general performance of the economy is a challenge to the successful practice of public sector talent management in Zimbabwe. When the economy is not performing well, employees in the public sector specifically will leave their jobs looking for greener pastures outside the country. It also means that when the economy is not performing well, remuneration will not be matching with key skills and yet remuneration is a key aspect of a proper talent management model.

Table 1. Emerging themes

Subject matter	Rubric	Writer (s)	Year of Publication
Benefits of technology on talent retention	Transforming talent management as a game changer for firm competitiveness of Islamic banks	Samidi et al.	2023
	Organizational culture and employee retention: A comprehensive review.	Johnson and Brown	2022
	Total rewards and employee retention: The role of monetary and non-monetary compensation	Garcia, L., et al.	2022
Suitable technology for recruitment and selection.	An Integrative Framework of Talent Management and Systems: Identifying Future Possibilities	Sucharita and Thakurta	2023
	Talent management: a critical literature review and research agenda for public sector human resource management	Kravariti and Johnston	2019
Talent management challenges	Leadership talent mindset as a catalyst for talent management and talent retention: The case of a Botswana local government institution	Barkhuizen and Masale	2022
	Human Resources Management Practices in Enhancing Knowledge Retention in the Registrar's Department at NUST, Zimbabwe	Ntini and Dhewa	2023
	Talent Management-War for Talents	Stuss	2020

continued on following page

Table 1. Continued

Subject matter	Rubric	Writer (s)	Year of Publication
	Systemic Issues with US Army Talent Management and Retention	Pinigis	2023
	Human resources for health talent management contribution: A case for health systems strengthening in the public health sector	Nkala et al.	2021
	Retention strategies of healthcare professionals as a tool for effective service delivery in the Zimbabwean health sector	Kanyumba and Msosa	2020
	Staff retention realities at Zimbabwe revenue authority (ZINARA) Manicaland Region, Zimbabwe	Chikwature and Makamache	2020
	Multi-level challenges in talent management in a post COVID-19 future: Examining the banking sector in Vietnam	Thanh Dang et al	2023

Source: (Authors, 2024)

DISCUSSION

This chapter sought to determine the benefits of technology on talent retention in the public sector, ascertain the suitable technology for recruitment and selection and explore the talent management challenges in the public sector. A systematic literature review of the literature was conducted, and the research field was mapped using the theme-oriented approach as suggested (Leidner, 2018). Beyond question, adopting digital technologies is associated with reduced labour cost, effective workforce management and increased productivity.

Recruitment in the public sector is a critical process, and technology has proven to be beneficial in improving its effectiveness. The study found that leveraging technology, such as online job portals and applicant tracking systems, streamlines the recruitment process in Zimbabwe. These technologies enable efficient job posting, resume screening, and applicant tracking, resulting in a larger pool of qualified candidates and reduced recruitment timelines. This improved recruitment process enhances the chances of attracting high-quality talent to the public sector.

Furthermore, technology can play a significant role in talent retention in the public sector in Zimbabwe as revealed by the study. It was revealed that the use of technology tools, such as performance management systems and employee engagement platforms, positively impacts employee satisfaction and commitment. These tools provide a platform for transparent performance evaluation, timely feedback, and recognition, which contribute to improved job satisfaction and retention rates.

In terms of professional development, the study revealed that learning management technology has offered new opportunities for skills enhancement in the Zimbabwean public sector. This is so because by providing accessible and cost-effective learning opportunities, technology-enabled platforms have empowered public sector employees to acquire new skills and knowledge necessary for career growth. The availability of these resources demonstrates the commitment of public sector organizations in Zimbabwe to employee development and retention.

The use of technology in data management and decision-making has also been a significant finding in enhancing recruitment and retention in the public sector of Zimbabwe. The study emphasizes the role of data analytics tools in improving workforce planning and informed decision-making. By leveraging data on employee performance, turnover, and engagement, public sector organizations can identify trends and patterns, enabling them to proactively address talent gaps and implement retention strategies.

Moreover, the adoption of artificial intelligence technology could transform communication and collaboration in the public sector of Zimbabwe. Our research highlights the impact of collaboration tools and digital communication platforms in fostering teamwork and knowledge sharing. These technologies facilitate seamless communication, even in geographically dispersed teams, and promote a culture of collaboration, which contributes to employee satisfaction and retention. Additionally, technology is instrumental in enhancing employee engagement and recognition in the public sector of Zimbabwe. Findings indicate that the use of technology-based employee recognition platforms and social intranets helped to improve the overall work culture in the public sector. These platforms provide channels for acknowledging and appreciating employee contributions, fostering a sense of belonging and loyalty, thereby increasing employee retention rates.

Overall, the study findings as extrapolated from various studies highlight the significant benefits of leveraging technology to enhance public sector recruitment and retention in Zimbabwe. These findings include improved recruitment processes, increased employee satisfaction and commitment, enhanced professional development opportunities, data-driven decision-making, improved communication, and collaboration, as well as enhanced employee engagement and recognition. By embracing technology effectively, public sector organizations in Zimbabwe can attract and retain talented individuals, ultimately contributing to the overall success of the sector.

CONCLUSION

Embracing technology in public sector talent management in Zimbabwe is of paramount importance. Several findings from the sources consulted in this chapter highlight a positive impact of technology in talent management. Moreover, social media platforms have emerged as a valuable tool for recruitment and selection. Social media platforms, such as LinkedIn, Facebook, and Twitter, provide access to a large pool of potential candidates and enable recruiters to showcase job opportunities. Artificial intelligence (AI) and machine learning (ML) technologies have also shown promise in recruitment and selection. Notwithstanding the aforesaid benefits, various challenges related to talent retention were noted as affecting all forms of organisations at the international level. Talent management is a serious problem that is not being handled properly even by developed countries. Several organisational leaders fail to support talent management models through watertight policies and finances. The general performance of the economy is a challenge to the successful practice of public sector talent management in Zimbabwe. When the economy is not performing well, employees in the public sector specifically will leave their jobs looking for greener pastures outside the country. It also means that when the economy is not performing well, remuneration will not be matching with key skills and yet remuneration is a key aspect of a proper talent management model.

RECOMMENDATION AND DIRECTION FOR FURTHER RESEARCH

The benefits of technology on talent retention and suitable technology on recruitment and selection identified by the systematic integrative review are real despite differences in the economic development of countries in which the benefits are experienced. In Zimbabwe, some of these benefits are hard to recognize due to either non-implementation or poor performance of the economy. To address some of the persistent bureaucratic ills related to technology adoption in the public sector, the researchers recommend the Zimbabwean government partner with other private sector organisations and donor communities to come up with good talent management practices supported by reward plans.

The review of documents pointed to a lack of both qualitative and quantitative empirical studies to document the benefits of digital transformation in public sector HRM in Zimbabwe. This is because few public sector organisations in Zimbabwe have successful talent management models and business practices. The results of this study can be replicated in other contexts to further mixed-method studies on digital transformation and its impact on talent management in Zimbabwean public sector organisations.

The researchers used two databases and the World Wide Web for literature search to identify talent management, retention strategies and use of technology articles. Therefore, future researchers can use more than two databases and do ancestry searches to find out more information about the benefits and challenges associated with technology in talent management in the public sector. Ancestry search would assist in revealing key patterns of talent management and technology adoption, benefits, and problems, and further add credibility to the study findings.

Human resource practitioners and other managers responsible for people management and production processes can be informed on key challenges associated with talent management through this study. Thus, evidence-based decision-making and policy formulation are enabled in organizational operations. Conducive operational laws can be developed to minimize talent mobility which adversely affects public sector organisations from digitalising talent management for effective service delivery. Noting several complexities in digitalising talent management in the Zimbabwean public sector, the researchers suggest mixed-method and longitudinal empirical studies to be carried out for each observed theme. Such studies would provide a clear picture of the trends and patterns of modern talent management practices. Possible strategies for the menacing challenges can be found when empirical evidence is abundant.

REFERENCES

Acar, P. (2016). Theoretical journey of talent management: Egalitarian and elitist approach. *Pressacademia*, 3(3), 284–284. 10.17261/Pressacademia.2016321984

Al Jawali, H., Darwish, T. K., Scullion, H., & Haak-Saheem, W. (2022). Talent management in the public sector: Empirical evidence from the Emerging Economy of Dubai. *International Journal of Human Resource Management*, 33(11), 2256–2284. 10.1080/09585192.2021.2001764

Balcerzyk, R., & Materac, J. (2019). Talent management as a concept of human capital management. *Scientific Papers of Silesian University of Technology. Organization and Management Series*, 2019(133), 7–18. 10.29119/1641-3466.2019.133.1

Barkhuizen, E. N., & Masale, R. L. (2022). Leadership talent mindset as a catalyst for talent management and talent retention: The case of a Botswana local government institution. *SA Journal of Human Resource Management*, 20. Advance online publication. 10.4102/sajhrm.v20i0.1914

Barney, J. B. (2014). How marketing scholars might help address issues in resource-based theory. *Journal of the Academy of Marketing Science*, 42(1), 24–26. 10.1007/s11747-013-0351-8

Becker, G. (1965). *Human capital: A theoretical and empirical analysis, with special reference to education*. University of Chicago Press.

Chikwature, W., & Makamache, W. (2020). Staff Retention Realities at Zimbabwe Revenue Authority ZINARA) Manicaland Region, Zimbabwe. *European Journal of Research and Reflection in Management Sciences*, 8(1), 34–52.

Cohen, D., & Soto, M. (2007). Growth and human capital: Good data, good results. *Journal of Economic Growth*, 1(3), 113–207. 10.1007/s10887-007-9011-5

Dang, N. T. T., Nguyen, T. Q., Kok, S. K., & Ha, V. D. (2023). Multi-level challenges in talent management in a post COVID-19 future: Examining the banking sector in Vietnam. *Cogent Business & Management*, 10(3), 2251198. Advance online publication. 10.1080/23311975.2023.2251198

Denning, S. (2022, February 9). What Is The Digital Age And What Does It Mean? *Forbes*.

Enwereji, P. C., & Emmanuel, U. D. (2022). Talent Management Practices in the South African Public Service. *Khazanah Sosial*, 4(3), 417–433. 10.15575/ks.v4i3.19708

Falletta, S. V., & Combs, W. L. (2020). The HR analytics cycle: A seven-step process for building evidence-based and ethical HR analytics capabilities. *Journal of Work-Applied Management*, 13(1), 51–68. 10.1108/JWAM-03-2020-0020

Fauzian, N. R., Prasojo, E., Muslim, M. A., & Wangsaatmaja, S. (2024). DIGITALISED TALENT MANAGEMENT IN PUBLIC SECTOR: A LESSON LEARNED FROM THE WEST JAVA PROVINCIAL GOVERNMENT. *Journal of Law and Sustainable Development*, 12(2), e2559. 10.55908/sdgs.v12i2.2559

Frese, M., & Rauch, A. (2001). Entrepreneurship, Psychology of. In *International Encyclopedia of the Social & Behavioral Sciences* (pp. 4552–4556). Elsevier., 10.1016/B0-08-043076-7/01420-0

Garcia, L.. (2022). Total rewards and employee retention: The role of monetary and non-monetary compensation. *Human Resource Management Journal*, 52(4), 567–582.

Gillies, D. (2015). Human Capital Theory in Education. In *Encyclopedia of Educational Philosophy and Theory* (pp. 1–5). Springer Singapore., 10.1007/978-981-287-532-7_254-1

Jake, S. (2022, August 15). *New Technologies in Talent Management.* CODEPWR.

Johnson, R., & Brown, A. (2022). Organizational culture and employee retention: A comprehensive review. Journal of Applied Organizational Studies. *Journal of Applied Organizational Studies*, 36(3), 421–439.

Kanyumba, B., & Msosa, S. K. (2020). RETENTION STRATEGIES OF HEALTHCARE PROFESSIONALS AS A TOOL FOR EFFECTIVE SERVICE DELIVERY IN THE ZIMBABWEAN HEALTH SECTOR. *Eurasian Journal of Business and Management*, 8(2), 51–62. 10.15604/ejbm.2020.08.02.001

Kravariti, F., & Johnston, K. (2020). Talent management: A critical literature review and research agenda for public sector human resource management. *Public Management Review*, 22(1), 75–95. 10.1080/14719037.2019.1638439

Kravariti, F., Tasoulis, K., Scullion, H., & Alali, M. K. (2023). Talent management and performance in the public sector: The role of organisational and line managerial support for development. *International Journal of Human Resource Management*, 34(9), 1782–1807. 10.1080/09585192.2022.2032265

Kutcher, A. M., & LeBaron, V. T. (2022). A simple guide for completing an integrative review using an example article. *Journal of Professional Nursing*, 40, 13–19. 10.1016/j.profnurs.2022.02.00435568452

Leidner, D. (2018). Review and Theory Symbiosis: An Introspective Retrospective. *Journal of the Association for Information Systems*, 19(06), 552–567. 10.17705/1jais.00501

McKenzie, J. (2023). *Grey literature: What it is & how to find it.* Simon Fraser University.

Meshram, R.MESHRAM. (2023). THE ROLE OF ARTIFICIAL INTELLIGENCE (AI) IN RECRUITMENT AND SELECTION OF EMPLOYEES IN THE ORGANISATION. *Russian Law Journal*, 11(9s). Advance online publication. 10.52783/rlj.v11i9s.1624

Mhlanga, D., Shava, E., & Dzingirai, M. (2023). Harnessing State Capability in Embracing the Fourth Industrial Revolution: Is Zimbabwe Prepared? (pp. 239–254). 10.1007/978-3-031-28686-5_12

Milukutu, A., & Siachisa, M. (2023). Assessing the Impact of Digital Transformation on Employee Performance in the Public Sector: A Case Study of Zambia's Ministry of Health Headquarters (2017-2022). *International Journal of Humanities, Social. Sciences and Education*, 10(9), 118–126. 10.20431/2349-0381.1009013

Mjulwa, S. (2023). *TALENT MANAGEMENT AS AN ADMINISTRATIVE TOOL TO ENHANCE SERVICE DELIVERY: A CASE OF O.R. TAMBO DISTRICT MUNICIPALITY*. DURBAN UNIVERSITY OF TECHNOLOGY.

Mudimu, C. (2013). *An evaluation of talent management system in the Zimbabwean Health Care Industry: A case of Parirenyatwa Group of Hospitals*. University of Zimbabwe.

Muduli, A., & Trivedi, J. J. (2020). Social media recruitment: the role of credibility and satisfaction. *Evidence-Based HRM: A Global Forum for Empirical Scholarship, 8*(2), 237–251. 10.1108/EBHRM-08-2019-0069

Mutadzakupa, B. (2023). *A TOURISM EMPLOYEE TALENT MANAGEMENT FRAMEWORK FOR HOTEL EMPLOYEE RETENTION IN ZIMBABWE*. University of South Africa.

Mutsagondo, S., & Khumalo, N. (2023). "E-skills scarcity and the digital records management landscape in Zimbabwe." *Library Philosophy and Practice (e-Journal*. Nguyen, H., Groth, M., & Johnson, A. (2023). How Display Rules Influence Turnover in Healthcare Teams and the Moderating Role of Team Negative Affective Tone. *Journal of Service Research*, 109467052311760. Advance online publication. 10.1177/10946705231176070

Njerekai, C. (2020). An application of the virtual reality 360° concept to the Great Zimbabwe monument. *Journal of Heritage Tourism*, 15(5), 567–579. 10.1080/1743873X.2019.1696808

Nkala, B., Mudimu, C., & Mbengwa, A. (2021). Human resources for health talent management contribution: A case for health systems strengthening in the public health sector. *World Journal of Advanced Research and Reviews*, 9(2), 192–201. 10.30574/wjarr.2021.9.2.0062

Ntini, V., & Dewah, P. (2023). Human Resources Management Practices in Enhancing Knowledge Retention in the Registrar's Department at NUST, Zimbabwe. *Regional Journal of Information and Knowledge Management*, 8(1), 60–75.

Potočnik, K., Neil, R., Marise, B., & Nikolaou, I. (2021). Paving the way for research in recruitment and selection: Recent developments, challenges and future opportunities. *European Journal of Work and Organizational Psychology*, 30(5), 1–16. 10.1080/1359432X.2021.1904898

Samidi, S., Maarif, M. S., Saptono, I. T., & Arsyianti, L. D. (2023). Transforming talent management as a game changer for firm competitiveness of Islamic banks. *Cogent Business & Management*, 10(3), 2257590. Advance online publication. 10.1080/23311975.2023.2257590

Sembiring, E., & Damayanti, N. (2023). TALENT ATTRACTION, TALENT RETENTION, AND TALENT MANAGEMENT AS A MEDIATING ON ORGANIZATION PERFORMANCE. *Ultima Management : Jurnal Ilmu Manajemen*, 15(1), 58–76. 10.31937/manajemen.v15i1.3125

Stuss, M. M. (2020). TALENT MANAGEMENT – WAR FOR TALENTS. *Proceedings of the 11th Business & Management Conference,* Dubai. 10.20472/BMC.2020.011.013

Tapiwa, G. G., Pedzisai, P., Bernard, N., & Mervis, C. (2022). Digitalisation of Human Resources Systems and Process Necessary for Public Sector Transformation in Zimbabwe. In *Transformational Human Resources Management in Zimbabwe* (pp. 61–74). Springer Nature Singapore., 10.1007/978-981-19-4629-5_5

Thakurta, R. (2024). A work system theory perspective on talent management and systems. *Systems Research and Behavioral Science*, sres.3007. Advance online publication. 10.1002/sres.3007

Tsamados, A., Aggarwal, N., Cowls, J., Morley, J., Roberts, H., Taddeo, M., & Floridi, L. (2022). The ethics of algorithms: Key problems and solutions. *AI & Society*, 37(1), 215–230. 10.1007/s00146-021-01154-8

Utami, H., & Alamanos, E. (2023). *Theory Hub Book.*

Wegrich, K. (2024). Public sector. In *Encyclopedia Britannica.*

Compilation of References

Abane, J. A., & Brenya, E. (2021). The relationship between organizational environment antecedents and performance management in local government: Evidence from Ghana. *Future Business Journal*, 7(1), 1–17. 10.1186/s43093-020-00049-2

Abdel Azem Mostafa, H., Hassan EL-Sayed. Mahfouz, H., & Mohammed Araby Ebraheem, S. (. (2021). Effect of Educational Program about Talent Management for Nursing Managers on Their Job Affiliation and Organisational Excellence. *Egyptian Journal of Health Care*, 12(2), 718–740. 10.21608/ejhc.2021.170481

Abdeldayem, M. & Aldulaimi, S. 2020. Trends And Opportunities Of Artificial Intelligence In Human Resource Management: Aspirations For Public Sector In Bahrain.

AbdulKareem, A. (2024). Investigating ICT adoption and public value of e-recruitment in the public sector: The role of social media use. *International Journal of Public Sector Management, 37*(2), 284-304. https://doi.org/10.1108/IJPSM-10-2023-0307

Abugabel, A. 2023. The Impact of Digital Transformation on Sustainable Development: The Mediating Role of Development of Human Resources Management Practices "An Empirical Study on Private Hospitals. *Journal of Alexandria University for Administrative Sciences,*https://doi.org/10.21608/acj.2023.294133

Acar, P. (2016). Theoretical journey of talent management: Egalitarian and elitist approach. *Pressacademia*, 3(3), 284–284. 10.17261/Pressacademia.2016321984

Adekunle, A. A. (2018). Digital HR, public service and sustainable governance. *IOSR Journal of Humanities and Social Science (IOSR-JHSS), 23*(12), 61-65.

Adenugba, A. A., Fadoju, O., & Akhuetie, R. E. (2017). Non-meritocratic factors and the recruitment process in Oyo State Civil Service, Nigeria. *African Sociological Review/Revue Africaine de Sociologie, 21*(2), 115-133.

Adero, F. A., & Odiyo, W. O. (2020). Employee Characteristics, Contemporary Human Resource Management Practices and Organisation Effectiveness. *International Journal of Business Management, Entrepreneurship, and Innovation*, 2(2), 1–18. 10.35942/jbmed.v2i2.111

Adisa, T. A. & Mordi, C. 2022. *HRM in the Global South: A Critical Perspective,*https://doi.org/10.1007/978-3-030-98309-3

African Tax Administration Forum. (2021). Case Study: Uganda Revenue Authority's Digital Transformation. Available at: Revenue mobilisation through tax transparency (ataftax.org) [Accessed 21 December 2023]

African Union. (2020). *The Digital Transformation Strategy for Africa*. African Union.

African Union. (2021). *Digital transformation strategy for Africa (2020-2030)*. Retrieved from https://au.int/en/documents/20200518/digital-transformation-strategy-africa-2020-2030

Aggarwal, V., & Sharon, S. D. (2017). Digital human resource management. *Gyan Management Journal*, 11(2), 23–27.

Agostino, D., Bracci, E., & Steccolini, I. (2021). Accounting and accountability for the digital transformation of public services. *Financial Accountability & Management*, 38(2), 145–151. 10.1111/faam.12314

AGSA [Auditor General of South Africa] (2020). *Our Vision.* Available at https://www.agsa.co.za/AboutUs/OurVision .aspx (last accessed 20 January 2024).

Agustian, K., Pohan, A., Zen, A., Wiwin, W., & Malik, A. J. (2023). Human Resource Management Strategies in Achieving Competitive Advantage in Business Administration. [ADMAN]. *Journal of Contemporary Administration and Management,* 1(2), 108–117. 10.61100/adman.v1i2.53

Ahmed, H. K. (2016). The impact of Talent management on the competitive advantage in the organisations. *UAE Proceedings of 37th ISERD International Conference,* Abu Dhabi, UAE, 6th June 2016.

Ahmed, U., Kura, K. M., Umrani, W. A., & Pahi, M. H. (2019). Modelling the Link Between Developmental Human Resource Practices and Work Engagement: The Moderation Role of Service Climate. *Global Business Review.* Advance online publication. 10.1177/0972150919837813

Aisa, R., Cabeza, J., & Martin, J. (2023). Automation and aging: The impact on older workers in the workforce. *The Journal of the Economics of Ageing,* 26, 100476. 10.1016/j.jeoa.2023.100476

Al Aina, R., & Atan, T. (2020). The Impact of Implementing Talent Management Practices on Sustainable Organisational Performance. *Sustainability (Basel),* 12(20), 8372. 10.3390/su12208372

Al Awadhi, T. H., & Muslim, S. B. (2023). Reviewing the relation between human resources practices, talent management and succession planning in UAE public sector. *Information Sciences Letters,* 12(4), 1271–1283. 10.18576/isl/120442

Al Jawali, H., Darwish, T. K., Scullion, H., & Haak-Saheem, W. (2022). Talent management in the public sector: Empirical evidence from the Emerging Economy of Dubai. *International Journal of Human Resource Management,* 33(11), 2256–2284. 10.1080/09585192.2021.2001764

Al Shikhy, A., Makhbul, Z. M., Rawshdeh, Z. A., Arshad, R., & Ali, K. A. M. (2019). Dispositional resistance to change and user resistance behaviour to use human resources information systems in the healthcare sector: The moderating role of conscientiousness. [IJRTE]. *International Journal of Recent Technology and Engineering,* 8(4), 565–572.

Alade, S. (2023). Design and Implementation of a Web-based Document Management System. *Information Technology and Computer Science,* 2, 35–53.

Al-Alawi, A. I., Messaadia, M., Mehrotra, A., Sanosi, S. K., Elias, H., & Althawadi, A. H. (2023). Digital transformation adoption in human resources management during COVID-19. *Arab Gulf Journal of Scientific Research,* 41(4), 446–461. 10.1108/AGJSR-05-2022-0069

Albert, O. (2009). Whose e-governance? A critique of online citizen engagement in Africa. *African Journal of Political Science and International Relations,* 3(4), 133–141.

Aldoseri, A., Al-Khalifa, K., & Hamouda, A. (2023). A road-map for integrating automation with process optimisation for AI-powered digital transformation. *Preprints*.org.

Aleksandrova, S. V. (2023, September). Implementation of Digital Technologies in Production Processes. In *2023 International Conference on Quality Management, Transport and Information Security, Information Technologies (IT&QM&IS)* (pp. 104-108). IEEE. 10.1109/ITQMTIS58985.2023.10346533

Al-hassi, A. (2021). *Digital transformation in higher education institutions and its role in achieving sustainable development (reality and obstacles)* (Unpublished thesis). Misr University for Science and Technology, Cairo, Egypt.

Alhazemi, A. (2017). Critical Analysis and Current Challenges Facing HRIS Adoption in Arab Countries Case of Saudi Arabia. *International Journal of Heritage. Tourism and Hospitality,* 11(2), 143–16.

Ali, E., & Elias, H. Potential Application of HR Analytics to Talent Management in the Public Sector: a Literature Review. *2023 International Conference on Cyber Management and Engineering, CyMaEn 2023*, 2023. 8-11 https://doi.org/10.1109/CyMaEn57228.2023.10051107

Ali, M. S., Abdalgani, S. A., & Dahlan, D. (2023). Assessing the Effectiveness of 360-Degree Performance Appraisal System to Enhance Employees' Productivity in Jordanian Listed Banks. In *Artificial Intelligence (AI) and Finance* (pp. 164–174). Springer Nature Switzerland. 10.1007/978-3-031-39158-3_15

Ali, Z., Valk, T. J., Bjerre-Christensen, T., Brandt, S., Isberg, A. P., Jensen, M. L., Helledi, L. S., Kaas, A., Thomsen, S. F., Andersen, A. D., & Robert Zibert, J. (2021). Exploring decentralized glucose and behaviometric monitoring of persons with type 2 diabetes in the setting of a clinical trial. *Journal of Diabetes Science and Technology*, 17(1), 117–124. 10.1177/1932296821104565634553637

Alkashami, M. (2023). Human Resource Information Systems (HRIS) in the 21st Century: A Critical Appraisal: . *Baltic Journal of Law & Politics, 16*(1), 375-388.10.2478/bjlp-2023-0000026

Alkhalaf, T. (2023). The effect of ability, motivation and opportunity (AMO) on SMEs' innovation performance. *Creativity and Innovation Management, 33*(1), 21-38. https://doi.org/10.1111/caim.12578

Alkhalil, Z., Hewage, C., Nawaf, L., & Khan, I. (2021). Phishing attacks: A recent comprehensive study and a new anatomy. *Frontiers of Computer Science*, 3, 563060. 10.3389/fcomp.2021.563060

Almatrooshi, B., Singh, S. K., & Farouk, S. (2016). Determinants of organisational performance: A proposed framework. *International Journal of Productivity and Performance Management*, 65(6), 844–859. 10.1108/IJPPM-02-2016-0038

AlMunthiri, O., Bani-Melhem, S., Mohd-Shamsudin, F., & Raziq, M. M. (2023). Fostering innovative behaviours of public sector employees: The potency of innovation-based HR practices, risk propensity and error tolerance. *. *International Journal of Public Sector Management*, 37(2), 159–182. 10.1108/IJPSM-08-2023-0242

Alpopi, C. (2019). Sustainable e-Governance and Human Resource Development European. *Journal of Sustainable Development*, 8(5), 16–20.

AL-Qassem. A. H., Agha, K., Vij, M., Elrehail, H., & Agarwal, R. (2023, March). Leading Talent Management: Empirical investigation on Applicant Tracking System (ATS) on e-Recruitment Performance. In 2023 international Conference on Business Analytics for Technology and security (ICBATS) (pp. 1-5). IEEE.

AlSaadoon, A. (2020). *A Design Research Approach to Enhance the Peer-to-peer Recognition and Appreciation Among Employees and Develop a Better Relationship to Boost Employee Motivation.* California (Doctoral dissertation, The Claremont Graduate University).

Alvarenga, A., Matos, F., Godina, R., & Matias, CO, J. (. (2020). Digital transformation and knowledge management in the public sector. *Sustainability*, 12(14), 5824. 10.3390/su12145824

Ammons, D. N., & Roenigk, D. J. (2015). Performance management in local government: Is practice influenced by doctrine? *Public Performance & Management Review*, 38(3), 514–541. 10.1080/15309576.2015.1006461

Ammons, D. N., & Roenigk, D. J. (2020). Exploring devolved decision authority in performance management regimes: The relevance of perceived and actual decision authority as elements of performance management success. *Public Performance & Management Review*, 43(1), 28–52. 10.1080/15309576.2019.1657918

Amudavi, E. L. (2018). Revolutionary Impact of the Advancement of Information Communication Technology (ICT) on the HRM Function. *International Journal of Innovative Information Systems & Technology Research*, 6(2), 1–7.

Anand, J., & Radha, S. (2020). E-Recruitment: An Advantage Over Traditional Recruitment. *International Journal of Advanced Research in Management, Architecture. Technology and Engineering*, 6(4), 1–15.

Anderson, M. H., & Lemken, R. K. (2023). Citation context analysis as a method for conducting rigorous and impactful literature reviews. *Organizational Research Methods*, 26(1), 77–106. 10.1177/1094428120969905

Androniceanu, A., Georgescu, I., & Sabie, O. M. (2022). The impact of digitalization on public administration, economic development, and well-being in the EU countries. *Central. European.Public Administration Review*, 20(2), 9–31.

Angrave, D., Charlwood, A., Kirkpatrick, I., Lawrence, M., & Stuart, M. (2016). HR and analytics: Why HR is set to fail the big data challenge. *Human Resource Management Journal*, 26(1), 1–11. 10.1111/1748-8583.12090

Anlesinya, A., Amponsah-Tawiah, K., & Dartey-Baah, K. (2019a). Talent management research in Africa: Towards multilevel model and research agenda. *African Journal of Economic and Management Studies*, 10(4), 440–457. 10.1108/AJEMS-12-2018-0371

Ansell, C., & Torfing, J. (2021). *Public governance as co-creation: A strategy for revitalizing the public sector and rejuvenating democracy*. Cambridge University Press. 10.1017/9781108765381

Armstrong, M., & Taylor, S. (2020). *Armstrong's handbook of human resource management practice*. Kogan Page Publishers.

Aroge, S. T., & Hassan, M. A. (2011). The responsibility of human resource management and development professionals in the development of low-skilled workers in the Nigeria public sector. *International Journal of Business and Management*, 6(11), 227–233.

Aro-Gordon, S. (2016). Leveraging Information Technology for Effective Performance Appraisal in the Nigerian Public Service. *SDMIMD Journal of Management, 7*(2).

Arora, M., Prakash, A., Mittal, A., & Singh, S. 2022. Moderating Role of Resistance to Change in the Actual Adoption of HR Analytics in the Indian Banking and Financial Services Industry. *Evidence-Based HRM a Global Forum for Empirical Scholarship,*https://doi.org/10.1108/EBHRM-12-2021-0249

Arundel, A., Bloch, C., & Ferguson, B. (2019). Advancing innovation in the public sector: Aligning innovation measurement with policy goals. *Research Policy*, 48(3), 789–798. 10.1016/j.respol.2018.12.001

Auditor General. (2017). *Auditor General's Report of State-Owned Enterprises 2017*. Government Printers.

Auditor General. (2023). *Report of the Auditor General on Appropriation accounts, finance and revenue statements and fund accounts for the year ended December 31, 2022*. Government Printers.

Auditor General. (2023). *Report of the Auditor-General for the financial year ended December 31, 2020, on local authorities*. Government Printers.

Auditor General. (2023). *Report of the Auditor-General for the financial year ended December 31, 2022 on state owned enterprises and parastatals*. Government Printers.

Auriacombe, C. J. (2016). Towards the construction of unobtrusive research techniques: Critical considerations when conducting a literature analysis. *African Journal of Public Affairs*, 9(4), 1–19.

Ayakwah, A., Damoah, I. S., & Osabutey, E. L. C. (2021). Digitalization in Africa: The Case of Public Programs in Ghana. In Abugre, J.B., L.C. Osabutey, E., P. Sigué, S. (Eds.) *Business in Africa in the Era of Digital Technology. Advances in Theory and Practice of Emerging Markets* (pp.7-25). Cham: Springer.

Babbie, L. (2014). *The Basics of Social Research*. Wadsworth: Cengage Learning.

Babbie, E. R. (2007). *The practice of social research.* Thomson Wadsworth.

Bagozzi, C. (2007). The legacy of technology acceptance model and a proposal for paradigm shift. *Journal of the Association for Information Systems*, 8(4), 244–254. 10.17705/1jais.00122

Bahiroh, E., & Imron, A. (2024). Innovative Human Resource Management Strategies in the Era of Digital Transformation. [PRODUCTIVITY]. *Management Studies and Business Journal*, 1(2), 154–162. 10.62207/6wnrgj39

Baku, A. A. (2022). Digitalisation and new public management in Africa. In R.E. Hinson, N. Madichie, O. Adeola, J… (Eds.), *New Public Management in Africa: Contemporary Issues* (pp.299-316). London: Palgrave Macmillan Cham. 10.1007/978-3-030-77181-2_12

Bal, Y., Bozkurt, S., & Ertemsir, E. (2022). The importance of using human resources information systems (HRIS) and a research on determining the success of HRIS. In *Strategic Human Resource Management at Tertiary Level* (pp. 197-209). River Publishers

Balcerzyk, R., & Materac, J. (2019). Talent management as a concept of human capital management. *Scientific Papers of Silesian University of Technology. Organization and Management Series*, 2019(133), 7–18. 10.29119/1641-3466.2019.133.1

Bankins, S. (2021). The ethical use of artificial intelligence in human resource management: A decision-making framework. *Ethics and Information Technology*, 23(4), 841–854. 10.1007/s10676-021-09619-6

Banu, S. R. (2019). Hr digital transformation. *Journal of The Gujarat Research Society*, 21(13), 946–951.

Barkhuizen, E. N., & Masale, R. L. (2022). Leadership talent mindset as a catalyst for talent management and talent retention: The case of a Botswana local government institution. *SA Journal of Human Resource Management*, 20. Advance online publication. 10.4102/sajhrm.v20i0.1914

Barkhuizen, N., & Gumede, B. (2021). The Relationship Between Talent Management, Job Satisfaction and Voluntary Turnover Intentions of Employees in a Selected Government Institution. *SA Journal of Human Resource Management*, 19. Advance online publication. 10.4102/sajhrm.v19i0.1396

Barney, J. B. (2014). How marketing scholars might help address issues in resource-based theory. *Journal of the Academy of Marketing Science*, 42(1), 24–26. 10.1007/s11747-013-0351-8

Bawalla, O. G., & Rufai, D. O. (2021). Technological Advancement: Issues, Challenges and Perspectives for Human Resource Practice in Nigeria. *KIU Journal of Social Sciences*, 7(3), 47–55.

Bechter, B., Brandl, B., & Lehr, A. (2022). The Role of the Capability, Opportunity, and Motivation of Firms for Using Human Resource Analytics to Monitor Employee Performance: A Multi-level Analysis of the Organisational, Market, and Country Context. *New Technology, Work and Employment*, 37(3), 398–424. Advance online publication. 10.1111/ntwe.12239

Becker, G. (1965). *Human capital: A theoretical and empirical analysis, with special reference to education.* University of Chicago Press.

Beeri, I., Uster, A., & Vigoda-Gadot, E. (2019). Does performance management relate to good governance? A study of its relationship with citizens' satisfaction with and trust in Israeli local government. *Public Performance & Management Review*, 42(2), 241–279. 10.1080/15309576.2018.1436074

Bejakovic, P., & Mrnjavac, Z. (2020). *The Importance of Digital Literacy on the labour market. Employee Relations.* [Online] Retrieved from: https://www.researchgate.net/publication/ 340515952_The_importance_of_digital_literacy_on_the_labour_market. (Accessed on 27 February 2024).

Belizón, M. J., & Kieran, S. (2021). Human Resources Analytics: A Legitimacy Process. *Human Resource Management Journal*. Advance online publication. 10.1111/1748-8583.12417

Bella, K. M. J., Ramyasri, M. D., & Vijayashree, P. (2023). Revolutionizing HR Management: Embracing Technology for Enhanced Efficiency and Employee Engagement. *International Journal of Scientific Research in Modern Science and Technology*, 2(3), 28–34.

Benbunan-Fich, R., Desouza, K. C., & Andersen, K. N. (2020). IT-enabled innovation in the public sector: Introduction to the special issue. *European Journal of Information Systems*, 29(4), 323–328. 10.1080/0960085X.2020.1814989

Ben-Gal, H. C. (2019). An ROI-based Review of HR Analytics: Practical Implementation Tools. *Personnel Review*, 48(6), 1429–1448. Advance online publication. 10.1108/PR-11-2017-0362

Bengtsson, C., & Bloom, M. (2017). Human Resource Management in a Digital Era. *LUP Student Papers, 0-30.*

Betchoo, N. K. (2016, August). Digital transformation and its impact on human resource management: A case analysis of two unrelated businesses in the Mauritian public service. In *2016 IEEE International Conference on Emerging Technologies and Innovative Business Practices for the Transformation of Societies (EmergiTech)* (pp. 147–152). IEEE. 10.1109/EmergiTech.2016.7737328

Bhanumathi, P., Jeevitha, R., & Rema, V. (2023). Embedding Technology in Human Resource Management. In *Managing Technology Integration for Human Resources in Industry 5.0, 1-19.* IGI Global.

Bhebhe, N. (2023, February). The government insists on performance contracts for council bosses. *Chronicle (Philadelphia, Pa.)*, 17, •••. https://www.chronicle.co.zw/government-insists-on-performance-contracts-for-council-bosses/

Biea, E. A., Dinu, E., Bunica, A., & Jerdea, L. (2023). Recruitment in SMEs: The role of managerial practices, technology and innovation. *European Business Review*, 36(3), 361–391. 10.1108/EBR-05-2023-0162

Bilgic, E. (2020). Human Resources Information Systems: A Recent Literature Survey, In M.A. Turkmenoglu, M.A. & B. Cicek, B. (Eds.), *Contemporary Global Issues in Human Resource Management* (pp. 73-87), Leeds: Emerald Publishing.

Bissola, R., & Imperatori, B. (2018). HRM 4.0: The digital transformation of the HR department. In *Human Resource Management and Digitalization. The Effects of Industry 4.0 on Human Resource* (pp. 51-69). Routledge.

Biyela, A. C., Nzimakwe, T. I., Mthuli, S. A., & Khambule, I. (2018). Assessing the role of intergovernmental relations in strategic planning for economic development at local government level: A case study of Umkhanyakude District Municipality. *Journal of Gender* [JGIDA]. *Information and Development in Africa*, 7(2), 221–239. 10.31920/2050-4284/2018/v7n2a11

Boakye, A., & Ayerki Lamptey, Y. (2020). The Rise of HR Analytics: Exploring Its Implications from a Developing Country Perspective. *Journal of Human Resource Management*, 8(3), 181. 10.11648/j.jhrm.20200803.19

Bojang, M. B. S., & Bwando, W. (2018). *E-municipality applications in local government: Prospects and challenges*, A paper presented at 3600 with youth 4th international student conference, Manisa, 3rd–4th April 2018.

Bondarouk, T., Parry, E., & Furtmueller, E. (2017). Electronic HRM: Four decades of research on adoption and consequences. *International Journal of Human Resource Management*, 28(1), 98–131. 10.1080/09585192.2016.1245672

Bonilla-Chaves, E., & Palos-Sanchez, P. (2023). Exploring the evolution of human resource analytics: A bibliometric study. *Behavioral Sciences, 13*(3), 244. https://doi.org/10.3390/bs13030244

Bonnet, D., & Westerman, G. (2020). *The new elements of digital transformation.* Cambridge, MA. *MIT Sloan Management Review*, 4(2), 34–48.

Botlhoko, T. S. (2017). *Promoting effective financial accountability in local government in the North West Province: Developing operational guidelines for Municipal Public Accounts Committees.* Unpublished doctoral thesis. Bloemfontein: Central University of Technology.

Bourgon, J. (2015). Leadership for Change, Innovation for Results: A New Synthesis. Paper presented at the Distinctively Public Sector: The Case for a New Synthesis of Public Administration, Queensland, Australia.

Bourke, J., & Crowley, F. (2015). The role of HRM and ICT complementarities in firm innovation: Evidence from transition economies. *International Journal of Innovation Management*, 19(05), 1550054. 10.1142/S1363919615500541

Bowen, G. A. (2009). Document Analysis as a Qualitative Research Method. *Qualitative Research Journal*, 9(2), 27–40. 10.3316/QRJ0902027

Bozkus, K. (2023). Organisational Culture Change and Technology: Navigating the Digital Transformation. In Sarfraz, M., & Hassan Shah, W. U. (Eds.), *Organisational Culture - Cultural Change and Technology* (pp. 1–22). Intechopen.

Brabete, V. (2023). Assessing and forecasting current and future trends of ict employment in european enterprises. *Brain Broad Research in Artificial Intelligence and Neuroscience*, 14(4), 1–40. 10.18662/brain/14.4/489

Brown, M. I. (2022). Investigating the promise and pitfalls of pulse surveys. *Industrial and Organizational Psychology: Perspectives on Science and Practice*, 15(1), 137–149. 10.1017/iop.2021.124

Brunetto, Y., & Beattie, R. (2020). Changing role of HRM in the public sector. *Public Management Review*, 22(1), 1–5. 10.1080/14719037.2019.1645876

Bryson, J., Crosby, B., & Stone, M. (2015). Designing and implementing cross-sector collaborations: Needed and challenging. *Public Administration Review, 75*(5), 647-663. https://doi.org/10.1111/puar.12432

Budhwar, P., Chowdhury, S., Wood, G., Aguinis, H., Bamber, G. J., Beltran, J. R., Boselie, P., Lee Cooke, F., Decker, S., DeNisi, A., Dey, P. K., Guest, D., Knoblich, A. J., Malik, A., Paauwe, J., Papagiannidis, S., Patel, C., Pereira, V., Ren, S., & Varma, A. (2023). Human resource management in the age of generative artificial intelligence: Perspectives and research directions on ChatGPT. *Human Resource Management Journal*, 33(3), 606–659. 10.1111/1748-8583.12524

Budhwar, P., Malik, A., De Silva, M. T., & Thevisuthan, P. (2022). Artificial intelligence–challenges and opportunities for international HRM: A review and research agenda. *International Journal of Human Resource Management*, 33(6), 1065–1097. 10.1080/09585192.2022.2035161

Caligiuri, P., & Dragoni, L. (2019). Developing global leadership talent. In Collings, D., Scullion, H., & Caligiuri, P. (Eds.), *Global talent management* (2nd ed.).

Calvard, T. S., & Jeske, D. (2018). Developing human resource data risk management in the age of big data. *International Journal of Information Management*, 4(3), 159–164. 10.1016/j.ijinfomgt.2018.07.011

Camngca, V. P., Amoah, C., & Ayesu-Koranteng, E. (2024). Underutilisation of information communication and technology in the public sector construction project's implementation. *Journal of Facilities Management*, 22(1), 1–20. 10.1108/JFM-10-2021-0128

Cappelli, P. (2008). *Talent on demand: Managing talent in an age of uncertainty.* Harvard: Harvard Business Press.

Castro, C., & Lopes, C. (2022). Digital government and sustainable development. *Journal of the Knowledge Economy*, 13(2), 880–903. 10.1007/s13132-021-00749-2

Cavanagh, J., Walker, M., Pariona-Cabrera, P., Bartram, T., & Halvorsen, B. (2022). Health Services in Australia and the Impact of Antiquated Rostering Practices on Medical Scientists: A case for HR Analytics and Evidenced-Based Human Resource Management. *Personnel Review*. Advance online publication. 10.1108/PR-09-2021-0690

Chang, Y. J. (2023). *Building an effective hiring and smooth employee boarding process: company X*. Turku and Salo (Master's Thesis, Turku University Of Applied Sciences).

Chan, J. Y., Chai, W. X., Koh, C. K., Ngo, S. L., & Teh, L. L. (2020). *The impact of talent attraction, talent development and talent retention on job satisfaction in hospitality industry*. Universiti Tunku Abdul Rahman.

Chapano, M., Mey, M. R., & Werner, A. (2022). Adoption of Digital Strategies Across the Human Resource Value Chain. *SA Journal of Human Resource Management*, 20. Advance online publication. 10.4102/sajhrm.v20i0.1992

Chapano, M., Mey, M. R., & Werner, A. (2023). Perceived Challenges: Unfounded Reasons for Not Forging Ahead With Digital Human Resource Management Practices. *SA Journal of Human Resource Management*, 21. Advance online publication. 10.4102/sajhrm.v21i0.2085

Chapano, M., Mey, M. R., & Werner, A. (2023). Value Derived from Digitalised Human Resource Management: Perspectives from South Africa. [-pages.]. *African Journal of Employee Relations*, 47, 29. 10.25159/2664-3731/10914

Charles, K., & Onouha, B. C. (2020). *Entrepreneurial Talent Management and Organisational Agility of Construction Firms in Rivers State.*

Chashi, K., & Mwanza, B. G. (2022). The Influence of the Fourth Industrial Revolution on Human Resource within the Zambian Banking Sector. SSRN *Electronic Journal*. 1-16. 10.2139/ssrn.4190617

Chaturvedi, V. (2023). Role of Cognitive Technology for Improving Human Resource Management Experience: A Multi-Dimensional Perspective. *Data Science and Intelligent Computing Techniques; Nanda, SJ, Yadav, RP, Eds*, 13-25.

Chen, S., Lee, A. Y., & Ahlström, D. (2019). Strategic Talent Management Systems and Employee Behaviors: The Mediating Effect of Calling. *Asia Pacific Journal of Human Resources*. Advance online publication. 10.1111/1744-7941.12229

Chen, Z. (2023). Artificial intelligence-virtual trainer: Innovative didactics aimed at personalised training needs. *Journal of the Knowledge Economy*, 14(2), 2007–2025. 10.1007/s13132-022-00985-0

Chen, Z. (2023). Collaboration among recruiters and Artificial Intelligence: Removing human prejudices in employment. *Cognition Technology and Work*, 25(1), 135–149. 10.1007/s10111-022-00716-036187287

Chesney, T. (2006). An acceptance model for useful and fun information systems. *Human Technology*, 2(2), 225–235. 10.17011/ht/urn.2006520

Chethana, K. M., & Noronha, S. D. (2022). *A Descriptive Study of Talent Management Practices Followed by Wipro LTD*. International Journal of Case Studies in Business It and Education., 10.47992/IJCSBE.2581.6942.0221

Chigora, P., Poshai, L., & Mcilo, A. (2022). Challenges with Online Teaching and Learning Under Covid-19 Lockdown in Selected Zimbabwean Universities. *Journal of Public Administration and Development Alternatives*, 7(2), 36–49. 10.55190/RDHC9092

Chikomba, A., Rodrigues, A., & Ngoepe, M. (2021). Management of digital records in selected financial services parastatals in Zimbabwe. *Information Development*, 37(2), 245–257. 10.1177/0266666920906858

Chikumira, T. (2024, March 9). New ICT policy documents a game changer – Govt. *ZBC News*. https://www.zbcnews.co.zw/featured/new-ict-policy-documents-a-game-changer-govt/

Chikwariro, S., Bussin, M. & De Braine, R. (2021). Reframing performance management praxis at the Harare city council, *SA Journal of Human Resource Management/SA*. 19(0), a1438. https://doi.org/.10.4102/sajhrm.v19i0.1438

Chikwature, W., & Makamache, W. (2020). Staff Retention Realities at Zimbabwe Revenue Authority ZINARA) Manicaland Region, Zimbabwe. *European Journal of Research and Reflection in Management Sciences*, 8(1), 34–52.

Chilunjika, A., Intauno, K., & Chilunjika, S. R. (2022). Artificial Intelligence and public sector human resource management in South Africa: Opportunities, challenges, and prospects. *SA Journal of Human Resource Management*, 20(0), a197212. 10.4102/sajhrm.v20i0.1972

Chitumba, P., & Mupanedemo, F. (2024, March 8). Harness ICT to improve service delivery. *The Herald*. https://www.herald.co.zw/harness-ict-to-improve-service-delivery/

Chiware, M., & Vyas-Doogapersad, S. (2021). Assessing results-based personnel performance system in the Ministry of Home and Child Care, Zimbabwe. *Research in Business & Social Science*, 11(7), 321–330.

Chiwawa, N., & Wissink, H. (2024). Effective strategy execution for enhanced service delivery in South African municipalities. *Africa's Public Service Delivery and Performance Review*, 12(1), a741. 10.4102/apsdpr.v12i1.741

Choto, T. B., & Poshai, L. (2023). The Politics and Public Administration nexus in the practice of Football Administration in Zimbabwe. *Administrative Theory & Praxis*, 45(4), 1–17. 10.1080/10841806.2023.2282924

Choung, M., & Manamela, M. G. (2018). *Digital inequality in rural and urban settings: Challenges of education and information in South African youth context*. [Online] Retrieved from: https://www.researchgate.net/publication/333132846_Digital_Inequality_in_ Rural_and_Urban_settings_Challenges_of_Education_and_Information_in_South_African_Youth_Context. (Accessed on 19 January 2024).

Cho, W., Choi, S., & Choi, H. (2023). Human Resources Analytics for Public Personnel Management: Concepts, Cases, and Caveats. *Administrative Sciences*, 13(2), 1–22. 10.3390/admsci13020041

Christian, C. C. (2022). Artificial intelligence in human resources management and human resource accounting in Nigerian public sector. *Management and Human Resource Research Journal, 11*(01).

Christ, K. L., & Helliar, C. V. (2021). Blockchain technology and modern slavery: Reducing deceptive recruitment in migrant worker populations. *Journal of Business Research*, 131, 112–120. 10.1016/j.jbusres.2021.03.065

Chugunova, M., & Danilov, A. 2022. Use of Digital Technologies for HR Management in Germany: Survey Evidence. SSRN *Electronic Journal,*https://doi.org/10.2139/ssrn.4010539

Citrin, J. M., & DeRosa, D. (2021). *Leading at a distance: Practical lessons for virtual success*. John Wiley & Sons.

Civil Service College Uganda. (2018). Report on Public Sector Recruitment Practices. Available at: Annual Report 2018 - 2019 Civil Service College Annual Report for the Year Ended 31 March 2019 - DocsLib [Accessed 12 January 2024]

Clarke, A. (2017). Digital government units: What are they, and what do they mean for digital era public management renewal? *International Public Management Journal*, 23(3), 358–379. 10.1080/10967494.2019.1686447

Clarke, A., Lindquist, E., & Roy, J. (2017). Understanding governance in the digital era: An agenda for public administration research in Canada. *Canadian Public Administration*, 60(4), 457–475. 10.1111/capa.12246

Clarke, M., & Scurry, T. (2020). The role of the psychological contract in shaping graduate experiences: A study of public sector talent management programmes in the UK and Australia. *International Journal of Human Resource Management*, 31(8), 965–991. 10.1080/09585192.2017.1396545

Coculova, J., & Tomčíková, Ľ. (2021). *Innovative Human Resource Management Practices for the Talent Management Implementation*. Marketing and Management of Innovations., 10.21272/mmi.2021.4-04

Cohen, D., & Soto, M. (2007). Growth and human capital: Good data, good results. *Journal of Economic Growth*, 1(3), 113–207. 10.1007/s10887-007-9011-5

Collings, N., Nyberg, A. J., Wright, P. M., & McMackin, J. (2021). Leading through paradox in a COVID-19 world: Human resources comes of age. *Human Resource Management Journal*, 31(4), 819–833. 10.1111/1748-8583.12343

Colombari, R., & Neirotti, P. (2023). Leveraging Frontline Employees' Knowledge for Operational Data-Driven Decision-Making: A Multilevel Perspective. *IEEE Transactions on Engineering Management*, •••, 1–12.

Colonnelli, E., Prem, M., & Teso, E. (2020). Patronage and selection in public sector organizations. *The American Economic Review*, 110(10), 3071–3099. 10.1257/aer.20181491

Conte, F., & Siano, A. (2023). Data-Driven Human Resource and Data-Driven Talent Management In internal and Recruitment Communication Strategies: An empirical Survey on Italian Firms and Insights for European Context. *Corporate Communications*, 28(4), 618–637. Advance online publication. 10.1108/CCIJ-02-2022-0012

Coombs, C., Hislop, D., Taneva, S. K., & Barnard, S. (2020). The strategic impacts of Intelligent Automation for knowledge and service work: An interdisciplinary review. *The Journal of Strategic Information Systems*, 29(4), 101600. 10.1016/j.jsis.2020.101600

Council of Europe. (2019). Public ethics: fighting nepotism within local and regional authorities. Available at: ES274310_PREMS 072519 GBR 5001 Combattre le nÃ©potisme au sein des pouvoirs locaux et rÃ©gionaux TXT BAT A6.pdf (coe.int) [accessed 22 December 2023]

Creswell, J. W. (2014). *Research design*. Sage Publications, Inc.

Creswell, J. W., & Creswell, J. D. (2018). *Research design: Qualitative, quantitative and mixed methods approaches* (5th ed.). SAGE.

Curzi, Y. (2023). High-performance work systems and firm innovation: The moderating role of digital technology and employee participation. Evidence from Europe. *Management Research Review, 47*(13), 51-67. https://doi.org/10.1108/MRR-11-2022-0751

da Silva, L. B. P., Soltovski, R., Pontes, J., Treinta, F. T., Leitão, P., Mosconi, E., de Resende, L. M. M., & Yoshino, R. T. (2022). Human resources management 4.0: Literature review and trends. *Computers & Industrial Engineering*, 168, 108111. 10.1016/j.cie.2022.108111

Dabić, M., Maley, J. F., Švarc, J., & Poček, J. (2023). Future of digital work: Challenges for sustainable human resources management. *Journal of Innovation & Knowledge*, 8(2), 100353. 10.1016/j.jik.2023.100353

Daher, M. M., & Ziade, F. (2024). Technology, Workforce, and the Future of Sustainable Work. In *Navigating the Intersection of Business, Sustainability and Technology* (pp. 119–136). Springer Nature Singapore.

Dahlbom, P., Siikanen, N., Sajasalo, P., & Järvenpää, M. (2019). Big Data and HR Analytics in the Digital Era. *Baltic Journal of Management*, 15(1), 120–138. Advance online publication. 10.1108/BJM-11-2018-0393

Dalayga, B., Baskaran, S., & Mahadi, N. (2021). *Talent Development Practices:* A Revisit as an Imperative for Talent Retention. *International Journal of Academic Research in Business & Social Sciences*, 11(2), 330–348. 10.6007/IJARBSS/v11-i2/8578

Dang, N. T. T., Nguyen, T. Q., Kok, S. K., & Ha, V. D. (2023). Multi-level challenges in talent management in a post COVID-19 future: Examining the banking sector in Vietnam. *Cogent Business & Management*, 10(3), 2251198. Advance online publication. 10.1080/23311975.2023.2251198

Das, B. K., & Rajini, G. (2023). Leadership development through 360-degree multi-rater feedback—An experience sharing of need, approach, roll-out, and the impact. *Environment and Social Psychology*, 9(2), 1–20. 10.54517/esp.v9i2.2000

De Vries, M. S. (2016). *Understanding public administration.* Bloomsbury Publishing. 10.1007/978-1-137-57546-3

Debasis, D. (2019). Internet of Things (IoT): The new paradigm of HRM and skill development in the fourth industrial revolution (industry 4.0). *IUP Journal of Information Technology*, 15(4), 7–30.

Debrah, E., Effah, J., & Owusu-Mensah, I. (2019). Does the use of a biometric system guarantee an acceptable election's outcome? Evidence from Ghana's 2012 election. *African Studies*, 78(3), 347–369. 10.1080/00020184.2018.1519335

Deloitte. (2020). *Global human capital trends 2020: The social enterprise at work: Paradox as a path forward*. Deloitte Insights. Retrieved from https://www2.deloitte.com/us/en/insights/focus/human-capital-trends/2020.html

Deloitte. (2022). Government Trends 2022. Available at: 2022 Government Trends | Deloitte Insights [Accessed 12 January 2024]

Deng, H., Duan, S. X., & Wibowo, S. (2022). Digital technology driven knowledge sharing for job performance. *Journal of Knowledge Management*, 2(5), 1–14. 10.1108/JKM-08-2021-0637

Denning, S. (2022, February 9). What Is The Digital Age And What Does It Mean? *Forbes.*

Denzin, N. K., & Lincoln, Y. S. (2003). *A handbook of qualitative research.* Sage Publications.

Department of Public Service and Administration (DPSA). (2007) Employee performance management and development System. Available from: https://www.dpsa.gov.za/dpsa2g/documents/ep/2007/EPMDS.pdf (Accessed: 11 May 2024).

Department of Public Service and Administration (DPSA). (2021). Employment practice. Available from: https://www.dpsa.gov.za/dpsa2g/documents/sms/2021/sms_30_06_2021.pdf (Accessed: 11 May 2024).

Department of Public Service and Administration. (1995). White Paper on the Transformation of the Public Service Pretoria: DPSA

Department of Public Service and Administration. (1995). *White Paper on the Transformation of the Public Service.* Pretoria: DPSA

Department of Public Service and Administration. (1997). White Paper on Transforming Public Service Delivery (Batho Pele White Paper) Pretoria: DPSA

Department of Public Service and Administration. (1997). *White Paper on Transforming Public Service Delivery (Batho Pele White Paper).* Pretoria: DPSA

Department of Public Service and Administration. (2023). Address by the Department of Communications and Digital Technologies Deputy Director-General For Information Society & Capacity Development, Mr Mlindi Mashologu, at the Digital Government Workshop at Microsoft Campus, Johannesburg. 6 September 2023. Retrieved from https://www.gov.za/news/speeches/communications-and-digital-technologies-digital-government-workshop-06-sep-2023

Desouza, K. C., Denford, J. S., & Krishnamurthy, R. (2019). How the US federal communications commission managed the process of IT modernization. In Urbach, N., & Röglinger, M. (Eds.), *Digitalization cases. Management for professionals* (pp. 411–428). Springer., 10.1007/978-3-319-95273-4_22

Dhanalakshmi, R., Cherukuri, D. M., Ambashankar, A., Sivaraman, A., & Sood, K. (2023). Smart Analytics and AI for Managing Modern Performance Management Systems. In *Smart Analytics, Artificial Intelligence and Sustainable Performance Management in a Global Digitalised Economy,110, 243-263.* Emerald Publishing Limited. 10.1108/S1569-37592023000110B016

Di Carlo, D. (2023). Beyond neo-corporatism: State employers and the special-interest politics of public sector wage-setting. *Journal of European Public Policy*, 30(5), 967–994. 10.1080/13501763.2022.2036791

Di Giulio, M., & Vecchi, G. (2023). Implementing digitalisation in the public sector. Technologies, agency, and governance. *Public Policy and Administration*, 38(2), 133–158. 10.1177/09520767211023283

Di Mascio, F., & Natalini, A. (2013). Context and mechanisms in administrative reform processes: Performance management within Italian local government. *International Public Management Journal*, 16(1), 141–166. 10.1080/10967494.2013.796263

Dick, E. (2021). *Current and potential uses of AR/VR for equity and inclusion. Information Technology and Innovation Foundation, 1-12.* ITIF Publications.

Diez, F., Bussin, M. & Lee, V. 2019. *Fundamentals of HR analytics: A manual on becoming HR analytical,*https://doi.org/10.1108/9781789739619

Dixit, S., & Arrawatia, M. (2018). The impact of talent management on job satisfaction and employee performance in public sector banks of Rajasthan. *International Journal of Creative Research Thoughts*, 6(1), 425–435.

Dobson, P., Myles, J., & Jackson, P. (2007). Making the case for critical realism: Examining the implementation of automated performance management systems. [IRMJ]. *Information Resources Management Journal*, 20(2), 138–152. 10.4018/irmj.2007040109

Du Plooy-Cilliers, D., & Davis, C. (2014). *C & Bezuidenhout. Research matters* (1st ed.). Juta and Company Ltd.

Du Toit, D.F.P., van der Waldt, G., Bayat, M.S & Cheminais, J. (1998). *Public Administration and Management for effective governance*. Juta & Co Ltd: Kenwyn – South Africa.

Dube, V. (2022). Mayors, council chairpersons sign performance contracts. *The Sunday News*. 1 May 2022. https://www.sundaynews.co.zw/mayors-council-chairpersons-sign-performance-contracts/

Duggineni, S. (2023). Impact of Controls on Data Integrity and Information Systems. *Science and Technology*, 13(2), 29–35.

Dunleavy, P., Margetts, H., Bastow, S., & Tinkler, J. (2006). New public management is dead—Long live digital-era governance. *Journal of Public Administration: Research and Theory*, 16(3), 467–494. 10.1093/jopart/mui057

Dutta, D. 2018. Social Media and Technology Trends in HRM: Cases in Recruitment and Talent Management. https://doi.org/10.5772/intechopen.79342

Dwiputrianti, S., Sutiyono, W., Suryanto, A., Rachmawati, T., & Purba, C. O. (2023). *Understanding Indicators of Talent Acquisition and Retention of Different Generations in Building Talent Management: A Case Study of DKI Jakarta Provincial Government*. Policy & Governance Review., 10.30589/pgr.v7i1.646

Economic Commission for Africa. (2003). *Public sector management reforms in Africa: Lessons learned*. Economic Commission for Africa.

Edwards, M. R., Charlwood, A., Guenole, N., & Marler, J. (2022). HR analytics: An emerging field finding its place in the world alongside simmering ethical challenges. *Human Resource Management Journal*. Advance online publication. 10.1111/1748-8583.12435

Eikebrokk, T. R., & Olsen, D. H. (2020). Robotic process automation and consequences for knowledge workers; a mixed-method study. In *Responsible Design, Implementation and Use of Information and Communication Technology: 19th IFIP WG 6.11 Conference on e-Business, e-Services, and e-Society, I3E 2020, Skukuza, South Africa, April 6–8, 2020* [Springer International Publishing.]. *Proceedings*, 19(Part I), 114–125.

Elhanafy, E., & El Hessewi, G. (2021). Effect of talent management training program on head nurses leadership effectiveness. *Egyptian Journal of Health Care*, 12(4), 351–361. 10.21608/ejhc.2021.199134

Elrehail, H. HR Analytics and Future of Work: A Systematic Literature Review. *2nd International Conference on Business Analytics for Technology and Security, ICBATS 2023*, 2023. https://doi.org/10.1109/ICBATS57792.2023.10111370

Enaifoghe, A. (2021). Digitalisation of African Economies in the Fourth Industrial Revolution: Opportunities for Growth and Industrialisation. *African Journal of Development Studies*, 11(2), 31–53.

Enwereji, P. C., & Emmanuel, U. D. (2022). Talent Management Practices in the South African Public Service. *Khazanah Sosial*, 4(3), 417–433. 10.15575/ks.v4i3.19708

Erin, O., Adegboye, A., & Uwuigbe, U. (2024). Public sector transparency and sustainable development: A focus on Sub-Saharan Africa. *Journal of Public Affairs*, 24(1), e2885. 10.1002/pa.2885

Eurostat. (2023) Digitalisation in Europe - 2023 edition, Retrieved April 19, 2024,fromhttps://ec.europa.eu/eurostat/web/interactive-publications/digitalisation-2023

Eyamu, S., Wanyama, S. B., Ndanyi, D. M., & Sansa, A. (2021). A Critical Analysis of New Public Management, Human Resource Practices and Operational Performance in Uganda's Public Sector. *Journal of Human Resource Management*, 9(4), 102–114.

Fagarasan, C., Cristea, C., Cristea, M., Popa, O., & Pisla, A. (2023). Integrating Sustainability Metrics into Project and Portfolio Performance Assessment in Agile Software Development: A Data-Driven Scoring Model. *Sustainability (Basel)*, 15(17), 13139. 10.3390/su151713139

Fajana, S., Owoyemi, O., Elegbede, T., & Gbajumo-Sheriff, M. (2011). Human resource management practices in Nigeria. *Journal of Management and Strategy*, 2(2), 57–62. 10.5430/jms.v2n2p57

Falletta, S. V., & Combs, W. L. (2020). The HR analytics cycle: A seven-step process for building evidence-based and ethical HR analytics capabilities. *Journal of Work-Applied Management*, 13(1), 51–68. 10.1108/JWAM-03-2020-0020

Falloon, G. (2020). From digital literacy to digital competence: The teacher digital competency (TDC) framework. *Educational Technology Research and Development*, 68(5), 2449–2472. 10.1007/s11423-020-09767-4

Fatile, O. J., & Igbokwe-Ibeto, C. J. (2012). Nigerian public sector and the challenges of human capital development: The way forward. *Scottish Journal of Arts. Social Sciences and Scientific Study*, 1(2), 11–23.

Fauzian, N. R., Prasojo, E., Muslim, M. A., & Wangsaatmaja, S. (2024). DIGITALISED TALENT MANAGEMENT IN PUBLIC SECTOR: A LESSON LEARNED FROM THE WEST JAVA PROVINCIAL GOVERNMENT. *Journal of Law and Sustainable Development*, 12(2), e2559. 10.55908/sdgs.v12i2.2559

Fenwick, A., Molnar, G., & Frangos, P. (2024). Revisiting the Role of HR in the age of AI: Bringing humans and machines closer together in the workplace. *Frontiers in Artificial Intelligence*, 6(1272823), 1–10. 10.3389/frai.2023.127282338288334

Ferlie, E. (2017, March 29). The New Public Management and Public Management Studies. *Oxford Research Encyclopedia of Business and Management.* Retrieved 23 Apr. 2024, fromhttps://oxfordre.com/business/view/10.1093/acrefore/9780190224851.001.0001/acrefore-9780190224851-e-129.

Fernandez, V., & Gallardo-Gallardo, E. (2020). Tackling the HR digitalization challenge: Key factors and barriers to. *Competitiveness Review*, 31(1), 162–187. 10.1108/CR-12-2019-0163

Fiias, O. C., & Augustine, A. C. (2020). Promoting Human Resource Management Practice in Public Organisations in Nigeria. *SGI-Journal of Social Science and Humanities*, 2(5), 118–128.

Filippus, K., & Schultz, C. (2019). Exploring Talent Management Execution in the Ministry of Justice in the Namibian Public Sector. *SA Journal of Human Resource Management*, 17. Advance online publication. 10.4102/sajhrm.v17i0.1162

Fitzgerald, M.. (2014). Embracing digital technology: A new strategic imperative. *MIT Sloan Management Review*, 55(2), 1.

Flynn, N. (2002). *Public Sector Management*. Prentice Hall.

Frese, M., & Rauch, A. (2001). Entrepreneurship, Psychology of. In *International Encyclopedia of the Social & Behavioral Sciences* (pp. 4552–4556). Elsevier., 10.1016/B0-08-043076-7/01420-0

Fryer, K., Antony, J., & Ogden, S. (2009). Performance management in the public sector. *International Journal of Public Sector Management*, 22(6), 478–498. 10.1108/09513550910982850

Gabara, N. (2024). *DPSA finalising Digital Policy framework to drive public service transformation.* Retrieved from https://www.dpsa.gov.za/thepublicservant/2024/03/15/dpsa-finalising-digital-policy-framework-to-drive-public-service-transformation/

Gabryelczyk, R. (2020). Has covid-19 accelerated digital transformation? initial lessons learned for public administrations. *Information Systems Management*, 37(4), 303–309. 10.1080/10580530.2020.1820633

Galanti, T., De Vincenzi, C., Buonomo, I., & Benevene, P. (2023). Digital Transformation: Inevitable Change or Sisable Opportunity? The Strategic Role of HR Management in Industry 4.0. *Administrative Sciences*, 13(2), 1–19. 10.3390/admsci13020030

Gallardo-Gallardo, E., Thunnissen, M., & Scullion, H. (2020). Talent management: Context matters. [REMOVED HYPERLINK FIELD]. *International Journal of Human Resource Management*, 31(4), 457–473. 10.1080/09585192.2019.1642645

Gani, N. (2024). Optimising human resource information systems in the context of MSME technology management. *Jurnal Informasi Dan Teknologi, 6*(1), 302-309. https://doi.org/10.60083/jidt.v6i1.519

Garcia, L.. (2022). Total rewards and employee retention: The role of monetary and non-monetary compensation. *Human Resource Management Journal*, 52(4), 567–582.

Ghazzawi, K., & Accoumeh, A. (2014). Critical success factors of the e-recruitment system. *Journal of Human Resources Management and Labor Studies*, 2(2), 159–170.

Gibson, A. (2024). Agile workforce planning. In Harper, S. M., & Marshall, C. J. (Eds.), *Strategic workforce planning: Concepts, theories, and applications** (pp. 116–139). Oxford University Press., 10.1093/oso/9780197759745.003.0007

Gilch, P. M., & Sieweke, J. (2021). Recruiting digital talent: The strategic role of recruitment in organisations' digital transformation. *German Journal of Human Resource Management*, 35(1), 53–82. 10.1177/2397002220952734

Gil-Garcia, J., Dawes, S., & Pardo, T. (2017). Digital government and public management research: Finding the crossroads. *Public Management Review*, 20(5), 633–646. 10.1080/14719037.2017.1327181

Gillies, D. (2015). Human Capital Theory in Education. In *Encyclopedia of Educational Philosophy and Theory* (pp. 1–5). Springer Singapore., 10.1007/978-981-287-532-7_254-1

Gintova, M. (2023). Understanding public servants' perspectives on return to office and digital government: Lessons learned from Canada. *Transforming Government People Process and Policy, 18*(1), 118-130. https://doi.org/10.1108/TG-07-2023-0091

Girisha, M., & Nagendrababu, K. (2019). E-Human resource management (E-HRM): A growing role in organizations. *International Journal of Management Studies*, 6(1/5), 98–104.

Glaister, A., Amri, A., & Spicer, D. (2019). Talent management: Managerial sense making in the wake of omanization. *International Journal of Human Resource Management*, 32(3), 719–737. 10.1080/09585192.2018.1496128

Glenn, T. (2012). The state of talent management in Canada's public sector. *Canadian Public Administration*, 55(1), 25–51. 10.1111/j.1754-7121.2012.00204.x

Glyptis, L., Christofi, M., Vrontis, D., Del Giudice, M., Dimitriou, S., & Michael, P. (2020). E-Government implementation challenges in small countries: The project manager's perspective. *Technological Forecasting and Social Change*, 152, 119880. 10.1016/j.techfore.2019.119880

Gobble, M. M. (2017). The Datification of Human Resources. *Research Technology Management*, 60(5), 59–63. 10.1080/08956308.2017.1348143

Gomathy, D. (2024). Human resource management: Case study with solutions. *International Journal of Scientific Research in Engineering and Management, 08*(03), 1-11. https://doi.org/10.55041/IJSREM23383

Govender, I. G., & Reddy, P. S. (2014). Monitoring and Evaluation in Local Municipalities: A Case Study of KwaZulu-Natal Province. *Administration Publica*, 22(4), 160–177.

Government of Zimbabwe. (2013). *Constitution of Zimbabwe Amendment 20, Act 2013*. Government Publishers.

Government of Zimbabwe. (2015). *Civil service report*. Government Printers.

Government of Zimbabwe. (2016). *National Informational Communication Technology Policy*. Government Printers.

Government of Zimbabwe. (2016). *Zimbabwe National Policy for Information and Communications Technology*. Government Publishers.

Government of Zimbabwe. (2017). *Public Procurement and Disposal of Public Assets Act* [Chapter 22:23]. Government Printers.

Government of Zimbabwe. (2018). *2018 National Critical Skills Audit Report*. Government Printers.

Government of Zimbabwe. (2018). *Vision 2030: "Towards a Prosperous & Empowered Upper Middle Income Society by 2030"*. Government Printers.

Government of Zimbabwe. (2018). *Vision 2030: Towards a Prosperous & Empowered Upper Middle Income Society by 2030*. Government Publishers.

Government of Zimbabwe. (2020). *National Development Strategy 1 - January 2021 - December 2025*. Government Printers.

Government of Zimbabwe. (2020). *National Development Strategy 1 January 2021 – December 2025: Towards a Prosperous & Empowered Upper Middle Income Society by 2030*. Government Publishers.

Government of Zimbabwe. (2022). *Performance contract*. Government Printers.

Greasley, K., & Thomas, P. (2020). HR Analytics: The Onto-epistemology and Politics of Metricised HRM. *Human Resource Management Journal*, 30(4), 494–507. Advance online publication. 10.1111/1748-8583.12283

Grinell, J. R., & Unrau, Y. (2005). *The qualitative research approach in research methods for social workers. Peosta.* Eddie Bowers Publishing.

Gromyko, I. (2024). Organisational support for leadership and teamwork in international virtual project teams. Vilnius (Doctoral dissertation, Vilniaus Universitetas).

Gupta, P. 2023. HR analytics: An effective tool for performance management and business development. *HR Analytics in an Era of Rapid Automation.*https://doi.org/10.4018/978-1-6684-8942-0.ch008

Haak-Saheem, W., & Festing, M. (2020). Human resource management–a national business system perspective. *International Journal of Human Resource Management*, 31(14), 1863–1890. 10.1080/09585192.2017.1423366

Habbal, A., Ali, M. K., & Abuzaraida, M. A. (2024). Artificial Intelligence Trust, risk and security management (AI trism): Frameworks, applications, challenges and future research directions. *Expert Systems with Applications*, 240, 122442. 10.1016/j.eswa.2023.122442

Hadebe, T. P. S. (2021). *Employee performance management and development system at the Kwa-Zulu Natal Provincial Department of Public Works*. Thesis (MPA)-Stellenbosch University, Available from: https://scholar.sun.ac.za/server/api/core/bitstreams/fabd4c7a-1ca1-44b7-9621-a5c0a5507742/content (Accessed 25 February 2024).

Hague, R., Harrop, M., & McCormick, J. (2019). *Comparative government and politics* (11th ed.). Red Globe Press.

Halid, H., Yusoff, Y. M., & Somu, H. (2020). The relationship between digital human resource management and organizational performance. *Advances in Economics, Business and Management Research*, Series volume number 141. First ASEAN Business, Environment, and Technology Symposium (ABEATS 2019) (pp. 96-99). Atlantis Press.

Halid, H., Yusoff, Y., & Somu, H. (2020). The relationship between digital human resource management and organisational performance. https://doi.org/10.2991/aebmr.k.200514.022

Halid, H., Halim, S. N. A., & Ravesangar, K. (2022). Human resource management practices in the digital era. In *Technological Challenges: The Human Side of the Digital Age* (pp. 109–158). Springer International Publishing. 10.1007/978-3-030-98040-5_5

Hall, J. L., Shin, G., & Bartels, C. E. (2022). Measuring the effect of performance management in local economic development policy: The case of tax increment finance districts in the Dallas-Ft. Worth metroplex. *Local Government Studies*, 48(4), 628–654. 10.1080/03003930.2020.1869544

Hanekom, P. (2020). *Covid-19 exposes South Africa's digital literacy divide*. Mail &Guardian. p. [Online] Retrieved from: https://mg.co.za/opinion/2020-09-08-covid-19-exposes-SouthAfricas-digital-literacy-divide (Accessed on 09 March 2024).

Hannah, M., Heyns, E., & Mulligan, R. (2020). Inclusive infrastructure: Digital scholarship centers and the academic library liaison. *Portal (Baltimore, Md.)*, 20(4), 693–714. 10.1353/pla.2020.0033

Haque, M. A., & Nishat, S. S. (2022). *The Impact of HRM Digitalization on Employee Performance in the RMG Industry of Bangladesh*. European Journal of Business Management and Research., 10.24018/ejbmr.2022.7.4.1540

Hartono, S., Tjahyadi, R., & Cassandra, C. (2021, August). Analysis of Employee and Manager Self Service Module on SAP Portal (A Case Study Approach). In *2021 International Conference on Information Management and Technology (ICIMTech), 1*, 93-98. IEEE. 10.1109/ICIMTech53080.2021.9535090

Harvard Business Review. (2021). Insights on Digital Transformation. Available at: The Essential Components of Digital Transformation (hbr.org) [Accessed 12 January 2024]

Hashiyana, V., Ujakpa, M. M., Suresh, N., Mukaya, K. T., & Mukupi, B. (2021, May). E-Recruitment System: A Case of Namibian Government. In *2021 IST-Africa Conference (IST-Africa)* (pp. 1-8). IEEE.

Haswani, F., Erlita, Y., & Rika, . (2023). Integrating extensive and intensive reading worksheets on digital platforms. [Journal of Applied Linguistics and Literature]. *JOALL*, 8(2), 415–432. 10.33369/joall.v8i2.28043

He, T. (2024). Digital health integration for noncommunicable diseases: Comprehensive process mapping for full-life-cycle management. *Journal of Evidence-Based Medicine, 17*(1), 26-36. https://doi.org/10.1111/jebm.1258

Heeks, R., & Bailur, S. (2007). Analyzing e-government research: Perspectives, philosophies, theories, methods, and practice. *Government Information Quarterly*, 24(2), 243–265. 10.1016/j.giq.2006.06.005

He, J., Morrison, A. M., & Zhang, H. (2021). How High-Performance HR Practices and LMX Affect Employee Engagement and Creativity in Hospitality. *Journal of Hospitality & Tourism Research (Washington, D.C.)*, 45(8), 1360–1382. Advance online publication. 10.1177/1096348021996800

Henry, L. (2019). *Bridging the urban-rural digital divide and mobilizing technology for poverty eradication: Challenges and gaps.* [Online] Available from: https://www.un.org/ development/desa/dspd/wp-content/uploads/sites/22/2019/03/ Henry-Bridging-the-DigitalDivide-2019.pdf (Accessed on 14 February 2024).

Henry, L. M., Hansen, E., Chimoff, J., Pokstis, K., Kiderman, M., Naim, R., Kossowsky, J., Byrne, M. E., Lopez-Guzman, S., Kircanski, K., Pine, D. S., & Brotman, M. A. (2024). Selecting an Ecological Momentary Assessment Platform: Tutorial for Researchers. *Journal of Medical Internet Research*, 26(1), e51125. 10.2196/5112538175682

Hood, C. (1991). A public management for all seasons? Public administration, pp. 69, 3–19.

Hood, C., & Jackson, M. (1992). *The New Public Management: A recipe for disaster.* In: Hazard Management and Emergency planning: Perspectives on Britain. London – James and James.

Hoogervorst, J. A., Koopman, P. L., & Flier, H. V. D. (2002). Human resource strategy for the new ICT-driven business context. *International Journal of Human Resource Management*, 13(8), 1245–1265. 10.1080/09585190210149501

https://www.undp.org/south-africa/blog/election-drama-promoting-civic-participation-among-youth-through-industrial theatre (Accessed on 20 February 2024).

Hujran, O., Alarabiat, A., Al-Adwan, A. S., & Al-Debei, M. (2023). Digitally transforming electronic governments into smart governments: SMARTGOV, an extended maturity model. *Information Development*, 39(4), 811–834. 10.1177/02666669211054188

Ikyanyon, D., Johnson, P., & Dawson, J. (2020). Institutional context and human resource management in Nigeria. *Employee Relations*, 42(1), 1–16. 10.1108/ER-03-2017-0056

Inakefe, G. I., Bassey, V. U., Ikeanyibe, O. M., Nwagboso, C. I., Agbor, U. I., Ebegbulem, J., Mbonu, F. I., & Ike, G. U. (2023). Digital Literacy and E-Governance Adoption for Service Delivery in Cross River State Civil Service. [IJEGR]. *International Journal of Electronic Government Research*, 19(1), 1–23. 10.4018/IJEGR.328327

International Labour Organization. (2020). Guidelines on Fair Recruitment. Available at: FAIR III brochure (ilo.org) [Accessed 12 January 2024]

Islam, M. T., & Tamzid, M. (2023). Artificial Intelligence in Human Resource Management. *the Book "Management Education for Achieving Sustainable Development Goals in the Context of Bangladesh*, 61-80.

Ivarsson, F., & Svahn, F. (2020). *Digital and conventional matchmaking–similarities, differences and tensions.* In *Proceedings of the 53rd Hawaii International Conference on System Sciences*, Maui, HI. 10.24251/HICSS.2020.727

Jacobs, E. (2021). *Moving from Access to Accessibility: The Deception of the Digital Divide in Development.* [Online] Retrieved from: https://www.za.undp.org/content/ south_africa/en/home/blog/2021/moving-from-access-to-accessibilit y--the-deception-ofthe-digita.html

Jake, S. (2022, August 15). *New Technologies in Talent Management.* CODEPWR.

Järlström, M., Saru, E., & Pekkarinen, A. (2023). Practices of sustainable human resource management in three Finnish companies: Comparative case study. *South Asian Journal of Business and Management Cases, 12*(1), 31-51. https://doi.org/10.1177/22779779231154656

Jasni, N. N., Mahadi, N., Yaakop, A. Y., & Baskaran, S. (2022). *People Analytics: An Evidence-Based Approach in Managing Employees.* International Journal of Academic Research in Progressive Education and Development., 10.6007/IJARPED/v11-i3/15086

Jayaraman, S., Talib, P., & Khan, A. N. (2018). Integrated Talent Management Scale: Construction and Initial Validation. *SAGE Open*, 8(3). Advance online publication. 10.1177/2158244018780965

Jayasena, S. D. N. S., Rajasekera, J., & Wenkai, L. (2023). Talent Management for Enhancing the Efficiency of Human Resources in the Public Sector of Sri Lanka: A Comparative Study. *Kelaniya Journal of Human Resource Management*, 18(2), 1–11. 10.4038/kjhrm.v18i2.108

Jimoh, L. A., & Kee, D. M. H. (2022). Talent Management: The Way Out of Poor Task Performance. *Industrial and Commercial Training*, 54(4), 623–636. Advance online publication. 10.1108/ICT-03-2022-0016

Johansson, J., & Herranen, S. (2019). *The application of artificial intelligence (AI) in human resource management: Current state of AI and its impact on the traditional recruitment process.* Retrieved from http://www.diva2:1322478/FULLTEXT01.pdf (Accessed on 11 February 2024).

Johnson, R., & Brown, A. (2022). Organizational culture and employee retention: A comprehensive review. Journal of Applied Organizational Studies. *Journal of Applied Organizational Studies*, 36(3), 421–439.

Johnstone, S. (2023). Human resource management in recession: Restructuring and alternatives to downsizing in times of crisis. *Human Resource Management Journal, 34*(1), 138-157. https://doi.org/10.1111/1748-8583.12512

Joseph, J., & Williams, R. (2022). A retrospective analysis: ICT for improved municipal service delivery amidst COVID 19: ICT and Municipal Service Delivery'. *EUREKA: Social and Humanities*, 2(1), 70–85. 10.21303/2504-5571.2022.002284

Junita, A. (2021). The Creative Hub: HR Strategic Function in The Digital Age. .10.2991/aer.k.210121.031

Kamalakannan, D. (2024). The integration of digital transformation with human resource management – a theoretical point of view. *International Journal of Scientific Research in Engineering and Management, 08*(02), 1-13. https://doi.org/10.55041/IJSREM28895

Kamal, M., & Lukman, Z. (2017). The effects of talent management on performance management. *International Journal of Academic Research in Business & Social Sciences*, 7(9), 372–385.

Kambur, E., & Yildirim, T. (2023). From traditional to smart human resources management. *International Journal of Manpower*, 44(3), 422–452. 10.1108/IJM-10-2021-0622

Kangethe, A. T. W., Njoroge, P. M., Wangombe, C. W., Munyi, C. M., & Njeru, R. G. (2022). Leveraging on Technology and Job Performance in the Public Service: A Study of Department of Finance and Economic Planning, Embu County Kenya. *International Journal of Academic Research in Business & Social Sciences*, 12(11), 2798–2813. 10.6007/IJARBSS/v12-i11/15744

Kanyumba, B., & Msosa, S. K. (2020). RETENTION STRATEGIES OF HEALTHCARE PROFESSIONALS AS A TOOL FOR EFFECTIVE SERVICE DELIVERY IN THE ZIMBABWEAN HEALTH SECTOR. *Eurasian Journal of Business and Management*, 8(2), 51–62. 10.15604/ejbm.2020.08.02.001

Kapitanov, V. A., Osipova, O., & Chikileva, L. S. 2021. Promising Areas for Developing HR Managers' Competencies in the Digital Age. *SHS Web of Conferences,*https://doi.org/10.1051/shsconf/20219101016

Kariuki, P., & Reddy, P. (2017). Operationalising an effective monitoring and evaluation system for local government: Considerations for best practice. *African Evaluation Journal*, 5(2), 1–8. 10.4102/aej.v5i2.240

Karwehl, L. J. & Kauffeld, S. 2021. Traditional and New Ways in Competence Management: Application of HR Analytics in Competence Management. *Gruppe Interaktion Organisation Zeitschrift Für Angewandte Organisationspsychologie (Gio),*https://doi.org/10.1007/s11612-021-00548-y

Kellogg, K., Valentine, M., & Christin, A. (2020). Algorithms at work: The new contested terrain of control. *The Academy of Management Annals*, 14(1), 366–410. 10.5465/annals.2018.0174

Kentenyingi, R. (2022). Closing the growing digital skills gap in Uganda. Available at: https://www.uncdf.org/article/7859/closing-the-growing-digital-skills-gap-in-uganda [Accessed 15 April 2024]

Ketolainen, N. (2018). *Digitalization of human resources – the transformation journey into an automated and data-driven service organization.* Master thesis, University of Applied Sciences Haaga, Helsinki, Finland.

Kettl, D. F. (1997). The global revolution in public management: Driving themes, missing links. *Journal of Policy Analysis and Management*, 16(3), 446–462. 10.1002/(SICI)1520-6688(199722)16:3<446::AID-PAM5>3.0.CO;2-H

Khanyile, M., Nzimakwe, T.I. & Mthuli, S.A. (2021). Challenges of Innovations in Participatory Governance in uMshwathi Local Municipality in Kwazulu-Natal. *Journal of Public Administration, 56*(4.1), 972-985.

Khatri, M. R. (2023). Integration of natural language processing, self-service platforms, predictive maintenance, and prescriptive analytics for cost reduction, personalisation, and real-time insights customer service and operational efficiency. *International Journal of Information and Cybersecurity*, 7(9), 1–30.

Khawaja, S., & Khalid, S. U. (2022). Retooling governance for improving public service delivery: Case study of right to public services commission, Khyber Pakhtunkhwa – Pakistan. *Governance: An International Journal of Policy, Administration and Institutions*, 35(2), 421–436. 10.1111/gove.12607

Khera, S., & Gulati, K. (2012). Human resource information system and its impact on human resource planning: A perceptual analysis of information technology companies. [IOSRJBM]. *IOSR Journal of Business and Management*, 3(6), 6–13. 10.9790/487X-0360613

Khoreva, V., Vaiman, V., & Van Zalk, M. (2017). Talent management practice effectiveness: Investigating employee perspective. *Employee Relations*, 39(1), 19–33. 10.1108/ER-01-2016-0005

Khunoethe, H., Reddy, P. S., & Mthuli, S. A. (2021). Performance Management and the Integrated Development Plan of the Msunduzi Municipality in South Africa. *NISPAcee Journal of Public Administration and Policy*, 14(2), 161–187. 10.2478/nispa-2021-0019

Kiadaliri, A., Dell'Isola, A., Lohmander, L., Hunter, D., & Dahlberg, L. (2023). Assessing the importance of predictors of adherence to a digital self-management intervention for osteoarthritis. *Journal of Orthopaedic Surgery and Research, 18*(1). https://doi.org/10.1186/s13018-023-03562-6

Kiggundu, M. N. (2017). Alternative service delivery in Africa: The case for international regional organisations. *Africa's Public Service Delivery & Performance Review*, 4(2), 283–311. 10.4102/apsdpr.v4i2.114

Kimathi, L. (2017). Challenges of the devolved health sector in Kenya: Teething problems or systemic contradictions? *Africa Development. Afrique et Developpement*, XLII(1), 55–77.

Kim, S., Wang, Y., & Boon, C. (2021). Sixty years of research on technology and human resource management: Looking back and looking forward. *Human Resource Management*, 60(1), 229–247. 10.1002/hrm.22049

Kirtzalidou, A. (2023). Factors Affecting Human Resource Motivation in The Public Sector. Thessaloniki (Master's Thesis, International Hellenic University).

Klepić, I. & Klepić, Z. 2023. The Influence of Determination of the Required Competencies on the Business Performance of Small and Medium Enterprises. https://doi.org/10.20867/thi.26.5

Köchling, A., & Wehner, M. C. (2020). Discriminated by an algorithm: A systematic review of discrimination and fairness by algorithmic decision-making in the context of HR recruitment and HR development. *Business Research*, 13(3), 795–848. 10.1007/s40685-020-00134-w

Koch, T., Gerber, C., & De Klerk, J. J. (2018). The impact of social media on recruitment: Are you LinkedIn? *SA Journal of Human Resource Management*, 16(1), 1–14. 10.4102/sajhrm.v16i0.861

Konateh, H., Duramany-Lakkoh, E., & Udeh, E. (2023). Cost and administrative effectiveness of recruitment and selection practices on public service delivery in public sector institutions. *European Journal of Business Management and Research, 8*(2), 21-30. https://doi.org/10.24018/ejbmr.2023.8.2.1814

Kozjek, T., & Franca, V. (2020). *Talent Management in the Public Sector*. Central European Public Administration Review., 10.17573/cepar.2020.2.03

Krasivskyy, O., Pirozhenko, N., Samborska, O., Harbusiuk, V., & Inozemtseva, O. (2023). A Model for Implementing Digital Personnel Management in Security and Safety for Engineering Enterprises. *International Journal of Safety and Security Engineering*, 13(3), 519–526. 10.18280/ijsse.130314

Kravariti, F., & Johnston, K. (2019a). Talent management: A critical literature review and research agenda fo r public sector human resource management. *Public Management Review*, 22(1), 75–95. 10.1080/14719037.2019.1638439

Kravariti, F., Tasoulis, K., Scullion, H., & Alali, M. K. (2023). Talent management and performance in the public sector: The role of organisational and line managerial support for development. *International Journal of Human Resource Management*, 34(9), 1782–1807. 10.1080/09585192.2022.2032265

Kruyen, P. M., & Sowa, J. E. (2023). Essential but ignored: Including blue-collar government workers into human resource management research. *Public Personnel Management*, 52(4), 521–542. 10.1177/00910260231187540

Kshetri, N. (2021). Evolving uses of Artificial Intelligence in human resource management in emerging economies in the global South: Some preliminary evidence. *Management Research Review*, 44(7), 970–990. 10.1108/MRR-03-2020-0168

Kuhlmann, S. (2010). New public management for the classical continental European administration. *Public Administration*, 88(4), 1116–1130. 10.1111/j.1467-9299.2010.01869.x

Kumar, A., & Priyanka, S. (2013). Understanding the evolution of technology acceptance. *International Journal of Selection and Assessment*, 1(2), 24–38.

Kumar, L. (2014). *Research methodology*. Sage Publications.

Kumar, M. D., Yap, A. C. T., Govindarajo, N. S., Tamah, A., & Sharma, V. (2024). Intelligent Industry 4.0: Artificial Intelligence and Robotic Process Automation as Tendsetters. In *AI and Data Analytics Applications in Organisational Management* (pp. 249–273). IGI Global.

Kumar, S. R. (2021). The Impact of Talent Management Practices on Employee Turnover and Retention Intentions. *Global Business and Organizational Excellence*. Advance online publication. 10.1002/joe.22130

Kumar, V., Alshazly, H., Idris, S. A., & Bourouis, S. (2021). Evaluating the impact of COVID-19 on society, environment, economy, and education. *Sustainability (Basel)*, 13(24), 13642. 10.3390/su132413642

Kutcher, A. M., & LeBaron, V. T. (2022). A simple guide for completing an integrative review using an example article. *Journal of Professional Nursing*, 40, 13–19. 10.1016/j.profnurs.2022.02.00435568452

Kuwali, D. (2024). Accountable Governance: Fighting Corruption in Africa. In Kuwali, D. (Ed.), *Corruption Proofing in Africa* (pp. 221–234). Routledge. 10.4324/9781003326649-21

Labour Guide. (2023). Employment Equity Act. Retrieved January 26, 2014, From https://labourguide.co.za/employment-equity/employment-equity-act

Ladimeji, O. A. (2020). The Fourth Industrial Revolution and Nigeria: A Policy Conundrum and High Stakes for the Future of the African Continent. *Think (London, England)*, 83(1).

Lapuente, V., & van de Walle, S. (2020). The effects of new public management on the quality of public services. *Governance: An International Journal of Policy, Administration and Institutions*, 33(3), 461–475. 10.1111/gove.12502

Larkin, J. (2017). HR digital disruption: The biggest wave of transformation in decades. *Strategic HR Review*, 16(2), 55–59. 10.1108/SHR-01-2017-0006

Lauer, T. (2020). *Change management: fundamentals and success factors*. Springer Nature.

Laurim, V., Arpaci, S., Prommegger, B., & Krcmar, H. (2021). Computer, whom should I hire?–acceptance criteria for artificial intelligence in the recruitment process. In *Proceedings of the 54th Hawaii International Conference on System Sciences,* 5495-5504. Scholar Space. 10.24251/HICSS.2021.668

Leavy, P. (2014). *The Oxford handbook of qualitative research*. Oxford University Press. 10.1093/oxfordhb/9780199811755.001.0001

Lederer, A. L., Maupin, D. J., Sena, M. P., & Zhuang, Y. (2000). The Technology Acceptance Model and World Wide Web. *Decision Support Systems*, 29(2), 269–282. 10.1016/S0167-9236(00)00076-2

Ledger, T., & Rampedi, M. (2019). Mind the gap: Section 139 interventions in theory and in practise. [Online]. Available at: https://pari.org.za/reports

Leidner, D. (2018). Review and Theory Symbiosis: An Introspective Retrospective. *Journal of the Association for Information Systems*, 19(06), 552–567. 10.17705/1jais.00501

Leskina, E. I. 2022. Digital Talent Management for Human Capital Development. https://doi.org/10.15405/epsbs.2022.01.62

Likhitkar, P. & Verma, P. 2019. HR Value Proposition Using Predictive Analytics: An Overview. https://doi.org/10.1007/978-981-13-9330-3_15

Lin, L.-H., & Wang, K.-J. (2022). Talent Retention of New Generations for Sustainable Employment Relationships in Work 4.0 Era—Assessment by Fuzzy Delphi Method. *Sustainability (Basel)*, 14(18), 11535. Advance online publication. 10.3390/su141811535

Liu, M. (2021). An Empirical Study on Talent Management Strategies of Knowledge-Based Organisations Using Entrepreneurial Psychology and Key Competence. *Frontiers in Psychology*, 12, 4615.

Loevinsohn, B. (2008). Performance-based contracting for health services in developing countries: A toolkit. https://documents.worldbank.org/curated/en/649511468314708749/Performance-based-contracting-for-health-services-indeveloping-countries-a-toolkit

Lu, J. (2015). The performance of performance-based contracting in human services: A quasi-experiment. *Journal of Public Administration: Research and Theory*, 26(2), 277–293. 10.1093/jopart/muv002

Lukaszewski, K. M., Stone, D. L., & Johnson, R. D. (2016). Impact of human resource information system policies on privacy. *AIS Transactions on Human-Computer Interaction*, 8(2), 58–73. 10.17705/1thci.00079

Lumunon, D. F., Massie, J. D., & Trang, I. (2021). The Effect of Training, Digital Transformation, and Work Motivation on Employee Performance during the Covid-19 Period: A Study on Culinary UMKM Employees in Manado City. *Central Asian Journal of Literature Philosophy and Culture*, 2(8), 22–37.

Luu, T. T. (2018). Engaging Employees With Disabilities in Vietnamese Business Context. *Employee Relations*, 40(5), 822–847. Advance online publication. 10.1108/ER-06-2017-0134

Mabuza, J. (2020). [Impact on digital transformation. A research report submitted to the Faculty of Commerce, Law and Management, University of the Witwatersrand, Master of Management in the field of Digital Business. From wiredspace.wits.ac.za.]. *COVID*, 19, •••.

Macedo, R. R. d., Veloso, E. F. R., Pinsky, V. C., & Trevisan, L. N. (2023). *Career Management in Digital Age: A Study of Leadership's Competencies and Practices Applied for IT Professionals*. Revista De Administração Da Ufsm., 10.5902/1983465969082

Madhani, P. M. (2022a). Human Resources Analytics: Leveraging Human Resources for Enhancing Business Performance. *Compensation &amp. Compensation and Benefits Review*, 55(1), 31–45. 10.1177/08863687221131730

Magoro, P. (2015). Performance Management Agreements for Senior Managers in the Makhuduthamaga Local Municipality: A Case of Their Usage in Service Delivery. *Journal of Public Administration*, 50(si-1), 700–711.

Maharani, M. & Wang, G. 2022. The Use of Gamification for Pre-Recruitment System in Tax Consulting Company. *Journal of Information Systems and Informatics,*https://doi.org/10.51519/journalisi.v4i3.320

Majam, T., & Jarbandhan, D. B. (2022). Data-driven human resource management in the Fourth Industrial Revolution (4IR). *Africa's Public Service Delivery & Performance Review*, 10(1), a588. 10.4102/apsdpr.v10i1.588

Makasi, S. S. (2022). *Perspectives on the implementation of the Performance Management and Development System in the Department of Social Development in Eastern Cape.* Masters of Public Administration, University of the Western Cape. Available from: https://etd.uwc.ac.za/bitstream/handle/11394/3029/Makas_MPA_2011.pdf?sequence=1 (Accessed: 25 February 2024).

Mamokhere, J. (2019). An assessment of reasons behind service delivery protests: a case of Greater Tzaneen Municipality, *Journal of Public Affairs*. 20(2). [Online]. Available at: https://onlinelibrary.wiley.com/doi/abs/10.1002/pa.2049

Mansyur, N. A. (2023). The challenges of personnel management for public service organizations in the era of technological disruption in Indonesia. *Journal of Management and Administration Provision*, 3(3), 81–92. 10.55885/jmap.v3i3.287

Margherita, A. (2022). Human resources analytics: A systematization of research topics and directions for future research. *Human Resource Management Review*, 32(2), 100795. Advance online publication. 10.1016/j.hrmr.2020.100795

Marhil, M., Masaud, K., & Majid, N. (2023). The mediating role of job satisfaction on the relationship between human resources management strategies and employees performance in Waha Oil & Gas Company in Libya. *American Journal of Economics and Business Innovation, 2*(1), 63-69. https://doi.org/10.54536/ajebi.v2i1.1437

Marler, J. H., & Boudreau, J. W. (2017). An evidence-based review of HR Analytics. *International Journal of Human Resource Management*, 28(1), 3–26. 10.1080/09585192.2016.1244699

Martínez-Peláez, R., Ochoa-Brust, A., Rivera, S., Félix, V. G., Ostos, R., Brito, H., Félix, R. A., & Mena, L. J. (2023). Role of digital transformation for achieving sustainability: Mediated role of stakeholders, key capabilities, and technology. *Sustainability (Basel)*, 15(14), 11221. 10.3390/su151411221

Martín-Hernández, P. (2023). Artificial Intelligence: The Present and Future of Human Resources Recruitment and Selection Processes. *Engineering Proceedings*, 56(1), 188–202.

Martinus, M. S. (2022). The Paradigm Shift from Traditional Public Administration to Sustainable Public Administration. *African Journal of Development Studies (formerly AFFRIKA Journal of Politics, Economics and Society), 12*(2), 99-129.

Masenya, M. J., Mokoele, N. J., & Makalela, K. I. (2018). Performance management as a mechanism to effective public service delivery in South Africa. *African Journal of Public Affairs*, 10(4), 106–117.

Masilela, L., & Nel, D. (2021). The role of data and information security governance in protecting public sector data and information assets in national government in South Africa. *Africa's Public Service Delivery and Performance Review*, 9(1), 385. 10.4102/apsdpr.v9i1.385

Masri, N., & Suliman, A. (2019). Talent management, employee recognition and performance in research institution. *Studies in Business and Economics*, 14(1), 127–140. 10.2478/sbe-2019-0010

Matimbwa, H. (2023). Human Resource Information System Applications: Insights from Local Government Authorities in Tanzania. *Ruaha Journal of Business. Economics and Management Sciences*, 6(1), 87–100.

Matli, W., & Ngoepe, M. (2020). Capitalizing on digital literacy skills for capacity development of people who are not in education, employment or training in South Africa. *Sabinet African Journals,* 3(7), 44-58 https://journals.co.za/doi/abs/ 10.1080/20421338.2019.1624008

Maurya, K., & Agarwal, M. (2018). Organisational talent management and perceived employer branding. *The International Journal of Organizational Analysis*, 26(2), 312–330. 10.1108/IJOA-04-2017-1147

Mawela, T., Ochara, N. M., & Twinomurinzi, H. (2017). *E-government implementation: A reflection on South African Municipalities*. Available at: http://www.scielo.org.za/pdf/sacj/v29n1/09. pdf. (Accessed on 20 February 2024).

Mazurchenko, A., & Maršíková, K. (2019). Digitally-powered human resource management: Skills and roles in the digital era. *Acta Informatica Pragensia*, 8(2), 72–87. 10.18267/j.aip.125

Mbiza, S. (2021). ICT Innovations Propel Local Development: Where are Zimbabwean ICT Technopreneurs? [WJRR]. *World Journal of Research and Review*, 12(6), 16–20. 10.31871/WJRR.12.6.7

McCaffry, R., & Sexton, L. (2018). *Improving government performance through effective talent management.* Unpublished research report, Vol. 4, Association of International Certified Professional Accountants, Durham, NC, US.

McCartney, S., & Fu, N. (2022). Bridging the Gap: Why, How and When HR Analytics Can Impact Organizational Performance. *Management Decision*, 60(13), 25–47. Advance online publication. 10.1108/MD-12-2020-1581

McKenzie, J. (2023). *Grey literature: What it is & how to find it.* Simon Fraser University.

McKinsey & Company. (2020). The next chapter: Driving technology leadership in the public sector. Available at: McKinsey & Company Article [accessed 05 January 2024]

McKinsey & Company. (2021). *The future of work after COVID-19*. Retrieved from https://www.mckinsey.com/featured-insights/future-of-work/the-future-of-work-after-covid-19

Mehale, K. D., Govender, C. M., & Mabaso, C. M. (2021). Maximising training evaluation for employee performance improvement. *SA Journal of Human Resource Management*, 19(0), 1–11. 10.4102/sajhrm.v19i0.1473

Meiyanti, R., Utomo, B., Sensuse, D. I., & Wahyuni, R. (2018, August). e-Government challenges in developing Countries: A literature review. In *2018 6th International Conference on Cyber and IT Service Management (CITSM)* (pp. 1-6). IEEE.

Mello, D. M. (2015). Performance management and development system in the South African public service: A critical review. *Journal of Public Administration*, 50(si-1), 688–699.

Mello, D. M. (2020). Exploring the use of information and communication technology in the implementation of a performance management and development system in the South African public service. *African Journal of Governance and Development*, 9(2), 585–598.

Memon, M., Soomro, N., & Qazi, S. W. (2024). Mapping Digital Recruitment Tools Using Advanced Convergent Qualitative Meta-integration. *Vision: The Journal of Business Perspective*, 09722629231220989.

Mer, A., & Virdi, A. S. (2023). Navigating the paradigm shift in HRM practices through the lens of artificial intelligence: A post-pandemic perspective. *The Adoption and Effect of Artificial Intelligence on Human Resources Management, Part A*, 123-154.

Mer, A., & Srivastava, A. (2023). Employee Engagement in the New Normal: Artificial Intelligence as a Buzzword or a Game Changer? In *The Adoption and Effect of Artificial Intelligence on Human Resources Management, Part A* (pp. 15–46). Emerald Publishing Limited. 10.1108/978-1-80382-027-920231002

Mergel, I. (2016). Agile innovation management in government: A research agenda. *Government Information Quarterly*, 33(3), 516–523. 10.1016/j.giq.2016.07.004

Mergel, I. (2019). Digital service teams in government. *Government Information Quarterly*, 36(4), 101389. 10.1016/j.giq.2019.07.001

Mergel, I. (2021). Open innovation in the public sector: drivers and barriers for the adoption of Challenge. gov. In *Digital Government and Public Management* (pp. 94–113). Routledge. 10.4324/9781003258742-6

Mergel, I., Edelmann, N., & Haug, N. (2019). Defining digital transformation: Results from expert interviews. *Government Information Quarterly*, 36(4), 101385. 10.1016/j.giq.2019.06.002

Meru, A. K., & Kinoti, M. W. (2022). Digitalisation and public sector service delivery in Kenya. In Adeola, O., Edeh, J. N., & Hinson, R. E. (Eds.), *Digital Service Delivery in Africa: Platforms and Practices* (pp. 229–248). Springer International Publishing. 10.1007/978-3-030-83909-3_10

Meshram, R.MESHRAM. (2023). THE ROLE OF ARTIFICIAL INTELLIGENCE (AI) IN RECRUITMENT AND SELECTION OF EMPLOYEES IN THE ORGANISATION. *Russian Law Journal*, 11(9s). Advance online publication. 10.52783/rlj.v11i9s.1624

Metz, T. (2022). African Ethics and Public Governance: Nepotism, Preferential Hiring, and Other Partiality. In K, Ogunyemi, I. Adisa & R.E. Hinson (Eds.), *Ethics and Accountable Governance in Africa's Public Sector, Volume I. Palgrave Studies of Public Sector Management in Africa* (pp.109-129). Cham: Palgrave Macmillan.

Mhlanga, D., Shava, E., & Dzingirai, M. (2023). Harnessing State Capability in Embracing the Fourth Industrial Revolution: Is Zimbabwe Prepared? (pp. 239–254). 10.1007/978-3-031-28686-5_12

Mhlanga, D., Shava, E., & Dzingirai, M. (2023). Harnessing State Capability in Embracing the Fourth Industrial Revolution: Is Zimbabwe Prepared? In The Fourth Industrial Revolution in Africa: Exploring the Development Implications of Smart Technologies in Africa (pp. 239-254): Springer.

Mhlanga, D., & Moloi, T. (2020). COVID-19 and the digital transformation of education: What are we learning on 4IR in South Africa? *Education Sciences*, 10(7), 1–11. 10.3390/educsci10070180

Midiwo, J. (2016). Influence of Human Resource Information Systems on the Performance in Kenyan Public Universities (Doctoral dissertation, Jomo Kenyatta University of Agriculture and Technology).

Mikalef, P., Conboy, K., Lundström, J. E., & Popovič, A. (2022). Thinking responsibly about responsible AI and 'the dark side' of AI. *European Journal of Information Systems*, 31(3), 257–268. 10.1080/0960085X.2022.2026621

Milukutu, A., & Siachisa, M. (2023). Assessing the Impact of Digital Transformation on Employee Performance in the Public Sector: A Case Study of Zambia's Ministry of Health Headquarters (2017-2022). *International Journal of Humanities, Social. Sciences and Education*, 10(9), 118–126. 10.20431/2349-0381.1009013

Ministry of Public Service. (2019). Public Service Digital Strategy. Available at: Ministry of Public Service Strategic Plan 2015/2016 – 2019/2020 – Ministry of Public Service [Accessed 20 December 2023]

Mitchell, A. (2023). Collaboration technology affordances from virtual collaboration in the time of COVID-19 and post-pandemic strategies. *Information Technology & People*, 36(5), 1982–2008. 10.1108/ITP-01-2021-0003

Mitosis, K. D., Lamnisos, D., & Talias, M. A. (2021). Talent Management in Healthcare: A Systematic Qualitative Review. *Sustainability (Basel)*, 13(8), 4469. 10.3390/su13084469

Mjulwa, S. (2023). *TALENT MANAGEMENT AS AN ADMINISTRATIVE TOOL TO ENHANCE SERVICE DELIVERY: A CASE OF O.R. TAMBO DISTRICT MUNICIPALITY*. DURBAN UNIVERSITY OF TECHNOLOGY.

Mkhize, L. N., Nzimakwe, T. I., & Mthuli, S. A. (2021). Bureaucrats' views on performance management in a KwaZulu-Natal Provincial Government Department. *Administratio Publica*, 21(1), 83–101.

Mobideen, H., Allahawiah, S., & Alomari, K. M. (2019). The Impact of Human Resources Information Systems on Human Resources Selection and Recruitment Strategy: An applied study on Arab Potash Company in the Hashemite Kingdom of Jordan. *International Journal of Advanced Trends in Computer Science and Engineering*, 8(5), 2475–2484. 10.30534/ijatcse/2019/93852019

Mofolo, M. (2012). Strengthening performance management system implementation in South African municipalities. *Africa's Public Service Delivery & Performance Review*, 1(1), 73–86. 10.4102/apsdpr.v1i1.25

Mogbojuri, B. O. (2024). Unlocking the Potential: Artificial Intelligence and Machine Learning in Human Resources Information Systems. *IEEE-SEM Publications*, 12(3).

Mohammed, A. Q. (2019). HR ANALYTICS: A MODERN TOOL IN HR FOR PREDICTIVE DECISION MAKING. *Journal of Management*, 10(3). Advance online publication. 10.34218/JOM.6.3.2019.007

Mohana, S., M, R. K. & Subramanyam, P. N. V. B. 2021. Talent Management Practices and Sustainable Organizational Performance in Cement Industry. *Journal of Management and Science*, https://doi.org/10.26524/jms.11.24

Mohangi, P., & Nyika, F. (2023). Performance management implementation in local government: A literature review of relevant international literature. *Public Administration Journal*, 13(1), 75–86.

Mohanty, S., & Mishra, P. C. (2020). Framework for understanding Internet of Things in human resource management. [Top of Form]. *Revista ESPACIOS*, 4(1), 1–12.

Mokgolo, M. M., & Dikotla, M. (2023). Ethical violations: Shortlisting and interviewing processes in the South African public service. *Africa's Public Service Delivery & Performance Review*, 11(1), a648. 10.4102/apsdpr.v11i1.648

Molino, M., Cortese, C. G., & Ghislieri, C. (2020). The promotion of technology acceptance and work engagement in industry 4.0: From personal resources to information and training. *International Journal of Environmental Research and Public Health*, 17(7), 2438. 10.3390/ijerph17072438322601 42

Moloi, D. (2023). *The Case for Immediate Action on Public Sector Digital Transformation is urgently needed.* Retrieved from https://www.dpsa.gov.za/thepublicservant/2023/09/06/the-case-for-immediate-action-on-public-sector-digital-transformation-is-urgently-needed/

Moodley, M. (2016). *Employee performance management and development system at King Edward V111 hospital as a tool for service delivery.* Master of Business Administration, University of KwaZulu-Natal. Available from: https://researchspace.ukzn.ac.za/server/api/core/bitstreams/2dbf411e-e12d-407a-b940-41d369f13bf3/content (Accessed: 25 February 2024).

Moran, R. (2023). An investigative analysis of how influential leadership and change management strategies were during the transitional phase to a Technological University.

Morgan, H. (2022). Conducting a qualitative document analysis. *The Qualitative Report*, 27(1), 64–77.

Mosca, M. (2020). *Digitalization of HRM: A study of success factors and consequences in the last decade*. University of Twente.

Moynihan, D. P., & Pandey, S. K. (2010). The big question for performance management: Why do managers use performance information? *Journal of Public Administration: Research and Theory*, 20(4), 849–866. 10.1093/jopart/muq004

Mthuli, S. A. (2018). *A Systems thinking exploration of the challenges facing Maritime Education and Training: The case of public higher education institutions in KwaZulu-Natal* (Doctoral dissertation, University of KwaZulu-Natal). Available at: https://researchspace.ukzn.ac.za/items/be891477-102b-4d1f-b66d-b5675dc45d18 (Accessed: 6 May 2024).

Mthuli, S. A., Singh, N., & Reddy, P. S. (2023a). Political Leadership and *Ubuntu* for Public Sector Performance in South Africa. In *African Leadership: Powerful Paradigms for the 21st Century* (pp. 27-43). Emerald Publishing Limited.

Mthuli, S., Singh, N., & Reddy, p. (2022). Political leadership for improved. *Lessons from Political Leadership in Africa: Towards Inspirational and Transformational Leaders*, 15.

Mthuli, S., Singh, N., & Reddy, P. (2023b). Eroding efficiency and effectiveness: the impact of corruption on public sector performance in South Africa. In *The Nexus between Poverty and Corruption: Quo Vadis?* (pp.153. 176). Cambridge Scholars Publishing.

Mthuli, S. A., Ruffin, F., & Singh, N. (2022). Define, Explain, Justify, Apply'(DEJA): An analytic tool for guiding qualitative research sample size. *International Journal of Social Research Methodology*, 25(6), 809–821. 10.1080/13645579.2021.1941646

Mtuwa, S., & Chiweza, A. L. (2023). Implications of Corruption on Public Administration in Malawi. *Journal of Humanities*, 31(1), 91–112. 10.4314/jh.v31i1.5

Mudimu, C. (2013). *An evaluation of talent management system in the Zimbabwean Health Care Industry: A case of Parirenyatwa Group of Hospitals*. University of Zimbabwe.

Muduli, A., & Trivedi, J. J. (2020). Social media recruitment: the role of credibility and satisfaction. *Evidence-Based HRM: A Global Forum for Empirical Scholarship, 8*(2), 237–251. 10.1108/EBHRM-08-2019-0069

Mugari, I., Chigwandaza, G. S., & Obioha, E. E. (2023). Citizens' perspectives on the form, contributory factors and impacts of white-collar crimes on local authorities in Zimbabwe. *Cogent Social Sciences*, 9(2), 2248750. 10.1080/23311886.2023.2248750

Mukamurenzi, S., Grönlund, Å., & Islam, M. S. (2019). Challenges in implementing citizen-centric e-government services in Rwanda. *Electronic Government, an International Journal, 15*(3), 283-302.

Mukuze, K. (2023). *Developing a predictive model for human capital analytics adoption in Zimbabwean State Universities.* Chinhoyi (Doctoral dissertation, Chinhoyi University of Technology).

Mukuze, K., Chavunduka, D., Manuere, F., & Ndhlovu, P. (2023). An Integrative Review of HR Analytics Implementation. *Management and Economics Research Journal*, 9(1), 1–7. 10.18639/MERJ.2023.9900076

Mukwawaya, O. Z., Proches, C. G., & Green, P. (2021). Perceived Challenges of Implementing an Integrated Talent Management Strategy at a Tertiary Institution in South Africa. *International Journal of Higher Education*, 11(1), 100. Advance online publication. 10.5430/ijhe.v11n1p100

Mulgan, G., & Albury, D. (2003). Innovation in the public sector. Strategy Unit, Cabinet Office, *1*(1), 40-. Available from: https://www.urban-response.org/system/files/content/resource/files/main/innovation-in-the-public-sector.pdf (Accessed: 25 February 2024).

Murenzi, P., & Olivier, B. (2017). E-government challenges faced by selected district municipalities in South Africa and Rwanda. *Administratio Publica*, 25(1), 141–171.

Musakuro, R. (2022). TALENT MANAGEMENT PRACTICES IN A SELECTED SOUTH AFRICAN HIGHER EDUCATION INSTITUTION. *Problems and Perspectives in Management*, 20(1), 532–542. 10.21511/ppm.20(1).2022.42

Musakuro, R. N., & De Klerk, F. (2021). Academic talent: Perceived challenges to talent management in the south african higher education sector. *SA Journal of Human Resource Management*, 19, 1–13. 10.4102/sajhrm.v19i0.1394

Muscalu, E. (2014). *Anca, e.* HR ANALYTICS FOR STRATEGIC HUMAN RESOURCE MANAGEMENT.

Musopero, O., & Lee, G. (2021). Examining the Challenges of Implementing Merit-based Civil Servant Recruitment in Zimbabwe. *International Journal of Public Administration and Management Research*, 6(2), 84–99.

Mutadzakupa, B. (2023). *A TOURISM EMPLOYEE TALENT MANAGEMENT FRAMEWORK FOR HOTEL EMPLOYEE RETENTION IN ZIMBABWE*. University of South Africa.

Mutegi, F. M. (2021). Influence of Strategic Human Resource Practices on Public Service Delivery of Huduma Centres in Kenya (Doctoral dissertation, KeMU).

Mutsagondo, S., & Khumalo, N. (2023). "E-skills scarcity and the digital records management landscape in Zimbabwe." *Library Philosophy and Practice (e-Journal.* Nguyen, H., Groth, M., & Johnson, A. (2023). How Display Rules Influence Turnover in Healthcare Teams and the Moderating Role of Team Negative Affective Tone. *Journal of Service Research*, 109467052311760. Advance online publication. 10.1177/10946705231176070

Muzanenhamo, A., & Rankhumise, E. (2023). Human resource management and digitalisation in a South African public enterprise. [IJIAS]. *Indonesian Journal of Innovation and Applied Sciences*, 3(1), 31–37.

Muzanenhamo, A., & Rankhumise, E. (2023). Human resource management and digitalization in a South African public enterprise. *Indonesian Journal of Innovation and Applied Sciences*, 3(1), 31–37. 10.47540/ijias.v3i1.692

Mwakatumbula, H., & Moshir, G. (2020). *Digital skills for gig workers in digital platforms. Digital Skills Insights.* [Online] Retrieved from: https://www.researchgate.net/publication/344927745_Digital_skills_for_gig_workers_in_digital_platforms (Accessed on 29 January 2024).

Mzezewa, T. (2019). *State of staff turnover & retention in municipalities of South Africa.* Unpublished research report. Johannesburg: LGSETA

Nachit, M., & Okar, C. (2020). Digital transformation of human resources management: A roadmap. Paper presented at the 2020 IEEE International Conference on Technology Management, Operations and Decisions (ICTMOD). 10.1109/ICTMOD49425.2020.9380608

Nachit, H., & Belhcen, L. Digital Transformation in Times of COVID-19 Pandemic: The Case of Morocco (July 7, 2020). Available at *SSRN*: https://ssrn.com/abstract=3645084 or http://dx.doi.org/10.2139/ssrn.3645084

Naidoo, R. & Ndlovu, S. W. 2022. Stickiness Impediments in Digital HRM. https://doi.org/10.24251/HICSS.2022.638

Nair, K. (2019). Overcoming today's digital talent gap in organisations worldwide. *Development in Learning Organisations an International Journal, 33*(6), 16-18. https://doi.org/10.1108/DLO-02-2019-0044

Nalubega, T., & Uwizeyimana, D. E. (2019). Public sector monitoring and evaluation in the Fourth Industrial Revolution: Implications for Africa. *Africa's Public Service Delivery and Performance Review*, 7(1), 1–12. 10.4102/apsdpr.v7i1.318

Napathorn, C. 2020. How Do MNCs Translate Corporate Talent Management Strategies Into Their Subsidiaries? Evidence From MNCs in Thailand. *Review of International Business and Strategy,*https://doi.org/10.1108/RIBS-04-2020-0043

Napierala, J., & Kvetan, V. (2023). Changing job skills in a changing world. In *Handbook of Computational Social Science for Policy* (pp. 243–259). Springer International Publishing. 10.1007/978-3-031-16624-2_13

Nardo, M., Forino, D., & Murino, T. (2020). The evolution of man–machine interaction: The role of human in Industry 4.0 paradigm. *Production & Manufacturing Research*, 8(1), 20–34. 10.1080/21693277.2020.1737592

National Information Technology Authority-Uganda (NITA-U). (2019). National IT Survey Report. Available at: Final NITA-U ANNUAL REPORT FY2019-20 Ver.1.2 Final Report -2020-08-04.pdf [Accessed 12 Jan. 2024]

National Information Technology Authority-Uganda (NITA-U). (2020). National IT Survey Report. Available at: National IT Survey Report 2022 - Final.pdf (nita.go.ug) [Accessed 2January 2024]

National Planning Agency. (2020). National Development Plan III (NDP III). Available at: NDP-3-Report.pdf (health.go.ug) [Accessed 10 January 2024].

National Planning Authority. (2020). National Development Plan III (2020/21 – 2024/25). Available at: THIRD NATIONAL DEVELOPMENT PLAN (NDPIII) 2020/21 – 2024/25 - Ministry of Health | Government of Uganda [Accessed 04 January 2024]

National Planning Commission. (2012). *National Development Plan 2030: Our Future – Make it Work.* The Presidency.

Nattrass, N. (2020). In defence of exploratory research: A reply to critics. *South African Journal of Science, 116*(SPE), 1-36

Ndebele, I. (2021). *Management's support and implementation of electronic document and records management systems in government departments.* Durban (Doctoral dissertation, Durban University of Technology).

Ndou, M. M., Mofokeng, J. T., & Khosa, D. (2021). *Exploring the Role of Management in the Implementation of Talent Management.* Technium Social Sciences Journal., 10.47577/tssj.v26i1.4887

NDP. (2012). Ten Year Review of the National Development Plan: 2012-2022. https://www.nationalplanningcommission.org.za/assets/Documents/Ten%20Year%20Review%20of%20the%20National%20Development%20Plan_26%20September%202023.pdf

Nel-Sanders, D., & Malomane, A. P. (2022). Challenges and best practices for e-municipalities'. *Africa's Public Service Delivery and Performance Review*, 10(1, a646), 1–15. 10.4102/apsdpr.v10i1.646

Ngqobe, F., Fourie, D. J., & Tshiyoyo, M. (2021). Performance management and accountability practices in South African municipalities: Critical Considerations. *Administratio Publica*, 29(3), 109–128.

Nguimkeu, P., & Okou, C. (2021). Leveraging digital technologies to boost productivity in the informal sector in Sub-Saharan Africa. *The Review of Policy Research*, 38(6), 707–731. 10.1111/ropr.12441

Nguyen, C. M. A., & Ha, M. T. (2023). The interplay between internal communication, employee engagement, job satisfaction, and employee loyalty in higher education institutions in Vietnam. *Humanities & Social Sciences Communications*, 10(1), 1–13. 10.1057/s41599-023-01806-837361101

Nhede, N. T., Mazenda, A., & Masiya, T. (2022). The South African public service and the Fourth Industrial Revolution. *Africa's Public Service Delivery and Performance Review*, 10(1), 420. 10.4102/apsdpr.v10i1.420

Nicholas, S. (2021). *Talent Management and Organisational Performance Correlation of Faculty at Community Colleges in Southern California*. ProQuest.

Nicolás-Agustín, Á., Jiménez, D., & Maeso-Fernandez, F. (2021). The role of human resource practices in the implementation of digital transformation. *International Journal of Manpower, 43*(2), 395-410. https://doi.org/10.1108/IJM-03-2021-0176

Nicolás-Agustín, D., Ramírez-Correa, P. E., & Alfaro-Perez, J. (2021). Digital workforce planning and management in the public sector: Drivers, strategies, and challenges. In Tan, B. B. T., & Dahlin, P. A. (Eds.), *Digital transformation in public sector organisations** (pp. 101–120). Springer.

Njerekai, C. (2020). An application of the virtual reality 360° concept to the Great Zimbabwe monument. *Journal of Heritage Tourism*, 15(5), 567–579. 10.1080/1743873X.2019.1696808

Njoku, E., Ruel, H., Rowlands, H., Evans, L., & Murdoch, M. (2019). An Analysis of the contribution of e-HRM to sustaining business performance. In Bissola, R., & Imperatori, B. (Eds.), *HRM 4.0 For Human-Centered Organizations*. Emerald Publishing Limited. 10.1108/S1877-636120190000023003

Nkala, B., Mudimu, C., & Mbengwa, A. M. (2021). *Human Resources for Health Talent Management Contribution: A Case for Health Systems Strengthening in the Public Health Sector*. World Journal of Advanced Research and Reviews., 10.30574/wjarr.2021.9.2.0062

Nocker, M., & Sena, V. (2019). Big Data and Human Resources Management: The Rise of Talent Analytics. *Social Sciences (Basel, Switzerland)*, 8(10), 273. Advance online publication. 10.3390/socsci8100273

Nosike, C. J. (2023). Deployment of modern digital technologies and ICTs in Public Sector HRM: Benefits and challenges. [IJAAS]. *Interdisciplinary Journal of African & Asian Studies*, 9(3), 1–13.

Novac, C., & Ciochină, R. S. (2017). The Impact of The Digital Era on Human Resources Management. Social Media as Recruiting Environment for Potential Candidates. *Management and Leadership*, 2017, 97–107.

Ntini, V., & Dewah, P. (2023). Human Resources Management Practices in Enhancing Knowledge Retention in the Registrar's Department at NUST, Zimbabwe. *Regional Journal of Information and Knowledge Management*, 8(1), 60–75.

Ntshakala, T., & Nzimakwe, T. I. (2017). Performance auditing as a mechanism for effective service delivery in the South African local government. *Journal of Public Administration and Development Alternatives*, 2(1), 67–81.

Nurlina, N., Situmorang, J., Akob, M., Quilim, C. A., & Arfah, A. (2020). Influence of e-HRM and human resources service quality on employee performance. *The Journal of Asian Finance. Economics and Business*, 7(10), 391–399.

Nyagadza, B., Pashapa, R., Chare, A., Mazuruse, G., & Hove, P. K. (2022). Digital technologies, Fourth Industrial Revolution (4IR) & Global Value Chains (GVCs) nexus with emerging economies' future industrial innovation dynamics. *Cogent Economics & Finance*, 10(1), 1–15. 10.1080/23322039.2021.2014654

Nyakudya, S., Jamboa, N., Madududu, P., & Manyise, T. (2024). Unlocking the potential: Challenges and factors influencing the use of ICT by smallholder maize farmers in Zimbabwe. *Cogent Economics & Finance*, 12(1), 2330431. Advance online publication. 10.1080/23322039.2024.2330431

Nyathi, M., & Kekwaletswe, R. (2023). Realizing employee and organizational performance gains through electronic human resource management use in developing countries. *African Journal of Economic and Management Studies*, 14(1), 121–134. 10.1108/AJEMS-11-2021-0489

Nyikadzino, T. (2024). President Mnangagwa launches three ICT policies to boost the country's digital economy. *State of the Nation*. 8 March 2024.

Nyikadzino, T. (2024, March 8). President Mnangagwa launches three ICT policies to boost the country's digital economy. *State of the Nation*. https://stateofthenation.co.zw/2024/03/08/president-mnangagwa-launches-three-ict-policies-to-boost-the-countrys-digital-economy/

Nyikadzino, T., & Vyas-Doorgapersad, S. (2022). Zimbabwe's transition to a devolved system of government: Critical factors for success. *Africa's Public Service Delivery and Performance Review*, 10(1), a604. 10.4102/apsdpr.v10i1.604

Nyikadzino, T., & Vyas-Doorgapersad, S. (2023). Collaborative governance in Zimbabwe's urban local authorities: Challenges and consideration for improved service delivery, *Social Sciences. The Humanist Educator*, 4(3). Advance online publication. 10.25273/she.v4i3.18059

Nzimakwe, T. I. (2012). Transforming the public service through e-government: Challenges for the future. *Africanus*, 42(1), 56–68.

Nzimakwe, T. I. (2015). Adopting Innovation Strategies to Enhance Service Delivery. *Administratio Publica*, 23(2), 57–72.

Nzimakwe, T. I. (2018). Mobile technology innovations for improved governance and enhanced service delivery in South Africa. *Administratio Publica*, 26(4), 115–132.

Nzimakwe, T. I., & Pillay, P. (2010). Information and communication technology. *Administratio Publica*, 18(1), 124–138.

Obermayer-Kovács, N., Csizmadia, T., & Banász, Z. (2022). Companies on thin ice due to digital transformation: The role of digital skills and human characteristics. *International and Multidisciplinary Journal of Social Sciences, 11*(3), 88-118. https://doi.org/10.17583/rimcis.10641

Odegov, J., Malakhova, E., & Garnov, A. (2019, February). Digitalization of Business Processes in Human Resources Management of Russian Industrial Enterprises. In *International Conference Communicative Strategies of Information Society (CSIS 2018)* (pp. 93-97). Atlantis Press. 10.2991/csis-18.2019.19

OECD. (2019). *Measuring the Digital Transformation: A Roadmap for the Future*. OECD Publishing., 10.1787/9789264311992-

Ofoma, C. (2021). Digitalization driven public service and service delivery: The Nigeria's experience. *Journal of Public Administration. Finance and Law*, 10(22), 73–80.

Ogedengbe, D. E., James, O. O., Afolabi, J. O. A., Olatoye, F. O., & Eboigbe, E. O. (2023). Human Resources In The Era of The Fourth Industrial Revolution (4ir): Strategies and Innovations In The Global South. *Engineering Science & Technology Journal*, 4(5), 308–322.

Ogedengbe, D. E., James, O. O., Afolabi, J. O. A., Olatoye, F. O., & Eboigbe, E. O.Damilola Emmanuel Ogedengbe1Oladapo Olakunle JamesJennifer Osayawe Atu AfolabiFunmilola Olatundun OlatoyeEmmanuel Osamuyimen Eboigbe. (2023). Human Resources in the Era of the Fourth Industrial Revolution (4IR): Strategies and Innovations in the Global South. *Engineering Science & Technology Journal*, 4(5), 308–322. 10.51594/estj.v4i5.617

Ojogiwa, O. T., Sokfa, F. J., & Qwabe, B. R. (2023). Exploring the Capabilities of the Fourth Industrial Revolution for Improved Public Service Delivery in Nigeria. *International Journal of Environmental, Sustainability, and Social Science*, 4(4), 952–962.

Okeke-Uzodike, O. E., & Subban, M. (2015). Public sector recruitment policies: Efficiency, effectiveness and consequences. *Problems and Perspectives in Management*, 13(1), 26–34.

Okemwa, O. (2016). *Developing digital information literacy at institutions of higher learning in Sub Saharan Africa: Opportunities and Challenges.* [Online] Retrieved from: http://ir.mksu.ac.ke/handle/123456780/4306. (Accessed on 25 February 2024).

Okolie, U. C., & Irabor, I. E. (2017). E-recruitment: Practices, opportunities and challenges. *European Journal of Business and Management*, 9(11), 116–122.

Olaitan, O. O., Issah, M., & Wayi, N. (2021). A framework to test South Africa's readiness for the fourth industrial revolution. *South African Journal of Information Management*, 23(1), 1–10. 10.4102/sajim.v23i1.1284

Olsen, J. P. (2017). *Democratic accountability, political order, and change: Exploring accountability processes in an era of European transformation*. Oxford University Press. 10.1093/acprof:oso/9780198800606.001.0001

Ontrup, G., Schempp, P. S. & Kluge, A. 2021. Choosing the Right (HR) Metrics: Digital Data for Capturing Team Proactivity and Determinants of Content Validity. *Journal of Organizational Effectiveness People and Performance*, https://doi.org/10.1108/JOEPP-03-2021-0064

Onyango, G. (2020). Legislative oversight and policy-reforms in "unsettled" political contexts of public administration. *International Journal of Public Administration*, 43(3), 213–228. 10.1080/01900692.2019.1627556

Opoku, F. K., Kwao, I. T., & Johnson, A.-P. (2023). Human Resource Policies and Work–life Balance in Higher Education: Employee Engagement as Mediator. *SA Journal of Human Resource Management*, 21. Advance online publication. 10.4102/sajhrm.v21i0.1939

Orga, C. C., & Ogbo, A. I. (2012). Evaluating the challenges of human resource management in Nigeria. *European Journal of Business and Management*, 4(13), 78–86.

Osborne, D., & Gaebler, T. (1992). *Reinventing Government: How the Entrepreneurial Spirit is Transforming the Public Sector*. Addison Wesley.

Osborne, S. P. (2006). The new public governance? *Public Management Review*, 8(3), 377–387. 10.1080/14719030600853022

Osborne, S. P. (2010). *The New Public Governance? Emerging perspectives on the theory and practice of public governance*. Routledge. 10.4324/9780203861684

Osborne, S. P., Cucciniello, M., Nasi, G., & Zhu, E. (2022). Digital transformation, artificial intelligence and effective public services: Challenges and opportunities. *Global Public Policy and Governance*, 2(4), 377–380. 10.1007/s43508-022-00058-7

Osborne, S. P., Radnor, Z., & Nasi, G. (2012). A New Theory for Public Service Management? Toward a (Public) Service-Dominant Approach. *American Review of Public Administration*, 43(2), 135–158. 10.1177/0275074012466935

Oyebanji, B. K., & Kassim, R. N. M. (2017). Technology (ICT) Perception of Employee Towards E-HRM Practices in Public Sectors: A Case Study of Nigeria. *World Journal of Research and Review*, 4(6), 262790.

Padma, S. (2023). Securing Organisational Sustainability: The Vitality of Succession Planning in Indian Public Sector Enterprises. *International Development Planning Review*, 22(2), 187–195.

Palos-Sánchez, P. R., Baena-Luna, P., Badicu, A., & Infante-Moro, J. C. (2022). Artificial intelligence and human resources management: A bibliometric analysis. *Applied Artificial Intelligence*, 36(1), 2145631. 10.1080/08839514.2022.2145631

Pandey, A., Grima, S., Pandey, S., & Balusamy, B. (Eds.). (2024). *The Role of HR in the Transforming Workplace: Challenges, Technology, and Future Directions*. CRC Press.

Pandeya, G. P., & Oyama, T. (2019). Revitalizing local government performance management: Further dissecting the role of socioeconomic status and social mobilization policy. *Local Government Studies*, 45(6), 869–892. 10.1080/03003930.2019.1585817

Pandita, D., & Ray, S. (2018). Talent management and employee engagement–a meta-analysis of their impact on talent retention. *Industrial and Commercial Training*, 50(4), 185–199. 10.1108/ICT-09-2017-0073

Pang, K., & Lu, C. (2018). Organisational motivation, employee job satisfaction and organisational performance: An empirical study of container shipping companies in Taiwan. *Maritime Business Review*, 3(1), 36–52. 10.1108/MABR-03-2018-0007

Pantelidis, I. (2019). Digital human resource management. In *Human Resource Management in the Hospitality Industry* (pp. 337–352). Routledge. 10.4324/9780429441400-21

Paramita, D. (2020). *Digitalization in talent acquisition: A case study of AI in recruitment.* Masters Thesis. Uppsala Universitet, Sweden.

Parkar, A., Srivastava, A., Kaur, A., Geo, A., Bandopadhyay, S., & Sinha, P. (2021). Digitization in Human Resource-Literature Review and Future Research Agenda. *SAMVAD*, 22(0), 21–29. 10.53739/samvad/2021/v22/164043

Parliamentary Information Service. (2022). The Skills Development Act. Retrieved March 26, 2014, From https://static .pmg.org.za/docs/2000/appendices/000229SDASummary.htm

Parliamentary Monitoring Group [PMG]. (2020). *Report on Intervention in Msunduzi Local Municipality.* Available at https://pmg.org.za/tabled-committee-report/595/ (last accessed 20 January 2024).

Parra, C. M., Gupta, M., & Mikalef, P. (2021). Information and communication technologies (ICT)-enabled severe moral communities and how the (Covid19) pandemic might bring new ones. *International Journal of Information Management*, 57, 102271. 10.1016/j.ijinfomgt.2020.102271

Pasara, T., & Garidzirai, R. (2020). The boomerang effects: An analysis of the pre and post dollarisation era in Zimbabwe. *Economies*, 8(32), 1–20. 10.3390/economies8020032

Pathirane, L., & Blades, D. W. (1982). Defining and measuring the public sector: Some international comparisons. *Review of Income and Wealth*, 28(3), 261–289. 10.1111/j.1475-4991.1982.tb00617.x

Patterson, E. (2023). Reducing the gap between rhetoric and reality: Use of digital service standards for public service innovation through digital transformation in Australia. *Australian Journal of Public Administration, 82*(4), 557-589. https://doi.org/10.1111/1467-8500.12615

Pearse, N. J., & Williams, Q. W. (2009). Organizational Culture and the Implementation of Performance Management. *Administratio Publica*, 17(1), 28–42.

Performance contract for the Human Capital Development Director, Harare City Council.

Phahlane, M. M. (2023). Electronic Human Resource Management (e-HRM) in a South African Organization. In *Enhancing Employee Engagement and Productivity in the Post-Pandemic Multigenerational Workforce* (pp. 156-170). IGI Global

Piabuo, S. M., Piendiah, N. E., Njamnshi, N. L., & Tieguhong, P. J. (2017). The impact of ICT on the efficiency of HRM in Cameroonian enterprises: Case of the Mobile telephone industry. *Journal of Global Entrepreneurship Research*, 7(1), 7. 10.1186/s40497-017-0063-5

Pillai, R., & Sivathanu, B. (2022). Measure what matters: Descriptive and predictive metrics of HRM-pathway toward organisational performance. *International Journal of Productivity and Performance Management*, 71(7), 3009–3029. 10.1108/IJPPM-10-2020-0509

Poister, T. H. (2010). The Future of Strategic Planning in the Public Sector: Linking Strategic Management and Performance. *Public Administration Review*, 70(s1), s246–s254. 10.1111/j.1540-6210.2010.02284.x

Pollitt, C., & Bouckaert, G. (2004). *Public Management Reform: A Comparative Analysis*. Oxford University Press. 10.1093/oso/9780199268481.001.0001

Poshai, L. (2017). *A critical assessment of the e-readiness status of Zimbabwe's public sector institutions: Exploring the Registrar General Department's level of preparedness to utilise the passport application system (2012-2016)* (Masters dissertation, University of Zimbabwe).

Poshai, L., Chilunjika, A., & Intauno, K. (2023). Examining the institutional and legislative frameworks for enforcing cybersecurity in Zimbabwe. *International Cybersecurity Law Review*, 4(4), 431–449. 10.1365/s43439-023-00093-y

Poshai, L., & Vyas-Doorgapersad, S. (2023). Digital Justice Delivery in Zimbabwe: Integrated Electronic Case Management System Adoption. *South African Journal of Information Management*, 25(1), a1695. 10.4102/sajim.v25i1.1695

Potočnik, K., Neil, R., Marise, B., & Nikolaou, I. (2021). Paving the way for research in recruitment and selection: Recent developments, challenges and future opportunities. *European Journal of Work and Organizational Psychology*, 30(5), 1–16. 10.1080/1359432X.2021.1904898

Prabhu, U., Fathima, Y., Sathyanarayana, N., Srikumar, M. S., & Cavaliere, L. P. L. (2024). Emerging Digitalization Trends in Human Resource Management. In *Data-Driven Intelligent Business Sustainability* (pp. 214–234). IGI Global.

Prakash, K., Reddy, A., & Yasaswi, R. (2021). AI-powered HCM: The analytics and augmentations. https://doi.org/10.5772/intechopen.100475

Prasad, S. (2023). Blockchain and Data Privacy in Human Resource Management. *3rd International Conference on Advance Computing and Innovative Technologies in Engineering (ICACITE)*

Prebreza, B. (2021). *Towards a blended working environment*. Thuringia, Erfurt (Master's Thesis, University of Applied Sciences Ltd.).

Profiroiu, C. M., Negoi ă, C. I., & Costea, A. V. (2023). Digitalization of public administration in EU member states in times of crisis: The contributions of the national recovery and resilience plans. *International Review of Administrative Sciences*, 90(2), 336–352. 10.1177/00208523231177554

Prokopenko, O., Garafonova, O., & Zhosan, H. (2023). Digital tools in human resource management: how digitisation affects personnel management. *Socio-economic relations in the digital society, 4*(50), 84-94.

Public Procurement and Disposal of Public Assets Authority (PPDA). (2020). Report on e-Government Procurement System. Available at: PPDA-Annual-Report-2020-2021.pdf [Accessed 12 January 2024]

Public Service Commission. (2024). *Report on Digitisation of Human Resources Processes in the Public Service*. Pretoria: The Public Service Commission Retrieved from https://www.psc.gov.za/documents/reports/2024/Report_on_Digitisation_of_Human_Resource_Management_Processes_in_the_Public_Service.pdf

Pulakos, E. D. (2004). *Performance Management: A roadmap for developing, implementing and evaluating performance management systems*. Society for Human Resource Management (SHRM) Foundation: United States of America.

Pulakos, E. D., & O'Leary, R. S. (2011). Why is performance management broken? *Industrial and Organizational Psychology: Perspectives on Science and Practice*, 4(2), 146–164. 10.1111/j.1754-9434.2011.01315.x

Qamar, Y., & Samad, T. A. (2021). Human Resource Analytics: A Review and Bibliometric Analysis. *Personnel Review*. Advance online publication. 10.1108/PR-04-2020-0247

Rademacher, U., & Grant, T. (2019). Out of Africa: A new perspective on digitalisation in Africa. *Journal for Technology Assessment in Theory and Practice*, 28(2), 41–47. 10.14512/tatup.28.2.s41

Raghavan, M., Barocas, S., Kleinberg, J., & Levy, K. (2020, January). Mitigating bias in algorithmic hiring: Evaluating claims and practices. In *Proceedings of the 2020 conference on fairness, accountability, and transparency* (pp. 469-481). 10.1145/3351095.3372828

Rahi, S. (2023). Fostering Employee Work Engagement and Sustainable Employment During COVID-19 Crisis Through HR Practices, Employee Psychological Well-Being and Psychological Empowerment. *Industrial and Commercial Training*, 55(3), 324–345. Advance online publication. 10.1108/ICT-04-2022-0023

Rahman, M., & Aydin, E. (2020). Benefits, barriers and risks–the role of technology in e-HRM implementations in public sector organisations: Evidence from Bangladesh. *International Journal of Human Resources Development and Management*, 20(3-4), 252–268. 10.1504/IJHRDM.2020.107976

Raja-Santhi, A., & Muthuswamy, P. (2023). Industry 5.0 or Industry 4.0 S? Introduction to Industry 4.0 and a peek into the prospective Industry 5.0 technologies. [IJIDeM]. *International Journal on Interactive Design and Manufacturing*, 17(2), 947–979. 10.1007/s12008-023-01217-8

Rakhy, K. S., & Vijayan, S. (2018). Digitalisation in Human Resource Management Process, the Opportunity for the Competence Management in Retail Sector. *International Journal of Pure and Applied Mathematics*, 119(12), 2569–2581.

Rakolobe, M. (2019). Politicised public service and corruption in Lesotho. *The Strategic Review for Southern Africa*, 41(1), 97–121.

Ramachandran, R., Babu, V., & Murugesan, V. P. (2023). Human resource analytics revisited: A systematic literature review of its adoption, global acceptance and implementation. *Benchmarking*. Advance online publication. 10.1108/BIJ-04-2022-0272

Ramírez, J. G. C. (2024). AI in Healthcare: Revolutionising Patient Care with Predictive Analytics and Decision Support Systems. *Journal of Artificial Intelligence General science (JAIGS)* 3006-4023, 1(1), 31-37.

Rana, G., Sharma, R., & Goel, A. K. (2018). *Unraveling the Power of Talent Analytics: Implications for Enhancing B usiness Performance. Business Governance and Society*. Springer International Publishing., 10.1007/978-3-319-94613-9_3

Ranson, S., & Stewart, J. (1994). *Management for the Public Domain: Enabling the Learning Society*. Macmillan Press Ltd. 10.1007/978-1-349-23787-6

Rasmussen, T., & Ulrich, D. (2015). Learning from practice: How HR analytics avoids being a management fad. *Organizational Dynamics*, 44(3), 236–242. 10.1016/j.orgdyn.2015.05.008

Reddy, P., Nemec, J., & de Vries, M. S. (2015). The State of Local Government. *Public Policy and Administration*, 14(3), 160–176. 10.5755/j01.ppaa.14.3.13430

Reina, R., & Scarozza, D. (2021). Human Resource Management in the Public Administration. In Decastri, M., Battini, S., Buonocore, F., & Gagliarducci, F. (Eds.), *Organisational Development in Public Administration* (pp. 61–101). Palgrave Macmillan. 10.1007/978-3-030-43799-2_3

Republic of South Africa. (1998). *White Paper on Local Government.* Cape Town: Government Printers.

Reunamäki, R., & Fey, C. F. (2023). Remote agile: Problems, solutions, and pitfalls to avoid. *Business Horizons*, 66(4), 505–516. 10.1016/j.bushor.2022.10.003

Rex, T., Bhattacharya, S., Narayanan, K., & Budhwar, P. (2020). *Opportunities and Barriers in the Practice of Human Resource Analytics. Human & Technological Resource Management (HTRM): New Insights int o Revolution 4.0.* Emerald Publishing Limited., 10.1108/978-1-83867-223-220201004

Rodgers, W., Murray, J. M., Stefanidis, A., Degbey, W. Y., & Tarba, S. Y. (2023). An artificial intelligence algorithmic approach to ethical decision-making in human resource management processes. *Human Resource Management Review*, 33(1), 100925. 10.1016/j.hrmr.2022.100925

Roffia, P., & Dabić, M. (2023). The role of management control and integrated information systems for the resilience of SMEs. *Review of Managerial Science, 18*(5), 1353-1375. https://doi.org/10.1007/s11846-023-00657-6

Rönnblom, M., Carlsson, V., & Öjehag-Pettersson, A. (2023). Gender equality in Swedish AI policies. What's the problem represented to be? *Review of Policy Research, 40*(5), 688-704. https://doi.org/10.1111/ropr.12547

Roy, J. (2017). Smart cities in Canada: An examination of progress and impediments in Halifax, Canada. *International Journal of Services Technology and Management*, 23(5-6), 361–380. 10.1504/IJSTM.2017.088944

Rupeika-Apoga, R., Petrovska, K., & Bule, L. (2022). The effect of digital orientation and digital capability on digital transformation of SMEs during the COVID-19 pandemic. *Journal of Theoretical and Applied Electronic Commerce Research*, 17(2), 669–685. 10.3390/jtaer17020035

Rusilowati, U., Narimawati, U., Wijayanti, Y. R., Rahardja, U., & Arif, O. (2024). Optimizing Human Resource Planning through Advanced Management Information Systems: A Technological Approach. *Aptisi Transactions on Technopreneurship* (ATT), 72–83.

Ruwende, I. (2017). Performance contracts for council heads. *The Herald.* 24 May, 2017.

Rykun, E. (2019). *Artificial intelligence in HR management – What can we expect? Retrieved* from https://thebossmagazine.com/ai-hr-management/ (Accessed on 10 January 2024).

Saad, A., & Itika, J. (2024). An Investigation of the Transformation Process from Manual to E-Recruitment in Tanzania Public Service. *Journal of Public Policy and Administration*, 9(1), 1–19. 10.47604/jppa.2254

Saadatmand, M., Safaie, N., & Dastjerdi, M. (2022). Presenting a Structural Model of Digitalised Talent Management in a New Age: A Case Study on the Mobile Telecommunication Industry in Iran. *SA Journal of Human Resource Management*, 20. Advance online publication. 10.4102/sajhrm.v20i0.1894

Sadik-Zada, E. R., Gatto, A., & Niftiyev, I. (2022). E-government and petty corruption in public sector service delivery. *Technology Analysis and Strategic Management*, 34(4), 1–17. 10.1080/09537325.2022.2067037

Sakarina, S., Ena, Z., Cakranegara, P. A., & Surahman, S. (2022). Digital Transformation in Human Resource Management in the Industrial Age 4.0. *Quantitative Economics and Management Studies*, 3(5), 750–756. 10.35877/454RI.qems1067

Sakib, M. (2023). Industry 4.0 and its implications on human resource management practices: A systematic literature review and bibliometric analysis. *Dhaka University Journal of Management, 15*(1&2). https://doi.org/10.57240/DUJMV15A8

Sakka, F., El Maknouzi, M. E. H., & Sadok, H. (2022). Human resource management in the era of artificial intelligence: Future HR work practices, anticipated skill set, financial and legal implications. *Academy of Strategic Management Journal*, 21(1), 1–14.

Salau, O. P., Osibanjo, A., Adeniji, A., Falola, H., Igbinoba, E., Atolagbe, T., & Ogueyungbo, O. (2020). Crystalising employment quality and behavioural outcomes of employees in the public service. *Heliyon*, 6(12), 1–11. 10.1016/j.heliyon.2020.e0561933364474

SALGA [South African Local Government Association] (2012). A Municipal Guide/Roadmap to successful ICT governance. Available at: https://www.salga.org.za/Documents/Municipalities/Municipla%20Focus/Municipal%20ICT/SALGA_ICT-Governance-Guidelines_revised_June2012_v1_2.pdf Accessed 23 January 24.

Salvadorinho, J., & Teixeira, L. (2023). Happy and Engaged Workforce in Industry 4.0: A New Concept of Digital Tool for HR Based on Theoretical and Practical Trends. *Sustainability (Basel)*, 15(3), 2781. 10.3390/su15032781

Sambo, N. M., & van der Waldt, G. (2022). A strategic framework for Public Performance Management and Development System implementation: The case of the National Department of Human Settlements. *Administratio Publica*, 30(2), 86–107.

Samidi, S., Maarif, M. S., Saptono, I. T., & Arsyianti, L. D. (2023). Transforming talent management as a game changer for firm competitiveness of Islamic banks. *Cogent Business & Management*, 10(3), 2257590. Advance online publication. 10.1080/23311975.2023.2257590

Sánchez, M. (2020). University e-readiness for the digital transformation: The case of universidad nacional del sur. *Revista Gestão & Tecnologia*, 20(2), 75–97. 10.20397/2177-6652/2020.v20i2.1848

Sánchez-Marín, G. (2023). Linkages between high-performance work practices and family-centered goals: Implications for financial performance in family firms. *Journal of Small Business and Enterprise Development, 31*(1), 126-151. https://doi.org/10.1108/JSBED-03-2023-0117

Saputra, A., Wang, G., Zhang, Z., & Behl, A. (2021). The Framework of Talent Analytics Using Big Data. *The TQM Journal*. Advance online publication. 10.1108/TQM-03-2021-0089

Sarker, M. N. I., Wu, M., & Hossin, M. A. (2018, May). Smart governance through bigdata: Digital transformation of public agencies. In *2018 international conference on artificial intelligence and big data (ICAIBD)* (pp. 62-70). IEEE.

Satispi, E., Rajiani, I., Murod, M., & Andriansyah, A. (2023). Human resources information system (HRIS) to enhance civil servants' innovation outcomes: Compulsory or complimentary? *Administrative Sciences, 13*(2), 32. https://doi.org/10.3390/admsci13020032

Saunders, M., Lewis P., & Thornhill, A. (2019). Research Methods for Business Students: Pearson Education Limited. Eight editions.

Saurombe, M., Barkhuizen, N., & Schutte, N. (2017). *Exploring the determinants of a talent value proposition for sustainable higher education institutions: A conceptual paper.* Winter London Business Research Conference. London: Proceedings of 2017 Winter London Business Research Conference.

Saxena, M., Bagga, T., Gupta, S., & Mittal, A. (2022). Employees' Experiences of Accepting and Adopting HR Analytics: A Phenomenology Study. *The Open Psychology Journal*, 15(1), e187435012208040. Advance online publication. 10.2174/18743501-v15-e2208040

Schäfer, M. (2018). The fourth industrial revolution: How the EU can lead it. *European View*, 17(1), 5–12. 10.1177/1781685818762890

Scholkmann, A. B. (2021). Resistance to (digital) change: Individual, systemic and learning-related perspectives. *Digital transformation of learning organizations*, 219-236.

Schultz, C. M. (2021). The future and the role of human resource management in South Africa during the Fourth Industrial Revolution. *SA Journal of Human Resource Management*, 19, 11. 10.4102/sajhrm.v19i0.1624

Sebastian, I. M., Ross, J. W., Beath, C., Mocker, M., Moloney, K. G., & Fonstad, N. O. (2020). How big old companies navigate digital transformation. In *Strategic information management* (pp. 133–150). Routledge. 10.4324/9780429286797-6

Semaihi, S. O. 2023. Talent Management and Performance in the Public Sector: The Mediating Role of Line Managerial Support. *Journal of Organizational Effectiveness People and Performance*, https://doi.org/10.1108/JOEPP-09-2022-0274

Sembiring, E., & Damayanti, N. (2023). TALENT ATTRACTION, TALENT RETENTION, AND TALENT MANAGEMENT AS A MEDIATING ON ORGANIZATION PERFORMANCE. *Ultima Management : Jurnal Ilmu Manajemen*, 15(1), 58–76. 10.31937/manajemen.v15i1.3125

Semyachkov, K. A. (2019). May. Digital economy in developing countries: problems and prospects. In *1st International Scientific Conference" Modern Management Trends and the Digital Economy: from Regional Development to Global Economic Growth"(MTDE 2019)* (102-106). Atlantis Press.

SEND-Ghana. (2015). *Bringing development to the doorsteps of citizens*. Ghana News Agency.

Senona, M. E. (2017). *The relationship between talent management and job satisfaction among teachers in Limpopo Province: A case of Maleboho East Circuit*. Unpublished Masters Dissertation. Southern Business School.

Senyo, P. K., Effah, J., & Osabutey, E. L. (2021). Digital platformisation as public sector transformation strategy: A case of Ghana's paperless port. *Technological Forecasting and Social Change*, 162, 120387. 10.1016/j.techfore.2020.120387

Setianingrum, H. W., Bisri, B., Widyastuti, T., & Fitra, S. (2023). Virtual reality technologies in a dynamic change of human resources management. [JMAS]. *Journal of Management Science*, 6(4), 673–678.

Setyawan, A., & Nelson, A. (2020). Factors Affecting Talent Management Strategies in Construction Companies. *Almana: Jurnal Manajemen Dan Bisnis*, 4(3), 392–397. 10.36555/almana.v4i3.1479

Shahaab, A., Khan, I. A., Maude, R., Hewage, C., & Wang, Y. (2023). Public service operational efficiency and blockchain–A case study of Companies House, UK. *Government Information Quarterly*, 40(1), 101759. 10.1016/j.giq.2022.101759

Shah, G., Memon, N., & Tunio, G. (2021). Need for Talent Management and Investigating Its Impact on Organisational Performance of Higher Education Institutes. *International Review of Management and Business Research*, 10(1), 168–182. 10.30543/10-1(2021)-13

Shaikh, M. (2021). Determining the Relationship between Human Resource Practices, Employee Well-Being, and Organisational Performance. *RJ International Journal of Management Studies*, 1(1).

Shariuda, M. A., El Tanany, S. & Maraiyesa, Y. 2018. Building Capacity of Government Leaders in Egypt/

.

Sharma, M., Luthra, S., Joshi, S., & Kumar, A. (2022). Analysing the impact of sustainable human resource management practices and industry 4.0 technologies adoption on employability skills. *International Journal of Manpower*, 43(2), 463–485. 10.1108/IJM-02-2021-0085

Sharma, P. (2023). Innovations in Human Resource Management: Adapting to the Future of Work. *Journal of Informatics Education and Research*, 3(2), 1–11.

Shava, E. & Doorgapersad, S. V. 2021. Talent management: A'recipe'for public service delivery in the fourth industrial revolution. *International Journal of Research in Business and Social Science (2147-4478),* 10, 138-148

Shava, E. (2022). Survival of African governments in the Fourth Industrial Revolution. Africa and the Fourth Industrial Revolution: Curse or Cure? 125–144.

Shava, E. 2022. Talent Management: A 'Recipe' for Public Service Delivery in the Fourth Industrial Revolution. *International Journal of Research in Business and Social Science (2147-4478),*https://doi.org/10.20525/ijrbs.v10i8.1504

Shava, E., & Ndebele, N. C. (2023). Data marginalization in South Africa: A quest for inclusive digital participation. *Social Sciences and Education Research Review*, 10(2), 122–131.

Sheehan, M., Grant, K., & Garavan, T. (2018). Strategic talent management: A macro and micro analysis of current issues in hospitality and tourism. *Worldwide Hospitality and Tourism Themes*, 10(1), 28–41. 10.1108/WHATT-10-2017-0062

Shipena, D. (2019). *A study of talent management practices in the Namibian Police Force.* Unpublished Masters dissertation. Krugersdorp: Southern Business School.

Shirase, R., Chhibber, P., & Narkhede, A. (2023). Factors Affecting the Successful Digitalisation of Human Resources. In P., Tyagi; N., Chilamkurti; S., Grima… (Eds.), *The Adoption and Effect of Artificial Intelligence on Human Resources Management, Part A* (pp. 99-105). Leeds: Emerald Publishing Limited. 10.1108/978-1-80382-027-920231005

Shopola, A. M., Mukonza, R., & Manyaka, R. K. (2024). Consultocracy in South African public service: A case of repositioned public administration curricula. *Africa's Public Service Delivery and Performance Review*, 12(1), a747. 10.4102/apsdpr.v12i1.747

Shopola, M. A., Mudau, J., & Mukonza, R. M. (2021). Public administration and management training in South African technical and vocational education and training colleges: Unpacking its relevance in the contemporary time. *African Journal of Development Studies*, 2021(Special Issue (1)), 199–218. 10.31920/2634-3649/2021/sin1a11

Shruthi, K., & Poornima, A. S. (2023, September). A Transparent and Privacy-Preserving Job Search Platform Built on the Ethereum Blockchain Framework. In *2023 IEEE 2nd International Conference on Industrial Electronics: Developments & Applications (ICIDeA)* (pp. 235-242). IEEE.

Shukla, A., Mishra, L., & Agnihotri, A. (2023). A Comprehensive Review of the Effects of Digital Technology on Human Resource Management. *Technology. Management and Business*, 31, 7–19. 10.1108/S1877-636120230000031002

Sidoti, B. J., Walsh, L. L., Parsley, K. M., Callis-Duehl, K., Hove, A. A., Liu, H., Uzcategui, M., Sternad Zabukovšek, S., Jordan, S., & Bobek, S. (2023). Managing Document Management Systems' Life Cycle in Relation to an Organisation's Maturity for Digital Transformation. *Sustainability*, 15(21), 1–35.

Siemens, A. (2017). *African Digitalization Maturity Report 2017.* [Online] Retrieved from: https://www.readkong.com/page/african-digitalization-maturity-report-2017-digital – asset. (Accessed on 26 April 2024).

Singh, G., Tiwari, P., & Garg, V. (2023). HRM Digitalisation: Exploring Success and Outcomes. In P., Tyagi; N., Chilamkurti; S., Grima… (Eds.), *The Adoption and Effect of Artificial Intelligence on Human Resources Management, Part B* (pp. 199-219). Leeds: Emerald Publishing Limited.

Singh, A., & Sahoo, D. M. K. (2023). Revolutionizing Recruitment: Harnessing the Power of Technology. *Iconic Research and Engineering Journals*, 6(12), 1343–1355.

Singhavi, C., & Basargekar, P. (2020). *Re-imagining diffusion and adoption of information technology and systems: A continuing conversation* (pp. 650-661). [Online] Retrieved from: www.researchgate.net/publication/347648779 _Implementing_ICT_at_School_Level_Facto rs_Affecting_Teachers'_Perceived_Proficiency. (Accessed on 8 April 2024).

Singh, P. S. J., Oke, A. E., Kineber, A. F., Olanrewaju, O. I., Omole, O., Samsurijan, M. S., & Ramli, R. A. (2023). A mathematical analysis of 4IR innovation barriers in developmental social work—A structural equation modeling approach. *Mathematics*, 11(4), 1–7. 10.3390/math11041003

Singh, S. (2017). E-Recruitment: A new dimension of human resource management in India. *International Journal of Advance Research in Computer Science and Management Studies*, 5(3), 99–105.

SITA. (2023). Digital Transformation Strategic Plan. From https://www.sita.co.za/sites/default/files/Strategic%20Plan %202020-2024.pdf

Škudienė, V., Vezeliene, G., & Stangej, O. (2020). Transforming human resource management: innovative e-HRM value creation for multinational companies. In *Innovation Management* (pp. 140–166). Edward Elgar Publishing. 10.4337/9781789909814.00021

Smith, S. R., & Smyth, J. (1996). Contracting for services in a decentralized system. *Journal of Public Administration: Research and Theory*, 6(2), 277–296. 10.1093/oxfordjournals.jpart.a024311

Smowtech. (2022) Recruitment and selection: What are they, and what are their differences? Retrieved January 25, 2023, From https://smowl.net/en/blog/recruitment-selection-definition-differences/

Sokolow, A. (2020). *South Africa's Fourth Industrial Revolution limited by lack of computer literacy, access.* MEDILL Reports Chicago. [Online] Retrieved from:https://news.medill.northwestern.edu/chicago/south-africas-fourth -industrialrevolution-limited-by-lack-of-computer-literacy-access (Accessed on 28 February 2024).

Soomro, K. A., Kale, U., Curtis, R., Akcaoglu, M., & Bernstein, M. (2020). Digital divide among higher education faculty. *International Journal of Educational Technology in Higher Education*, 17(2), 1–16.

Sosu, J.N. (2020). Performance management in Ghana's local government: A case study of Ada East District Assembly. *Commonwealth Journal of Local Governance* 2019, 22: 7376. https://doi.org/10.5130/cjlg.vi22.7376

Sousa, M. J., & Rocha, Á. (2019). Skills for disruptive digital business. *Journal of Business Research*, 94, 257–263. 10.1016/j.jbusres.2017.12.051

South African Government. (2022). *South African e-Government strategy 2022-2025*. Retrieved from https://www .gov.za/documents/e-government-strategy-2022-2025

South African Local Government Association (SALGA). (2018). *Municipal Managers Forum.* Pretoria: SALGA.

South African Local Government Association (SALGA). (2020). *2nd Annual Local Government Talent Management Seminar.* Pretoria: SALGA.

Sposato, M. (2024). Editorial. *Strategic HR Review, 23*(1), 40-42. https://doi.org/10.1108/SHR-02-2024-204

Sripathi, K., & Madhavaiah, C. (2018). Are HR professionals ready to adopt HR analytics? A study on analytical skills of HR professionals. *Journal of Advanced Research in Dynamical and Control Systems*, 10, 303–308.

Stachová, K., Papula, J., Stacho, Z., & Kohnová, L. (2019). External partnerships in employee education and development as the key to facing industry 4.0 challenges. *Sustainability, 11*(2), 345. https://doi.org/10.3390/su11020345

St-Hilaire, W. (2024). The public sector value-based management: Effect of the digital matrix on the optimisation of resources for micro-organisations. *SEDME (Small Enterprises Development Management & Extension Journal) a Worldwide Window on MSME Studies, 51*(1), 17-26. https://doi.org/10.1177/09708464231223485

Stone, R. J., Cox, A., Gavin, M., & Carpini, J. (2023). *Human resource management.* John Wiley & Sons.

Strohmeier, S. (2020). Digital human resource management: A conceptual clarification. *German Journal of Human Resource Management*, 34(3), 345–365. 10.1177/2397002220921131

Strohmeier, S. (2020). Smart HRM–a Delphi study on the application and consequences of the Internet of Things in Human Resource Management. *International Journal of Human Resource Management*, 31(18), 2289–2318. 10.1080/09585192.2018.1443963

Stuss, M. M. (2020). TALENT MANAGEMENT – WAR FOR TALENTS. *Proceedings of the 11th Business & Management Conference,* Dubai. 10.20472/BMC.2020.011.013

Subbaiah, D. (2024). AI-powered strategies for talent management optimization. *Journal of Industrial Engineering Research, 4*(2). https://doi.org/10.52783/jier.v4i2.848

Susan, E. (2019). Human Resource Management. Adara. *Journal of Islamic Education Management*, 9(2), 952–962.

Suta, P., Lan, X., Wu, B., Mongkolnam, P., & Chan, J. H. (2020). An overview of machine learning in chatbots. *International Journal of Mechanical Engineering and Robotics Research*, 9(4), 502–510. 10.18178/ijmerr.9.4.502-510

Sutcliffe, M., & Bannister, S. (2020). *Research on the 4th Industrial Revolution: Implications for Local government in the context of skills development Final Report.* City Insight. Available at https://cdn.lgseta.co.za/resources/ research_and_reports/2019%20%E2%80%93%202020%20research%20projects/research%20project%20-%20 4th%20industrial%20 revolution%20in%20the%20local %20govt%20sector.pdf. Accessed 8 March 2024.

Tan, E. (2021). *A conceptual model of the use of AI and blockchain for open government data governance in the public sector.* Retrieved from https://soc.kuleuven.be/io/ digi4fed/doc/d-3-2-1-a-conceptual-model-of-the-use-of-ai-and.pdf (Accessed on 11 March 2024).

Tangi, L., Janssen, M., Benedetti, M., & Noci, G. (2020). Barriers and drivers of digital transformation in public organizations: Results from a survey in the Netherlands. In *Electronic Government: 19th IFIP WG 8.5 International Conference, EGOV 2020, Linköping, Sweden, August 31–September 2, 2020* [Springer International Publishing.]. *Proceedings*, 19, 42–56.

Tapiwa, G. G., Pedzisai, P., Bernard, N., & Mervis, C. (2022). Digitalisation of Human Resources Systems and Process Necessary for Public Sector Transformation in Zimbabwe. In *Transformational Human Resources Management in Zimbabwe* (pp. 61–74). Springer Nature Singapore., 10.1007/978-981-19-4629-5_5

Tate, M., Bongiovanni, I., Kowalkiewicz, M., & Townson, P. (2018). Managing the "fuzzy front end" of open digital service innovation in the public sector: A methodology. *International Journal of Information Management*, 39, 186–198. 10.1016/j.ijinfomgt.2017.11.008

Tensay, A. T., & Singh, M. (2020). The nexus between HRM, employee engagement and organisational performance of federal public service organisations in Ethiopia. *Heliyon*, 6(6), 1–15. 10.1016/j.heliyon.2020.e0409432577549

Thakur, A. (2024). Implementation of Artificial Intelligence in Human Resource Management in Asia-Pacific. In *Exploring the Intersection of AI and Human Resources Management* (pp. 30–46). IGI Global.

Thakurta, R. (2024). A work system theory perspective on talent management and systems. *Systems Research and Behavioral Science*, sres.3007. Advance online publication. 10.1002/sres.3007

The Herald. (2019, August 6). Editorial comment: E-recruitment of nurses will bring fairness. The *Herald*. https://www.herald.co.zw/editorial-comment-e-recruitment-of-nurses-will-bring-fairness/

The Herald. (2020, November 6). State enterprises' reform will benefit all. *The Herald*. https://www.herald.co.zw/editorial-comment-state-enterprises-reform-will-benefit-all/

The Sunday News. (2020, September 6). ICTs skills slow uptake worries Govt. *The Sunday News*. Retrieved from https://www.sundaynews.co.zw/icts-skills-slow-uptake-worries-govt/

Theresianto, S. (2017). *Activity-Based Workplace Design: An Australian Perspective*. Sydney (Doctoral dissertation, The University of New South Wales, Sydney).

Thimmanna, A. V. N. S., Naik, M. S., Radhakrishnan, S., & Sharma, A. (2024). Personalised Learning Paths: Adapting Education with AI-Driven Curriculum. [EEL]. *European Economic Letters*, 14(1), 31–40.

Thobejane, G., van der Heever, H., & Mokgatle, M. (2022). Knowledge, Understanding and Satisfaction with the Implementation of the Performance Management System at a District Hospital in the Madibeng Subdistrict, South Africa. *International Journal of Environmental Research and Public Health*, 19(1), 14461. 10.3390/ijerph19211446136361341

Thomas, G. (2020). Digital Maturity of HR in SMEs. *European Journal of Economics and Business Studies*, 6(1), 56–62. 10.26417/ejes.v6i1.p56-62

Thomas, M. A., Cipolla, J., Lambert, B., & Carter, L. (2019). Data management maturity assessment of public sector agencies. *Government Information Quarterly*, 36(4), 101401. 10.1016/j.giq.2019.101401

Tiwari, A., Vaghela, S., Nagar, R., & Desai, M. (2019). Applicant tracking and scoring system. *International Research Journal of Engineering and Technology*, 6(4), 320–324.

Todisco, L., Tomo, A., Canonico, P., & Mangia, G. (2023). The bright and dark side of smart working in the public sector: Employees' experiences before and during COVID-19. *Management Decision, 61*(13), 85 102. https://doi.org/10.1108/MD-02-2022-0164

Tomar, P., & Kaur, G. (2019). *Green and smart technologies for smart cities*. CRC Press. 10.1201/9780429454837

Tracy, S. J. (2019). *Qualitative research methods: Collecting evidence, crafting analysis, communicating impact*. John Wiley & Sons.

Transparency International. (2020). Corruption Perceptions Index. Available at: 2020 Corruption Perceptions Index - Explore the… - Transparency.org [Accessed 30 December 2023]

Tripathi, N. G., & Goel, M. (2022). Citisen-Centric Smart Planning: Case Study San Diego, California. In *Smart Master Planning for Cities: Case Studies on Domain Innovations* (pp. 271–300). Springer Nature Singapore. 10.1007/978-981-19-2386-9_8

Tsamados, A., Aggarwal, N., Cowls, J., Morley, J., Roberts, H., Taddeo, M., & Floridi, L. (2022). The ethics of algorithms: Key problems and solutions. *AI & Society*, 37(1), 215–230. 10.1007/s00146-021-01154-8

Turesky, E. F., Smith, C. D., & Turesky, T. K. (2020). A call to action for virtual team leaders: Practitioner perspectives on trust, conflict and the need for organisational support. *Organizational Management Journal*, 17(4/5), 185–206. 10.1108/OMJ-09-2019-0798

Turnea, E. S., & Aruştei, C. C. (2023). Augmenting HRM through enhancing the benefits of digital transformation. *Cross Cultural Management Journal*, 2, 105–111.

Turner, T. S., Creighton, S., Nudurupati, S., & Bititci, U. (2004). Implementing a Web enabled performance measurement system. *Measuring Business Excellence*, 8(2), 40–54. 10.1108/13683040410539427

Udovita, P. (2020). Conceptual review on dimensions of digital transformation in modern era. *International Journal of Scientific and Research Publications*, 10(2), 520–529. 10.29322/IJSRP.10.02.2020.p9873

Uganda Bureau of Statistics. (2020). Statistical Abstract. Available at: 11_2020STATISTICAL__ABSTRACT_2020.pdf (ubos.org) [Accessed 10 December 2023]

Uganda Communications Commission. (2020). Communications Market Performance Report. Available at: UCC-September-2020-Market-Intelligence-Report.pdf [Accessed10 January 2024]

Uganda Public Service Commission. (2021). Annual Report. Available at: Consolidated Annual Inspection and PAIPAS Report FY 2021-22.pdf [Accessed 12 January 2024]

Uganda Public Service Standing Orders. (2020). Available at: https://publicservice.go.ug/download/the-uganda-public-service-standing-orders-2021-edition/ [Accessed 12 Jan. 24]

Ukeje, I. O., Ndukwe, C., Emma, C., Ogbulu, U., & Onele, J. C. (2020). Public service recruitment practices and implications for sustainable development in Ebonyi State, Nigeria. *International Journal of Public Administration*, 43(4), 361–372. 10.1080/01900692.2019.1636394

United Nations Development Programme. (2023). Uganda's Digital Transformation Journey. Available at: Uganda's Digital Transformation Journey | United Nations Development Programme (undp.org) [Accessed 15 April 2024]

United Nations E-Government Survey. (2020). E-Government in the Digital Era: Challenges and Opportunities. United Nations. Available at: Regional Challenges and Opportunities | United Nations iLibrary (un-ilibrary.org) [accessed 15 December 2023]

United Nations. (2020). E-Government Development Index. Available at: EGOVKB | United Nations > About > Overview > E-Government Development Index [Accessed 12 January 2024]

Upadhyay, P. (2024). Industry 4.0 Inducing Paradigm Changes in Human Resources. In *The Role of HR in the Transforming Workplace* (pp. 1-9). Productivity Press.

Utami, H., & Alamanos, E. (2023). *Theory Hub Book*.

Vaiman, V., & Collings, D. G. (2023). *GLOBAL TALENT MANAGEMENT: Past, Present, and Future* (7th ed.). Readings and Cases in International Human Resource Management., 10.4324/9781003247272-3

Van der Waldt, G. (2014). Implementation challenges facing Performance Management Systems in South African Municipalities: Selected cases. *Administratio Publica*, 22(2), 132–152.

Van der Westhuizen, E. J. (Ed.). (2016). *Human resource management in government: A South African perspective on theories, politics and processes*. Juta and Company, (Pty) Limited, Capetown.

Van Hoye, G., Van Hooft, E. A., Stremersch, J., & Lievens, F. (2019). Specific job search self-efficacy beliefs and behaviors of unemployed ethnic minority women. *International Journal of Selection and Assessment*, 27(1), 9–20. 10.1111/ijsa.12231

Varma, A., Budhwar, P. S., & DeNisi, A. (Eds.). (2023). *Performance management systems: A global perspective*. Taylor & Francis. 10.4324/9781003306849

Väyrynen, H., Helander, N., & Jalonen, H. (2022). Public innovation and digital transformation. https://doi.org/10.4324/9781003230854

Veale, M., & Brass, I. (2019). *Administration by Algorithm? Public Management Meets Public Sector Machine Learning* In: Algorithmic Regulation (Karen Yeung and Martin Lodge eds., Oxford University Press, 2019), Available at *SSRN*: https://ssrn.com/abstract=3375391

Vears, D. F., & Gillam, L. (2022). Inductive content analysis: A guide for beginning qualitative researchers. *Focus on Health Professional Education: A Multi-disciplinary Journal, 23*(1), 111-127.

Veglianti, E., Trombin, M., Pinna, R., & De Marco, M. (2023). Customised Artificial Intelligence for Talent Recruiting: A Bias-Free Tool? In *Smart Technologies for Organisations: Managing a Sustainable and Inclusive Digital Transformation* (pp. 245–261). Springer International Publishing. 10.1007/978-3-031-24775-0_15

Velsberg, O., Westergren, U. H., & Jonsson, K. (2020). Exploring smartness in public sector innovation – creating smart public services with the Internet of Things. *European Journal of Information Systems*, 29(4), 350–368. 10.1080/0960085X.2020.1761272

Verlinden, N. (2023). HR trends report Preview. From https://www.linkedin.com/posts/neelie-verlinden_aihr-hr-trends-2023-activity-7008096578326392832-bO63

Verma, S., Rana, N., & Meher, J. R. (2024). Identifying the enablers of HR digitalization and HR analytics using ISM and MICMAC analysis. *The International Journal of Organizational Analysis*, 32(3), 504–521. 10.1108/IJOA-01-2023-3611

Vey, K., Fandel-Meyer, T., Zipp, J. S., & Schneider, C. (2017). Learning & Development in Times of Digital Transformation: Facilitating a Culture of Change and Innovation. *International Journal of Advanced Corporate Learning*, 10(1), 22. 10.3991/ijac.v10i1.6334

Vezi, M. J. (2017). *Nurses' Perceptions of Employee Performance Management and Development System (EPMDS) at a selected hospital in Durban, eThekwini District in KwaZulu-Natal.* Master's Degree in Nursing Administration, University of KwaZulu-Natal. Available from: https://researchspace.ukzn.ac.za/server/api/core/bitstreams/7581b2e9-a4b9-46ac-90e3 a799952cf356/content (Accessed: 25 February 2024).

Vial, G. (2021). *Understanding digital transformation: A review and a research agenda.* Managing Digital Transformation. 10.4324/9781003008637-4

Vignesh Saravanan, K., Jothi Thilaga, P., Kavipriya, S., & Vijayalakshmi, K. (2023). Data Protection and Security Enhancement in Cyber-Physical Systems Using AI and Blockchain. In *AI Models for Blockchain-Based Intelligent Networks in IoT Systems: Concepts, Methodologies, Tools, and Applications* (pp. 285–325). Springer International Publishing. 10.1007/978-3-031-31952-5_13

Vilčiauskaitė, B., Savanevičienė, A., & Navickas, V. (2020). *Managing Older Talents in the Context of Aging Society.* Economics & Sociology., 10.14254/2071-789X.2020/13-4/13

Vrontis, D., Christofi, M., Pereira, V., Tarba, S., Makrides, A., & Trichina, E. (2022). Artificial intelligence, robotics, advanced technologies and human resource management: A systematic review. *International Journal of Human Resource Management*, 33(6), 1237–1266. 10.1080/09585192.2020.1871398

Vyas-Doorgapersad, S. (2022). The Use of Digitalization (ICTs) in Achieving Sustainable Development Goals. *Global Journal of Emerging Market Economies*, 14(2), 265–278. 10.1177/09749101211067295

Wadhwa, S., Wadhwa, P., & Khalique, F. (2024). Explorative Study on Understanding the Human-Centred Design to Nurture the Employee Experience. In *Humanising Businesses for a Better World of Work* (pp. 109–126). Emerald Publishing Limited. 10.1108/978-1-83797-332-320241008

Wang, J., Bai, W., & Liu, Y. (2022). Optimization for the human resources management strategy of the IoT industry based on AHP. *Computational Intelligence and Neuroscience, 2022*, 1-10. https://doi.org/10.1155/2022/3514285

Wang, L., Zhou, Y., & Zheng, G. (2022). Linking digital HRM practices with HRM effectiveness: The moderate role of HRM capability maturity from the adaptive structuration perspective. *Sustainability (Basel)*, 14(2), 10–23. 10.3390/su14021003

Wang, Y. (2021). When artificial intelligence meets educational leaders' data-informed decision-making: A cautionary tale. *Studies in Educational Evaluation*, 69, 100872. 10.1016/j.stueduc.2020.100872

Warnich, S., Carrell, M. R., Elbert, N. F., & Hatfield, R. D. (2018). *Human resource management in South Africa.* (6th Edition). South Western Cengage learning.

Warrick, D. D. (2023). Revisiting resistance to change and how to manage it: What has been learned and what organisations need to do. *Business Horizons*, 66(4), 433–441. 10.1016/j.bushor.2022.09.001

Weber, M. (2023). Bureaucracy. In *Social theory re-wired* (pp. 271–276). Routledge. 10.4324/9781003320609-33

Wegrich, K. (2024). Public sector. In *Encyclopedia Britannica.*

Wheeler, K., & van de Haterd, B. (2024). *Talent Acquisition Excellence: Using Digital Capabilities and Analytics to Improve Recruitment.* Kogan Page Publishers.

Wiblen, S., & McDonnell, A. (2020). Connecting 'talent' meanings and multi-level context: A discursive approach. *International Journal of Human Resource Management*, 31(4), 474–510. 10.1080/09585192.2019.1629988

Wirtz, B. W., & Müller, W. M. (2023). An integrated framework for public service provision in smart cities. *International Journal of Public Sector Performance Management*, 11(3), 310–340. 10.1504/IJPSPM.2023.130260

Word Bank. (2023). https://www.worldbank.org/en/country/zimbabwe/overview (accessed on 6 March 2024).

World Bank. (2021). *World development report 2021: Data for better lives*. Retrieved from https://www.worldbank.org/en/publication/wdr2021

World Bank. (2021). Digital Economy for Africa (DE4A) Initiative. Available at: Digital Economy for Africa Initiative (worldbank.org) [Accessed 12 January 2024]

World Bank. (2021). World Development Report 2021: Data for Better Lives. Available at: World Development Report 2022: FINANCE for an Equitable Recovery (worldbank.org) [Accessed 12 Jan. 24]

World Economic Forum. (2020). The Future of Jobs Report 2020. Available at: WEF_Future_of_Jobs_2020.pdf (weforum.org) [accessed 11 January 2024]

Wright, V. (2019). Reshaping the state: the implications for public administration. In *The State in Western Europe* (pp. 102–137). Routledge. 10.4324/9781315037479-6

Wurim, B. P. (2012). Talent management and employee productivity in public sector organizations of Nigeria. *Journal of Management and Corporate Governance*, 4(1), 1–13.

Yarger, L., Cobb Payton, F., & Neupane, B. (2020). Algorithmic equity in the hiring of underrepresented IT job candidates. *Online Information Review*, 44(2), 383–395. 10.1108/OIR-10-2018-0334

Yaro, I. (2014). Recruitment and selection in the Nigerian public service: Nature, challenges and way forward. *British Journal of Economics. Management and Trade*, 4(7), 1005–1017.

Yeo, M., Ananthram, S., Teo, S. T., & Pearson, C. A. (2015). Leader–member exchange and relational quality in a Singapore public sector organisation. *Public Management Review*, 17(10), 1379–1402. 10.1080/14719037.2013.806573

Yiga, I., & Wandiba, A. (2017). Recruitment and Selection Process and Local Government Performance in Kiboga District, Uganda. *KIU Journal of Social Sciences*, 2(2), 71–82.

Yiu, C. (2012). The big data opportunity: Making government faster, smarter and more personal. The Policy Exchange:London. Available at: http://ict-industry-reports.com.au/wp-content/uploads/sites/4/2013/05/2012-The-Big-Data-opportunity-in-Government-UK-Policy-Exchange-July-2012.pdf (Accessed: 09 May 2024).

Yoon, B. S. (2019). The Role of Civil Service and the Human Resource Management Policies Required for the Government of the Future. *Public Service Excellence in the 21st Century*, 169-202.

Zaharee, M., Lipkie, T., Mehlman, S. K., & Neylon, S. K. (2018). Recruitment and Retention of Early-Career Technical Talent. *Research Technology Management*, 61(5), 51–61. 10.1080/08956308.2018.1495966

Zainee, I. A., & Puteh, F. (2020). Corporate social responsibility impact on talent retention among Generation Y. *Gestão*, 27(4), 369–392. 10.1108/REGE-06-2019-0070

Zavyalova, E., Sokolov, D., Kucherov, D. & Lisovskaya, A. 2022. The Digitalization of Human Resource Management: Present and Future. *Foresight and Sti Governance,* https://doi.org/10.17323/2500-2597.2022.2.42.51

Zeidan, S. & Itani, N. 2020. HR Analytics and Organizational Effectiveness.

Zhang, J., & Chen, Z. (2023). Exploring human resource management digital transformation in the digital age. *. *Journal of the Knowledge Economy*. Advance online publication. 10.1007/s13132-023-01214-y

Zinyama, T. (2021). Systemic corruption in Zimbabwe: Is the human factor the missing link? *African Journal of Public Affairs*, 12(1), 132–152.

Zinyama, T., Nhema, A. G., & Mutandwa, H. (2015). Performance management in Zimbabwe: Review of current issues. *Journal of Human Resources Management & Labour Studies*, 3(2), 1–27. 10.15640/jhrmls.v3n2a1

Zuiderwijk, A., Chen, Y.-C., & Salem, F. (2021). Implications of the use of AI in public governance: A systematic literature review and research agenda. *Government Information Quarterly*, 38(3), 34–78. https://doi.org/. giq.2021.10157710.1016/j

About the Contributors

Elvin Shava is a Senior Lecturer of Public Governance at the University of KwaZulu-Natal where he teaches Advanced Public Service Delivery, Public Sector Human Resource Management including Subnational Governance and Development. Further, he supervises postgraduate students and is a member of the South African Association of Public Administration and Management (SAAPAM). He is also a Review Editor for the Frontiers' Journal in Sustainable Cities. Dr Shava's current research interests revolve around Digital and Smart governance where he explores how Information Communication Technologies (ICTs), and related digital technologies can be used effectively to transform education, communities and public administration in South Africa and other low-income countries. Dr Shava has extensively published articles in reputable peer-reviewed journals and presented his research at various local and international conferences.

Nduduzo C Ndebele is a senior lecturer in the Discipline of Public Governance at the University of KwaZulu Natal. He teaches both undergraduates and postgraduates students and supervise at honours, masters and PhD level. Prior to joining academia, he served as a Human Resource Practitioner for the KwaZulu Natal Department of Health. His research focus areas are Public Sector Human Resources, Public Health Policy, South Africa Higher Education and Digital Governance in Local Government.

Lewis Edwin Chigova is a postdoctoral research fellow at the North-West University's Afrocentric Governance of Public Affairs. Lewis' research interests include public sector innovation, public Governance and local Governance studies

Anuoluwapo Durokifa holds a Ph.D. in Public Administration from the University of Fort Hare. She is an academic and a researcher who is passionate about South Africa/ Africa's development and growth. Her research interests include: Sustainable development, public policy, monitoring and evaluation, gender equality, development, African leadership and of recent tech policy. Dr Durokifa is currently with the School of Public Management, Governance and Public Policy, University of Johannesburg.

Andrew Enaifoghe (PhD) is a university lecturer, author and enthusiastic academic researcher. He is a passionate lecturer/ educator with experience in developing and implementing diverse curriculums covering a wide range of subjects related to the field of specialization. He is highly skilled at motivating students through positive encouragement and re-enforcement of concepts via interactive classroom instruction and observation. successful in helping students develop strong literacy, numeracy, social and learning skills. He has strong research experience in social sciences and humanities. His research interest is multi-disciplinary / trans-disciplinary, and through his experience in research, he has learned the ability to translate and contextualize complex research theories to a variety of audiences. He thrives in both independent and collaborative work environments.

Idris Olayiwola Ganiyu is a senior lecturer at York St John University, Yorkshire, United Kingdom, and a doctor of philosophy in human resource management with extensive and diverse teaching, research, and industry experience. Analytical Research Specialist with expertise in experimental HR research, business process analysis, and data collection, modelling, and analysis. Leads the design of innovative research projects to contribute valuable insights and advancements in the field. Employs a range of instructional methods and techniques to meet different student learning styles and needs. Effective supervisor and mentor to master- and doctoral-level students. Expert in various data analysis methods, techniques, and tools. Team collaborator with strong communication, interpersonal relations, and problem-solving skills.

Costa Hofisi is a full professor at North-West University. He is the Director of the Afrocentric Governance of Public Affairs research entity.

Thokozani Ian Nzimakwe is currently employed as an academic in the School of Management, IT, and Governance at the University of KwaZulu-Natal, South Africa. He holds a doctoral degree in Public Administration and Management from the University of KwaZulu-Natal. Before joining academia, he was in the public service for 14 years in various government departments. His research interests are local governance, public sector accountability, public finance, ICT, and public sector reforms. He has published widely in scholarly journals, contributed to various book chapters, and has attended and delivered papers at national and international conferences. He worked as a Lecturer at Mangosuthu University of Technology. He started his career in 1988 when he joined the Department of Health. Between 1999 and 2001 he was seconded to the Compliance Division of the KwaZulu-Natal Gambling Board. In 2002 he was appointed as a Lecturer in the Department of Public Administration and Management at Mangosuthu University of Technology in Umlazi, Durban. In January 2007 he joined the then School of Public Administration and Development Management of the University of KwaZulu-Natal. He has more than 20 years in academia.

Kudakwashe Intauno is a student at the University of Duisburg-Essen in Germany. His current research focuses on smart governance.

Vivence Kalitanyi holds a Ph.D. in Management from the University of the Western Cape (UWC). He is an Associate Professor at the University of Johannesburg where he lectures entrepreneurship, operations management, research methodology, and E-commerce. He holds an NRF rating category C and widely publishes articles in accredited journals and book chapters. He supervises Honours, Masters, and Ph.D. students. His research interest involves mainly entrepreneurship, migrant entrepreneurship, and operations management. He is the author of a book, journal articles, and book chapters. He attends national and international conferences to present his research works. He mentors novice researchers in the Department of Business Management of his University. His hobby involves reading current socio-politico and economic affairs from around the world, hence he possesses a good understanding of these fields. He is a member of the Editorial Board for the Journal of Business and Economics in the 4th Industrial Revolution (JBE4IR).

Siphiwe Mandina has 12 years' experience in lectureship in Marketing Management coupled with marketing experience in the media, manufacturing and transport sectors. She has research interests in Services marketing, Brand management, destination branding and competitiveness. Siphiwe Mandina is also a Marketing Strategy and Service Marketing Consultant.

RaymondMapuranga is a dedicated and accomplished lecturer in the field of Human Resource Management. With a passion for teaching, research and a commitment to academic excellence. Mr. Mapuranga completed his undergraduate studies in HRM at a prestigious university, where he graduated with honors and masters. His exceptional academic performance and strong interest in understanding human relations led him to pursue a Ph.D. in HRM a programme he is yet to finish. For his doctoral studies, Mr. Mapuranga is focusing his research on employee resourcing strategies and how they can be manipulated for improved organisational performance. He has published in scopus indexed journals and other accredited journals and appeared for conference presentations in various platforms

Abigail Maravanyika is the Assistant registrar human resource management at the Reformed church university. Is a holder of a Master of Science Degree in HRM. Area of interest is employee well being and gender inclusivity in management. She has over five years experience in managerial role and is responsible for policies the institution.

Sindy Mbele UKZN graduate and HR Executive with more than 15yrs of multinational experience in business integration; talent acquisition; building and maintaining a high-performance culture; talent management; leadership development; succession management; key talent retention; and transformation.

Syanda A. Mthuli holds a doctorate in Administration (Public Administration) and a Master of Commerce (Leadership Studies). He is a Senior Lecturer in the Discipline of Public Governance within the School of Management, Information Technology and Governance at the University of KwaZulu- Natal. He has over a decade of experience in the higher education sector from various universities in South Africa and is also the founder and Director of the Southern Africa Centre for Research and Institutional Development (SACRID). His research interests and publications are in bureaucracy performance, political leadership and competition, social science research methods, participatory governance, community economic policy - development and environmental administration.

Kebiat Mukuze is a lecturer at Midlands State University in Zimbabwe in the department of Human Resource Management with over five years experience in research and has published work in scopus indexed journals, WEB of science and other reputable journals. Area of specialty in research is Human Capital Analytics.

About the Contributors

Misheck Musaigwa is a Postdoctoral Research Fellow at the University of Johannesburg, with more than a year and a half of experience in the field. Specializing in digital transformation, Misheck is at the forefront of research that explores the intersections of technology, management, and industry innovation. His work particularly focuses on the implications and applications of Industry 4.0. In addition to his research, Misheck is deeply committed to academic responsibilities that include teaching and mentoring postgraduate students. This role enables him to share his rich expertise and cultivate the research skills of the next generation of scholars, significantly enhancing their academic and professional trajectories. Misheck holds a Ph.D. in Management from the University of KwaZulu-Natal, where he developed a profound understanding of digital transformation processes within industries.

Ayler Beniah Ndraha, S.STP., M.Si., is a scholar and practitioner in the field of government studies who has made significant contributions to Human Resource Management (HRM). Known for integrating profound academic knowledge with rich practical experience, Dr. Ndraha provides deep insights and practical solutions in human resource planning. With a strong educational background, Dr. Ayler Beniah Ndraha holds a Bachelor of Applied Science in Government Studies (S.STP), a Master of Science (M.Si), and a Doctorate in Government Studies (DIP), all obtained from the Institute of Domestic Government (IPDN) in Jatinangor-Bandung. His work experience in various government institutions such as Bappeda, BKPSDM, Kominfo, and Kesbangpol provides a solid foundation for understanding organizational dynamics and governance practices in collaboration with empirical practice. Dr. Ndraha's contribution to the book "Digital Transformation in Public Sector Human Resource Management" is evident through the chapter titled "Digital Workforce Planning and Management in the Public Sector." In this chapter, he provides a comprehensive guide for public sector professionals, scholars, and policymakers, exploring the challenges and opportunities of digital transformation in HRM. By emphasizing talent management, technological integration, and strategic decision-making, he inspires proactive approaches to thrive in the digitally-driven landscape. Through integration of insights from the African public sector, Dr. Ndraha highlights the importance of aligning digital strategies with ethical considerations and leveraging technological capabilities. Ultimately, the chapter aims to empower public sector entities to adapt and succeed in the digital era, fostering organizational resilience and long-term success while addressing societal needs. Currently, Dr. Ndraha is an active Civil Service Lecturer at Universitas Nias. Despite being relatively young, he has contributed to various seminars and scholarly discussions at regional, national, and international levels, sharing valuable insights into governance dynamics and human resource management. His expertise and dedication to advancing government studies and deep understanding of human resource management make him a significant figure in inspiring and guiding future generations in this field.

Tawanda Nyikadzino is a post-doctoral researcher in the School of Public Management, Governance and Public Policy at the University of Johannesburg. Tawanda holds a PhD in Public Management and Governance (University of Johannesburg, South Africa), a Master of Public Administration and a BSc (Hons) in Administration (University of Zimbabwe), and a Research Methodology Certificate (University of Witwatersrand, South Africa). He specialises in public management, devolution and decentralisation reforms, local government management and public policy. He has published over 15 peer-reviewed book chapters and journal articles with internationally accredited publishers. Tawanda has more than nine years of experience working as a researcher and educator in tertiary institutions and has vast research and consultancy experience. Tawanda has done several consultant jobs for national and international organisations. He has participated as a lead researcher in UNICEF and UNDP projects.

Ojogiwa, Oluwaseun Temitope holds a PhD in Public Administration from the University of KwaZulu-Natal. She is a Postdoctoral Fellow for the NRF/SARChI Chair in Sustainable Rural Livelihoods in the University of KwaZulu Natal, South Africa. Her research focuses on public service innovations, sustainable rural development and local economic development.

Alexander Markey Oluka holds a PhD in Management Sciences specialising in Business Administration from Durban University of Technology and has over a decade of experience in academia and the accounting industry. Currently pursuing a Master of Digital Entrepreneurship at the European New School of Digital Studies in Germany. Dr Oluka is an esteemed lecturer and experienced supervisor at Regenesys Business School and MANCOSA. His interest focuses on finance, accounting, and digital transformation in business, particularly in emerging markets. He has published extensively in internationally accredited journals, providing insights into strategic financial management, tax compliance, and technological advancements. An active participant in international conferences, Dr Oluka bridges academic research and industry practices, enriching both fields with his work.

Leon Poshai is a Lecturer in the Department of Governance and Public Management at the Midlands State University (MSU) in Zimbabwe. He holds a BSc Honours in Public Administration, a Master of Public Administration from the University of Zimbabwe and a PhD in Public Administration from the University of the Western Cape (UWC). His current research is focused on digital governance, smart cities and Public Sector Management Information systems.

Andrisha Beharry Ramraj, senior lecturer at the University of KwaZulu-Natal, holds a PhD in Management studies majoring in management, leadership and governance. Furthermore, she holds a Post Graduate Diplomas in Higher Education and Human Resources Management. In 2004 and 2005, she received NRF scholarships to complete her Honours and Masters degrees, respectively. She has presented at local and international conferences in the areas of Management, Leadership, Marketing, Human Resources management, Global Business and Entrepreneurship. She has published in the fields of Leadership, Entrepreneurship, Human Resources and Business Management. She recently published book chapters on entrepreneurial sustainability and employee wellness and leadership across the globe. In 2016 and 2017, she received best presentation awards for the best paper delivered at conferences. She serves on the Teaching and Learning committee within the University of KwaZulu Natal (UKZN) and served as the Bachelor of Business Administrator Programme Manager (Self-Funding Teaching Programme) for one term. She teaches across levels within the Discipline of Management and Entrepreneurship, from entry-level to masters level. She is keen on developing undergraduate curriculum transformation within the discipline. Redesigning curricula to suit the dynamics of modern teaching in the world, and enabling sustainability and digitisation is fast becoming her passion. Having realised her desire for higher education, Dr Beharry served as an expert advisor for the Student Society of Entrepreneurship (CAVE) based at UKZN. Further to this, she shares her expertise as a research expert for the Centre of Entrepreneurship.

Standa Sani is a visionary entrepreneur and leader with a diverse academic background in business management, law, and technology. With qualifications including a Bachelor of Commerce in Business Management, Master of Tech in Strategy & Innovation, Bachelor of Substantive Law, Master in Human Rights, Peace & Development, and a Postgrad Degree in Procedural Law, he combines multidisciplinary knowledge to drive transformative change. Standa's expertise spans strategy, innovation, law, and human rights, enabling him to create sustainable solutions and make a positive impact. Through his ventures, he leverages his academic qualifications to shape the future and drive innovation at the intersection of business, technology, law, and social impact.

Elvin Shava is a Senior Lecturer of Public Governance at the University of KwaZulu-Natal where he teaches Advanced Public Service Delivery, Public Sector Human Resource Management including Subnational Governance and Development. Further, he supervises postgraduate students and is a member of the South African Association of Public Administration and Management (SAAPAM). He is also a Review Editor for the Frontiers' Journal in Sustainable Cities and currently the Editor of this book: Digital Transformation in Public Sector Human Resource Management. Dr Shava's current research interests revolve around Digital and Smart governance where he explores how Information Communication Technologies (ICTs), and related digital technologies can be used effectively to transform education, communities and public administration in South Africa and other low-income countries. Dr Shava has extensively published articles in reputable peer-reviewed journals and presented his research at various local and international conferences.

Blessing Takawira is an accomplished Supply Chain Management Specialist and academic with over a decade of experience in procurement, strategic leadership, and education. He holds a PhD in Business Management from the University of Johannesburg and excels in enhancing supply chain operations and academic excellence. Currently a Postdoctoral Research Fellow at the University of Johannesburg, he conducts advanced supply chain and business management research, collaborates with industry leaders, and publishes scholarly articles. Additionally, Dr Takawira is an Independent Expert at Tshwane University of Technology and a Senior Business Supply Chain Management Specialist at Pace International Trading Pty Ltd. He lectures and supervises postgraduate and doctoral students and has developed module guides for Mancosa.

Xolani Thusi, holds the PhD in Public Administration as the highest qualification and He works as a Senior lecturer at University of Limpopo (UL). His research interests are mainly application of public policies and sustainable public service delivery. As an emerging scholar he is in alignment within UL motto: Finding Solutions for Africa.

Shikha Vyas-Doorgapersad is appointed as a Full Professor, School of Public Management, Governance and Public Policy at University of Johannesburg, South Africa. Her previous lecturing experience includes International College for Girls (India); University of Zululand, and North-West University (South Africa). She holds degrees of M.A., M.Phil., and Ph.D. in Public Administration from the University of Rajasthan (India). Her research interests are in Public Policy, Gender Issues, and in Municipal Governance. She has presented research findings at international conferences world-wide. She has authored two books (University Book House, Jain Prakhan Mandir [Publishers in India]), Editor of three books (Taylor and Francis, Routledge [Publishers in New York]); contributed chapters in books and have published articles in national and international accredited journals. She serves as Editor-in-Chief, Guest Editor, Associate Editor, Editorial Board Member, and reviewer to South African and international journals. She is a member of the International Advisory Board and International Scientific Committees to various conferences world-wide. She is serving as an Adjunct Research Professor in the School of Business and Management of Uganda Technology and Management University. She is appointed as a Visiting Professor at the Riara School of Business, Riara University in Kenya. She serves as External Moderator/Examiner for MAs and PhDs for several universities in South Africa. She has published more than 100 articles in scientific journals.

Beauty Zindi a Post Doctoral Research Fellow in the School of Management, Governance and Public Policy within the College of Business and Economics at the University of Johannesburg in South Africa. She obtained her Doctor of Public Administration degree at the University of Fort Hare. She has published her research in the form of book chapters and journal articles in reputable peer reviewed journals. Her research interests are in supply chain management and public sector human resource management.

Index

Symbols

4IR 1, 2, 4, 5, 6, 18, 40, 41, 85, 86, 94, 130, 131, 132, 133, 134, 136, 137, 138, 140, 141, 143, 144, 160, 185, 186, 188, 190, 194, 196, 197, 200, 202, 213, 240, 242, 244, 245, 256, 263

A

Advancements 1, 2, 23, 25, 26, 30, 33, 37, 43, 44, 46, 51, 60, 62, 81, 91, 94, 97, 116, 118, 121, 122, 131, 138, 146, 157, 185, 188, 190, 194, 196, 204, 205, 206, 208, 210, 213, 214, 268
African Bureaucracies 1, 2, 4, 6, 8, 9, 10, 11, 12, 13, 14, 15, 115, 116
Algorithmic bias 60, 62, 72, 97, 119, 124, 156
Algorithmic Biases 115, 152, 154, 157
Analytics 5, 9, 16, 23, 25, 27, 28, 30, 32, 34, 36, 38, 58, 61, 62, 63, 66, 67, 68, 69, 72, 73, 76, 77, 78, 80, 81, 83, 85, 86, 87, 89, 90, 91, 92, 93, 94, 95, 96, 97, 98, 99, 100, 101, 102, 103, 104, 105, 106, 107, 108, 109, 110, 111, 112, 113, 131, 134, 135, 137, 138, 139, 140, 147, 149, 150, 156, 187, 192, 232, 260, 267, 268, 272, 274
Artificial Intelligence 2, 5, 9, 10, 11, 12, 16, 17, 18, 20, 21, 23, 30, 35, 40, 47, 61, 62, 63, 78, 81, 82, 83, 84, 85, 86, 87, 88, 89, 98, 104, 107, 108, 117, 125, 127, 128, 131, 142, 143, 144, 146, 150, 151, 155, 159, 160, 188, 194, 203, 209, 221, 232, 256, 260, 264, 265, 268, 269, 272, 275
ayler 21

C

Challenges 1, 2, 3, 5, 9, 10, 12, 13, 15, 17, 18, 19, 21, 22, 24, 25, 26, 28, 29, 30, 31, 32, 33, 35, 36, 39, 48, 53, 55, 56, 57, 60, 61, 62, 65, 70, 71, 73, 74, 75, 76, 78, 80, 81, 83, 84, 86, 91, 92, 94, 95, 96, 97, 99, 101, 103, 104, 105, 108, 109, 111, 112, 115, 116, 117, 118, 119, 120, 121, 122, 123, 124, 127, 128, 130, 131, 132, 133, 135, 136, 137, 138, 140, 142, 143, 144, 145, 146, 148, 149, 152, 154, 155, 156, 158, 159, 160, 162, 164, 166, 172, 173, 174, 175, 177, 179, 182, 183, 184, 186, 189, 190, 192, 194, 195, 196, 197, 198, 199, 203, 204, 206, 207, 208, 213, 215, 217, 218, 219, 232, 233, 239, 240, 241, 244, 245, 248, 249, 250, 251, 252, 257, 259, 260, 263, 264, 265, 267, 268, 269, 270, 271, 272, 273, 274, 276
Compatibility 60, 61, 65, 71, 79, 81

D

Data-Driven Decision-Making 11, 21, 22, 23, 24, 25, 26, 27, 30, 31, 61, 62, 65, 67, 69, 75, 76, 77, 81, 83, 94, 105, 115, 116, 136, 202, 267, 269, 272
Devolution 162, 174, 179, 180
Digital 1, 2, 3, 4, 5, 6, 8, 9, 10, 12, 13, 14, 15, 16, 17, 18, 19, 20, 21, 22, 23, 24, 25, 26, 27, 28, 29, 30, 31, 32, 33, 34, 35, 36, 37, 39, 40, 41, 42, 43, 44, 45, 46, 47, 48, 49, 50, 51, 52, 53, 54, 55, 56, 57, 58, 59, 60, 61, 62, 63, 65, 66, 67, 69, 70, 71, 72, 73, 75, 76, 77, 79, 80, 81, 82, 83, 84, 85, 87, 88, 89, 91, 94, 95, 96, 97, 98, 99, 101, 107, 108, 109, 110, 111, 112, 114, 115, 116, 117, 118, 119, 120, 121, 122, 123, 124, 125, 126, 127, 128, 130, 131, 132, 133, 134, 135, 136, 137, 138, 139, 140, 141, 142, 143, 144, 145, 146, 147, 148, 149, 150, 151, 152, 153, 154, 155, 156, 157, 158, 159, 160, 161, 162, 163, 165, 166, 171, 175, 178, 179, 185, 186, 187, 188, 189, 190, 191, 192, 193, 194, 195, 196, 197, 198, 199, 200, 201, 202, 203, 204, 206, 208, 209, 210, 211, 212, 213, 214, 215, 217, 220, 222, 223, 225, 226, 227, 228, 229, 230, 231, 232, 233, 239, 240, 241, 242, 243, 244, 245, 246, 247, 248, 249, 250, 251, 252, 253, 254, 255, 256, 257, 258, 259, 260, 261, 262, 263, 264, 265, 266, 271, 272, 273, 274, 275, 276
Digital Age 22, 24, 26, 37, 39, 42, 43, 48, 49, 55, 57, 73, 89, 95, 110, 111, 114, 144, 187, 199, 202, 203, 204, 206, 217, 232, 240, 250, 258, 259, 260, 263, 265, 274
Digital Divide 1, 3, 14, 20, 41, 60, 62, 119, 121, 122, 124, 138, 152, 154, 156, 157, 159, 245, 250, 251
Digital Hiring 43, 116, 117, 118, 119, 120, 121, 124, 134, 145, 146, 147, 148, 149, 150, 151, 152, 153, 154, 155, 156, 222, 223, 260, 263
Digital HRM 25, 26, 27, 33, 43, 48, 54, 59, 61, 76, 80, 81, 97, 99, 101, 112, 130, 131, 132, 133, 134, 136, 137, 138, 139, 140, 161, 197, 244, 248, 251, 252, 253
Digitalisation 1, 2, 3, 4, 5, 8, 9, 12, 14, 15, 16, 17, 18, 19, 20, 39, 42, 44, 47, 50, 52, 53, 55, 84, 97, 99, 101, 116, 117, 118, 121, 123, 124, 130, 131, 132, 133, 134, 136, 138, 140, 166, 198, 199, 200, 202, 203, 204, 206, 208, 209, 210, 211, 212, 213, 214, 215, 223, 241, 242, 276
Digital transformation 3, 6, 12, 16, 17, 20, 21, 22,

23, 24, 25, 26, 27, 28, 29, 30, 31, 32, 33, 34, 35, 36, 37, 39, 40, 41, 42, 43, 44, 45, 46, 47, 48, 49, 50, 51, 52, 53, 54, 55, 56, 57, 58, 59, 60, 61, 62, 63, 80, 81, 82, 84, 85, 88, 89, 91, 95, 96, 97, 98, 99, 107, 114, 115, 116, 117, 118, 119, 120, 121, 122, 123, 124, 125, 126, 127, 128, 130, 131, 133, 134, 136, 137, 138, 139, 140, 144, 145, 146, 147, 150, 156, 158, 159, 161, 162, 163, 166, 175, 185, 186, 187, 188, 189, 190, 191, 193, 195, 196, 197, 198, 199, 200, 201, 202, 203, 209, 214, 215, 222, 223, 231, 232, 233, 239, 240, 241, 242, 243, 244, 245, 246, 247, 248, 249, 250, 251, 252, 253, 254, 256, 257, 258, 260, 261, 263, 264, 265, 273, 275

digital workforce 21, 22, 23, 24, 25, 26, 27, 28, 29, 30, 31, 32, 33, 35, 37, 79, 222, 244

Digitization 150, 157, 188, 189, 196, 197, 220

E

e-Human Resource Management 255

Electronic Performance Monitoring 210, 213

Employee Retention 90, 103, 105, 227, 270, 272, 275, 276

Employee satisfaction 32, 60, 61, 63, 81, 252, 271, 272

Ethics 18, 58, 60, 62, 72, 82, 125, 167, 246, 247, 277

H

HR Analytics 90, 91, 92, 93, 94, 95, 96, 97, 98, 99, 100, 101, 102, 103, 104, 105, 106, 107, 108, 109, 110, 111, 112, 113, 135, 232, 274

HRM 12, 13, 16, 19, 20, 21, 22, 23, 24, 25, 26, 27, 28, 30, 31, 33, 37, 39, 40, 41, 42, 43, 44, 45, 46, 47, 48, 49, 50, 51, 52, 53, 54, 55, 57, 58, 59, 60, 61, 62, 63, 65, 66, 67, 68, 69, 70, 71, 72, 73, 75, 76, 77, 78, 79, 80, 81, 85, 86, 87, 88, 91, 93, 94, 95, 97, 98, 99, 100, 101, 105, 107, 109, 112, 117, 121, 122, 125, 130, 131, 132, 133, 134, 135, 136, 137, 138, 139, 140, 141, 142, 143, 144, 145, 146, 148, 149, 150, 151, 154, 156, 157, 158, 161, 185, 186, 187, 189, 190, 197, 199, 200, 202, 203, 204, 207, 208, 210, 211, 212, 213, 214, 216, 219, 220, 221, 239, 240, 241, 242, 243, 244, 245, 246, 248, 249, 250, 251, 252, 253, 255, 260, 261, 263, 265, 273, 276

Human Capital 23, 24, 25, 34, 45, 50, 52, 58, 86, 95, 101, 102, 110, 131, 136, 142, 170, 171, 183, 232, 240, 261, 274, 275

Human Resource Management 1, 2, 3, 9, 10, 11, 14, 16, 17, 18, 19, 20, 21, 22, 23, 24, 25, 27, 30, 33, 34, 35, 36, 37, 39, 40, 41, 42, 45, 46, 47, 48, 49, 52, 53, 54, 56, 57, 58, 59, 60, 63, 79, 82, 83, 84, 85, 87, 88, 89, 92, 99, 100, 101, 102, 104, 107, 108, 109, 110, 111, 112, 113, 114, 115, 116, 117, 125, 126, 127, 130, 131, 142, 143, 144, 158, 159, 160, 161, 181, 185, 186, 188, 189, 190, 194, 196, 197, 198, 199, 200, 201, 202, 203, 204, 210, 214, 216, 217, 220, 221, 226, 233, 235, 236, 237, 240, 254, 255, 256, 257, 258, 260, 261, 263, 269, 270, 274, 275

Human Resources 3, 16, 17, 18, 19, 20, 24, 25, 26, 27, 29, 30, 31, 32, 33, 35, 36, 37, 42, 43, 45, 47, 49, 50, 51, 52, 53, 56, 57, 59, 61, 63, 82, 83, 85, 86, 87, 88, 91, 93, 103, 104, 107, 108, 109, 110, 111, 112, 118, 125, 131, 142, 143, 144, 145, 146, 148, 162, 165, 175, 184, 185, 188, 189, 190, 191, 197, 199, 203, 216, 219, 223, 232, 235, 239, 240, 241, 242, 243, 244, 246, 248, 249, 255, 256, 257, 261, 269, 270, 271, 276

I

Information systems 16, 24, 25, 26, 33, 34, 36, 54, 55, 59, 63, 82, 86, 101, 111, 125, 126, 158, 161, 191, 198, 199, 204, 206, 216, 218, 221, 243, 245, 249, 251, 256, 257, 268, 275

Innovation 4, 10, 13, 17, 23, 24, 26, 28, 29, 30, 33, 34, 35, 36, 37, 40, 41, 42, 44, 51, 52, 53, 54, 57, 58, 59, 66, 73, 82, 84, 95, 98, 99, 103, 119, 124, 125, 126, 128, 130, 131, 134, 140, 141, 144, 153, 157, 160, 161, 177, 186, 188, 189, 194, 196, 197, 200, 201, 202, 204, 211, 216, 219, 221, 232, 235, 243, 244, 245, 250, 251, 254, 256, 265, 270

Interagency collaboration 42, 60

L

Local Government 2, 59, 66, 129, 146, 152, 156, 158, 160, 161, 162, 163, 164, 165, 166, 167, 168, 169, 170, 171, 172, 173, 174, 175, 176, 177, 178, 179, 180, 181, 182, 183, 184, 206, 207, 208, 212, 216, 217, 220, 230, 234, 237, 256, 270, 274

M

Management 1, 2, 3, 5, 7, 8, 9, 10, 11, 14, 15, 16, 17, 18, 19, 20, 21, 22, 23, 24, 25, 26, 27, 28, 29, 30, 31, 32, 33, 34, 35, 36, 37, 39, 40, 41, 42, 44, 45, 46, 47, 48, 49, 50, 51, 52, 53, 54, 55, 56, 57, 58, 59, 60, 61, 62, 63, 64, 65, 66, 67, 68, 69, 70, 72, 73, 74, 75, 76, 78, 79, 80, 81, 82, 83, 84, 85, 86, 87, 88, 89, 90, 91, 92, 93, 94, 95, 96, 97, 98, 99,

100, 101, 102, 103, 104, 105, 106, 107, 108, 109, 110, 111, 112, 113, 114, 115, 116, 117, 125, 126, 127, 128, 130, 131, 132, 133, 134, 135, 136, 139, 140, 142, 143, 144, 145, 147, 148, 155, 156, 157, 158, 159, 160, 161, 162, 163, 164, 165, 166, 169, 170, 171, 172, 173, 175, 177, 178, 179, 181, 182, 183, 184, 185, 186, 188, 189, 190, 191, 193, 194, 195, 196, 197, 198, 199, 200, 201, 202, 203, 204, 205, 206, 208, 210, 211, 212, 213, 214, 216, 217, 218, 219, 220, 221, 222, 223, 224, 225, 226, 227, 228, 229, 230, 231, 232, 233, 234, 235, 236, 237, 238, 240, 241, 242, 243, 244, 245, 246, 247, 249, 251, 252, 253, 254, 255, 256, 257, 258, 259, 260, 261, 262, 263, 264, 265, 267, 268, 269, 270, 271, 272, 273, 274, 275, 276

Management Information System 214

Municipalities 66, 145, 146, 147, 148, 149, 150, 151, 152, 154, 155, 156, 157, 160, 166, 173, 181, 183, 184, 212, 217, 218, 220, 223, 224, 230, 233, 236

N

Nepotism 1, 2, 7, 11, 18, 117, 118, 125, 130, 131, 134, 192, 196, 198

Nigeria 2, 5, 9, 31, 131, 132, 134, 137, 138, 139, 140, 142, 143, 144

O

Ongoing monitoring 60, 77

Organisational Performance 24, 29, 30, 32, 34, 50, 75, 77, 86, 88, 92, 93, 95, 97, 98, 99, 101, 102, 103, 105, 106, 136, 171, 179, 210, 224, 228, 230, 231, 235, 237, 267

P

People Performance and Organisational Performance 224

Performance Contracts 162, 163, 164, 166, 167, 168, 169, 170, 171, 172, 173, 174, 175, 176, 177, 178, 179, 180, 181, 184, 207

Performance Evaluation 28, 30, 51, 78, 80, 90, 102, 103, 104, 105, 194, 197, 202, 203, 204, 206, 208, 209, 210, 211, 212, 213, 214, 215, 271

Performance Management 3, 11, 23, 27, 28, 31, 37, 46, 47, 60, 61, 62, 63, 66, 67, 68, 75, 81, 83, 86, 88, 89, 91, 96, 97, 98, 99, 103, 109, 131, 133, 134, 135, 136, 140, 162, 163, 164, 165, 166, 169, 170, 171, 172, 173, 175, 179, 181, 182, 183, 184, 189, 193, 202, 203, 204, 205, 206, 208, 212, 213, 216, 217, 218, 220, 221, 223, 224, 234, 235, 236, 241, 244, 245, 271

Processes 1, 2, 3, 4, 5, 6, 7, 8, 9, 10, 11, 12, 13, 14, 15, 18, 19, 21, 22, 23, 24, 25, 26, 27, 28, 30, 31, 37, 41, 44, 45, 47, 49, 50, 61, 64, 65, 66, 67, 73, 75, 76, 78, 79, 81, 82, 87, 92, 93, 97, 98, 99, 101, 102, 103, 104, 105, 106, 115, 116, 117, 118, 119, 120, 121, 122, 123, 124, 131, 134, 135, 136, 139, 140, 144, 145, 146, 148, 149, 150, 151, 152, 153, 155, 156, 157, 162, 164, 166, 171, 172, 173, 175, 181, 183, 185, 186, 187, 189, 190, 191, 193, 194, 195, 196, 197, 198, 204, 210, 213, 224, 226, 229, 231, 232, 234, 241, 243, 244, 245, 246, 248, 249, 251, 257, 259, 261, 264, 265, 267, 268, 269, 272, 273

public sector 1, 2, 3, 4, 5, 6, 7, 8, 9, 10, 11, 12, 13, 14, 15, 16, 17, 18, 19, 20, 21, 22, 23, 24, 25, 26, 27, 28, 29, 30, 31, 32, 33, 34, 35, 36, 37, 39, 40, 41, 42, 43, 44, 45, 46, 47, 48, 49, 50, 51, 52, 53, 54, 56, 57, 58, 60, 61, 62, 63, 64, 65, 66, 67, 68, 69, 70, 71, 72, 74, 75, 76, 77, 78, 79, 80, 81, 82, 83, 84, 85, 86, 87, 89, 90, 91, 92, 93, 94, 95, 96, 97, 99, 100, 101, 102, 103, 104, 105, 106, 107, 108, 109, 110, 113, 115, 116, 117, 118, 119, 120, 121, 122, 123, 124, 125, 126, 127, 128, 130, 131, 132, 133, 134, 135, 136, 137, 138, 139, 140, 141, 142, 143, 144, 145, 146, 148, 149, 151, 154, 156, 157, 161, 163, 166, 168, 182, 185, 186, 187, 188, 189, 190, 191, 192, 193, 194, 195, 196, 197, 198, 199, 200, 202, 203, 204, 205, 206, 207, 208, 209, 210, 211, 212, 213, 214, 215, 216, 217, 219, 220, 221, 223, 228, 231, 232, 233, 235, 236, 239, 240, 241, 242, 243, 244, 245, 246, 247, 248, 249, 250, 251, 252, 254, 256, 259, 260, 261, 262, 263, 264, 265, 267, 268, 269, 270, 271, 272, 273, 274, 275, 276, 277

Public sector HRM 21, 22, 25, 39, 40, 41, 42, 43, 44, 45, 46, 47, 49, 50, 52, 57, 60, 61, 62, 63, 65, 66, 67, 68, 69, 70, 71, 72, 75, 76, 77, 78, 79, 80, 81, 91, 94, 95, 97, 99, 105, 117, 121, 122, 132, 133, 134, 136, 139, 140, 141, 143, 145, 146, 148, 149, 151, 154, 156, 157, 185, 203, 204, 207, 210, 211, 212, 213, 214, 241, 243, 246, 250, 251, 252, 263, 265, 273

Public Sector Human Resources Management 47, 145, 197

Public Service 4, 6, 7, 8, 9, 18, 19, 20, 35, 36, 40, 41, 42, 43, 44, 45, 46, 47, 48, 49, 54, 55, 56, 66, 85, 86, 87, 88, 89, 95, 100, 106, 113, 117, 118, 119, 120, 121, 123, 126, 128, 132, 135, 136, 139, 140, 142, 143, 144, 149, 160, 181, 182, 183, 184, 186, 188, 189, 190, 191, 195, 196, 202, 203, 204, 207,

209, 210, 211, 212, 213, 214, 216, 218, 219, 222, 223, 224, 225, 231, 232, 233, 234, 239, 240, 241, 242, 243, 244, 245, 249, 250, 251, 252, 254, 255, 256, 257, 264, 274

R

Recruitment And Selection 1, 2, 3, 4, 5, 6, 7, 8, 9, 10, 11, 12, 13, 14, 15, 18, 23, 35, 78, 85, 98, 116, 129, 131, 139, 140, 144, 145, 150, 186, 189, 190, 191, 196, 201, 214, 227, 234, 241, 244, 248, 249, 260, 265, 268, 269, 270, 271, 272, 273, 275, 276

S

Service Delivery 4, 5, 6, 9, 18, 19, 20, 28, 31, 35, 40, 41, 42, 43, 44, 47, 50, 51, 52, 57, 62, 65, 76, 78, 85, 86, 94, 95, 100, 104, 106, 113, 115, 116, 117, 121, 122, 123, 126, 132, 136, 143, 146, 149, 150, 154, 159, 160, 162, 173, 175, 177, 178, 179, 181, 183, 184, 187, 190, 195, 202, 203, 204, 205, 206, 208, 209, 211, 212, 213, 214, 218, 219, 222, 223, 224, 225, 228, 230, 231, 232, 233, 234, 239, 240, 242, 243, 244, 247, 250, 251, 252, 254, 255, 256, 262, 271, 273, 275

South Africa 2, 5, 6, 7, 12, 17, 22, 31, 32, 39, 40, 41, 55, 57, 83, 84, 85, 90, 104, 108, 111, 115, 130, 134, 142, 145, 146, 151, 152, 154, 156, 159, 160, 161, 162, 166, 173, 175, 183, 185, 188, 190, 191, 192, 195, 197, 200, 201, 202, 203, 204, 205, 206, 207, 208, 209, 210, 211, 212, 213, 214, 215, 216, 217, 218, 219, 221, 222, 223, 230, 233, 236, 237, 239, 240, 241, 242, 243, 244, 245, 250, 251, 252, 257, 276

South African Government 22, 28, 36, 191, 195, 223, 230, 231, 242

Sustainable Development 17, 37, 48, 84, 107, 125, 131, 144, 158, 161, 164, 199, 242, 244, 246, 249, 274

T

Talent Management 11, 16, 21, 23, 25, 26, 27, 28, 29, 30, 31, 32, 33, 36, 37, 46, 55, 66, 75, 76, 82, 90, 91, 92, 93, 94, 95, 96, 97, 98, 99, 100, 101, 102, 103, 104, 105, 106, 107, 108, 109, 110, 111, 112, 113, 132, 139, 140, 144, 204, 222, 223, 224, 225, 226, 227, 228, 229, 230, 231, 232, 233, 234, 235, 236, 237, 259, 260, 261, 262, 263, 264, 265, 267, 268, 269, 270, 271, 272, 273, 274, 275, 276

Technological adaptation 187

Technological Advancement 28, 44, 46, 47, 130, 138, 142, 208, 214

Technologies 2, 4, 5, 9, 10, 14, 15, 19, 20, 21, 22, 23, 25, 26, 27, 28, 30, 31, 37, 39, 40, 41, 43, 44, 45, 46, 47, 50, 51, 52, 54, 55, 57, 58, 60, 61, 62, 63, 64, 66, 67, 68, 70, 71, 72, 73, 77, 78, 79, 80, 81, 82, 84, 88, 89, 95, 97, 98, 99, 108, 115, 116, 117, 119, 121, 123, 127, 131, 133, 134, 135, 136, 137, 138, 139, 140, 143, 145, 146, 147, 148, 149, 150, 152, 153, 155, 156, 157, 160, 166, 179, 185, 187, 188, 189, 190, 193, 194, 197, 200, 202, 203, 209, 210, 211, 213, 214, 215, 220, 221, 227, 232, 239, 240, 242, 243, 244, 245, 247, 248, 249, 250, 252, 254, 255, 256, 259, 260, 263, 264, 265, 266, 268, 269, 271, 272, 275

Technology 1, 2, 3, 4, 6, 8, 9, 12, 13, 14, 15, 16, 19, 20, 22, 23, 26, 27, 28, 32, 33, 34, 40, 41, 42, 43, 44, 45, 46, 47, 48, 49, 50, 51, 52, 53, 55, 56, 58, 60, 61, 62, 63, 68, 70, 71, 72, 73, 74, 75, 76, 77, 78, 79, 80, 81, 82, 83, 84, 85, 86, 87, 88, 91, 97, 99, 100, 101, 102, 103, 104, 105, 107, 109, 116, 117, 118, 119, 122, 123, 124, 125, 126, 127, 130, 131, 132, 133, 134, 135, 136, 137, 139, 140, 142, 143, 144, 145, 146, 147, 148, 149, 150, 151, 152, 154, 155, 156, 157, 158, 159, 161, 166, 171, 175, 178, 181, 182, 186, 187, 189, 190, 192, 193, 194, 197, 199, 201, 202, 203, 204, 206, 207, 209, 210, 211, 216, 217, 218, 219, 231, 232, 233, 238, 241, 242, 243, 244, 245, 247, 248, 249, 250, 251, 255, 256, 259, 260, 262, 263, 264, 265, 267, 268, 269, 270, 271, 272, 273, 274, 275

Transformation 3, 5, 6, 8, 12, 16, 17, 20, 21, 22, 23, 24, 25, 26, 27, 28, 29, 30, 31, 32, 33, 34, 35, 36, 37, 39, 40, 41, 42, 43, 44, 45, 46, 47, 48, 49, 50, 51, 52, 53, 54, 55, 56, 57, 58, 59, 60, 61, 62, 63, 80, 81, 82, 84, 85, 87, 88, 89, 91, 95, 96, 97, 98, 99, 107, 114, 115, 116, 117, 118, 119, 120, 121, 122, 123, 124, 125, 126, 127, 128, 130, 131, 133, 134, 136, 137, 138, 139, 140, 144, 145, 146, 147, 150, 156, 158, 159, 161, 162, 163, 166, 169, 175, 183, 185, 186, 187, 188, 189, 190, 191, 193, 195, 196, 197, 198, 199, 200, 201, 202, 203, 207, 209, 214, 215, 222, 223, 231, 232, 233, 239, 240, 241, 242, 243, 244, 245, 246, 247, 248, 249, 250, 251, 252, 253, 254, 255, 256, 257, 258, 260, 261, 263, 264, 265, 273, 275, 276

U

universitas nias 21

Unsettled Context 163

Z

Zimbabwe 1, 2, 5, 6, 7, 8, 14, 17, 18, 19, 20, 60, 65, 83, 104, 162, 163, 164, 167, 171, 172, 173, 174, 177, 180, 181, 182, 183, 184, 239, 240, 241, 246, 247, 248, 249, 250, 251, 252, 255, 256, 257, 259, 260, 262, 263, 264, 265, 269, 270, 271, 272, 273, 274, 275, 276

Ensure Quality Research is Introduced to the Academic Community

Become a Reviewer for IGI Global Authored Book Projects

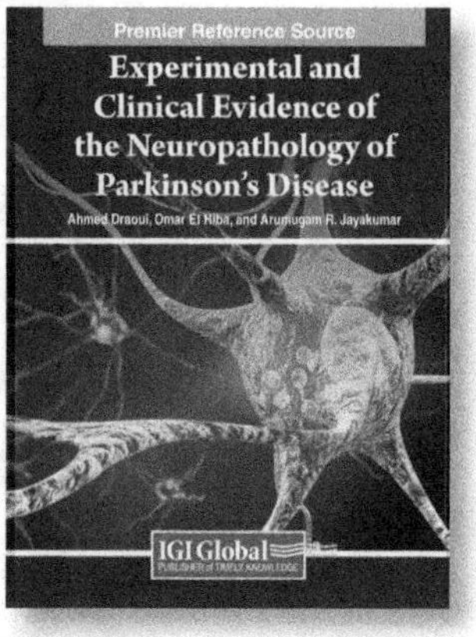

The overall success of an authored book project is dependent on quality and timely manuscript evaluations.

Applications and Inquiries may be sent to:
development@igi-global.com

Applicants must have a doctorate (or equivalent degree) as well as publishing, research, and reviewing experience. Authored Book Evaluators are appointed for one-year terms and are expected to complete at least three evaluations per term. Upon successful completion of this term, evaluators can be considered for an additional term.

If you have a colleague that may be interested in this opportunity, we encourage you to share this information with them.

www.ingramcontent.com/pod-product-compliance
Lightning Source LLC
LaVergne TN
LVHW060419300926
849162LV00006B/1467
* 9 7 9 8 3 6 9 3 2 8 8 9 7 *